# Flash™ 5

# Graphics, Animation, and Interactivity

**James L. Mohler, M.S.Ed.**

**ONWORD PRESS**

**THOMSON LEARNING**™

Australia   Canada   Mexico   Singapore   United Kingdom   United States

**ONWORD PRESS**

™

**THOMSON LEARNING**

# Flash™ 5: Graphics, Animation, and Interactivity
## by James L. Mohler, M.S.Ed.

**Business Unit Director:**
Alar Elken

**Acquisitions Editor:**
James Gish

**Developmental Editor**
Daril Bentley

**Editorial Assistant:**
Jaimie Wetzel

**Executive Marketing Manager:**
Maura Theriault

**Managing Editor:**
Carol Leyba

**Executive Production Manager:**
Mary Ellen Black

**Senior Production Coordinator:**
Toni Hansen

**Art/Design Coordinator:**
Rachel Baker

**Illustrator:**
Nicole Reamer

**Cover Design:**
Cummings Advertising

**Technology Project Manager**:
David Porush

Printed in Canada
1 2 3 4  5 6 XXX 04 03 02 01 00

For more information contact
OnWord Press
an imprint of Thomson Learning,
PO Box 15015,
Albany, NY 12212-5015

Or find us on the World Wide Web at
http://www.onwordpress.com

For permission to use material from this text or product, contact us by
Tel    (800) 730-2214
Fax   (800) 730-2215
www.thomsonrights.com

**Library of Congress Cataloging-in-Publication Data**

Mohler, James L.
    Flash 5: graphics, animation, and interactivity / James L. Mohler.
       p. cm
    includes index
    ISBN: 0-7668-2909-X
    1. Computer graphics 2. Computer animation 3. Flash (Computer file) 4. Web sites—Design. I. Title

T385.M632 2000
006.6'96—dc21                    00-047543

## About the Author

James L. Mohler is an Associate Professor in the Department of Computer Graphics at Purdue University. He has authored or coauthored 13 texts related to multimedia and hypermedia development, presented over 30 papers and workshops at national and international conferences, and written numerous articles for academic and trade publications. He has been awarded several teaching awards at Purdue University and was recently chosen as a Fulbright Distinguished Chair in Multimedia. Mr. Mohler has been awarded several teaching awards and currently serves as webmaster for the School of Technology at Purdue University, lead developer for the Interactive Multimedia Development specialization within the department, webmaster for the Purdue University Virtual Visit web site, and executive editor for the *Journal of Interactive Instruction Development.*

He also enjoys serving as Praise and Worship Leader at Living Word Ministry Center in Frankfort, Indiana. James and his wonderful wife Lisa have three children, Meisha Danielle, Christian Alexander, and Treyton James. He can be contacted via email at *jlmohler@tech.purdue.edu.*

## Acknowledgments

I would like to especially thank the wonderful team at Delmar for all their support on this book. The author is only a part of a much larger team, and thanks go to acquisitions editor Jim Gish (one of the best I have worked with), project manager Carol Leyba and development editor Daril Bentley (thanks for your patience and help in pulling this out in time), senior production coordinator Toni Hansen, executive production manager Mary Ellen Black, and editorial assistant Jaimie Wetzel.

I would also like to thank the many readers at Amazon and elsewhere who were so supportive of the Flash 4 edition of this book.

Finally, I would like to thank my wonderful wife Lisa, who has been patient and loving while I have spent endless hours in the office.

*This book is dedicated to my students—past, present, and future.*
*It is you who keep me "sharpening the saw."*

# Contents

# Introduction

Those of us who are part of the information age, involved with web development and its expansion, are lucky to have experienced the birth and growth of this transient communication media. Much like early pioneers, we are continuing to push the hardware, software, and any other technological resources we can get our hands on to the limit—seeing just how much we can do with it, and how much it will handle. Often in both corporations and educational institutions it means seeing how much we can do with how little intervention and resources.

Although the rate of change can be alarming to some, we should consider ourselves lucky to have been able to be a part of one of the largest explosions of technology in the twentieth century. Many would say, "Heck, I've been using the Net for twenty or so years," but let's put this into perspective. There is a big difference between a couple hundred universities and organizations using the "Net" versus the vast millions using it today. In addition, communicating via the Net "back then" was very cryptic and difficult. Sure, communication occurred, but oh was it ugly! Today, things are more standardized and easier than 10 years ago, but there is still a significant amount of technical skills that are required.

The largest amount of growth and development of the Internet has occurred within the last 10 years. Sources state that today nearly 2000 new users get on the Net each month. Aside from the number of surfers on the web, the number of web sites alone has increased from just over 1000 in the early 1980s to close to 10 million today. Ten years ago, who would have imagined Internet access and services available to virtually every in-home user? Not to mention tagging an Internet feeder line onto your incoming television cable line or through a satellite link. It is extremely exciting to be a part of the rapidly evolving world of the Internet.

Of all the things the Web can be, probably the one that encourages me most is its ability to be so many things to so many people. Flash is a technology that is changing, and will continue to change, what we consider "delivering over the Web."

There are not many technologies I have gotten excited enough about to write a book on. When HTML first came out, I was excited and decided to focus my efforts on learning this "new technology," and writing a book.

My co-author and I had about 30 days to learn, consume, and regurgitate as much as we could about HTML. We were coaxed into riding the wave of technology, and I am grateful I could ride along with an experienced surfer.

However, this book is different from others I have written. I have spent more time on this book—writing, revising, reviewing, and testing in the classroom. This book has been about nine months in development, and I can truly say that this book is a compilation of everything I know about Flash. With this book, I have had a luxury unavailable in the past—time.

I hope you enjoy using and learning from this book. Flash is a wonderful tool, and I foresee that it will continue to evolve and become more useful as time progresses.

## Audience

This book is designed for educators, students, and practitioners in the field who really want to get "up close and personal" with Flash. I have been very disappointed with books that were supposed to cover the range of Flash capabilities, only to be a rehash of the tutorials, with very limited explanations and examples. Similarly, there are many books that provide complex examples but provide little in the way of explanation. If you learn best by dissecting and figuring things out for yourself, those books may be worth their money. But I think you will find, as I have, that having to dissect things and figure them out on your own takes more time than well-documented, simpler examples.

I have designed this book for people who really want to learn how Flash works. The examples are designed to educate you, not provide you with a quick fix. Within the pages of this book you will find referenced examples from cover to cover. Starting with the basics, you begin hands-on work in Chapter 2. By chapters 15 and 16, you examine strings of ActionScript and JavaScript that only a code junky could love. By the time you complete this book, you will know how Flash works and how to go about creating your own Flash movies and Flash-based web sites.

## Philosophy and Approach

The author's greatest strength is that he is an educator first and a developer second. Most of his time is spent finding ways to help people learn and understand how computer graphics and programming works. The philosophy is to go beyond simple button pushing and rote techniques to focus on the larger picture. When someone understands how something works, they can use that knowledge to do much more than reemploy some code or some technique laid out before them. They can apply what they have learned to another problem or another context much broader than the original content presented.

The goal and reason for sometimes-lengthy explanations in this text is to provide you the knowledge derived of many hours of testing, and of many successes and failures. Someone once said that there is no substitute for "drive time" when it comes to learning a new technology or a new piece of software. This is true of any learning situation. Beware of books that suggest that you can learn a software package in hours. You can learn techniques in a matter of hours, but do you really understand what you are doing, and could you replicate it in another context? Probably not. This is the reason for the thorough explanations throughout this book, intended to help you really understand what it is you are doing, and what the software is doing.

Complex examples are often too unwieldy for learners to break down and understand what is actually going on as they are trying to follow them. Thus, many of the examples in this book focus on a single concept, and thus appear simple. The person looking for a quick fix might prefer another approach, but the best way to describe a feature is to separate it and talk about it out of context, so that you understand what the feature does. You can then integrate that learning into a more complex project. That is the philosophy that drives, and the approach taken in, this book.

Finally, the approach taken in the previous (Flash 4) edition of this book was well received. That same tutorial approach is used in this edition, but this edition differs in that it incorporates many more exercises, as well as a significantly greater and more detailed amount of material devoted to Flash 5 programming capability. In the words of those who have commented, "it's like having a teacher right there." That is the greatest compliment the previous edition could have received, because it indicates that the goal of the book was achieved. The goal of this book has been to improve on and expand that achievement.

 **NOTE:** As you work through Chapter 6, and other chapters that deal with ActionScript, realize that there are two types of denotations for actions (see Glossary). The first is the general action name (as listed in the Toolbox list), such as Go To, Play, Stop, and so on. The second is the form of the code associated with action names (as shown in the interface Action list), such as *gotoAndPlay* and *gotoAndStop*, or *play( )* and *stop( )*. The text follows these styles for the two types of denotation. Furthermore, scripting code items (such as *gotoAndStop*) are case sensitive, so pay special attention to the capitalization used.

# ▪ ▪ ▪ Book Features and Conventions

The sections that follow discuss the major features of this book. This edition includes two color inserts, a tear-out quick-reference card of keyboard shortcuts to Flash commands, and a companion CD-ROM.

 **NOTE:** *In addition to files in support of the text, the companion CD-ROM contains trial versions of Macromedia Flash, Swift3D, and Vecta3D. See the section "About the Companion CD-ROM," at the end of this introduction, and Appendix H for more information.*

## Color Inserts

Two color inserts show graphics discussed within chapters, most of which are associated with examples and exercises. These are graphics for which color is particularly important or beneficial. In addition, they show the range of Flash graphics in application. Cross references point from the text to the respective color insert graphic, and you will find that these renderings help illuminate the text discussion. The inserts are located at two points in the book, and are labeled insert A and insert B. Cross references in the text indicate the respective insert.

## Quick-reference Card

The tear-out quick-reference card at the back of the book contains Flash commands, by category, and their associated "quick keys." This feature is convenient in that you can quickly find that command you do not quite remember. In addition, the use of shortcut keys is an important aspect of becoming more proficient in Flash.

## Glossary, Appendices, and Index

You will find at the back of the book an extensive glossary of Flash-specific terms, as well as general terms related to the areas of functionality Flash incorporates. The glossary serves as a study in its own right. Eight appendices offer information and look-up tables associated with topics covered in chapters (see the table of contents). A thorough index covers all text content, including entries that allow you to locate conceptual material.

## Text Conventions

Italic font in regular text is used to distinguish certain command names, code elements, file names, directory and path names, and similar items. Italic is also used to highlight terms and for emphasis.

The following is an example of the monospaced font used for examples of command statements and computer/operating system responses, as well as passages of programming script.

```
var myimage = InternetExplorer ? parent.
cell : parent.document.embeds[0];
```

The following are the design conventions used for various "working parts" of the text. In addition to these, you will find that the text incorporates many exercises, examples, and sidebars. All of these elements are easily distinguishable and accessible. Sidebar material highlights or supplements topics discussed in the text.

 **NOTE:** *Information on features and tasks that requires emphasis or that is not immediately obvious appears in notes.*

 **TIP:** *Tips on command usage, shortcuts, and other information aimed at saving you time and work appear like this.*

 **WARNING:** The warnings appearing in this book are intended to help you avoid committing yourself to results you may not intend, and to avoid losing data or encountering other unfortunate consequences.

 **CD-ROM NOTE:** *These notes point to files and directories on the companion CD-ROM that supplement the text via visual examples and further information on a particular topic.*

# Version Specificity and Prerequisites

The files found on the companion CD-ROM are specific to Flash 5 and are not backward compatible. If you have an older version of Flash, you will not be able to open the Flash files. However, there is a 30-day trial version of Flash 5 located in the Macromedia folder on the companion CD-ROM. Feel free to install it to get up and running with the exercise files.

As to prerequisites, the book really has none. Indeed, prior experience in a vector or raster image editor would be helpful, but it is not imperative. Similarly, prior experience in programming will make writing your own ActionScript and JavaScript easier. However, you will find that this book covers all aspects of both using Flash and getting you up and running with ActionScript.

# About the Companion CD-ROM

The companion CD-ROM located at the back of the book is one of the most important things about this book. There are well over 50 example files you will be prompted to use throughout the book. You will find that the CD-ROM is PC and Macintosh compatible, and versions of the example files exist for both platforms, as do the trial versions of Macromedia Flash, Swift3D, and Vecta3D. For PC users, there is an additional trial software available called SwiSH.

 **NOTE:** *See also Appendix H, which provides a complete directory structure of the content of the companion CD-ROM.*

Because some operations in Macromedia Flash, particularly the Control | Test Movie command, require Flash to write to the drive of the computer, you may find it more helpful to copy the instructional example files to a local drive. If you are on a PC, an installation routine is available that allows you to install all files, or individual chapters as you need them. If you are on a Macintosh, you will need to copy the chapter files manually by dragging and dropping them to a local drive.

If you choose not to copy the files to a local drive from the very start, to be able to use Control | Test Movie in Flash, at some point you will have to save the files to a local drive. A *Read Me* file is located on the CD-ROM that details this information. On the PC side, the *Read Me* file details how to run and use the setup program.

part one:

# The
# Application

chapter

1

# Flash on the Horizon

## ▪▪▪ Introduction

The Web is dramatically morphing in appearance every day, and no end is in sight to its evolution. Some people complain of the rate of change. However, many believe the Web is paving the way for faster and better communication, thanks to the wealth of these emerging technologies. Thankfully, we are moving away from pages filled with endless streams of text with limited aesthetic appeal. With the use of tools such as Flash, developers are polishing their web sites with sophisticated animations and vector-based graphics that please the visual sense and communicate more effectively.

With a wealth of web technologies, you may question where Macromedia Flash fits in and why it is so important. After all, new technologies and new acronyms for the Web are a daily occurrence. Like many developers striving to break into (or keep up with) the web arena, you may tire of the "latest and greatest" advent for the Web. With so many technologies being released and revised, it is difficult to get excited about "another technology." But as soon as you have seen any one of the many web sites that contain full-screen animation, sound, or interactivity, you will appreciate the implications and excitement that surround Macromedia Flash.

Web developers have seen many technologies come and go, and many more will undoubtedly follow. Nevertheless, once in a while a particular technology emerges that has the potential to change the way we work. Macromedia Flash is a perfect example of such a technology, and the good news is that it will likely be around a while because of the advantages it offers, not to mention its proliferation into so many web sites. An added benefit is that once you learn the basics of Flash, you can do almost anything with it.

The latest release of Flash has some very exciting features to offer, but before you explore them, you need to look at Flash in context. This chapter highlights the implications of static and dynamic vector graphics on the Web. It describes how Flash is a force for change in the type and amount of web content being delivered. This chapter is not intended to be a lengthy conceptual overview but a presentation of important concepts for those who have chosen to begin learning to create web sites using Flash.

If you are an experienced developer, this chapter is probably old hat for you, and you will likely skip past it. That is quite all right. But to provide adequate context for all, this chapter is designed to provide an overview of Flash's context in the web development cycle, as well as a little bit of relevant information to provide a base level of understanding.

Regardless of whether you are a new or experienced surfer, you will undoubtedly see web content continue to evolve into an increasingly dynamic and interactive environment. In its relatively short existence (in human years), the Web has quickly migrated from a predominantly text-based environment to one that is now incomplete without graphics and aesthetic design components. For your site to be noticed, there had better be something more than a static image and some static text. Interactivity and dynamism, the crux of the next phase of the web revolution, are the elements that will make your site stand out. As a developer, it will be exciting to witness and take part in these changes.

Aside from an overview and a little history, in this chapter you will also review the predominant features of Flash and the numerous things that can be done with it. This chapter also provides a cursory introduction to the main features of Flash 5, as well as a perspective on the integration issues surrounding implementation, such as what can be delivered, and how. Discover how Flash compares with other emerging technologies, as well as with other Macromedia packages.

 **NOTE:** *Realize that this discussion is designed as a quick overview. You may want to consult Chapter 5 of the* Using Flash 5 *book that came with your software for further information concerning integration with other Macromedia packages.*

If you are new to Flash but familiar with other Macromedia authoring software, you will discover that Flash differs significantly from Director and Authorware because its main focus is on vector elements. At the conclusion of this chapter, you will examine some of these differences.

# Objectives

In this chapter, you will:

- Discover current trends in web design
- Learn some "rules of the road" for graphics in web pages
- Note the important things you should consider about developing for the Web
- Acknowledge the context and importance of vector graphics
- Examine the main features of Macromedia Flash
- Contrast Flash with other web technologies
- Discover how Flash can be used in conjunction with other graphics programs

# The Current State of the Web

First and foremost, the Web is a communication tool. Throughout history, many technologies have impacted communication. From the moveable-type printing press to the desktop computers of today, many technological advances have revolutionized how we are impacted by a message, how vividly that message is portrayed, and the cost associated with broadcasting the message. The Web provides one of the most cost-effective means of providing real-time, instantly accessible information, as indicated in figure 1-1 (see also color plate A-1). The Web continues to drastically change the way we deliver, receive, and consume information.

Understand that the Web is by no means the first revolutionary communication media. Nevertheless, it is a medium that has evolved and been made available to masses of people with the shortest amount of development time. Inventions such as the printing press, telegraph, phonograph, telephone, and television have indeed greatly impacted communication, but in each case over a much broader timeline. Since 1994, the Web has exploded. Today, business, education, government, and people everywhere are using the Web as their principal means of communication. Most sources indi-

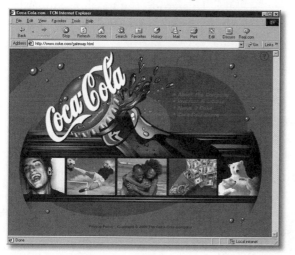

*Figure 1-1 More and more companies are choosing the Web for the delivery of real-time information, and Flash has become a standard delivery vehicle (http://www.coke.com/). See also color plate A-1.*

*Figure 1-2 Before 1994, marketing sites were taboo! (http://www.nike.com/). See also color plate A-2.*

cate that web content will double over the next 5 to 10 years, which is encouraging for those of us who do, and who want to do, web development.

Why was 1994 such a critical year? Before that point, the Web was an academic-only environment and was largely text based. Advertisements, marketing (see figure 1-2 and color plate A-2), and personal web sites were unheard of, even considered "unethical" or "illegal." With the release of the Web to corporate, business, and personal use, the landscape has changed significantly in a very short time. Today, many of the technologies used across the Web are a result of use by the public at large.

At its roots, the Web was designed as a universal medium. The primary goal was to create a mass of information that could be readily received by any connected user without a specific tie to any single software application, program, or platform. The interpreter, or the browser, had to be able to read a single defining file and present (or "render") the content on the fly for the user. The language developed to do this was Hypertext Markup Language (HTML). This crude (by today's standards) language was a subset of a more elaborate markup language called Standard Generalized Markup Language (SGML).

 **NOTE:** *SGML has a broad history. SGML was designed so that developers could tag bits of information that could be used for search engines in multimedia. SGML is still in use today and is most often applicable to extremely large products, such as electronic dictionaries and encyclopedias. SGML is a larger set of rules, called a Document Type Definition (DTD).*

HTML allowed developers to "mark up" their content with special tags that could be interpreted on the fly. This tagging language offered the support of graphics via Graphic Interchange Format (GIF), already common due to the use of CompuServe and other online services, and the Joint Photographic Experts Group (JPEG) format. The underlying vehicle for delivering all content was to be simple by design, providing almost anyone the ability to communicate with this new medium.

As brilliant as this scheme was, it was designed by scientists and academia. In most cases, these individuals were more concerned with delivery, accessibility, and readability from anywhere than how the content looked. Graphics and the aesthetic appearance of pages were secondary and deemed less important. Thus, the first version of HTML provided very limited means for truly designing web pages.

Keep in mind that HTML was designed as a loosely defined language. Most of the tags describe the general way in which an element such as a string of text, a table, a form, or an image should be rendered. However, HTML does not specifically define exact placement, nor does it give a precise definition of the type of information presented.

This is the reason you see so many extended "tag sets" and additional technologies used in combination with HTML, such as Dynamic HTML (DHTML) and Cascading Style Sheets (CSS). These extensions strive to make up for the shortcomings and limitations of HTML in terms of aesthetic control and content extension. Even more important, newer technologies such as Extensible Markup Language (XML) and Extensible Stylesheet Language (XSL) may eliminate the need for HTML altogether, but it will be quite some time before this transition is complete.

As HTML has matured, more and more tags and attributes have been added to make it a more designer-friendly structure. As a matter of fact, nearly 50 percent or more of the features added (as well as those that are termed "emerging technologies") have been aimed at increasing the graphical nature of the Web. Most pages before 1995 were aesthetically numbing. Today, it is difficult to find pages that are not aesthetically pleasing. Of course, there are still pages that are not up to current visual standards (*http://www.webpages thatsuck.com/*), but they are not as prevalent. From both good and not-so-good examples, we are learning what constitutes effective web design.

As more and more designers aim content at the Web, the rules of the road are getting defined—through experience, if nothing else. The genre (the "web look," if you will) is beginning to evolve and stabilize. Rather than looking like a traditional, static publication in digital form, web pages are taking on their own persona and are diverging from their traditional "page-oriented" roots.

Although some traditional rules apply, web design is somewhat peculiar. Web design is unique in that it adds two components not available in traditional documents: interactivity and dynamism. *Interactivity* is defined as the ability of the user to choose the information to be viewed. *Dynamic components* generally include animated graphics and video, with or without sound, as well as content that changes to meet the user's needs in real time. Let's examine some of the "standards" that prevail as they relate to web graphics and web design.

**NOTE:** *You could argue that navigation is a common element between traditional and digital design. However, interactivity and navigation are not really the same thing. Designing effective web pages and sites combines several areas of knowledge, not the least of which include traditional graphic design principles and human-computer interface (HCI) design principles.*

## Some Rules of the Road for Visuals

One of the most difficult things for those new to the web arena is determining the most effective places for graphics in a web page. Most are aware of the importance of using graphics, but are uncomfortable making decisions concerning where to use them and how to create and implement them. Using concepts such as clustering, eye flow, and composition and layout, the designer focuses on making site designs that are easier to interpret. In the application of graphics to any particular purpose, you must determine if a graphic will:

- *Enhance, complement, supplement, or complete content that cannot be adequately described or explained with text.* Often graphics are used to supplement or replace certain parts of text-based material. A single well-designed graphic can eliminate several paragraphs of text, and an animated graphic much more. The primary use of graphics is for content purposes. Graphics used in this way also increase attention, motivation, comprehension, and interpretation, as indicated in figure 1-3.

- *Present items such as buttons, button bars, and icons to allow for navigation.* Graphically based components present an easier, more effective, and often more efficient means of interacting with the computer. Icons, menus, and other WIMP-based (Windows, Icons, Menus, and Pointers) constructs can help the end user in navigating information by presenting a more logical, interpretable, and user-friendly structure for interaction, as indicated in figure 1-4 (see also color plate A-3).

- *Create a visual flow with directional, helper, and "filler" graphics.* Unlike traditional media, such as textbooks, most web pages have unique

*Figure 1-3 The most frequent use of graphics is for content purposes (http:// www.tech.purdue. edu/resources/map/).*

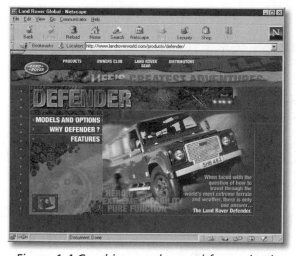

*Figure 1-4 Graphics are also used for navigation (http://www.landroverworld.com/). See also color plate A-3.*

elements and original content structures. Knowing where to look for navigation and content usually requires visual direction of attention. With texts, rules are learned early in life as to the navigation of a book, as well as the rules for reading. With web pages and sites, more visual assistance may be needed. Therefore, graphics are often used to direct attention and eye flow, and create a visual construct for interpretation. Using graphics to direct attention allows you to easily find navigation items and quickly access the content to be assimilated, as indicated in figure 1-5.

**TIP:** *Typically, the elements that make a web design "too busy" are the graphics used for eye flow or direction. Remember that negative space (white space) is good because it balances your layout. Often beginning page designers fill every nook and cranny of a page with text or graphic elements. This also applies to Flash animations and components. When you are designing, make sure you leave adequate breathing room for the elements in your design. Negative space is often as effective as positive space, as indicated in figure 1-6.*

Aside from the primary uses of graphics for content, navigation, and eye flow, graphics should also follow guidelines within web designs, such as the following:

*Figure 1-5 Graphics can also be used for design and to direct attention (http://www.kodak.com/go/ontheroad/).*

• When used for content purposes, graphics should always aid in communication. Use graphics to display something that cannot be adequately communicated with text, or to add more clarity to the content being discussed. Often static or dynamic images are used to display visual or spatial relationships, overcome lan-

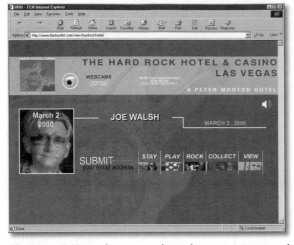

*Figure 1-6 Negative space is as important as positive space in almost every type of design (http://www.flashoutlet.com/view/hardrockhotel/).*

guage barriers, add credibility, involve reluctant readers, or aid in interpretation. They can also eliminate the need for lengthy blocks of text.

• Graphics should never overshadow or distract the audience from the message you are communicating. Every graphic placed within a product must have purpose. Inserting graphics to add flair generally distracts the audience from the message at hand. Too many dancing bullets or other active elements are usually detrimental when used in mass. In addition, static elements, when used in large quantities, can be equally numbing. Assets used in web pages should help the user better navigate and interpret the content, as well as direct his or her attention.

• Graphics contribute to the overall tone of the product. The tone of a web site is often conveyed by the graphics. Additionally, the evaluation of any given site, even if the content is not significantly graphically based, is most often derived from the quality and use of graphics. Graphics must be designed around the expectations of the audience, and with the communicative goal in mind.

• The audience's impression is not only based on what is being shown in the graphic but on its size, quality, orientation, placement, and processing requirements. Generally, the graphically challenged are concerned only with what appears in the graphic. Yet, these other attributes significantly contribute to the evaluation of a particular graphical asset. Related to size and quality, especially on the Web, is the proportional file size of a particular graphic. Modem-based web surfers who encounter a web page with a large cumulative file size will likely cancel the download if it takes more than a couple of minutes. Even with a vector-based tool such as Flash, file size can still be an important issue.

Understanding the issues related to the use and delivery of graphics is as important as understanding how to create them. Before continuing with the context of graphics on the Web, let's look at some of the global advantages and disadvantages of web communication.

## Advantages of Web Delivery

The Web provides several unique advantages over other modes of communication, such as traditional publications and even digital publications such as CD-ROM and DVD. Of all the media that can be used for multimedia content, none is more fluid than the Web. The Web is dynamic in both its editability and in the range of media elements that can be implemented within it. Similarly, web content is accessible almost everywhere and, when a connection can be established, is accessible at all hours of the day and all days of the year.

You probably need no convincing of the advantages the Web offers in delivering a wide variety of information. However, a few cautionary notes (some rationalism, if you will) are in order as the web design craze and the mad rush of Flash development is occurring.

First, no matter what technology you choose for content delivery, you must always examine how frequently the information changes and how you plan to manage to keep up with it. Whether one medium or the other is most appropriate for the information depends on how fluid the information is. A key to attracting and keeping users is ensuring that information is fresh. Concerning the stability of information, too often people believe that one technology or the other (such as print, Web, or CD-ROM) is the answer for everything. "Just put it on the Web" is the cry that is heard. But rationally you have to consider whether you are just posting information to be posting information.

In addition, when and where information may be needed is also important. There are times when CD-ROM media may be advantageous over web media, or vice versa. There are still computer users out there that are not connected to the Web. Furthermore, there may be times when traditional print-based publications are best for a particular situation. Always choose the technology based on the need and the given resource limitations. Keep a balance among time, task, and resources.

Finally, this book is indeed about Macromedia Flash and all of the wonderful things you can do with it. But do not put blinders on when it comes to development. Seldom will you develop web content in a vacuum, and seldom will a single technology meet every need out there. As a matter of fact, putting all of your development effort into a single piece of technology, no matter how good that technology is, can be detrimental in the long run.

Definitely Flash is a key technology on the Web today, but it should not be the only tool in your tool bag. To be able to keep up with the rate of change on the Web, you should be versed in many things and, moreover, should understand how to integrate technologies and push them to work together. The most successful web developers are not only masters of specific technologies but gurus of the means by which those technologies are integrated and used together.

## Disadvantages of Web Delivery

It would be wonderful if all of our creative endeavors were boundless, but as with every technology, there are limitations. When dealing with multimedia on the computer, half the battle is finding ways to overcome the technical hindrances imposed on our ideas.

With the Web, your primary limitation is bandwidth. Secondary limitations include proprietary technologies and plug-ins, browser inconsistencies, display differences, and author and content validity. Nonetheless, your biggest battle in designing for the Web is dealing with the limits imposed on what you can deliver through that narrow pipe leading to your audience. Indeed, connections are getting better, but there is still a proliferation of users accessing via slow connections, particularly when you look at a global audience.

You must design around the end user; that is, according to their limitations and their needs. In general, delivery of computer media is always limited by the weakest link, and thus you always design around the lowest common denominator. With so much information available on the Web, if users do not find what they are looking for in the first few minutes of the experience, they will go somewhere else. Therefore, any site that requires an eternity to download, has an endless introduction with no skip button, or sends the user on search forays will likely be avoided.

One of the characteristics of good web developers is that they determine (or have in mind) the lowest common technological denominator among the intended audience before they even touch a computer. A good web designer knows a lot more than what looks good. He or she also thinks logically about what can be delivered to that audience in a reasonable fashion.

Statistically speaking, in relation to a normal or bell curve, the people you should design around are the middle 68 percent of your users, as indicated in figure 1-7. They are generally more alike than they are different. You should not design for the upper 16 percent, because they are the advanced users and will more than likely exceed your expectations in hardware, software, and skills. If you design for them, you eliminate 84 percent of your audience from viewing your site.

For example, say you are designing an e-commerce site targeting middle-aged users. This audience probably consists largely of in-home users who are not likely to pay a lot for web connections (thus, modem users) and who probably do not have a lot of computer experience (the 68 percent).

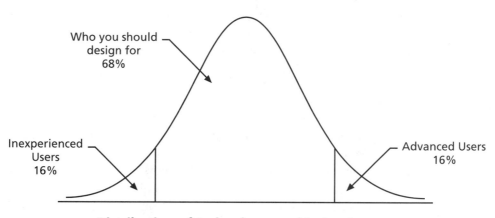

Who you should design for 68%

Inexperienced Users 16%

Advanced Users 16%

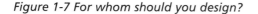

**Distribution of technology enabled web users**

*Figure 1-7 For whom should you design?*

A very small minority of them (the upper 16 percent) may be the exact opposite: fast connections and a lot of experience. If you design for the advanced users, you probably will not sell much, because you are ignoring the majority of users. You must design for the middle section of users, who are more alike than they are different. If you design for the middle 68 percent, you can be assured that in reality 84 percent (the middle and the upper range) of users will be able to access and use your site.

Now let's discuss the lower 16 percent. The lower 16 percent will always be behind the technology curve. They are the ones who may be using an archaic browser, may be afraid of downloading a plug-in due to "viruses," or for whatever reason cannot or will not make use of your site. Often regardless of the accommodations you make in your web sites, the lowest 16 percent of users will never have the technology or skills to view and use your site. You cannot please or accommodate everyone. The best web sites will be able to satisfy and accommodate the 84 percent. Prior to starting a site design, always try to establish what the majority of your users will have and will be able to view.

## *The Nuts and Bolts of Connections and Speeds*

High-quality audio, video, animation, and graphics typically require much bandwidth to download, display, and play back effectively. But in reality, anything you intend to push over the Web requires some knowledge of file sizes, connections, and speeds to design those assets effectively.

For example, a single high-resolution raster graphic at 640 x 480 pixels can require up to a 900-kilobyte-per-second data rate to be delivered without any noticeable lapse of download time. One minute of acceptable-quality, compressed audio (22.05 kHz, 8-bit, monaural) can require download speeds of up to 1.3 megabytes per second, whereas 15 seconds of compressed video (with audio) at 160 x 120 pixels requires 900 kilobytes per second. The higher the quality of media element, the longer it takes to download or view from the Web. File weight (size) is directly proportional to user wait.

Table 1-1 shows the common connection speeds for end users, as well as how long it takes to download 100 kilobytes of data. The importance of this table is that devices often claim a high connection rate or bandwidth when presented in marketing literature. Yet, actually the data rate is what is important. Similarly, if you are familiar with CD-ROM development, it is helpful to have a "feel" for the comparison of the speeds of CD-ROMs and network connections.

*Table 1-1 Web Connection Types and Rates*

| Connection | Data Rate | Bandwidth | Time per 100 KB (sec.) |
|---|---|---|---|
| 14.4 modem | 1.8 KB | 14.4 kb | 55 |
| 28.8 modem | 3.6 KB | 28.8 kb | 27 |
| 33.6 modem | 4.2 KB | 33.6 kb | 23 |
| 56K modem | 7 KB | 56 kb | 14 |
| ISDN | 7-16 KB | 56-128 kb | 14-6 |
| Frame relay | 7-64 KB | 56-512 kb | 14-1.5 |
| T1 | 32-193 KB | 256-1,544 kb | 3.1-.5 |
| 1X CD | 150 KB | 1.2 mb | .66 |
| DSL | 188 KB | 1.5 mb | .53 |
| Cable modems | 188 KB | 1.5 mb | .53 |
| 2X CD | 200 KB | 1.6 mb | .5 |
| 4X CD | 450 KB | 3.6 mb | .22 |
| 10X CD | 1.2 MB | 9.6 mb | .08 |
| Ethernet | 1.25 MB | 10 mb | .08 |
| 16X CD | 2.4 MB | 19.2 mb | .04 |
| 24X CD | 3.6 MB | 28.8 mb | .02 |
| T3 | 5.5 MB | 44 mb | .01 |
| USB | 12 MB | 96 mb | .0083 |
| Firewire | 100-400 MB | 800 mb-3.2 gb | .001-.00025 |

If you have done this type of work, you realize that even moderate multimedia sound and video capability requires speeds of 200 KBps or greater for adequate playback. Thus, devices appearing further up in the chart (see table 1-1) will provide unacceptable results, such as video that plays erratically or audio that inadvertently pauses. As it relates to Flash development, such connections require that you use preloaders in your movies so that those inadvertent pauses are not apparent (see Chapter 10).

 **TIP:** *You can easily calculate bandwidth from data rate, or vice versa. This allows you to determine how long it will take to download a certain amount of content over a particular connection. Given a bandwidth, divide by 8 to obtain the data rate. Then divide the file size by the data rate. Given a data rate, multiply by 8 to determine the bandwidth.*

It must be noted that the connection speeds shown in table 1-1 assume that a single user is connected to the data source. As more individuals attempt to access a site, the data rate is split across the number of multiple connections. This means that even though the user can download data at 188 KBps (assuming a 1.5-mbps connection) the server that is supplying the data may be serving 100 other users at the same time. This decreases the actual amount of data being served to each individual. In this instance, the server may become a "weak link" due to the number of connected users.

### *Overcoming Limitations*

When dealing with networking technologies, much development has taken place. Many companies are striving to create the solution to the bandwidth problem. Realize that the real solution to this problem is probably a combination of several methods, not just one. From a theoretical vantage, there are three ways to increase the speed of a network:

- Increase the number of physical cables or connections on the Internet so that there are more routes on which data may travel.

- Increase the quality of the physical cabling or connections on the Internet so that more data may be pushed through it.

- Decrease the file size of the data being transferred on the Internet.

Realize that development money is being spent in all three of these areas, because whoever creates the best solution has a tremendous opportunity. Many telecommunications companies are spending millions of dollars trying to increase the speed of their network through more cabling and higher-quality cabling. Yet, these first two methods for augmenting speed are the most expensive and the most time consuming. It can take massive amounts of effort and time to replace cabling, not to mention the cost of high-quality cables such as fiber optics. Additionally, increasing cabling throughout the Internet can be quite complex when you consider the various interconnections that must be made.

Therefore, many companies are focusing on finding new and ingenious ways for designers and developers to deliver high-quality media assets that have smaller file sizes. Finding ways of decreasing digital file sizes is much cheaper than other methods. This technique also distributes the cost of increasing network speed across a broader range of the population. Rather than a single company, such as MCI/WorldCom or another telecommunications company, having to replace thousands of miles of cabling, individual developers can reduce their content size and increase network speed at a much lower cost.

Technologies that are able to decrease file size while maintaining quality are a hot commodity. Additionally, technologies that can deliver more than just static graphics are vitally important to all content providers, not the least of which are publishers. Ultimately, publishers are in the process of evolving to use the new media available to them. Although none have stopped creating traditional texts, many are extending their repertoire of distribution means to include the Web and CD-ROM. However, the publishing arena is one that is familiar with ever-changing technologies.

## The Issue of Planning

Regardless of medium, the main purpose of any publication is to educate, entertain, inform, or persuade the audience. Being able to communicate in each of these areas requires knowledge of how to pull it off effectively. Most often, web designers are given content to put on the Web, making the task a little easier. Sometimes they need to develop the content or coordinate content development among a group of individuals. In either case, the main purpose behind providing content is to communicate.

As most developers know, rule number one in multimedia and hypermedia development is that content is king. Poorly designed content can never be masked. Slick graphics, dancing bullets, and animated elements cannot mask poor content. It is like dressing up the exterior or interior of a house with a cracked foundation with the intent of selling it. It will not sell because the footing on which everything else rests is unstable. The same is true of poor content. As the foundation from which communication occurs, all content is supported by elements that enhance and clarify.

By definition, for communication to occur, a sender must send a message, and a receiver must receive and comprehend the message. *Environmental "noise"* is an important factor that can impact the communication process. In web communication, noise is something with which we are most concerned. Noise is anything that disrupts communication by distracting the receiver and inhibiting reception of the message. Noise can result from the sender in the form of poor content. It can occur in the communication channel through a hefty page that takes an eternity to download. It can also develop on the receiver's end by incompatible client software.

We see a lot of noise on the Internet. Many people on the Web have things to say; however, due to noise, their message is not received. In the information age, we must understand that people are inundated with information. When a message is blocked or surrounded with noise, it may be misunderstood, misinterpreted, or ignored outright. For maximum impact, a site must communicate clearly, effectively, and precisely.

In reality, creating a product that communicates effectively (be it book, periodical, CD-ROM, or web site) requires the use of careful planning so that the product itself is successful. How well the message is conveyed to and received by the audience determines the success of a product. For the most part, creating a good web site can be summed up in one word: *planning*!

Most sites fail because issues that were not considered during conception arise. People instantly jump behind their computers and start pushing pixels and spewing code, inevitably creating, in most cases, horrid sites. Problems with browsers, platforms, fonts, and so on will snafu this quick method of creating a web site. There is no replacement for time spent planning a site.

 **TIP:** *One of the best tools for site planning is paper and pencil. Use thumbnails, flowcharts, and storyboards to help you define and refine your ideas.*

As you develop a site, you also must be concerned with providing good content, no matter what tools and technologies you use. You must also ascertain whether you can adequately provide what your audience wants. Plan and acquire the technologies necessary to be able to deliver what you are envisioning. Sometimes the obvious choice is the technology right in front of you!

## The Emergence of Vector Graphics

One of the most revolutionary inventions for graphics in the traditional publishing industry was the advent of vector-based illustrations. As many will attest, the same problems indicative of graphics on the Web have plagued desktop publishers for many years. It is common for high-resolution raster images to bring computers, networks, and printers to a slow crawl because of the amount of data they contain. Even with some of the best compression techniques, pixel-by-pixel image definitions still require a vast amount of data for high-quality output on any device, not just over the Web.

This was the purpose for vector graphics. Vector graphics emerged as a "new" way of creating graphics consisting of small, mathematically based objects. Because vector drawings consisted of objects instead of pixels, high-resolution printing capability was available without the severe overhead of bulky raster file sizes. Vector elements such as points, lines, arcs, and polygons were defined using a language called PostScript. Instead of defining a line as a series of colored picture elements, or pixels (raster), PostScript could be used to define a line as two connected points in 2D Cartesian space.

The interconnected line could have any number of attributes, such as thickness, style, or color. This resulted in a tremendous difference in file size. The vector line would only require about 5 K to define the two points, whereas raster would require 20 or 30 K to define the same line represented by 25 or 30 pixels. In the end, the comparison of files showed that vector was more flexible and typically required one-quarter the storage space of a comparable raster image.

In addition to minute sizes, vector files provide an illustration form with a resolution that can be easily adjusted based on the output device. Consequently, adjusting vector graphic resolution results in no change in file size, which is a definite difference from a world used to dealing with raster images. Based on this attribute, PostScript or vector graphics are called device independent. Their resolution can be changed to match any output device.

## Vector, for the Display?

Although vector graphics have been widely used for print-based media for many years, it was not extensively used on the Web until recently. Vector drawings were never designed for 72-dpi display media, such as that used for multimedia or hypermedia. Therefore, when displayed on a monitor, most vector graphics look very poor. Aliased edges, as shown in figure 1-8, typically negate any other advantages to using them in display media.

However, PostScript illustrations can now be as much at home on the Web as anywhere

*Figure 1-8 Aliased edges typify vector drawings displayed on the screen.*

*Figure 1-9 Scaleable images, small file sizes, and superb quality are attributes of vector graphics for the Web (*http://www.disney.com/*).*

else, due to the inclusion of automatic anti-aliasing in Flash. The added benefits of scaleable images, small file sizes, interactivity, and a range of other features are causing an explosion of vector graphics use on the Web, as indicated in figure 1-9. Flash has been the driving force behind the emergence of vector graphics on the Web, with more than 274 million users worldwide to the date of this writing. You can check the current statistics at *http://www.macromedia.com/software/player_census/contents.html.*

Although Flash is one of the main vehicles of delivering vector graphics today, there are several formats that are being proposed as a standard format for web graphics. These include WebCGM, Scalable Vector Graphics (SVG), and Vector Markup Language (VML). Which format will emerge as the standard remains to be seen.

WebCGM is an ISO standard metafile format. Metafile simply means that the format can store raster data, vector data, or both. CGM files are a common file format used for technical illustration and technical documentation. In Chapter 11, CGM format is used to extract vector data from Pro/ENGINEER for use in Flash. Although WebCGM has potential, there are currently no browsers or authoring environments that support it. For more information on WebCGM, visit *http://www.w3.org/TR/REC-Web CGM/.*

The SVG format is a specification being developed by a World Wide Web Consortium (W3C) working group composed of a variety of leading companies, including Microsoft, Adobe, and Macromedia. SVG is slated to be a modular XML tag set for vector graphics in ASCII-based text format that will provide detailed descriptions of vector graphics so that they can be viewed by a variety of applications. Look for the SVG format to emerge over the coming months. Currently, there are no indications that browsers are preparing for SVG support. Similarly, it appears that SVG is more of a competitor to Adobe's PDF format than Flash SWF. Nonetheless, for more information on the SVG format, visit *http://www.w3.org/TR/WD-SVG.*

The VML format is an XML-based format for vector graphics developed by Microsoft. It is currently supported by Microsoft Internet Explorer

5 and higher, but is ignored by other browsers. For more information, examine *http://msdn.microsoft.com/standards/vml/*.

## The De Facto Standard for Web-based Vector Graphics

Formerly called FutureSplash Animator, Macromedia Flash is a full-featured package that allows a variety of element creations. From still images and animated segments to buttons and full-blown scripting, Flash can be used to create objects that were once typically integrated as raster images.

# A Brief History of Flash

Just for a record of the real history of Flash, the source code for Macromedia Flash was actually created by a small company called FutureWave Software, Inc., in 1996. Based on a vector illustration product called SmartSketch that they had developed, FutureWave demonstrated its new FutureSplash Animator 1.0 product at the January 1997 Macworld Expo in a small booth at San Francisco's Moscone Center.

Soon after, FutureWave, SmartSketch, and FutureSplash Animator all disappeared, or so it seemed. Macromedia purchased FutureSplash and renamed it Flash. SmartSketch was sold to Broderbund Software, who has incorporated its features into some of their PrintShop range of products. Although such buyouts frequently spell doom for small inventive products, Macromedia's purchase of FutureSplash Animator and the marketing that has been devoted to it is one of the main reasons it has had such an impact on the Web.

Ease of transporting files from one program to another is a typical question when working with graphics packages. Exporting vector illustrations into Flash is a one-step process, because a variety of file formats can be imported into the program. This is a significant benefit to designers, publishers, authors, and educators, regardless of content specialization.

Porting vector images into Flash and adding animation or sound effects can be done quite effortlessly. With the new integration of a special FreeHand import feature, relative to FreeHand 9 files, importing vector drawings are much better in the latest version of Flash. Similarly, Flash 5 now supports the import of PNG files directly from Fireworks, with preservation of Fireworks objects.

Flash's newer features also include Bezier tools, MP3 import, draggable guides, customizable shortcut keys, shared libraries, Web-native printing, the Movie Explorer, ActionScript development tools, and internal XML and HTML support. Throughout this book, you will see a great number of these features in use. First, however, an overview of Flash's base-level features seems appropriate.

## Anti-aliasing

Using Flash as an illustration tool has several significant advantages because of its vector nature. The first major advantage of Flash-based illustrations is the ability to display any range of elements with anti-aliased edges. Complex blends, minute details, 8-bit transparency, and animated objects are automatically anti-aliased at any size, as indicated in figure 1-10.

*Figure 1-10 Flash images can contain complex blends and fills that are anti-aliased for that "bitmap" look at any size (*http://www.matchlogic.com/*).*

Flash also includes a feature that allows the audience to easily zoom in and take a closer look at your illustrations, using the right mouse button. Because the drawing elements are vector based and resolution independent, they can remain anti-aliased and have that "bitmap" look at whatever size they are viewed. Additionally, you can turn off the automatic anti-aliasing for faster performance on slower machines. Flash 5 offers three settings for playback quality: low, medium, and high.

Another advantage of Flash movies is that any portion of a graphic can be included as a hyperlink to another site or page. Because an entire Flash illustration consists of vector objects, each object can be individually assigned to a particular URL without the use of external programming or code. All of the needed information is contained within the Flash image itself, rather than in the HTML file.

As a final note about Flash images, hardcopy printouts are "print quality." New functions in Flash 5 make printing easier than ever. Unlike raster images on the Web (which are usually 72 dpi), the print quality of a Flash image will equal the quality of the user's printer. No matter what the DPI capability of the printer, the Flash image will output at the current resolution of the printer.

You might ask why this is important. In the digital age, many of us dream of the paperless office. Even with a tool such as the Web, we still print out 90 percent of the information we want to keep, even if it will likely be accessible on the Web tomorrow. Using Flash images in your site will help ensure that your images print out with higher quality from the Web than raster images.

## Animation

The second major aspect of Flash, one that is most often highlighted, is the capability to create vector-based animations. Typically, animation on the Web is either based on GIF files, scripting languages such as JavaScript, or programming languages such as Java. However, Flash provides a completely vector-based environment for creating animations.

Most other methods are based on raster images, meaning that they take significantly longer to download, with no particular method available for overcoming the problem of file size. From full-screen to icon-sized animations, any dimensional size range can be included with web sites that use Flash. Yet, Flash also provides the ability to import raster images, bringing creation and development capabilities full circle.

**NOTE:** *Based on research performed by NPD, 97 percent of web browsers worldwide have the Flash Player installed, which translates to more than 274 million people that can view Flash immediately. The Flash Player is preinstalled on most computers, including those with Windows 95/98 and 2000, IE 4 and higher, Netscape 4.5 and higher, AOL 4.0 and higher, and Mac OS 8 and higher. For more information, visit* http://www.macromedia.com/software/flash/survey/whitepaper/.

## Interactivity

Probably the most exciting thing about Flash is that developers now have the ability to create true graphical user interfaces and interactive components on the Web. Often information is difficult to navigate due to a lack of a usable interface. Because every site is different, the user must learn to use and navigate each individual site that exists. User interfaces for sites do not negate the learning factor; they simply make learning to navigate a site easier.

Flash excels at being able to deliver rich graphics for realistic-looking user interfaces, as shown in figure 1-11 (see also color plate A-4). From buttons and slider bars to complex and original elements, authors can now create a unique experience

*Figure 1-11 Graphical user interfaces may be used on the Web, making navigation more intuitive and user friendly (*http://www.tech.purdue.edu/resources/map/mapv2/). See also color plate A-4.*

for the users of their site without the tremendous file size overhead typically associated with raster graphics. Internally, Flash offers two complex features, FlashScript and ActionScript. These can be used to create anything from very simple to complex interactive environments.

## Sound

One of the most intriguing things about Flash is its ability to integrate sound. For most sites that use audio, synchronization of the audio with the visual data is easier because the audio is contained inside the Flash file. Using the timeline in Flash, which works much like Director's timeline, the developer simply associates the sound with a particular object or frame. When the object or frame is encountered, the sound is played.

Sound files used within authored Flash movies are stored within the SWF file format. Inside the Flash file, sounds can be compressed with one of the newest (and hottest) technologies, MP3, as well as standard ADPCM compression. MP3 offers tremendous compressibility, making it possible to create long-playing animations with voice-overs or music with smaller files. Moreover, because the audio is stored inside the SWF file, there are no external references or additional HTML code needed. Flash 5 can import WAV, AIFF, AU, and MP3 files.

## Other Features in Flash 5

Aside from the main capabilities, Flash also allows several other capabilities. Throughout this book, you will be looking at all of these. Nevertheless, as a preview, realize that with Flash you have the tools to develop a variety of elements, such as the following:

- *Use an assortment of tools to create any range of drawings, from simple to complex.* If you have experience in other vector- or even raster-based tools, you will quickly be able to start drawing. Although Flash provides the typical vector Pen tool, where you can work with Bezier points, you will find that editing Flash vectors is much easier than other environments, because you are not limited to working with point-based vectors.

- *Create vector elements that have transparency.* One of the difficult aspects of most vector tools is that creating transparent objects, such as glass, is often challenging. With Flash's unique environment, you can specify any range of transparency, from 100 percent opaque to 100 percent transparent.

- *Easily create buttons and menus using Flash symbols.* One of the tricky elements on the Web is creating a realistic button. Often you must create two or three different raster images to represent the different operational states of each button. Then you have to tie it together with JavaScript or some other technology. With Flash, buttons and menus are created internally as a single file. Simply define your button states as a symbol. Then share those buttons among the various files that use them via a shared library. It really is that easy! If you are familiar with Flash 4, you will find that Flash 5's new Smart Clips feature makes creating complex interface components, such as drop-down menus, much easier.

- *Want to use editable text fields, but not sure of using HTML forms and the intricacies involved?* Flash allows you to create editable text fields within your movies. Data can then be gathered and used in client- or server-side scripting using the traditional POST or GET actions. In the past, form elements had to be separate from your Flash movies. With Flash, they can be directly integrated within your movies.

- *Create tweened animations for motion, shape blends, or opacity blends.* Do you want to create a circle that morphs to a square? Or an opaque object that vanishes into nothingness? Flash allows you to set up tweened animations with not only motion but all other attributes of objects.

- *Although vector is great, there may be times you need that photo-realistic image in your site.* Sure, you could place it directly into your HTML code, but you can also import it into Flash. Flash provides some handy tools for working with bitmaps, as well as nifty integration with tools such as FreeHand and Fireworks. You can combine both raster and vector objects into one Flash file and still benefit from compression and streaming.

- *Do you want to use a font but are not sure if the users will have it on their machine?* The common solution for using custom fonts on web pages is to create a bitmap and insert it into a page. But because bitmaps add to the amount of time it requires to download the page, an easier method is to let Flash do the work for you. Use any font you want in a Flash file, place it in your page, and it will come out right every time, regardless of browser or platform.

- *One of the most significant additions to Flash 4 was the ability to perform custom scripting.* Flash 5 is even better, with an expanded set of Actions, as well as ActionScript (very similar to JavaScript), a debugging tool, and an ActionScript editor. You can now create complex behaviors that were not possible in earlier versions of the product. It is truly one of the best enhancements to Flash 5. If you are a programmer, you will like this aspect of Flash 5.

- *Flash 5 adds a very significant component: the Movie Explorer.* One of the difficulties in Flash 4 was organizing and finding assets in a movie. The Movie Explorer allows you to sort and view hierarchical document structure to efficiently analyze and edit even the most complex projects.

In addition to these features, and the list could go on, Flash supports a wide variety of other helpful items, such as internal HTML and XML support, QuickTime 4 import/export, bandwidth profiling, standalone projectors, and other features discussed in later chapters.

## If You Can Dream It...

In the past, imagination was severely limited by raster file sizes. Now, almost anything you dream up can be integrated on the Web. Well, almost anything.

Throughout this book, you will take a look at a wide variety of samples, in addition to learning how Flash works. Along the way, you will discover that there are fewer creative limitations using Flash because you are using a vector-based tool.

## ▪ ▪ ▪ Example Flash Sites

Before continuing, take a break and examine some of the sites that are using Flash. Visiting these sites will provide a context for the exercises and examples you will be seeing later in this book. Before jumping to the sites found on the companion CD-ROM, ensure that you have the latest version of the plug-in from Macromedia's site:

*http://www.macromedia.com/shockwave/download/*

If you have purchased and installed Flash, the plug-in is probably already installed. You can find out by accessing Netscape's Help menu and selecting About Plug-ins. This will show the plug-ins currently installed for your browser. If you are using Internet Explorer and do not have the plug-in, when you access a page that contains a Flash element, Internet Explorer will automatically prompt you to download the needed plug-in.

 **CD-ROM NOTE:** *To sample the sites, access the* F5gai/chapter1/ *folder on the companion CD-ROM and open the file* sites.html *into your browser. Access the sites in the list to see that vast array of Flash implementations currently on the Web.*

# ▪ ▪ ▪ Flash and Other Software Programs

One of the most important aspects of any software application is integration with other programs. As you read earlier, Flash provides a number of import and export paths that allow you to use images and drawings from other programs in your Flash movies. Although this book focuses on Flash, it is imperative that other software programs are briefly acknowledged.

## Director and Authorware

Director and Authorware are two of Macromedia's other programs that can be used with Flash. Both software programs are aimed at creating interactive multimedia CD-ROMs. However, via Shockwave, both Director and Authorware movies can be "Shocked" and used on the Web.

 **NOTE:** *Realize that Shockwave is a general term used by Macromedia to denote movies that are web-ready. A Shockwave movie could be generated from Director, Authorware, or Flash. The program from which the movie is generated determines what can be done in it.*

Many differences exist between Director and Authorware. Director is a time-based authoring environment, whereas Authorware is an interaction-based program. Director was designed for complex multimedia products. Therefore, it excels at synchronizing graphical components with audio components. However, because of its scripting language Lingo, Director is not easy for a novice to use.

Alternatively, Authorware was designed with ease-of-use in mind. It was primarily designed so that educators could easily create education and training CD-ROMs without extensive knowledge of multimedia programming.

Nonetheless, both Director and Authorware movies can use Flash movies. If you create a Flash animation (or other component), you can import it into Director or Authorware for playback on a CD-ROM or on the Web (via Shockwave). For web authoring, the main component is Flash. Yet, if you need the additional capabilities that either Director or Authorware provides, you can import your Flash movies and use them with both programs.

Director 8.0 can currently import and use Flash 4 elements. With the release of version 5 of Flash, look for a Director Xtra in the near future that will import Flash 5 movies. Director 7 can only utilize Flash 4 movies. Similarly, Director 6.5 and earlier, as well as Authorware, can only use Flash elements. Flash provides the ability to save in various versions when you export the movie. However, saving in older Flash formats does limit some of the Flash capabilities you can use.

# FreeHand and Illustrator

Macromedia FreeHand and Adobe Illustrator are competing vector illustration packages. Both allow very complex vector illustrations to be created, and both are widely used in the publishing industry. Although they both provide the traditional Bezier controls, drawings created in either may be ported to Flash.

A new feature in Flash 5 is the ability to import FreeHand files directly into Flash. In version 4, you had to export out of FreeHand as an SWF and then open into Flash. When you import a FreeHand graphic, the file's layers, text blocks, library symbols, and pages are all maintained in Flash, making FreeHand an excellent choice to complement Flash development.

 **NOTE:** *Additionally, when importing FreeHand files into Flash you will find that arrowheads, line styles, PostScript fills, and other special items are now supported by version 5. See Chapter 3 for more information about importing and exporting files.*

Macromedia FreeHand can also directly export to the Flash SWF format. FreeHand is generally preferable over Illustrator because it has two very useful features for generating SWF files: vector transparency and Release to Layers. FreeHand's vector transparency is automatically transferred to the corresponding SWF file. Thus, what was transparent in FreeHand will also be transparent in Flash. FreeHand's Release to Layers Xtra lets you build animations from FreeHand blends quickly. Because Flash can import EPS (Encapsulated PostScript) files and Adobe Illustrator (AI) files, drawings created in Illustrator can also be imported, animated, and used within Flash.

# Photoshop and PhotoPaint

Although it is not necessary to have a raster imaging application to work with Flash, you can import raster images from almost any paint program. Adobe Photoshop and Corel PhotoPaint are two of the most common, but you could also use images from a shareware application such as LView Pro or PaintShop Pro. In Chapter 3, you will examine how raster images may be used within Flash. For now, realize that any paint program that can create standard file formats such as JPEG, TIF, or GIF can be used in conjunction with Flash.

# Flash and QuickTime 4.0

One of the significant additions to Flash 4 was the direct support of importing and exporting QuickTime 4. In release 4 of QuickTime, Apple licensed and integrated the Flash Player code into the QuickTime video format. This allows all of the benefits of Flash elements to be combined with the already existing benefits of QuickTime. QuickTime movies can now include Flash graphics, animation, and interactivity. Flash can be used to add custom navigational controls, text effects, animation, and titling to your digital video movies stored in the QuickTime format.

# Flash and Other Technologies

Although Flash is a fully featured, standalone program, it can also be used in conjunction with other technologies on the Web. The following sections focus on other emerging technologies. This is far from a comprehensive look at these technologies. In fact, entire volumes are devoted to explaining how to use them.

Nevertheless, descriptions of these technologies are provided here. Similarities or differences from Flash are also noted. You will find that because Flash can do so many things, it competes with many of these technologies in one way or another. However, in most instances, Flash can be used in conjunction with these technologies to create extremely complex sites.

## JavaScript, JScript, and VBScript

To add to the functionality available in the browser, several scripting languages have been developed by Microsoft and Netscape. JavaScript, JScript, and VBScript are all scripting languages that give added functionality to web pages. With these languages, you can control specific features of the browser and web page, such as the status line, browser windows, and even content within a page.

Netscape created JavaScript, whereas Microsoft created JScript and VBScript. Problems arise, however, because competing companies created these languages. Some features are not compatible across both major browsers. For example, some features of JavaScript will not work in Internet Explorer, and features of JScript and VBScript will not work in Netscape. In an effort to make life easier for developers, the World Wide Web Consortium (W3C) developed an underlying standard called ECMAScript, based on elements found in both manufacturers' technologies.

 **NOTE:** *One of the most difficult things about all these web technologies revolves around ensuring that they work in both the major browsers. Whenever you use JavaScript, JScript, or VBScript, you must test the pages in both browsers. Often you must test the pages in multiple versions as well. One of the most critical aspects of web development is testing, testing, testing.*

JavaScript and VBScript are vital to working with Flash components. In the latter chapters of this book, you will be learning how to combine Flash elements with JavaScript and VBScript to communicate from one Flash movie to another. Although this text is not a comprehensive volume on either of these scripting languages, you will at least learn the JavaScript and VBScript commands that work with Flash. If you have a further interest in JavaScript or VBScript, check out the following links:

- **For JavaScript:**

  ~ *http://www.serve.com/hotsyte/*

  ~ *http://javascript.internet.com/*

  ~ *http://www.javascripts.com/*

  ~ *http://www.jsworld.com/*

  ~ *http://webdeveloper.com/javascript/*

- **For VBScript:**

  ~ *http://msdn.microsoft.com/scripting/*

  ~ *http://builder.com/Programming/VBScript/*

  ~ *http://vbscript.superexpert.com/*

- **For Jscript:**

  ~ *http://msdn.microsoft.com/scripting/*

- **For ECMAScript:**

  ~ *http://www.ecma.ch/*

  ~ *http://webreview.com/wr/pub/98/09/11/feature/*

## Java and CGI

Java and CGI are advanced programming languages for the Web. They provide a variety of advanced functions from simple formatting of text via a form to complete application development.

Java is a language created by Sun that allows the developer to create a program that is platform independent. This means that a program can be written once and run anywhere. Java can be used to create entire applications, as well as serve as the operating system for servers. It is a very powerful language that has almost limitless application.

CGI, on the other hand, stands for Common Gateway Interface and is a method of providing communication (a gateway) between two dissimilar technologies. For example, a CGI script can be used to preprocess data coming from a form before it is sent on to an e-mail address or some other location. A CGI script can also be used to create a gateway between a database program and Java. CGI can be used for a variety of purposes and can be created in a variety of languages, such as C, C++, and PERL. Its main purpose is to provide a means of transferring data from one object to another, while allowing the data to be massaged along the way.

Realize that there is a significant difference between the scripting languages (JavaScript, VBScript, and JScript) and the programming languages (Java and CGI). Although someone with little programming experience could probably pick up and use the scripting languages quickly, the programming languages are much more involved and have a much higher learning curve. Java and CGI require prerequisite knowledge in other languages, such as C and C++. More information on Java and CGI can be found at the following sites:

- *http://dir.yahoo.com/Computers_and_Internet/Programming_ Languages/Java/*

- *http://dir.yahoo.com/Computers_and_Internet/Internet/World_ Wide_Web/CGI___Common_Gateway_Interface/*

## Dynamic HTML (DHTML)

Dynamic HTML (DHTML) was created by Netscape and Microsoft as a means of making web pages interactive and more responsive to the variety of end user display variables that may exist. For example, you can create pages that are more consistent across browsers and platforms. Additionally, you can include content that changes, depending on browser, location, and so on.

Both Netscape and Microsoft use a similar approach, but their implementations differ. Netscape's method offers a <LAYER> tag that is used in conjunction with JavaScript and Style Sheets. Microsoft uses VBScript and JScript (Microsoft's version of JavaScript) with Cascading Style Sheets and ActiveX. Both methods allow the user to add more interactive elements and control X, Y, and Z positioning of elements within the web page, which represents a definite advantage to the designer.

The important part is the Z axis (depth), which allows for layers within a browser, much like drawing, illustration, and page layout programs. Before DHTML, there were only two functional layers in the browser, the background of the body (<BODY background="mybkrd.gif">) and the layer, consisting of elements within the body.

DHTML is the web designer's dream, providing the ability to completely control positioning along three axes. In this aspect, DHTML is competition because Flash also provides the ability to create layered compositions. However, whereas Flash layers are contained within the Flash movie, DHTML creates the layers dynamically in the browser. For more information on DHTML, visit the following sites:

- *http://dynamicdrive.com/*
- *http://developer.netscape.com/tech/dynhtml/resources.html*
- *http://www.dhtmlzone.com/*
- *http://www.insideDHTML.com/*
- *http://www.webcoder.com/*

## Cascading Style Sheets

Cascading Style Sheets (CSS) are a means of creating a generalized description of formatting that can be applied on the fly to a series of web pages within a site. For example, if you have a series of pages that uses common elements, you could define a style sheet that contains the definitions for the consistent elements. The style sheet allows custom formatting and exact placement of web page items far beyond the limited means provided by HTML tables and frames.

Similar to the DHTML, CSS competes with Flash in that it allows direct and accurate page placement. Although it is beyond the scope of this book, Macromedia offers the same style sheet approach for Flash movies through a product called Generator. For more information on Cascading Style Sheets, visit the following sites:

- *http://www.w3.org/TR/REC-CSS2/*
- *http://builder.cnet.com/Authoring/CSS/*
- *http://www.microsoft.com/truetype/css/gallery/*
- *http://jaring.nmhu.edu/notes/cascade.htm*
- *http://www.webreview.com/universal/resources/CSS.htm*

## ActiveX and Active Server Pages

ActiveX uses system- or operating-system-level components to support the additional features required by the browser. Microsoft's original goal was to provide system-level components that could be installed with the OS, rather than always having to rely on plug-ins (which is what Netscape does).

Using system-level components allows other applications, not just browsers, to have access to the "plug-in" capabilities. For example, PowerPoint or Word could use Flash components via an ActiveX control. Internet Explorer (IE) exclusively uses ActiveX components. Instead of using plug-ins, IE uses ActiveX components to support Flash, Shockwave, digital video movies, and other extended features of web pages.

On the other hand, Active Server Pages (ASP) are an extension to Microsoft's HTTP server software, Microsoft Internet Information Server

(MIIS). ASP allows you to create a customized delivery of materials to the people that view your site. You can determine their browser, platform, connection speed, and a wealth of other variables, and then deliver appropriate information. ASP is often used to link databases defined in Access or SQL to web pages so that information is dynamically pulled from the database for page generation. For more information about Active Server Pages or ActiveX, check out the following sites:

- *http://www.aspsite.com/*
- *http://www.microsoft.com/*

## Summary

This chapter predominantly focused on the global issues surrounding Flash and web development in general. You have read about current design trends, as well as the primary uses and rules for graphics in web pages. You also examined the primary advantages and disadvantages of web delivery.

As noted, it is vital to understand the importance of vector graphics on the Web, and why Flash is having such an impact in the web community. In this chapter, you also read about Flash's main features, how it compares to other technologies, and how it can be used with other programs. Now that you have looked at these issues, in the remainder of this book you will get down to business and start designing and creating in Flash.

# Getting Familiar with Flash

### ▪ ▪ ▪ Introduction

Now that you have a little background, it is time to start working with Flash. Just like any application, it may take you some time to get used to the interface and the numerous ways you can perform many of the functions. As you read and work your way through the chapters, you will undoubtedly become very familiar with Flash.

Before you begin to work on a project, it is imperative that you are clear on what you want to do. It is surprising the number of people that sit in front of the computer and believe they will magically stumble into a masterpiece. This seldom happens. With any computer-based tool, it is important to know where you are going before you start doodling in the application. This is especially relevant when using authoring programs, because these programs can do so many things in so many ways. Absolutely, you must have a plan of attack.

This chapter begins by taking a cursory look at the various steps of the development cycle and what happens during each stage. No matter how small or large the site, always *at least* mentally note the various stages of site development. Due to the focus of this book, this chapter will review the major aspects within the development process.

This chapter concludes with a tour of Flash. When starting projects in Flash, several environmental variables may need to be modified. Additionally, it is important to have a strategy for developing Flash animations, as there are several modes of operation and ways of making files more efficient and effective.

# ■ ■ ■ Objectives

In this chapter, you will:

- Review the development process for creating interactive, dynamic sites
- Look at the browser and acknowledge its impact on your development of Flash movies and animations
- Observe the Flash interface and note the various tools with which you will work
- Learn to set up the Flash environment for starting movies and animations from scratch
- Examine Flash timelines
- Learn about tools within Flash that can make development of your screens easier
- Discover sources of help that are provided with the software and from other sources

# ■ ■ ■ Creating Dynamic Sites

An essential element in web presentations includes the ability to interact with the information. Dynamism causes throngs of people to hoard to the Web. Unlike a traditional document, a person using the Web can choose where he or she wants to go. Information no longer has to be digested in a linear fashion or in a method preconceived by the author.

One of the keys of effective interactive products and effective web sites is nonsequential design. By designing all pages nonlinearly (that is, with alternate paths that can be chosen), the end user is presented with a customizable environment. Even so, navigation through the content of a web site must be designed so that it occurs logically, clearly, and concisely. Present what the user needs when he or she needs it. The focus and pertinent information must be clearly evident or noticeable.

The biggest difficulty people have with developing interactive media is breaking out of linear thinking. We are so used to creating linear documents, such as brochures and books. As a result, it can sometimes be challenging to arrange information nonsequentially. Breaking this habit is the most difficult aspect of creating effective web sites.

The design of the information in your site is as important as the graphics and media elements you choose to place in them. Nonsequential thinking is required to produce tools that use any nonsequential schemata. Interactive design requires nonlinear thinking, as well as creativity and thinking outside the box.

Nonlinear structure permits a site to be user-centered, allowing the user to choose where he or she wants to go. This is why the interactive design and navigation is so important. You will find that many sites deemed exceptional exhibit interactive design that is logical and easy to navigate. A lot of this is a result of planning, creative thinking, and following a reproducible development process.

Just like the development of any other communication media, you can follow a defined process to create web documents that effectively communicate. Whenever a document, book, or other published product is created, the people involved painstakingly follow a well-defined process that is often refined along the way (and from project to project), with trial and error a component of that process.

When creating a document such as a brochure or flyer, the audience and message must be defined. Determine how best to fit and deliver the message to that audience, just as the material in a book centers on the needs of its audience.

Web-based delivery is no different from traditional publishing in this regard. However, with hypermedia you have many more options, many more elements, and often a wider audience. Adapting the wide variety of media elements (such as text, graphics, sound, and video) so that they effectively communicate can be very challenging. Yet, the entire process can be described as consisting of four basic steps: planning, design, development, and implementation, as shown in figure 2-1. Basing your production on these steps will help you communicate effectively through your site.

## Planning

The development of a web site begins with planning. In most instances, there are five aspects of a site you must define: content, audience, development system, delivery system, and functionality.

Content is king in multimedia development. Simply put, multimedia is all about communication. The success of a web site is based on how well the content and graphics communicate the intended message to the user.

There is a precarious balance between graphic quality and content quality. Even with great graphics, poor content can never be dressed up. Similarly, good content can never communicate as effectively with poor graphics. The first step in developing a good communication tool is analysis of the content and graphics you intend to provide and ensuring the quality of those elements for communication.

When examining content in regard to planning, keep the audience as your focus. All good web sites are audience centered. What does your audience expect to see at your site? What will attract them? What will repel

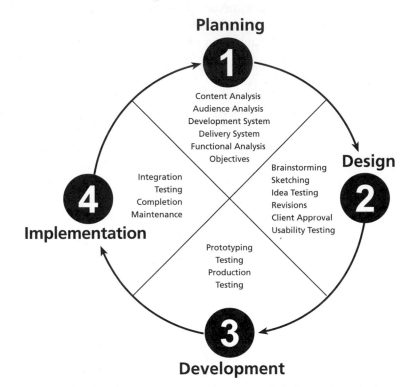

*Figure 2-1 The development process for successful, dynamic web sites.*

them? The point in identifying and analyzing the audience is to tailor the web site and its content to the audience's needs.

Beyond the content and the audience, consider also your resources, such as software, hardware, and personnel. This may include time and money as well. More and more corporations are creating web development groups, rather than having a single individual create the entire site. Typically these groups include individuals from several departments, who are often oblivious to collaborative resources. The primary aspects of concern for the development system are the applications, platform, tools, and other resources that may be used. Looking at these items in a group setting increases everyone's awareness of collaborative resources and makes for a more efficient and effective development process.

One of the wonders of the Web is its universal nature. Indeed, the audience is important, and you must consider what they will be looking for from your site. Nevertheless, another important aspect of the audience is the system from which they will view your site. This includes giving consideration to the hardware the user will be employing to access the Web. This is the most frequently overlooked part of the development process.

The main concerns in the delivery system include what type of network access the user has, what platform they are using, and the typical machine configuration they will be using. Additionally, concerns about accessibility of plug-ins and players must also be considered. You must keep in mind that they may be viewing through rose-colored glasses. Limitations on the user's end may prevent you from implementing certain technologies or require that you make allowances for other limitations.

After looking at the content, audience, development, and delivery variables, you should have a rather good grip on what your site is all about and what content it will probably contain. To finish your planning, you must examine the details surrounding implementation. Begin by making sketches of page layouts (which leads into the design phase) and flow-chart sketches of the overall layout.

You should also at this stage produce written documentation noting the specifics of the elements of the functional analysis previously described. This documentation will serve as a roadmap for where the site is headed. It will also help when making crucial design decisions. By planning, you will be able to truly design a site with most, if not all, of your variables identified. More often than not, unsuccessful attempts at web design are a result of poor or insufficient planning.

## Design

For many people, the design portion of the development process is one of the most difficult tasks. Coming up with new and refreshing ideas to attract your audience takes time. There are a wide variety of things you could and may want to do.

During the design process, several tasks will be completed; some concurrently, and others in series. As a continuation of the functional analysis, the design and layout of pages will be solidified and may even be implemented as a prototype. Understand that the initial design phase is often an experimental (trial-and-error) process. Several design iterations for a particular page or the entire site may be necessary. Throughout the design process, ideas will be generated, tested, and evaluated.

 **TIP:** *When working as a freelance designer, the design phase often requires that the client view many iterations of a site. Eventually, the client will choose one of the designs or a combination thereof for the site. Once this has occurred, it is a good idea to get the client to sign off on the design. This solidifies in writing that the client approves the design and wants to begin production.*

One of the serious aspects of multimedia and hypermedia design is called feature creep. Feature creep is a never-ending design cycle during which the client continually requests changes or additions to be made during production. Inevitably this stalls production, and increases rework and production time while reducing your profit margin. Having the client sign a written document stating that the design is approved will reduce feature creep, production time, and rework.

## Development

True production begins after much work and planning has taken place. It may seem like a lot of work up front, and it is. Successful sites do not just happen. A tremendous amount of planning is involved when creating any good communication medium. It is in the development phase that everything seems to come together. If you are working as a freelance web consultant or as part of a development group, it is at this point you will see most of the site materialize.

In the development phase, all pages are completed in terms of content and any other special features the web site includes, such as back-end programs, web databases, and Shocked components. The site is also extensively tested for errors during this phase, using an off-line or secondary server.

 **NOTE:** *Keep in mind that time spent planning is not wasted. The planning that goes into web site development is a long-term investment that will pay off once the site is completed. Jumping into development (which is where most of us want to start) is not a good idea. Successful sites are always the result of effective planning.*

## Implementation

Once the web site has been completed off-line, the last part of setting up the site is moving it to your web server. Working off-line provides a means of testing the site before making it live on the Web. Additionally, when you move the site to a live server, testing should occur a second time. It is absolutely vital that you do some type of testing. More than likely you will be checking for errors throughout the development and implementation phases. Testing should occur in all browsers (and versions of browsers) the target audience may use to view the site. Due to differences in browsers and browser versions, the only way to be sure the site will work is to test, test, and then test some more.

 **TIP:** *To ensure compatibility with various browsers and versions of browsers, you should try to test your site in as many browsers as possible. At the very least, testing should be done in a version of Netscape and a version of Internet Explorer (IE). It can be assumed that this covers about 75 to 85 percent of the browsers being used.*

Both IE and Netscape can be installed on a single computer. Additionally, multiple Netscape versions can run on a machine without a lot of difficulty. For example, the author uses six versions of Netscape for testing purposes, to ensure that pages will work on older versions.

However, installing multiple versions of IE is more difficult. Due to the way IE is integrated into the operating system, generally one version is all you can have on your computer. Nonetheless, at least test in one version of Netscape and one version of IE to ensure cross-browser compatibility.

# ▪ ▪ ▪ Acknowledging the Browser Variable

The Web we enjoy today is an idea that has been around for quite some time. Many individuals are credited with defining, refining, and enhancing the idea of a worldwide communication system, even though most of the general public has a perception that it is a "new thing."

Vannevar Bush first conceived two of the fundamental constructs of the Web shortly after World War II. Bush became the father of the terms *hypertext* and *hypermedia*. In the mid 1960s, Ted Nelson later refined the concepts in relation to a computer-based hypertext communication system that was platform independent, universal, and multiprotocol capable.

The year 1989 saw the first real definition of what we know as today's Web, via a proposal written by Timothy Berners-Lee concerning this type of communication in regard to general information about particle accelerators and experiments among the CERN organization. From there, additional contributors, such as Marc Andreessen (Mosaic for X Windows) and even publishers such as O'Reilly, helped foster the new fledgling technology called the Web. The commercialization that followed caused the Web and the web browser to evolve rapidly over time into a tool that can be used to browse masses of pages and a broad range of media elements.

While continuing to expand and enhance the capabilities of the web browser, we are constantly faced with the possibility of losing its universal nature. Anyone who has created pages and used any extension technology (from basic scripting to advanced technologies) has had to deal with the curse of the web browser. That is, compatibility is a primary issue when you start using anything more than basic HTML.

The differences among implementations of browsers and among browser versions are examined throughout this book. It is vital to understand that as the complexity of media elements and coding increases, it becomes increasingly more difficult to ensure compatibility. A certain amount of compatibility is lost to achieve greater extensibility. This is one major reason testing is critical. Compatibility is examined in this book in terms of its relationship to implementations of Flash. However, as you are developing, compatibility should always be a consideration in the back of your mind.

# The Grand Tour

If you are familiar with other Macromedia tools (particularly Director, or in some ways Dreamweaver), you may find Flash's interface somewhat recognizable. As a time-based program, Flash's interface is divided into several distinct areas that provide various capabilities. The Flash work area consists primarily of the toolbar, the timeline, the stage, and a variety of floating panels, as shown in figure 2-2. Also shown in figure 2-2 are the standard shortcut menu and the Launcher bar. The Launcher bar is new to Flash 5 and is similar in function to the item of the same name found in Dreamweaver.

## The Toolbar

The Flash 5 toolbar is divided into four sections: Tools, View, Colors, and Options, as shown in figure 2-3. The Tools section contains the tools used to draw and paint objects on the stage, as well as the tools for

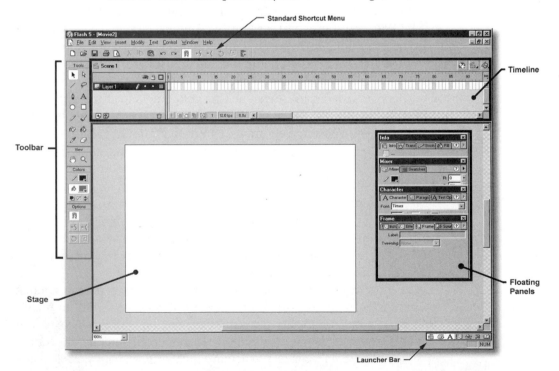

*Figure 2-2 The Flash interface includes the toolbar, timeline, stage, and floating panels.*

selecting objects or portions of objects to be modified. The View section provides access to the Hand (pan) and Zoom tools, and the Colors section provides access to current line and fill colors.

At the bottom of the toolbar is the Options section, which shows the optional settings for the current tool. These options, which were called modifiers in the previous version, allow you to choose the way a tool behaves. For example, select the Brush tool and settings relevant to it appear in this area, such as Brush Mode, Brush Size, Brush Shape, and Lock Fills, as shown in figure 2-3. Note that as different tools are selected, the options change. Only options that apply to the currently selected tool appear in this area.

 **NOTE:** *When working with tools in the next chapter, keep an eye on the available options, because they indicate the current settings for a particular tool, as well as what control you have over the tool.*

## The Timeline

The timeline is used to lay out animations and interactive elements over time. The timeline permits the creation of frame-by-frame animation (similar to traditional cel animation), as well as tweened animation. Tweened animations are created by defining keyframes that are the key positions, sizes, orientations, and colors of objects and then assigning those frames to what is termed a *motion tween*. The computer then automatically generates the in-between frames, called tweens. You can also create morph-type animation using *shape tweening*. Chapter 4 goes into more depth on the subject of creating both cel and tweened animation in Flash.

*Figure 2-3 The Flash 5 toolbar is divided into four sections: Tools, View, Colors, and Options.*

Before moving on, it should be noted that Flash's timeline allows the creation of layered drawings similar to vector and raster programs such as FreeHand or Photoshop. Much like other programs, Flash layers can be turned off (hidden), locked (so you do not accidentally change them), and rearranged. You will also find that you can set the elements on a layer to a specific color, to make it easier to distinguish which items are on which layers as you work.

The concept of layering is pretty common in graphic applications. Each layer is like an acetate sheet that contains nothing until you start drawing on it. Layers allow you to assign the elements in your drawing to logical groupings that permit you to structure the drawing for manipulation. Layers also provide the ability to animate several items at one time, even though they look like they are one "flat" composite. In the timeline, three major types of layers can be defined: drawing layers (called Normal), Guide layers, and Mask layers. You will read more about layers in Chapter 4. For now, realize that when it comes to animation, as well as movie organization, layers are vitally important.

**NOTE:** *As you start working with Flash and begin progressing through the exercises in the book, get into the habit of using layers and paying special attention to how they are used for organizational purposes in examples and exercises.*

## The Stage

Most often, Flash files are displayed in the browser. However, Flash also allows you to create projector files that can be played apart from the browser in a player. Nonetheless, the stage is the area that will appear in the browser or in the Flash Player. Although it is the timeline that defines sequencing and timing, the stage visually shows the position and orientation of those objects. It is similar to a theatrical performance, consisting of two elements: a script (the definition of things to take place in the movie) and a stage (where the action takes place). This analogy, used in Director, also applies to Flash.

For example, when authoring a movie, you choose a particular place you want something to occur in the movie, say frame 5. You set the timeline at that point and then place the items you want to appear at that point onto the stage. Thus, while authoring you concurrently use the stage and timeline, placing objects on the stage at various points in the timeline. In the next chapter, on drawing and adding elements to movies, you immediately start to see how this works.

**TIP:** *Flash supports many typical GUI capabilities. For example, you can "tear off" the toolbar, as well as the standard shortcut menu of icons at the top of the screen (see figure 2-2 for location), and place it wherever you want on your screen. You can also detach the timeline, which is particularly useful if you have a dual monitor system. When the timeline is in its default "docked" location, the separation border between the stage and the timeline can be sized by click-dragging it up or down so that more layers can be viewed in the timeline.*

## Floating Panels

The fourth part of the Flash work area is the various floating panels used to access and control a variety of things. The panels are arranged into logical sets of items that are generally used together. However, you can also change this arrangement. You access these panels in the Window menu, as well as the Window | Panels submenu.

The floating panels are in many ways a new feature of Flash 5 and are an evolution of the Inspector palette found in version 4. Many of the panels simply provide quicker access to controls, rather than having to go deep into a menu structure or having to select a tool in the toolbar.

The strange thing about the new panels is their arrangement in the Window menu, which at first glance may appear to be a hodgepodge. However, as you become more familiar with Flash 5 you will develop a sense of the logic of their arrangement. By default, four panel sets are automatically visible upon starting Flash:

- *Info, Transform, Stroke,* and *Fill:* This set of panels is used to work with objects on the Stage.

- *Mixer* and *Swatches:* Provides the ability to quickly access the color mixer and allows you to save swatches (pre-mixed colors).

- *Character, Paragraph,* and *Text Options:* These panels give you immediate access to settings for text objects.

**NOTE:** *These three panel sets are discussed in Chapter 3.*

- *Instance, Effect, Frame,* and *Sound:* These let you immediately access the properties of instances and frames, which you will learn about later. You will begin examining these panels in Chapters 4 and 5.

You do not necessarily need to accept the default arrangement of panels. You can customize the panel collections by dragging any individual panel to another set of panels. This is similar to the functionality found in other Macromedia tools, as well as other tools, such as Adobe Photoshop. You can also collapse the panels using the controls in the upper right corner of each set of panels.

Additionally, Flash 5 allows you to save your panel arrangements as well as their placement on screen. Notice the Window | Save Panel Arrangement option. By selecting this, you can name and save your panel arrangements however you choose. Once you name and save a panel, it will appear in the Window | Panel Sets submenu. If you wish to delete a panel set, access the *Flash 5/Panel Sets* folder on your hard drive and delete the name of the panel set you wish to delete. In addition to the panels displayed by default, you should also be aware of the other miscellaneous panels found in the Window | Panels menu:

- *Align panel:* Align allows you to quickly align or distribute objects on the stage.

- *Clip Parameters panel:* This provides access to information concerning smart clips, a new feature that allows you to more easily create complex interactive components such as drop-down menus and radio buttons.

- *Scene panel:* This panel allows you to manage the scenes in your movie.

 **NOTE:** *If you have the server product Macromedia Generator installed, you will also see a Generator panel option. This gives you access to information pertinent to items used with Generator objects.*

Continuing with the Window menu, note the Window | Toolbars submenu. It gives access to:

- *Main:* This turns the standard shortcut menu (figure 2-2) on and off.

- *Status:* This turns the status bar at the bottom of the screen on and off. The status bar will give you instructions when you roll over a tool or screen item.

- *Controller:* This feature works similar to digital video controllers, such as the QuickTime or Media Player controller, by providing a standard cassette tape or VCR-type controller for quick playback and rewinding of movies as you are authoring.

Also in the Window menu, notice the other two groups of commands directly beneath the "panels" section. These give you access to some very important items:

- *Movie Explorer:* Movie Explorer is one of the most useful additions to Flash 5 because it allows you to quickly view all elements in the movie, as well as perform a certain amount of editing on those elements. You will begin examining the Movie Explorer in Chapter 8, and continue to use it throughout the rest of the book.

- *(Object) Actions:* To have an object do something, you assign "actions" to it. The Actions panel is used to create, modify, and assign actions to objects. Chapter 6 explores the use of the Actions panel.

- *Debugger:* For both programmers and designers, one of the difficulties in authoring movies is ensuring that the movie plays properly. The Debugger provides the capability to analyze what is happening within a movie as it is playing and, as its name implies, helps you debug your movies. The Debugger is introduced in Chapter 13, and several subsequent chapters explore its use in detail.

- *Output:* This feature provides feedback about movies when they are compressed and prepared for integration into web pages. For more details regarding how this feature works, see Chapter 9.

- *Library:* Special Flash components called "symbols" (reusable components) are accessed through libraries. For specifics on creating, importing, and using symbols in libraries, as well as why they are important, see Chapter 5.

- *Common libraries:* You can create your own libraries, but Flash comes with several default libraries you can employ as you are learning to build movies. As you will see in Chapter 5, using symbols from these libraries is relatively easy, and you can eventually add your own libraries to this list if you want.

 **NOTE:** *For now, do not worry about remembering all of the panels and what each one does. All you need to know at this point is where the panels are accessed. Each of these panels is discussed in detail throughout the course of the book.*

# Setting Up Your Work Environment

As previously noted, Flash provides many options for customizing the work environment. Some of these options adjust the default settings for the application. Others modify default settings for the file on which you are currently working. The next couple of sections examine ways of customizing the work environment, including settings related to movie files.

## Preferences

Several of Flash's operating parameters can be customized using the Preferences option. Flash 5 now provides all environment settings in a single tabbed dialog box. In the prior version of Flash, the environment settings were found in two places, Preferences and the Assistant. Now, you will find all settings in the Preferences option in the Edit menu.

### General

The General tab of the Preferences dialog box, shown in figure 2-4, allows adjustments to be made to General environment variables, including:

- *Undo Levels:* This option specifies the number of consecutive Edit | Undo commands you can execute. The maximum is 300.

- *Printing Options:* This feature disables Postscript output when printing. Only select this when encountering problems printing Flash files. This option is only available in Windows.

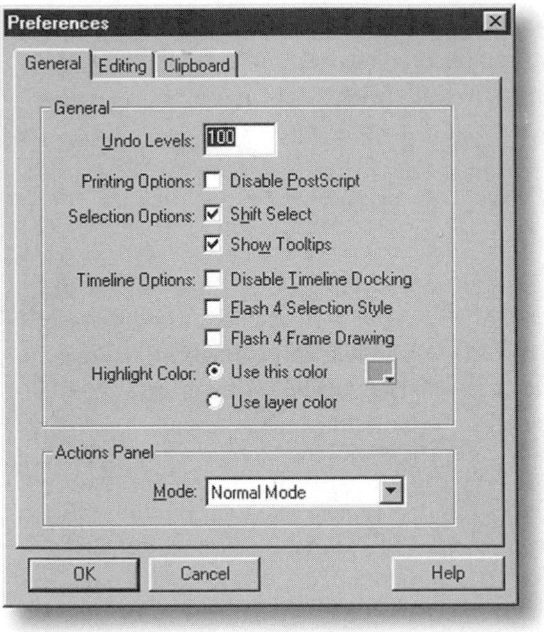

Figure 2-4 The Preferences dialog box allows you to customize general, editing, and clipboard settings.

- *Selection Options:* This area defines how multiple objects are selected. By default, this checkbox is selected, which means that you must press the Shift key to select multiple objects. If you prefer Flash 3's default method, in which clicking on multiple objects automatically adds them to a selection, deselect this option.

  ~ Tooltips can also be turned off in the Selection Options area. A Tooltip is the descriptor that appears when you hold the cursor over a tool or item in the work area.

- *Timeline Options:* This checkbox allows you to define whether the timeline can be "docked" above the stage area. When Timeline Docking is enabled (the checkbox is not checked), the timeline is inserted above the stage. The default is enabled docking.

~ If you are familiar with Flash 4, you will remember that selecting, moving, and copying frames was anything but easy (at least as you were learning). In Flash 5, Macromedia has made Flash's timeline more like Director in that when you select a keyframe, the keyframe and its copied frames behave as a single unit and are more easily selected. This means you do not have to click and drag across a bunch of frames to select a segment. If you choose, you can revert to Flash 4's method of frame selection by enabling the Flash 4 Selection Style.

~ Again, if you are familiar with version 4, you will recall that its timeline displays blank keyframes with a hollow circle. In Flash 5, blank keyframes are no longer identified this way. They are simply white frames with lines at their left edges. There are no hollow circles. Similarly, the last copied keyframe of an object in the timeline now displays with a small rectangle in it, denoting the "end of the sprite." This is an attempt to make Director's timeline and Flash's timeline more alike. However, if you prefer the Flash 4 method of frame identification, you can select the Flash 4 Frame Drawing option, which will make the version 5 timeline look like the version 4 timeline.

If you are a Flash 4 user migrating to version 5, it is recommended you resist the temptation of turning on the previous two Preference options. Realize that future versions of Flash will probably mimic Director even more than version 5. It would be better to get used to the "new timeline" now than to wait until Flash 6 and be forced to do so (these options may not be available in future versions). In addition, once you get used to this method of selection and frame identification, you will probably like it more and become even more productive.

- *Highlight Color:* This Preference option allows you to determine what color is used for highlighting. You may select a color or allow the layer color to be used.

- *Actions Panel:* When you are working with actions using the (Object) Actions panel, there are two modes of operation: Normal and Expert. This Preference option determines which is the default mode when the Actions panel is opened.

### Editing

The Editing tab, shown in figure 2-5, provides settings for the Pen tool, which is a new tool to Flash, as well as various drawing parameters, such as the following:

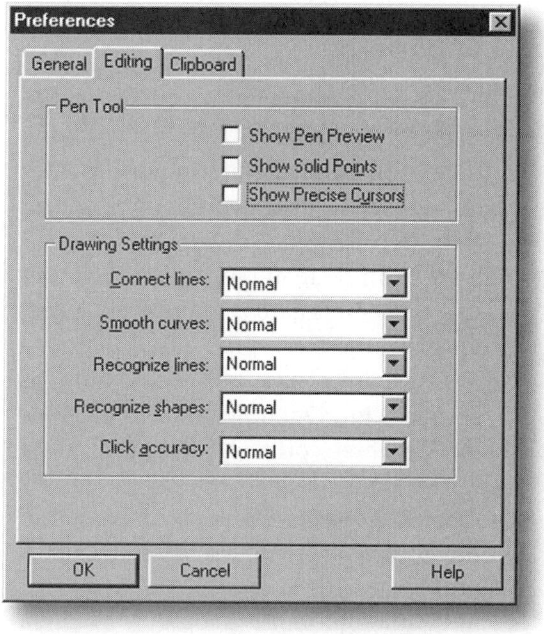

- *Show Pen Preview:* This allows you to preview line segments as you draw them. If you enable this feature, once you have selected the first point, Flash will display a preview of the line segment as you move the cursor around the screen.

- *Show Solid Points:* In reality, this setting determines whether Flash Bezier points work like FreeHand or like Illustrator. FreeHand displays deselected points as hollow, and selected points as solid. Illustrator is the opposite. If you are familiar with FreeHand, leave this option deselected. If you are familiar with Illustrator, you may want to select this option to make the environment more like what you are used to.

*Figure 2-5 The Editing tab allows you to establish defaults for the Pen tool and various drawing settings.*

- *Show Precise Cursors:* This setting changes the Pen tool cursor to an X, for precise drawing.

- *Connect Lines:* This option controls the distance required before a line or other entity snaps to a point.

- *Smooth Curves:* This specification determines the smoothing algorithm when using the smooth modifier associated with certain drawing tools.

- *Recognize Lines:* This feature sets the accuracy of line recognition.

- *Recognize Shapes:* This option controls the accuracy of shape recognition.

- *Click Accuracy:* This feature defines the accuracy of mouse movements and clicks.

Flash can automatically recognize certain shapes. In the next chapter, on drawing, you will understand how curve, line, and shape recognition works. It is pretty cool, but sometimes it can be detrimental. For example, when drawing certain shapes, Flash may try to automatically smooth or recognize the object when you do not want it to. When beginning to draw with Flash, remember that adjustments can be made to the smoothing and recognition functions via the Preferences option.

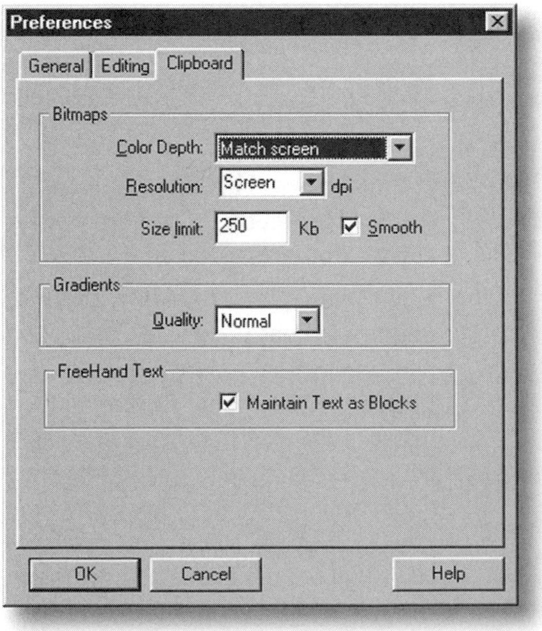

## Clipboard

Flash can include bitmaps either through the clipboard or by importing them. In comparison, importing files provides the user with more control. However, by using Preferences, adjustments can be made regarding the input of a pasted bitmap, as well as how vector elements are copied out of Flash.

As shown in figure 2-6, the Bitmaps section allows modifications to be made to the three primary attributes of a raster element from the clipboard. By default, pasted bitmaps are matched to the current screen color depth and current screen resolution (72 PPI).

Although most people work in a screen depth greater than 8-bit, if you do work at 8-bit, a pasted image will appear

*Figure 2-6 Adjustments can be made regarding the input of a pasted bitmap, as well as how vector elements are copied out of Flash using the Clipboard tab.*

grainy if the Color Depth option is set on Match Screen. In such a case, the Color Depth option should be changed to at least 16-bit (64 thousand colors) or 24-bit (16.7 million colors). Generally, the default settings in the Bitmap section should not need to be changed.

One caution, however, has to do with the Size Limit option. If you have difficulty pasting a bitmap from the clipboard, examine the Size Limit setting. If what you are pasting is greater than the size limit, it may look poor or not be pasted. The Size Limit setting may need to be increased. The Size Limit setting prevents the importing of images that are tremendously large, which, even in Flash, could be detrimental.

Ultimately, when adjusting settings in the Bitmaps section, you must find a balance between bit depth (color fidelity) and file size. The higher the bit depth, the larger the resulting Flash files. Most often, file size will be your biggest concern. Yet, there may be times when you will want to ensure a certain level of color depth.

 **TIP:** *For optimum file size, use few (if any) bitmaps. If you must use bitmaps, some trial and error may be needed to get an appropriate balance between file size and bit depth.*

The following are the remaining options within the Preferences window.

- *Gradients:* This area controls the quality of vector gradients copied from Flash for pasting into other programs.

- *FreeHand Text:* Controls how text blocks are pasted from FreeHand. If this option is not selected, text is pasted as vector outlines.

In addition to these options, the Macintosh version of Flash provides two other options for the user:

- *PICT Settings:* This option determines whether the clipboard is stored as vector or raster.

- *Gradients:* This feature controls the quality of PICT gradients stored on the clipboard.

## Keyboard Shortcuts

A new feature of Flash 5, which also exists in FreeHand, is the ability to create your own customized set of keyboard shortcuts for commands and features in Flash. By default, Flash uses its own built-in shortcuts. Yet, you can modify the existing shortcuts, save sets of shortcuts, rename and delete sets, or select pre-defined keyboard shortcuts for making Flash work like other applications, such as FreeHand, Fireworks, Illustrator, or Photoshop.

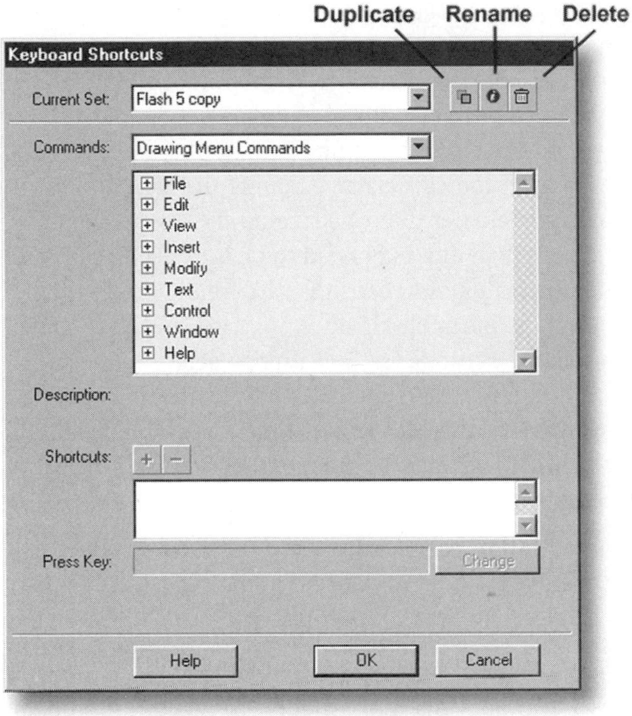

Duplicate   Rename   Delete

*Figure 2-7 Use the Keyboard Shortcuts dialog box to edit the keyboard shortcuts in Flash.*

To modify shortcuts, use the Edit | Keyboard Shortcuts option to open the dialog box shown in figure 2-7. Note that you cannot change the existing default shortcuts. To create your own set, you must first duplicate one of the existing sets and then modify the settings within the duplicated set. Once you have duplicated a set, select an item in the Commands section of the dialog, select the Press Key field, and press the keyboard combination you want for the item. The dialog box will indicate whether there are conflicting shortcuts. Use the Rename and Delete buttons to perform those actions on a shortcut set.

# ▪▪▪ Getting Started in Flash

As you have read, the timeline organizes and controls the placement and display of elements over time. You place elements on the stage and define when they appear within the timeline.

However, if you had to build every movie, regardless of length, using a single timeline, you would end up with very long timelines. Thus, Flash provides the ability to create multiple timelines, called *scenes*, to help you maintain shorter timelines. Before you look at scenes, realize that each timeline consists of three important parts: frames, layers, and the playhead.

## Parts of a Timeline

Frames or cels (in terms of traditional cel animation) are laid out along the timeline, corresponding to the times various objects appear on the stage. In animation, a frame is actually a single instance in time. The compilation of frames creates the animation when it is played. An exercise in working with a Flash file follows, but first read the following CD-ROM note.

**CD-ROM NOTE:** *You may choose to work from the CD-ROM or from the hard drive. It is recommended, however, that you install or copy the files to a hard drive or other writable media. As you get into the later chapters, having the files installed on a hard drive will make working with the files easier. One particular function in Flash, the Test Movie command, requires that Flash be able to write to the drive. If you work exclusively from the CD-ROM, the Test Movie option will not be able to function. The CD-ROM has a setup program you can use to install the files to your hard drive on a PC. On a Macintosh, simply copy the F5gai folder to a local drive. If you have not done so, it is recommended that you do so now.*

 ## CD-ROM Exercise

To begin working with a sample Flash file, open the file *ch02_01.fla* located in the *F5gai/chapter2/* folder, installed from the companion CD-ROM. As you read the following paragraphs, experiment with the sample file. To play the animation, use Control | Play or press the Enter key.

Figure 2-8 shows an example movie with several frames in the timeline. Note that the movie contains five layers. Each layer contains a different

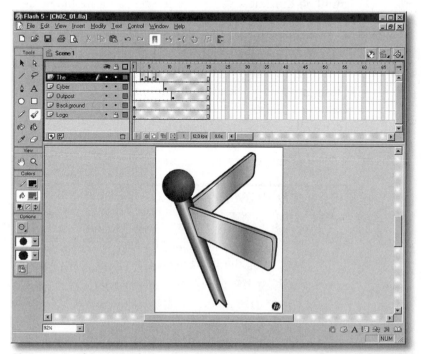

*Figure 2-8  The example is a movie that contains many frames and layers.*

component that appears on the stage over time. Think of a frame in a Flash movie as the smallest unit of time in the movie. Remember that layers are like acetate sheets that provide a means of organizing elements in your movie. The small red indicator (shown over frame 1 in figure 2-8) indicates the frame being viewed. You can move the playhead to a different frame by click-dragging the playhead or by simply clicking once in any frame in the timeline. As you do so, you see the "state" of the elements on the stage at the chosen instance in time.

## Multiple Timelines: Scenes

If frames could be placed only along a single timeline in Flash, it would be quite a limiting tool. Either the timeline would be very long or you would have to jump from one movie to another in order to create lengthy (or "long-playing") movies.

However, Flash allows the developer to work with multiple timelines within a single movie. This provides a means of organizing different scenes within a single, self-contained movie. It also helps keep timeline lengths manageable. Appropriately, each timeline in a movie is called a scene. Each scene may contain its own set of layers and objects.

As shown in figure 2-9, the name of the scene being viewed is displayed in the left of the Edit Path. Typically, when you design movies with multiple timelines, you will add scenes to the movie as you progress linearly through the development process. However, using the Scene panel, scenes can be created or added in any order, can have any name, and can even be rearranged after they are created.

Figure 2-9 also shows an example movie that contains multiple scenes. Flash provides quick access to the scenes stored in a movie using the Scene button in the right-hand side of the Edit Path. Clicking on this button reveals the scenes available in the movie. You can easily switch to any scene by clicking on its name in the list. Again, the current scene is indicated in the left of the Edit Path.

### CD-ROM Exercise

To see a sample movie that has multiple scenes, open the file *ch02-02.fla* located in the *F5gai/chapter2* folder, installed from the companion CD-ROM. To see (and hear) the movie play, use Control | Test Movie.

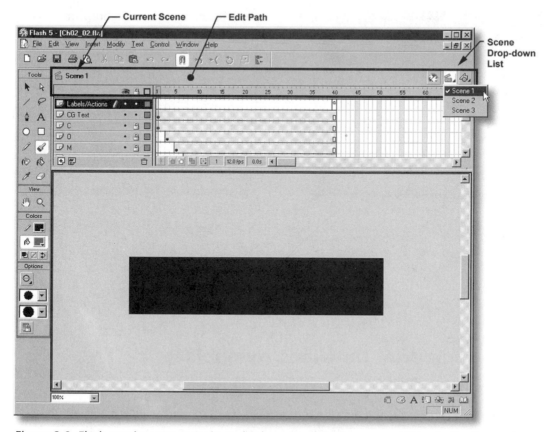

*Figure 2-9  Flash movies may contain multiple scenes, which are accessible via the Scene drop-down list in the right side of the Edit Path. The current scene is displayed in the left side of the Edit Path.*

**WARNING:** To be able to use Test Movie, the Flash file must reside on a writable drive. If you open the file directly from the companion CD-ROM and try to use Test Movie, you will receive an error message. Although you can save the files as needed to a hard drive and then use Test Movie, due to the proliferation of files you will be working on, it may be faster if you just install or copy the exercise files to your hard drive. See the *Read Me* file on the companion CD-ROM for more information.

When creating movies, scenes can be easily added and deleted using the Insert | Scene and Insert | Remove Scene menu options. When you add a scene to a movie, you will be prompted to name it. Scene names can be modified using the Modify | Scene menu option. You can also use the

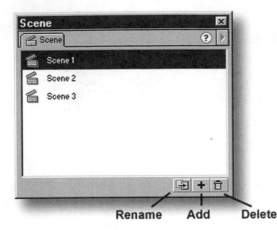

Rename        Add        Delete

*Figure 2-10 The Scene panel can be used to add, delete, rename, or duplicate a scene.*

Scene panel, shown in figure 2-10. It can be used to quickly add, delete, rename, or even duplicate a scene in the movie.

Scenes are a very good organizational tool. When viewing the sample files distributed with Flash, you will find that most, if not all, use scenes. You may be asking, "If I break up my movie into scenes, how do I get from one scene to another?" Chapter 6 explains how Flash allows you to easily (and automatically, if necessary) jump from one scene to another using actions.

**TIP:** *When planning movies, creation and organization will be much easier if the content is divided into chunks so that multiple scenes can be created. This helps keep the number of frames in a single timeline from becoming too lengthy.*

## Special Timelines: Symbols

In movies with multiple scenes, there may be a particular element (such as a logo or a graphical button) that will appear in more than one scene. As the developer, you may want to also use these repetitive elements in multiple frames within a single scene. If copies of a logo element were pasted on the stage in multiple locations within a movie, the file size would increase due to the repetitively defined elements. Symbols are the solution to this problem. With symbols, for example, you can define an object once and then reuse it throughout a movie, without any additional file size being added.

Flash allows special timelines to be defined within a movie that can be used numerous times without having to create multiple copies of the same object. They are called symbols, and are nothing more than special timelines within a movie. Just about anything can be a symbol. Yet, all Flash symbols fall into one of three categories: a *graphic,* a *button,* or an entire animated timeline, called a *movie clip.* Symbols are also generated when you import a bitmap graphic or sound clip.

You will learn more about symbols and how they can be used later in this book. Just realize that using symbols is vitally important. You can create movies much more efficiently by reducing the number of repetitive objects by defining, using, and reusing symbols. In addition, symbols offer other capabilities, which are examined more closely in Chapter 5.

Many of the sample movies included with Flash, as well as those included with this book, use symbols. Unlike prior versions of Flash, symbols are accessed using the Symbol List button located in the upper right of the timeline next to the Scene Drop-Down List button (figure 2-9). However, consider the following Tip.

 **TIP:** *Just as you can select a scene from the Scene List for viewing, you can access any user-generated symbol using the Symbol List button. To access all symbols in a movie, including bitmaps and sounds, use the Window | Library command. The Library is where all symbols are stored for easy access.*

# ⬛⬛⬛ Movie Properties

Just as Preferences allows you to set parameters for the Flash environment, the Movie Properties menu option allows modifications to be made to certain parameters of movie files themselves. If the Modify | Movie menu option is selected, the Movie Properties dialog box is presented, as shown in figure 2-11. Here, you can set several of the current movie's properties.

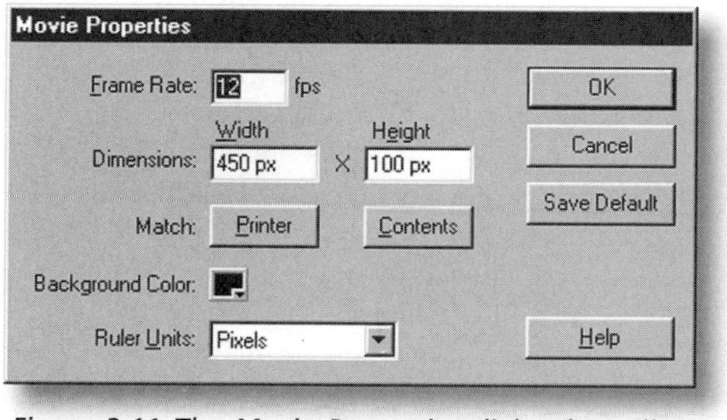

*Figure 2-11 The Movie Properties dialog box allows modifications to be made to certain parameters of movie files.*

The Movie Properties options include:

- *Frame Rate:* This feature controls the rate at which the movie plays. The frame rate is specified in frames per second (fps).

- *Dimensions:* This option defines the size of the stage. You may specify pixel or inch measurements, with sizes ranging from 18 x 18 to 2880 x 2880 pixels (or .25-inch x .25-inch to 40-inch x 40-inch).

- *Match:* This feature allows the stage dimensions to be automatically set to match the printer or the content of the stage.

- *Background Color:* This sets the color for the background of the stage.

 **TIP:** *The background color of the stage is one of the most important items in the Movie Properties dialog box. The background color of the stage may be set to any currently defined solid color. In order to define colors, you must use the Window | Colors dialog*

*box. Chapter 3 discusses how to define solid colors using the Color dialog box, as well as the Mixer panel.*

- *Ruler Units:* This option sets the default units used within your movie.

# ▪ ▪ ▪ Viewing Options

The viewing options within Flash are similar to other drawing and painting programs. Flash provides several optional elements that can make working with the stage and your objects easier, including the quality settings, interface components, and other miscellaneous view options.

## Quality

The first item for discussion is the quality settings found within the center portion of the View menu: Outlines, Fast, Anti-alias, and Anti-alias Text. The default setting for quality is Anti-alias.

Because Flash is a vector-based tool, you can interactively control the quality of the display as you work. The redraw speed can vary, depending on the quality setting in the View menu, in addition to the RAM and video RAM of the computer. The fastest redraw speed is provided via the Outline setting. This shows only the outlines of the vector elements in the movie, without fills or line styles, as shown in figure 2-12 (see also color plate A-5). This is similar to Keyline viewing mode in FreeHand. The Fast setting shows fills and text, but does not anti-alias anything. The Anti-alias and Anti-alias Text settings show all fills and line styles. The only difference is that Anti-alias Text also shows text on the stage as anti-aliased.

You may want to adjust the quality settings as you work. For example, to see if two lines intersect, set the quality to Outlines. Additionally, when drawings become quite complex, you may want to create your graphics in Fast or Anti-alias mode to speed up redraws. The quality set-

*Figure 2-12 The various View menu quality settings can be interactively controlled (see also color plate A-5).*

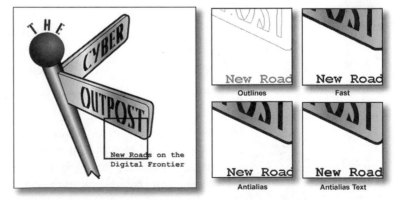

ting chosen will vary, depending on what you are trying to do, the speed of the computer, and the complexity of your drawing.

 **TIP:** *Both the quality setting within the authoring environment and the playback quality for web pages can be specified. This allows a significant amount of flexibility for individuals browsing the Web on slower computers or older browsers. In Chapter 9, you will take a closer look at adjusting the playback quality, using HTML attributes in the < EMBED > and < OBJECT > tags.*

## Interface Components

In many of the sample files that come with Flash, you will find that some are "missing" the timeline. Within the View menu, the timeline can be turned on or off using the Timeline option. For example, in the Lessons sample files (found under Help | Lessons), the timeline is turned off. To view how this or other movies are created, turn on the timeline to review how they were created. Additionally, the Work Area option will toggle the area around the stage on or off. If you draw off the edge of the stage, turning on the Work Area option will reveal the objects that fall off the stage.

Located in the Window menu is the Toolbar submenu and the Tools option. These settings control the default state of Flash as it starts. Use the options to configure what items you would like to see when you start Flash. For example, deselecting the Tools option will cause the toolbar to be turned off by default when a new file is started or opened.

## Miscellaneous View Options

Aside from the quality and interface component settings, the View menu includes several other options worth noting:

- *Goto:* This setting allows the user to quickly jump between scenes.
- *Zoom* and *Magnification:* These allow you to quickly zoom in and out. You can also use the Zoom control drop-down list at the bottom of the work area for this purpose.

For those migrating from Flash 4, note that the Show Frame option and the Show All option are buried in the Magnification submenu. The Show Frame feature sets the zoom level to display the boundaries of the current frame. The Show All setting zooms to reveal any and all objects, including those that may be in the work area (called the Paste Board in FreeHand and Illustrator).

- *Rulers:* This option displays rulers along the edges of the stage in the current units. Remember that the default units are set via the Modify | Movie Properties dialog box.

- *Grid:* This submenu provides access to Show Grid, which turns the stage grid on and off; Snap to Grid, which determines whether the selection and drawing tools snap to the grid; and Edit Grids, where you can modify all the properties of the grid, including spacing, color, and accuracy.

- *Guides:* Guides are a new feature in Flash 5. The Guides submenu provides access to Show Guides; Lock Guides, which prevents existing guides from being inadvertently moved; Snap to Guides; and Edit Guides, where you can modify all the properties of the guides, including color and accuracy.

- *Snap to Objects:* This option determines whether objects snap to other objects or the grid. Snap sensitivity is set in the Preferences dialog box.

- *Show Shape Hints:* Shape hints are used for shape tweening and allow you to control how one object morphs to another. Shape tweening is discussed in detail in Chapter 4.

- *Hide Edges:* The Hide Edges option allows you to edit objects without viewing their highlighting. This way, as you are editing, you can see how objects will appear in their final state. The closest analogy to this is Photoshop's capability of hiding selection edges.

- *Hide Panels:* Quickly hides any and all panels currently on the screen.

## Sources of Help and Assistance

Since Flash 4, developers have generated a tremendous number of sources of information, several of which you may find helpful in your quest. One word of caution, however: not all the sources that exist are necessarily accurate or easy to decipher. Before you look at other sources, first become familiar with the materials that come with the Flash software. The software installation CD-ROM is a good place to start, because not all of the materials on the CD-ROM are automatically installed. The CD-ROM is full of many sample movies and helpful bits of information. Additionally, the Help system installed with the software is a good reference when creating movies.

 **TIP:** *Because the Flash Help menu is HTML based, you may want to create bookmarks in your browser for quicker access. While in Flash, clicking on the options in the Help menu will automatically open the computer's default browser. Browser bookmarks tied to the help menus are particularly useful if you have several of the latest Macromedia products, such as Director, Authorware, or Dreamweaver. You can access any of the help menus without having the software open.*

**CD-ROM NOTE:** *The Web is home to many Flash-oriented development sites. Located in the* F5gai/chapter2/ *folder installed from the companion CD-ROM is a file named* developer.html. *Use this listing of references to examine the developer resources available.*

Two web sites you may wish to visit are the CGT Q&A Repository and the support site for this book. The Repository is found at the following address:

*http://www.tech.purdue.edu/cg/resources/q&a2/*

The support site for this book is found at the following address:

*http://www.tech.purdue.edu/textbooks/fgai2e/*

The CGT Q&A is a web site the author uses at Purdue University. Students post questions online, and the author, in return, answers them online. Although the site includes more than just information about Flash, you may find it useful while learning Flash. In addition, do not be afraid to post a question or two as they arise.

 **NOTE:** *The support site for the book will post miscellaneous items, additional resources, and book errata. You may also wish to contact the author at* jlmohler@tech.purdue.edu. *Although he may not be able to respond to every question or comment, he will try.*

# ■ ■ ■ **Summary**

This chapter examined in detail the hypermedia development process. The two most important aspects of developing successful sites are planning and testing. These cannot be ignored if you expect to develop a site that attracts your audience and successfully communicates your message. In addition, this chapter explained the Flash interface components and how movie timelines are constructed. Subsequent chapters will continue to focus on the various aspects of Flash and how to create stimulating content using it.

chapter

# 3

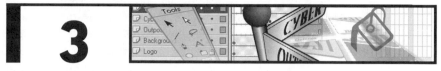

# Drawing and Painting Tools

## ▪ ▪ ▪ **Introduction**

If you have ever used vector-based tools to create illustrations, you will find that some of Flash's procedures for drawing are somewhat familiar. If you have extensive experience drawing in these programs, you may be able to quickly browse this chapter and proceed to Chapter 4.

Be forewarned, however: Even to an experienced illustrator, some the tools in Flash may seem peculiar or out of place. For example, why is a Paint Bucket, a Dropper, an Eraser, and a Lasso tool in a vector program? These are tools that typify raster programs, not vector programs. Even with some similarities, Flash is probably unlike any vector program you have worked with.

This chapter begins by looking at the primary differences between Flash and typical vector-based drawing programs, providing a foundation on which to build. It is hoped you have at least doodled in vector programs such as Macromedia FreeHand, Adobe Illustrator, CorelDraw, or Deneba Canvas. If you have not, you are still on level ground, as this chapter takes a ground-zero approach to Flash's drawing and painting tools.

Even with the addition of the Pen tool to Flash 5, you may find drawing in Flash difficult. Editing is easier, but starting from scratch with Flash's drawing tools may not provide the breadth of control available in other vector packages.

Although this chapter presents a bottom-up approach, realize that if you want to create complex drawings, or if you have extensive experience in FreeHand or Illustrator, you may find it easier to compose images in those packages. You can then import the images into Flash. The chosen method will depend on your experience but, ultimately, it may be faster (and more profitable) to construct in FreeHand or Illustrator and animate in Flash.

Directly following the comparison of Flash to other vector applications, this chapter examines Flash's tools one at a time. While learning tools and techniques, you will be working with, building upon, and creating a variety of illustrations. In several instances, you will be directed to use files from the companion CD-ROM. Open and work with these files while progressing through the chapter to see applied examples. As suggested in the previous chapter, you will find it easier to work with the exercise files if you install or copy them to your hard drive.

# ▪ ▪ ▪ **Objectives**

In this chapter, you will:

- Discover the primary differences between traditional vector illustration packages and Flash
- Examine the drawing tools Flash uses to create images
- Look at the drawing and painting tools and how they can be used to create fills, lines, and other entities
- Find out how to use the Text tool to add, manipulate, and modify text
- Learn to use selection and editing tools
- Understand and use concepts such as transformations, alignment, and grouping
- Find out more details about importing and exporting files
- Learn the various methods of saving Flash files

# ▪ ▪ ▪ **Traditional Vector Versus Flash**

Because many people involved in web development come from other publishing areas, particularly the desktop publishing arena, it seems appropriate to note the major differences between Flash and other vector programs. Although the following is not an exhaustive list (you may find other differences that are important or relevant), it is a good place to start. Some of these disparities include these features:

- In general, Flash does not require the use of control or Bezier points for drawing and editing. When beginning to create and edit objects in Flash, you will not find the control points that are characteristic with vector objects. Flash allows objects to be created and edited "naturally" without having to select points. In addition, Flash objects can be manipulated in whole or in part without "cutting" or knife tools. Yet, Flash 5 does provide one new tool, the Pen tool, which allows you to work with Bezier points if you like. So, although you are not forced to work with Bezier points, you can when you need added control over vector lines and arcs.

- Fills are not attached to objects such as polygons or lines. Instead, fills are created with a Paint Bucket, and line colors and styles are defined with the Ink Bottle. Fills become separate and distinct objects rather than being connected to a closed polygon. Accordingly, you can edit a fill object just like a line. To generate fills, polygons do not have to be closed.

- Nongrouped and nonsymbol elements overlaid on one another will delete other elements of dissimilar color or merge with elements of a similar color. This feature is akin to working on a single layer in a raster editor. Painting in one object deletes the previously existing object behind it.

- Flash offers shape recognition, which means that elements do not have to be drawn perfectly. With the Straighten and Smooth tools, you can quickly and easily turn wavy lines into straight lines, or a roughly drawn ellipse or rectangle into a perfect circle or square.

 **NOTE:** *At this point, the differences offered here are cursory descriptions. Applied examples of these statements are discussed in the sections that follow. It may be useful to review this section after reading the entire chapter.*

Flash is unusual in its hybrid nature. The following sections examine the tools available in Flash. Some resemble vector tools, and others perform more like raster tools. Regardless of similarity, all tools create, edit, or manipulate vector objects. In certain cases, they can also be used to "edit" bitmaps, as you will see.

## ▪ ▪ ▪ Zooming, Selections, and Transformations

When beginning to work in Flash, the first thing to examine is the toolbar. In Chapter 2, the toolbar was identified in the left-hand side of the screen. The options section changes when different tools are selected, and indeed some tools have no options. Figure 3-1 shows the toolbar with its various tools identified. The purpose and functionality of each tool is covered in the following sections.

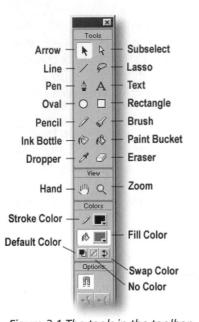

Figure 3-1 The tools in the toolbar can be relocated, detached from their default position on the left-hand side of the screen.

**TIP:** *If you forget what a tool icon represents, place your cursor over the icon for 1 to 2 seconds. The application will reveal a description. You can also look at the status line of the Flash interface (lower left-hand bar at the bottom of the screen) for details about what the tool does.*

In addition, each tool has a keyboard shortcut, which is also revealed by holding the cursor over a tool's icon. The tear-out card at the end of this book provides a quick reference for keyboard shortcuts.

Before continuing, open Flash. A new file will automatically load. Drag the cursor over the tools in the toolbar to view the context text that exhibits the name of the tool and its keyboard shortcut. Notice that the status line also describes what each tool does.

## Zooming and Panning

As a recap from Chapter 2, recall that the View menu provides a Magnification submenu that can be used for zooming. A zoom control drop-down is also located at the bottom of the work area. The toolbar also provides the Zoom tool, used to zoom in and out of a drawing. It also has the Pan button (the "hand" icon), which is used for panning.

If you click on the Zoom tool, the options section reveals the "zoom in" (plus sign) and "zoom out" (minus sign) buttons. To pan, click on the Pan button or hold down the spacebar and click-drag on the stage. Regardless of the tool selected, holding down the spacebar will provide the ability to pan the drawing area. Of course, you can also pan using the scrollbars at the side and bottom of the stage.

Even though the Zoom tool can be selected in the toolbar, it would be wise to get accustomed to using quick keys for magnifying in order to become faster at drawing in Flash. To zoom and pan without use of the Zoom tool, use the keyboard commands specified in table 3-1.

Table 3-1 PC and Macintosh Zooming and Panning Keyboard Commands

| Function | PC | Mac |
|---|---|---|
| Zoom In | Ctrl+spacebar | Command+spacebar |
| Zoom Out | Ctrl+Alt+spacebar | Command+Option+spacebar |
| Pan | Spacebar | Spacebar |

Note also the shortcut keys associated with the View menu's zoom settings. These keyboard shortcut commands are specified in table 3-2.

*Table 3-2 Shortcut Keyboard Commands for View Menu Zoom Settings*

| Command | PC | Mac |
|---------|------|-----------|
| 100% | Ctrl+1 | Command+1 |
| Show Frame | Ctrl+2 | Command+2 |
| Show All | Ctrl+3 | Command+3 |

Finally, observe the Zoom Control (drop-down menu) option below the stage scrollbar in the lower left. Here you can select a zoom level from the drop-down menu or enter your own numerical value. The following CD-ROM exercise provides you with an opportunity to practice using keyboard shortcuts for zooming.

 ### CD-ROM Exercise

To see how magnifying works, open the file *ch03_01*.fla located in the *F5gai/chapter3/* folder, installed from the companion CD-ROM. For the time being, ignore the content and practice zooming, using the keyboard shortcuts listed in tables 3-1 and 3-2.

## Working with the Arrow Tool

The Arrow tool provides several important capabilities. Clicking on the Arrow tool reveals the following options, as shown in figure 3-2:

- Snap to Objects (Magnet) controls whether or not objects snap to one another while drawing and editing.
- Smooth and Straighten control the shape-recognition features of elements.
- Rotate and Scale allow transformations to be performed on objects currently displayed on the stage.

### Moving Endpoints and Shaping Objects

Before examining the Arrow tool options and how they work, a review of how the Arrow tool is used to modify elements in drawings is in order. As mentioned at the beginning of this chapter, Flash does *not* force you to use control points for editing. It actually allows you to work with either points (using the Subselect tool) or natural drawing capabilities (using the

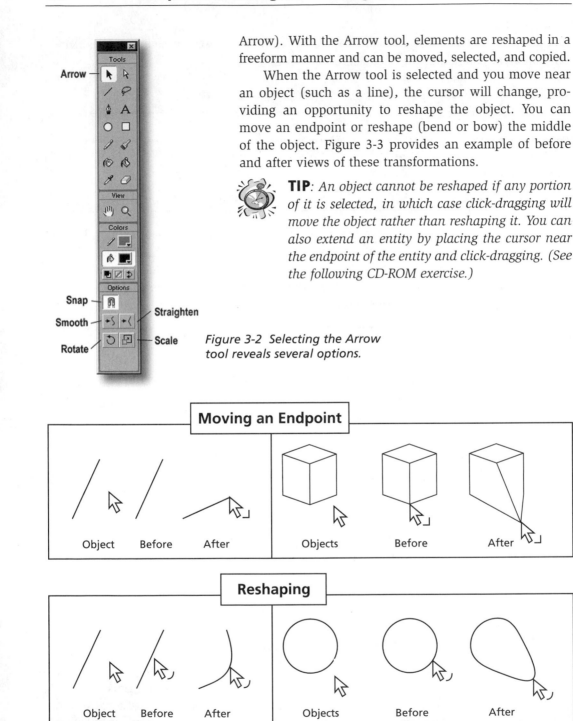

Arrow

Snap

Smooth — Straighten

Rotate — Scale

*Figure 3-2 Selecting the Arrow tool reveals several options.*

Arrow). With the Arrow tool, elements are reshaped in a freeform manner and can be moved, selected, and copied.

When the Arrow tool is selected and you move near an object (such as a line), the cursor will change, providing an opportunity to reshape the object. You can move an endpoint or reshape (bend or bow) the middle of the object. Figure 3-3 provides an example of before and after views of these transformations.

**TIP**: *An object cannot be reshaped if any portion of it is selected, in which case click-dragging will move the object rather than reshaping it. You can also extend an entity by placing the cursor near the endpoint of the entity and click-dragging. (See the following CD-ROM exercise.)*

## Moving an Endpoint

Object    Before    After         Objects    Before    After

## Reshaping

Object    Before    After         Objects    Before    After

*Figure 3-3 Reshaping objects using the Arrow tool makes element modification easier when accuracy is not that important.*

### CD-ROM Exercise

To see how reshaping functions work, open the file *ch03_01.fla* located in the *F5gai/chapter3/* folder, installed from the companion CD-ROM. Try the following:

- Move the endpoints of the line or curve.
- Bend the center of the line or curve.
- Stretch or modify the box and circle.

## Selections and Moving Objects

Aside from reshaping objects, you can also move all or part of an object to another location on the stage. This is another way in which Flash differs from traditional vector-based drawing. To move an object in Flash, it must first be selected before you can click-drag it to a new location.

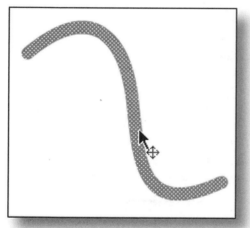

When selected, all objects in Flash can also be moved, or "nudged," using the arrow keys on the keyboard. Once an object is selected, pressing the arrow key moves the object a pixel at a time in the direction of the arrow. If you hold down on an arrow key, the object will scoot across the screen. Holding the Shift key down moves the object 8 pixels per key press.

When an object (or part of an object) is selected, a pattern is displayed over the object. This signifies that the object is selected. When the cursor is moved near a selected object, the move mode of the cursor is represented as an arrow, as shown in figure 3-4. (See the following CD-ROM exercise.)

*Figure 3-4 When moving objects using the Arrow tool, a pattern is displayed over the object.*

### CD-ROM Exercise

To see how moving objects with the Arrow tool works, open the file *ch03_02.fla* located in the *F5gai/chapter3/* folder, installed from the companion CD-ROM. Select and move the elements from the upper row to the lower row.

By default, to select multiple items on the stage you must hold the Shift key down, as in packages such as FreeHand or Illustrator. Yet, if you prefer the older method, where simply clicking on multiple objects selects them, you can use the Preferences to set up Flash 5 to work this way. Remember that this setting can be changed in the Edit | Preferences | General tab using the Selection Options. If the Shift Select checkbox is selected, it will make Flash's selection groups work more like FreeHand or Illustrator, in that the Shift key must be held down to add to a selection.

If you want to select everything on the current layer, use Select All (Ctrl + A on the PC or Command + A on the Mac). To deselect everything, press the Esc key or click on a blank spot on the stage.

As previously mentioned, one of the unusual things about Flash is that when filled objects are created, such as a square with a red fill, the fill is not attached to the lines. Additionally, line segments do not have to be joined to add a fill. To some extent, areas do not even have to be closed to fill them. Flash can automatically fill in gaps that are present. This is one significant difference between Flash and other illustration programs.

Fills are editable objects, just like the lines that surround them. Until you get used to this, it may seem odd and cause some frustration. It is important to note this distinction, particularly if you want to move both an object and its fill at the same time. Select the lines that bound the polygon, as well as the fill within the polygon, if you want to move them both.

At times, you may want to quickly select all line segments that constitute a polygon, instead of having to select each segment individually. To do this, such as with the four line segments that constitute a square, double click on any one of the line segments. All of the other line segments will be selected. If a set of segments has a fill, double clicking on the fill selects the fill and the line segments that surround it. (See the following CD-ROM exercise.)

---

## CD-ROM Exercise

To see how moving lines and fills works, open the file *ch03_03.fla* located in the *F5gai/chapter3/* folder, installed from the companion CD-ROM. Move the objects from the upper row to the lower row. By varying what is selected, you can move just the lines that form the polygon, just the fill, or both at the same time.

While working with selections when using the Arrow tool, be careful when holding down the Ctrl key as you drag a selected object. If you hold down the Ctrl key while dragging with the Arrow tool, a copy of the object will be created and moved, rather than the original object. When Flash is copying, the cursor will show a white plus sign as you drag an element. Those who are accustomed to using the Ctrl key in FreeHand or Illustrator (to quickly revert to the Arrow tool) may find this feature troublesome. However, it can be resolved by an immediate "undo."

### Understanding Grouping and Overlays

As you are beginning to see, Flash definitely has a different way of working. However, there are some functions, such as grouping, that should be familiar from other packages. Working with groups in Flash is just like working with them in FreeHand or Illustrator. Groups allow several objects to be selected, grouped, and transformed (moved, rotated, or scaled) as a single entity. At any point, the collection can be ungrouped to split it back into its component objects.

To group objects, select several objects and use the Modify | Group menu option (or Ctrl + G on the PC or Command + G on the Mac). To ungroup, use the Modify | Ungroup command (or Ctrl + Shift + G on the PC and Command + Shift + G on the Mac).

 **TIP:** *To select a group, simply click on it. To delete a group, select it and press the Delete key.*

Ungrouped objects in Flash have the peculiar nature of deleting or merging with other objects on the same layer when you overlap them. This is particularly true in terms of fills, as seen in figure 3-5 (see also plate A-6). When viewing figure 3-5 (a-1), note the two separate objects in the first cell. If the ungrouped object is moved over the top of the other ungrouped object and deselected, as in figure 3-5 (a-2), the forward object deletes the object behind it. When you move the object back to its original position, as shown in figure 3-5 (a-3), notice the "knockout" that is left in the background object.

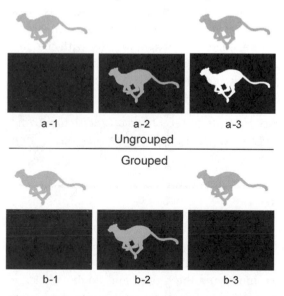

a-1   a-2   a-3
Ungrouped

Grouped

b-1   b-2   b-3

*Figure 3-5 The results of ungrouped (a) and grouped (b) objects moved over one another (see also color plate A-6).*

In the example displayed in figure 3-5 (a), the ungrouped objects are different colors. Thus, the shape of the upper object is knocked out of the lower object. If the objects were the same color, the two objects would meld or merge (a Boolean union) to create a single object. Think of the example shown in the progression of figure 3-5 (a) as a Boolean subtraction caused by the difference in color.

The deletion effect shown in series figure 3-5 (a) can be overcome through the use of groups. When objects are grouped, as shown in the progression in figure 3-5 (b), the knockout (or merging) effect does not occur.

**NOTE:** *One of the most difficult things to become accustomed to as you learn to draw and paint in Flash is its additive and subtractive property. However, it will help if you get into the habit of using groups as you acquaint yourself with the drawing editor. (See the following CD-ROM exercise.)*

### CD-ROM Exercise

Learn more about the additive and subtractive property by opening the file *ch03_04.fla* located in the *F5gai/chapter3/* folder, installed from the companion CD-ROM. Follow the instructions and move the objects to see the results.

As a final note on groups, it should be mentioned that the objects that constitute a group may be edited without continually grouping and ungrouping the objects. By double clicking on a group with the Arrow tool, all other objects in the drawing will dim slightly, leaving only items for the specified group 100-percent opaque. At this point, anything in the group can be edited. You can delete elements, add elements such as lines or fills, or rearrange elements that are part of the group. Once finished, double clicking again restores the stage to its original state, with the elements recomposed as a single, grouped element with the changes made. The CD-ROM exercise that follows provides practice in modifying elements within a group.

**NOTE:** *The double-click trick for groups only works with the Arrow tool. The Subselect tool cannot be used to double click on a group for editing.*

### CD-ROM Exercise

Practice modifying elements within a group. Open the file *ch03_05.fla* located in the *F5gai/chapter3/* folder, installed from the companion CD-ROM. Follow the instructions by double clicking on the group, modifying the group, and double clicking again.

When working with the drawing and painting tools later in this chapter, keep in mind that the Ink Bottle, Paint Bucket, Eraser, and Dropper (designed to modify existing elements on the stage), as well as the Subselect and Pen tools, will not work on grouped objects. For these tools to work, objects have to be ungrouped. The double-click trick that permits the modification of grouped objects becomes very important when you want to edit groups using these tools.

### Snap, Smooth, and Straighten

As previously mentioned, several options appear when the Arrow tool is selected. Three of these are Snap (Magnet), Smooth, and Straighten. The Snap option forces one object to snap to another. This is helpful when you are trying to get endpoints to line up or objects to snap to specific locations. By default, the Snap modifier is on.

Do not forget that the sensitivity of the snap function can be adjusted in the Edit | Preferences | Editing tab. Connect Lines and Click Accuracy affect the snap function.

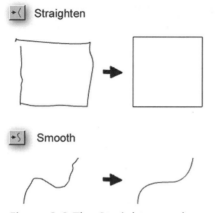

Unlike prior versions, Flash 5 will constrain lines to a horizontal, vertical, or 45-degree increment (independent of the Snap modifier), when the Shift key is pressed. If Shift is held down while drawing or moving objects, the objects will automatically constrain as you draw.

One of Flash's convenient features is its ability to dynamically smooth (simplify curves) and straighten (remove curves) common shapes. For instance, lines that are roughly square (but not perfect) can be corrected using the Straighten modifier to make them into a perfect square, as shown in figure 3-6. Similarly, objects that resemble other standard shapes can be straightened into common shapes or smoothed into more organic forms. For practice using the Smooth and Straighten modifiers, see the following CD-ROM exercise.

*Figure 3-6 The Straighten and Smooth options can be used to quickly adjust objects.*

### CD-ROM Exercise

View up close how the Smooth and Straighten modifiers work. Open the file *ch03_06.fla* located in the *F5gai/chapter3/* folder, installed from the companion CD-ROM. Follow the instructions to smooth and straighten the objects shown.

**NOTE:** *Flash's Smooth and Straighten functions are affected by the current zoom level. Thus, the extent of adjustment these commands make is dependent on the zoom level.*

### Rotate and Scale

The Rotate and Scale options allow you to transform individual objects and groups. When you click on the Scale option, handles appear at the edges and corners of the selected object, as shown in figure 3-7.

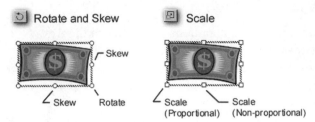

Rotate and Skew

Skew

Skew     Rotate

Scale

Scale
(Proportional)

Scale
(Non-proportional)

*Figure 3-7 The Scale option provides handles for proportional and disproportional scaling, whereas the Rotate option provides handles for rotating or skewing.*

Moving a corner handle scales the object proportionally, whereas moving a side handle scales the object disproportionally along a single axis.

Similarly, when you select the Rotate option, handles appear on the edges and corners of the object. However, with the Rotate option, corner handles are used for object rotation and side handles for skewing. The CD-ROM exercise that follows provides practice in scaling, rotating, and skewing objects.

### CD-ROM Exercise

To take a closer look at how the Scale and Rotate options work, open the file *ch03_07.fla* located in the *F5gai/chapter3/* folder, installed from the companion CD-ROM. Follow the instructions to scale, rotate, and skew the object shown.

## More Transformations

When examining the Flash drawing tools, a few notable items should be mentioned. Similar to other drawing programs, Flash's Modify | Transform menu options provide the ability to perform the previously discussed transformations, in addition to these functions:

- *Scale:* This option is the same as the Scale modifier.
- *Rotate:* This feature is identical to the Rotate modifier.
- *Scale and Rotate:* This command allows entry of numerical values for scaling and rotation.
- *Rotate 90° CW:* This item rotates the object 90 degrees clockwise.
- *Rotate 90° CCW:* This function automatically rotates the object 90 degrees counterclockwise.
- *Flip Vertical:* This mirrors the object across a horizontal axis.
- *Flip Horizontal:* This option mirrors the object across a vertical axis.

In Flash 5, you can also access information about an object or about transformations using the Info and Transform panels, respectively. Use the Window | Panels submenu to open these panels.

With the Info panel, shown in figure 3-8 (a), you can enter a new stage position for an object using a specific X-Y location, or a new size by entering a height or width. In the Transform panel, shown in figure 3-8 (b), you can numerically transform an object's scale, rotation, or skew by entering values in the fields and clicking on the Copy and Apply Transform button.

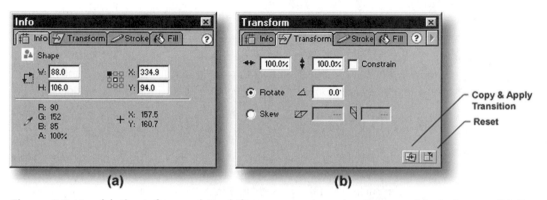

Figure 3-8 Use (a) the Info panel to define a new stage location or object size, or (b) the Transform panel to enter a numerical value for scaling, rotation, or skew.

### Arranging Groups

In the Modify menu, you should also note the Arrange submenu. Arranging allows you to change the Z-ordering of grouped objects in the current layer. Within a single layer, multiple groups can be overlaid on top of one another, similar to other drawing programs. Although the stage looks like a flat drawing, it is not. Some objects are closer to the screen, and others are farther away, as shown in figure 3-9. Using commands such

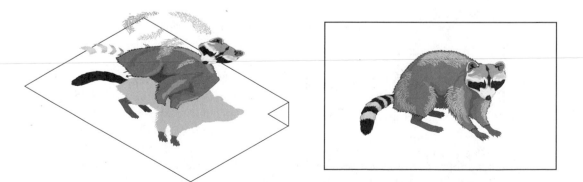

Figure 3-9 Objects are overlaid to create the appearance of a flat image.

as Move to Front and Move to Back allows you to selectively arrange your grouped objects so that they appear the way you want.

The Arrange commands will not work on ungrouped objects. Keep in mind the additive and subtractive nature of ungrouped objects, mentioned earlier in this chapter.

 **TIP:** *Use combinations of the Ctrl (Command), Shift, and Arrow keys to quickly perform the Arrange submenu commands.*

The Arrange submenu also provides a Lock and Unlock feature, which allows you to lock items at their current size and in their current position on the stage. Note that once an object is locked, it cannot be selected.

 **NOTE:** *If you do not have an object selected, the menu options in the Transform and Arrange submenus will be inactive.*

## Working with the Subselect Tool

A very helpful addition to Flash 5 is the Subselect tool. One of the existing features of Flash that has been nice for beginners, and yet one of its pitfalls, is the "natural drawing" tools. Flash 4 shielded the end user from having to deal with the typical control points of the vector environment.

Although it is nice to be able to use the Arrow tool for editing in a freeform manner (particularly for new users), many of us are used to dealing with Bezier curves and the control points that are typical of FreeHand, Illustrator, and other illustration tools. In fact, precise construction of vector drawings is very difficult when you cannot add points to a line and when you cannot adjust the control handles of a Bezier curve. Thus, Macromedia has now exposed the control points of Flash objects through the Subselect tool and the Pen tool. The following examines the Subselect tool.

When you select the Subselect tool, you will not find any options appearing in the toolbar. However, when you select on a vector element on the stage, the control points of the element will be revealed. When dealing with lines, control points will appear on the endpoints of lines, as shown in figure 3-10 (a). When you select a curve, the points appear. Selecting a point on a curve reveals curve handles, as shown in figure 3-10 (b). If you click-drag the curve handles, the curve will change. Note that deselected points are displayed as hollow squares, whereas selected points are shown as black squares.

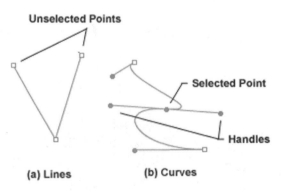

**Unselected Points**

**Selected Point**

**Handles**

**(a) Lines**

**(b) Curves**

*Figure 3-10 When you use the Subselect tool, (a) control points appear at the end of lines and (b) points and curve handles appear on arcs and circles (see also color plate A-7).*

When the control points of a line are revealed with the Subselect tool, you can move a point by click-dragging on it to select and move it, or you can move the entire line by clicking on the middle of it. When working with an arc or circle, the control points will appear with small balance handles attached to them. If you adjust the balance handles, the curve will change. Click-dragging a point will move it. When using Subselect, you can select on a point and press the Delete key to get rid of it. Similarly, you can hold down the Shift key and select multiple points along a line, arc, or circle to modify them all at once. However, there is one caveat.

The Subselect tool works nicely except that in most vector editors, you can select multiple points along a path and then click-drag them to move them all at once. In Flash, this does not appear to work without use of the keyboard. If you try to click-drag a set of selected points, only the current point will move.

The following CD-ROM exercise demonstrates this problem. With the cube that is to be "squished," you should be able to select all of the points at the top of the cube and then click-drag them down. If you try it, you will see that you can only click-drag a single point. To "squish" the cube, select all of the points and then use the arrow keys to nudge the set of points down.

### CD-ROM Exercise

Examine the new Subselect tool by opening the file *ch03_08.fla* located in the *F5gai/chapter3/* folder, installed from the companion CD-ROM. Follow the instructions to modify the objects.

The combination of the Arrow tool and Subselect tool in Flash provides complete control of your vector creations. Where accuracy is not a necessity, or where you need to perform general editing such as deleting line segments, use the Arrow tool. When you need complete control over an element, such as accurately controlling a Bezier curve, use the Subselect tool.

## Working with the Lasso Tool

As you look at selections and basic editing facilities, it is the Lasso tool that stands out as one of the more difficult, yet rewarding, of the advanced tools. The vector elements in Flash are editable in a manner similar to that associated with raster editors. When using the Lasso tool, this becomes quite evident. Figure 3-11 illustrates the challenge of removing an image for use in another file. Unfortunately, when the image is all on one layer and has no groups, there has been some "melding" and "subtracting," such as in the example in figure 3-5.

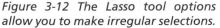 Lasso Tool

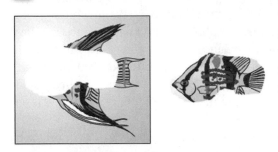

*Figure 3-11 The Lasso tool is ideal for correcting mistakes and making irregular selections.*

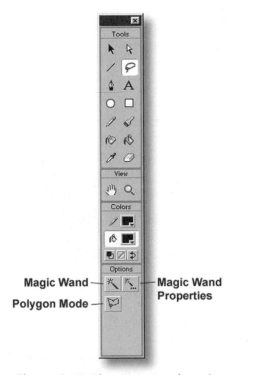

Magic Wand — Magic Wand Properties

Polygon Mode —

*Figure 3-12 The Lasso tool options allow you to make irregular selections.*

Removing an element in a flattened drawing is a perfect job for the Lasso tool. The Lasso assists most often in the process of correcting mistakes resulting from not using groups or layering. However, in some instances, the Lasso tool can also be used to make complex selections. The Lasso tool allows you to select an irregular area that can then be moved or copied to a new location or file.

The Lasso tool has several specialized options. Many of these operate in a manner similar to features in Adobe Photoshop. Figure 3-12 shows the Lasso tool options, which include the Magic Wand and Polygon Mode. When you are working with the Lasso tool, you can add a new area to an existing selection by holding down the Shift key. Unfortunately, subtractions cannot be made from an existing selection, as in Photoshop. Neither can you save selections.

When working from a bitmap, you can use the Magic Wand option to quickly select adjacent color areas. Use the Magic Wand properties to adjust the sensitivity of the Magic Wand. The Threshold option controls the number of adjacent colors included in the selection, and the Smoothing option controls the roughness of the generated selection.

The normal Lasso tool allows you to make a freeform selection, as shown in figure 3-13 (a). With Polygon Mode selected, the freeform selection is constrained to being made with straight lines, as shown in figure 3-13 (b).

As you are making selections with the Lasso tool, you can easily switch between Lasso modes (freeform versus polygon) using the Alt key. If you begin in freeform mode, pressing the Alt key activates polygon mode. Pressing Alt again reverts back to freeform mode. The functionality of the Lasso tool is comparable to the Lasso tool in Macromedia Fireworks.

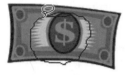 

     (a) Normal             (b) Polygon Mode

*Figure 3-13 The Polygon Mode option allows you to make freeform selections consisting of straight lines.*

You can also delete areas selected with the Lasso tool. Flash works unlike most vector drawing tools in this aspect. Try out this feature in the following CD-ROM exercise.

### CD-ROM Exercise

Get a close look at how the Lasso Tool works. Open the file *ch03_09.fla* located in the *F5gai/chapter3/* folder, installed from the companion CD-ROM. Follow the instructions to use the Lasso tool to select the fish and copy it to a new location or file.

# ∎∎∎ Painting, Drawing, and Editing Tools

To this point, the focus of this chapter has been on the methods of selecting and transforming objects that already exist on the stage. The drawing, painting, and editing tools add to the wealth of functionality available in Flash. Drawings can be quickly created using these tools, particularly with the addition of the Pen tool.

## Working with the Line Tool

Among the most basic of elements you will want to create are lines. However, if you are familiar with version 4, one of the first things you will notice is that the Line tool no longer has options (such as Stroke and Style) that appear at the bottom of the toolbar. These are now accessed through the Stroke panel, where you set the current color, style, and height of the line you are about to draw.

The current stroke attributes for all of the tools (including Line, Pencil, Oval, Rectangle, Ink Bottle, and the new Pen tool) are accessed through the Stroke panel, shown in figure 3-14. Use Window | Panels | Stroke to open the panel. The relocation of these stroke attributes is a somewhat significant change from version 4, and may take a little getting used to.

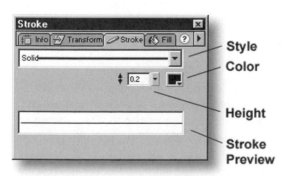

*Figure 3-14 Stroke attributes are now accessed via the Stroke panel.*

The CD-ROM exercise that follows provides practice that will help familiarize you with this new interface.

### CD-ROM Exercise

Open the file *ch03_10.fla* located in the *F5gai/chapter3/* folder, installed from the companion CD-ROM. Use the Stroke panel and Line tool to practice creating lines with various stroke styles, widths, and colors.

The Stroke panel will also allow you to create custom stroke styles, such as your own sizes for dashed lines, and so on. However, you should minimize the number of custom styles used, as they can increase file size when used in large quantities.

## Working with the Oval Tool

The Oval tool can be used to create filled or unfilled ellipses and circles. When you select the Oval tool, again the Stroke panel is used to set the stroke color, height, and style. In the same manner, the fill attributes for

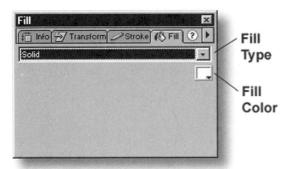

Figure 3-15 Fill attributes are now accessed in the Fill panel.

the Oval tool (as well as for the Rectangle, Brush, and Paint Bucket tools) are accessed through the Fill panel, shown in figure 3-15. You access the Fill panel via Window | Panels | Fill, which offers four types of fills: Solid, Linear Gradient, Radial Gradient, and Bitmap.

Figure 3-15 shows the panel with Solid as the selection for type. Depending on the type of fill you select, the lower part of the panel will change. The creation of custom colors (including gradients and bitmap fills) and the use of the Mixer and Swatches panels are covered later, in the section "Working with Colors."

 **TIP:** *If you want to draw a perfect circle with the Oval tool, hold down the Shift key as you draw.*

Although most of the attributes for Strokes and Fills are confined to the panels of the same name, you can still access and set stroke color and fill color in the toolbar using the Colors section of the toolbar, shown in figure 3-16. All other attributes associated with strokes and fills are now set in their respective panels.

Directly beneath the controls for Stroke and Fill color in the toolbar are three small but important buttons (figure 3-16). The leftmost button, Default

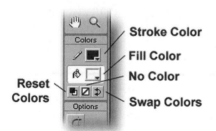

*Figure 3-16 Three small but very important buttons in the Colors section of the toolbar.*

Colors, resets the stroke and fill colors to their default (black and white), and the rightmost button, Swap Colors, switches the colors currently assigned to stroke and fill colors (similar to what you can do in Photoshop with the Foreground and Background colors). The middle button, No Color, is special.

When drawing items such as ovals and rectangles, it is important to note how you create an oval (or circle) with no fill and how you create an oval fill (or circle) with no line. The middle button, No Color, is important because it is what provides this capability. If you wish to create an oval with no fill, select the Oval tool, and then click on the Fill color in the Colors section. Click on the No Color button to set the fill to no color. Use a similar process for creating a fill with no line. The following CD-ROM exercise provides practice in creating different types of ovals.

## CD-ROM Exercise

Open the file *ch03_11.fla* located in the *F5gai/chapter3/* folder, installed from the companion CD-ROM. Use the Stroke panel and Line tool to practice creating ovals with various stroke styles, widths, and colors. Try creating at least one circle without a fill and one circle fill without a line.

## Working with the Rectangle Tool

As with the Oval tool, the attributes for the stroke and fill characteristics of the Rectangle tool are set in the Stroke and Fill panels. However, there is one exception: the Round Rectangle Radius option, which appears in the toolbar options when the Rectangle tool is selected. Figure 3-17 shows the location of this item. Clicking on the Round Rectangle Radius button accesses a dialog box in which you can enter a radius for the rectangle's corners. The CD-ROM exercise that follows provides practice in working with the Line, Oval, and Rectangle tools.

**Round Rectangle Radius**

*Figure 3-17 The Round Rectangle Radius button appears in the toolbar options when the Rectangle tool is selected.*

**TIP:** *As you are in the process of drawing a rectangle, you can adjust the rectangle's radius by pressing the up arrow or down arrow.*

 ### CD-ROM Exercise

Get a better idea of how the Line, Oval, and Rectangle tools work. Open the file *ch03_12.fla* located in the *F5gai/chapter3/* folder, installed from the companion CD-ROM. Follow the instructions to create the entities suggested.

 **TIP:** *If you want to draw a perfect square with the Rectangle tool, hold down the Shift key as you draw.*

## Working with the Pencil Tool

The Pencil tool allows you to draw freeform lines. Again, the Stroke attributes set in the Stroke panel apply to this tool. You will also note that

Figure 3-18 The Pencil Mode option appears when the Pencil tool is selected.

the Pencil Mode option of the Pencil tool appears in the toolbar options, as shown in figure 3-18. Use the Pencil Mode options to define the following types of lines:

- *Straighten:* This feature automatically forces the line you draw to be composed of straight-line segments.

- *Smooth:* This option will automatically simplify drawn segments, attempting to make a smooth arc.

- *Ink:* This selection leaves lines exactly as they are drawn. No smoothing or straightening occurs.

In Flash, you do not always have to be concerned with drawing exactly what you want the first time. The Smooth and Straighten modifiers associated with the Arrow tool can always be used to smooth or straighten a line. In addition, with the added control it provides, you may find the new Pen tool more advantageous when constructing line or arc segments. See "Working with the Pen Tool" later in this chapter for more information.

## Working with the Brush

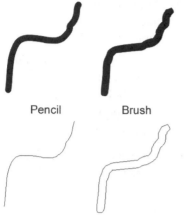

Pencil          Brush

*Figure 3-19 The difference between a Pencil and Brush object is revealed when viewed in Outline mode.*

Aside from drawing individual lines with the Pencil tool, the Brush tool can be used to draw wider strokes. Predominantly the Brush is used to fill enclosed areas with color by painting in the fill.

Although the visual difference between elements drawn with the Pencil and Brush may seem minute on screen, a more detailed look reveals why you might use one over the other. As shown in figure 3-19, a curve drawn with the Pencil and a curve drawn with the Brush are not alike. The biggest difference between these elements is that objects created with the Pencil are individual strokes with a thickness. Brush objects are really closed polygons, which can be seen when the viewing mode is changed to Outlines. The following CD-ROM exercise provides practice in working with the Pencil and Brush tools.

### CD-ROM Exercise

To learn more about the differences between the Pencil and Brush tools, open the file *ch03_13.fla* located in the *F5gai/chapter3/* folder, installed from the companion CD-ROM. Follow the instructions to manipulate the entities as suggested.

When you select the Brush tool, you will find that four items appear in the toolbar options, as shown in figure 3-20. These options are Brush Mode, Size, Shape, and Lock Fill, which are described in the sections that follow.

### Brush Modes

Similar to the Pencil modes, the Brush modes determine how paint is applied with the brush. You can apply paint in a "normal" manner, inside a fill, behind other objects, and so on. The options of Brush Mode are Paint Normal, Paint Fills, Paint Behind, Paint Selection, and Paint Inside. Figure 3-21 shows sample images of the three most commonly used Brush modes (see also color plate A-8). See the following CD-ROM exercise for greater familiarity with Brush Mode.

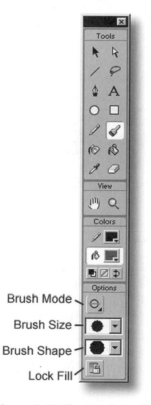

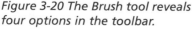

*Figure 3-20 The Brush tool reveals four options in the toolbar.*

Original

Paint Normal

Paint Fills

Paint Behind

*Figure 3-21 The Brush modes allow you to paint in a variety of ways (see also color plate A-8).*

The various Brush modes perform the following functions:

- Paint Normal draws on top of any existing lines or fills.

- Paint Fills affects only fills on the stage, leaving lines unchanged.

- Paint Behind renders behind any existing lines or fills.

- Paint Selection makes drawing occur within the selected fill only.

- Paint Inside paints only the fill area where you began the stroke. Paint Inside will not go over lines. If nothing exists where you start painting, nothing will be applied.

### CD-ROM Exercise

To better understand the Brush modes, open the file *ch03_14.fla* located in the *F5gai/chapter3/* folder, installed from the companion CD-ROM. Follow the instructions to paint in various modes.

### Locking Fills

The Lock Fills button in the toolbar options is a useful feature that locks the angle, size, and origin of the current gradient or fill. This button permits you to easily extend an existing fill into adjacent areas of the drawing. When using the Dropper tool (which allows you to pick up a line, fill, or gradient color), Lock Fill is automatically selected.

When using the various drawing and painting tools, you can always tell if Lock Fills is on by looking closely at the cursor. When this option is on, a small padlock is displayed as part of the cursor.

Eraser Mode — Faucet

Size & Shape

*Figure 3-22 The Eraser options provide a means of deleting all objects or selected objects in a drawing.*

*Figure 3-23 The Eraser modes control what is erased (see also color plate A-9).*

# Working with the Eraser

The Eraser tool in Flash provides a means of deleting all objects or selected objects from a drawing. The Eraser tool provides three options, as shown in figure 3-22. These modifiers are Eraser Mode, Eraser Shape, and Faucet. If you want to start your drawing over, double clicking on the Eraser tool will clear the entire canvas. If you accidentally erase your drawing, you can use Edit | Undo to restore it.

## *Eraser Modes and Shape*

As with previous tools, the Eraser Mode option provides settings that control what the Eraser will affect. You can perform a "normal" erase, as well as erase only specific elements. Figure 3-23 shows the results of the commonly used Eraser modes on an image (see also color plate A-9). The Eraser Shape modifier permits the size and shape of the Eraser to be changed.

The Eraser Mode options are the following. To experiment with the Eraser modes, see the following CD-ROM exercise.

• Erase Normal deletes both lines and fills.

• Erase Fills erases fills only.

• Erase Lines gets rid of lines only.

• Erase Selected Fills removes portions of a selected fill.

Original

Erase Normal

Erase Selected Fill

Erase Fills

- Erase Inside deletes inside an object. The inside is defined by where you start erasing within the bounds of the lines of a closed shape.

The eraser will only work on objects that are ungrouped. If an object is grouped, you can double click on it with the Arrow tool for editing, instead of using Modify | Ungroup. Once you have double clicked on it, you can then use the eraser. Double clicking again restores the group with the changes. To completely erase a grouped object, select it and press the Delete key.

### CD-ROM Exercise

To find out more about the Eraser modes, open the file *ch03_15.fla* located in the *F5gai/chapter3/* folder, installed from the companion CD-ROM. Follow the instructions to erase in various modes and see their effects.

### Faucet

The Faucet option allows you to quickly erase large areas of color within your drawings. For example, if you wanted to replace one of the large filled areas shown in figure 3-24, the Faucet option would be most effective. With the Faucet selected, you could click once and the entire filled area would be erased. See the following CD-ROM exercise for practice in using the Faucet option.

*Figure 3-24 The Faucet option allows you to erase filled areas in one click.*

### CD-ROM Exercise

Understand how to use the Faucet modifier better by opening the file *ch03_16.fla* located in the *F5gai/chapter3/* folder, installed from the companion CD-ROM. Follow the instructions to erase the filled areas.

## Working with Colors

The Colors section of the toolbar has not been discussed previously so that you could first become familiar with some of the more basic tools. At this time, turn your attention to working with colors in Flash. Later, you will continue looking at the remainder of Flash's tools.

In general, there are two ways to define and use colors in Flash. In the first method, you use the Mixer Panel to define colors that are stored as swatches, which are accessible via the Swatches panel. If you want to use a custom color, you must first mix and store the color before you can use it. Much like a traditional artist, swatches give you quick access to the colors in your movie, allowing you to reuse them whenever and wherever you want, without having to continually mix values. Swatches in Flash are akin to Swatches in Photoshop in this regard.

The only problem with using swatches is that there are times when you may just want to quickly define and use a single color and not have to go through the process of mixing a color and storing it as a swatch. Thus, Flash gives you a second means of defining color through a feature called the Color dialog box. These two items are really separate entities. That is, when you mix colors with the Color dialog box, they are not automatically added as swatches. Similarly, swatch colors are not automatically accessible via the Color dialog box.

You might view use of the Colors dialog box as an exception to the use of swatches. There will seldom be a time you will not want to store a color you use as a swatch, so the Colors dialog box may seem like an unnecessary duplication in the software. Additionally, there is not a significant amount of time difference between the two methods of defining and using color. Regardless, Macromedia has included both methods, even though 99 percent of the time you will likely use the swatch method.

## Color Swatch Lists

Let's begin by examining the swatch list as it appears when you use the Flash tools. You have seen in the tools examined to this point that the stroke and fill colors, located in the Colors section of the toolbar, are the current colors used by the painting and drawing tools. When you start drawing, whatever colors are shown in the Colors section of the toolbar are the one's the tool draws or paints with. The current Stroke color and Fill color can also be accessed via the Stroke panel or the Fill panel.

You select a swatch from the drop-down color palette in the toolbar's Colors section to change the current color for the stroke or the fill of a tool. The drop-down color palettes for the stroke and fill colors contain the same color matrices as the drop-down color palettes everywhere in the program. You will find this list in several places, including the Movie Properties dialog box, the Character panel, the Swatches panel, the Fill panel, the Stroke panel, and so on. Really anywhere you may need to select a color, you will find the same drop-down color palette available.

The drop-down color palette contains a color matrix (or list of colors), which shows all colors currently defined and available in the environment. The default colors shown in figure 3-25 are based on the "web-safe" colors. However, you can add your own colors to this list (see also color plate A-10). To select a stroke or fill color for one of Flash tools, you simply select on it in the list with the dropper that appears when you pop open the list.

For example, if you wanted to select a specific color for an oval's line and fill, you would select the Oval tool and then click on the stroke swatch in the Colors section of the toolbar, which pops open the palette list. Click on a color and it is selected for the stroke. Set the fill by clicking on the fill swatch and selecting a color. When selecting stroke or fill colors for the Oval or the Rectangle tool, you should notice the No Color button located in the upper left of the pop-up list (figure 3-25). Select this swatch to assign no color to the stroke or fill. This allows you to create fills without lines, or lines without fills.

As previously mentioned, you can add your own colors to the drop-down color palette. This is performed via the Mixer panel, which you will examine shortly. However, inquisitive readers probably noticed the Color Dialog button shown in figure 3-25. Remember that the Color dialog operates independently of the drop-down color palette and the Mixer panel. It is basically a means of quickly creating a color for use without having to create a swatch. Let's review the Color dialog box and then return to the swatches and how you can add your own colors to the color palette.

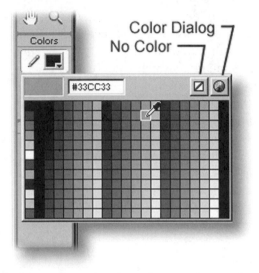

Figure 3-25 The drop-down palette of colors for the stroke and fill buttons includes a No Color option (see also color plate A-10).

### The Color Dialog Box

The key to working with color in Flash is understanding that there are two ways of defining solid colors to be used with a stroke or fill: via swatches and via the Color dialog box. Within the Mixer panel, you can define a color and then save it as a swatch so that you can reuse it later from the drop-down list. The Colors dialog box also allows you to quickly define a color. However, it does not give you the option of saving the color as a swatch in your drop-down palette.

Begin examining the Colors dialog box by clicking on the Color button in the Stroke or Fill drop-down lists, shown in figure 3-25. Clicking on the Color button opens the Color dialog box, shown in figure 3-26 (see also color plate A-11).

Once the Color dialog box is open, note that it gives you access to the set of default colors defined for the environment. Keep in mind that these are independent of the swatches shown in the drop-down list. Clicking on any of the colors in the Colors dialog sets the current color to the one you have selected. Clicking on OK will allow you to start using the color as the stroke or fill.

Color Space     Value Bar

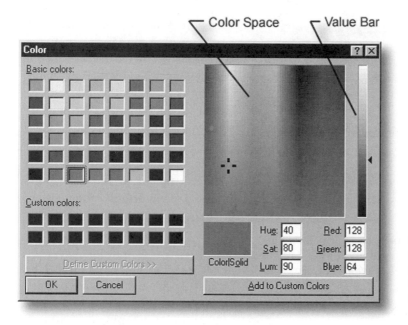

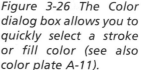

*Figure 3-26 The Color dialog box allows you to quickly select a stroke or fill color (see also color plate A-11).*

### Creating Custom Colors

In the Colors dialog box, you can also create your own custom color. To do this, adjust the parameters of one of the already-existing basic colors or start from scratch (black) and define your own new color.

To start from scratch, you begin by clicking on one of the boxes under Custom Colors. To modify one of the existing default colors to create a new color, click on a color box under the Basic colors set. In either case, use the Color Space and Value controls to visually adjust the color, or use the HSL or RGB fields to modify the numerical values. Once you get the color you want, click on the Add to Custom Colors button to add the color to the Custom Colors section. Then click on OK to set the stroke or fill color to your newly defined color. Keep in mind that the color is not automatically added to the drop-down color list that is based on saved swatches.

 **TIP:** *Although the Color dialog box provides a quick means of playing with color, colors defined there do not automatically show up in the drop-down color palette. You can force them to appear in the drop-down color palette using the Mixer palette's menu. Once you have defined a color using the Color dialog box, access the Mixer and select Add Swatch from its menu.*

### Mixer and Swatches Panels

Probably the most efficient means of creating colors is to use the Mixer panel. Use Window | Panels | Mixer to open the mixer panel, shown

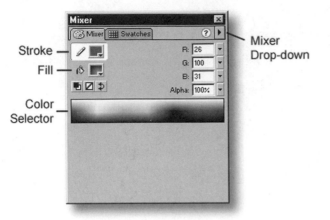

Stroke

Fill

Color
Selector

Mixer
Drop-down

*Figure 3-27 The Mixer panel allows you to define the solid colors used for strokes and fills, as well as colors used as the basis for gradient fills (see also color plate A-12).*

in figure 3-27 (see also color plate A-12). Within the Mixer panel, you define solid colors to be used for strokes and fills, as well as colors to be used within a gradient fill.

The color matrix that appears within the stroke and fill drop-down color palettes include 228 default colors. The first column (12 colors) includes the base colors generally used for interface components within an operating system. The next column and the last column are simply visual separators. The middle 216 colors are browser-safe colors, or colors that should be used if you are designing around an 8-bit (256-color) environment.

In the Mixer panel, click on either the Stroke or Fill section to make it active. In figure 3-27, the Stroke section is active, so any color selected will be for the stroke. To define a color, you can select a color in the Color Selector; enter a series of RGB values in the R, G, and B, fields; select an existing swatch from the color matrix in the drop-down color palette; or open the Color dialog box button in the color matrix of the drop-down color palette.

 **TIP:** *If you want to work with HSB (hue, saturation, and brightness) or HEX (hexadecimal) values in the Mixer, instead of RGB values, use the Mixer panel drop-down menu to change the entry type (figure 3-28). For more information about hexadecimal colors, see Appendix C.*

## The Alpha Field

You may be wondering, "What is the purpose of the Alpha field?" The Alpha slider allows you to define the level of transparency (or opaqueness) of a color. Flash supports 8 bits of transparency for any defined color. Thus, a color could have 256 levels of transparency. However, the slider is based on percentages, so the actual number of levels is 100. The important point is that a color could be 53 percent transparent, 1 percent transparent, or 93 percent transparent. This provides a tremendous amount of flexibility when creating graphics for the Web.

Transparent *.gif* files, which only offer 1-bit transparency, pale by comparison. In a transparent *.gif*, a pixel is either 100 percent transparent or 100 percent opaque. There are no gradations or variations of transparency allowed. The next chapter focuses on animation and it discusses the use of the Alpha feature for creating objects that have varying levels of transparency.

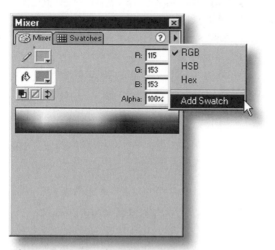

Figure 3-28 Use the Mixer drop-down menu to set the field type (RGB, HSB, or HEX), and to add the current color as a swatch.

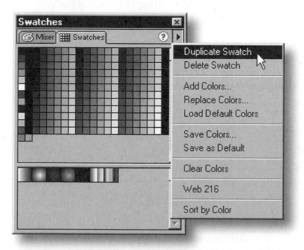

Figure 3-29 The Swatches panel shows all of the currently defined colors and gradients defined in the movie file (see also color plate A-13).

Once you have defined a stroke or fill color in the Mixer, you can easily add the color to the Swatches panel from the Mixer. This is advantageous because colors added as a swatch can be accessed via the drop-down color palette. In the Mixer, to add the current color as a swatch, select Add Swatch from the Mixer drop-down menu, shown in figure 3-28.

Changes made to the Swatch color list, that is if you add or delete swatches from the list, are stored in the Flash movie file. Thus, the custom colors you make for a given file are stored within it. Flash will start up with the same default start-up colors each time you start a new file.

Now that you understand how to create your own colors and add them as a swatch, examine the Swatches panel, shown in figure 3-29 (see also color plate A-13). Use Window | Panels | Swatches to open the panel if it is not currently displayed. Basically, the Swatches panel reveals all of the solid colors and gradient fills that have been defined for the current movie file. The colors shown in the Swatches panel are the same as those shown in the drop-down color palette for the stroke and fill colors, as well as everywhere else that there is a drop-down color palette. Think of the Swatches panel as the master control for the stored or saved colors and gradients that are available in your movie.

In the Swatches panel, clicking on a color from the drop-down color palette in the list makes it the current color for either the stroke or fill, depending on which is the currently selected item in the Colors section of the toolbar. However, more important is the Swatches drop-down menu, shown in figure 3-29. In addition to being able to duplicate and delete existing swatches in the palette, you can manipulate collections of swatches. The menu shown in figure 3-29 reveals that you can Add, Replace, and Save palettes of colors from Flash. You can also revert to the default start-up set of colors or replace the default colors with a palette of your own. This allows you to manage sets of colors that apply to a series of movies.

Flash stores saved palettes in its own proprietary format, denoted with a *.clr* extension (*.fclr* on the Mac). Thus, you can save a palette of custom colors you have created and import it into another Flash file. You can also export your Flash colors to a Photoshop *.act* file, which can then be imported into Photoshop's Swatches palette. Additionally, you can import color palettes from other sources. Flash allows you to import colors from its own *.clr* format, Photoshop's *.act* format, or from an existing *.gif* graphic.

Also in the menu shown in figure 3-29, you see three other options: Clear Colors, Web 216, and Sort by Color. The Clear Colors option lets you delete all colors in the Swatches panel color list, leaving only black and white. The Web 216 option allows you to load the default 216 web-safe colors. These are the default start-up colors that are loaded when you first begin using Flash. Even if you use the Save as Default option to replace the default colors, you can always get back to the 216 web-safe colors using the Web 216 option. The Sort by Color option sorts the colors in the Swatches panel color list by luminosity.

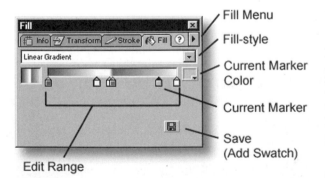

Figure 3-30 You now create gradients fills, as well as solid and bitmap fills, in the Fills panel (see also color plate A-14).

## Creating Gradient Fills

One of the significant changes in Flash 5 is the addition of the Fill panel. In the previous versions of Flash, you mixed solid fills and gradient fills in the same dialog box. In Flash 5, however, you create gradients in the Fill panel, shown in figure 3-30 (see also color plate A-14). Solid colors, as you have already seen, are mixed in either the Mixer panel or in the Colors dialog box.

To create a fill, open the Window | Panels | Fill panel. Use the Fill-style drop-down to select the type of fill you want to create. The options of the dialog are None, Solid, Linear Gradient, Radial Gradient, and Bitmap. Solid gradients simply require you to select the color, from the drop-down list, to use. Gradients, however, require a little more work.

**NOTE:** *Bitmap gradients are discussed later in this chapter.*

When you select the Linear or the Radial Gradient option, the panel will look similar to that shown in figure 3-30. You use the Edit Gradient Range markers to define the beginning and ending colors for the gradient. If you click on one of the markers, a drop-down color palette will appear to the right of the gradient range. Select a color if you wish to change the color.

You can add more markers and colors to the gradient by clicking near the bottom of the gradient bar and setting the color. Once you have a gradient you like, to add it to the Swatch list, click on the Add Swatch button at the bottom of the gradient panel, or use the Add Swatch option in the Fill drop-down menu. The fill you have defined can now be used with the Paint Bucket, Oval, Rectangle, and other tools.

If you click on a gradient in the Swatches panel, the Mixer panel fill values will appear blank. Thus, if at anytime you go to the Mixer panel and find that the RGB fields for the fill are blank, it means you currently have a gradient selected in the Fill panel.

You can change the fill style, the arrangement of the color markers in a gradient, or other color options of an existing gradient swatch at any time. Selecting a gradient swatch in the Swatches panel will transfer the swatches settings to the Fill panel automatically, allowing you to modify the settings for the gradient. However, gradients that already exist on the stage will not be affected unless the items are refilled. The next chapter covers how gradients that use transparency are created and used. This includes gradients that progress from opaque colors to transparent colors.

## Working with the Paint Bucket

Now that you know how to work with colors and define fills, you can take a look at using those elements with the Paint Bucket. You can easily add a solid or gradient fill to an area. In order to create a fill, the set of lines does not necessarily have to be a closed polygon, as you will see in the following section. The Paint Bucket offers three options that control its behavior, as shown in figure 3-31. These are Gap Size, Lock Fill, and Transform Fill, discussed in the sections that follow.

Gap Size

Lock Fill — Transform Fill

*Figure 3-31 The Paint Bucket provides three options: Gap Size, Lock Fill, and Transform Fill.*

### Gap Size

When using Gap Size, polygons do not have to be completely closed in order to be filled. Gaps are one of the most difficult things to deal with in most vector drawing programs. Fortunately, Flash can automatically "close gaps" so that fills can be applied. This does not mean, however, that it adds a line to close the gap, as you will see.

 **TIP**: *Because Flash works so program-specifically with fills, it may be more efficient to import line drawings from other packages and then render them in Flash. Complex drawings with many fills are often easier to render in Flash than in traditional vector illustration packages.*

Gap Size presents several options for filling, all of which focus on the size of gaps you want Flash to ignore. To close the gaps manually, select the Do Not Close Gaps option. The Gap Size option is very effective for complex drawings or for line drawings imported from other sources. To experiment with the Gap Size option, see the following CD-ROM exercise.

 ### CD-ROM Exercise

To find out more about the Gap Size option, open the file *ch03_17.fla* located in the *F5gai/chapter3/* folder, installed from the companion CD-ROM. Try the various settings on the objects shown.

### Lock Fill and Transform Fill

The Paint Bucket provides two other useful options for working with fills: Lock Fill and Transform Fill. Lock Fill works in a manner similar to the Lock Fill option used with the Paint Brush tool. It allows you to select a fill and extend that fill into a new area. Transform Fill, however, is a feature that you can use to rotate or scale a fill that has been applied to an area, as shown in figure 3-32.

Select        Rotate        Scale

*Figure 3-32 Using the Transform Fill option.*

After an area has been filled with a gradient, it can be easily rotated or scaled using Transform Fill. As shown in figure 3-32, the corner handles that appear on the fill allow it to be rotated. The side handle that appears allows you to scale the fill within the area. The center handle allows you to move the fill. As the cursor moves near these handles, it will change to indicate that the transformation is available. Using the Transform Fill option, fills can be shaped to fit almost any area. To practice working with the Transform Fill option, see the following CD-ROM exercise.

### CD-ROM Exercise

Learn more about the Transform Fill modifier. Open the file *ch03_18.fla* located in the *F5gai/chapter3/* folder, installed from the companion CD-ROM. Use the Transform Fill option to adjust the fills applied to the objects.

## Working with the Ink Bottle

When working with fills, you can change their color, orientation, and other characteristics by simply refilling them. However, you use the Ink Bottle to change the characteristics of lines.

To change the color of a line or set of lines, click on the Ink Bottle tool and, in the Stroke panel, set the characteristics for the style, height, and color of the line. Click on the line or lines you want to change and they will be changed to match the settings you establish in the Stroke panel.

When lines intersect, Flash automatically recognizes them as line segments instead of continuous lines. Theoretically, and in terms of vector programs such as FreeHand or Illustrator, lines are automatically "broken" (or "cut") when they intersect.

The advantage of this Flash feature is that lines do not have to be trimmed back. Just select them in order to delete them. However, the negative aspect is that when you want to change a line's color or style, you have to apply the change across each segment that constitutes the line. To get several segments to fill at once, double click on them and then use the Ink Bottle on the selection. For practice using the Ink Bottle tool, see the following CD-ROM exercise.

### CD-ROM Exercise

Discover more information about using the Ink Bottle tool. Open the file *ch03_19.fla* located in the *F5gai/chapter3/* folder, installed from the companion CD-ROM. Use Ink Bottle and the settings in the Stroke panel to adjust the characteristics of the lines in the drawing.

## Working with the Dropper

The Dropper tool, much like similar tools found in raster editors, allows you to select the line and fill characteristics of a particular object so that it may be applied to another object. This tool is particularly handy for editing a work in progress.

Line          Fill

*Figure 3-33 The Dropper's cursor indicates the item being sampled.*

The Dropper tool has no options. After selecting the Dropper, dragging the cursor over an object reveals the characteristics you are about to pick up: line or fill. Figure 3-33 shows the difference between the two cursors. Once you click on a fill or line, the Paint Bucket or Ink Bottle is selected. Using the characteristics (acquired by the Dropper) in the Paint Bucket or Ink Bottle, you can modify other elements in your drawing to match one another. See the following CD-ROM exercise for practice in using the Dropper tool.

When you select the Dropper tool, the Lock Fill button is automatically active in the Fill tool. This allows you to quickly and easily extend or continue a fill into other areas of your drawing.

### CD-ROM Exercise

To find out more about the Dropper tool, open the file *ch03_20.fla* located in the *F5gai/chapter3/* folder, installed from the companion CD-ROM. Use the Dropper to render the object on the right by picking up line and fill characteristics from the rendering on the left. Once you pick up a fill from the object on the left, you must deselect Lock Fill.

## Working with the Pen Tool

As previously mentioned, the Pen tool and the Subselect tool are two of the latest additions to the Flash tool set. Granted, one of the advantages of Flash was, and still is, its natural drawing tools. However, users familiar with other vector drawing programs long for greater control; that is, access to control points.

When you select the Pen tool, you will find no options in the toolbar. To use this tool, you begin by clicking points on the stage. If you use a single click, the pen tool will add straight-line segments. If you click-drag as you add an element, handles will appear, creating Bezier curve segments. By varying single clicks and click-drags, you can create continuous strokes consisting of straight and Bezier segments. Double clicking a point will end the stroke you are creating. You can also hold down the Ctrl key (the Option key on the Mac) and click to end the line.

Remember that by default the Pen tool does not show the stroke as it is being created. You can use the Edit | Preferences | Editing tab to turn on the Show Pen Preview option. This allows you to see what you are drawing as you draw it. In addition, for greater accuracy, you can turn on Show Precise Cursors in the Editing tab.

In addition to creating strokes, you can use the Pen tool to add, subtract, and modify stroke points on existing line and arc segments. You can use the Pen tool to subtract a point from a straight segment between two points. However, one drawback is that you cannot add a point to a straight segment. To subtract a point, click with the Pen tool on the desired line to make it active. Then move the Pen tool close to an existing point. The cursor will change to reveal a minus sign. Click on the point and it will be removed from the segment.

 **TIP:** *With the Pen tool selected, if you hold down the Ctrl key (the Option key on the Mac), you can select a Bezier point and then work with its balance handles to modify the curve.*

The Pen tool also offers two functions in regard to Bezier segments. First, you can add points to a Bezier segment by moving the Pen tool over the segment and clicking. Unlike other vector environments, however, you cannot click-drag to instantly move the Bezier handles. Rather, you click to add the point, and then hold down the Ctrl key (PC) or the Option key (Mac) to select the point and change the position of its handles.

The second thing you can do is turn a Bezier point into a straight-segment point (an angle). If you move the Pen tool over an existing Bezier point, the cursor will change to reveal a small angle icon. If you click on the point, it is turned into a straight-segment point (a sharp angle). The angle created is based on the angle segment between the two line segments. For practice in working with the Pen tool, see the following CD-ROM exercise.

 ### CD-ROM Exercise

To learn more about the Pen tool, open the file *ch03_21.fla* located in the *F5gai/chapter3/* folder, installed from the companion CD-ROM. Use the Pen tool to create and modify the segments shown.

## Working with the Text Tool

Text is supported by effective graphics, and vice versa. Flash provides very accurate control of text elements, and a relatively designer-friendly environment that incorporates control over font, style, size, color, alignment, kerning, and other text characteristics.

### Remember: It Is Vector!

One of the things you must keep in mind is that almost any font on your system may be used within your movies. In the past, custom fonts for use in a web page had to be rendered as raster elements. Flash, on the other hand, allows any TrueType font to be integrated without worry. Web-ready Flash movie files (*.swf*) automatically include the necessary information to define the font. Therefore, in terms of translation to your audience, you can use any font on your system.

 **TIP:** *Adobe PostScript I fonts may be used easily on the Macintosh without significant problems. However, on the PC, fonts used with Adobe Type Manager (also known as PostScript fonts) may cause problems when you create your web-ready files. Therefore, avoid using Adobe Type Manager fonts on the PC.*

### Working with Text

When you click on the Text tool, you will not find any options listed. Like several other interface elements, text attributes are now housed in panels. There are three panels that directly relate to text objects: Character, Paragraph, and Text Options.

Once you have clicked on the Text tool, begin entering text by clicking on the stage. Doing so reveals a text box with a flashing I-beam cursor. The text you enter is displayed in the box at the point of the cursor. As you type, the text box automatically jumps to the next line when you reach the far right side of the text box. You will also notice a small white box at the upper right of the text box, as shown in figure 3-34. Click and drag this handle to increase or decrease the width of the text box.

Text box handle

This a sample text box

*Figure 3-34 Adjust the text box width by click-dragging the text box handle.*

### CD-ROM Exercise

To learn to insert text, open the file *ch03_22.fla* located in the *F5gai/chapter3/* folder, installed from the companion CD-ROM. Use the Text tool to add text to the file as instructed.

It is easy to edit any aspect of text that has been entered. To make changes to what has been entered into the text box, double click on the text to edit it. To change the formatting of the text, select the text box and then use the Character, Paragraph, or Text Options panel. The panels are described in the sections that follow.

## The Character and Paragraph Panels

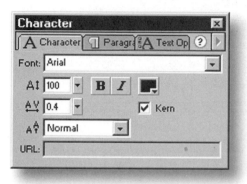

*Figure 3-35 The Character panel is used to modify the character attributes of entire blocks of text, as well as of words and phrases.*

A text block's font, size, color, tracking kerning, and style (bold and italic) are modified using the Character panel, shown in figure 3-35. These options are used to adjust the attributes of entire blocks of text, or of individual words and phrases within a block of text. To edit the attributes of an entire block of text, select the block of text and then adjust the appropriate options in the Character panel. To edit an individual portion of text, double click on the text block with the Text tool and use the I-beam cursor to select a word or phrase. Then modify the settings in the Character panel. Anytime you double click on a block of text, the Text tool is automatically made active.

**NOTE:** *When double clicking on a block of text, make sure to use the I-beam to select a word or phrase before changing the settings in the Character panel. If you only double click and try to change the option (without making a text selection), no visible changes will be seen in the text. A selection must be made before the changes can be applied.*

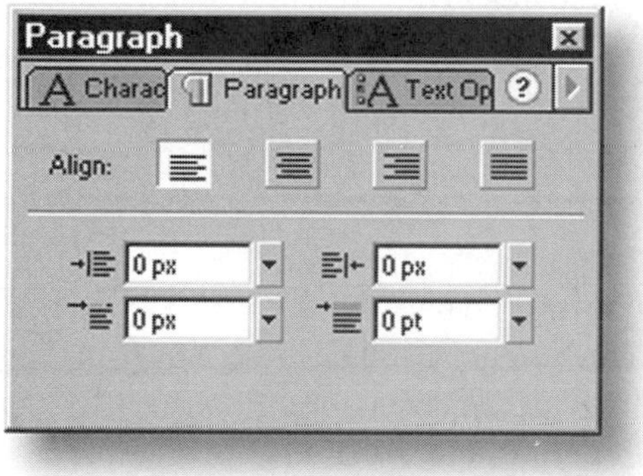

**Paragraph**

*Figure 3-36 The Paragraph panel is used to modify text alignment, margins, and line spacing.*

In addition to font characteristics, a wide range of paragraph properties can also be adjusted and applied to blocks of text using the Paragraph panel, shown in figure 3-36. This panel allows you to adjust text alignment (justification), margins, indentation, and line spacing. As you adjust the sliders for these options, the changes are displayed in real time on the screen. To use these features, select a block of text and then use the Paragraph panel.

The default units for paragraph properties are determined by settings in the Ruler Units option. Ruler Units can be changed using the Modify | Movie menu option.

Aside from the Character and Paragraph panels, many of the text formatting features can be accessed using the following Text menu options. For greater familiarity with the Character and Paragraph panels, see the CD-ROM exercise that follows.

- *Font:* Specifies the font face.
- *Size:* Determines the font size in points.

- *Style:* Controls font attributes, including normal, superscript, subscript, bolding, and italicizing.

- *Alignment:* Determines the justification.

- *Tracking:* Adjusts the amount of spacing between characters (kerning).

- *Character, Paragraph, Options:* Opens the respective panel.

 **CD-ROM Exercise**

Take a closer look at how the Character and Paragraph panels work. Open the file *ch03_23.fla* located in the *F5gai/chapter3/* folder, installed from the companion CD-ROM. Use the panels to change the characteristics of the text.

On occasion, you may want to start with a font, but then want to modify the letters in a customized manner. For example, if you have text that says "Drip" that you want to make look like it is dripping, you are not limited to just the fonts you have. You can convert any text to outlines and then edit it using the various painting and drawing tools.

To convert text to outlines in Flash (similar to Convert to Paths in FreeHand), select a text block and use Modify | Break Apart. Once you break text apart, it loses its text features, such as the ability to change a word or phrase. However, note that breaking apart large quantities of text can drastically increase the size of your movie files. Only break text apart for special effects, and do so sparingly. The CD-ROM exercise that follows provides practice in using the Modify | Break Apart functionality.

 **CD-ROM Exercise**

Learn more about modifying text. Open the file *ch03_24.fla* located in the *F5gai/chapter3/* folder, installed from the companion CD-ROM. Use Modify | Break Apart, and then use the drawing or painting tools to modify the look of the text.

## Text Options Panel

The Text Options panel, shown in figure 3-37, allows you to create both static and dynamic text elements, as well as elements that are changeable by the end user. The default setting is Static. Text objects worked with under the Dynamic and Input options can be specified as able to be manipulated or otherwise dependent on other data in the file (such as a variable), or dependent on the user. There are many things that you can do with the settings under the Dynamic and Input options.  However,

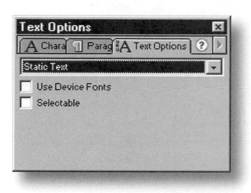

*Figure 3-37 The Text options panel allows you to create text objects that are either static (default) or dynamic, as well as objects changeable by the user.*

you do not want to dive in too quickly. Chapters 6 and 14 cover dynamic and editable text fields in more detail.

# Other Editing Features

To this point, this chapter has covered the various tools used for selecting, drawing, painting, and editing. Flash's other editing features include rulers, grids, and guides; the Align panel, the Curves command, the Shapes submenu, and the Break Apart command. These features are discussed in the sections that follow.

## Rulers, Grids, and Guides

It goes without saying that any good computer graphics package includes features that help the user draw and paint accurately. Three options you should be aware of are Rulers, Grids, and (with Flash 5), Guides. Each of these is accessed via the View menu.

When the Rulers option is activated, you can now click-drag guides onto the stage, in a manner similar to packages such as FreeHand, Illustrator, and Photoshop. The only odd thing about the Grids and Guides options is that the Snap to Grids and Snap to Guides options are buried in their respective submenus, whereas the Snap to Objects option is found in the main View menu. That these snap functions are not all found in the same, immediately available location is somewhat of a nuisance when trying to check which snaps are turned on. Nonetheless, Flash has matured in that it now provides all three of these vital drawing aids.

## Align Panel

While drawing, it is often helpful to be able to align several objects or to equally space objects across a given area. Much like other vector editors, Flash provides a utility that will quickly allow you to align or space objects consistently, without having to use a grid, snap, or rulers. If you

Figure 3-38 The Align panel allows you to align or space objects consistently.

select multiple objects and open the Align panel, shown in figure 3-38, you can quickly align or distribute the selected objects.

**TIP:** *Quickly open the Align panel by using Ctrl + K on the PC or Command + K on the Mac.*

In addition to aligning objects (Align) and distributing objects (Space Evenly), Flash can size several objects so that their heights or widths (or both dimensions) match, all in one operation. Additionally, you can align objects to one another and justify them on the page (stage) at the same time. The Match Size feature is particularly useful when creating web interfaces. This causes all selected elements to be aligned and sized to match one another. To explore the Align feature, see the following CD-ROM exercise.

**TIP:** *You cannot use Lock in conjunction with Align, as you can in programs such as FreeHand or Illustrator. Once an object is locked, it cannot be selected. You must use Modify | Arrange | Unlock All to be able to select the item that was locked.*

### CD-ROM Exercise

To find out more about the Align feature, open the file *ch03_25.fla* located in the *F5gai/chapter3/* folder, installed from the companion CD-ROM. Use Align to try different configurations to see what they do. Pay particular attention to Match Size and what it does.

## Optimizing Curves

As mentioned in the first chapter, file size is an important consideration when creating web documents. Even though Flash is a vector drawing tool, complex drawings and movies can push the limits of reasonable delivery. Therefore, even with Flash, file size as regards object creation must be monitored to make sure your files are as small as possible.

Flash offers the Modify | Optimize menu option, which smoothes curved lines and fill outlines by reducing the number of points used to define them. This can significantly reduce the size of a file in very complex drawings.

To use this feature, which is similar to the Smooth modifier, select an element and then access the Modify | Optimize menu option, which accesses the Optimize Curves dialog box, shown in figure 3-39. Using the slider, specify the degree of smoothing desired. Realize that this is often a

*Figure 3-39*
*The Optimize Curves dialog box is a utility that smoothes curved fills and lines.*

trial-and-error process. The results of curve optimization depend on the curves selected and the current zoom level.

The Optimize Curves dialog box provides two options in addition to the slider that controls the level of smoothing. The Use Multiple Passes option allows the optimization process to be repeated until the curve can no longer be optimized. This is similar to the process of multiple smoothing operations. The *show totals message* option displays an alert box that provides information about the optimization process. Use this data to determine how much smoothing has occurred.

Optimize Curves is just one way of creating small and efficient Flash files. Other means of "working smart" and optimizing your files for distribution are covered in Chapter 9.

## Shapes Submenu

The Modify | Shapes submenu contains several useful options. These are Convert Lines to Fills, Expand Fill, and Soften Fill Edges. These options are discussed in the sections that follow.

### Convert Lines to Fills

The Convert Lines to Fills option takes all selected lines and converts them to fills, as if they had been painted with the paintbrush. The width of the fill is determined by the thickness associated with the line before employing the Convert Lines to Fills option.

The Convert Lines to Fills option is useful for special effects, such as filling a line with a gradient. Convert Lines to Fills also makes it possible to erase part of a line. In some respects, this option works in a manner similar to breaking text apart. However, converting many of the lines in a drawing to fills will significantly increase the size of your movie files. Therefore, use this feature sparingly.

### Expand Fill

The Expand Fill option allows you to quickly expand or inset a fill by a specified distance per the current drawing units. This option does not work on lines, grouped elements, or symbols, but does allow you to quickly expand

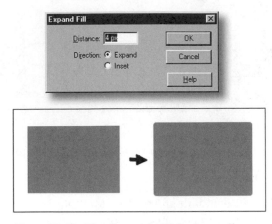

Figure 3-40 *The Expand Fill feature allows you to expand or inset singular filled areas.*

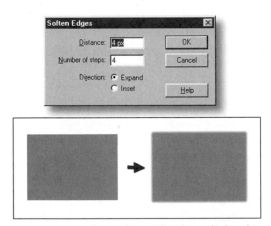

Figure 3-41 *The Soften Fill Edges dialog box allows you to create drop shadow effects.*

a fill area. If you select a fill and use Expand Fill, the fill will grow or shrink by the extended value. For example, if you expand a rectangular fill by 10 pixels, the rectangle grows in size and its corners become rounded, as shown in figure 3-40.

### Soften Fill Edges

The Soften Fill Edges option allows you to create special elements, such as soft-edged drop shadows. With a fill selected, you can use the Soften Fill Edges option to generate a series of repeating elements that expand and become more transparent. Similar to the Expand Fill option, the Soften Fill Edges option works best with a single fill that has no line style.

To use Soften Fill Edges, select a fill and then access Modify | Shape | Soften Edges to open the Soften Fill Edges dialog box, shown in figure 3-41. Use the Distance field to enter the amount of expansion (or inset), and the Number of Steps field to define the number of steps in the area. Figure 3-41 shows an example of the effect of the Soften Fill Edges option.

Depending on the number of steps you specify in the dialog box, file size may vary drastically. The Soften Edges option adds several outline elements to your file to create the drop shadow effect.

## Breaking Items Apart

In the "Working with the Text Tool" section, the Break Apart command was used to convert text to its representative lines and arcs for editing with the painting and drawing tools. The Break Apart command is also useful for functions such as breaking symbols and bitmaps. The following section discusses how bitmaps can be used in Flash and how the Break Apart command applies to them. Chapter 5 covers in more detail the process of breaking and working with symbols. Realize that the Break Apart command applies to more than just text, and has both positive and negative effects.

# ■ ■ ■ ■ Importing and Exporting Graphic Files

Many users frequently want to import files from other software packages. Accordingly, Flash supports a variety of file formats for the PC and Mac platforms. Table 3-3 provides details on common file formats supported by Flash for import. As indicated in the table, support of some of these formats is limited to either the PC or the Mac platform.

*Table 3-3 File Formats Supported by Flash for Import*

| File | Extension | Type | Compression | Windows | Mac |
|------|-----------|------|-------------|---------|-----|
| Adobe Illustrator (6.0 or lower) | .eps, .ai | Metafile (usually vector) | N/A | Yes | Yes |
| Audio Interchange File Format | .aif | Sound | Varies | No* | Yes |
| AutoCAD DXF | .dxf | 2D Vector | N/A | Yes | Yes |
| Bitmap (Windows) | .bmp | Raster | None | Yes | No |
| Enhanced Windows Metafile | .emf | Metafile | N/A | Yes | No |
| Flash Player | .swf | Metafile | N/A | Yes | Yes |
| FreeHand (7, 8, or 9) | .fhX | Metafile (usually vector) | N/A | Yes | Yes |
| FutureSplash Player | .spl | Metafile | N/A | Yes | Yes |
| GIF and Animated GIF | .gif | Raster | Lossless | Yes | Yes |
| JPEG | .jpg | Raster | Lossy | Yes | Yes |
| MP3 | .mp3 | Sound | Mpg | Yes | Yes |
| PICT | .pct | Metafile | Lossless | Yes | Yes |
| PNG | .png | Raster | Lossless | Yes | Yes |
| Flash Player | .swf | Metafile | N/A | Yes | Yes |
| Windows Waveform | .wav | Sound | PCM | Yes | No* |
| Windows Metafile | .wmf | Metafile | N/A | Yes | Yes |

*\* See the following Note.*

**NOTE:** *If you have QuickTime 4 installed on your system, you will be able to do some additional things. First, .aif and .wav files can be imported on either platform. Additionally, with QuickTime 4 installed, Flash can also import MacPaint files (.pntg), Photoshop files (.psd), Macintosh Pict bitmap files (.pct) on the PC, QuickTime images and movies (.qtif and .mov), Silicon Graphics files (.sai), Targa raster files (.tga), and TIFF images (.tif).*

Flash supports vector, raster, metafile, sound, and video formats. Metafile formats can contain information that is raster, vector, or both simultaneously. In some cases, Flash may not support a particular format. However, copying and pasting may allow images or other files to be transferred from one package to another. As noted in Chapter 2, the Edit | Preferences dialog box contains several options that control the quality of elements passed from the clipboard into Flash. You may need to adjust these settings to adequately paste from the clipboard.

## Importing and Using Bitmaps in Flash

Flash allows you to use raster graphics within your files in various ways. As logic dictates, the more raster graphics in a Flash file, the larger the resulting file size. Granted, due to bitmap compression, file sizes will not grow as quickly as in other formats, but sticking too many raster images into a Flash file will make the size grow.

Within Flash, you can use bitmaps as movie elements, fills, or templates for creating vector elements. To import a raster graphic, use the File | Import menu option. The graphic will be automatically placed on the stage. You should ensure that your raster images are pre-sized to fit the Flash movie before importing. Sizing images in Flash may result in poorer visual quality and larger file sizes. This is much like using the HEIGHT and WIDTH attributes of the HTML < IMG > tag to size images (covered in Chapter 9). Size all raster images before importing.

When importing bitmap graphics in Flash, use Windows *.bmp* files on the PC and *.pct* files on the Mac. If you import bitmaps, do so using formats that are not lossy compressed. Flash's compression will be most effective (as it relates to size and visual quality) if you import uncompressed graphics or lossless compressed images, as opposed to images already compressed with lossy compression (such as *.jpg*).

As a second note, Flash supports the import of a series of images. For example, if you have a series of bitmaps you wish to use as a small animation, import them automatically by naming them properly. As long as the files reside in the same folder and have file names that end with a sequence of numbers (such as *myfile001, myfile002*, and so on), Flash will import the series automatically. When sequential images are imported, they occur in successive frames of the current layer. Individual imported bitmaps are also placed in the current layer.

 **NOTE:** *Animated .gif files can be easily imported into Flash. When imported, each .gif frame becomes a separate Flash frame. Again, be careful of the number of raster images you import into Flash. Bitmap images can increase file size quickly.*

A final note concerning importing bitmaps is that Flash preserves an image's alpha channel (transparency) settings. If you create an image in Photoshop or other raster editor, transparency of backgrounds remains intact when you import them. This allows raster elements, such as a picture of a button with a drop shadow, to be imported without having to worry about anti-alias halos. Because the edges of the drop shadow would be partially transparent, and because Flash supports that transparency, you would not have to deal with the anti-alias halos commonly associated with such images.

### Using Trace Bitmap

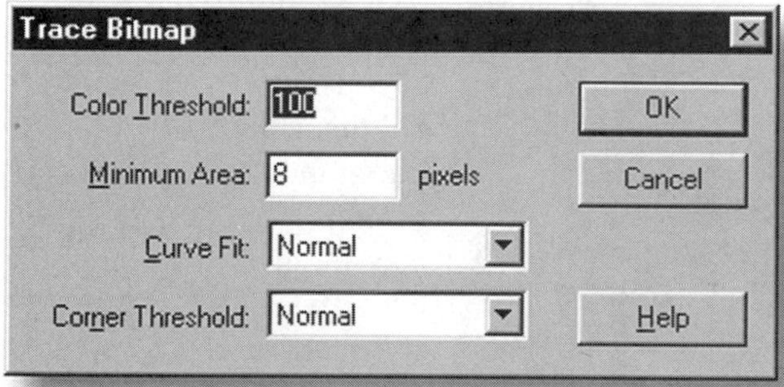

Use the Trace Bitmap feature to convert bitmaps to a vector representation. As with all raster-to-vector processes, it is not perfect. Most often, the best representation results in an image with a watercolor-type look. However, by tracing a bitmap instead of allowing the bitmap to remain in the file, file size can often be reduced.

*Figure 3-42  The Trace Bitmap dialog box contains features that control how bitmaps are converted to vector images.*

To use the Trace Bitmap feature, import a raster image and select it. Use the Modify | Trace Bitmap menu option. You will be presented with the Trace Bitmap dialog box, shown in figure 3-42. The Trace Bitmap dialog box options provide the following controls over tracing:

- Color Threshold determines the overall accuracy of the tracing. It does this by comparing two pixels. If the difference between the two RGB values is less than the color threshold, Flash sees the pixels as the same color.

- Minimum Area controls the number of adjacent pixels compared at one time.

- Curve Fit specifies how smoothly outlines are drawn.
- Corner Threshold affects whether sharp edges are retained or smoothed.

 **TIP 1:** *To get the best representation possible from the Trace Bitmap feature, use the following specifications:*

- *Color Threshold = 100*
- *Minimum Area = 1*
- *Curve Fit = Pixels*
- *Corner Threshold = Many Corners*

 **TIP 2:** *If you just cannot get the trace the way you want, simplify the image in Photoshop or other raster editor. You can often achieve and image that can be more successfully traced by reducing the colors (such as reducing 24-bit to 8-bit) or by simplifying the image using posterization tools.*

Although it may take a couple of iterations to get satisfying results, you may find that the Trace Bitmaps feature is a neat way of creating a custom look, as shown in figure 3-43 (see also color plate A-15). However, depending on the complexity of the trace and the number of tracings you do, file size may dramatically increase. File size should always be a consideration. To explore the Trace Bitmap feature, see the following CD-ROM exercise.

Original                              Traced Bitmap

*Figure 3-43  This is an example of the best-case representation of the bitmap from the Trace Bitmap command (see also color plate A-15).*

## CD-ROM Exercise

To see how the Trace Bitmap feature works, open the file *ch03_26.fla* located in the *F5gai/chapter3/* folder, installed from the companion CD-ROM. Use Modify | Trace Bitmap with a variety of settings to see the results.

## Breaking Apart Bitmaps

When dealing with bitmaps, you can use the Modify | Break Apart menu option to sample colors from a bitmap and to use a bitmap as a fill. By breaking up an image, certain drawing tools can affect the raster image or can be used in combination with the image.

When you fill a shape with a bitmap, the shape becomes what is commonly called a "clipping path." This is similar to clipping paths in Photoshop or the Paste Inside feature of FreeHand. Clipping paths show only the part of the inserted element that falls inside the closed path.

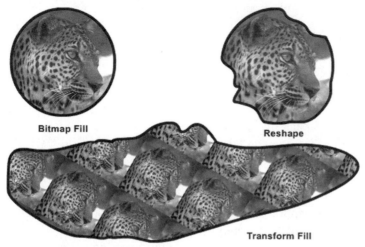

Bitmap Fill

Reshape

Transform Fill

Figure 3-44 shows an example of a bitmap that has been broken apart. Using the Dropper, the bitmap was sampled (clicked on with the Dropper) to define the bitmap as a fill. A circle was then drawn and bitmap-filled using the Paint Bucket. As the circle is reshaped, the interior image tiles and repeats within the area.

When a bitmap fill is stretched, the image automatically tiles

*Figure 3-44 Breaking apart a bitmap allows it to be reshaped, and to act as a fill.*

across the fill area. Use the Transform Fill modifier of the Paint Bucket to rotate or scale the image, just as if it were a solid or gradient fill.

## Final Notes Concerning Bitmaps

In conclusion, it is meaningful to mention these final important issues:

- Once a bitmap has been broken apart, you may use the Dropper to sample the bitmap for use as a fill with the other Flash tools.

- Bitmaps pasted from other applications are generally embedded. You must break them apart to use them.

- When you import a bitmap, it is defined as a symbol. If you trace and then delete the bitmap, you must make sure you also delete the symbol. See Chapter 5 for more information about bitmap symbols.

- Ultimately, bitmaps should be used sparingly. If you decide to use a bitmap in Flash, make it as small as possible. On the Web, file size is the biggest limitation.

## Importing Vector Graphics into Flash

For importing vector graphics into Flash, you will find that FreeHand is the best choice. Flash automatically recognizes the layers in a FreeHand file. Additionally, FreeHand offers the particularly useful features Blend (which will create iterative steps between two shapes) and Release to Layers (which will automatically separate a blend to separate layers). These supplementary features in FreeHand make creating Flash animations and movies faster. FreeHand also provides the ability to convert CYM(K) files to RGB with decent color fidelity.

Importing vector graphics into Flash is performed using the File | Import menu option. When you import a vector graphic, the image is brought into Flash as a group in the current layer.

# Saving Flash Files

When you save a Flash file, it will have the native *.fla* file extension. These can be opened back into Flash and edited. However, when preparing a movie for the Web, use the File | Export Movie menu option, which prepares web-ready Shockwave Flash files with an *.swf* file extension. When an *.swf* file is created, the option of "protecting" it so that it cannot be opened back into Flash for editing is provided. Some Flash *.swf* files can be opened; some cannot. It depends on whether or not the file is protected. Exporting *.swf* files is covered in more depth in Chapter 9.

Although most of the time you will simply be exporting out as an *.swf* file for use on the Web, Flash does provide other means of exporting movies to other applications. Flash provides the ability to save in AVI (Video for Windows), QuickTime, Animated GIF, and sequenced static formats such as JPEG and EMF.

Additionally, Flash provides the ability to save templates for use with Macromedia's server-based product, Generator. Generator allows the developer to create Flash movies in which content changes and is customized to the viewer. For more information about Generator, see Appendix D.

# Summary

This chapter covered Flash's various selection, drawing, painting, and editing tools. This chapter also examined how bitmap graphics can be imported and used in Flash. The next chapter continues by looking at layering and animation in Flash. It discusses how traditional cel animation is created, and examines more advanced keyframe and tweening-type animations.

chapter

# 4

# Cel and Keyframe Animation

### ▪▪▪ Introduction

In the early 1900s, J. Stewart Blackton and Emile Kohl were the first to create what later became known as *animation*. Albeit crude, their work inspired several other well-known artists of the time to begin dabbling with new technologies for creating multiframe sequences. Through the inventions of Thomas A. Edison and the experimental works of many other people, cel animation was born.

The first animation studios quickly emerged. Centered in New York, the animation industry started to blossom. Yet, decades passed before an enterprising individual named Walt Disney introduced his Mouse. Using additional enhancements such as sound, Disney created clever animations that were little more than series of strung-together images.

Animation has advanced rapidly, but many early techniques and planning aids of the 1930s are still widely used. Even though the technology has evolved tremendously, the need for basic animation planning has not. Developing ideas and storyboarding is still vitally significant.

This chapter starts with a brief introduction to the tools and techniques for planning animation. With preplanning, the amount of time it takes to create animations can be significantly reduced, regardless of the tool used. This chapter focuses on two very important aspects of Flash: using layers and creating animation. This chapter will demonstrate that Flash is a very robust tool as it relates to both of these capabilities.

# ▪▪▪ Objectives

In this chapter, you will:

- Learn the basic concepts and principles involved in animation creation
- Examine the Flash object hierarchy and how the stage, overlays, and layers are interrelated
- Learn how to use all aspects of layers in your Flash files
- Learn how to work with frames to create animation
- Discover the cel animation tools found in Flash
- Learn how to create keyframe animation
- Use layer guides to create constrained elements
- Create shape, motion, and transparency animations

# ▪▪▪ Animation Theory and Principles

Animation is one of the most fascinating visual phenomena known. It tricks the human eye and gives the perception of "life" within the single frames that constitute the animation. The concept of animation is simple, but the effects perceived can be much more intricate.

## The Illusion

An animation creates illusions by flashing a series of images so quickly that the eye cannot distinguish between each individual image or cel, as shown in figure 4-1. A single frame's content represents a single instance of time in the animation. During playback, the images blend together in time to create the perception of change. This occurs because of a visual phenomenon called *persistence of vision*, in which the eyes and brain continue to perceive an image even after the image has been removed.

*Figure 4-1  Displaying multiple images with small changes across them creates the perception of movement.*

To see an example of persistence of vision, look at a fluorescent or bright color for a minute or two and then look at a blank, white page. Notice that your eyes will still perceive the color on the blank page even though it is not there. More than likely, the image will appear with less intensity, but it is a noticeable phenomenon for most people. This residual effect is the main reason that animations can be produced.

**NOTE:** *For more information on the human eye and perception, check out* The Joy of Visual Perception: A Web Book, *by Peter K. Kaiser, on-line at* http://www.yorku.ca/eye/.

When dealing with animation, remember that it is really nothing more than a series of images with content that changes. Each frame represents a single instance in the total time of the animation. In the traditional setting, each frame is first created as a drawing. Then it is rendered and photographed in its proper time position (relative to the other frames). Therefore, traditional animation is a result of multiple, traditionally constructed images. Digital animation is nothing more than the same concept duplicated on the computer.

## Cel and Keyframe Animation

To understand the concept of keyframe animation, you must comprehend the sequence involved in creating a traditional animation. The process of traditional animation usually began with an idea of a writer or animator. Then, a storyboard of the animation was created showing the story line and the actions of the characters or objects. Even today, it is common to create storyboards before production. The animation storyboard is a sketch that shows what the individual frames in the animation will contain, as shown in figure 4-2.

Considering that most animation consists of several hundred frames, it is impractical to draw every frame from the animation in the storyboard. Therefore, the storyboard usually contains only the main actions of the animation (or primary actions), called the *keys* or *keyframes*.

 **NOTE:** *Even when using digital tools, storyboarding is still a very important process. Seldom are animations created without prior planning using storyboards. It may be tempting to sit down and immediately start creating, but creation time will decrease and you will have more clarity of thought if storyboarding is done first!*

PANEL ROTATE ON CLICK OF BUTTON

LOWER PANEL ROTATE DOWN TO REVEAL TEXT

POWER-UP FLASHES SCREEN ELEMENTS

*Figure 4-2  The animation storyboard shows the key actions (keys or keyframes) in the animation.*

During the traditional process, when the storyboard was created, the master artist drew the keyframes. Also called in-betweens or "tweens," the remaining intermediate frames were created by several apprentice (or "blue-collar") artists. Sometimes as many as a hundred tween artists were needed on feature-length projects. Thus, the laborious part of creating animations was the production of tweens.

After the frames were drawn, they were then painted and still photographed to create film animation. To produce the movements in the animation, each frame was drawn on a separate piece of acetate. Sometimes a single frame consisted of several sheets of acetate. Usually each moving item in the animation, also called a *sprite*, required a distinct piece of acetate. By varying the combinations of acetate sheets, each frame was then photographed. The combination of frame photographs produced a final animation that gave the perception of movement, due to changes in the elements from frame to frame, when it was played back.

When beginning to learn Flash as an animation tool, it is best to start by creating cel animation. Every frame change is generated through this process. Note that the application provides several tools, such as *Onion-skinning*, to allow animation creation to be a quick process. Onion skinning allows you to see transparent versions of neighboring frames so that you can adjust the current frame. A carryover from traditional cel animation, onion-skinning is a useful technique for getting the timing of characters and objects correct.

If Flash could only create cel animations, the program would not be that impressive, because many cel-based animation programs already exist. In addition, cel animation is extremely time consuming. This is the biggest negative factor. For this reason, Flash also includes keyframe animation capabilities. This is where the real power lies. Typically, keyframe animations significantly decrease the amount of time spent developing animations.

 **TIP:** *Although cel animation is time consuming, some animation designs can only be produced using cel techniques. Anytime you can use keyframe techniques, you should. However, there may be times when you have to revert to cel animation methods.*

# ■■■ Understanding the Flash Object Hierarchy

Flash provides a logical hierarchy for the arrangement of elements in the drawing environment. As previously mentioned, grouped and ungrouped elements interact in different ways. The sections that follow examine the drawing hierarchy more closely, providing a broader understanding of the drawing environment, which includes more than just groups.

## Overlay and Stage Levels

To understand the Flash hierarchy, realize that four organizational levels exist within a movie: the stage level, the overlay level, the layer, and the scene. Figure 4-3 shows a representation of this hierarchy in more detail. Regardless of the number of grouped or ungrouped elements, each layer consists of a stage level and an overlay level. A scene consists of one or more layers.

 **NOTE:** *The previous chapter examined working within a single layer using groups and overlays, without dealing with layers. However, by understanding more about the use of layers, you will be able to efficiently create animations and drawings.*

In figure 4-3 (a), notice that each layer consists of an overlay level and a stage level. The stage level contains ungrouped objects, such as lines and fills, as well as items that have been broken apart, such as bitmaps or text blocks. The overlay level contains grouped elements, unbroken bitmaps, and text.

Yet, on the screen, as shown in figure 4-3 (b), it is difficult to visually perceive this hierarchy until interaction with the objects begins. Also note that scene 1 consists of layers 1, 2, and 3. Thus, each movie can have multiple scenes, each of which has its own set of layers. Again, each layer has both an overlay level and a stage level. The following are examples of how this hierarchy affects the drawing environment in Flash. Exercise 4-1, which follows, highlights the differences between overlays and groups.

- Grouped objects suddenly appear in front of ungrouped objects after grouping. If you have two ungrouped objects, grouping one will bring it in front of the ungrouped object.

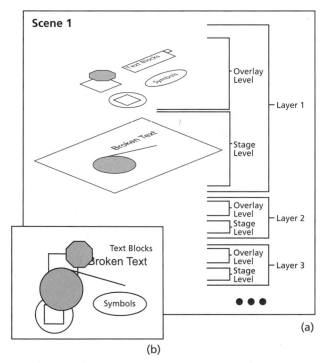

*Figure 4-3 The Flash object hierarchy (a) describes why the environment behaves the way it does, but (b) visually you may not perceive the hierarchy.*

- A grouped object cannot be sent behind an ungrouped object. The Arrange commands only apply to objects within the overlay level, not between the overlay and stage level. Thus, a grouped object cannot be sent behind an ungrouped object. Nor can an ungrouped object be arranged in front of a grouped object.

- Objects that are grouped do not interact (subtract or union), as do ungrouped objects. When an object is grouped, it moves from the stage level to the overlay level. Objects on the overlay level do not interact (subtract or union) with one another.

- Broken text objects, as well as bitmap and fill objects, interact with other fills and objects in the drawing. Because all of these elements reside on the stage level, interaction (subtract or union) occurs.

- Objects that are ungrouped suddenly begin subtracting from other objects. When you ungroup an object, it moves from the overlay level to the top of the stage level, where it is allowed to interact with other ungrouped objects.

### Exercise 4-1 Exploring Overlays and Groups

To see the distinction between overlays and groups, perform the following steps.

1. Start a new file in Flash.

2. Use the Oval tool to draw a filled oval on the stage.

3. Use the Rectangle tool to draw a filled rectangle of a different color. Do not overlap the rectangle on the oval. Note that because neither is grouped, oval and rectangle both exist on the stage level.

4. Select the oval outline and its fill (double click on the oval fill to quickly select both) and group them. This moves the oval line and fill from the stage level to the overlay level.

5. Move the grouped oval so that it overlaps the rectangle. Note that the oval is visually in front of the square.

6. Try to use the Modify | Arrange | Send to Back menu command with the oval selected. The oval will not move behind the rectangle because the oval is on the overlay level. When trying to move the rectangle to the front, notice that because the rectangle is on the stage level the Arrange menu commands are dimmed.

   **NOTE:** *The Arrange commands can never be used on ungrouped objects.*

7. Double click on the rectangle fill (which also selects its lines) and group it. When you group the rectangle, it moves in front of the oval because the rectangle was translated from the stage level to the overlay level during grouping. Anytime you group an element, it will appear at the top of the overlay level.

8. Deselect the rectangle and select the oval.

9. Use Modify | Arrange | Move to Front. Because the oval and rectangle are now both on the overlay level, you can rearrange them at will using the Modify | Arrange menu commands.

10. Select both the oval and the rectangle.

11. Select the Modify | Ungroup menu option and click on a blank spot on the canvas to deselect both the rectangle and oval.

12. Try to select the rectangle or oval and move it. Notice that part of the object you selected has been erased. When both entities were ungrouped, they both translated back to the stage level. Once on that level, deselecting caused an interaction (subtract or union) of the elements.

Since nothing in the drawing environment exists that specifically says "this is the overlay level" or "this is the stage level," the distinction between the two may seem contrived. However, theoretically the distinction describes the way grouped and ungrouped objects behave, as well as how they are defined in the application and resulting movie.

The biggest distinction between these two theoretical levels is that the stage level contains ungrouped and broken elements, and the overlay level contains grouped elements, text objects, and symbols. In addition, ungrouped elements interact (subtract or add), depending on fill and line colors, whereas grouped elements do not.

 **NOTE:** *It is vitally important to understand these distinctions between the overlay and the stage levels before moving on to layers.*

## Layers

To better understand the overlay and stage levels, it is important to take a look at layers. When building drawings, you will undoubtedly want to create items on various layers. Each layer in Flash contains its own special elements, and is distinct and separate from other layers, just as objects between the stage and overlay level are separate and distinct. The following sections take a closer look at how layers can be used to organize drawings. When creating animations, the use of layers will become more important and more apparent.

## Working with Layers

You use the timeline area of the interface to work with layers in Flash. Up to this point, the discussion of layers has concentrated on working within a single layer to make it easier to deal with the drawing environment.

Layers are displayed as individual channels (or rows) within the timeline. Objects on layers higher in the layer order display in front of objects on layers lower in the layer order. In figure 4-4, for example, objects on layer 1 would be displayed in front of objects on layer 3.

Flash's layer ordering is the same as FreeHand, Illustrator, and Photoshop. Uppermost layers are higher in the stage order. Director, however, is the exact opposite. In Director, uppermost layers (channels) are furthest back in the stage order. Note the small button at the far right of the timeline bar (labeled in figure 4-4). Clicking on this button (Modify Frame View) reveals a drop-down menu that lets you customize the way the timeline is displayed.

If there are many frames in a movie, you can use this drop-down to reduce the width of the frames to allow more of them to be viewed within the timeline area. To view more layers, you can either drag the bottom

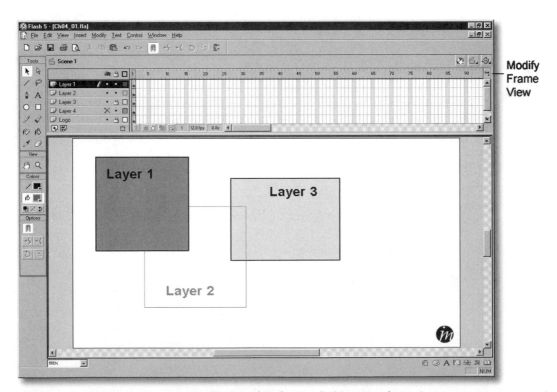

*Figure 4-4 Objects on layer 1 are displayed in front of objects on layer 3.*

of the timeline down the screen or, if you have multiple monitors, detach the timeline altogether and place it in a second monitor.

## Layer States

When looking at a layered movie, the first things you will notice are the small icons and dots to the right of the layer names. These icons and dots indicate the current state of the layer. Above layer 1 in figure 4-5, you see three icons. The "eye" indicates whether the layer is hidden. The "padlock" indicates whether the layer is locked. The small rectangle indicates the preview color for the layer. An examination of figure 4-5 reveals the following:

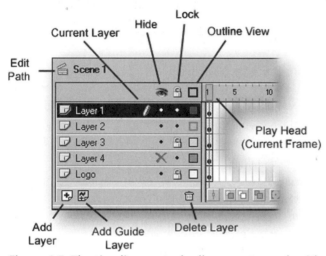

Figure 4-5 The timeline controls allow you to work with the layers in your movie scene. See also color plate B-1.

- The small pencil icon indicates that layer 1 is the current layer. This means that anything drawn or pasted into the movie will be placed on that layer. Only one layer can be the current layer. When a layer is the current layer, it is also identified by black shading.

- The square in layer 2 (which is red) indicates that it is currently in Outline mode. As you read in Chapter 2, you can use the View menu to change the display quality of your drawing as you work. You can also change the display quality for an individual layer. Here, layer 2 has been set to red outlines. Although the items on layer 2 are simple, understand that by-layer outlining is usually used when a particular layer contains complex elements that take a while to redraw. You can speed up performance by setting layers (ones with complex elements) to Outline mode. Note also that there are a variety of colors you can use for outlining.

- The padlock icon in layer 3 specifies that it is locked. When a layer is locked, the items on the layer are visible, but you cannot select, edit, or move items on that layer. This is helpful when you are creating complex images or animations and want to see an item but not select it.

- The X icon in layer 4 indicates that the layer is hidden, in which case none of the elements on that layer can be seen or edited.

To change the state of any given layer, you simply click on the dots under the eye, padlock, or rectangle. This is a refreshing change from earlier versions of Flash. By being able to directly access the layer states, you can work much more quickly. Note that layers can have multiple states. For example, a layer could be in Outline mode, as well as locked. Additionally, the current layer can be locked or hidden. However, if the current layer is locked or hidden and you try to draw or paste, Flash will prompt you that it cannot draw or paste until a layer is assigned as the correct layer.

 **NOTE:** *To be able to paste or draw, the current layer must be unlocked and visible.*

Pay close attention to the layer states when beginning to work with layers. Invariably, at some point you will start drawing only to find that you are on the wrong layer. It happens to everyone. Just keep in mind that anything drawn or pasted is created on the current layer. The sections that follow discuss how to add, delete, and manipulate layers. For practice in working with the Layer modes, see the following CD-ROM exercise.

 **TIP:** *You can quickly hide all layers by holding down the Ctrl key (Option on the Mac) and clicking in any layer, under the eye icon. If you hold down the Alt key (Command on the Mac) and click under the eye, all layers except the one you clicked in will be hidden. This same trick works for locking or outlining layers.*

---

 *CD-ROM Exercise*

To see how the Layer modes work, open the *file ch04_01.fla* located in the *F5gai/chapter4* folder, installed from the companion CD-ROM. This file contains five layers currently set to various modes. When opening the file, you may have to adjust the separation line between the timeline and stage to view all of the layers.

Adjust the various layer states. Additionally, experiment with elements on specific layers by making a layer current and then drawing on it. Turn the layers on and off to see that the elements were placed on the current layer.

### Adding, Deleting, and Modifying Layers

Adding, deleting, and modifying layers is a relatively easy task due to the Add Layer and Delete Layer buttons found in the bottom of the timeline. Use them to add and delete layers (see figure 4-5). The Add Guide Layer button, shown in figure 4-5, is discussed in more detail later in this chapter.

To add a layer, click on the Add Layer button. The layer will be inserted above the currently selected layer. You can also use the Insert | Layer menu option, which will instead add a layer at the bottom of the timeline. To remove a layer, select the layer you want to delete and click on the Delete Layer button. Note that when you add layers they are given a default name. Renaming is accomplished by double clicking on the layer name or by selecting the layer and using Modify | Layer, which opens the Layer Properties dialog box, shown in figure 4-6. Here you can adjust any of the layer's properties. As you can see, this is where you determine the color used when the layer is set to Outline mode.

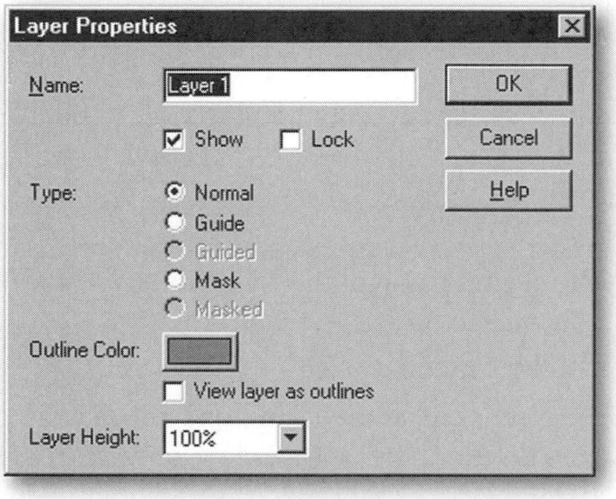

The Layer Height drop-down list (see figure 4-6) allows you to adjust the display height of the layer in the timeline. As you will see in later chapters, when you add sound, actions, labels, or comments to a layer, they are represented in the timeline. Adjusting the height of the timeline makes reading the timeline easier when a layer or keyframe has such elements associated with it.

After some layers have been created in your drawing, you may want to rearrange their order. To move a layer higher in the ordering, click and drag it to where you want it located. Use click-drag to move layers up and down in the timeline.

In addition to the functionality previously described, Flash offers a context menu that can be used to quickly perform many of these operations. Figure 4-7 shows the context menu, accessed by right-clicking on a layer. The CD-ROM exercise that follows provides further practice in working with layers.

*Figure 4-6   The Layer Properties dialog box shows you all attributes of a selected layer.*

*Figure 4-7   Using the layer's context menu to access its options.*

## CD-ROM Exercise

To continue examining how layers work, open the file *ch04_01.fla* located in the *F5gai/chapter4* folder, installed from the companion CD-ROM. Perform the following steps. You will discover that working with layers is relatively easy.

1. Click on the Insert Layer button to add a new layer to the drawing. Note that when adding a layer, the new layer becomes the current layer and is added above the currently selected layer.

2. Double click on the default name of the layer you just created and enter a new name for it.

3. Draw some elements on the new layer.

4. Delete layer 3 by selecting it and clicking on the Delete Layer button. When deleting, the layers below shift up in the layer order.

5. Click-drag on layer 2 in the timeline and move it to the top of the layer order. Note that because layer 2 is now at the top of the layer order, its rectangle appears in front of all other items on the stage.

6. Select the rectangle labeled layer 1 on the stage. When you select it, notice that frame 1 turns black. When selecting items on the stage, the frames associated with those items turn black, indicating in which layer and frames they reside. If multiple items that occur on multiple layers are selected, frames respective to each item and layer will appear black.

When you select an item on the stage that is not on the current layer, the item's layer becomes the current layer. As long as the item is visible and not locked, selecting an item makes its layer the current layer.

**NOTE:** *The steps that follow are vitally important because they are where most confusion concerning layers comes into play.*

7. Set the state of all layers to visible and unlocked by right-clicking on any layer and selecting Show All in the context menu. This makes all layers visible and unlocked.

8. Use Edit | Select All (Ctrl + A or Command + A) to select all items. When you do a select all, all items on all layers are selected, in addition to items that may be on the current

layer. The only way to keep items in other layers from being selected is to lock their respective layers.

9. Deselect the items by clicking in a blank spot on the stage.

10. Select the square on layer 1 and use Modify | Ungroup (Ctrl + Shift + G or Command + Shift + G) to ungroup it. Repeat this for the square on layer 2. Hide the remaining layers.

11. Select several items that make up the objects contained on layers 1 and 2. When multiple layers are set to Normal, their elements can be selected. Generally, this ability is what causes confusion when making selections. If you do not get in the habit of locking or hiding layers, making specific selections in a multilayer movie may be difficult.

12. Examine one more thing concerning layers. Notice that the elements on layers 1 and 2 are ungrouped. Although these elements still reside on their respective layers, they are ungrouped on those layers. Use Modify | Select All (Ctrl + A or Command + A) to pick all of the elements. Frames in layers 1 and 2 will turn black, indicating that the selected elements are contained on those layers.

13. Use Modify | Group to group the elements. After this step, note that two groups are created. Selected elements on layer 1 are grouped and remain on layer 1. Selected elements on layer 2 are grouped and remain on layer 2. When items from multiple layers are grouped, groups are created for each layer. Other programs, such as FreeHand, shift all elements to a single layer. Flash, however, does not.

In a multilayer movie, when an object is selected, the frames associated with the object and its layer turn black. If multiple layers are visible and unlocked, be careful so as not to inadvertently select items you do not intend to manipulate.

 **NOTE:** *The only way to keep from selecting objects unintentionally is by locking the layer (or locking the object).*

## Layer View Modes

When working with complex drawings in which there are many layers, remembering which objects are on which layers can be complicated. As drawings become more complex, making selections becomes more difficult, and the screen redraw time requires more processing.

To speed up drawing, computation, and selection time, change the View mode of a layer. Similar to the View | Outlines menu option, the View modes allow only outlines to be seen. However, instead of being applied to the entire movie environment, the Layer View modes only affect a single layer. This allows you to set different layers to distinct colored outlines. The outlines can be set to Red, Orange, Blue, and so on within the Layer Properties dialog box (see figure 4-6). This can be very helpful for increasing the redraw speed and simplifying the selection process when working with complex drawings. The following CD-ROM exercise provides practice in working with Layer View modes.

### CD-ROM Exercise

See how Layer View modes work by reopening the file *ch04_01.fla* located in the *F5gai/chapter4/* folder, installed from the companion CD-ROM. Try changing the View mode for the various layers to see what it does.

### Special Layers: Masks and Guides

Within your movies two special types of layers can be created: mask and guide layers. Masks allow everything on the layer to be hidden directly beneath the mask, except in cases where the placed object is filled. This is similar to Paste Inside in FreeHand or Layer Grouping (Clipping Groups) in Photoshop. Guide layers, on the other hand, allow specific paths for animations to be defined. Later in this chapter, you will find examples of these types of layers and how they relate to animation creation.

# ▪ ▪ ▪ Creating a Basic Animation in Flash

The animation examples that follow are quite simple. While continuing to build on concepts, you will learn how to create more complex animations. The first sample is the Cyber Outpost image, shown in figure 4-8. The goal of this animation is to make the words *The Cyber Outpost* appear on the screen. Use this simple example as an introduction to basic animation and frame concepts in Flash in the following CD-ROM exercise.

### CD-ROM Exercise

Open the file *ch04_02a.fla* located in the *F5gai/chapter4* folder, installed from the companion CD-ROM. Realize that the image shown in figure 4-8 has already been created. Your task will be to animate it. To render your own version of the image for

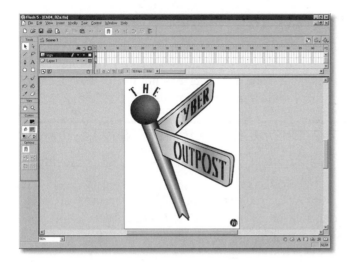

Figure 4-8 A basic example to help you get familiar with frame identifiers and frame-by-frame animation in Flash.

practice, the file *ch04_02b.fla* contains only lines. In this file, you can color your own version of the Cyber Outpost image to be animated.

## Creating Layers

In regard to the previous CD-ROM exercise, upon starting the movie file, recognize that the file has a single layer and a single frame, as shown in the timeline. The text elements are broken apart and grouped. You can see this if you click on them. You want to first create some layers for each of the elements to help organize the movie. It is easier to make objects appear on the stage if they are distinguished by layer. Use the Insert Layer button to produce three more layers for a total of four, as shown in figure 4-9.

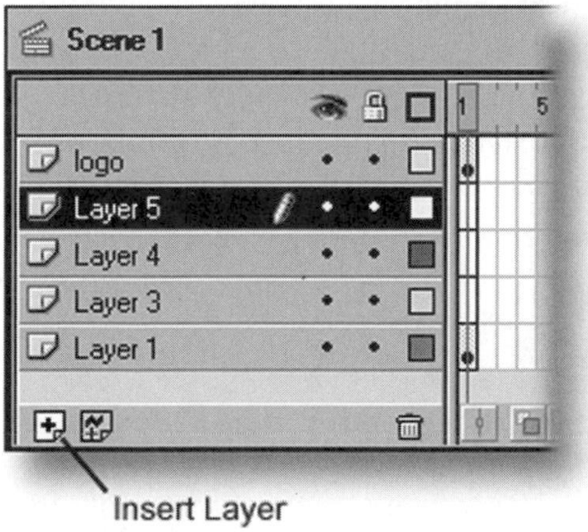

## Naming Layers

Once you have some layers, you will need to name them. It is important to name layers because the more layers you get, the easier it is to become confused about which object is on what layer. Rename each layer, as follows, by double clicking on the layer's name in the timeline:

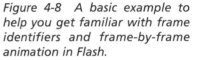

Insert Layer

Figure 4-9 Adding layers to a file is accomplished using the Insert Layer button.

- Name layer 1 *Background*.
- Name layer 3 *The*.
- Name layer 4 *Cyber*.
- Name layer 5 *Outpost*.

## "Moving" Objects to a New Layer

You now want to move the elements from the Background layer to each of the named layers you created. To do this, use the cut and paste options to move the objects from one layer to another. In exercise 4-2, which follows, you will position each object on the appropriate layer.

### Exercise 4-2 Moving Elements to a New Layer

The steps that follow take you through the process of moving elements to a new layer.

1. Click on the Arrow tool. Select the *The* text. Frame 1 in the Background layer turns black, indicating that the text resides on that layer.

2. Use Edit | Cut (Ctrl + X or Command + X).

3. Click on layer The to make it the current layer. Remember that when you paste or draw, elements are placed on the current layer. Clicking on a layer makes it the current layer, as indicated by the pencil icon next to the layer.

4. Use Edit | Paste In Place (Ctrl + Shift + V or Command + Shift + V) to insert the object in the exact stage position it was cut from. If you used the default paste procedure (Ctrl + V or Command + V), the object would be placed in the center of the stage.

5. Repeat this process and place the *Cyber* text on the Cyber layer and the *Outpost* text on the Outpost layer.

6. After moving the objects to their appropriate layers, if it happens that the background layer is "hiding" the other layers, click-drag the Background layer to the bottom of the layer order so that you can see the text components.

7. Save the file, as you will continue working with it in material to follow.

## Working with Frames

With the objects already separated onto layers, the next step is to start working with frames. Working with the timeline's frames can be a little disconcerting at first. Nevertheless, once you get the hang of it, the process will become second nature.

# Identifiers

One of the goals of Flash 5 was to make the interface more consistent with other Macromedia products, particularly Director. One of the significant changes is that sets of frames that contain objects are now called sprites, which act as singular units. In prior versions, frames did not act as a single unit.

 **TIP:** *Although not recommended, if you prefer the Flash 4 method of frame identification and manipulation, you can use the Preferences to make the Flash 5 timeline behave like Flash 4. Enable the Flash 4 Frame Drawing checkbox to make identification like version 4. Enable Flash 4 Selection Style to make frame selection like version 4.*

Due to this change, there are now five basic frame representations that can exist in the timeline, as shown in figure 4-10. The first layer, Blank Frames, shows the representation for a set of frames that contain no objects. When creating animations in Flash, you build from the left of the timeline using blank frames. If you want an object to appear at, for example, frame 10, you insert blank frames up to and including frame 10 and then place a keyframe. This process is discussed in more detail later in the chapter.

The second layer shown in figure 4-10, named Static Sprite, shows a sprite that simply exists on the stage, beginning at frame 1 and ending at frame 15. Note that it begins with a keyframe, which is an initial definition of objects' respective locations, sizes, orientations, and colors. A black circle identifies a keyframe. The sprite extends to frame 15, in which there is the endframe indicator (a small, hollow rectangle).

Sprites in the timeline are completely adjustable as far as their starting point (keyframe) and duration (endframe) are concerned. This is a significant change from Flash 4. You can click-drag a keyframe to move the point at which the objects (represented by the keyframe) appear on the stage. Similarly, you can click-drag the endframe indicator to change the duration of the sprite, which is the amount of time the objects appear on the stage. Clicking on the center of a sprite selects

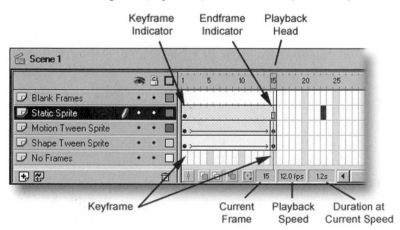

*Figure 4-10 The various frame identifiers assist the user in the development and identification of frames. See also color plate B-2.*

all frames associated with it. When an entire sprite is selected, you can click-drag it to another location in the timeline.

The third and fourth layers (Motion Tween Sprite and Shape Tween Sprite, respectively) are the two types of tweened animation. Notice that both types of tween sprites begin and end with a keyframe. As with static sprites, you can click-drag these keyframes to adjust starting time and duration. (Static sprites are discussed in detail later in the chapter.) Finally, the last layer has no frames defined.

View the working file for the Cyber Outpost animation. Notice that four keyframes exist: one on each layer. Keyframes are frames that define primary position, orientation, or size of objects on the stage. In the timeline, keyframes containing graphical components are displayed as a filled black dot. Again, frames that do not have graphical elements in them ("blank keyframes") are displayed as white areas. By continuing with the exercises, you will see how the frame identifiers change during the creation of the animation.

Editing objects on the stage affects the nearest left keyframe. If the playback head is between a keyframe indicator and an endframe indicator, the objects in the keyframe are modified.

 **NOTE:** *Pay close attention to where the playback head is located when editing (moving, rotating, or scaling) objects on the stage.*

## Adding and Deleting Frames

Continue with the example you were working on to learn more. The Cyber Outpost animation will occur over 20 frames. The background of the animation stays the same over those 20 frames, whereas the remaining three layers will change to create the animation.

To begin, add copied frames to the background so that it exists on the stage as the movie plays. Frames can be inserted into the timeline using the context menu, the Insert menu, or the mouse and timeline. You will see how to perform all three methods.

Add some frames to the Background layer by selecting the first frame of the Background layer and right-clicking with the mouse. In the context menu that pops up, select Insert Frame. This adds a copied frame to the Background layer, as shown in figure 4-11. Note that many commands can be executed on the selected frame in the context menu.

 **TIP:** *To bring up the context menu when using a Macintosh and single-button mouse, hold down the Ctrl key and click and hold on a frame.*

In addition to using the context menu, frames may also be added using the Insert menu. First, click on frame 2 in the Background layer. Use the

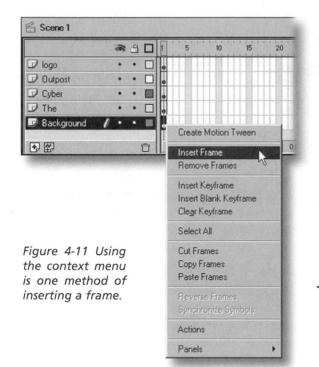

*Figure 4-11 Using the context menu is one method of inserting a frame.*

Insert | Frame menu option to insert a frame. You can also quickly add frames by selecting a specific frame in the time-line and pressing the F5 function key. Often the quickest method of adding frames to an animation is to drag the frame to a specific location in the time-line. For example, click-drag on frame 3 in the Background layer and drag the frame out to frame 20, as shown in fig-ure 4-12.

Once the Background layer is extended, do the same thing on the other three layers, all at once. Click in frame 1 of the "logo" layer, hold down the Shift key, and click on the other three keyframes. This will select a sin-gle frame across all four layers, as shown in figure 4-13. Then press and hold the F5 key to move the frames out to frame 20.

Note that when a sprite has an end-frame indicator (meaning that there are at least two frames in the sprite), you can click-drag on the endframe indicator to extend the sprite duration. When there is only a single keyframe in the sprite, click-dragging it will move the keyframe, as opposed to extending its duration.

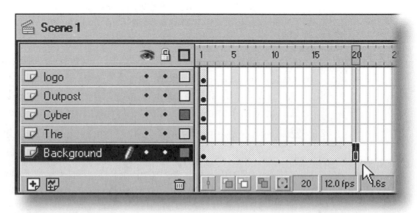

*Figure 4-12 When the endframe indicator is shown on a sprite, you can click-drag it to extend the duration of a sprite.*

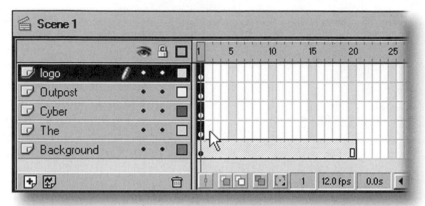

*Figure 4-13 You can select a frame across multiple layers by holding down the Shift key and clicking on frames in different layers.*

# Working with Blank Frames and Keyframes

To finish the animation, you will insert some keyframes and delete some elements so that each of the text components appears on the stage at two frame increments. Exercise 4-3, which follows, takes you through this process.

## Exercise 4-3 Inserting Keyframes and Deleting Elements

To make each text component appear on the stage at two frame increments, perform the following steps.

1.  Begin by clicking on frame 3 of the The layer. The entire sprite will be selected and the playhead will move to frame 3. Right-click and select Insert Keyframe from the context menu. Repeat this process in frames 5 and 7, as shown in figure 4-14.

With the keyframes in place, you next need to modify the text contained in each keyframe. You will change the text element so that the first keyframe has no text, the second displays the T, the third shows Th, and the fourth reveals The.

2.  Select the first sprite in the The layer by clicking on frames 1 and 2 while holding down the Shift key.

When a sprite consists of just two frames, to select the entire sprite you must click in the keyframe and the endframe while holding down the Shift key. When a sprite consists of more than two frames, clicking in the middle of the sprite selects all frames associated with it.

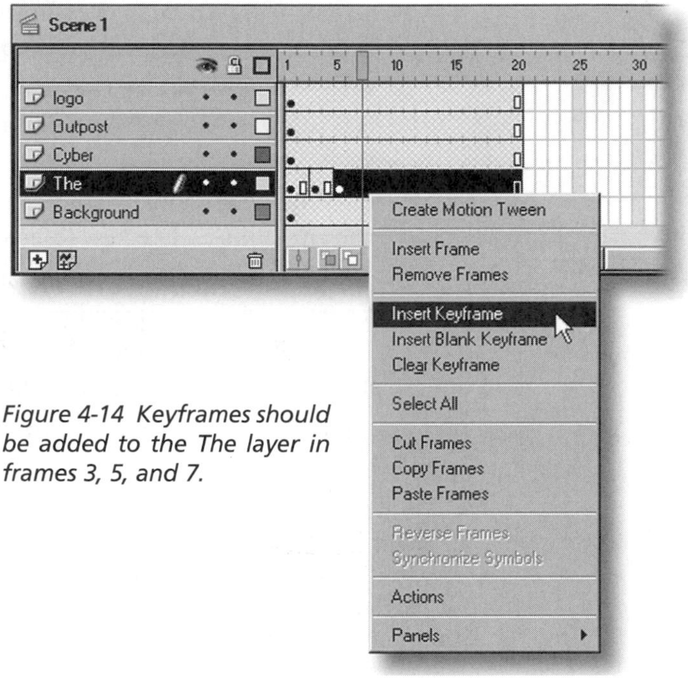

*Figure 4-14 Keyframes should be added to the The layer in frames 3, 5, and 7.*

3.  Press the Delete key to remove the text from the stage and the definition of it in the timeline. Note that the frame identifier changes to a blank frame representation.

When creating animations, you have to build frames from the left, and you cannot have blank areas (with no frames) in the timeline. For entities such as the T for the second key to appear on the stage at frame 3, blank frames must be built to that point. You cannot simply insert a keyframe at frame 3 with nothing in front of it.

**NOTE:** *Always build frames from the left.*

Unlike programs such as Director, "blank" spaces (no frames) cannot be placed between sets of frames. To make an element appear or start at a particular time, build blank frames to that point and then enter a keyframe.

4.  Click on frame 3 in layer The.
5.  Ungroup the text using Modify | Ungroup.
6.  Delete the *h* and *e*.
7.  Repeat this process in frame 5 by removing the *e*.
8.  Once this is completed, use the Control | Rewind and Control | Play menu options to view the animation.

9.  To finish the animation, you will modify the Cyber and Outpost layers so that they appear on the stage at the appropriate time.

10. Select frame 9 in the Cyber layer and right-click to insert a keyframe.

11. Click between frame 1 and frame 9 (to select the sprite) and press the Delete key, to delete the *Cyber* text.

12. Repeat this process for the Outpost layer by adding a keyframe in frame 11, and removing the *Outpost* text in the first sprite. Use the Rewind and Play options in the Control menu to view the final animation.

Because timing in Flash is affected by the Frame Rate setting of the movie and the number of frames to be played, you can speed up or slow down the animation you just created by adjusting the playback speed of the movie or by adding or deleting frames. Adjust the playback rate of an animation through the Modify | Movie Properties dialog box to change the overall playback speed.

Alternatively, to change the playback speed of a specific portion of an animation, add or delete frames as needed. In the example you created, change the timing of any of the elements by clicking the playhead to a specific location (click where the numbers are). Then use Insert | Frame or the F5 function key to add frames.

In general, playback rates can be set higher than the default of 12. However, the number of elements, the view quality settings, and the playback machine for the animation affect the maximum playback speed.

 **CD-ROM NOTE:** *A completed example of the Cyber Outpost animation is found in the* F5gai/chapter4 *folder, installed from the companion CD-ROM. The file is named* c04_02c.fla. *Open this file if you want to compare your results with the example.*

## Cel Animation Tools

In the previous example, the simple animation displays items on the stage at different times. Using similar techniques combined with Flash's cel animation tools, movement can be created. The instructions in this section will help you create another cel-type animation. However, this time some useful "traditional" tools will be highlighted, as well as interesting frame manipulation techniques. Figure 4-15 shows the image with which you will be working. See the following CD-ROM exercise to begin this process.

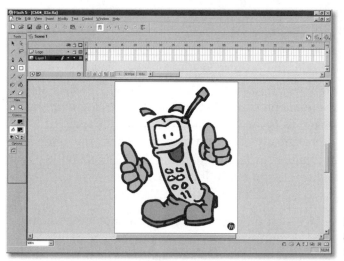

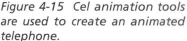

*Figure 4-15 Cel animation tools are used to create an animated telephone.*

## CD-ROM Exercise

Open the file *ch04_03a.fla* located in the *F5gai/chapter4* folder, installed from the companion CD-ROM. Follow along and create the example animation described in this section. As with the previous exercise, if you would rather render your own version of the image for practice, the file *ch04_03b.fla* contains only lines. By beginning with this file, you can color your own version of the phone. Similarly, a finished version of the animation is also found on the companion CD-ROM (*ch04_3-D.fla*). Look at the finished version to know what you are about to create.

To begin this animation, you will first layer the items. In this exercise, you will animate the hands, eyebrows, and eyes of the telephone. The steps that follow take you through the process of creating separate layers for each of these items.

1. Name the existing layer Background.

2. Create three new layers and give them each a name: Hands, Eyebrows, and Eyes.

3. Select the objects that constitute the right hand. Group them, cut them, and paste them in place on the Hands layer.

4. Repeat this process for the left hand. Place it on the Hands layer as well.

5. Select the objects that constitute the right eyebrow and group them. Cut and paste these elements in place on the

Eyebrows layer. Repeat the process for the left eyebrow and place those elements on the Eyebrows layer as well.

6. Select the right eye, group it, and put it on the Eye layer. Repeat with the process for the left eye, placing it on the Eye layer as well.

7. Complete the process by extending the duration of all five sprites out to frame 15. Set the playhead to frame 1 if it is not there already (click on frame 1 where the timeline frame numbers are), and then use the F5 function key to move the duration out to frame 15.

8. Save your work.

With the objects on different layers, start animating by working with the eyes and eyebrows first. In the finished animation, the eyes will move from side to side and the eyebrows up and down. The following steps take you through the process of animating the eyes and eyebrows:

1. Insert a keyframe in frames 2, 3, and 4 in the Eyes and Eyebrows layers.

 **TIP:** *You can add the keyframe to both layers at the same time by clicking in a frame in one layer, holding down the Shift key, and clicking in the same frame in the second layer. Then use the F6 function key to insert a keyframe.*

2. Move the playhead to frame 2. Using the Arrow tool on the stage, move the eyes on the stage so that they look toward the left. Then move the playhead to frame 3 and move the eyes so that they look toward the right, again using the Arrow tool. Leave frame 4 in the original position.

3. Move the playhead to frame 2 and, using the arrow keys, move the left eyebrow down on the stage. In frame 3, move the right eyebrow down. Again, leave frame 4 alone.

4. Using Control | Rewind and then Control | Play, play the animation to see what you have created.

5. While the animation played, you probably noticed that it was so quick that it was hard to see what was happening. To slow it down a little, add some frames. Move the playhead to frame 1. Use function key F5 to insert one frame. Repeat this process in the other two keyframes in which the eyes and eyebrows move.

6. Play the animation to see what you have created. Adjust the positioning of the elements to get the image to look the way you want. To alter an object, pick the respective keyframe and layer corresponding to the object, select the object on the stage, and then move the object. Do not forget that you can use the arrow keys to nudge the objects, instead of click-dragging. If you want to rotate the eyebrows a little, you can use the Arrow tool modifiers or the Transform panel to help you.

7. Save what you have completed thus far.

## Creating the Frame-by-Frame Movement

The previous steps were nothing more than an extension of the steps used in the Cyber Outpost animation. The only difference is that you adjusted stage position rather than the time at which the object appeared.

Now you will animate the hands of the phone. This is a little trickier because the motion needs to be smooth across three frames. In exercise 4-4, which follows, you will begin by roughly positioning the hands.

### Exercise 4-4 Animating an Object

To begin animating the hands of the telephone, perform the following steps.

1. Insert keyframes in frames 10 and 11 of the Hands layer.

2. Move the playhead to frame 10. Use the Arrow tool to move and rotate the left hand and right hand, as shown in figure 4-16.

*Figure 4-16 The hands are moved and rotated into position. See also color plate B-3.*

**TIP:** *When rotating objects, the default location for the center of rotation is the center of the object. This can be changed by using the Modify | Transform | Edit Center menu option. After selecting this menu option, move the small plus sign to change the center point for rotation.*

Move the playhead to frame 11. Move and rotate the hands a little more, as shown in figure 4-17. With the hands appropriately positioned, notice that the motion of the animation may not be as smooth as you would like. Flash provides a special tool called Onion-skinning that can help you arrange the elements so that they animate more smoothly. This is how figures 4-16 and 4-17 were created.

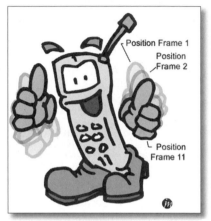

*Figure 4-17 The hands are moved and rotated a little more. See also color color plate B-4.*

## Onion Skin and Onion Skin Outlines

The Onion Skin and Onion Skin Outlines buttons, shown in figure 4-18, allow you to create frame-by-frame animations by showing a representation of before and after frames beside the current frame. Surrounding frames are shown transparently with the current frame.

When you click on the Onion Skin button, two small markers (called, surprisingly, onion markers) appear around the playhead, as shown in figure 4-18. Move the onion markers to reveal more or fewer frames concurrently on the stage. When building frame-by-frame animations, you can turn Onion Skin on to see the frames around the current frame. However, you can only

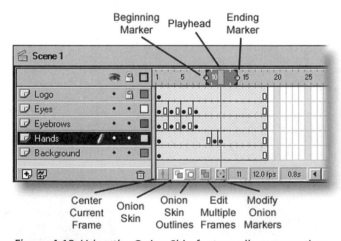

*Figure 4-18 Using the Onion Skin feature allows smoother animations to be created in Flash. See also color plate B-5.*

edit (move, rotate, scale) within the current frame, which is displayed opaque. Semitransparent objects are not editable. In Onion Skin mode, you can move the playhead to the point (frame) you want to edit while still being able to see the frames immediately adjacent to it.

## Using Onion Skin

In exercise 4-5, which follows, you will use the Onion Skin feature while continuing to work on the phone animation. The Onion Skin Outlines button is similar to the Onion Skin button except that instead of showing transparent objects for the neighboring frames, it shows the surrounding frames as outlines.

---

### *Exercise 4-5 Using the Onion Skin Function*

To practice using the Onion Skin feature, perform the following steps.

1. Click on the Onion Skin button in the timeline. Adjust the positions of the hands so that they appear to move smoothly. Onion Skin mode becomes more important in regard to the number of frames you have to compare.

2. Once you are finished modifying your animation, turn off the Onion Skin mode by clicking on the Onion Skin button.

3. Play your movie to view the changes you made.

4. Save the file.

Before you begin using the tweening features of Flash, it is important to review a few other concepts, including copying and pasting frames, reversing frames, and editing multiple frames. The sections that follow explore these processes.

## Copying, Pasting, and Reversing Frames

In the same manner items on the stage are copied and pasted, completed frames can be copied from one position to another in the timeline. When you copy a frame, all objects within that frame are copied. Similarly, when you paste, all items are pasted.

However, note that copy and pasting frames is not necessarily the same thing as copying and pasting objects on the stage. Understanding this difference is important.

**NOTE:** *Pay special attention to whether you have been instructed to copy and paste in the timeline (frames) or on the stage (objects).*

In the telephone animation, you created three hand positions. Using those keyframes you created, in the reverse order, you can make the hands return to their original position. This allows the animation to be looped without having to manually position the hands on the stage. The CD-ROM exercise that follows takes you through this process.

### CD-ROM Exercise

If you have been following along to this point, continue to use the file on which you have been working. Alternatively, load the sample file *ch04_03c.fla* from the *F5gai/chapter4* folder, installed from the companion CD-ROM. Begin by generating a reverse sequence for the hands.

**NOTE:** *If you were just working with Onion Skin, make sure you have turned it off.*

1.  Hold down the Ctrl key (Command on the Mac) and right-click on frame 1 in the Hands layer. Holding down the Ctrl key while clicking on a frame allows you to select the specific frame instead of the entire sprite. Select the Copy Frames option from the context menu.

2.  Hold down the Ctrl key (or Command) again and right-click on frame 12 in the Hands layer. Select Paste Frames in the context menu. The keyframe copied from frame 1 is now pasted in frame 12.

3.  Holding down the Ctrl (or Command) and Shift keys simultaneously (Ctrl to select an individual frame and Shift to do a multiple selection), select frames 10 and 11 in the Hands layer. Right-click and select Copy Frames from the context menu.

4.  Hold down the Ctrl key (or Command) and right-click in frame 13. Select Paste Frames in the context menu. The two frames you just copied should now be in frames 13 and 14.

5.  When you pasted the frames, the endframe of the last sprite may have protruded out a frame or two. Finish the process by click-dragging endframes of the sprites on the other layers to extend them out to the same duration as the Hands layer.

6.  Play your animation. Notice that the animation is not quite right yet. You need to reverse the order of frames 12, 13, and 14 to make it look right.

7.  Hold down the Ctrl (or Command) and Shift keys simultaneously, and click on frames 12, 13, and 14 to select all three.

**TIP:** *You can quickly select multiple adjacent frames by clicking on a frame (with the Ctrl or Command key held down), and then pressing Shift and clicking again. This is similar to using click-Shift-click to select multiple lines of text in a word processor.*

8. Use Modify | Frames | Reverse to reverse or right-click on one of the selected frames, and then select Reverse Frames from the context menu. This reverses the sequence of the frames. However, you will notice that the duration of the sprite in frame 12 is not right. Let's fix it.

When you use reverse frames, it actually reverses the sprites, not just the frames. The sprite in frame 12 was originally at the end and was greater than a single frame. Thus, when you reverse it, the sprite stays the exact same length. There are a number of ways of correcting this. For example, prior to performing the reverse, you could copy the keyframe in frame 1 and paste it in frame 15. Alternatively, you can fix the duration of the sprite after the fact, as you will do in the next few steps.

 **NOTE:** *Be careful of what you select when using Reverse Frames. It is easy to accidentally select the wrong frames (or wrong layers).*

9. Click-drag the endframe in frame 17 back to frame 12.

10. Hold down the Ctrl (or Command) and Shift keys simultaneously and select frames 18 and 19. Click-drag the selection back to frames 13 and 14.

11. Hold down the Ctrl key (or Command), click on frame 14, and use the F5 function key to move the endframe out. See the following Tip to delete the blank frames at the end of the sprite.

 **TIP:** *Quickly delete blank frames by selecting them and pressing the Backspace key.*

12. Play the animation. Notice that the hands move back and forth in a more natural progression.

13. Save your file.

 **TIP:** *To make the animation loop when it reaches the end, use the Control | Loop Playback menu option.*

# Edit Multiple Frames: Sizing Entire Animations

A common question people ask is how to scale an entire animation once it has been created. As simple as it may sound, scaling the telephone animation requires you to select all elements on all layers at one time, across multiple frames.

Flash provides a feature similar in function to Onion Skin, called Edit Multiple Frames, which allows you to view the content of a number of frames at the same time. Unlike Onion Skin, in the Edit Multiple Frames mode all objects are shown as opaque and are editable at the same time.

 **NOTE:** *If Edit Multiple Frames and Onion Skin are enabled, Edit Multiple Frames overrides Onion Skin.*

Because all objects are opaque, it is difficult to tell what is on each layer. In addition, it is easy to mistakenly move the wrong objects, so you do have to be cautious using this feature. However, Edit Multiple Frames is the most simple means of scaling all objects in a movie at the same time. See the following CD-ROM exercise for practice in using the Edit Multiple Frames feature.

 **TIP:** *Keep the Edit Multiple Frames mode from affecting a particular layer by hiding or locking the layer.*

---

 ### CD-ROM Exercise

For this exercise, use the file you have been working with or open the file *ch04_03-D.fla* located in the *F5gai/chapter4* folder, installed from the companion CD-ROM. Begin working with Edit Multiple Frames by performing the following steps.

1. Click on the Edit Multiple Frames button (see figure 4-19).

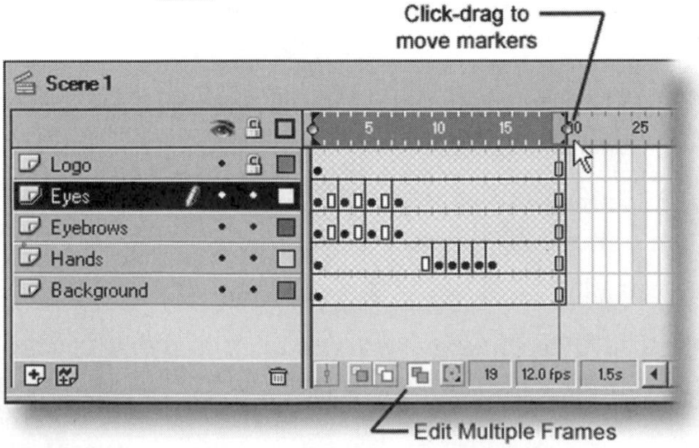

*Figure 4-19 The beginning and ending markers can be moved while in Edit Multiple Frames mode. See also color plate B-6.*

2.  Move the beginning and ending markers in the timeline so that they include the frames that require editing, which in this case is all frames in the animation. Move the pointers so that they are at the beginning and ending frames of the timeline, as shown in figure 4-19.

3.  Click on the stage and use Edit | Select All to select all elements of all frames.

4.  Click on the Arrow tool and select the Scale option.

5.  Click-drag the scale handles on the outer edge of the selection to scale the items.

If your purpose is to scale all objects in the movie, make sure you get them all. If you scale and notice that you missed something, use Edit | Undo and try performing the Select All again.

6.  Deselect the objects by clicking on a blank spot in the canvas.

7.  Click on the Edit Multiple Frames button again to turn it off.

8.  Play the animation to see the results. The only difference is that the animation is now smaller!

 **TIP:** *Remember that you can also use the Transform panel to scale objects numerically.*

Although the telephone animation is quite simple, it has covered several of the basic concepts you will need to understand before you create more complex animations. Sometimes cel animation techniques are the only way of solving an animation problem or of implementing a certain design. However, Flash would be quite limiting if cel were the only method of creating animations. The next section examines tween animation, which is a very powerful capability. Tweening allows much flexibility and makes creating complex animations easier.

**NOTE:** *For more examples of creating special effects, see Chapter 12.*

# ▪ ▪ ▪ Tweened Motion Animation

As is evident from the last section, creating frame-by-frame animations is quite tedious. Although it is good to know, cel animation requires tremendous amounts of time when creating complex animations. This section examines Flash's tweening ability. With tweens you can create animations that center on movement, rotation, scaling, and color (called a *motion tween*), or on shape blends (morphs), called a *shape tween*. You also can produce special guides and mask layers that can be helpful with specific animation tasks.

## Overlay Objects for Tweened Animation

To this point, you have been working with groups, frames, layers, and scenes directly and indirectly. Your repertoire should also include symbols. Chapter 2 identified a special type of timeline called a *symbol*. Symbols are important for file efficiency. Yet, symbols are also very important for motion tweens. Actually, any overlay object (including text, bitmaps, and groups) can be used for tween animation. Realize that stage-level elements cannot be used with motion tweens. This excludes anything that is not grouped or is not a symbol.

Whereas layers and groups are important organizational tools, symbols are important for tween animation and file efficiency. Even though motion tweening in Flash can be performed on other elements, when working with more complex movies, symbols should always be used. As you start the next chapter, you will also see that symbols are important if you want to use the Movie Explorer.

In prior drawings and animations, data was added to the file anytime an object was created or copied to the stage. In the telephone animation from the last section, anytime a keyframe was created, a duplicate copy of objects in your drawing was produced. Flash provides a more efficient means of building reusable components, called symbols. You can reuse symbols over and over without adding multiple copies (redundant data) to your movies.

The three types of symbols are graphics, buttons, and movie clips. This chapter deals with graphic symbols used as static, reusable graphics. Graphic symbols do not necessarily have to be static, but they do have some limitations compared with movie clip symbols. Chapter 5 explores these issues in more detail. In this chapter, you will look at the basics of creating graphic symbols and using them in the main movie timeline for motion tweens.

## Creating a Graphic Symbol

To show how motion tweens work, exercise 4-6, which follows, involves the creation of a simple ball that moves across the screen. It provides a basis for more complex tweened animation examples later.

### Exercise 4-6 Creating a Motion Tween

To begin creating a motion tween, perform the following steps.

1.  Start with a new file in Flash. Use the Oval tool to create a circle with a gradient fill. You may want to use the Paint Bucket's Transform Fill option to move the center point for the gradient so that it looks more like a 3D ball.

2.  Delete the line around the circle.

3. Make a symbol out of the "ball." Select the ball with the Arrow tool and use Insert | Convert to Symbol (or function key F8).

4. A dialog box will pop up, requesting a name for the symbol and information regarding the type of symbol you are about to create. Enter a name and select Graphic for the Behavior. Click on the OK button to make the ball a symbol.

5. Once the symbol is created, you can work with it on the stage. However, you cannot edit it with the painting and drawing tools in the main movie. To edit a symbol, such as changing its color or fill, you access the symbol's timeline. To do this, select the symbol on the stage and use Edit | Edit Symbols.

6. Once you do this, the upper left of the stage area indicates that you are currently in the symbol's timeline and not the main movie's timeline (figure 4-20). While working on a symbol, you can use the painting and drawing tools on the symbol. See how this works by filling the ball with a different gradient. Jump back to the main movie timeline by clicking on the link next to the symbol's name in the upper left. This area is called the Edit Path. When you return to the scene, notice that the fill of the symbol has changed.

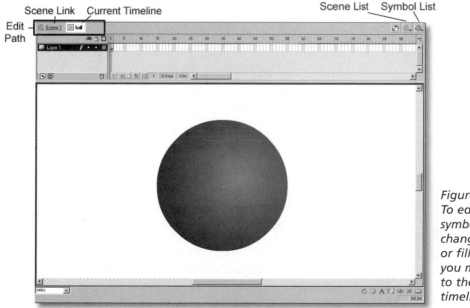

Figure 4-20
*To edit a symbol, such as changing line or fill colors, you must switch to the symbol's timeline.*

Although you used Edit | Edit Symbols, there are other methods for editing a symbol. When you right-click on a symbol in the main timeline, you can choose to Edit, Edit in Place, or Edit in a New Window in the context menu. Edit switches you to the symbol's timeline. Edit in Place can be used if you need to refill or edit the bitmap characteristics on the stage. In this mode, the timeline of the symbol is not shown. Edit in a New Window opens a new Flash window for editing the symbol. This is handy for multiple monitor configurations.

## Working with Instances

When a symbol is placed on the stage of a movie, it is called an *instance*. In simple terms, an instance is a reference to a symbol. In traditional computer terms, the symbol is the data and the instance is a reference to the symbol. You can modify the size, shape, location, and orientation of symbol instances without affecting the actual symbol data. Thus, instances of the same symbol can have various sizes, shapes, locations, and orientations within the same movie.

Flash's symbol, library, and stage relationship is very similar to the relationship among Director's cast member, cast, and stage. The symbol is the data; the instance is the reference to the symbol. Continue in exercise 4-7, which follows, with the example and animate the ball using a motion tween. You begin by setting up the two key positions of the ball on either side of the stage.

### Exercise 4-7 Setting the Stage

To establish the two key positions of the ball on either side of the stage, perform the following steps.

1.  In the timeline, move frame 1 to frame 20 to extend the duration of the instance on the stage.

2.  Move the playhead to frame 1 and move the ball to the left side of the screen.

3.  Hold down the Ctrl key, right-click in frame 20, and select Insert Keyframe from the context menu.

4.  With the playhead in frame 20, define a new position for the ball somewhere on the right side of the screen.

5.  Save your file.

 **TIP:** *If you prefer to use numerical values for instance placement on the stage, you can use the Info panel to define the location of the instance in frame 20. Entering values into the X or Y fields will move the currently selected object.*

## Setting Up the Tween in the Frame Panel

In the timeline, tweening automatically creates interpolated frames (in-between frames) between two keyframes. Size, position, orientation, and color of the two surrounding keyframes can be automatically tweened. You have already created two keyframes in your sample file. The difference between the two keyframes is the location of their instances on the stage. At this point, all you have to do is tell Flash to "tween" between these instances to create an animation of the ball moving across the stage. The CD-ROM exercise that follows takes you through this process.

### CD-ROM Exercise

For this exercise, use the file you have been working with or open the file *ch04_04a.fla* located in the *F5gai/chapter4* folder, installed from the companion CD-ROM. A finished example of the animation is also available (*ch04_04b.fla*). Set up the tween between two keyframes by performing the following steps.

1. Select the sprite by right-clicking on any frame between 2 and 18. Notice the Create Motion tween shortcut in the menu. You could use this to quickly create the tween. However, you should know where you can manually set it up. Select the Panels | Frame option in the context menu to open the Frame panel. You could also use Window | Panels | Frame.

2. In the Frame panel, set the Tweening drop-down to Motion, as shown in figure 4-21.

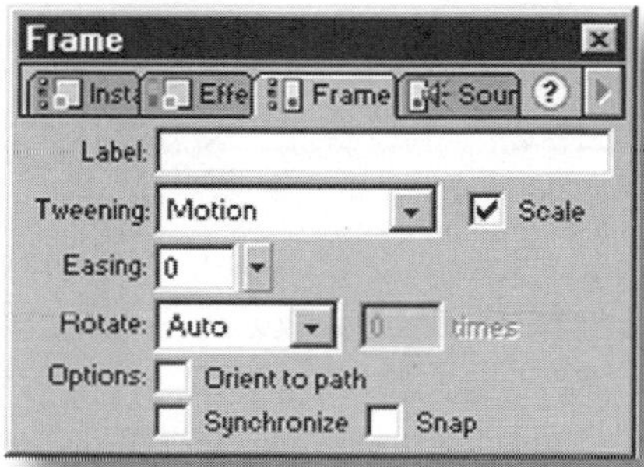

When setting up tween animations, you can actually right-click on any part of the sprite to set up the tweening. However, when working with multiple layers, make sure you select the correct sprite. Even the best user occasionally selects the wrong layer when dealing with numerous layers.

*Figure 4-21 The Frame panel is where you define that the sprite should be assigned to motion tween.*

3. Once you have set the Tweening drop-down, note that the area between the two keyframes is represented with a blue background and an arrow. This frame identifier denotes motion tween animation, as shown in figure 4-22 (a). If the

tween is not successful, for whatever reason, the timeline will display the frames as a dashed line, as shown in figure 4-22 (b).

(a) Successful tween

(b) Unsuccessful tween

*Figure 4-22 The Tween frame identifier shows that a tween animation was (a) successfully applied or (b) unsuccessfully applied. See also color plate B-7.*

4.  Play back the movie to see the animation that has been automatically created.

 **TIP:** *Use the Enter key as a shortcut to start and stop animations, rather than the Control menu.*

When working with basic tween animation, you should keep the following in mind.

- *Motion tweening only works on symbols, text, bitmaps, or groups.* Tweening has no effect when objects are individual elements residing on the stage level. If tweening is applied to objects on the stage level, the timeline will represent the tween as a dashed line with no arrows. Additionally, when the animation is played, nothing will happen.

- *Tweening only works on individual symbols, text elements, bitmaps, or groups.* To tween several items at once, each must reside on an individual layer.

- *Tweening is a frame property.* To set up tweening, you must right-click in the sprite and use the Frame panel. Alternatively, you can use the Modify | Frame (Ctrl + F or Command + F) menu option to open the Frame panel.

- *Tweening is often a quick means of setting up animations.* However, realize that once a tween has been created, you can define additional keyframes by using a right-click in the tween. This allows you to further modify and tweak a sequence. For example, in the previous example, you could make the ball "bounce" by selecting frame 10 and pulling the ball down on the stage. The tweening would then be occurring between three keys instead of two.

In addition to the Tweening property, frames can be assigned label, sound, and action properties. The Labels field is found in the Frame panel. Sounds and actions have their own panels. Chapter 6 discusses how labels and actions are assigned to frames. Chapter 7 describes working with the Sound panel.

## Other Tween Settings in the Frame Panel

In addition to the default settings, you have control over the following aspects of the tween, as shown in figure 4-22. The CD-ROM exercise that follows provides practice in using the Scale, Rotate, and Easing options.

- *Scale:* Assuming the size of an instance changes between two keyframes, this setting determines whether the size of the object is tweened.

- *Easing:* Often when creating animation, you may want an animated object to speed up or slow down during its tween. Easing allows you to adjust the speed of the tween. Ease In slows the beginning of the tween, whereas Ease Out slows the end of the tween.

- *Rotate:* This option specifies whether the object rotates during the tween. It also allows you to set the number of times the object rotates during the tween.

- *Orient to Path:* When the instance is asymmetric in shape, the Orient to Path option determines how the object travels along a path. See the section "Understanding Guide Layers" in this chapter for more information regarding the effects of this setting.

- *Synchronize:* If the number of frames in a graphic symbol's animation is not an even multiple of the scene's timeline, the symbol animation may play sporadically. The Synchronize option restarts the graphic symbol when the scene loops.

- *Snap:* This forces the motion tween to follow the guide associated with the layer. You will read more about guide layers later in this chapter.

### CD-ROM Exercise

View how the Scale, Rotate, and Easing options work. Open the file *ch04_04b.fla* located in the *F5gai/chapter 4* folder, installed from the companion CD-ROM. Adjust the tweening options for the ball.

## Using the Effects Panel

Motion tweens alone are a nifty feature of Flash. As you have seen, you can use a motion tween to animate position, location, and size using the Frame panel. However, you can do one other thing when you are using motion tweening. The "color" properties of a symbol instance can be adjusted on the stage, thus making it possible to animate the instance as part of a motion tween. This is how you make objects appear and disappear during a movie, as well as create a wide range of other effects.

The term *color* is used broadly here, covering the ability to adjust brightness (amount of black or white applied to an instance), tint (the pureness of the symbol), and alpha characteristic (opacity). Flash also provides a mechanism for modifying all three of these characteristics simultaneously. In the following CD-ROM exercise you can take a closer look at how this works.

 **NOTE:** *The Effects panel will only work on symbols. It has no effect on groups, text objects, or stage-level objects.*

### CD-ROM Exercise

See how effects can be animated using motion tweens. Open the file *ch04_05a.fla* located in the *F5gai/chapter4* folder, installed from the companion CD-ROM. Follow along with the exercise. The completed file is named *ch04_05b.fla*.

Figure 4-23 shows the example with which you will be working in exercise 4-8, which follows. You will use the Alpha option in the Effect panel to make objects disappear by setting the first keyframe to 100 percent alpha (also the default) and the last keyframe to 0 percent. In this example, you will make objects 1 and 3 go from 100 percent opaque in frame 1 to 100 percent transparent in frame 20. Object 2 will go from 100 percent transparent to 100 percent opaque.

### Exercise 4-8 Creating a Color-effect Animation

To create a color-effect animation, perform the following steps.

1.  Move the playhead to frame 20 so that you are working in keyframes in frame 20.

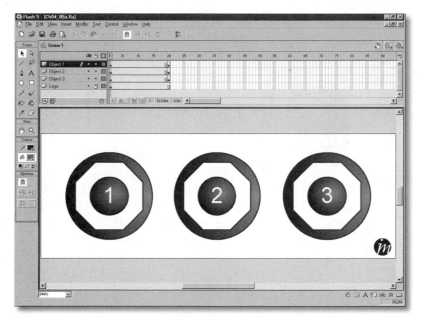

*Figure 4-23 A tweened effect can be created by modifying the alpha levels of a symbol instance.*

Recall that because effects are instance properties they will work only on symbol instances. Thus, they are applied to the objects on the stage rather than to frames in the timeline. However, make sure you are in the right frame before applying the effect.

2. Right-click on object 1 on the stage. Select the Panels | Effect option in the context menu to open the Effect panel.

3. Click on the drop-down menu and select Alpha.

4. At frame 20, object 1 needs to totally disappear; therefore, set the slider next to the drop-down menu to 0, as shown in figure 4-24. Object 1 should disappear on the stage.

5. Move the playhead to frame 1 and click on object 2 on the stage. Set the instance's Alpha to 0 in the Effect panel.

6. Repeat the process on object 3 and set its Alpha to 0. Make sure to move the playhead to frame 20 before adjusting the Alpha. Otherwise, the

*Figure 4-24 The Effect panel allows the "color" attributes of the symbol instance to be set.*

instance in frame 1 will be changed instead of the instance in frame 20.

7.  Now that you have applied effects to the symbol instances in various frames, quickly assign the motion tween by right-clicking somewhere between frames 2 and 18 on each of the sprites in each layer. Select Create Motion Tween in the context menu.

8.  Play the animation to see the effect of the motion tweens on the applied effects.

You can change the Brightness, Tint, or Alpha setting during any tween. Use varying combinations of the three during any tween animation using the Advanced option. Keep in mind that objects can also change size, location, or orientation at the same time as an effect. Each of these effects means different things in terms of the effect they can create or manipulate, as follows. To explore these other effects, see the CD-ROM exercise that follows.

*   *Brightness* is the lightness or darkness of an instance. The instance is lightened by adding white and darkened by adding black.

*   *Tint* is actually the saturation or purity of the instance. Using the Tint option allows you to overlay percentages of other colors over the instance. This changes the purity of the instance, more accurately known as saturation.

*   *Alpha* describes the level of opaqueness or transparency of the instance. By varying the opacity, such as reducing the Alpha setting to 0, the object disappears.

*   *Advanced* allows any combination or all of the other three effects to be changed at the same time, so that tint and alpha changes can be made at the same time.

### CD-ROM Exercise

If it is not already, open the file *ch04_05a.fla* located in the *F5gai/chapter4* folder, installed from the companion CD-ROM. Try some of the other effects to see how they can be used to create animations.

## Understanding Guide Layers

Earlier in this chapter, the simple ball animation example was used to help explain basic motion tweening. However, the result was not very realistic. This section examines guide layers and how they can be used to constrain tweened instances to a path. See the following CD-ROM exercise to begin to explore guide layers.

## CD-ROM Exercise

Learn about guide layers. Open the file *ch04_06a.fla* located in the *F5gai/chapter4* folder, installed from the companion CD-ROM. The completed file is named *ch04_06b.fla*.

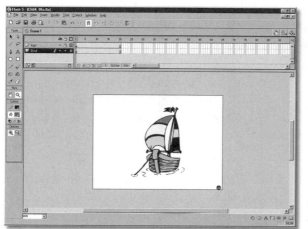

When creating animations in which you want an object to travel along a specific path, guide layers are very helpful. In exercise 4-9, which follows, use a guide layer to define a path for the boat, shown in figure 4-25, to travel along. When creating a guide layer, draw the path you want the object to travel on, just like drawing any other object.

*Figure 4-25 This is the boat you will animate using a guide layer.*

## Exercise 4-9 Using Guide Layers

To practice using guide layers, perform the following steps.

1. Make the boat a graphic symbol by selecting it and using the F8 function key. Although you could work with it as is (because it is a group), it is best to always work with symbols whenever possible.

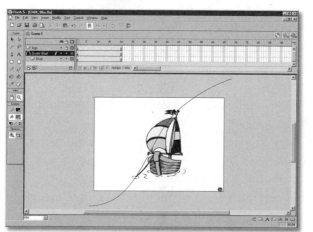

2. Extend the duration of the boat and logo symbols out to frame 20.

3. With the *Guide: Boat* layer as the current layer, click on the Add Guide Layer button, shown in figure 4-25.

4. With *Guide: Boat* as the current layer, draw a line across the screen, as shown in figure 4-26. Because you want the line to extend well beyond the stage, you may have to zoom out so

*Figure 4-26 A path for the boat needs to be created on the new* Guide: Boat *layer.*

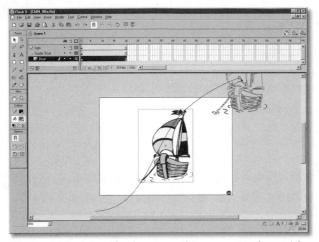

*Figure 4-27 Drag the boat until it snaps to the guide layer.*

that you can see more of the work area. In addition, make sure to use the Smooth modifier for smoothing the path of the Pencil, or use the Pen tool.

5. Select the Arrow tool and make sure the Snap (Magnet) option is on.

When using guide layers, be aware of the state of the Snap option. Even if the Arrow tool is not selected, you will find a Snap button in the standard toolbar above the timeline.

6. Select the Boat and click-drag it to the path, as shown in figure 4-27. You may want to click on the symbol's insertion point (small crosshairs) and snap the insertion point to the path.

 **TIP:** *Keep in mind that you can change the center point for a symbol instance using Modify | Transform | Edit Center.*

7. Right-click in frame 20 in the Boat layer and select Insert Keyframe.

8. Drag the boat to the lower left of the screen. By click-dragging from the insertion point, it will continue to snap to the line. You may have to lock the guide layer so that you do not accidentally grab the endpoint of the line.

9. Set up the tweening. Right-click on a frame between 2 and 18 in the Boat layer. Select the Create Motion Tween option.

10. Play the animation to see the results.

11. Modify the Boat so that it appears to be coming toward the screen. Place the playhead in frame 1.

12. In frame 1, scale the boat instance down using the Arrow tool on the stage, or by using the Transform panel. The boat instance should scale around its center point.

13. To make it more realistic, turn off the path by clicking under the eye in the guide layer. An X indicates that the layer is hidden.

14. Use the Enter key to play the animation.

The Orient to Path option in the Frame panel was mentioned earlier in the chapter. To see what it does, right-click on the tween you just created (in the timeline) and select the Panel | Frame option. In the panel, enable the Orient to Path option by clicking on the checkbox. Replay the animation to view the results. Notice how the Boat now rotates to remain perpendicular to the path. Guide layers give you tremendous freedom when creating animations. The following is a list of things to consider about guide layers:

- Once a tween object has been created, it can always be modified. As long as the tween has the Snap option selected in the Frame panel, the object will travel along the path during the animation.

- Closed polygons, such as ellipses or rectangles, can be used as guide layers also. However, when using closed polygons for guides, you will inevitably have to use more keyframes in the tweened object to ensure it moves in the proper orientation around the path. For an example of this, see Chapter 12.

- You could adjust any of the other instance properties (including color effect) during the tween, just as you set up a scale during the tween animation you just performed. Anything you define in the keys related to position, size, orientation, or color will be tweened.

- A guide layer can be applicable to multiple elements. In prior versions of Flash, each layer had to have its own layer guide. Now you can use a single layer guide for multiple layers.

## Understanding Mask Layers

Similar to masks in other packages, mask layers offer the ability to use one layer as a mask for another layer. When combining masks with tweened animation, you can get a variety of special effects. The CD-ROM exercise that follows provides practice in working with mask layers.

 *CD-ROM Exercise*

Learn about layer masks. Open the file *ch04_07a.fla* located in the *F5gai/chapter4* folder, installed from the companion CD-ROM. Notice the basic text elements and a red circle, as shown in figure 4-28. If you play the animation, you will see that a tweened animation has been set up in which the circle passes over the text. At this point, if you make the circle a mask for the layer beneath it, the resulting effect is that of a spotlight passing over the text. Set up the layer mask by performing the following steps:

*Figure 4-28 Two layers are needed for creating a simple spotlight effect.*

1.  Right-click on the Spotlight layer (on the layer name, not the sprite in the layer) and select Mask from the context menu. This option defines the layer as a mask, and the layer beneath it as masked.

2.  Press the Enter key to play the animation. Notice that the text only appears where the opaque fill passes over it.

When a layer is going to be used as a mask, it really does not matter what color (hue) the objects on the layer are, nor does it matter what the Alpha (transparency) setting of those objects are. When a layer is a mask, it is 100 percent opaque. Chapter 12 describes methods of overcoming this limitation.

3.  To make the animation just a little more interesting, insert a layer beneath the Text layer and name it Background.

4.  As with guides, mask layers can be used to mask multiple layers. Thus, be careful that the new layer is not inserted as a mask. If so, right-click on the layer name and select Properties in the context menu. Change the Type from Masked to Normal. Click on OK.

5.  Right-click on frame 1 of the Text layer and use Copy Frames in the context menu.

6.  Right-click on frame 1 in the Background layer and select Paste Frames.

7.  Click on the text on the stage and change its color to about 50 percent gray using the Fill Color option in the Colors section of the toolbar.

8.  Press the Enter key to play the animation and see the effect.

By combining motion tweening and masks, you can create unique effects. Chapter 12 continues to examine a variety of effects that can be created using motion tweening, guide layers, effects, and mask layers.

# ••• **Beyond Basic Motion: Tweened Shapes**

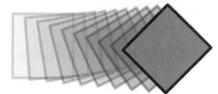

Just as motion tweening can be applied to overlay objects, shape tweening can be used on stage-level objects. Shape tweening allows elements to be created that morph from one object to another, as shown in figure 4-29.

*Figure 4-29 Shape tweening allows you to produce elements that morph from one thing to another. (See also color plate B-8.)*

## Using Shape Tweening

Shape tweening is created in a manner similar to motion tweening, except that it uses stage-level objects instead of overlay objects. You define keyframes for shape tweening, just as you do for motion tweening. Realize that shape tweening works only with singular objects. If you want multiple objects to tween (morph) at the same time, they have to be on separate layers. To further explore shape tweening, see the following CD-ROM exercise.

 *CD-ROM Exercise*

Learn more about shape tweening. Open the file *ch04_08a.fla* located in the *F5gai/chapter4* folder, installed from the companion CD-ROM. The completed file is named *ch04_08b.fla*. You will create a shape tween using the author's initials. Each letter will morph to the next in a circular manner. This animation could be easily looped on a web page. However, if you want, you can create your own file and use your own initials. When adding your own text, break it apart before trying to perform the shape tween. Shape tweens work only on stage objects. Begin creating a shape tween by performing the following steps:

1. Right-click on the first sprite in layer 1 and select Panels | Frame to bring up the Frame panel.

2. Select Shape in the Tweening drop-down. You can accept the default settings for the Shape Tweening options, as shown in figure 4-30.

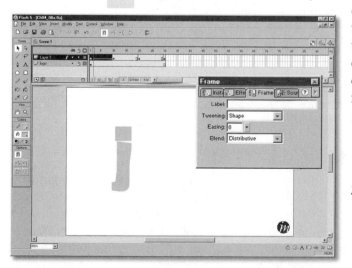

*Figure 4-30 Default settings for the Shape Tweening options.*

When Shape Tween is selected, two Blend options are available for your morphing animations: Distributive and Angular. Distributive attempts to create intermediate shapes that are smoother and more irregular. Angular attempts to preserve corners and straight lines. Therefore, use Angular only for shapes that have sharp corners and straight lines.

3. Repeat this process for the remaining sprites in layer 1. Consider trying some different settings in the Frame panel to see their effect.

4. Press the Enter key to play your animation. To turn on looping, use the Control | Loop Playback option.

5. When you play back the animation, notice that it pauses slightly due to the last keyframe, which is a copy of the first. To fix this, right-click on frame 29 and select Insert Keyframe.

6. Right-click on frame 30 and select Remove Frame.

7. Click-drag the endframe indicator in the Logo layer back to frame 29.

8. Replay the animation to see the effect.

Once a shape (or motion) tween has been set up, you can insert and delete keyframes within the tween. However, in the last step of the previous exercise, you first inserted a keyframe next to the existing keyframe *before* deleting the last keyframe. Had you deleted the last keyframe first, the last tween would not have worked. For tweens to be maintained after creation, they must have a keyframe at the beginning and at the end. If either keyframe is deleted, the tween will not work.

Depending on the letters used in the last exercise, you probably noticed that at least one of the letters did not morph quite right. To control what points in the starting keyframe are morphed to points in the ending keyframe, use Shape Hints.

 **TIP:** *Blend color in a shape tween, too. Just fill the shapes with different colors, and the color will "morph" as well.*

## Shape Hints

Shape hints provide control over complex or awkward morphs by presenting labels (points) used to perform the interpolation of frames. Even simple shape blends can benefit from shape hints, as shown in figure 4-31. By synchronizing the points on the beginning and ending keyframe objects, you control how the object goes through its metamorphosis. Shape hints are useful for basic morphs as well as more complex ones, such as morphing one bitmap to another.

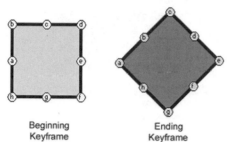

Beginning          Ending
Keyframe          Keyframe

*Figure 4-31 Shape hints allow you to control shape metamorphosis. (See also color plate B-9.)*

For any shape tween, 26 shape hints (points) can be defined. In the starting keyframe, shape hints are yellow. In the ending keyframe, they are green. Additionally, shape hints are red when they have not been defined. For practice in working with shape hints, see the following CD-ROM exercise.

## CD-ROM Exercise

Learn more about shape hints. Open the file *ch04_09a.fla* located in the *F5gai/chapter4* folder, installed from the companion CD-ROM. The completed file is named *ch04_09b.fla*. In this example, you will morph some simple objects. Before beginning, play the animation to see how it is currently morphing.

1.  Begin by selecting the first keyframe in the shape tween.

2.  Use Modify | Transform | Add Shape Hint (Ctrl+H or Command+H). A small, red circle with the letter *a* appears. Red shape hints indicate that they have not yet been defined.

3.  Click-drag the shape hint to the first point identification point, as shown in figure 4-32.

4.  Click on the ending keyframe and define the point. The point defined in the first keyframe will morph to the point defined in the ending keyframe. Notice also that the shape hint has turned green, meaning that it has

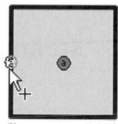

*Figure 4-32 Click-dragging the shape hint.*

been identified in the beginning and ending frame. If it remains red, this indicates a problem.

5.  Play the animation and see the difference the shape hint has made.

6.  Return the playhead to frame 1 and use Modify | Transform | Add Shape Hint (Ctrl+H or Command+H) to add another point.

7.  Define the point in the beginning and ending keyframes. Repeat this process until the morph is the way you want it.

8.  Play the animation and see the difference the shape hints have made.

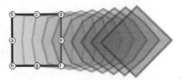

*Figure 4-33 Eight shape hints perform the shape tween in this example.*

9.  In this exercise, 8 shape hints should be sufficient, as shown in figure 4-33. Remember that a maximum of 26 shape hints can be used for each shape tween.

If you define the shape hints and then decide results are not satisfactory, use Modify | Transform | Remove All Hints to delete them. This reverts to the original shape tween. Additionally, you can remove an individual hint by right-clicking on it and selecting Remove Hint from the context menu. You can hide the shape hints by deselecting the View | Show Shape Hints menu option.

If you are a FreeHand user, realize that you can also use FreeHand's blending capability to quickly and easily create frame-by-frame shape morphs. If you use the Blend Xtra in FreeHand, a second Xtra (Release to Layers) can be used to move each blend step to a separate layer. When you export the Flash file from FreeHand, select the Animate Across Layers option to define each layer as a Flash frame. Although you do not have as much control over FreeHand blends as you do with Flash shape hints, this is another way of creating shape blends using Macromedia tools.

## ∎ ∎ ∎ Summary

This chapter covered many fundamental concepts regarding the creation of animations in Flash. Layers and symbols are two of the most important efficiency features of Flash, no matter what you are creating. Although the animations created were very basic, they demonstrated the functionality of cel animation, motion tweens, color effects, guides, masks, and shape tweening.

Building on these fundamentals, you will be able to create almost any type of animation using vector elements. If you are really interested in more complex animation techniques, jump to Chapter 11 or 12 right away. However, make sure to return or you will miss the real power of Flash: interactivity!

# chapter 5

# Symbols and Libraries

## ∎ ∎ ∎ Introduction

The last chapter introduced you to how graphic symbols work as they relate to motion tweens. Indeed, symbols are a powerful facility within Flash. You can create reusable components with them, adding little in the way of file size. Symbols allow you to overcome the negative aspects of adding multiple copies of the same object in your file. As mentioned in the previous chapters, small file sizes are very important for efficient web delivery. Thus, symbols allow you to significantly reduce file sizes. Additionally, realize that you are not limited to graphic symbols only. Two other types of symbols, buttons and movie clips, also exist.

This chapter examines the pertinent points related to creating symbols and using libraries. The latter portion of this book supplies applied examples of symbols incorporated into various tasks.

## ∎ ∎ ∎ Objectives

In this chapter, you will:

- Discover the importance of using symbols within your movies
- Find out when and where symbols should be used
- Learn how to create graphic, button, and movie clip symbols
- Understand the difference between the standard libraries and the current library
- Figure out how to open other movies as libraries and how to insert symbols from other movies

- Learn to use the Movie Explorer to examine the structure of your movies
- Find out about shared libraries and how a single library can share its symbols across multiple files

# The Power of Symbols and Libraries

As you have read, a movie may contain multiple timelines used for different purposes. Scenes are main timelines within a movie and allow you to divide your movie into defined sections. When you create elements in a particular frame on the stage, the elements are defined; therefore, they increase the file size. If you have an object that appears in multiple frames, as shown in the example in figure 5-1, the data of the object must be written several times within the file. With the ability to create symbols, this redundant data is unnecessary. When a symbol is used, the data is defined once. All "copies" of the object that appear in the stage are then referenced to the symbol. These "copies" are called *instances*.

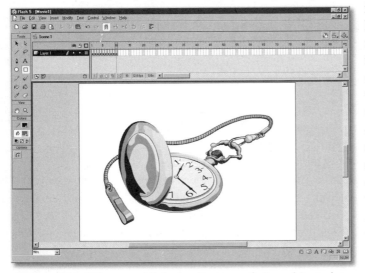

Figure 5-1 *When multiple keyframes of the object data exist, the file is unnecessarily large; symbols can be used to reduce the file size.*

Converting static, repetitive objects to graphic symbols significantly reduces the resulting Flash file. In the example shown in figure 5-1, the original file (with multiple copies of the object) was 288 KB. After converting the object to a symbol and creating references to (or, instances of) the symbol, the file size was reduced to 46 KB. As you can see, the use of symbols is imperative to maintaining small file sizes.

# Creating Graphic Symbols

Symbols can be created a couple of ways, depending on whether or not the items are already in the movie. The last chapter described the first of these methods. If you already have existing items on the stage you want to make into a symbol, select these objects on the stage and use Insert | Convert to Symbol. This process converts the selected items into a symbol.

Since Flash will convert selected items on the stage to a symbol, you must carefully make your selections. If you accidentally have items on the stage selected and employ Insert | Convert to Symbol, the selected items will become part of the newly created symbol.

 **NOTE:** *The technique of selecting objects on the stage and converting them to symbols is usually only effective for generating graphic and button symbols.*

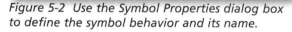

*Figure 5-2  Use the Symbol Properties dialog box to define the symbol behavior and its name.*

Most often, symbols are used from the very beginning of movie creations. To create a new symbol within a movie, use Insert | New Symbol (Ctrl + F8 or Command + F8). This process opens the Symbol Properties dialog box, shown in figure 5-2. Define the symbol's behavior (type) and its name in this dialog box.

 **TIP:** *Generally, any time an object (or set of objects) is to be reused in your movie, you will want to make it into a symbol, rather than creating it in a movie scene timeline. Indeed, in most of the movies you create, almost everything may be made of symbols. In fact, this approach is recommended as the most efficient method of developing movies.*

## ▪ ▪ ▪ Symbol Behaviors (Types)

When working with symbols, each is defined by a behavior and a name. The behavior defines the type of symbol. Alternatively, the name can actually be anything, but should generally be unique, as well as something easily identifiable by you.

It is a good idea to develop a standard way of labeling your symbols. Different types of symbols are uniquely defined in the library by icons that you will learn about later. However, throughout the examples in this book, you will find MC on the end of a name for movie clips, and other conventions peculiar to the author. Particularly in complex movies, consistency in symbol naming is key.

**TIP:** *Try to adopt some personal way of identifying your movie symbols. On the end of your symbol name, add MC for movie clips, _b for buttons, and _g for graphics.*

Once a movie contains some symbols, you can interactively switch between the movie scenes and any existing symbols. At any time, you can edit, delete, or create more symbols. To edit a symbol, use Edit | Edit Symbols

Edit Path ⎯

⎯ Current Symbol Name

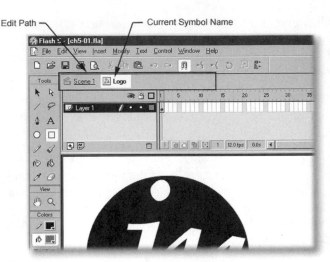

*Figure 5-3   To edit a symbol you must access the symbol's timeline.*

(Ctrl + E or Command + E on the Mac), or use the Symbol List button in the upper right of the screen to choose the symbol on which you want to work.

As discussed in the last chapter, you can also right-click on a symbol in the stage (if it exists in the current frame) and select Edit, Edit in Place, or Edit in Window. Once you are accessing a symbol, the symbol name appears in the upper left of the screen, as shown in figure 5-3. The area in the upper left shows the current scene or symbol, and is called the *Edit Path*.

**CD-ROM NOTE:** *To examine a movie that contains symbols, open the file ch05-01.fla located in the* F5gai/chapter5/ *folder, installed from the companion CD-ROM. Use the Symbol List button to examine the symbols in the file.*

As you begin working with symbols, be careful that you know whether you are working in a movie scene or in a symbol. Particularly as you are getting started, it is all too easy to begin and suddenly find yourself working in the wrong timeline!

# ▪ ▪ ▪ Different Symbols, Different Purposes

Flash provides three types of symbols, discussed in the sections that follow. These are graphic, button, and movie clip symbols. Each of these has a timeline that behaves in a certain manner. The main difference between each type of symbol is in the manner in which it plays through its timeline and how it behaves in the main movie timeline. Thus, each serves a different purpose and has some special functionality. You will also see in the sections that follow how each symbol is used within a movie.

Realize that you can easily change a symbol's Behavior (type) property in the Library panel. A symbol that is defined as a graphic can be "redefined" as a button or movie clip, although you usually have to do some editing in the symbol if you make this type of change. The important thing is that just because the symbol was originally defined one way does not mean that its definition cannot be modified. It is not uncommon to change a symbol's behavior during the development of a movie. Later in this chapter you will see how to use the Library panel to perform this function.

## Graphic

A graphic symbol has its own timeline and may have any number of layers. Although you have used graphic symbols for static elements, they can include animation. However, graphic symbols cannot include button symbols, interactivity, or sound. Furthermore, a graphic symbol that contains animation stops when the main movie it is inserted into stops. This feature is what makes it different from a movie clip symbol.

Graphic symbols are typically meant for items that will be used in the main movie's timeline for frame-by-frame or tween animation. As you saw in the previous chapter, symbols, particularly graphic symbols, are vital in making tween animation work.

Additionally, graphic symbols may be integrated into other symbols. Realize that you can create compound or nested symbols. Many symbols can be used within other symbols. Later chapters offer a variety of examples of graphic symbols used in other symbols, such as buttons and movie clips. Once you have finished this chapter, see chapters 12 and 14 for more details.

 **TIP:** *Most of the time you will use movie clips for symbol-based looping animations. Yet if you use a graphic symbol for animation, sometimes the symbol animation will cut off or stop before it is able to complete a loop, due to the brevity of the main movie. Use Modify | Frames | Synchronize Symbols to automatically adjust the synchronization between a graphic symbol loop and a main movie segment.*

## Buttons

Buttons are another type of symbol. As the name implies, button symbols provide the ability to create a symbol that automatically behaves like a pushbutton control. Flash makes it very easy to produce these controls in that it provides special frames for the up, over, down, and hit states of the button. (States are discussed later in this chapter.) By placing objects in these frames, a push button's functionality is automatically created.

In reality there are many things you can do with a button, and you are not limited to using push buttons. Flash 5 provides the capability to create very complex interactive controls much more easily than prior versions. However, you do not create these controls with just a button symbol. Rather, they are an extension of the movie clip symbol, and are called *smart clips*.

Because smart clips require extensive knowledge of symbols, actions, and ActionScript, discussion and examination of this topic is provided in Chapter 14. Do not worry; you will see examples of smart clips later. For now, just realize that they are for the creation of complex interactive components.

## Movie Clips

The third type of symbol, and quite possibly the most powerful, is the movie clip. A movie clip is a symbol in which the entire timeline plays when it is placed inside the main movie. A movie clip can contain almost anything and is different from a graphic symbol in that its animation continues to play even after the main movie into which it is inserted stops.

Movie clips are like having a Flash movie play inside another Flash movie. The entire timeline of the movie clip can be used to set up animation. The movie clip can then be inserted into the main movie, taking up only one frame in the main movie. Additionally, a movie clip could be inserted into a button's over state to create a button that animates when the user rolls over a button symbol. With movie clips, the possibilities are almost endless, as you will learn in this and the following chapters.

In some regards, movie clips in Flash are similar to film loops in Macromedia Director. Movie clips, however, have other special features, such as the ability, using a *tellTarget* action, to be told to play, stop, or go to a frame. At its base level, though, a Flash movie clip is analogous to a Director film loop. As previously mentioned, Flash 5 includes a special type of movie clip symbol called a smart clip. In Flash 4, creating custom interface elements, such as drop-down menus, was quite difficult. In Chapter 14, you will take an extensive look at smart clips, including how to create them and use them.

# ∎ ∎ ∎  Understanding Libraries

The term *library* as it is used within Flash may be, to some extent, a misnomer for those who are familiar with libraries in other packages. Indeed, Flash symbols that exist in one file may be used in any other file. In this regard, every Flash file can be a library. Yet in most other packages, a library is a "special" file that can only be used as a library; it cannot be used for other purposes.

In Flash, however, *every* file that has symbols can function as a library. By using the File | Open as a Library menu option, any Flash file that contains symbols can be made to yield its components for reuse in another file. Additionally, symbols you want to share across multiple movies can now be defined in a single, shared library, rather than having copies of those symbols in each movie file. You can use the File | Open as a Shared Library menu option to work with shared components. Setting up a library of shared symbols is relatively easy, as you will discover in this chapter. First, however, let's begin with the basics of libraries.

## Opening Files as a Library and Importing Symbols

You can easily access symbols from any Flash file. Any Flash file that contains symbols can be opened as a library while you work. The symbols can be "imported" into the current file by simply dragging and dropping them into the current file. In the following CD-ROM exercise, you will open one of the startup files and import some symbols from another file to see how this works.

The Library panel allows you to perform myriad maintenance tasks and gives you quite a bit of information, such determining what types of symbols are in the library, how many times a symbol has been used, and when the symbol was last modified. You can also create groups of symbols in folders, for easier management. The CD-ROM exercise that follows shows you how to import symbols from another file.

### CD-ROM Exercise

To import symbols from another file, perform the following steps.

1.  For this exercise, open the file *ch5-02.fla* from the *F5gai/chapter5* folder, installed from the companion CD-ROM.

2.  Use File | Open as a Library and select the file *library.fla* in the *F5gai/chapter5* folder, installed from the companion CD-ROM. Doing so will open the Library window, as shown in figure 5-4.

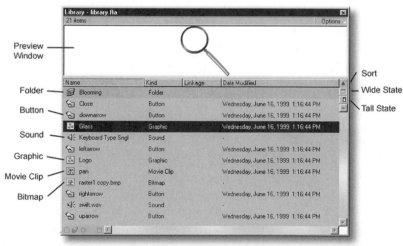

*Figure 5-4 When a file is opened as a library, the Library panel opens, revealing the symbols in the file.*

As shown in figure 5-4, three buttons exist above the vertical scroll bar of the Library window: Sort Direction, Wide State, and Narrow State (view). Flash libraries can now be sorted by any of the headings listed to the left of the Sort Direction button. Sort Direction determines whether the items are shown as ascending or descending. Note that Sort Direction only applies when you are in Wide State view mode.

The Wide State and Narrow State view mode buttons affect the width and amount of data shown in the library. In Wide State view, the Library window can be sized, and shows more than just the name of the symbol. The Narrow State view restricts the width of the window to the name only, but allows variable height of the window.

3. Once the library is open, notice the small icons in the list, which indicate the behavior or type of symbol (see figure 5-4). Begin by inserting a graphic symbol. Scroll down the list, find the "glass" symbol, and click on it.

4. To place the "glass" symbol into the current movie, click-drag in the preview window or on the symbol's name and drag the instance of the symbol to the stage so that it is inserted into the current movie.

Once a graphic symbol is placed on the stage, small crosshairs will be present at the center of the symbol. This is the registration point of the graphic symbol. When creating a graphic symbol, you can control where the symbol objects appear in relation to the registration point. Generally, the registration point will be either in the center or aligned to a part of the element.

5. Symbols placed on the stage can be modified in various ways. You can scale, deform, move, or change color effects without affecting the actual symbol's data. This is because the representation on the stage is an instance or reference to the symbol, as opposed to the data itself. As a demonstration of this, use the Scale modifier of the Arrow tool, or the Transform panel, to disproportionately scale the symbol down on the stage.

6. Use the Window | Library panel to open the current file's library. Notice that the symbol in the current file has not changed. It is the instance (or reference) on the stage that has changed.

7. Use Ctrl + L to close the current file's library.

You can group symbols into folders for easier management. To access the symbols within a folder, double click on the folder to expand it. To collapse an expanded folder, double click on it. When you create your own movies, get into the habit of using folders in the library. In large movies with a lot of symbols, organization via folders is key.

8.  In the *library.fla* Library window, double click on the Blooming folder to expand its content. Click on the Blooming Movie clip. When you do so, the movie clip will appear in the small preview window. You can use the small Play button in the upper right portion of the preview window to preview the movie clip. Click-drag the movie clip to the stage and scale it down a little.

9.  At this point, play the movie to see what happens. Go to the Control menu, where you will see that Play Movie is inactive. When you insert a movie clip symbol on the stage, from that point on you must use Control | Test Movie to see the movie clip play.

10. Insert a simple button from the library. If you closed the *library.fla* panel when you tested the movie, use File | Open as a Library again to open the *library.fla* file.

11. Scroll down and find the Close button. Click-drag it to the stage.

12. To see the button work, access the Control | Enable Buttons menu option. When authoring movies, you must enable this option to see buttons "work." Once enabled, you can roll the mouse over and click on the button to see it work.

13. You have seen how to import a graphic, button, and movie clip into your movie. Symbols can also be used in other symbols to create compound or nested symbols. With the *library.fla* file open as a library, click-drag the symbol named Pan into the movie. This is a movie clip symbol that has four buttons inserted into it. If Enable Buttons is on, note that the buttons do not work. Because the button symbols are nested within a movie clip symbol, you must use Control | Test Movie to get these buttons to work.

As you have seen, getting symbols from other files is relatively easy. The ability to drag and drop symbols from other files is very powerful indeed. Yet, realize that when you import symbols from other files they become part of the file you drag them into. To see this at work, continue with the following steps.

14. If the *library.fla* Library panel is currently open, close it.

15. In the open file, access the Symbol List button. Note that all of the symbols you imported from the *library.fla* file are now part of the current file.

16. Save this file to your computer as *mylibrary.fla* and then close it.

17. Start a new, blank file.

18. Use Open as a Library and select the *mylibrary.fla* file you just saved.

19. At this point, you could start the process of importing symbols into the new, blank canvas again by dragging them from *mylibrary.fla* to this new file.

Symbols are powerful in that they can be reused over and over, just by importing them from existing files. In this way, you can work like the programmer who creates small components that can be reused from application to application. After some time, you can create and collect many reusable components that will reduce your production time.

As you have read in this section, opening external libraries of symbols and using their components is pretty easy. You can set up your own libraries of common elements by creating a Flash file that contains myriad symbols with no elements in the main movie timeline.

## Accessing the Current Movie Library

Aside from using symbols from other files, understand that while you are working on a file, you can access the file's own symbols and place them on the stage. Follow along with this next CD-ROM exercise to better understand this concept.

 **NOTE:** *It is vital that you understand access to external libraries versus the internal library that exists in the currently open file. Window | Library is used to access the current file's library. File | Open as a Library is used to open an external file's library. Do not get these confused.*

Perform the following CD-ROM exercise to place the symbols that exist in the currently open file on the stage.

 ### CD-ROM Exercise

To place a file's internal symbols on the stage, perform the following steps.

1. To work through this exercise, open the file *ch5-03.fla* located in the *F5gai/chapter5/* folder, installed from the companion CD-ROM.

2. Begin by using Insert | New Symbol.

3. Enter *oval* as the symbol name and *graphic* as the behavior.

4. Draw an oval on the stage and then click on the Scene 1 link in the Edit Path to return to the main timeline. Note when you do so that although you created a new symbol in the library of the file, an instance of the symbol was not placed on the stage.

5. Use Window | Library (Ctrl + L or Command + L) to open the current movie's library of symbols. As you can see, the symbol you just created is in the library, as well as two folders.

6. Click-drag the "oval" symbol you just created to the stage.

7. Find the Sphere Movie symbol (in the *Sphere Objects* folder) and click-drag it to the stage.

8. Double click on the *Wow* folder in the library window to expand it, and add the Blooming Movie symbol to the stage.

9. Use Control/ | Test Movie to see the results.

Students often ask, "Why make an issue of something so simple?" That is, why focus on placing symbols on the stage from the library? Quite frankly, as you start adding symbols to the library (either by constructing new symbols, copying and pasting, or whatever) invariably new users think that by adding a symbol to the library it automatically appears on the stage. Wrong! The only time a symbol will automatically appear in both places is if you use Convert to Symbol on objects already in the main timeline.

 **NOTE:** *When you use the Insert | New Symbol option, it adds it to the library. You must then manually create an instance of it on the stage.*

## Using the Library Window

When you access the current file's library, there are several control buttons that appear, as shown in figure 5-5. Note the buttons along the lower left of the Library panel, which allow you to quickly add new symbols and folders, find out information about a particular symbol, and delete an existing symbol.

### Using the Shared Library

For the shared library to work, a web-ready SWF version of the library must be created, in addition to the SWF version of the movie file or files. By

New Symbol    New Folder    (Symbol) Properties    Delete

*Figure 5-5 The Library panel's Options menu and quick access buttons.*

default, the movie file SWF (into which shared components are placed) will look for the shared library SWF in its directory. For example, a file named *mymovie.swf* will by default look for its shared library in the same directory into which it is placed. However, you can change the directory location for the shared library using the Shared Library Properties option in the Options menu of the Library panel. This allows you to store a shared library in a single, common location.

For a moment, compare figures 5-4 and 5-5. When you opened the external file as a library (figure 5-4), note that the buttons in the lower left were inactive, indicating that you could not add, delete, or modify the folders or symbols in the external file.

Whenever you open an external file as a library or open a shared library (which you will read about in a minute), you cannot add or delete symbols or folders. You can make these types of modifications only in the current file's library. Thus, if you wish to modify the content of an external library or a shared library, you must open it directly into Flash, make the modifications, and resave it. Also note that when a shared or external library is opened, the background color of the panel (behind the symbol names) is grayed, also indicating that you cannot edit the library content.

## The Options Menu

Another note about figure 5-5 is the Option menu, which provides menu access to these and several other capabilities. The features of the Library Options menu include:

- *New Symbol:* Creates a new symbol by opening the New Symbol dialog box
- *New Folder:* Creates a folder into which you can place or group symbols
- *New Font:* Allows you to import a font description into the library
- *Rename:* Allows the developer to rename an existing symbol
- *Move to Folder:* Moves the selected symbol into a new folder
- *Duplicate:* Duplicates the selected symbol and allows you to define a new behavior for the symbol

- *Delete:* Deletes the symbol from the library

**WARNING:** You must be careful when deleting symbols from the library because this operation cannot be undone. When you try to delete a symbol, Flash will prompt you to ensure that you want to perform the action. The program will also indicate whether or not the symbol is currently in use. Consequently, deleting a symbol currently in use by a scene will cause all instances of the symbol in the scene(s) to disappear.

Small squares appear on the stage when a symbol that is needed has been deleted. Before deleting a symbol from the library, it is a good idea to check the usage count. The usage count shows how many times a symbol has been used in the movie. Thus it allows you to quickly figure out which symbols are not used in a movie. See also "Usage Count" in the following list.

 **TIP:** *If you need to delete multiple symbols or move multiple symbols to a folder, you can select multiple symbols in the Library panel by holding down the Shift key. You can then select Delete or Move to Folder from the Options drop-down menu in the Library panel.*

- *Edit:* Switches the editing environment to the selected symbol.
- *Edit With:* For symbols such as bitmaps or sounds, this option allows you to select the editor (external application) to be used to open a file so that you can edit the symbol within it.
- *Properties:* Brings up the Symbol Properties dialog box, where you can rename the symbol or change its behavior.
- *Linkage:* Reveals the Symbol Linkage Properties dialog box. This option is used with shared libraries.
- *Define Clip Parameters:* This option is used to define a smart clip.
- *Select Unused Items:* Allows you to easily find symbols not used by any of the movie scenes, so that you can delete them.
- *Update:* Allows you to automatically re-import (update) bitmap and sound symbols.
- *Play:* Allows you to play non-nested graphic and movie clip symbols.
- *Expand/Collapse:* Allow you to quickly expand or contract one or all folders.
- *Shared Library Properties:* This dialog is where you enter the URL for the location of a shared library.
- *Usage Count:* Usage counts tell you how many times a symbol is used in a movie. You can set the library to constantly update the counts using the Keep Use Counts Updated option, or you can manually update the counts as needed using the Update Use Counts Now option.

Remember that many of the Library Option menu commands are inaccessible when you are viewing an external or shared library. Most of the Options menu commands (as well as the New Symbol, New Folder, Symbol Properties, and Delete Symbol buttons at the bottom of the Library window), are disabled when you are viewing an external or shared library.

## Default Libraries

In the previous sections, you have observed how to import symbols from other files, as well as how to access the current movie's symbols. In addition to this, the Flash software includes several default libraries of symbols. These are accessed using the Window | Common Libraries submenu. You may want to access these to see what is available and to practice importing symbols from them.

You can customize the content of the default libraries that appear in the Common Libraries submenu. The files used by this menu are found in the *Program Files/Macromedia/Flash 5/Libraries* folder on the PC, or in the *Flash 5/Libraries* folder on the Macintosh. You can add and delete symbols from the existing libraries, or you can add your own libraries by copying Flash files that contain symbols to this folder.

## Shared Libraries

One of the most innovative features in Flash 5 is the ability to share libraries between groups of files. With this feature, sets of Flash movies that use the same interface components (such as buttons, sliders, and the like) and other symbols that may appear across multiple movies can now be made and used more efficiently. In the following few exercises you will learn how to create a library that has symbols to be shared, as well as how to utilize those symbols in another movie file. To make a shared library work, there are four general things you do:

- Create a Flash file that contains the symbols you wish to share across movies.

- Define the symbols in that library as components that should be shared, using the Linkage menu option in the Library panel, and save the file.

- Open the file as a shared library and place the items identified as shared components in the library into the new movie.

- Export both the shared library file and the movie file as a web-ready SWF file.

Let's begin looking at how you can use shared libraries by first opening an existing library and defining components it should share.

### Defining Components to Be Shared

You can take any flash file and identify the components in that library that should be shared. In the following CD-ROM exercise, you will identify the symbols that should be shared and then actually use them in another file. One important note is that if you have symbols that are nested inside one another (such as a movie clip that contains several buttons, or any other nested situation), you must set all of the components to "share," not just the single parent symbol. The exercise highlights this fact.

### CD-ROM Exercise

Open the file *library.fla* located in the *F5gai/chapter5/* folder, installed from the companion CD-ROM. Perform the following steps.

1. With the *library.fla* file open, access the Library panel.

2. Move the Library panel to the center of the screen and drag its borders out so that you can see all of the options, as shown in figure 5-6. Alternatively, you can click on the Wide button (below the Sort Direction button) to quickly maximize the panel.

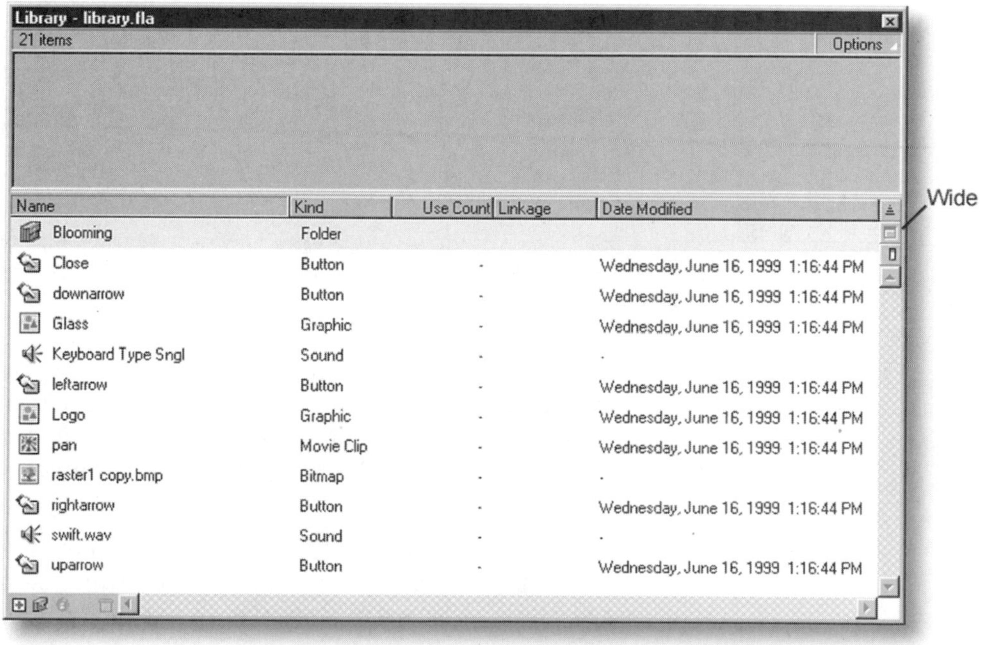

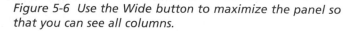

| Name | Kind | Use Count | Linkage | Date Modified |
|------|------|-----------|---------|---------------|
| Blooming | Folder | | | |
| Close | Button | - | | Wednesday, June 16, 1999 1:16:44 PM |
| downarrow | Button | - | | Wednesday, June 16, 1999 1:16:44 PM |
| Glass | Graphic | - | | Wednesday, June 16, 1999 1:16:44 PM |
| Keyboard Type Sngl | Sound | - | | |
| leftarrow | Button | - | | Wednesday, June 16, 1999 1:16:44 PM |
| Logo | Graphic | - | | Wednesday, June 16, 1999 1:16:44 PM |
| pan | Movie Clip | - | | Wednesday, June 16, 1999 1:16:44 PM |
| raster1 copy.bmp | Bitmap | - | | |
| rightarrow | Button | - | | Wednesday, June 16, 1999 1:16:44 PM |
| swift.wav | Sound | - | | |
| uparrow | Button | - | | Wednesday, June 16, 1999 1:16:44 PM |

*Library - library.fla* — 21 items — Options — Wide

*Figure 5-6 Use the Wide button to maximize the panel so that you can see all columns.*

3. In figure 5-6, note the Linkage column. When working with shared libraries, this column is used to indicate the current link status of the symbols. You will note that nothing is listed there currently, acknowledging that none of the symbols are currently set up as shared symbols. In this example you will set up the two button components as items to be shared. Begin by clicking on the Close button symbol and selecting Linkage from the Options menu. This will reveal the Symbol Linkage Properties dialog box, shown in figure 5-7.

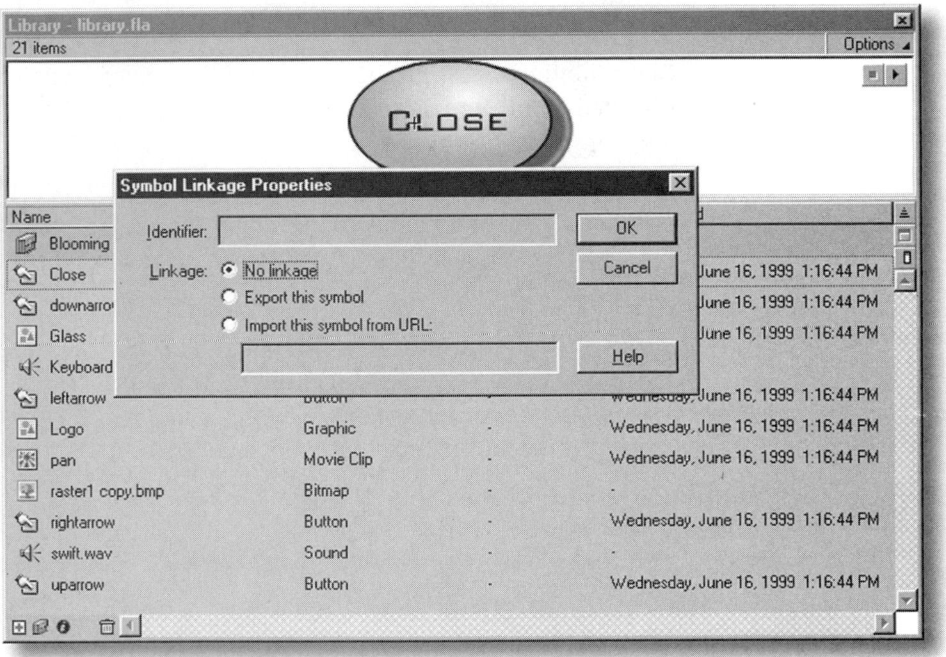

*Figure 5-7 The Symbol Linkage Properties dialog box is where you define that a symbol should be a shared element.*

4. In figure 5-7, note the default option, *No linkage*. Whenever you create symbols, they are not shared by default. To make an item a shared symbol, select the *Export this symbol* option. Go ahead and click on the *Export this symbol* option for the Close button symbol.

5. Once you have selected the *Export this symbol* option, you are required to enter a name for the symbol in the Identifier field. This name is how the file that uses the shared symbol will refer to it. It is also how you can use ActionScript to manipulate the object, which you will learn about in later chapters. For now, enter a name into the field and click on OK.

The *Import this symbol from URL* option in the Symbol Link Properties is for using shared symbols. You will read more about this in the next section.

6. Once you click on OK, note the change in the Linkage column that says that the symbol is now set to Export. You can quickly identify symbols that are set up for sharing by the Export option displayed in the Linkage column.

7. Now let's set up the other "button" element. Select the Pan movie clip, which is actually a movie clip that contains four other button symbols in the file.

8. Use the Linkage option and select the *Export this symbol* option in the Symbol Linkage Properties dialog box. Click on OK.

9. In addition to setting the parent symbol (Pan movie clip) for sharing, you must also set its child symbols for sharing. If you do not, the movie clip will be shared, but its child buttons will actually be copied to each file the Pan button is placed into, thus adding extraneous data to all files the pan button is inserted into. Set the down arrow, left arrow, right arrow, and up arrow symbols for sharing using the Linkage menu option, as you did with the prior two items.

10. Although you would normally set all symbols in a shared library to export, the remaining symbols will use their default, non-share setting for purposes of demonstrating something a little later. Save the file as *library_s.fla*. Additionally, select File | Export Movie to save the file as a web-ready SWF file (discussed in detail in Chapter 9).

11. In the Export dialog box, enter *library_s.swf* in the Filename field. Click on OK.

12. In the Export Flash Player dialog box, just click on OK.

## Using Shared Symbols

Now that you have set up a shared library, you can use the components from it in another file. Exercise 5-1, which follows, takes you through the process of working with a shared library.

 ### Exercise 5-1 Working with a Shared Library

To use the shared library you have set up, perform the following steps.

1.  Use File | New to begin a new Flash file.

2.  Use File | Open as Shared Library to open the file *library_s.fla*.

You can quickly tell the difference between a shared or external library and the current movie's library by the color of the background. If it is gray, the library is shared or external. If it is white, it is the current file's library.

In the shared library window, notice the Linkage column of the items you set as shared in the previous file, as shown in figure 5-8. This is a very important thing to pay attention to. Items that say Import will be brought in as shared components and will not change the file size of the current movie. Items that say nothing will be brought in and stored in the current movie's file (which adds to the file size). Drag the Close, Pan, and "glass" symbols onto the current file's stage.

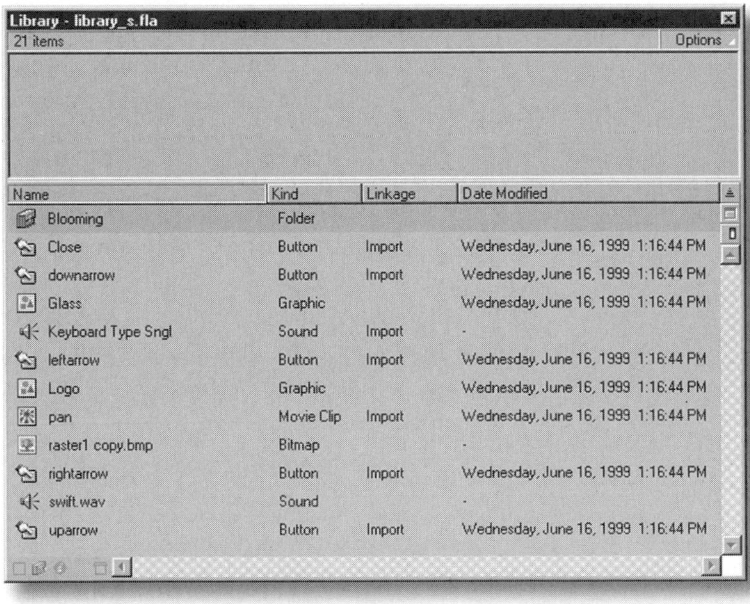

*Figure 5-8  When you open a file as a shared library, the Linkage column reveals which items are set up for sharing.*

3.  Close the shared library and open the current file's library.

4.  Notice in the library that the items that were set up for sharing are set on Import in the Linkage column. The "glass" symbol, which was not set up for sharing, has nothing in the Linkage column. This means that the current movie will import the shared components from the shared library at

run time. The other item, the magnifying glass, is simply duplicated data in the file and is not a shared component.

5. Before you leave this exercise, right-click on the Close button symbol in the Library panel and select Linkage in the context menu.

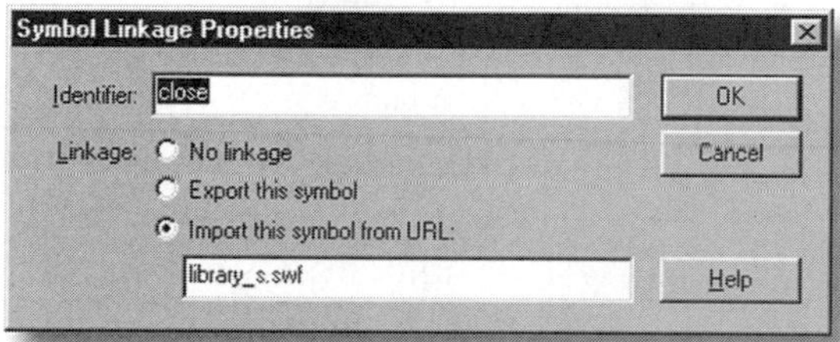

**Symbol Linkage Properties**

Identifier: close

Linkage:  ○ No linkage
          ○ Export this symbol
          ● Import this symbol from URL:
          library_s.swf

OK   Cancel   Help

*Figure 5-9 The element imported from the shared library is referenced by the identifier entered in the shared library.*

6. As shown in figure 5-9, notice that the identifier you set up in the shared library is displayed in the Identifier field. Also note that the selected Linkage radio button is *Import this symbol from URL* and that the name of the shared library SWF file is named here.

## Bitmaps, Sounds, and Fonts in Libraries

Two special elements automatically added to the library when they are imported are bitmap graphics and sounds. Additionally, you can import fonts into shared libraries to help reduce file sizes across sites that use numerous fonts in numerous movies.

Note that unlike vector-based graphic, button, and movie clip symbols, you cannot manually create bitmap, sound, or font symbols. There are no bitmap (paint) editor, sound editor, or font creation tools in Flash. Bitmap and sound symbols are created in the library as a result of importing a bitmap graphic from a tool such as PhotoShop, or a sound file generated from a sound editor such as Sound Forge or Bias Peak. Because of the file size of sound and bitmap elements, Flash allows you to compress them. Similarly, you may find the new shared library feature a helpful means of sharing these types of files across an entire site.

 **TIP:** *Once a sound or bitmap is in Flash, you can use the* Edit with *menu option (in the Library panel's Options menu) to open the symbol into an external application that exists on your machine.*

Concerning raster images, Flash provides the ability to determine the type of compression used through the library. If you access Properties in the Options menu with a bitmap symbol selected, the Bitmap Properties dialog box, shown in figure 5-10, is displayed. Figure 5-10 shows the JPEG option selected, but Flash also provides a PNG/GIF option.

To understand the difference between the PNG/GIF and JPEG options, you must know a little bit about compression. When examining image

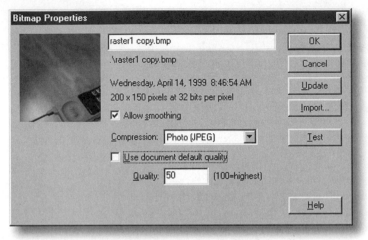

Figure 5-10 *The Bitmap Properties dialog box allows you to determine the type of compression used on the image.*

compression, two main types exist: *lossy* and *lossless*. Lossy files sacrifice or lose a certain amount of data to compress the file more, yielding smaller file sizes. Lossless does not.

Flash's PNG/GIF option uses lossless compression. It does not compress as much as the JPEG option but retains an exact replica of the original image in full detail. JPEG, on the other hand, is a lossy compression, meaning that the files are smaller. However, you may lose some of the detail in your image when using the JPEG option. When using the JPEG option, the developer determines the amount of data loss by entering a value in the Quality field. The lower the number, the greater the data lost (but the smaller the file).

## Experimenting with Compression

The compressibility of any raster graphic is determined by the number and amount of repetitive colors within the image. The greater the quantity of repetitive colors, the more the file can be compressed. Often, the best way to determine the appropriate type and, in the case of JPEG, quality for compression is through a little trial and error. Every image varies, and to determine the best method and quality means some experimentation.

 **NOTE:** *More information concerning bitmap compression settings is found in Chapter 9.*

In addition to the settings associated with raster graphics, sounds too have special compression options that can be set in the library. Flash offers a significant feature: the ability to utilize MP3 compression. MP3 is one of the most effective compression techniques for sound files, and can reduce even large and lengthy clips to a manageable size. Note that Flash also offers ADPCM compression, which is also a standard compression

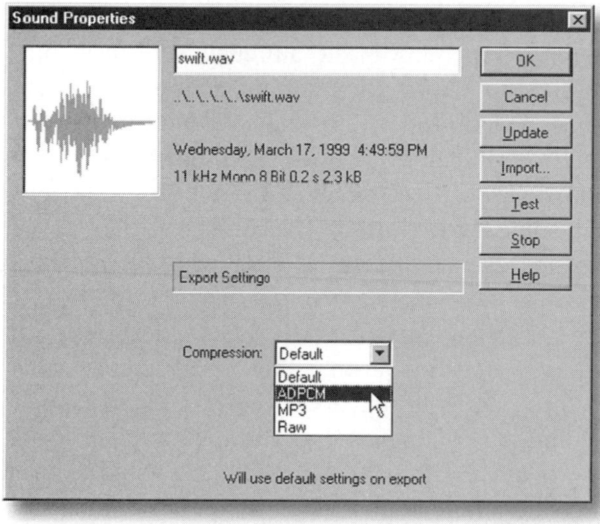

*Figure 5-11 The Sound Properties dialog box allows you to determine the type of compression for your sound files.*

technique. Select a sound file in the library and click on the Properties button to view the Sound Properties dialog box, shown in figure 5-11. The Export Settings Compression drop-down determines the type of compression used.

**NOTE:** *For more information on sound and compression settings in Flash, see chapters 7 and 9.*

## Font Symbols

A final note concerns fonts that are imported into a movie's library. Font symbols are generated as a result of importing into the library a font available to the system. For sites that utilize many fonts in movies, this is a nice feature.

However, if you are not using a shared library across your files, this feature will provide little benefit from the standpoint of file size in your web-ready movies. For example, say you have five movies that all use "Doodle" font. With no shared library, when saved as the web-ready SWF format, each of the movies will automatically include the complete description of the font and its characteristics in each of the five files.

If you were to import the font into each file's library, you would gain nothing, because whether or not the font file were stored in the FLA's library, the font description data would be automatically included in the SWF. This was one of the original "key features" of Flash web-ready files; that is, you did not have to worry about what fonts the users of your site had on their machine. Fonts used for design purposes would be displayed correctly because the font description was automatically included in the web-ready SWF.

Where importing fonts into a library is advantageous (from a file size perspective) is when there is a shared library. In the prior example, if the five movies use a shared library for common elements, and the "Doodle" font is in that shared library, when the SWF files are generated, the font will be written once to the shared library instead of in each of the movie files. Granted, a single font file may only be about 1 K in a single SWF file (not much of a file size savings), but if you had 10 to 12 fonts in 10 to 12 movies, the file size savings as a result of using fonts in a shared library becomes more important.

Regardless of file sizes, there is another way in which font symbols are advantageous. In the prior version of Flash, although SWF files automatically include font descriptions (and thus you do not have to worry about whether the user has the font or not), you did have to be concerned about the fonts in the native Flash authoring files (FLA). If it so happened that you authored with a particular font, removed the font from the system, and then tried to do some editing on the FLA files, the fonts in the FLA file got screwed up because they were no longer available to the authoring environment.

Thus, the ability to store font files in Flash files, independent of shared libraries, is advantageous, and is recommended. The one caveat is that you have to create a font symbol for any font you want to use in your design from the very beginning of your movie creation (or at least at the initial instance you plan to use the font in the movie). In exercise 5-2, which follows, you will create a font symbol in a file.

### Exercise 5-2 Creating a Font Symbol in a File

To practice creating a font symbol in a file, perform the following steps.

1.  Start a new Flash file using File | New.

2.  Open the file's library using Window | Library.

3.  Select New Font from the Options menu in the library.

4.  In the Font Symbol Properties dialog box, shown in figure 5-12, enter a name for the font and select the system font you want assigned from the Font drop-down. It is recommended that you use a name close to the actual font name. If you wish to include bold or italic versions of the font, check the Bold and Italic checkboxes.

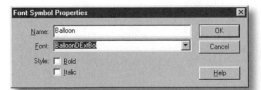

Figure 5-12  The Font Symbol Properties dialog box allows you to define a font symbol from the available system fonts.

5.  Close the library.

6.  On the stage, create a new text element with the Text tool and enter some text.

7.  Open the Character panel (Ctrl-T or Command-T).

8.  In the Font drop-down list, find the name you entered into your font symbol in the library and select it. Font symbols

are identified in the Font drop-down by a small asterisk (*)
that appears at the end of the font name.

 **NOTE:** *The key to using font symbols is in remembering
that you must define the font as a symbol and select in
the Character panel only fonts ending with an asterisk.*

## Summary of Library Concepts

To summarize this section concerning libraries, keep in mind the following important concepts. Again, be careful that you do not get the
Common Libraries submenu and the Window | Library menu options con-
fused as you work. The Common Libraries submenu accesses the default
libraries installed with Flash. The Window | Library menu option access-
es the current movie's library of symbols.

- Any Flash file that contains symbols can be opened as a library or
  set up as a shared library.

- Anytime you drag a symbol from another file (using Open as a
  Library), the symbol becomes part of the current file's library of
  symbols. Thus, you do not have to retain the originating file from
  which the symbols came. They are integrated into the file into
  which they are placed.

- To use a shared library, in the Linkage dialog box, you must first
  identify the symbols in the file you want to share.

- When you drag a symbol that is set up as a shared component, it
  is linked to the current file. If you open a library as a shared
  library and drag a symbol that is not set up as a shared component into the current file, the symbol becomes part of the current
  file's library of symbols and adds data to the file (similar to using
  Open as a Library).

- Use Window | Library to insert a symbol that exists in the current
  file to the current file's stage.

- Use the Window | Common Libraries submenu to open the
  default libraries installed with Flash.

- Save your own libraries to the *Flash 5/Libraries* directory for them
  to appear in the Common Libraries submenu.

- When you import a bitmap graphic or a sound into a file, the
  objects are automatically added to the current file's library. If you
  no longer need the bitmap or sound (i.e., it has been deleted from
  the stage), make sure you use Window | Library and delete the
  bitmap or sound symbol from the library too. Deleting a bitmap
  from the stage or a sound from a frame does not delete it from the

library. You must manually do this. It is always a good idea to use the Select Unused Items option from the Options menu in the Library panel to clean out unused symbols.

- Insert fonts that are used in a series of movies into a shared library to reduce the file size of your resulting web-ready movies.

- Insert fonts into individual movie files so that native FLA authoring files always have the necessary fonts, even if the font is removed from the system.

# ▪▪▪ Creating Buttons

To this point, you have been reading about symbols and have learned to create basic graphic symbols. In the next three sections, you will build a basic button that can be used as a simple interface component. The following CD-ROM exercise gets you started in creating a basic button.

### CD-ROM Exercise

To begin creating a basic button, perform the following steps.

1. Open the file *ch5-04.fla* located in the *F5gai/chapter5/* folder, installed from the companion CD-ROM. Within this folder are objects you will make into a button symbol, as shown in figure 5-13.

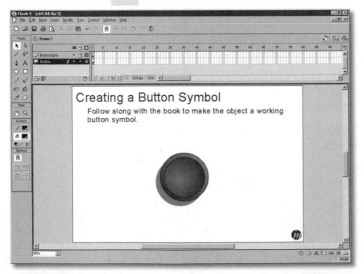

2. Select the button and the shadow (currently separate groups) to make these items a symbol using Edit | Convert to Symbol. Name the newly created symbol Button and set its behavior to Button.

Remember, if you accidentally create a symbol with the wrong behavior (that is, if it has a movie clip or graphic, rather than button behavior) you can easily change it. Access the Window | Library option and select the symbol. Select Properties from the Options menu and change the symbol's behavior. Then right-click on

*Figure 5-13 These are the objects you will convert into a button symbol.*

the stage and select Panels | Instance from the context menu. Change the Behavior drop-down to Button as well. When you have used Convert to Symbol, you must change the symbol's behavior in the library and on the stage. If you used New Symbol, you only have to change the behavior in the library.

3.  Switch to the new symbol's timeline using the Symbol List button.

In the Button symbol, notice that there are four tabs instead of a numbered timeline. These automatically appear at the top of a button symbol. They are synonymous with the four states of the object in relation to the mouse. The Up state is the normal state of the button, when the mouse is not affecting the button. The Over state is what the button looks like when the user rolls the cursor over it. The Down state shows how the button will be when the user clicks on it. The Hit state is the area that will react to the user's mouse. To create a button, you define the stage content for each state.

4.  In this example, you will leave the Up and Over states as they currently appear. However, you must still build the timeline from left to right. Thus, you need to extend the sprite in the Up frame to the Over frame. Right-click on the Up frame in the timeline and select Insert Frame. This creates a copy of the Up frame in the Over frame.

5.  In the Down frame, right-click and use Insert Keyframe.

6.  In the Hit frame, right-click and use Insert Keyframe.

7.  Click in the Down frame to modify the elements on the stage.

To make the button look like it is pressing in, you will rotate the button 180 degrees and nudge the shadow up and over. This simulates the action of the button pressing in by changing the highlights and shadow for the button.

8.  Use the Transform panel to rotate the button 180 degrees. You may have to click on the stage (to deselect the button and shadow) and then select the button only.

9.  To make the button look more realistic, you need to move the shadow on the down press. Select the shadow object in the Down frame.

10. Use the arrow keys to shift the shadow up 5 pixels and to the right 5 pixels.

11. Now you need to optimize the Hit frame. All you need in the Hit frame of a button is a basic fill. If you optimize your

buttons by removing extraneous objects, your file sizes will be smaller. Select in the Hit frame, and then use Edit | Select All and then Ungroup. Click in a blank area of the canvas to deselect.

12. Again, for the Hit area for the button, the only element you want is the main part of the button. Delete all fills and lines except for the outermost circle that defines the button, by selecting each item and pressing the Backspace or Delete key.

13. Fill the outermost circle with black and then select and delete the line that surrounds it.

14. Switch back to Scene 1 of the movie. You will note that because you used Convert to Symbol to create the symbol, it is already on the stage. If you had used Insert | New Symbol, you would have to use Window | Library to drag and drop the newly created symbol onto the stage.

15. Use Control | Enable Simple Buttons and place the cursor over the button. Try clicking on it to see if it works. In Chapter 7, you will learn to add sounds to any button state.

 **CD-ROM NOTE:** *A finished version of the button, named* ch5-04s.fla, *is located in the* F5gai/chapter5 *folder, installed from the companion CD-ROM.*

You can perform a wide range of functions with buttons. Buttons do not just have to look and behave like a traditional push button. The possibilities are quite endless. Even 3D buttons can be implemented, as can be seen in the Button library found under the Windows | Common Libraries option. In addition, Chapter 14 discusses how to create more complex buttons and menus using combinations of techniques, such as hidden areas (buttons that have invisible up, down, and over states, called triggers).

# ··· Creating Movie Clips

Movie clips are by far one of the most powerful features of Flash. With them, you can create a wide variety of things, not least of which are animated buttons. This section discusses when to create and use a movie clip symbol.

## When to Use Movie Clips

One of the most difficult things for new Flash developers to develop a sense of is when and where to use the various types of symbols, particularly movie clips. Keep in mind that movie clips are different from a movie scene in that, as a symbol, a movie clip only requires one frame in the main movie, even though a movie clip might consist of several frames. Additionally, movie clips differ from graphic symbol animations in that movie clips continue to play even if the main movie's timeline stops.

Generally, anytime you want a reusable animation to continue playing after the main movie has stopped, a movie clip is your best bet. By using a special movie action called *tellTarget*, you can stop a movie clip in midstream (see Chapter 8). Additionally, movie clips can be used to create arrangements of music and sound effects that are then overlaid in a scene. This capability of Flash is highlighted in Chapter 7. Finally, movie clip symbols allow very complex interactive components to be created through smart clips, which are discussed in Chapter 14.

## Creating and Using a Movie Clip

The simplest example of why you would use a movie clip is in the case of an animated button. In the following CD-ROM exercise, you will create a button that has an animated Over state. The animation will be created using a movie clip, which itself is based on a static graphic symbol. It is common to create a series of nested symbols, such as inserting a graphic and movie clip symbol into a button symbol.

### CD-ROM Exercise

**CD-ROM NOTE:** *To view the solution before starting, open the file* ch5-05s.fla *located in the* F5gai/chapter5 *folder, installed from the companion CD-ROM. Use Test Movie to preview the finished animation.*

To create a button with an animated Over state, perform the following steps.

2.  Open the file *ch05-05.fla* located in the *book/chapter5* folder, installed from the companion CD-ROM.

3.  Use Insert | New Symbol to create a new symbol named Spinner Movie. Set the behavior to Movie Clip.

4.  Use Window | Library to open the current movie's library to create the content for the Spinner Movie symbol from the other symbols. You will notice that there are already a couple other symbols in the file.

5.  Click-drag the Spinner graphic symbol to the stage. Position the crosshairs of the symbol on the existing stage crosshairs. Use the arrow keys to nudge the symbol.

6.  Create a tween animation that is 10 frames long by extending the sprite to frame 10.

7. Hold down the Ctrl key (Command in Mac), right-click on frame 10, and select Insert Keyframe.

8. With the symbol selected in frame 10, open the Transform panel and rotate the symbol 90 degrees.

9. Right-click on frame 1 and select Panels | Frame from the context menu.

10 Set the Tweening drop-down to Motion, and set the Rotate drop-down to Clockwise, 1 time.

11. To test while in the movie clip, select Control | Play.

 **NOTE:** *Realize that Control | Play works here because you are testing the movie clip timeline, as opposed to testing the movie clip.*

12. Insert the Spinner Movie into the Over state of the button. Use the Symbol List button to select the Button symbol.

13. Insert a keyframe in the Over, Down, and Hit frames of the Button symbol.

14. In the Down frame, rotate the button to give the appearance that the button is pressed.

15. In the Hit state, remove all elements except for a black fill in the largest circle (similar to the previous exercise).

16. Move the playhead to the Over frame. Then use Window | Library to open the current movie's library (if it is not already open).

17. Select the Spinner Movie from the library and click-drag it into the Over frame.

18. Align the registration point of the Spinner Movie clip with the existing button graphic using the arrow keys.

19. You have just added a movie clip to a button. Before you can "see" what you have done, you must place the button in the main movie.

20. Switch back to Scene 1 and drag the Button symbol from the current movie's library to the stage.

21. Use Control | Test Movie to see the animated button.

Keep in mind that you must use Test Movie to test a movie that contains movie clips. Simply enabling buttons will not work when the button contains a movie clip. Also keep in mind when working with the Instance panel that when you have a tween set up and you want to go back and modify some aspect of the tween, you must select an individual frame in the tween and not the entire sprite. If the entire sprite is selected, the Instance panel will appear blank, showing no tweening properties. If you select a single frame in the tween, the panel will show you the tween properties.

# Avoiding and Fixing Symbol Problems

As you conclude this chapter, a couple of important points should be acknowledged as they relate to working with symbols in movies. Generally, these items seem to cause confusion among people learning how to use symbols. Therefore, they have been reserved for the end of this chapter in the hope that they will make more sense. Typically, if you are having difficulty with a symbol or a specific technique, one of these related issues is likely the root of the problem.

## The Instance Panel

As noted earlier, you can easily redefine a button or change its behavior by accessing the symbol's properties in the library. This is not an infrequent occurrence. Realize that every symbol has a basic behavior definition in the library. Similarly, when a symbol is placed on the stage from the library, the stage recognizes the symbol's currently defined behavior and records it. When any symbol is placed on the stage, you can check to see how the stage defines it by opening the Instance panel and selecting the instance on the stage. Doing this reveals the stage definition, as shown in figure 5-14.

The problem is that the symbol definition in the library and the stage's recognition of referred instance are independent of each other. If you change the behavior of the symbol in the library, you must manually tell the stage, using the Instance panel, that the symbol's definition has changed. In a scene, you do this by selecting the instance and opening the Instance panel. If you use Test Movie or Enable Simple Buttons in the Control menu, with no response from the symbols, check their definition on the stage.

Another set of items within the Instance panel is the quick buttons, identified in figure 5-14. Use the Swap button to exchange one symbol for another on the stage. Use the Edit Symbol button to quickly jump to the symbol's timeline for editing, and use the Duplicate button to create a copy of the currently selected symbol. The Edit Actions button is examined in more detail in the next chapter.

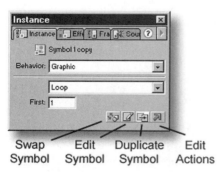

Swap    Edit    Duplicate    Edit
Symbol  Symbol  Symbol  Actions

*Figure 5-14  Selecting an instance and opening the Instance panel reveals the stage's definition of the instance behavior.*

## Compound or Nested Symbols

Symbols are not limited to singular creations. You can insert several symbols into another before inserting them into a scene. As you begin creating, as well as examining the examples in the later portion of this book, you will start to see the hierarchy of building effective symbols. For now, the following are some pointers as they relate to compound or nested symbols:

- Placing a button into a graphic symbol disables the button. The graphic of the Up state will display, but the button will not function.

- Placing a movie clip into a graphic symbol will allow the movie clip's animation to play, but any buttons or sounds will not function. The movie clip will loop as normal, however.

- A graphic or movie clip may be placed into a button's Up, Over, or Down state. This creates a button that has an animated state. To preview the animated state, you must use Test Movie. Enable buttons will only show the button states and not play the inserted movie clip.

- A graphic or button may be placed into a movie clip. When such a movie clip is inserted into a scene, Test Movie must be run to test the buttons.

## Breaking Symbols Apart

If you begin creating symbols and find that you need to break apart an instance of a symbol, so as to substantially change the instance, you can do so rather easily. Use Modify | Break Apart on a symbol instance to unlink the instance from the symbol into a collection of ungrouped lines and shapes. When you break apart a symbol instance, the process leaves the original symbol unchanged. Only the instance of the symbol is affected.

This process may be helpful if you have a series of buttons that are fundamentally the same, save one. You could use the button symbol to generate all instances and then simply break apart a single instance to create the custom version.

# ■ ■ ■ Summary

This chapter reviewed how symbols and the library could be used in Flash. While proceeding through the rest of this book, you will continue to see symbols used over and over. They are one of the most powerful features available in Flash. The next chapter looks at methods of adding actions to buttons, and how actions can be used to create interactivity.

chapter

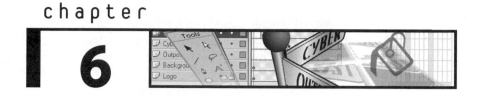

6

# An Introduction to Actions

## ▪▪▪ Introduction

Most sources, and even this book to some extent, highlight and tout the superior animation capability of Flash. Although Flash is definitely capable when it comes to animation, one of the most exciting aspects of Flash is its ability to use interactivity and internal scripting for content delivery. Animation and special effects are visually stimulating. However, the real point of the Web is efficiently and effectively communicating the information your audience wants. Getting to the information is half the battle amidst the mass of pages at most sites. Finding, or creating, the path of least resistance through effective interactions is critical.

Flash provides the ability to react to events and create interactivity through *actions*. Already you have seen that the button symbol can be used to generate a functioning button. Yet, thus far all you have read about is making the button work like a button visually. You have yet to connect the actions necessary to do something constructive with it. In this chapter, you will learn this and much more.

Realize that this chapter is just an introduction to what can be done with actions. The most significant thing about Flash 5 is the expansion of its internal scripting capabilities. As much as version 4 was for the designer, version 5 is for the programmer. Regardless of which camp you find yourself in, Flash 5 provides the best of both worlds. Indeed, you will find that concerning programming the possibilities within Flash 5 are endless. As has been true of Director for years, with Flash 5, as it relates to programming, there is not much you cannot do.

With that said, there is no way to present everything about actions or ActionScript in one chapter. An attempt would not do justice to what Flash 5 is really capable of. Therefore, much of the remainder of this book is devoted to examining various key aspects of ActionScript.

Chapter 13, in particular, provides the nitty-gritty of ActionScript from the programmer's perspective. Prior to that, the explanation of ActionScript is presented in small, consumable portions. This chapter begins by looking at the "basic actions," as well as how you apply those actions to objects.

# Objectives

In this chapter, you will:

- Find out what it means for an environment to be object oriented
- Examine the primary object and events within the Flash environment
- Explore the differences among frame, button, and movie clip events
- Examine each of the basic actions available and learn what each will do in a movie
- Discover the importance of labels
- Create an example movie that uses the Play, Stop, and Go To actions
- Examine how to use external navigation using the Get URL action
- Discover how you can use Tell Target to control movie clips within Flash
- Examine the Movie Explorer and see how you can use it to gain insight into the hierarchical structure of your movie

# What Does Object-oriented Mean?

Object-oriented programming (OOP) environments provide a logical way of creating computer software and developing multimedia materials. OOP languages were designed to more accurately model the real world than prior languages, as well as to allow faster development, greater quality, and enhanced modifiability of computer programs.

As the name implies, object-oriented programming provides certain objects that you, the developer, can interact with, control, and manipulate. Additionally, you as programmer can create your own objects, define how they behave, and then create instances of those objects within your environment.

As opposed to other methods of programming, object-oriented environments offer extensive flexibility. However, in multimedia authoring environments such as Flash and Director, the extent to which you can control and manipulate objects is dependent on the characteristics made accessible through the software (by the engineers that actually make the application). In many instances, there may be objects, but their characteristics may or may not be accessible by end users or programmers.

Generally, as the OOP languages inside authoring programs mature, more and more of the objects and their characteristics are made accessible to the multimedia developer. Director's Lingo language is a good example. Having matured over the past ten years, this language allows Director to outlast and surpass most, if not all, of its competitors. ActionScript, too, appears to be propelling Flash along a similar course. Yet, before diving into the nitty-gritty of ActionScript specifics (or even a cursory examination of basic actions in this chapter), you need to examine the foundation on which ActionScript is built: OOP fundamentals.

## Macromedia's Organization and Terminology

Two points need to be made about the discussion of actions, ActionScript, and OOP programming in general. First, the discussion here and throughout the book describes these items somewhat differently than the manner in which Macromedia does in its *Using ActionScript* reference. Rather than simply explaining individual commands and techniques in isolation, or simply regurgitating existing documentation in an applied example, the text seeks to help you understand more globally how object-oriented programming works.

Terminology in this book may also differ from Macromedia's use , mainly to avoid confusion in light of OOP terminology and other languages. This goes hand in hand with the fact that the organization of the actions within the Actions panel, which has its own functional logic, can be misleading in regard to the names of things.

Items of the Actions panel are grouped and named as they are to make things simpler for the person who really does not want to get into the nitty-gritty of programming and its lexicon. However, it is important to understand terminology as it is generally used in specific disciplines, such as programming. The point is to understand that there is a difference between how a software manufacturer organizes and labels items (for example, in this case for actions) and how the world of applications communicates. This will give you a clearer understanding of object-oriented programming, and a more fundamental understanding of the way ActionScript and the Flash environment work.

Two points need to be made about the sections that follow. If you learn how programming works in general, picking up a specific language is easier, and you will be able to do many advanced things, even if you do not know all of the syntactic language specifics. It is not enough that you know how to push buttons and use pre-built actions in Flash. You should understand the paradigm on which Flash, actions, and ActionScript is built. With that understanding, you will have a sense of how to go about doing just about anything with the tool.

## What Defines an Object?

One of the first questions that should come to mind is: What constitutes or defines an object in an object-oriented environment? What are the "characteristics" you can control, and how do you control them?

Simply put, objects have three things in common: *methods*, *properties*, and *event handlers*, each of which is defined by the object's *class*. The class is the primary structure that defines everything about an object: the object's methods (things the object can do), the object's properties (the necessary characteristics of the object), and the object's event handlers (things the object can react to). In reality, even handlers are nothing more than special methods. Yet, in most visual environments they are treated as distinct entities.

As a basic example, in general terms, you could create a class named *dog*. Within that class, you could define methods for the dog, such as *bark( );* and *wagtail( );*. You could create characteristics for the dog, such as *name*, *breed*, *height*, and *weight* (properties). You could also define events to which the dog would respond, such as *on seeCat*. You could then create an instance of your dog on the stage and make it do something by calling one of the methods you set up for the dog (*bark( );* or *wagtail( );*). Additionally, the dog could be made to do something particular in response to *on (seeCat)*, and you could have the properties of the dog (e.g., *height* and *weight*) change over time.

Although this example may seem rudimentary, it is important to conceptually understand that classes define objects by establishing methods, properties, and event handlers for the object. Various instances of objects, much like instances of symbols, are instantiated during the life of the program and can have various property values. Thus, you could use the *dog* class to define a multitude of difference instances of the dog, with various names, breeds, and so on. You could tell specific instances of the dog to bark or wag their tails. In addition, each might react at the same time, or individually, if they happened to see a cat!

You will find that understanding *what* actions to use depends on an understanding of the difference between properties and methods available in Flash. Generally, methods are distinguishable from properties in code by the parentheses that follow them. An understanding of *when* and *where* to use certain actions depends on an understanding of event handlers.

 **NOTE:** *It is vitally important that you understand these concepts. If necessary, take the time to write down the terms and definitions of* class, object, method, property, *and* event handler. *There is something about writing that helps you remember and understand. At*

*the least, you may want to bookmark this page so that you can return to this overview as necessary.*

## Flash Objects

In Flash, several objects are already defined for you to use, and you have been using them already. Note that you do not necessarily see the classes that define the objects, nor do you have to work with them directly in code. Even though you have been using the GUI tools to draw, paint, and animate, the OOP code objects do exist in the environment and they do affect the way Flash works. These are called environmental or intrinsic objects.

For example, the movie is an object. To prove this, what are some of the properties you have modified related to the movie already? Do frame rate, view quality, and background color ring a bell? A frame, a button, and a movie clip are also examples of objects. What are some of the properties of these objects with which you have worked?

Although OOP is not discussed at the beginning of this book, you can see how aspects of earlier chapters and exercises are related to it. Further, as you will see in later chapters, Flash also provides special ActionScript programming objects, such as the date, math, and selection objects. They provide special objects for you to work with in ActionScript code. These are called programming or extrinsic objects.

## Object Properties

Every object in an OOP environment has properties. *Properties* are simply characteristics of the object at a given instance in time. You can think of them as adjectives that describe an object. Realize that many of the properties of objects are not absolute. Some properties change over time, as a result of something in the environment or as a result of the programmer forcibly changing it. Some properties are only accessible in the authoring environment, such as the movie's frame rate and background color. In the run-time environment, these properties are fixed, which are often called *constants* or *literals*.

Some properties, such as view quality, are accessible and changeable during playback. They can be manipulated via ActionScript code. As you continue examining actions and ActionScript later in this book, you will learn about properties you can manipulate and those you cannot. For now, simply remember that properties are the characteristics (adjectives) that describe or contain information about the object.

## Object Methods

If properties are the adjectives that describe an object, methods are the action verbs for the object. As previously stated, methods are the definition of the things an object can do. In programming terms, methods are predefined functions that usually do something to or on behalf of the object. Generally, by simply calling a method, something happens.

One of the actions (methods) you will learn about is the "go to" action. It tells the main movie timeline to go to a specific frame or label in the movie. You call the method by simply attaching an action to a frame, button, or movie clip using the Actions panel.

The code contained within a method is usually transparent to the developer. All you have to do is call the method by stating its name. Methods normally require information when they are called. However, whether or not they need data obviously depends on what they are supposed to do. If there is needed data, it is called an *argument* or a *parameter*. In the "go to" example, when you call the method, it needs to know where you want it to go. That information, the frame or label reference, is known as an argument. In code, methods are generally called by typing the method name, followed by parentheses. Arguments or parameters are usually passed inside the parentheses. For the "go to" example, the code might look as follows:

```
goto(1) // to go to frame 1
or
goto("mylabel") // to go to the label called "mylabel"
```

 **NOTE:** *The double slashes in the previous code denote comments. This convention is used throughout this book. Anything following the double slashes (comments) would be ignored by Flash (or by the browser, if you are writing JavaScript).*

In its ActionScript documentation, Macromedia calls most of its basic actions commands. However, for purposes of clarity and consistency with OOP terminology, many of these "commands" are referred to in this text more precisely as methods, as is done in the previous example.

A little further clarification seems to be in order concerning terminology. In object-oriented programming, the goal of methods, functions, and commands are very similar: they all *do* something (action verbs). Methods and functions are usually related to doing something with or for a particular object. The key is that they are "linked" to an object. Commands, on the other hand, are usually code statements that tell the general environment to do something, independent of a specific object.

For example, if you tell a Flash movie to go to a specific frame, the "go to" is actually a method associated with the movie object. Macromedia calls this an action or a command, but it is in reality a method of the movie object. Somewhere behind the scenes, the movie object knows what it should do when you tell it to execute its "go to" method. Thus, methods are nothing more than predefined functions, or capabilities, for an object. Objects in all

OOP languages (such as Java, JavaScript, and Flash) have a certain number of predefined functions, called methods, that you can use.

> **NOTE:** *One of the things you should also understand is that often various objects will have a method of the same name. For example, in Flash, you can use a "go to" on the main movie as well as on a movie clip. Thus, both of these objects have a "go to" method defined.*

One final semantical note is that sometimes you will find that the terms *function* and *method* used interchangeably. However, to be accurate, methods are defined by a class. Thus, in the text of this book they are referred to as "predefined," because the class actually contains the description of what they are to do. On the other hand, the user defines functions by writing his or her own code for them. Functions allow the developer to add to an object functionality that does not already exist in the object's class. Hence, if a method does not exist, you write a function for whatever it is you want to do.

## Event Handlers

The final OOP construct to be examined is *event handlers*. They define the events in the environment that an object *can* respond to. Event handlers contain code segments, added by the developer, that "handle" the events (thus the name). Note that because an object can respond, this does not mean it will respond automatically. You have to add coding, either by adding predefined actions (methods and commands) or writing your own code (functions). The nice thing is that Flash now allows both in a very straightforward manner.

In any OOP environment, three things are required to get an object to do something: (1) the object must be able to respond to the event, (2) it must have code defined for what it should do when the event occurs (handler), and (3) the object must exist in the environment at the point the event occurs. Most coding problems for people new to Flash or Director (as well as other OOP environments) involve not keeping these three "rules" in mind. Let's take a closer look at what happens when an event occurs.

Almost everything in the Flash environment is a result of an event. When the playhead moves from one frame to another, an event occurs. When the user presses a key or clicks the mouse, events occur. When a movie clip is loaded or unloaded, again an event occurs. Thus, there are myriad events you can respond to.

Objects know that events occur because notifications are sent out from the environment stating that something has happened. The notification is called an *event message* (or simply *message*), which is sent out into the environment and acted upon by an object that can and will handle the event. If an object that can receive the message (can respond to the event) and has code (telling it what to do for the event) exists at the time of an event occurrence, the object receives the message, does its thing, and terminates the message. If no objects exist (no receiver for the event), the message is terminated and nothing happens.

In most environments, there is precedence for the manner in which messages can be received; that is, a hierarchy of sorts. For example, if two objects exist on the stage and both have programming to handle a particular event, only one can respond. Whichever object has precedence will intercept the message, do its thing, and terminate the message. In Flash, there are events for which precedence is important. We will return to this issue after you have examined the Flash objects and events.

 **NOTE:** *Make sure you read the section later on precedence. In Flash, messages do not terminate once they are received. More than one object can receive the same event message and inadvertently react.*

# ▪ ▪ ▪ Flash Objects and Events

The Flash environment has three objects that can react to events: the frame, the button, and the movie clip. In other words, these are entities to which you can assign actions. These objects can respond to two primary events: events related to the user (mouse or keyboard) and events associated with frames in the timeline. These two major events can be further subdivided into smaller component events. For example, the user event has eight subcomponents, including mouse and keyboard interaction, whereas the frame event has one. In the case of a frame event, when the frame is encountered, its actions execute.

The mouse subevents, on the other hand, include items such as Press, Release, Roll Over, and several others. Thus, you can assign various actions to each of these events, or one action to several of them. It is important to understand how an action is assigned to a frame or an instance of a symbol before you examine subevents in more detail.

## Frame and Instance Actions

Actions are assigned within Flash in two ways, depending on whether you want the actions to execute when the movie reaches a certain frame (a frame action) or when the user does something to a button (an instance action). Additionally, movie clips, which are also instances, can respond to frame or user events.

Right-clicking on a frame in the timeline and selecting actions in the context menu allows you to assign actions to a frame using the Frame Actions panel. When an action is assigned to a frame, the action will execute when the frame is encountered by the playhead.

**NOTE:** *When you designate an action to a frame, a lowercase letter a will appear in the nearest left keyframe. If adjacent frames are to have different actions, each frame must be a keyframe.*

Alternatively, to assign an action to a button or movie clip symbol, right-click on the symbol in the stage and select the Actions option from the context menu. This opens the Object Actions panel, shown in figure 6-1, which is very similar to the Frame Actions panel. Actions attached to instances of symbols on the stage are a property of the symbol instance, not the symbol itself. Thus, various instances of a symbol throughout a movie may have different actions.

 **TIP:** *As opposed to the lowercase letter a that appears in a frame when an action is assigned to it, there is no visual indicator that tells you that a symbol instance has an action. To find out whether or not an instance has an action, right-click on it and open the Actions panel.*

Figure 6-1 shows the Object Actions panel, with an action being assigned to a button. The Toolbox list on the left provides access to all available actions in Flash. The actions are organized according to usage. The groups include the following:

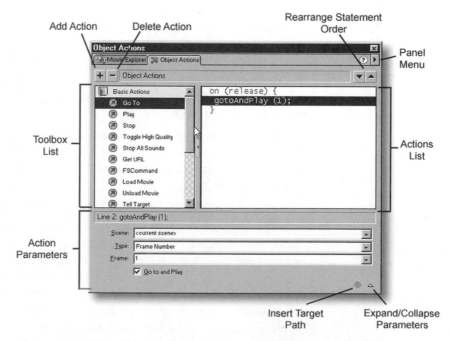

*Figure 6-1  The Object Actions panel and the Frame Actions panel are very similar. Both are used to assign actions to their respective objects.*

- *Basic actions:* These are predominantly simple navigation and interaction actions, which Macromedia commonly calls commands. These commands are all actually methods, except the *on MouseEvent* action, which is an event handler. Even the title, *on MouseEvent*, is a misnomer because it is this event handler that permits keyboard events. Nevertheless, the list includes most of the actions that were available in Flash 4's Action List. They are no doubt listed here for quick and easy access for those making the transition from Flash 4. The remainder of this chapter focuses on the actions listed in this group.

  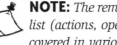 **NOTE:** *The remaining groups of actions shown in the Toolbox list (actions, operators, functions, properties, and objects) are covered in various chapters throughout the rest of the book.*

- *Actions:* This list contains all of the basic actions, as well as all of the new actions available in Flash 5. This list includes actions that could be classified as methods, commands, and event handlers.

- *Operators:* This list contains all of the operators available in Flash 5. Operators perform any number operations on values, as you will read about later.

- *Functions:* Functions, as defined by Macromedia (as well as the Core JavaScript Language Specification), are code segments that receive a value, do something to that value, and return the results. Thus, all of the actions here expect to receive data, do something to it, and return the value. Typically, these are also called methods. Functions are not usually predefined; rather, the programmer adds to the functionality already inherent in the object (defined by the class) by creating them.

- *Properties:* As you have already discovered, properties are the attributes of (adjectives that describe) objects. This list provides access to the properties you can extract and/or change during playback. Some are global (related to the movie as a whole; the movie object), and some are specific to particular objects (mainly movie clips).

- *Objects:* As you are programming, frequently you will want to work with specialized data to accomplish something specific, such as working with mathematic operations, dates, and so on. Therefore, special programming objects exist with their own predefined methods that you can use. For example, instead of having to manually construct an array (for those familiar with version 4, you can remember how fun this was), a special array object exists for your use. This group of objects provides quite a range of specialized objects, which you will learn about later in this book.

# Adding an Action

You add an action by either double clicking on an item in the Toolbox list on the left or by clicking on an action in the Toolbox list and clicking on the small plus (Add Action) button. As noted earlier, as far as organization is concerned, the Toolbox list is the same in the Object Actions and Frame Actions panels. However, you will find that certain actions are not applicable to frames or not applicable to objects. Actions that are not applicable to objects are grayed out in the Toolbox list. In exercise 6-1, which follows, you will attach an action to a button instance.

## Exercise 6-1 Attaching an Action to a Button Instance

To see how a basic action is attached to a button instance, perform the following steps.

1. Open Flash and start a new file.

2. Create a button symbol on the stage.

3. Right-click on the button and select Actions from the context menu.

   **TIP:** *You can also quickly open the Actions panel using Ctrl + Alt + A (Command + Option + A on Mac).*

4. In the Actions panel, double click on the Basic Actions group in the Toolbox list.

5. Double click on the Go To action.

6. Save this file so that you can return to it later.

Once you double click on an action in the Toolbox list, code is automatically added to the Action list. Let's examine the following code, which has been added to the Action list:

```
on (release) {
 gotoAndPlay(1);
}
```

As you read earlier, the coding or scripting that responds to an event is called an event handler (or *handler* for short) because it has code defined within it that "handles" the event. The handler begins with the event name, such as *on (release)*, as shown in the previous code. The things that are supposed to happen when the event occurs (that is, statements consisting of methods, functions, commands, and expressions) are grouped and appear between the curly braces. You will also find that the statements between the curly braces are terminated with semicolons (which are not required).

**NOTE:** *If you have ever peered at or worked with JavaScript coding, you will find that ActionScript is very similar. ActionScript is based on the Core JavaScript Language.*

Later in this book, you will return to examining code snippets from the Actions panel. However, before getting into code to deeply, because you need to examine the Actions panel a bit more. The Actions panel provides two modes of operation: Normal and Expert mode. In this chapter, you will work in Normal mode only, so that you can get the basic gist of how actions are assigned and how they work.

By default, the Actions panel is set on Normal mode and the panel menu provides access to this and other settings relative to the Actions panel, as shown in figure 6-2. When you start working in Expert mode in later chapters, you will examine the other options in the Actions panel menu in more detail. For now, just realize that the menu lets you set the mode for the Actions panel.

In Normal mode, you simply click on actions listed in the Toolbox list to add them to the Action list, as you did when you added the Go To action earlier. Note that when you click on various portions of the code in the Action list, options for the action are revealed in the lower part of the panel. These are called *parameters*, which, when an action requires them, are displayed and set in the lower part of the panel (see figure 6-1). Some

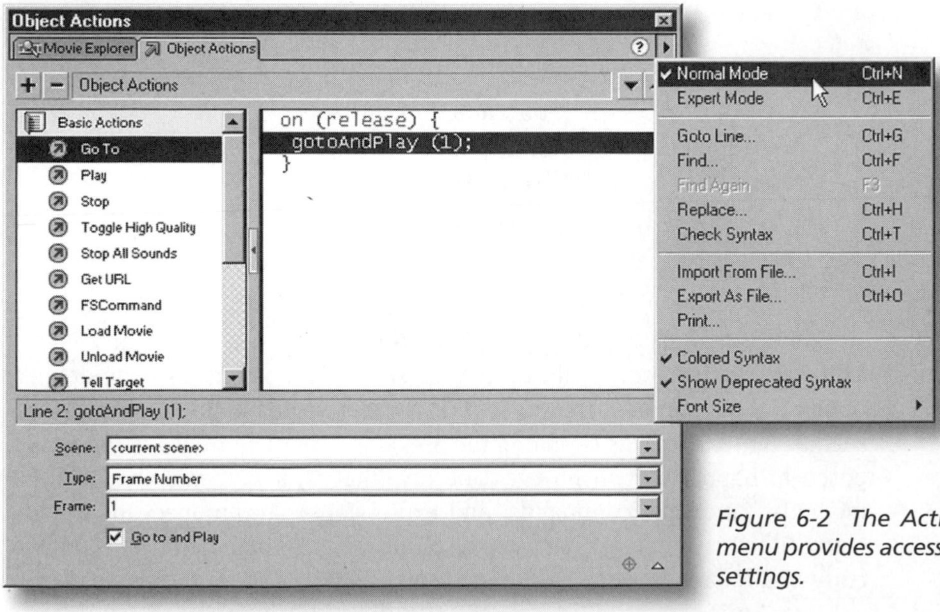

*Figure 6-2 The Actions panel menu provides access to various settings.*

actions have no parameters at all. The Go To action has three parameters you set. As you make selections from the drop-down menus, the code shown in the Action list changes to match your selections.

The Action list is one area of Flash that could definitely be improved. The problem with the Action list is that methods and event handlers are thrown together in one long list with little organization. The same problem exists in the other groupings. Rearrangement of the lists would make it easier to understand the action hierarchy in light of accepted OOP terminology.

Nonetheless, when you assign an action to a button (such as Play, Stop, or Go To), it is automatically inserted into the event handler *on (someevent)*, where *someevent* is a word such as *release*, *press*, and so on. This is the event that initiates the handler. All actions assigned to a button are automatically inserted inside an *on (someevent)* handler. Actions assigned to a movie clip are automatically inserted into an *onClipEvent (someevent)* handler, where *someevent* again is some word such as *load*, *enterFrame*, and so on.

However, when you insert an action into a frame, no *enterFrame* event handler appears. This is an assumed event and there are no multiple frame events, as in other applications. If you are used to programs such as Director (which has *prepareFrame*, *enterFrame*, *updateStage*, *exitFrame*, and other events), realize that Flash only has one event as it relates to a frame: the occurrence of the frame. Response to multiple frame events may be something to look for in future versions of Flash.

One thing that may seem confusing at first (particularly for those familiar with Director or other languages that allow event handlers) is the fact that the *on MouseEvent* action when entered into the Actions panel simply says "on (someevent)" not "on MouseEvent(release)" (or "on mouseUp" or "on mouseDown," like Director).

The title *on MouseEvent* is a carryover from Flash 3, which could not respond to the keyboard. A better name would be *on userEvent* because the action will detect both mouse and keyboard interactions. In lieu of renaming the action and having the code in the form of *on userevent (someevent)*, Macromedia has again left it as *on MouseEvent*, even though it is much more. Just keep in mind that it is for any user-generated event. In exercise 6-2, which follows, you will add multiple action to an instance.

## *Exercise 6-2 Adding Multiple Actions to an Instance*

Once you have added a single action to a button, you can continue adding more to the current handler. To see how this works, perform the following steps.

1. Open the file you were previously working with.
2. Click on the button you had created and open the Actions panel.

3. Click on the *gotoAndPlay (1);* code in the Action list.

4. Find the Stop All Sounds action in the Basic Actions list and double click on it.

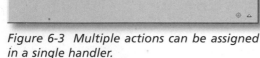

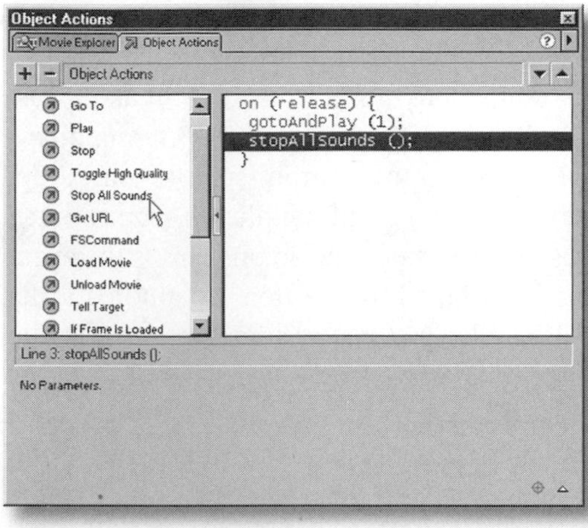

Note that when you double clicked on the Stop All Sounds action that it was added to the Actions list, as shown in figure 6-3. Once you start adding actions, you can add as many as you want to a single handler.

The order in which the actions occur is often important. What if you wanted all sounds to stop before going to another frame? You can easily change the order of actions in the list by continuing with the following steps.

5. Click on the Stop All Sounds action.

6. Use the Move Selected Action(s) Up button to place the Stop All Sounds action before the Go To action.

*Figure 6-3  Multiple actions can be assigned in a single handler.*

As you can see, the ordering of actions in the list is fluid and can be changed pretty easily. However, what if you want the button to stop the sounds when you roll over it and to go to another frame when you click it? Currently, both actions are assigned to occur on release. Let's modify the previous example so that it would do this. Continue with the following steps.

7. Click on the Stop All Sounds action.

8. Use the Move Selected Actions(s) Down button to move the Stop All Sounds action below the Go To action.

9. Click on the Move Selected Actions(s) Down button one more time. This causes a second handler to be created in the panel.

10. Click on the second *on (release)* statement. Note that the parameters for the action are displayed in the lower part of the Actions panel.

11. Deselect Release and select Rollover. Note the change in the code in the Action list, as shown in figure 6-4.

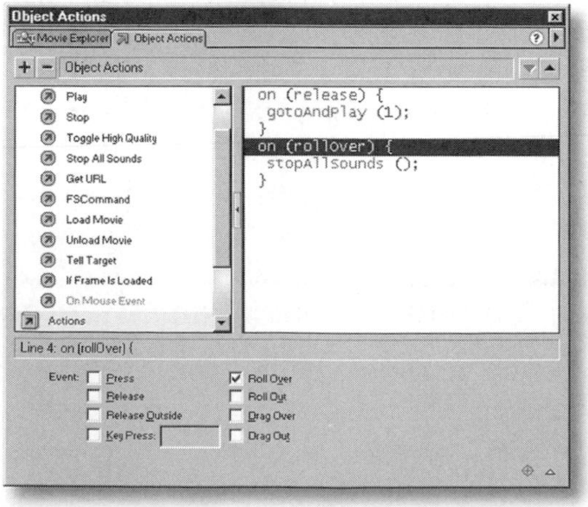

*Figure 6-4  Multiple handlers can be assigned in a single object.*

# Button Events

Before moving on, let's reflect on the button, frame, and movie clip subevents to which you can respond. Figure 6-5 shows the various events to which you can react with a button instance. Just as you can have multiple handlers assigned to an object, a single handler can be set up to handle multiple events. For example, you can specify that certain actions should respond to both a press and a release, as shown in figure 6-5. Thus, the actions contained within the handler will react on both press and release. In other words, it will execute the actions twice. For this reason, be careful using compound events in a single handler.

As it relates to *on MouseEvent*, actions can be set to take place when any one of the following scenarios occurs:

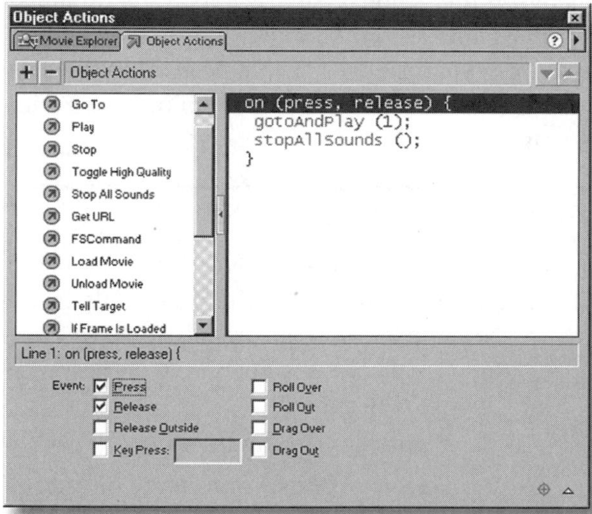

*Figure 6-5  Using multiple events in a single handler.*

- *Press:* Causes the actions to execute when the mouse button is pressed down.

- *Release:* Performs the actions when the mouse button is released inside the object.

- *Release Outside:* Implements the actions when the mouse button is released outside the object. However, the user would have had to have begun by clicking on the button.

- *Key Press:* Performs the actions when a particular key is pressed. To use the field, click the mouse in the field and press the key to which you want to respond. Note that not all keys or key combinations can be used. This option is generally limited to alphanumeric keys.

- *Roll Over:* Carries out the actions when the user rolls into or within the boundaries of the object.

- *Roll Out:* Executes the actions when the user rolls off the boundary of the object.

- *Drag Over:* Performs the actions only when the user drags across the object. This is generally used for an object such as a slider or scroll bar.

- *Drag Out:* Runs the actions only when the user drags outside the boundaries of the object.

# Frame Events

If you decide you want an action to execute based on a specific point in time within a movie, use a frame action. As mentioned earlier, frame actions are assigned by right-clicking in a frame and selecting Actions from the context menu that appears. Again, you can also double click in a frame, which will open the Actions and Sound panels, revealing the current state of the frame.

The only difference between the actions listed in the Frame Actions panel and the Object Actions panel is that the Toolbox list in Frame Actions has the *on MouseEvent* action inactive. The *on MouseEvent* event handler cannot be used in frames. In exercise 6-3, which follows, you will practice adding actions to frames.

## *Exercise 6-3 Adding Actions to Frames*

When creating frame actions, the only event you can respond to is entry into the frame itself. Thus, the action needs only to be assigned to a keyframe. To have a movie stop at a specific frame, perform the following steps.

1. Right-click on the frame.

2. Select Actions from the context menu that appears.

3. Double click on the Basic Actions group in the Toolbox list.

4. Double click on the Stop action to add it to the Action list.

The results of this action cause the movie to stop at the frame in which the action exists. Notice in figure 6-6 that the *enterFrame* handler is assumed, but is not shown; no *on* keyword is present and no curly braces are used.

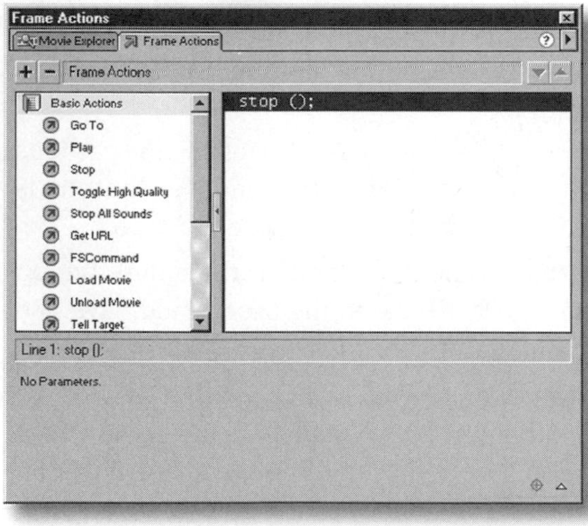

*Figure 6-6   When actions are assigned to frames, there is no on keyword, nor are there curly braces.*

# Movie Clip Events

Movie clip events are new in Flash 5. One of the biggest limitations in Flash 4 was the fact that you could only attach actions to buttons. Now you can also attach them to movie clip instances, practice of which is provided in exercise 6-4, which follows.

### Exercise 6-4 Attaching Actions to Movie Clip Instances

To attach an action to a movie clip instance, perform the following steps.

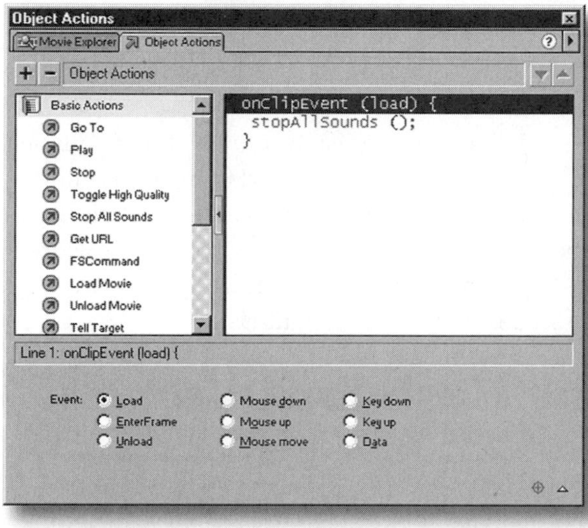

**Figure 6-7** *Actions can now be assigned to movie clip instances.*

1.  Start a new Flash movie and create a movie clip symbol.

2.  Right-click on the movie clip instance on the stage and select Actions from the context menu.

3.  In the Object Actions panel, select an action from the Toolbox list, such as Stop All Sounds.

If you followed along in the previous exercise, the Actions panel should look as it does in figure 6-7. Note that the event handler name for a movie clip is *onClipEvent* and that there are several specific events the movie clip can respond to, as shown in the bottom part of the panel.

When you attach actions to movie clips, you can have the actions respond to the following events:

*   *load:* This causes the actions to execute when the movie clip is loaded and appears on the stage.

*   *enterFrame:* This causes the actions to execute after the keyframe is played; that is, the keyframe in which the movie clip resides.

*   *unload:* Actions associated with this event are initiated in the first keyframe following the frame in which the movie clip was removed from the timeline.

*   *mouseDown:* This initiates the actions when the left mouse button is pressed.

*   *mouseUp:* This initiates the actions when the left mouse button is released.

*   *mouseMove:* This initiates the actions whenever the mouse is moved.

**TIP:** *Mouse position can now be tracked in version 5 using the _xmouse and _ymouse properties. Thus, you can have* *a movie clip that tracks the movement of the mouse and responds accordingly.*

- *keyDown:* Actions in movie clips linked to this event execute when a key is pressed.

- *keyUp:* Actions attached to movie clips linked to this event execute when a key is released.

- *data:* This initiates the actions whenever data is received into the movie clip from a *loadVariables* or *loadMovie* action.

Later in this book you will examine the use of movie clip actions in more detail. The one thing you should note is the overlap between button and frame events and movie clip events. When two objects can both react to an event, one or the other must have precedence. As you begin working with actions, and to a larger extent when you actually start writing your own code in Flash, precedence is an important issue.

## ▪ ▪ ▪ Precedence in the Flash Environment

Earlier in this chapter you read that in most OOP environments messages are terminated once an object intercepts them. Usually if two objects exist in the environment at the same time, and are both able to react to the same event, only one of those objects will be able to react. Which object reacts depends on a hierarchical precedence, or order, of messaging within the environment.

Because many people are familiar with Director, it serves as an example. In Director, there are two types of scripts that can be attached to objects on the stage: cast and sprite. Cast scripts are attached to the objects themselves (in Director's "library," called a *cast*), whereas sprite scripts are attached to the instances of objects on the stage.

 **NOTE:** *In Flash there is no equivalent of a cast script. That is, you cannot attach actions directly to symbols in the library. You can, however, place actions inside a symbol, which is very close to this functionality. Sprite scripts in Director are akin to attaching actions to a movie clip or button instance on the stage.*

In Director, both of these scripts can react to mouse events. One such event is *mouseUp*. If both a cast script and sprite script are attached to an object and have a *mouseUp* handler, only one of them will receive the event and do something. The second handler will not execute because the first automatically terminates the event message.

In Director, as it relates to mouse events, the sprite script has precedence and will be the script that executes and terminates the message. Unless you specifically tell the sprite script to pass the event onto the cast script, it will terminate the message and the second script will not execute. In essence, the second handler does not know anything has happened, because the first handler has terminated the message.

Flash, however, is a little bit different. First, event messages are not terminated. This means that if a situation exists in which multiple event handlers can react to an event message, they will both execute, and in a definite order.

Second, note that precedence was not even an issue in Flash 4 because there was no overlap in the events that could occur between a button and a frame. Now in Flash 5, you have hopefully noticed that the events associated with the movie clip coincide with events of frames and buttons. There is the potential for confusion if a movie clip and frame are set up to react to a specific event. The same is true of a movie clip that coincides with a button.

For example, a movie clip's actions can react to *enterFrame*. So do actions attached to a frame. Similarly, a movie clip can react to *mouseUp* and *mouseDown*, which coincide with a button symbol's press and release events. In both of these examples, if actions are attached to both items, both sets of actions will execute, with one set occurring before the other.

Thus, when setting up actions, you must acknowledge (1) that event overlap exists, (2) that both sets of actions will execute, and (3) which object's actions will occur first. In the following sections you will read about the cases of overlap that exist between the events handled by the various objects. These sections conclude with a quick summary that you can return to later in this book as you are performing more complex exercises.

 **NOTE:** *Anytime you are adding actions and you find something awry when you test the movie, make sure you consider the issues presented in the following sections. This is where logic concerning precedence becomes very important.*

## Movie Clip and Button Mouse Clicks

The first overlap exists between the *mouseDown* and *mouseUp* events in a movie clip and the *press* and *release* events of a button. Although named differently, in application these events are basically the same thing. Therefore, there is potentially a conflict between the two when you start attaching actions. At the least, you must be conscious of which occurs first when developing your movies.

In the following examples, you will examine some scenarios that display the precedence between a movie clip and button. As you begin to get into applied examples later in this book, you will be reminded of this section and of the precedence in the particular example. For now, you will examine base examples just to get the gist of how precedence is important in deciding where you attach actions and which objects receive events first (thus executing their actions first).

Note that the examples use the simple Trace action to bring up information in the Output window. It will basically reveal to you which object is reacting and in what order. Posting information to the Output window with the Trace action is a nice way of peering "behind the scenes" of a movie, but it is only effective for simple things. Later, you will see how to find out more comprehensive information using the Debugger. Nonetheless, do not be startled when you run the examples and the Output window opens and displays information. In the CD-ROM exercise that follows, you can practice previewing information in the Output window.

 ### CD-ROM Exercise

Open the file *ch6-01a.fla* located in the *F5gai/chapter6* folder, installed from the companion CD-ROM. Before you start messing with the file in the player, let's examine what actions are assigned to the objects.

1. Right-click on the button and select Actions from the context menu to open the Object Actions panel.

Notice that there are two handlers assigned to the button, one for *release* and the other for *press*. Basically, the Trace actions in the handlers are set up to provide information to the Output window when you test the movie. The information will reveal when the *press* and *release* handlers are executed.

2. With the Actions panel still open, click on the movie clip to reveal its actions. Similar to the button, the movie clip has two handlers with Trace actions. The handlers are set on *mouseUp* and *mouseDown*.

     **NOTE:** *The order of the handlers (*press *and* release *for the button;* mouseUp *and* mouseDown *for the movie clip) in the Actions panel is not important because each handler is set to a different event.*

3. Now use Control | Test Movie to open an SWF file into the player for testing.

4. Begin by clicking down and holding with the mouse on the button. When you do this, the Output window will open, revealing the text from the Trace action. Notice that the movie clip's *mouseDown* was executed before the button's *press*. Thus, the movie clip has precedence over the button. However, note that they both execute; the event message (*mouseDown*) is not terminated by the movie clip. This is a

significant difference from other OOP environments, particularly if you are used to the way Director works.

5. Now release the mouse button and notice again that the movie clip again has precedence over the button, in that the *mouseUp* from the movie clip is acknowledged before the *release* of the button.

6. With the movie still running, click anywhere in the movie, except on the button. Notice that the Output window shows that the *mouseDown* and *mouseUp* events attached to the movie clip execute regardless of where you place the mouse. Thus, *mouseDown* and *mouseUp* events attached to movie clips react to any mouse clicks in the environment. The mouse click does not have to be on the movie clip. In regard to buttons, however, for the actions associated with *press* and *release* to execute the mouse does have to be over the button.

 **TIP:** *You can clear the text in the Output window by selecting Clear from the Output window Options menu.*

Regarding the precedence of movie clips over buttons, the physical arrangement of the button and movie clip on the stage has no effect over the precedence. You may think that if the button where in front of the movie clip, it might affect the precedence, but it does not. For example, if a button overlaps a movie clip on the stage, the movie clip will still have precedence over the button, even if you click directly on the button. The following CD-ROM exercise provides an example of this precedence.

 ## CD-ROM Exercise

Open the file *ch6-01b.fla* located in the *F5gai/chapter6* folder, installed from the companion CD-ROM. *Ch6-01b.fla* shows that even if a button and movie clip overlap on the stage, the movie clip has precedence. Use Control | Test Movie to see the results.

Two additional examples are important to note. First, if a button is nested within a movie clip symbol, the movie clip will have precedence over the button. This is pretty logical, and given the prior examples, you would probably expect this. But what happens when a movie clip is nested within a button? The result may surprise you. If a movie clip is nested within a button, the movie clip will not be able to "hear" the mouse events at all. Sticking a movie clip in a button will in essence disable the movie clip's ability to react to the *mouseUp* and *mouseDown* events. The CD-ROM exercise that follows shows this principle in action.

### CD-ROM Exercise

Open the files *ch6-01c.fla* and *ch6-01d.fla* located in the *F5gai/ chapter6* folder, installed from the companion CD-ROM. *Ch6-01c.fla* shows that when a button is in a movie clip, the movie clip has precedence. *Ch6-01d.fla* shows that when a movie clip is in a button, the movie clip cannot respond. Use Control | Test Movie to see the results.

Another aspect of precedence between buttons and movie clips is when you create a drag-and-drop scenario; that is, a situation in which you can drag an element that exists on the stage (usually a movie clip). Movie clips can be set to react anytime the mouse moves, whereas a button can react to a drag off or drag over. As you saw in the prior examples, the movie clip has precedence in almost every case.

With issues concerning dragging, you will again find that the movie clip has precedence. Thus, if a button is set to react to a *dragOver* or dragOut while a movie clip is set to a *mouseMove*, the movie clip actions will override or take precedence over the button's actions. Both will still execute, but the movie clip actions will occur first.

## Movie Clip and Button Key Events

Movie clips and buttons can both respond to user interaction with the keyboard. The movie clip can respond to either a *keyDown* or *keyUp* event, whereas the mouse can only respond to a specific *keyPress*. When you start building items that should respond to key presses, the potential exists for uncertainty as to which (movie clip or button) will have precedence. See the following CD-ROM exercise for practice in determining what has precedence.

### CD-ROM Exercise

Open the file *ch6-02.fla* located in the *F5gai/chapter6* folder, installed from the companion CD-ROM. Let's take a look at what takes precedence when a movie clip and button both have key event handlers set up.

1.  Once you have opened *ch6-02.fla* into Flash, right-click on the button and select Actions in the context menu. Note that the button has two handlers, one for a simple *press* and one for *keyPress*. The *keyPress* event is set up to know when the user presses the P button.

2.  Click on the movie clip on the stage. Notice the handlers associated with it, which are set up to respond when a key is pressed and released (*keyUp* and *keyDown*).

**NOTE:** *Later in the book you will learn about the code being used to return the key by the Trace action (see the Message field in the exercise). Basically, the new Key object is being used to return the key's name.*

3. Use Control | Test Movie to open an SWF into the player.

4. Begin by pressing any key, except P, once on the keyboard. Note that the handlers associated with the movie clip return the key pressed in the Output window.

5. Press the P key once. Notice that the *keyDown* event associated with the movie clip has precedence over the *keyPress* event associated with the button.

6. Press and hold any key, except P. Notice in the Output window that the handler associated with the movie clip's *keyDown* event repeats continually while you hold the key.

As you have seen, because both buttons and movie clips can respond to the keyboard, precedence is important. Therefore, you would use the movie clip event to intercept or modify the entry of data from the keyboard. For example, when the user entered some data, you could intercept it with *keyDown* handler attached to a movie clip. You could also globally respond to any key on the keyboard using *keyUp*. With a button's *keyPress* event, however, you would use *keyPress* to set up quick-keys for the buttons in your movie.

## Movie Clip and Frame Events (*enterFrame*)

As with other objects that share events, precedence also exists when dealing with the movement of the playhead. Both the frames in the timeline and movie clips can be set up to respond to the *enterFrame* event. As already discussed, when you place actions in a frame, you do not see an *enterFrame* event. It is assumed. The movie clip, however, does have an *enterFrame* handler. The CD-ROM exercise that follows examines the relationship between frame events and movie clip *enterFrame* events.

 ### CD-ROM Exercise

Open the file *ch6-03.fla* located in the *F5gai/chapter6* folder, installed from the companion CD-ROM. Once you have *ch6-03.fla* open, click on the movie clip symbol and use the Actions panel to examine the action associated with it. Note that the movie clip symbol has a handler set to *enterFrame*.

1. Click on frame 1 of the Instructions layer and examine the action there. Note that is also set up to place information

in the Output window on the *enterFrame* (keep in mind that actions in frames are by default set to execute on *enterFrame*).

2. Use Control | Test Movie to play the movie. Let it play for about a second or two and then press the Escape key to stop it.

3. Examine the data in the Output window using the scroll bars. If you scroll up you will see that the action from the frame occurred before the action from the movie clip. You will also note that the movie clip occurred on every *enterFrame*, whereas the frame action executed only once.

4. Although it is not common to have a single-frame movie clip (where a movie clip is on screen for only one frame), this and the next step point out something important about the single-frame movie clip. Click in frame 1 of the Instructions layer and insert a frame so that it is two frames long.

5. Test the movie. Notice that the frame event can be made to continually repeat by looping. Notice also when this happens that the movie clip action does not get a chance to "chime in," because the movie is too busy executing the frame action.

The important thing to note about movie clip *enterFrame* events is that they are global. Anytime a movie clip with this event exists, the actions will execute for every frame the movie clip has on the stage. Frame actions, however, will only execute in the keyframe to which they are assigned. Thus, to repeat them you have to loop, or use the Go To action to return to the keyframe that has the action.

## Multiple Movie Clips

An interesting case of precedence exists if you have multiple movie clips in a single section of a movie. As you have seen, movie clip events are somewhat global in nature. Movie clips set to mouse events or key events execute their actions on every such event in the environment. The mouse does not necessarily have to be on the movie clip for the clip to respond to all key presses. Similarly, movie clips set to *enterFrame* events execute their actions on the entry of every frame. Therefore, the question arises, what happens when several movie clips are all set to the same event? What determines the precedence? Let's take a look. See the following CD-ROM exercise.

*CD-ROM Exercise*

Open the file *ch6-04.fla* located in the *F5gai/chapter6* folder, installed from the companion CD-ROM.

1. With the file open, begin by examining the actions attached to the three movie clips. Notice that each is assigned the *keyDown* event and uses the Trace action to indicate which one it is. A Tell Target action is used to control the movie clip. It tells the movie clip to go to the next frame (you will learn about this later in this chapter). For now, simply note that each action uses the *keyDown* event.

2. Use Control | Test Movie to start playing the movie. In the Output window, notice the order of the objects in regard to their response. MC1 is the upper left, MC2 is the upper right, and MC3 is the lower item. If they are set to respond to the *keyDown* event, what controls the order?

3. Click on MC2 (upper right).

4. Use Modify | Arrange | Move to Back.

5. Test the movie again. Note that the arrangement (in the layer) of multiple movie clips that share the same event determines the order of precedence. If you move an item to the front, it has higher precedence as far as the execution of its actions. An item further back in the arrangement has a lower priority concerning its actions.

A final note concerning arrangement and its effect on script execution is that this also applies across layers. As shown in the exercise, within a single layer, precedence is determined by arrangement. Similarly, if objects are spread across multiple layers, precedence is determined by layer order. Thus, the uppermost layer's actions would be executed before layers further back in the order. That is, layers further up in the timeline (layer 1 is in front of all others) have greater precedence.

## A Summary of Flash Precedence

In the prior sections you reviewed the issues of precedence that occur between frames, buttons, and movie clips.

- *Mouse clicks:* In general, the *mouseDown* and *mouseUp* events of a movie clip always have precedence over the *press* and *release* events of a button. All four will execute on a click, but the movie clip actions will always occur first. The only exception is when the movie clip resides within the button. In this case, the movie clip will not respond to clicks at all. Additionally, buttons only react when clicked on; movie clips react no matter where you click.

- *Button presses:* The *keyDown* and *keyUp* movie clip events are global in nature, meaning that any time a button is pressed, the actions execute. Button *keyPress* events only occur when a specific button is pressed. When a movie clip has key events and a button has key events, the movie clip's *keyDown* event will supercede the button's *keyPress* event.

- *EnterFrame:* Frame actions take precedence over movie clip actions assigned with the *enterFrame* event. Frame actions only execute when the keyframe to which they are assigned is encountered. Movie clip actions assigned to *enterFrame*, however, will repeatedly execute as long as the movie clip remains on the stage and the playhead is moving.

- *Multiple movie clips:* The arrangement of movie clips in the environment determines the precedence of script execution. If several movie clips share an event, the order of priority is determined by the arrangement. If items are on multiple layers, layer order determines precedence.

# ■ ■ ■ An Overview of Basic Actions

Most of Flash's basic actions are relatively straightforward, but some require more discussion than others. This section provides an overview of each basic action, what it does, and the information it needs to work. This section is followed by applied examples of the actions. Later chapters are devoted to discussing certain actions in greater detail. In fact, except for the chapter on 3D animation, the rest of this book is pretty much about actions, ActionScript, or JavaScript in one way or another.

## Go To

The most basic of the actions in Flash is the Go To action. This action can be used to jump to frames or labels in the current scene or in another scene. An important note is that the Go To action is limited to jumping to frames and scenes in the current movie.

To set up a Go To action, select the action from the Toolbox list and use the Scene drop-down list, shown in lower part of the Actions panel in figure 6-8, to select which scene you want to go to. The default is the current scene.

Then use Type drop-down list to choose whether you want to jump to a frame or a label. The Next and Previous Frame options are also available and their functions are as their names imply. Finally, you can also use

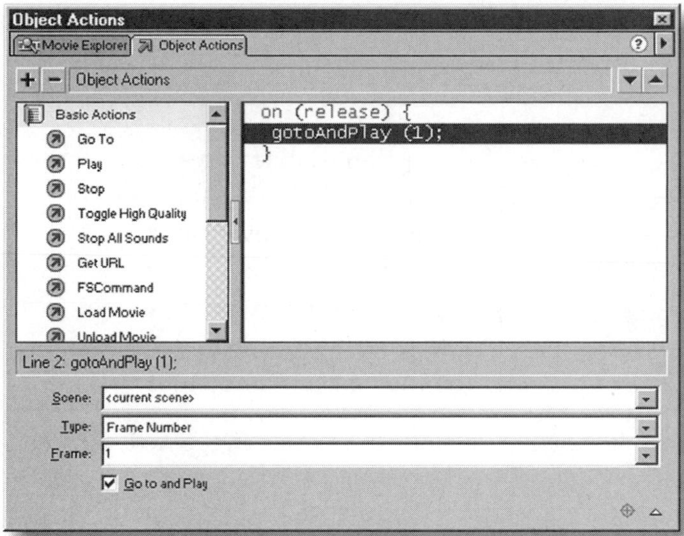

*Figure 6-8 When using the Go To action, you have the option to play or stop when the playhead reaches the new frame.*

ActionScript to construct a location to jump to using the Expression option.

Before broaching expressions, be cautioned about jumping to frames. Instead of jumping to specific frames, it is recommended that you set up your Go To actions with labels instead, by selecting Label from the Type drop-down list. Labels are generally better for setting up looping or "jump-to" locations. If frames are added to a movie, labels shift with the addition of frames. Absolute frame numbers do not. Using absolute frame numbers, such as specifically jumping to frame X, can cause problems if you add frames to the movie late in development. Labels are discussed further in the section "Working with Labels," which highlights this point.

The Expression option in the Type drop-down list allows you to enter data in the Frame field in a variety of ways. When in Normal mode, and when you select any of the other Type options, by default Flash assumes that everything you enter into the Frame field is a *string literal*. String literals are usually just basic text entries. The only time Flash will expect something else (that is, something that is not a string literal) is when you specifically select Expression from a drop-down list. Flash also expects an expression or number if you enable an Expression checkbox in many other actions.

When you choose to enter an expression, you enter ActionScript coding instead of reverting to basic string data. An expression can be used to perform a variety of tasks, such as concatenate two pieces of text to construct a movie location, construct a location based on a variable, or create a location in a movie (dynamically via a wide variety of methods).

Let's quickly look at some example locations that could be constructed using simple expressions. To use them, you select Expression in the Type drop-down in the Go To action. This allows you to enter a frame number, a label, or a target path with a frame number or label in the Frame field. Table 6-1 shows examples of the simple but valid expressions that could be used in the Frame field of the Go To action.

*Table 6-1 Valid Expression for the Go To Action*

| Type | Example | Description |
|------|---------|-------------|
| Frame number | 24 | Jumps to frame 24 in the current movie clip |
| Frame label | "Start" | Jumps to the frame label Start in the current movie clip |
| Target path and frame number | /mc1:24 | Jumps to frame 24 in the movie clip named mc1 |
| Target path and frame label | /mc1:Start | Jumps to the label Start in the movie clip named mc1 |

When you examine the Expert mode of working in the Actions panel, you will review the options for constructing expressions in more detail. Because expressions require greater knowledge of ActionScript, this is reserved for later in the book. Throughout this chapter, you will be focusing on using the default string literals by primarily using either drop-down lists or by entering some basic text into fields. However, the text points out where expressions are applicable. Most examples in this chapter are simple. However, do not be dismayed. You will see more complex examples before you finish this book.

A final item before moving on is the Go To and Play checkbox in the Go To action. When you use the Go To action, you have the options "go to the frame or label and stop" and "go to the frame or label and play" (see figure 6-8). By default, this action goes to the frame or label and plays. When disabled, the small checkbox at the bottom of the dialog box specifies that the movie will stop when it reaches the new frame or label.

## Play and Stop

The Play and Stop actions give you the ability to play or stop the movie at will. There may be times when you want to use these facilities for specific reasons. Additionally, you can direct these actions to specific movie clips within your main movie using the Tell Target action.

 **NOTE:** *For more information on the Tell Target action, see "Using Tell Target to Control Movie Clips" later in this chapter. For applied examples, see Chapter 8.*

## Toggle High Quality

The Toggle High Quality action allows you to adjust the View settings during playback at any given point. The action toggles anti-aliasing on and off. This facility is particularly useful if your audience is browsing your pages using older computers with a lower amount of video RAM, or if a movie is extremely detailed and complex.

# The Importance of Video RAM for Playback

The Toggle High Quality action is useful if you are designing for older computers that have video cards with less than 8 megabytes of RAM. The following explains why the video card and video RAM are so important in the playback of Flash movies.

As previously discussed, vector graphics are "mathematically" based in that they are descriptions of points, lines, arcs, fills, and objects to be displayed. Even though you see the graphical representation of those items on screen, the actual data in the file is written mathematically and describes objects, not pixel-based images.

However, to display those vector graphics on screen, the mathematical descriptions must be converted to point-by-point descriptions (a raster image) by the display card so that it can be rendered via the phosphor guns on a monitor. The process that occurs within the display card, rasterization, happens on the fly. Because vector graphics are "rasterized" on the fly by the video card, video RAM and video processor capability are much more important than RAM memory and the system processor.

Let's consider it another way to see it in comparison to bitmap graphics. Vector image data is delivered over the Web as math descriptions and then rasterized by the display card, resulting in small file sizes but greater overhead for the display card. You might say that the actual vector files are "post-rasterized" (after download). On the other hand, you might call true bitmap images that occur in web pages, such as GIF and JPEG, "pre-rasterized," because the actual rasterized image is delivered straight from the source.

The image is already rasterized. Therefore, the video processor really does not have to do much, except pump a large constant stream of data to the monitor. This is the reason for large file sizes and low computation requirements by the video card concerning raster graphics. Where raster graphics challenge the video card (as well as a network connection) is in the area of throughput (a bus issue). Where vector graphics challenge the video card is in the area of processing and working memory (video card capabilities).

Thus, when designing for older computers with base-level video cards (that is, older cards with 8 or less megabytes of video RAM), the ability to toggle quality can decrease the load placed on the card and, to a certain degree, help playback. If you are designing for such an audience, which is common in secondary or elementary schools as well as some businesses that only use their computers for word processing and the like, you may want to use the toggle high quality.

The visual quality will not be as slick because the anti-aliasing (which is "crunched" by the video processor) is basically turned off. However, speed of playback should increase. If you need to use this action, it is a good idea to test your movies on a comparable machine with a video card similar (as far as constraints are concerned) to what your audience will have.

## Stop All Sounds

As its name implies, the Stop All Sounds action does just that. As with other actions, you can use the Stop All Sounds action in combination with the Tell Target action to turn off specific sounds associated with specific objects. The Stop All Sounds action is not a permanent setting; that is, it does not permanently turn off the sound in the movie. It stops only the sound or sounds currently playing. Any sounds initiated later in the movie begin playing normally.

 **NOTE:** *For more information and applied examples of integrating sound, see Chapter 7. In that chapter, the Stop All Sounds action is used and explained further.*

## Get URL

The Get URL action is probably one of the most frequently used actions. With it, you can load a document specified at a URL into the current window that contains the Flash movie. Figure 6-9 shows the options presented when you select the Get URL action.

When using the default string literal approach, the Get URL field can contain relative or absolute URLs, as well as URLs in the form of a JavaScript statement or a mail statement. An absolute URL is one that contains the entire path and file name of the document to be loaded, such as the following:

```
http://www.tech.purdue.edu/cg/facstaff/jlmohler/
```

Relative URLs, on the other hand, are statements that define a new document based on the placement of the current document on a web server. Most often, specifying relative URLs provide a shorthand method of

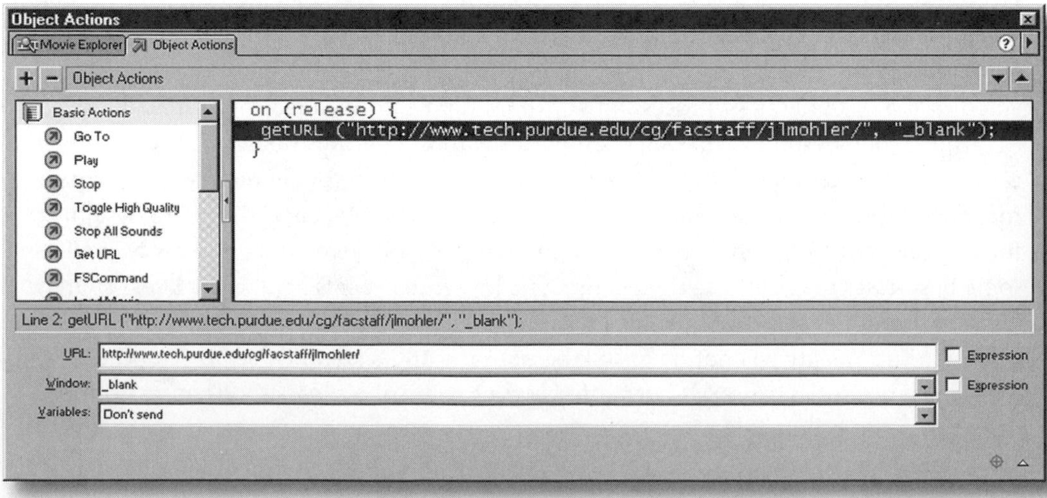

*Figure 6-9  The Get URL action provides the ability to load a new web page in the current browser.*

defining a new document to be loaded. Relative statements entered into the Get URL's URL field can include various things, as shown in Table 6-2.

*Table 6-2 Relative URL Entries for the Get URL Action*

| URL | Meaning |
|---|---|
| *myfile.html* | That *myfile.html* resides in the same directory or folder that contains the currently loaded document. |
| *../myfile.html* | That *myfile.html* resides in the parent folder of the folder in which the currently loaded document resides. In other words, *myfile.html* is one step backward in the directory structure. |
| *../../myfile.html* | That *myfile.html* resides two steps back in the directory structure. |
| */mystuff/myfile.html* | That *myfile.html* resides in a folder named *mystuff*, which is set up as a relative directory on the server. |

In addition to using HTTP URLs, you may also specify an e-mail address. This allows the Flash movie to open the user's default mail program with a new message to the location specified. To create a mail link in Flash, assign the Get URL field as *mailto:* followed by an e-mail address. For example, if an e-mail to *jlmohler@tech.purdue.edu* is desired, the URL would be *mailto: jlmohler@tech.purdue.edu*, as shown in figure 6-10.

As mentioned, you can use the URL field for the insertion of JavaScript commands. This is really a "back door" technique. Other actions, such as the FS Command action, are more suited to getting Flash to interact with JavaScript. Nonetheless, by entering *javascript:* in the URL field, you can call a JavaScript function using Get URL. For example, imagine that the following JavaScript function, which opens a simple dialog box, exists in the HTML page:

```
. . .
<SCRIPT>
<!–
function doalert()
{

window.alert('This
is an alert.')
}
//–>
</SCRIPT>
. . .
```

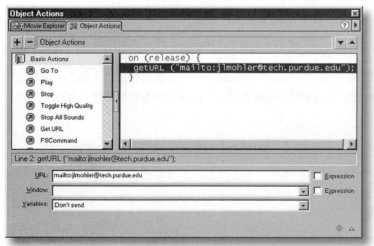

*Figure 6-10 You can insert an e-mail link into Flash, just as you can with HTML code.*

This function could be called from the Flash Get URL action using the following as the URL:

```
javascript:doalert()
```

As previously mentioned, using a JavaScript command in the Get URL action is not a preferred method of calling JavaScript functions, even though many sites use it. An FS command would be the preferred method. The reason is that the JavaScript command technique (calling a function in a URL) does not work in some older browsers, such as IE 3.X. Yet, it does work quite well in most 4.0 versions of Netscape and IE.

**NOTE:** *If you embed JavaScript functions in URLs, make sure you test extensively in multiple browsers and versions.*

The URL field in the Get URL action is an example of where you might want to use Flash's expression capabilities. Using it, you could create an expression that constructs the URL to be used from some entered text data and the string value in a variable, as shown in figure 6-11. In this manner, you could construct URLs on the fly based on the values of variables that exist within a movie. The expression capability adds unique potential to many of the actions, as you will continue to learn.

**CD-ROM NOTE:** *To see an example of these four types of Get URLs, open the HTML file* ch6-05.html *located in the* F5gai/chapter6/ *folder, installed from the companion CD-ROM. You may want to examine the FLA file to see the actions and how they are assigned to the buttons.*

To be able to test movies that use the Get URL action, you must do so within the browser. The Test Movie facility within Flash will not allow you

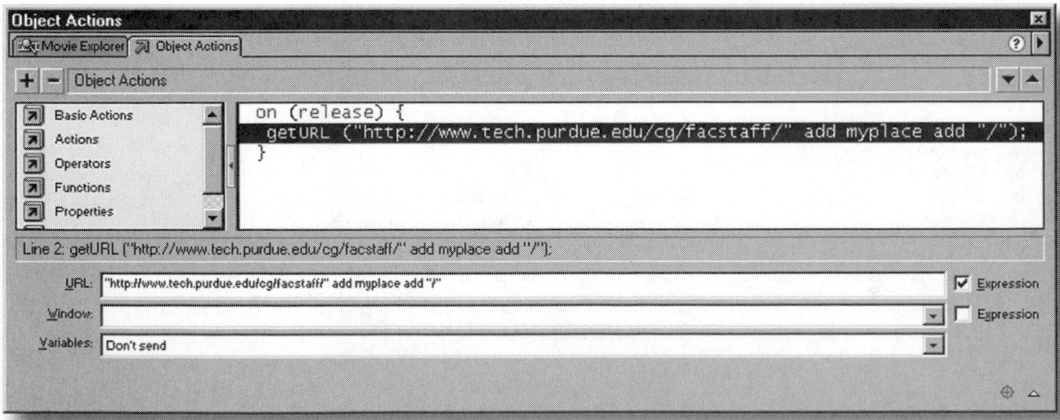

*Figure 6-11  An expression could be used to construct a URL from a string and the content of a variable.*

to see if your links to the Web, mail programs, and JavaScript work. Chapter 9 discusses how to use the Publish feature to quickly generate pages. To test relative URLs, the file must also be in the proper folder location to adequately test actions.

In addition to the URL field, the Get URL action allows you to use HTML window naming. The Window field in the Get URL action is used for targeting specific windows, usually when HTML frames are used. For example, if you had a frames page that had a named window called "content," you could specifically target the "content" window as the window to load the URL into. In addition, Flash provides the following four default HTML target names.

- *_self* opens the URL in the current window or frame.

- *_blank* opens the URL in a new browser window in front of the currently open window.

- *_parent* opens the URL in the parent of the current window. For example, in a frames document that contains two frames, the main document is the parent of either of the subframes.

- *_top* opens the URL in the topmost document. This is useful in situations where a frames document has many subframes or has nested frames.

 **NOTE:** *As with the URL field, expressions could also be used to construct targets based on variables.*

 **CD-ROM NOTE:** *To see a simple example of using the Target specification within the Get URL action, open the HTML file* frames.html *located in the* F5gai/chapter6/frames/folder, *installed from the companion CD-ROM. This shows an example of how to target named frame windows, as well as how to use the four default target specifications.*

 **NOTE:** *The use of named frames, nested frames, and targets is discussed in more detail in chapters 13 and 16.*

The final portion of the Get URL action is yet another important feature. The Variables drop-down list provides added flexibility for your movies by allowing you to pass variables from Flash (on the user's end) to the web server delivering the pages. This gives you the capability to very easily create form pages in Flash that pass their values to another technology on the server, such as CGI, ASP, and so forth.

Variables are nothing more than containers for data in memory. They allow you to store any range of data in your movies. An example is when you create a form field for the user to enter data. In Flash, variables are associated with the fields so that the data is stored and can be reused. Variables are discussed in the later chapters of this book.

By default, variables that exist in your movie are not passed to the subsequent pages that are loaded, denoted by the Don't Send option. However, when you choose to send the data in variables, you can use standard POST and GET methods to submit data from Flash to a server. When the server receives the information, it could use those values in a CGI script, a Java applet, an Active Server Page, or in myriad other technologies.

For example, imagine you created an editable text field into which the user submitted their name. The user's name could then be placed into a variable within Flash. You could use the Variable drop-down list to submit the user's name and other data to the server. The server could then use the user's name in the page, such as customizing the address for that particular name.

Fundamentally, the POST and GET methods are both means of transferring data from a web page (usually from a form) to a web server. Often technologies such as CGI scripts are used to interpret the data being sent from the browser. However, other server-side technologies, such as Microsoft Active Server Pages (ASP), may also intercept data being sent using a POST or GET, as you will see in a moment.

Both the POST and GET methods encode data as a set of name and value pairs. However, they do it a little bit differently, and the receiving technology usually has to use different techniques to extract the data. The GET method appends the data to the URL being accessed. A URL that is passing data with the GET method looks something like the following:

```
http://www.tech.purdue.edu/index.asp?fname=john&lname=smith
```

Here, the variables *fname* and *lname* are sent to the *index.asp* page residing on the server. The page could use the content of those variables in a variety of ways.

The difference between the GET and POST methods is not the way the data is encoded, but how the data is delivered behind the scenes. The GET method is sent as a query string (as previously discussed). The POST method is sent as part of the HTTP request, as if it were coming from a form. For example, imagine you had a field named *myname* in a Flash movie. If you used the GET method to send the data from the form to an Active Server Page (ASP), you would use code such as the following:

```
<% Response.Write Request.Query_String("myname") %>
```

This code would write the data from the Flash field to an HTML page. Thus, the GET method uses the ASP *Request* object to retrieve and utilize the data. Note that *Write()* method of the *Response* object simply tells ASP to write the data. If you used the POST method to send the data, you would use code such as the following to write the data from the field to an HTML page.

```
<% Response.Write Request.Form("myname") %>
```

 **CD-ROM NOTE:** *To see an example of either of these, use* Ch6-06.html *for an example of the GET method and* Ch6-07.html *for an example of the POST method. The native FLA files are in the* F5gai/chapter6 *directory, installed from the companion CD-ROM. The important thing is to look at the Get URL attached to the Send It button.*

For the examples cited in the previous CD-ROM Note, two ASP pages (copies of them are in the *chapter6* directory) have been set up that will receive the data from you and display it in the browser. However, you must be connected to the Internet for this example to work, as ASP is a server-side technology. Thus, the ASP pages must be running on a server that supports ASP for them to work. If you have a server that supports ASP, you could place the ASP files from the CD-ROM on your server and point the Get URL actions in the example files to the location on your server.

An important thing to remember concerning the two techniques is that the GET method is limited in the characters it can pass. For example, space characters are replaced with plus (+) signs, and other restricted characters are replaced with percentages (%). Thus, to use the passed data, the receiving technology (CGI, ASP, and so on) must interpret the data if spaces or other invalid characters have to be passed.

If you wish to use CGI or other technologies with Flash, you simply need to make sure which method (POST or GET) is required. Some technologies can use either and, indeed, POST is the most flexible of the two because it does not have character limitations and does not show the data it is passing in the URL, which often looks pretty messy.

## Microsoft's Active Server Pages (ASP)

ASP is a server-side technology that can pull data from many sources, including databases. It is also pretty easy to use; that is, once you get scripting under your belt. To a large extent, if you understand VBScript, you can write ASP. Additionally, many of the principles in this and other chapters related to OOP, Actions, and ActionScript apply to ASP as well.

For an in-depth look at ASP, see *ASP in a Nutshell* by A. Keyton Weissinger, published by O'Reilly. Just keep in mind that to use ASP your server must be set up to use it. Most NT boxes with MIIS have the capability already. UNIX boxes require additional software, such as Chili!Soft (*http://www.chilisoft.com/*), to be able to use ASP.

## FS Commands (FlashScript Commands)

As mentioned previously, using the Get URL action as a means of calling a JavaScript function (or using any other web technology) is not the preferred method. In general, you can use the FS Command action to send a message to whatever program is hosting or running the Flash Player. Thus, the FS Command action is the action you should use when you want to call a JavaScript or VBScript function from Flash. FS Command is an acronym for FlashScript Command, and it can actually be used to communicate to several things, including the Flash Player.

 **NOTE:** *Chapter 15 specifically covers the ins and out of using the FS Command action. Because it requires significant familiarity with scripting, this topic is reserved for the last chapter of the book. Several examples are presented there, showing the combination of JavaScript, VBScript mapping, and FS Commands.*

## Loading and Unloading Movies

The Load Movie action allows you to load one movie into another movie. Similar to the layering capability of Cascading Style Sheets (CSS) and Dynamic HTML (DHTML), the Load Movie action can display several movies at once, each of which is layered over the other. Similarly, loaded movies are layered and are identified by a level number.

**NOTE:** *The Load and Unload movie actions work in web page movies as well as those played within the Flash Player.*

When you use the Load Movie function, the primary movie defines the stage size, background color, and frame rate. The primary movie is identified as *_level0* in the hierarchy of movies. Subsequent movies that are loaded by the primary movie, using the Load Movie action, can be placed on specific layers, such as *_level1*, *_level2*, and so on. If you use the Load and Unload actions, you should design all movies with the same stage size, background color, and frame rate. The primary movie will override settings in movies lower in the hierarchy anyway.

If you use multilevel movies, the first instance of the Load Movie action will likely exist in a frame action. Subsequent use of the Load Movie action may be used in either object or frame actions. Loading a movie into a level that already has a movie in it replaces the original movie. For example, if *_level3* has a movie called "zapper" loaded into it, loading a movie called "zapper2" into *_level3* replaces the original movie "zapper" movie.

After selecting the Load Movie action, you are required to supply a URL for the movie, a location for the loaded movie, and parameters for how variables are to be passed to the new movie (figure 6-12). Similar to the Get URL action, the entered URL may be a relative or absolute. However, the entered URL must be representative of the file structure that exists during authoring and that which will exist during playback. You may find it easier to test with

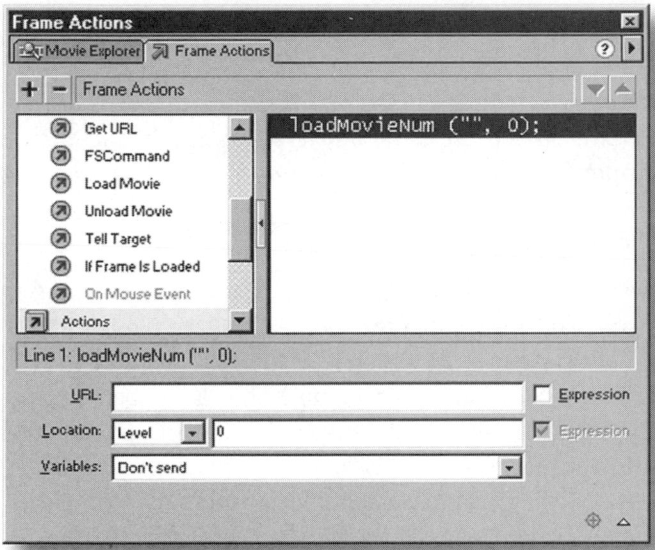

Figure 6-12 The Load Movie action allows you to load one movie into another, and requires several pieces of information.

all of your movies in the same directory, and then modify the URL entries for placement on a server.

**NOTE:** *If you use the Load Movie action, make sure you keep a note of the level on which the movies are loaded. The Unload Movie action allows you to specify only which level to unload, not which movie to unload.*

As with other actions, you can use expressions for the URL and Level or Targets (locations). Again, the ability to specify expressions in these fields allows you to construct their values based on variables and other data that exist at run time. This allows tremendous flexibility in your movies during playback.

**NOTE:** *For more information regarding loading and unloading movies, see Chapter 8.*

## Tell Target

Tell Target allows you to specifically direct commands to specific symbols. However, the Tell Target command works with movie clip symbols only. For example, you can tell a movie clip that exists within the main movie to stop or start playing. Additionally, you can use Tell Target to tell a specific movie clip that has sound in it to stop playing its sound. You can also direct commands to movie clips that exist in loaded movies. The Tell Target action provides a wide range of flexibility, as long as you follow the "rules." As to the rules, there are two:

- To be able to use Tell Target on a movie clip, the movie clip instance must be named. To do this, right-click on the symbol instance on the stage and open the Instance Panel (Ctrl+I or Command+I). In the Instance panel, enter a name in the Name field. This allows you to tell the object specific commands.

- The only objects that can receive actions from Tell Target are movie clips. For example, if you have a movie clip in a button that you want to talk to, by default you cannot. To use Tell Target, all of the nested symbols must be movie clips.

 **NOTE:** *Tell Target, briefly discussed later in this chapter, is a special action designed for use with movie clips. For its advanced uses, see Chapter 8.*

## If Frame Is Loaded

One of the interesting attributes of Flash SWF files (web-ready Flash files) is that they stream. This means that the moment a Flash file is partially downloaded, it can begin playing. However, let's say the first 50 frames of a movie do not take long to download, but frame 51 has some beefy component in it, such as a sound or bitmap. Because Flash streams, the first 50 frames are going to download pretty quickly and begin playing immediately. But what happens if the playhead reaches frame 51 before it is completely downloaded? You guessed it. The movie comes to a screeching halt!

The If Frame Is Loaded action is designed to overcome this problem. With it, you can set up a set of looping frames that repeatedly plays until a particular frame is loaded. When you set up these looping scenarios, called *preloaders*, really what you are trying to do is buy or occupy the user's time until the movie, or a portion of it, has loaded. The nice thing about this action is that there are several types of preloaders, all pretty much based on the same principle. Learn to set up one and you can do any of them. However, you need to be aware of some other concepts first. Thus, preloaders are discussed in detail in Chapter 10.

## ■ ■ ■ Working with Labels

As discussed in regard to the Go To action, Flash allows you to create looping segments and jump-to points for navigation using something called *labels* in the timeline. Rather than jumping to a frame using a Go To action, you can specifically identify a name for a movie location in the timeline and then jump to it while the movie plays.

 **NOTE:** *Labels in Flash work similarly to markers in Director.*

As previously mentioned, when it comes to jump-to points, labels are better than frames. When frames are deleted from the timeline, the number of frames deleted reduces the frame numbers that follow. Thus, any Go To actions hard referenced to a frame number get screwed up. This is why labels are preferred. When you use labels, and frames are deleted, the labels shift with the keyframe to which they are attached, meaning that labels are relative points (not absolute points) in the movie.

**NOTE:** *If you are making the transition from Flash 4 to Flash 5, you will note that comments are no longer inserted via the Frame panel (previously called the Frame Properties window). Comments are now directly added to ActionScript code, discussed later.*

When using labels and frame actions, it is usually best to create a layer that contains nothing but the labels, actions, and blank keyframes to which they are attached. In this way, you have the choice of deleting frames from other layers without disturbing the already defined actions and labels. This method is recommended and is demonstrated throughout the book.

## Adding Labels to a Movie

In exercise 6-5, which follows, you will add a label to a frame in the timeline. When you add a label to a keyframe, a small flag is displayed in the timeline, followed by the label name.

### Exercise 6-5 Adding a Label to a Movie

To add a label to a movie, perform the following steps.

1. Start a new Flash file.
2. Create a layer that will contain all of your labels (and frame actions). You might name this layer Labels/Actions.
3. Place a keyframe at the location you want to insert a label or comment. Here, you can simply use frame 1 by clicking in it.
4. Right-click on the blank keyframe and select Panels | Frame, or press Ctrl + F (Command + F), to open the Frame panel.
5. In the Frame panel, click on the Label field and enter the name for your label.

   **NOTE:** *If you add labels to a single frame, the label name will be hidden. However, the flag will still be displayed. You can roll the mouse over the flag and Flash will reveal the name of the label.*

6. You could now use the Go To action to jump to the label you just entered. When you add a label, a small red flag appears in the frame, with the name of the label following. However, if you added the label to frame 1 and it is only one frame long, you will not see the label name. Click in the frame and press the F5 function key to extend the sprite duration. This will reveal the name, as shown in figure 6-13.

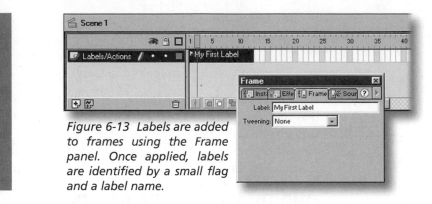

*Figure 6-13 Labels are added to frames using the Frame panel. Once applied, labels are identified by a small flag and a label name.*

## Applying Play, Stop, and Go To

Creating basic looping segments and navigation is easy to establish. To see how this is done, follow the instructions in the following CD-ROM exercise to create a simple movie.

### CD-ROM Exercise

Begin by opening the file *ch6-08.fla* located in the *F5gai/chapter6* folder, installed from the companion CD-ROM. Using this file, you will create an underwater scene with sets of fish that swim across the screen. The file already contains several symbols you will use.

1. Insert a layer above the Instructions layer named Labels/Actions.

2. Extend all sprites out to frame 20 by moving the playhead to frame 1 and using the F5 function key to extend them. You will create two looping segments: one in frames 1 through 10, and one in frames 11 through 20.

3. Add a keyframe in the Labels/Action layer at frames 10, 11, and 20.

4. Add a label, named Loop1, to frame 1. In frame 11, add a label named Loop2.

   **TIP:** *You can quickly call up the Frame panel using Ctrl + F or Command + F.*

   **NOTE:** *If you apply an action, label, or other frame change to the center of a sprite, it is applied to the leftmost keyframe that defines the beginning of that sprite.*

5. Add a Go To frame action to frames 10 and 20. Set the Go To action in frame 10 to label Loop1 by setting Type to Frame Label and Frame to Loop1. Notice that Action displays the current labels in the movie. Also select the Go To and Play checkbox at the bottom of the panel.

6. Repeat this for frame 20, setting the Label to Loop 2.

7. Save your file.

> **NOTE:** *Remember that double clicking on a frame immediately opens the Frame Actions panel and the Sound panel.*

At this point, if you used Control | Play to play the movie, you would see that the loop is not currently working. You must select Enable Simple Frame Actions from the Control menu. By doing so and using Play, the play head does loop, even though no animation has been set up yet.

8. To add the items that will loop in these frame segments, create a new layer, named Fish, above the Buttons layer.

9. Make layer Fish the current layer, if it is not already. Click in frame 1.

10. Use Window | Library to open the current movie's library and drag the symbol named Fish1 onto the stage.

11. Click-drag the endframe marker of the fish sprite (the rectangle in the timeline at the end of the fish you just placed) to frame 10.

12. Insert a keyframe in frame 10 of the Fish layer.

13. Set up a motion tween of the fish moving across the stage from right to left. If the animation is too fast, wait until you are done with the exercise to add more frames. If you want, you can play the movie to see the loop.

Now you will create another fish tween in the second loop area in the timeline, using the Fish2 symbol. Keep in mind that you cannot drag an item from the library to the stage if there is no keyframe in the frame you are dragging to.

14. Right-click on frame 11 in the Fish layer and add a blank keyframe.

> **NOTE:** *Step 14 is vitally important. If you have no keyframe in frame 11 in the Fish layer and you try to drag a symbol from the library, Flash will not let*

*you. The same is true if you try to draw in a frame with no keyframe.*

15. Drag the Fish2 symbol from the library to frame 11 and create a motion tween similar to the previous one. However, this time make the fish swim from left to right.

16. Save your file.

With the two sets of looping segments set up, add actions to the buttons so that you can navigate between the looping segments. Instead of Frame actions, you will add Instance actions to the two buttons that are already created.

17. Begin by adding a keyframe in the Button layer in frame 11.

18. Click on the sprite in the Buttons layer that extends from frame 1 to frame 10.

19. Right-click on the upper red button on the stage and select Actions.

20. In the Toolbox list, double click on the Go To action. Set it to go to Label Loop2. Make sure the Go To and Play checkbox is enabled.

21. Right-click on the lower red button and add a Go To action that goes to Label Loop2 as well. However, this time deselect the Go To and Play checkbox.

22. Click on the sprite that extends from frame 11 to frame 20 in the Buttons layer.

23. Change the text for the buttons so that it indicates that you will be going to the "1st" loop by double clicking on it and editing the text.

24. Assign the actions to the buttons. Set the upper button to Go To Label Loop1, with Go To and Play selected. Set the lower button to Go To Label Loop1, without Go To and Play selected.

25. Save your file.

Now you will add one more element so that you can highlight a significant thing about movie clips. As mentioned earlier, movie clips are special in that they continue to play even if the main movie timeline stops. Again, this is one way movie clip symbols differ from graphic symbols. Graphic symbols stop when the main movie timeline stops. Movie clips do not.

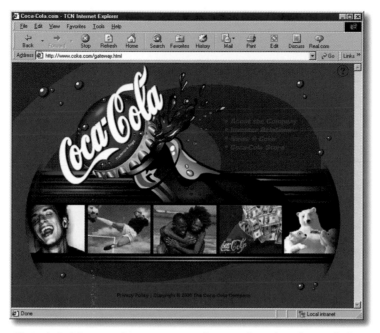

*Plate A-1 More and more companies are choosing the Web for the delivery of real-time information, and Flash has become a standard delivery vehicle (http://www.coke.com/).*

*Plate A-2 Before 1994, marketing sites were taboo! (http://www.nike.com/).*

*Plate A-3  Graphics are also used for navigation (http://www.landroverworld.com/).*

*Plate A-4  Graphical user interfaces may be used on the Web, making navigation more intuitive and user friendly (http://www.tech.purdue.edu/resources/map/mapv2/).*

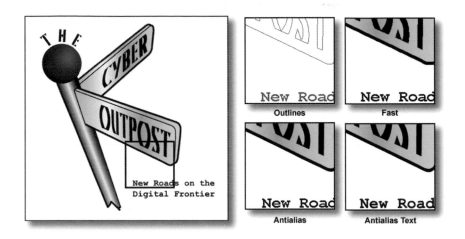

Plate A-5  The various View menu quality settings can be interactively controlled.

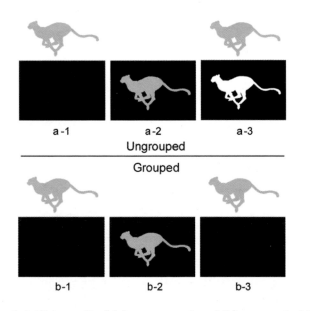

Plate A-6  The result of (a) ungrouped and (b) grouped objects moved over one another.

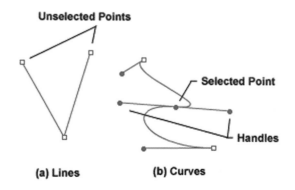

Plate A-7  *When you use the Subselect tool, (a) control points appear at the end of lines and (b) points and curve handles appear on arcs and circles.*

Original

Paint Normal

Paint Fills

Paint Behind

Plate A-8  *The Brush modes allow you to paint in a variety of ways.*

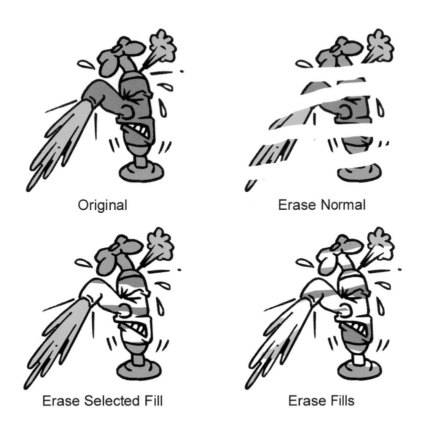

Original            Erase Normal

Erase Selected Fill            Erase Fills

*Plate A-9  The Eraser modes control what is erased.*

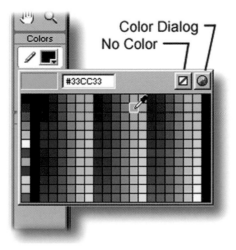

*Plate A-10  The drop-down palette of colors for the stroke and
fill buttons includes a No Color option.*

Color Space     Value Bar

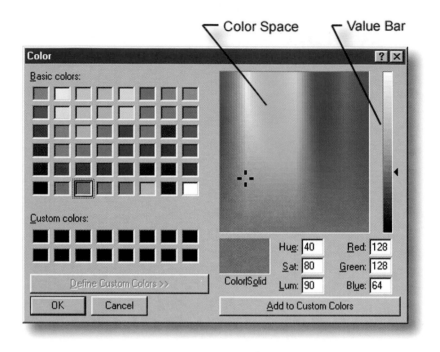

Plate A-11  The Color dialog box allows you to quickly select a
stroke or fill color.

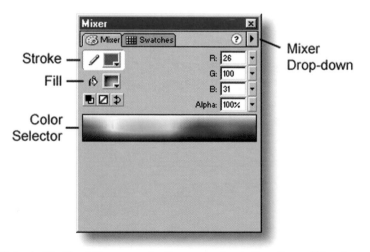

Plate A-12  The Mixer panel allows you to define the solid colors
used for strokes and fills, as well as colors used as the basis for
gradient fills.

Continue with the following steps to see that movie clips do indeed behave as discussed.

26. Create a new layer, named Bubbles, above the Fish layer.

27. Use Window | Library to open the current movie's library.

28. Find the movie clip named Bubbles and drag it to the Bubbles layer. Drag it down and to the left, just off the stage into the work area. You will find that the crosshairs (the registration point for the symbol) are up and to the right of the actual bubble graphics.

29. Place the movie clip's crosshairs in the center of the stage.

30. Save your file.

31. Select Control | Test Movie to view your creation.

If you use Test Movie and the sounds play back poorly, change the audio settings in the File | Publish Settings dialog box. Select the Flash tab and use the Audio Stream | Event Set buttons to set the properties so that the sample rate is higher. The Publish tab affects movies that are tested as well as published. Note that most of the sounds integrated into the sample FLA files of the companion CD-ROM are designed for 22 kHz mono.

 **CD-ROM NOTE:** *A completed version of the previous exercise is available. Access the file* ch6-08.fla *located in the* F5gai/chapter6 *folder, installed from the companion CD-ROM.*

As the movie is playing, use the Go To 2nd Loop (Play) button and the Go To 1st Loop (Play) buttons to see that the movie is jumping between the two loop points. In addition, use the Go To 2nd Loop (Stop) button and the Go To 1st Loop (Stop) buttons. Do you notice a difference between these two segments and what continues to play?

Realize that the Go To and Stop action (Go To without the Play checkbox selected) stops the main timeline of the movie, as it should. However, the Go To and Stop does not stop the Bubbles movie clip symbol. Movie clip symbols continue to play even if the main timeline of the movie stops. In essence, movie clip symbols play independently of the timeline. This is why the movie clip continues to play. If the bubbles symbol where a graphic symbol, notwithstanding the fact that the sound would not play, the bubbles would also stop when the main movie timeline stopped. In the next section, you will see how you can control a movie clip using the Tell Target action.

# ▪ ▪ ▪ Using Tell Target to Control Movie Clips

As demonstrated by the previous example, stopping the main movie timeline does not affect movie clip symbols. If the Bubbles movie clip were instead a graphic symbol, it would have stopped with the timeline. However, keep in mind that graphic symbols cannot include sound (which is why a graphic symbol was not used). Yet, you can use the Tell Target action to tell specific movie clips when to play and when to stop. You can even advance a movie clip forward and backward a frame at a time using Tell Target.

This section examines how Tell Target can be used within a movie to control other movie clips. The main thing to understand is that you can use Tell Target only on named instances of movie clips. This will become clearer as you work through the example. Macromedia states in its literature that the Tell Target action is deprecated in Flash 5 and that the *with* command should be used. This means that Tell Target is still supported in the Flash Player in Flash 5. However, this feature will likely not be present in the next version of Flash.

This chapter focuses on the use of Tell Target because it provides a nice way of becoming familiar with the movie hierarchy and methods of controlling movie clips. Unfortunately, that is its limitation; it only controls movie clips. Chapter 8 introduces the *with* action, a replacement for the Tell Target action. It is okay to use Tell Target right now, but do not get too comfortable with, as it will be replaced by the *with* action later in the book. As you wil find, there are only minor differences between the two actions.

## Using Tell Target

In the following CD-ROM exercise, you will use buttons within the main timeline of the movie to play, stop, and advance a small movie clip. The file you will begin working with already has some symbols inserted into it.

---

### CD-ROM Exercise

Begin by opening the file *ch6-09.fla* located in the *F5gai/chapter6* folder, installed from the companion CD-ROM.

1. Begin by creating a new layer called Labels/Actions above the Instructions layer.

Within the movie timeline, you will have to create two looping sections, similar to the last exercise. One will be used for playing the movie clip; the other will be used for the stopped and frame-by-frame advancing. By default, this example starts with the movie clip stopped.

As you have already seen, movie clips do not stop by default when the main timeline stops. In fact, movie clips automatically play and loop unless you add frame actions within the movie clip that tell it to do otherwise. Because this example has you play and stop a movie clip, two versions of the movie clip exist. One version includes no frame actions. The other has a stop action at each frame. You will understand why this is important a little later. You can see the two versions of the movie clip you will use by accessing the symbols. One version is labeled CD, whereas the other is named CD Stopped.

2. Extend all of the sprites out to frame 20.

3. In the Labels/Actions layer, insert a keyframe at frames 10, 11, and 20.

    **TIP:** *Instead of opening and closing the Actions panel all the time, you can minimize any panel by double clicking in its title bar. This will make it "skinny," so that it is not in the way.*

4. Add a label, named Stopped, to frame 1, and a label, named Playing, to frame 11.

5. Insert a Go To and Play action in frame 10 that goes to the label Stopped.

6. Add another Go To and Play action in frame 20 that goes to the label Playing.

7. Create a keyframe for frame 11 in the Buttons layer. Remember to hold down the Ctrl key (Command for Mac) while clicking on a frame to select a single frame.

8. In frame 11 in the Buttons layer, delete the Forward 1 Frame and Backward 1 Frame text and buttons. Then change the Play Clip text to Stop Clip by editing it, as shown in figure 6-14.

9. Use Window | Library to open the current movie's library.

10. Create a new layer named Clips.

11. Add a keyframe to frame 11 in the new layer.

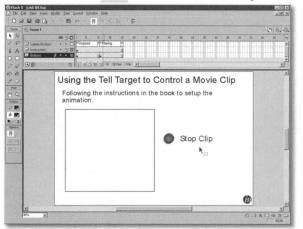

*Figure 6-14 Edit the elements at frame 11 in the Button layer.*

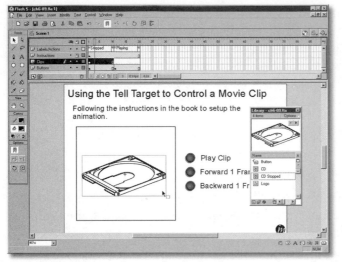

*Figure 6-15  Center the movie clip in the rectangle on the stage.*

12. In frame 1 of the Clips layer, insert the CD Stopped symbol within the rectangle on the stage. Visually center the movie clip's crosshairs in the center of the rectangle, as shown in figure 6-15.

13. Name the instance so that it can be targeted with buttons. To bring up the Instance panel, right-click on the symbol and then select Panel | Instance from the context menu.

14. Enter *Stopped CD* in the Name field. Now you can target ("talk to") this movie clip.

15. Click in frame 11 and insert the CD movie clip on layer Clips. Toggle the playhead between frames 10 and 11 to align the two symbols, or turn on Edit Multiple Frames to align the two elements. When jumping between the two looping segments in the main timeline, you do not want to see a positional jump between the two movie clips.

16. With the two symbols aligned, name the symbol you just inserted Playing CD, as you did with the other movie clip in step 14.

17. Set up the buttons so that they control the clip. Begin by moving the playhead to frame 1.

18. Right-click on the Play Clip button and open the Actions panel. Here, a Tell Target is not needed. All you want is to assign a Go To action to the Playing label in the main movie timeline. Therefore, insert a Go To and Play (the label is Playing) into the Actions panel.

19. Right-click on the Forward 1 Frame button on the stage. In the Actions panel, select Tell Target from the Toolbox list. It will automatically be placed inside a mouse event handler, as shown in figure 6-16.

As you get more experience, you can just write a target path into the Target field by typing it in. Here, you will use the

Insert Target Path editor to get you started. Stay tuned! At the end of this chapter you will return to this wonderful little dialog box, as it makes a really nice learning tool as it relates to learning about targets and relative versus absolute references.

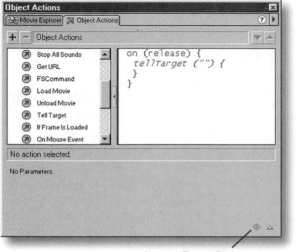

Insert a Target Path

*Figure 6-16 The Tell Target action is automatically inserted into a mouse event handler.*

20. Now you must tell it what to target. Click on the *tellTarget (" ")* { line in the Action list on the right and click in the Expression field. Click on the Insert a Target Path button (see figure 6-16) to open the Target Editor.

For the Insert a Target Path button to be active, clicking on the Tell Target line in the Action list is not enough. You must click on the Tell Target line in the Action list and then click the cursor in the Expression field, as if you were going to type some text.

21. In the Insert Target Path editor, note that the named instance (Stopped CD) appears in the preview window in the center. Click on the Stopped CD instance and its name will be added to the Target window, as shown in figure 6-17.

22. For now, do not worry about the items at the bottom of the Insert Target Path editor. Just click on OK and the content in the Target window will be added to the Target field in the Actions panel.

23. With the Tell Target action selected in the Action list, select Go To from the Toolbox list and double click on it. This inserts it into the Tell Target. Thus, the action will be directed to the object specified in the target.

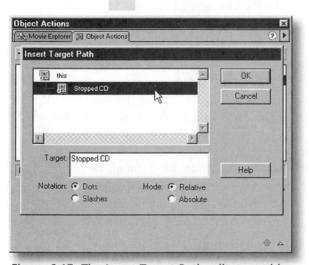

*Figure 6-17 The Insert Target Path editor provides a warm and fuzzy means of entering targets.*

```
Object Actions                                    [×]
[Movie Explorer][Object Actions]                 [?][▶]
[+][-] Object Actions                            [▼][▲]
┌─────────────────────┐  on (release) {
│🔊 Basic Actions    ▲│    tellTarget ("stopped CD") {
│📄 Actions          │      nextFrame ();
│ 🔊 break           │    }
│ 🔊 call            │  }
│ 🔊 comment         │
│ 🔊 continue        │
│ 🔊 delete          │
│ 🔊 do while        │
│ 🔊 duplicateMovieClip│
│ 🔊 else            │
│ 🔊 else if         │
│ 🔊 evaluate        │
│ 🔊 for           ▼│
└─────────────────────┘
Line 3: nextFrame ();
  Scene: [<current scene>            ▼]
   Type: [Next Frame                 ▼]
  Frame: [                           ▼]
     □ Go to and Play
                                  ⊕  ▵
```

*Figure 6-18  The Actions panel with the finished Tell Target that will control the movie clip.*

24. Click on the Go To action and set the Type to Next Frame. The Actions panel should look as it does in figure 6-18.

You should have noticed two things during this process. First, the Target Preview window can be used to find all of the available targets for the current button. If no targets appear, ensure that you named the movie clips on the stage or in your symbols. Second, the Go To Next Frame is automatically inserted between the Tell Target. Most of the available actions could be used within the Tell Target action.

25. Save your file.

26. Use the Actions panel to set up a Tell Target for the Backward 1 Frame button. Add the Tell Target, select the target, and then add the Go To, with Previous Frame selected.

27. Set up the action for the stop button in the playing loop. As with the Play button in the stopped section, a Tell Target is not needed here. Move the playhead to frame 11, right-click on the Stop button on the stage, and use the Actions panel to add a Go To (the label is Stopped) to the button.

28. Save your file again.

29. Use Control | Test Movie to see the results.

## Further Notes on Tell Target

The only problem you may find in the prior finished movie is if you are in the stopped section with the CD in its original starting position. If you try to use the Backward button, it will not work in that frame. Why? Because it was not programmed it to do it. When the movie clip is in the first frame, there is no previous frame. Similarly, if the movie clip is in its last frame and you tell it to go to the next frame, it will not work because there is no next frame. It can be done, however. Examine the movie file specified in the following CD-ROM note to see how this is done.

 **CD-ROM NOTE:** *To see how to make the previous movie smarter, open the file* ch6-09s_adv.fla *located in the* F5gai/chapter6 *folder, installed from the companion CD-ROM. Examine the actions associated with the forward and backward buttons.*

Although this movie is using Tell Target to change the current frame of the movie clip using the Go To action, a Tell Target can use any of the actions. As you will see in Chapter 7, using Tell Target with Stop All Sounds directed toward a particular movie clip may prove to be very useful. In the swimming fish example you did earlier, adding a name to the bubbles movie clip and an additional Tell Target handler (with a Stop action inside it) to the buttons would allow you to stop the bubbles movie clip, in addition to the existing Stop that applies to the main timeline.

 **CD-ROM NOTE:** *See if you can stop the bubbles from the previous example using the Tell Target action. Access the* file ch6-08s.fla *located in the* F5gai/chapter6 *folder, installed from the companion CD-ROM. Try stopping the bubbles movie clip.*

# ▪ ▪ ▪ Understanding the Movie Hierarchy

As you saw in the prior examples, and particularly if you looked at the advanced movie clip example (*ch6-09s_adv.fla*), being able to specifically target and talk to objects is one of the most crucial concepts in Flash. There are roughly 10 different actions that use targets, so it is pretty important. Understanding how to use Tell Target as well as the other actions starts with knowledge of the movie hierarchy.

Therefore, before concluding this chapter, a discussion of the movie hierarchy, as it relates to movie clips, is needed. In the prior examples you started dealing with the most basic of relationships, single movie clips within the timeline. However, there are much more complex situations that can exist, particularly when you start thinking about nested movie clips as well as layered movies (where movies are loaded into movies).

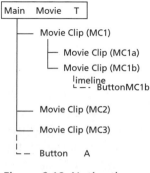

*Figure 6-19 Notice the hierarchy of symbols contained within an example movie.*

## Movies are Hierarchical!

Imagine that you have a movie with three movie clips and a button loaded into its timeline. The instances of the movie clips are named as MC1, MC2, and MC3. Remember that instance names are assigned to movie clips using the Instance panel's Name field. To make life more interesting, nested inside MC1 are two other movie clips, named MC1a and MC1b. MC1b also has a button in it. Figure 6-19 shows a graphical representation of this hierarchy.

Using the Tell Target command, the two buttons can be made to control any of the movie clips in the structure, as long as every movie clip instance is named. The most difficult part of the process is identifying the actual target specification.

## Absolute Versus Relative Targets

As you saw in the rotating CD movie clip example, it is relatively easy to have a button in the main timeline control movies that exist in the main timeline. However, realize that movie clips can be embedded or nested into other movie clips. Even with a structure such as that shown in figure 6-19, the Insert Target Path editor can reveal the target specification needed to point button A to movie clip MC1a. Figure 6-20 shows this.

In figure 6-20, note that the path editor is currently set on Absolute mode and Dot notation. Let's first deal with the issue of absolute and relative path names. To this point, the mode has not been discussed. Let's examine what the Absolute/Relative mode means.

When you want an object to talk to something else in an environment, you have to point the talking object to the receiving object based on either (1) the current object in the hierarchy or (2) a fixed point in the hierarchy. When you specify paths based on the object that is doing the taking, it is called *relative*; that is, where the receiving object is in relation to the talking object. If you specify the location of the receiving object based on a fixed point, it is called *absolute*. In Flash, the fixed point is the main movie timeline, and generally the only difference between the two is that relative usually requires less typing than absolute.

The only time relative versus absolute naming becomes very important is when you want to create reusable, self-contained movie clips. It also becomes important with smart clips. For example, let's say you set up a component you want to be able to drag and drop into other movies. If you use absolute paths, the component will not likely work unless you go back and modify the paths in relation to the new environment. If you use relative paths, clips can be made so that they are self-contained and not dependent on their hierarchical location in a movie.

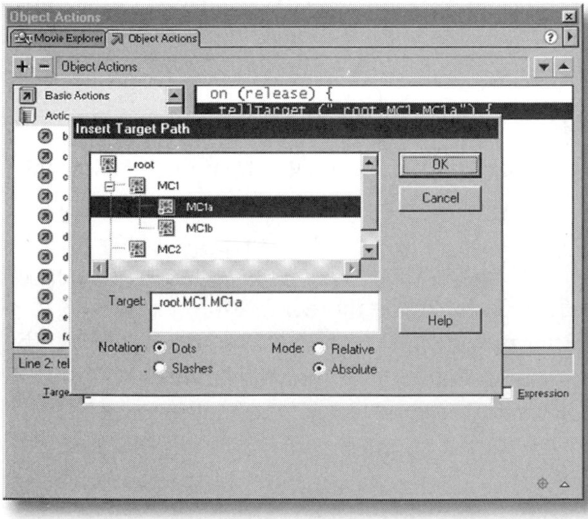

Relative versus absolute can be explained another way. An example you may be familiar with (where you deal with absolute versus relative paths) is the HREF attribute of the anchor tag in HTML. Let's say you have a home page that resides at the root level of your web site. The site URL is *http://www.somesite.com/*.

*Figure 6-20  The hierarchy of nested movie clips is displayed in the Insert Target Path editor.*

When you specify URLs off that home page, you can use either absolute or relative links.

Let's say you have a page (*newpage.html*) that resides in a folder (*myfolder*) at the root level of the server. You can use an absolute HEF based on a fixed point in the web structure. The HREF, then, would look as follows:

`http://www.somesite.com/myfolder/newpage.html`

However, you could also use a relative path, from the home page itself, and save a little typing. It would look as follows:

`myfolder/newpage.html`

Relative and absolute paths in Flash are basically the same thing and work in much the same way. Thus, in figure 6-20, the path is specified as an absolute path. Note that *_root* is the term used to identify the main movie timeline. The specification shown in the Insert Target Path could actually be used on any frame, button, or movie clip to control movie clip MC1a. The object this specification is attached to makes no difference because it is based on a fixed point, the main movie timeline, not on the talking object's location in the movie hierarchy.

 **CD-ROM NOTE:** *To see an example file that displays absolute paths, open the file* ch6-10.fla *located in the* F5gai/chapter6 *folder, installed from the companion CD-ROM. Examine the actions associated with button A and button MC1b.*

Now let's examine relative paths. When originally introduced, button A in this example was the object that was to control movie clip MC1a. If you wanted the path to be relative instead of absolute, it would be specified from button A's location in the movie hierarchy, as shown in figure 6-21.

In figure 6-21, notice the top-level object shown in the window in the middle. It says *this*, meaning the object you are currently attaching the action to. All other items in the list are specified according to the current object's location in the movie hierarchy.

If you refer to figure 6-19, notice that from where button A is located in the hierarchy, basically everything in the environment is visible to it. Thus, all of the movie clips show up in the Insert Target Path editor. But what happens if the button you want to target from is so deep in

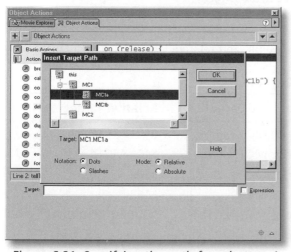

*Figure 6-21 Specifying the path from button A to movie clip MC1a using relative mode.*

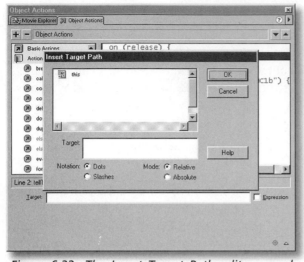

*Figure 6-22  The Insert Target Path editor reveals only objects that are deeper in the hierarchy, relative to the current object.*

the hierarchy that it cannot see the other items in the movie? For example, if you were to access button MC1b and use the Insert Target Path editor, nothing would show in the window (see figure 6-22).

Even though nothing shows up in the Insert Target Path editor, it does not mean you cannot control items backward or further up in the hierarchy from the current object. It just means you have to know and understand target paths well enough to be able to write them yourself. You will note that when you were dealing with absolute paths, you did not have to worry about this, because everything was always specified based on the main movie timeline (_root). When using absolute paths, everything will always show because everything will always be below the main movie timeline, at least from a hierarchical perspective.

Regardless of whether you are dealing with absolute or relative paths, remember that although you can use a Tell Target from a button, you cannot target *through* a button. For the Tell Target action to find the object, and actually any of the actions that use target paths, objects within the path of the target object must be movie clips. You cannot target movie clips that reside in buttons or graphic symbols. The entire path sequence has to be movie clips. This is primarily because they are the only symbols that can be named, and thus identified as objects you can talk to. Table 6-3, which follows, provides details on absolute and relative targets in dot syntax.

*Table 6-3 Absolute and Relative Targets in Dot Syntax*

| Target | From Object | Absolute Target | Relative Target |
|--------|-------------|-----------------|-----------------|
| MC1a | Button A | _root.MC1.MC1a | MC1.MC1a |
| MC1b | Button A | _root.MC1.MC1b | MC1.MC1b |
| MC2 | Button A | _root.MC2 | MC2 |
| MC3 | Button A | _root.MC3 | MC3 |
| MC1a | Button MC1b | _root.MC1.MC1a | _parent.MC1a |
| MC1b | Button MC1b | _root.MC1.MC1b | _parent.MC1b |
| MC2 | Button MC1b | _root.MC2 | _parent._parent.MC2 |
| MC3 | Button MC1b | _root.MC3 | _parent._parent.MC3 |

Table 6-3 is quite important, and you must compare it to figure 6-19 to get the gist of what is going on. Again, when specifying absolute paths, everything is referenced from the main movie timeline. Thus, all of the targets in the Absolute Target column begin with _root, regardless of which button it is attached to, and they are basically the same statements independent of button.

You specify relative targets, on the other hand, from a specific object. Notice the special term _parent, which refers to the parent timeline of the current object (in other words, one step up in the structure). Each time you specify _parent, you take one step back (up) in the movie clip (timeline) hierarchy, which can be done multiple times in a single target specification, as shown in the Relative targets column of table 6-3.

 **CD-ROM NOTE:** *To see an example file that displays relative paths, open the file* ch6-11.fla *located in the* F5gai/chapter6 *folder, installed from the companion CD-ROM. Examine the actions associated with button A and button MC1b.*

 **NOTE:** *Later in this book you will learn about the "this" keyword as well, which refers to the current timeline. In relation to figure 6-19, a* this *specified in movie MC1 would refer to MC1's timeline.*

## Slash Syntax Versus Dot Syntax

You should know something about dot syntax versus slash syntax as it relates to target paths. Slash syntax is a carryover from Flash 4, whereas dot syntax is new and is now the de facto standard. Even though dot syntax is the focus in most of this book, some relational information is in order so that users making the transition from Flash 4 will know the Flash 5 equivalents.

You have already learned a little bit about dot syntax and have seen how dots are used to identify target paths for movie clips. In addition to paths, dot syntax can be used to indicate the properties or methods related to an object or movie clip. Similarly, they can be used to identify variable information.

Slash syntax is similar to dot syntax. Much like navigating a DOS command line file structure, objects can simply be named to go deeper into the object hierarchy. Defining a path using slash syntax from a child object to a target located higher in a movie clip structure is done using a ../ before the movie clip you are trying to identify. The ../ tells Flash to look one step up in the movie clip structure. In essence, you could say that the ../ is akin to the _parent used in dot syntax. The dot syntax _root is similar to the _level0 parameter used with slash syntax. Table 6-4 shows equivalents between dot syntax targets and slash syntax targets.

*Table 6-4 Comparison of Dot and Slash Syntax with Target Paths*

| Target | From Object | Absolute (Dot) | Relative (Dot) | Absolute (Slash) | Relative (Slash) |
|--------|-------------|----------------|----------------|------------------|------------------|
| MC1a | Button A | _root.MC1.MC1a | MC1.MC1a | _level0/MC1/MC1a | MC1/MC1a |
| MC1b | Button A | _root.MC1.MC1b | MC1.MC1b | _level0/MC1/MC1b | MC1/MC1b |
| MC2 | Button A | _root.MC2 | MC2 | _level0/MC2/ | MC2 |
| MC3 | Button A | _root.MC3 | MC3 | _level0/MC3 | MC3 |
| MC1a | Button MC1b | _root.MC1.MC1a | _parent.MC1a | _level0/MC1/MC1a | ../MC1a |
| MC1b | Button MC1b | _root.MC1.MC1b | _parent.MC1b | _level0/MC1/MC1b | ../MC1b |
| MC2 | Button MC1b | _root.MC2 | _parent._parent.MC2 | _level0/MC2/ | ../../MC2 |
| MC3 | Button MC1b | _root.MC3 | _parent._parent.MC3 | _level0/MC3 | ../../MC3 |

 **CD-ROM NOTE:** *To see examples of the previous exercise files that show slash syntax with absolute and relative target paths, open the files* ch6-12.fla *and* ch6-13.fla *respectively, located in the* F5gai/chapter6 *folder, installed from the companion CD-ROM. Examine the actions associated with button A and button MC1b.*

This chapter only touched the surface of the capabilities of the Tell Target and scripting in general. Because Tell Target is an integral part of performing many advanced techniques, it will be revisited several times throughout the remainder of this book.

## ▪▪▪ Summary

This chapter examined basic actions and how they can be used to create interactivity within your movies. The Stop, Play, and Get URL actions will constitute much of what you need for basic sites. When you add to this the ability to control movie clips with the Tell Target action (as well as the boundless use of ActionScript and FS Commands that you will learn about later), there is almost nothing you cannot do with Flash. The next chapter begins examining how sound can be used within your movie.

chapter

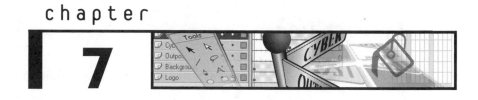

# 7

# Adding the Aural Element

## Introduction

Sound is one of the most important elements available on the Web today. Many information tools (even those independent of the Web) use text, graphics, and animation, but few use sound to its fullest potential. Although it should be a primary focus during development, sound is frequently the last aspect considered.

When reviewing various sites, particularly those with dynamic Flash elements, you will find that sound is a vitally important part of the sensory experience. If you strip a site of its aural attributes, something is noticeably missing. Music added to any visual media engages both sides of the brain and gives the audience a true multisensory experience.

Flash provides an advanced way of working with sound. For example, you can effortlessly insert short beeps and whistles associated with buttons in movies. Adding simple sounds to various states of a button is very easy. By using movie clips, you can also create complex music tracks that can be overlaid and controlled from the main movie timeline, just like any other movie clip. You can create sophisticated sound-based movie clips, just as complex hierarchical movie clip structures can be created with graphical data.

This chapter examines both the preparatory issues related to the integration of sound on the Web, as well as the specifics of how Flash deals with and uses aural data. You will learn to import sound and use Flash's Sound panel to adjust the way the sound is played back. Additionally, you will master using the Tell Target action described in the last chapter to control audio clips.

# ▪ ▪ ▪ Objectives

In this chapter, you will:

- Examine the primary issues related to computer-based audio
- Learn to sample sound from existing analog sources
- Find out how to import various sound formats into Flash
- Discover the difference between event and streaming sounds
- Explore the Sound panel in Flash and learn to use its settings and options
- Find out about ADPCM and MP3 compression and how they can be used in Flash

# ▪ ▪ ▪ Understanding Computer Audio

When dealing with digital sound, developers have two options for representing and distributing audio on the Web. Much like the choice for graphics (vector and raster), audio can also be represented in one of two ways: sampled or synthesized. Sampled sound includes WAV or AIFF files and is sometimes called *digitized* or *digital sound*, whereas synthesized sound is predominantly delivered via Musical Instrument Device Interface (MIDI) files. Vector and raster graphics can be used as an analogy for the similarities and differences between synthesized and digital audio.

## Types

The fundamental difference between sampled and synthesized sound is the way in which the audio is defined and played back. Any lengthy discussion of these differences requires an understanding of acoustical physics, but the basics are relatively simple.

When you create a sampled audio clip, you are engaging in the process of sampling, the conversion of analog data into a digital representation. Because audio is a time-based media, samples (audio states at instances in time) are captured from an analog source and then described digitally. Every pitch and volume characteristic at each instance in time is descriptively written in the file. A digital audio file is a description of multiple points over time, which form a sound curve that is approximated, based on certain digital settings at the time of sampling.

Theoretically, because analog data have an infinite level of descriptiveness, even the best digital recording is still only an approximation, but we can represent the totality of what the human ear can perceive. Even though the computer is limited to discrete, numerical representations, these imperfect representations are still enough for our limited receptors. That is, there is a point at which we usually do not notice missing data. Therefore, the sampled points describe instances in time at regular intervals, as shown in figure 7-1.

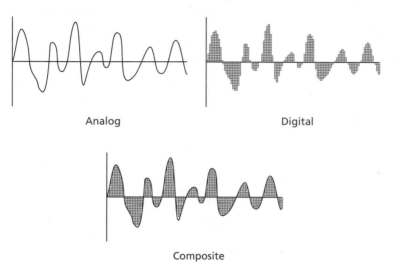

Analog

Digital

Composite

*Figure 7-1 The digital representation is only an approximation of the original analog audio clip.*

Synthesized sound (MIDI), on the other hand, describes audio much differently. Instead of describing the audio as digitized instances of time, at some base level, MIDI describes the various notes and instruments that should play at any given time. The MIDI description can also contain information such as sets of notes that should get louder or softer, as well as special effects such as distortion.

A special chip called a synthesis chip on the computer's sound card then interprets this description. The sound card generates the recreated sound in real time (thus, synthesis). Because MIDI is actually recreating the described audio (rather than playing back a recording), MIDI audio frequently sounds "fake" or "counterfeit." Advances have been made in MIDI technology, and it is getting increasingly difficult to distinguish synthesized sound from sampled sound.

 **NOTE:** *Because Flash cannot use MIDI sound, it will not be discussed further. Flash can only use digital audio. However, understand that the <EMBED> HTML tag can be used to integrate MIDI files directly into a web page.*

## Sampling Rate

To create digital audio, an analog source such as a cassette tape or CD-ROM is often used. When the analog audio is sampled, specific, equidistant intervals over time are captured and digitally recorded. The regularity of these capture points is called the *sampling rate*. It is measured in hertz or kilohertz. The higher the sampling rate, the denser the number of captured points and thus the more accurate or detailed the description of the audio.

Figure 7-2 shows an example of three captures using three different sampling rates. Notice that the highest sampling rate shown, 44 kHz, is extremely detailed (darker/denser) as compared to the lowest sample, 11 kHz. As logic dictates, a higher sampling rate results in a larger digital file.

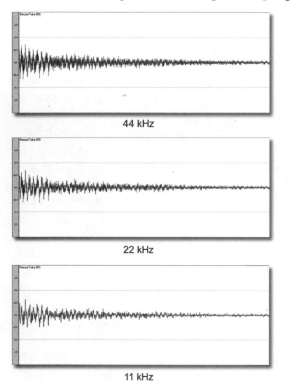

44 kHz

22 kHz

11 kHz

*Figure 7-2   These three samples of the same audio clip were captured at different sampling rates.*

Sounds that have a sampling rate of 44 kHz are said to be "CD quality." Most audio CD-ROMs use 44 kHz because this captures all sounds perceivable to the average human ear (22.1 kHz to 20 Hz). When you capture sounds or obtain them from stock galleries or other usable sources, they may be CD quality.

However, seldom will you use 44 kHz sounds in Flash. Due to the amount of detail in these files, you will generally down-sample these files to either 22 kHz or 11 kHz using sound software program so that they are adequate in size for web delivery. An alternative is to import the high-quality sound file into your Flash file and then down-sample the sounds when you generate your SWF files using Export Movie or Publish.

As the sampling rate of any digital audio clip decreases, the fidelity of the clip lessens. Because the sampling rate increases the amount of time between captures, certain high and low frequencies are lost in the recording. As the distance between samples becomes greater (a lower sampling rate), more and more frequencies are lost. This is how sampling rate affects the quality of a digital audio clip.

When working with sound on the computer, you must understand how sampling rate affects the clips you play back in Flash. Flash allows you to import and export 44-kHz sound files with movies. However, this is not efficient. Most computer speakers are not able to use or play back all that data, even though it may exist in the sound clip. Additionally, the size of 44-kHz sound files will drastically increase the size of your files. Generally, use 22-kHz or 11-kHz sound files in Flash. Employ a sound program, such as Sound Forge or Bias Peak (or even a basic sound program such as Sound Recorder in Windows) to down-sample your files.

Export Movie in the File menu allows you to adjust the sampling rate settings when generating SWF files for delivery. However, it is still preferable to down-sample the files before importing them into Flash so that your native FLA files are smaller. You might typically import 22-kHz sound files into Flash if that is the highest rate any of your sounds will have on the Web. However, if you are designing Flash files for CD-ROM delivery, 44 kHz may be acceptable. Use your best judgment and plan for the medium you intend to use for delivery.

## Bit Depth

Aside from sampling rate, digital audio has one other attribute that affects the sampled clip. At each captured instance in a digital audio clip, the computer must represent a captured point's amplitude using numbers. At a conceptual level, these numbers are represented as bits (or on and off states) in the computer. The more bits the computer can use to represent the "snapshot" of amplitude, the greater the degree of descriptiveness of that point. The number of bits the computer can use to describe any point (instance in time) is called *bit depth.*

If a visual comparison were made between representations of the same audio clip at 16 bit and 8 bit, you would see that the 16-bit file has a greater range of amplitudes, as shown in figure 7-3. Thus, bit depth affects a digital audio clip's dynamic range, which is the range between the loudest and softest audible level. The greater the bit depth, the larger the dynamic range and the more realistic the sound.

 **NOTE:** *Sampling rate and bit depth are independent of each other. However, they can affect each other. For example, an audio clip sampled with a high sampling rate and saved at a low bit depth may sound poor, even though it was sampled high.*

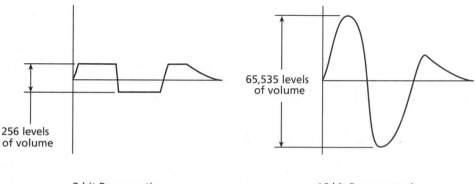

256 levels of volume

65,535 levels of volume

8-bit Represention

16-bit Representation

*Figure 7-3  8-bit and 16-bit sound clips have different levels of descriptiveness.*

## Sampling for Flash

For the sake of smaller file sizes, always try to use the lowest sampling rate and bit depth required for adequate presentation. Table 7-1 shows file size at various sampling rates and bit depths. As you can see, the higher the quality of sound, the greater the file size.

*Table 7-1  File Sizes per Sampling Rate and Bit Depth*

| Sampling | Bit Depth | Channels | File Size per 30 Seconds (MB) |
|----------|-----------|----------|-------------------------------|
| 44 | 16 | Stereo | 5.25 |
| 44 | 16 | Mono | 2.6 |
| 44 | 8 | Stereo | 2.6 |
| 44 | 8 | Mono | 1.3 |
| 22 | 16 | Stereo | 2.6 |
| 22 | 16 | Mono | 1.3 |
| 22 | 8 | Stereo | 1.3 |
| 22 | 8 | Mono | .65 |
| 11 | 16 | Stereo | 1.3 |
| 11 | 16 | Mono | .65 |
| 11 | 8 | Stereo | .65 |
| 11 | 8 | Mono | .325 |

When working, the most common sampling rate is 22 kHz, and the most common bit depth is 16 bit. Variation from these norms depends on the content being recorded or played back, as well as the expectations of the audience. Generally, music with many midtones may be adequately represented with 11 kHz, 8 bit. However, music with many highs or lows may not work well with these settings. Additionally, voice-over usually requires 22 kHz, 16 bit due to its dynamic qualities. Be prepared to do some "trial-and-error" work as you are learning what sampling rate and bit depth work best.

This discussion of audio attributes has purposely ignored multichannel sounds. When you record audio, there are usually two tracks: one for the left speaker and one for the right. You should avoid using multichannel sounds due to their impact on the size of your Flash files. Most sound programs can generate a single channel file from a multichannel file. If you want to incorporate special effects, such as panning from left to right or only playing on one speaker, you should use Flash's Sound panel to achieve this. The Sound panel offers this capability in the Effects drop-down menu, discussed in this chapter.

# ■ ■ ■  Sampling Digital Audio

Sampling audio on your PC or Mac is a relatively easy task, assuming you have a sound card that has an input jack and an appropriate software package. Most PCs and Macs have some type of system software that allows you to sample audio. However, the limits of what you can do are dependent on the utility. Regardless, you should be able to record and manipulate simple clips for use in Flash using what you have.

If you are looking for products to purchase for editing sound, programs such as Sound Forge for the PC or Bias Peak for the Macintosh are efficient for preparing audio for the Web. Although there are myriad packages available, these two products are likely to give you the most for your money. They are excellent for creating special effects.

If you want to create and composite multiple sounds to create mixed tracks, you may want to purchase Sonic Foundry's program Acid (*http://www.sonicfoundry.com*). This program is a tool that should be in every multimedia developer's arsenal.

The basic scenario for sampling audio is connecting an analog device such as a microphone or tape recorder to your computer. You will find that a microphone generally gives you the poorest results, particularly if it came with your machine. If you want to do serious microphone sound recordings, invest in a better microphone.

If you want to record audio using a tape recording or an audio CD-ROM, do not forget about copyright considerations. Although computers make it easy to use digitized elements, copyright issues are always a concern. Just because the musical score for a particular song may not have a copyright (or has a copyright that has expired) does not mean you can record it and use it for free. More than likely the group or individual performing the piece has certain rights. Often musical arrangements have multiple copyright considerations, both the musical score and the individual(s) performing it. Make sure you have the right to use any audio (or other media elements for that matter) you plan to employ.

1/4" Patch       1/8" Patch       RCA-Type

*Figure 7-4 Various types of audio connectors can be found on the back of the sound card Know which type yours has!*

To sample audio from a device such as a tape recorder or stereo, you need to interconnect the two devices so that the device is playing through the sound card of the computer. Find the output jack on the back of the sound card to see what type of jack it is. Most often, it is a patch-type connector. Figure 7-4 shows an example of the three main types of connectors: 1/4-inch patch, 1/8-inch patch, and RCA connector.

Next, examine the device from which you are recording. Look for a line-out connector. If none exists, you can use a headphone jack. Obtain a patch cable with the proper connectors for your card and device. These can usually be purchased for very little money at a local electronics store. After you have the cable and an established connection between your device and card, follow these suggestions for digitizing audio:

- Begin by checking the settings for the audio levels on the computer. Often, there are separate audio levels for the master volume, line in, CD-ROM, line out, and any other connections for the sound card. Set the volume of these on 50 percent if possible. Then, the volume can be controlled using the device's volume adjuster.

- Before playing any sound from the device, make sure the device volume level is on zero. Insert a tape or other media. Let it start playing. Then, increase the device volume to 1. This keeps you from overloading, blowing, or getting deafening feedback from the computer's speakers.

- Take a look within your recording software to see if adjustments can be made to the recording level. Both Sound Forge and Bias Peak provide a monitor level indicator, which is similar to a recording level indicator on a home stereo. If your software has monitor level indicators, as the audio plays through the card you will see the "LEDs" light up. You want the audio volume level to average at the lowest yellow. However, if the audio peaks in the red as it is playing, that is okay. You just do not want it to remain there for lengthy periods.

- When sampling audio, you are usually only able to record as much audio as you have disk space or memory. Some audio packages allow you to record only in RAM memory. Others write the audio directly to the hard disk during recording. Before purchasing any package, make sure it can record audio directly to the hard disk. If it cannot, you will be able to record only a couple of minutes of audio at a time. Both Sound Forge and Bias Peak allow you to record as much as you can store on your hard disk.

- Strive to sample your audio at the highest quality possible, such as 44 kHz, 16 bit, stereo. You can down-sample from this high-quality digital source before importing into Flash. If you have Sound Forge or Bias Peak, having a digital source file at the highest quality allows you to manipulate it by adjusting the lows or highs. You can also do a number of other things, such as add reverb, tremolo, or adjust EQ-type settings.

- Use the lowest quality sound needed in Flash. More than likely, the highest quality you should use is 22 kHz, 16-bit, mono-aural (single channel) sound clips. Lower-quality settings depend on the content of the clip itself. The only exception is if you plan to deliver your movie files via projector files on a CD-ROM. To reduce file sizes, try to deliver the lowest quality possible without degradation of the sound element.

Realize that you do not have to be an audio genius to create "hip" audio clips for your movies. Indeed, sampling clips is quite limited and often you have to be very cautious concerning copyright infringement. There are many programs that can make mixing and creating your own tracks quite effortless.

 **TIP:** *Programs such as Sonic Foundry's Acid are quite nice for those who know what sounds good, but are not musicians. If you need to generate music loops and effects, a program such as this is definitely worth the investment.*

# ···· Importing Sound into Flash

Importing and using sound in Flash is a two-step process. You begin by using File | Import to add the sound to the movie's library. You can then assign that sound clip to a frame in some timeline. Note that sounds are always added to frames, whether it is in the main timeline or in a symbol. Remember that graphic symbols will not play sounds that are assigned in them.

As noted earlier, Flash can import almost any sound quality. When importing sound, you can export an SWF movie for the Web with lower quality (down-sampled sounds). Thus, your native Flash files (FLA) can contain high-quality source sounds, whereas the exported movies (SWF) files can contain lower-quality sounds. If you are trying to create multiple movies appropriate for various connection speeds, the ability to store high and export low can be a useful facility.

In addition to various qualities, Flash 5 can now import a variety of file formats. Where Flash 4 was limited to Windows Waveform (WAV) and Audio Interchange File Format (AIFF), the new version can also import Sun audio (AU) and MP3 files. You should find that all of these formats are available on both the Macintosh and PC versions. On either platform you should also be able to use the QuickTime 4 import option. However, QuickTime 4 must be installed to be able to use these types of files. For practice in importing a sound, see the following CD-ROM exercise.

 **WARNING:** With all the hype concerning the MP3 audio format on the Web, including discussions of copyrights and the legalities associated with distributing them, always ensure you have the rights to use any sound files you decide to integrate into your movies. Although MP3 is the format causing the biggest stir, really with any sound you want to use you need to obtain permission. Even if the source you got it from says it is "royalty-free," do your homework. Avoid litigation by covering your bases!

### CD-ROM Exercise

To see how to import a sound for use in a file, open the file *ch7-01.fla* from the *F5gai/chapter7* folder, installed from the companion CD-ROM. To import a sound into file *ch7-01.fla*, perform the following steps.

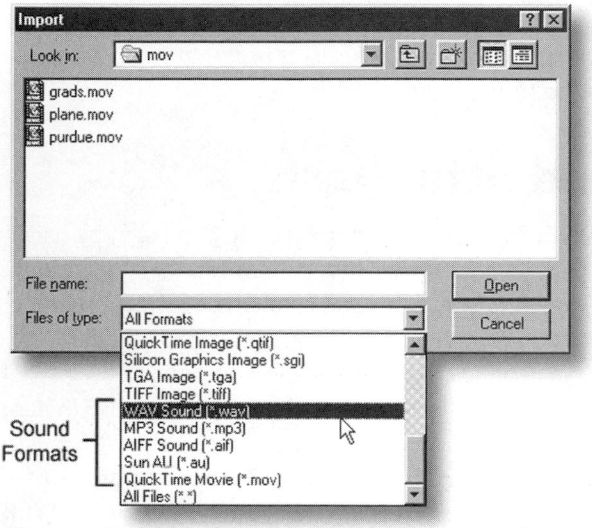

1. Select File | Import to reveal the Import dialog box, as shown in figure 7-5.

2. Notice the types of file you could import (WAV, AIF, AU, MP3 or MOV) from the Files of Type drop-down list, as shown in figure 7-5. You could also use the All Sound formats to see all valid sound formats that can be imported. Select WAV, AIF, or AU from the list.

3. Find the file called "beep" from the *F5gai/chapter7* directory. The file extension will depend on which format you have chosen to use.

*Figure 7-5 Select the audio file format in the Files of Type drop-down list.*

4. Double click on the file name in the window or click on the name and then on OK. Either technique adds the audio clip to the current movie's library.

5. Although you do not have to verify that it has been added to the library each time, go ahead and use Window | Library to open the library. Note that the file now exists in the library. However, it has not been assigned for use in the timeline yet.

6. Save your file.

   **NOTE:** *As with bitmap images, sounds you do not end up using in your movie should be removed from the current movie's library.*

One of the things you should note about the various sound formats is that there are many types of compression algorithms that can be used in them. Basic WAV and AIFF formats provide several, but the most common algorithm is PCM, which is the compression format Flash works with most easily. Therefore, if you try to import a WAV or AIFF file into Flash and it tells you it cannot read the file, convert the file to a PCM compressed WAV or AIFF file using a sound program such as Sound Forge or Bias Peak. You should then be able to import the file.

# Associating Sounds with Frames

Once a sound clip has been imported into a movie, assigning it to play in a particular frame (or frame in a symbol) is a relatively easy process. In either case, the sound is assigned using the Sound panel. The following CD-ROM exercise takes you through the process of assigning a sound to a frame.

 **TIP:** *To import a sound from another library, use either the Library menu or the File | Open option as a Library command to open a library. With the library open, select a sound symbol from the list and click-drag from the symbol preview to the stage. This adds the sound clip to the current movie's library.*

 ### CD-ROM Exercise

To see how to assign a sound to a frame in a file, open the file *ch7-02.fla* from the *F5gai/chapter7* folder, installed from the companion CD-ROM. If you did the prior exercise, you could continue using that file. In this exercise, you will assign the beep sound to a button press. You do this by attaching the sound to a frame in the button symbol. All sounds are assigned to frames. To assign the sound, perform the following steps.

1. Right-click on the button on the stage and select Edit in Place from the context menu.

2. Select the Down frame in the button layer.

   **NOTE:** *As Keep in mind that sounds are attached to frames, not to symbol instances.*

3. Right-click on the frame and select Panels | Sound from the context menu. You could also double click on the frame, which would open the Actions panel as well as the Sound panel.

4. In the Sound panel, change the Sound drop-down list to the beep sound.

5. Click on Scene 1 in the Edit Path to return to the main timeline.

6. Use Control | Enable Simple Buttons to enable the button.

7. Click on the button to verify that the sound does play.

Instead of Enable Simple Buttons, you could have used Test Movie. If you use Test Movie and the sounds are played back poorly, change the audio settings in the File | Publish Settings dialog box. Select the Flash tab and use the Audio Stream | Event Set buttons to set the properties. The Publish tab affects movies that are tested. Note that most of the sounds integrated into the sample FLA files on the companion CD-ROM are designed for 22 kHz mono.

When you assigned the sound in the exercise, you probably noticed the other options that were available in the Sound panel. The following sections describe the various options found there. Often the default values may work, particularly if you are using short event-based sounds. However, more complex creations will require adjustment of the optional settings in the Sound panel.

Yet, before looking at these options, you need to know about one other important thing. Synchronizing specific graphic components with lengthy sound components is a difficult task. For example, lengthy music clips to be synchronized with specific graphic events on the screen are very challenging, and often impossible to time exactly, given the wide performance differences that can exist on playback machines. As noted earlier in this book, the playback speed of Flash movies is highly dependent on the delivery computer.

Sound is a time-based medium, whereas the graphical components in Flash movies are frame based. This means that a sound must play consistently over time (time being a constant), regardless of machine performance. When you insert a sound in Flash, the sound will play consistently on every machine on which you play it. Unlike some digital video formats, AVI specifically, Flash does not drop portions of the sound if machine performance degrades. Thus, sound will always play back consistently.

However, the playback of graphical components is not based on a constant. The number of frames played back (per second) in a Flash movie varies depending on the performance of the playback machine. Thus, if sound and graphics are in a movie at the same time and the performance of the machine degrades, the sound will remain constant, whereas the graphic playback (output FPS) will vary. In this scenario, sound clips will be heard before their screen counterparts are visible. On machines that are faster than the development machine, graphics may occur on time or before they are needed. This is always the most troublesome aspect of creating synchronized graphics and audio in Flash.

However, all is not lost. Flash does offer some basic options for keeping synchronization somewhat consistent. It is not 100 percent exact, however. Consistency is a relative term and depends greatly on the performance difference between the development machine and the playback machine. The user's Internet connection type can also affect the perceived playback of a Flash movie. Nonetheless, the Sound panel provides several options, as discussed in the following section.

# ∎∎∎ The Sound Panel

Once you select a sound from the Sound drop-down, Flash displays the attributes of the sound clip below the Sound drop-down menu. Sampling rate (22 kHz), number of channels (Mono), bit depth (16 bit), length (0.3s), and

file size (15.2 kB) are all presented, as shown in figure 7-6. You also have several options within the Sound panel. The following sections discuss how each of these settings (Edit, Effect, Sync, and Loops) affects the playback of the sound.

## Sync: Event Versus Streaming Sounds

*Figure 7-6 The Sound panel offers several optional settings that affect the playback of the clip.*

The single most important setting in the Sound panel is the Sync drop-down. Within Flash, two types of sounds exist: *event* and *streaming*. The primary difference between these two types is that event sounds must be entirely downloaded before they can play, whereas streaming sounds can begin playing before they are entirely downloaded.

There is also a significant difference between these options concerning playback. Streaming sounds can be synchronized (at least as close as is possible in Flash) with the timeline. Event sounds, once started, play independently of the timeline. Let's examine these a little further.

An event sound plays when the keyframe to which it is attached is encountered. Once the keyframe is encountered, the sound plays in its entirety. If a loop value is entered in the Loop field (in the Sound panel), the looped sound continues to play even if the movie is stopped. Additionally, if the frame the event sound is attached to is encountered several times, multiple instances of the sound will play. The Start option in the Sync list is similar to the Event option except that only a single instance of the sound will play, even if the frame is encountered several times.

The Flash help file and the *Using Flash 5* book recites the exact opposite of the scenario just described. Testing (see the following CD-ROM note), shows that the Event Sync causes multiple instances to play, and that the Start Sync causes only one instance to play.

 **CD-ROM NOTE:** *To hear the difference between the Event and Start options, open and play the file* ch7-03.fla *located in the* F5gai/chapter7 *folder, installed from the companion CD-ROM. Use Test Movie to hear the difference.*

The Stop Sync option found in the Sync drop-down is really a misnomer and does not work as described by Macromedia. Instead, to stop a streaming sound, only extend the sound out in the timeline as far as you need it to play. When a streaming sound reaches the end of its sprite, it will stop. If you need to stop an event sound and there are no other sounds playing in the environment, use the Stop All Sounds action. If you need to stop an event sound and there are other sounds you want to continue playing, put the sound you want to stop in a movie clip. Then, when you want it to stop, use the Tell Target action to tell the sound movie clip to Stop All Sounds.

 **TIP:** *Most often, the Event and Start options are best for short sounds, such as a click for a button or other brief segments.*

Streaming sounds, as opposed to event sounds, do not have to be fully downloaded before they start playing. They begin playing almost immediately because the sound is divided into chunks that coincide with frames in the movie, called *interleaving*, much like digital video formats such as QuickTime (MOV) or Video for Windows (AVI).

Streaming clips allow you to begin playing a sound clip immediately, and provide the most accurate means of timing graphical components with aural ones in Flash. One negative aspect to streaming sounds is that if the machine performance degrades, the sound may stop playing until the next portion of aural data reaches the playback computer. For this reason, a preloader may be necessary.

 **CD-ROM NOTE:** *To see (and hear) an example created using the Stream option, open file ch7-04.fla located in the F5gai/chapter7 folder, installed from the companion CD-ROM. Understand that this file is rather large due to the music clip used within it. Thus, it would need quite a bit of optimizing before it would be ready for the Web.*

In general, it is best to use event sounds for short sounds, and streaming sounds for longer clips, such as background music. In either case, testing is a necessity due to the previously mentioned synchronization problems that can be encountered.

## Effect

The Sound panel includes several common special effects that may be quickly assigned to the sound clip. Earlier it was suggested that you import multichannel sounds because you can do this within Flash. This is what the Effect drop-down allows. Within Flash, you can quickly create fade-ins and fade-outs at the beginning and ending of your clips, as well as speaker panning. The effects in the drop-down include the following:

- *Left Channel:* Plays the entire sound in the left speaker channel.

- *Right Channel:* Plays the entire sound in the right speaker channel.
- *Fade Left to Right:* Makes the sound pan from the left speaker to the right speaker.
- *Fade Right to Left:* Makes the sound pan from the right speaker to the left speaker.
- *Fade In:* Sets up the beginning of the sound so that it fades in.
- *Fade Out:* Automatically fades out the end of the sound.
- *Custom:* Allows you to create your own custom effect by click-dragging the volume control using the Edit button.

When you select one of the effects from the Sound panel, the sound-editing controls of the clip are modified. The sound-editing controls are accessible via the Edit button, found in the Sound panel (see figure 7-6).

## Edit (Envelope)

If you apply an effect to a clip, or if you want to create your own custom effect, you click on the Edit button. When you click on the Edit button, you are presented with the Edit Envelope window, where you can use the sound-editing controls, as shown in figure 7-7. These controls allow you to define a volume, per left and right speakers, as well as control how much of the clip is played.

To adjust the volume of either speaker, click-drag the volume controls in the window, shown in figure 7-7. By adding multiple points within the preview window, fade-in and fade-out effects within the window are created, as shown in figure 7-8. If you were to select Fade In or Fade Out from the Effect drop-down, a similar set of points would be created for you automatically at the beginning or ending of a clip. Fade-ins and fade-outs on a single clip must be manually created.

To control clipping, in other words how long the clip plays, click-drag the In or Out points as needed. This allows you to play only a specified portion of a

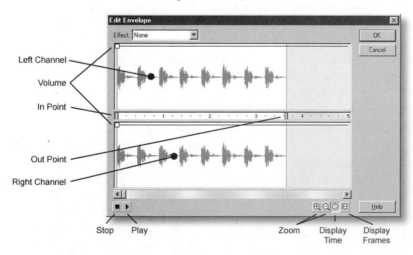

*Figure 7-7 The sound-editing controls are accessed via the Edit Envelope window.*

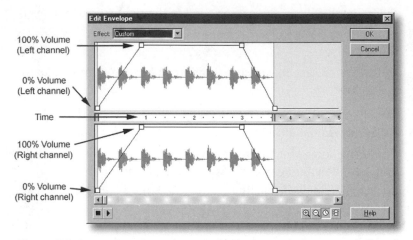

Figure 7-8  *By setting the volume in both channels from 0 to full and full to 0 creates a fade in and fade out.*

clip, even though the entire clip exists in memory. Note that even if you use clipping, the entire sound clip will be output in the resulting SWF. Thus, it would be more effective to edit the clip in a sound editor and import only the part you need.

Located below the preview window are controls for playing and stopping the sound, in addition to zoom controls and display options, as shown in figure 7-7. The Display Frames button is helpful when you are trying to synchronize a sound clip with specific graphical components in specific frames. Additionally, you normally use it with streaming sounds only, not event sounds, because only streaming sounds are "timed" or synchronized with the timeline. Event sounds play independently of the timeline. When you click on this button, the preview window shows the sound clip in relation to the current frames. The Display Time button, the default, shows the length of the sound clip in relation to time.

Keep in mind that audio and graphic synchronization may be dramatically impacted by the speed of the playback computer, as previously mentioned in this chapter. Thus, the terms timed and synchronized are here used loosely. You will find that Flash is not as accurate as Director in this regard.

When you select the Display Frames button, the playback speed is assumed to be the currently set frame rate (as defined in the Modify | Movie dialog box). Thus, the sound clip is displayed against the current frames, based on the movie frame rate. Yet, remember that sound is time based and will play consistently. The frame rate will vary, depending on the complexity of elements being displayed and the speed of the computer on which it is being played.

Although you can use the Display Frames button to help you synchronize audio and graphics, it is not 100 percent accurate. The best-case scenario when designing movies is to try to shoot for a target machine. Then, test, test, and test some more on both faster and slower machines. In reality, there is no way of creating an audio and graphics presentation for the Web using Flash that is 100 percent the same on every computer.

Machine performance, at least as far as video cards are concerned, varies too greatly. The only thing you can do is shoot for the middle 50 percent of the audience. They are more alike than they are different.

 **TIP:** *To remove a previously assigned sound from a frame, select the frame and use the Sound panel. Set the Sound drop-down list to None. If the sound is no longer being used, do not forget to delete it from the movie's library as well.*

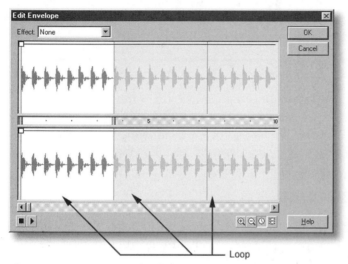

Loop

*Figure 7-9 Loops are displayed within the Edit Envelope window as grayed repetitions of the original.*

## Looping

The looping option within the Sound panel allows you to specify the number of loops you want the sound to play. The maximum number of loops is 999. Greater numbers entered in the loop field may cause unexpected results.

As you increase the number of loops, the Edit Envelope window shows the repetitions of the clip. If you switch the preview window to Display by Frames, you can see an approximation of how long the looping sound will play, as shown in figure 7-9.

# ▪▪▪ Flash Sound Settings

When you import a sound clip for placement into a movie, you can control the sound's default sampling rate and compression. Additionally, sound settings exist within the Publish Settings dialog box, where you can override the default settings that exist in the library.

Both of these options are helpful when creating multiple versions of files for delivery to various connection speeds. In addition, when trying to optimize file size, the ability to control sound quality is important. As it relates to file size, more than any other elements, bitmaps and sound drastically affect file size. Flash provides tremendous flexibility as you prepare movies for the Web or other means by allowing modification of the output quality of sound clips.

 **NOTE:** *To examine issues surrounding optimization as they relate to sounds, make sure you review Chapter 9.*

## Library Sound Properties

For each sound imported into your movie, default quality settings can be established, which are very similar to those identified for bitmaps in Chapter 3. As with bitmaps, sound clips are automatically added to the movie's library when you import them. The default quality settings take effect when the movie is exported. However, they can also be overridden when you export the SWF. For example, if you have a music clip that needs to have relatively high quality, combined with snippets and effects can be of lower quality, you can set these defaults in the current movie's library. The CD-ROM exercise that follows explores library properties further.

### CD-ROM Exercise

To learn about the library properties, open the file *ch7-05.fla* located in the *F5gai/chapter7* folder, installed from the companion CD-ROM. To set the default sampling rate and compression for a sound clip, perform the following steps.

1.   Use Window/Library to access the current movie's library.

2.   Find one of the sound clips in the symbol list and double click on its icon to open the Sound Properties dialog box.

3.   In the dialog box shown in figure 7-10, set the Compression option as desired. As different options are selected in the Compression drop-down, other related options will be shown. The settings established in the dialog box will be used as the default when the movie is exported (assuming you do not override them in the Publish Settings, Publish, or Export Movie operations).

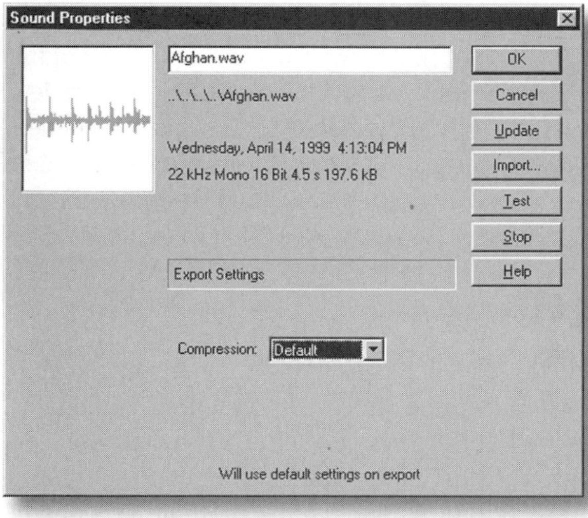

*Figure 7-10   The Sound Properties dialog box, accessed via the library, allows you to set the default compression settings for the sounds in your movie.*

In the dialog box shown in figure 7-10, aside from the OK, Cancel, and Help buttons, you see four buttons that can be very helpful when working in the library. The Test and Stop buttons allow you to test the sound clip while in the Sound Properties dialog box with the current settings. This is a nice method of hearing what the clip will sound like without having to jump out and use Test Movie or the other means of generating an SWF file.

The other two buttons are also helpful. The Import button allows you to replace the current sound with another sound, and the Update button allows you to automatically update the sound. The Update button is nice if you are working with a group of developers. Assuming the sound file resides in a shared area and was imported from that storage location, you can make changes to the external sound file and then click on the Update button to update the version in the Flash file. This allows you to work with "in-progress" sound clips.

## Compression Options

Flash offers three types of sound compression: linear (RAW), ADPCM, and MP3. The Default option is equivalent to no compression. If you plan to determine sound output settings when you generate your SWF files, you can leave the Sound Properties in the library set to Default and then set the properties when you output your SWF files.

The Raw option provides no real compression for your sound clips and is the default. When you select Raw from the Compression drop-down, you have control over the sampling rate and the number of channels in the sound. The Raw option simply inserts the sound into Flash files as raw clips defined in AIFF format.

One of the things you should notice as you are selecting different compression types is that the Sound Properties dialog box indicates the properties of the clip at the bottom of the dialog box. When selecting compressors, of particular interest is the percentage shown at the end. This shows how much you are reducing the clip by the options you are selecting.

When the ADPCM compressor is selected, you can set the sample rate and the bit rate of the clip (see figure 7-11). You have already seen (and heard) how sampling rate affects an audio clip through prior examples. The bit rate option controls the amount of compression applied to the clip. The lowest compression setting is 2 bit, and the highest is 5 bit. The results of the compression applied during export will depend on the similarity of amplitudes within the sound clip, much like the fact that the compression of a bitmap is based on the similarity of pixels in the image. More than likely, testing will be necessary to determine the best bit rate (compression) using ADPCM.

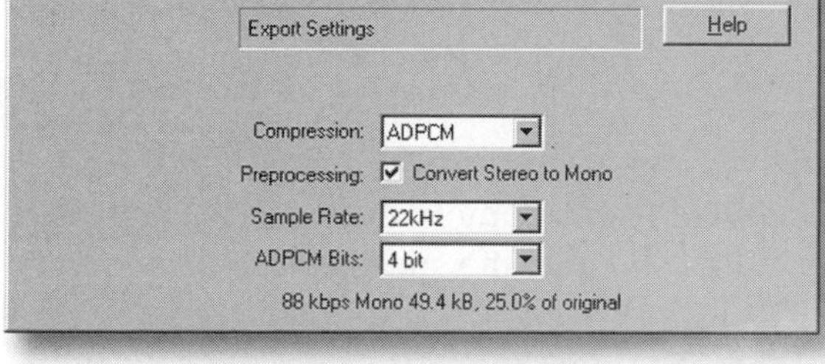

*Figure 7-11 The options provided when ADPCM is selected from the compression drop-down list.*

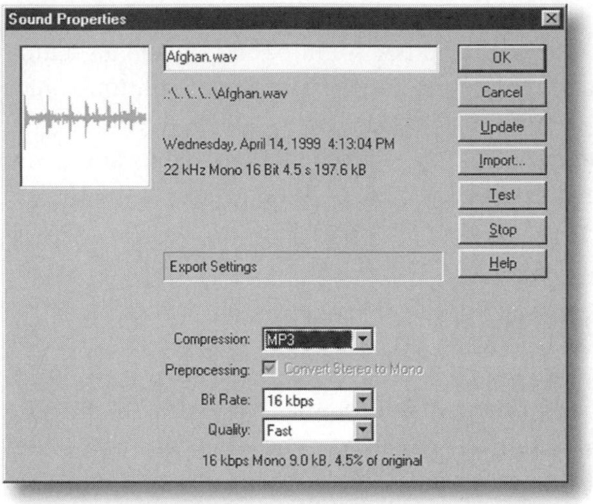

*Figure 7-12 Selecting MP3 compression provides control over preprocessing, bit rate, and quality.*

The last compression option, MP3, was introduced in Flash 4 and has taken the Web by storm. No doubt you have heard of the many copyright concerns regarding the MP3 format expressed by the recording industry, as well as its capabilities for compressing audio for end users. When you select the MP3 option, you can control preprocessing (channel control), bit rate, and quality, as shown in figure 7-12.

As with ADPCM compression, when you select the Convert Stereo to Mono checkbox, the sound clip is converted to a mono-aural clip. One thing you should note is that if the bit rate is set too low in an MP3, stereo sound is not possible. Thus, if you select a bit rate of 16 or 8, the Convert Stereo to Mono option is automatically selected.

The Bit Rate option allows you to determine the size of the chunks of data that are compressed. Much like JPEG compression in bitmap images, ADPCM and MP3 are both lossy compression schemes. This means that they sacrifice a certain amount of data to attain higher compressibility. The amount of data loss depends on the size of the chunks of data averaged (called subsampling) and the amount of averaging that occurs (called quantization).

The bit rate option controls the subsampling, and the quality option controls the quantization. It really does not matter whether you are discussing image compression and pixels or sound compression and amplitudes. The compression schemes in both select a block of information and then average the information.

In sound clips, the size of the block selected is chosen by the bit rate option. If you choose a smaller bit rate, the block of data is smaller and the compression will be less effective. If you choose a large bit rate, the data selection is larger and the compression will be more effective, at least from a file size standpoint.

As for the Quality setting, this option controls the amount of averaging that occurs within each selected block of information. The Quality settings range from Fast to Best and also affect the speed of playback on the delivery computer.

All of this regarding subsampling and quantization really says nothing of the aural quality of the clip. Regardless of the compression and options you choose, you will inevitably have to use trial and error to determine the best compressor for the job. The reason is that the compressibility of any digital file depends on the amount of redundant data in the file. Unless you are really into the basics of repetitive amplitudes of a file and have software to do that type of analysis, your best bet is to try the various compression options to get the optimum quality-to-file-size ratio.

## Export Movie Options

When exporting a movie to prepare it for distribution on the Web, you can assign sound compression options in File | Export Movie, as shown in figure 7-13. By default, the settings applied in this dialog box will only affect sounds that do not have properties assigned to them in the library. Sounds that already have defaults assigned to them in the library will use those settings. You can override the settings applied in the library by clicking on the Override Sound Settings checkbox. If this checkbox is selected, the settings assigned in the library will be ignored.

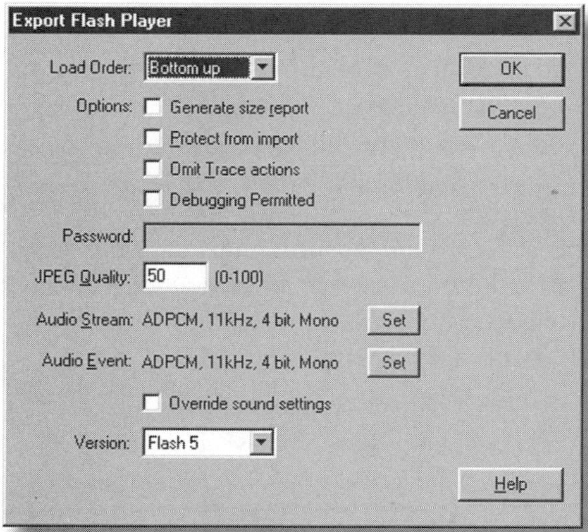

Flash now has two means of creating movies: File | Export Movie and File | Publish. The Publish feature allows you to output the standard SWF files, as well as HTML, GIF, Projector, and QuickTime movie files.

Both the Export Movie and Publish menu options derive their default settings from those established within the Publish Settings dialog box. The Publish Settings dialog box also affects movies that are executed through the Control | Test Movie option.

*Figure 7-13 The Export Movie dialog box provides the ability to override the default settings established in the library.*

 **NOTE:** *For more information concerning Export Movie options, see Chapter 9.*

# ▪▪▪ Using Stop All Sounds

As mentioned in Chapter 6, when using the Stop All Sounds action, all currently playing sounds are stopped. Yet, any sounds encountered after a Stop All Sounds action play normally. Use the Stop All Sounds action to stop a music loop before entering a new section or scene of your movie. This allows you to assign certain music loops to specific sections or scenes of your movie.

**CD-ROM NOTE:** *To see how the Stop All Sounds action works, open the file* ch7-06.fla *located in the* F5gai/chapter7 *folder, installed from the companion CD-ROM.*

You can also target movie clips that have music clips within them, telling them to Stop All Sounds. This is particularly useful when the Load Movie action is used.

 **CD-ROM NOTE:** *To see how the Stop All Sounds action works with Tell Targets, open the file* ch7-07.fla *located in the* F5gai/chapter7 *folder, installed from the companion CD-ROM.*

## ▪ ▪ ▪ Summary

This chapter examined the major concerns of using audio within your Flash movies. Obviously, sound is not something to ignore. In many cases, it is audio and small sound bites that complete and add interest to a site. Judiciously decide where, when, and how much sound to include. Too much sound use may make your site a bandwidth hog, whereas too little usage of sound does not satisfy the aural senses and makes the presentation boring. Synchronization is the trickiest part of sound in Flash. Allow enough time for testing when a significant amount of audio is incorporated within a movie, particularly streaming sound.

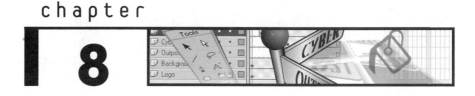

# Exploring Scenes and Multilevel Movies

## ▪ ▪ ▪ Introduction

Creating the internal structure for the various content pieces that constitute your web site can be one of the most difficult parts of designing an effective movie. Aside from managing all of the movie's pieces, how the content is divided should also be a main consideration. Will a single timeline work, or do you need multiple scenes? Additionally, would it be more effective to load movies into one another?

This chapter examines these issues, focusing predominantly on the Load and Unload movie structure. This chapter also reviews navigation issues concerning scenes, as well as the new Movie Explorer. Generally, scenes provide an effective means of structuring a movie that is self-contained, whereas multilevel movies (which use the Load Movie action) are practical for larger sites that require more files. The use of multiple movies also allows more individuals to work at the same time on a site, while also providing a means of concurrently updating the content.

## ▪ ▪ ▪ Objectives

In this chapter, you will:

- Discover how scenes can be used within a movie to structure your content based on the existing content

- Learn about the new Movie Explorer and how it can be used to examine movie components
- Create multilevel movies using the Load Movie and Unload Movie actions
- Learn to use the Tell Target action to communicate within multi-level movies

# Structuring Content for Flash

Designing Flash movies is much more than just sitting down behind the computer and "playing with the tool." Planning is an integral part of effectively using any tool. Much like an architect, half the battle for any designer is developing a plan. It is guaranteed that the individual digging the footer, pouring the concrete, or laying the blocks is thankful that the architect laid out a plan. Without a plan, each of these processes, as well as those that follow, would be less efficient, even impossible.

Flash provides the capability to organize your files. This book has already covered how symbols, layers, and groups work. These are primary methods of organizing Flash movies. Many of the decisions about what should be in a symbol, on a layer, or in a group require knowing where you are going with the design.

To use scenes and multiple movies, you need a plan to determine what is necessary. Do you need multiple scenes? Multiple movies? Or is a single timeline best? Generally, the content dictates which process is most appropriate.

As suggested elsewhere in this book, storyboards are important for you to know where you are going, even more so when using scenes and multiple movies. In the "real world," storyboards are a necessity for communication to the client and planning for the individual. Often, when schooling is involved, storyboards are deemed less important. Focus is often directed toward the end product rather than the process.

As you begin to use multiple scenes and movies to create sites that are more complex, it will become increasingly important that you have a plan to help you as you design. Storyboards, flowcharts, and even simple structural sketches will be vital. It is very easy to become confused when many symbols, scenes, or movies are part of your project. The use of scenes, multilevel movies, and even features such as the folder capability within the library, are an outgrowth of planning documents and sketches.

# Creating Multiscene Movies

Scenes are one tool for dividing your movie into logical chunks of content and segments. Although some may prefer to use symbols as the main scheme for chunking, scenes are worthy of mention. Scenes aid in the organizational process by helping you reduce the length of main movie timelines.

Just as you access your symbols using the Symbol List button, the Scene List button, shown in figure 8-1, can be used to access your scenes. Just as with symbols, clicking on each scene allows you to edit each one. The current scene is shown in the Edit Path. Keep in mind that every scene contains a timeline. Navigation can be established between timelines using the Go To action.

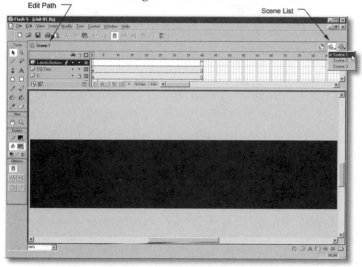

If you have a movie with many scenes and many symbols, be conscious of what you are working on. It is very easy to begin production and find you are working in the wrong place. Make sure you are observant of the Edit Path (see figure 8-1). Adopt a naming scheme to help reduce these types of errors. For example, all scene names could begin with an identifier, such as an asterisk or other symbol. Because both symbols and scenes start with the same letter, the use of S as an identifier is not recommended.

*Figure 8-1 Similar to accessing symbols, the Scene List provides access to the scenes in your movie.*

# Navigation Between Scenes

Chapter 6 examined the Go To action for developing navigation between sets of frames and creating looping segments. As you will recall, when the Go To action is selected, a frame or a label can be chosen as the jump-to point. When there are multiple scenes available, you can also jump to the scene, as well as a specific frame or label in the scene, as shown in figure 8-2.

 **TIP:** *If you want scenes to play one after another, insert an action in the last frame of one scene to jump to the first frame of another scene.*

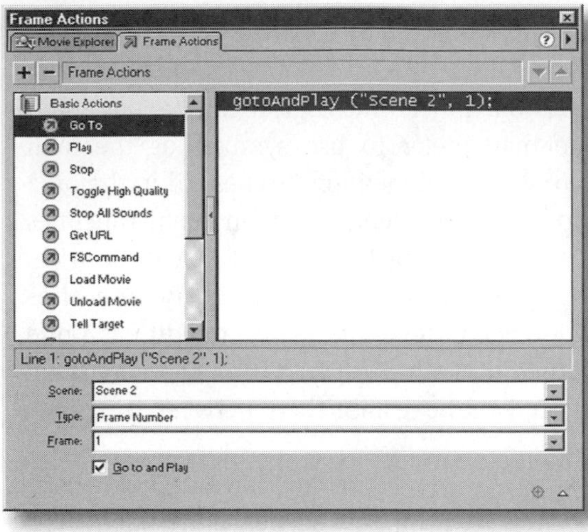

*Figure 8-2  When multiple scenes exist, you can jump to a frame or label in another scene.*

When using scenes to help organize movies and reduce the length of timelines, keep the following points in mind:

- To add scenes to your movie, use the Insert | Scene menu option. Generally, you will add scenes as needed. But again, to decide where scenes are appropriate depends on knowing what you are trying to create from the very start.

- When inserting a new scene, the scene is numerically labeled by default (that is, Scene 1, Scene 2, and so on). You can rename a scene using the Modify | Scene menu option, which brings up the Scene panel. Double clicking on a scene name allows you to change it.

- To delete a scene, use Insert | Remove Scene or use the Scene panel.
- Use the Scene List button to access various scenes, but be aware of which scene is currently being accessed. The Edit Path displays the current scene or symbol being edited.

Realize that the arrangement of the scenes (the order in which they are listed or the order in which they were created) does not affect what can be done with navigation between scenes. Regardless of their listed order, you can nonlinearly jump back and forth, navigating from one scene to any other that has been created.

 **CD-ROM NOTE:** *To examine how scenes can be used to divide a movie's content, open the file ch8-01.fla located in the F5gai/chapter8 folder, installed from the companion CD-ROM. This example is a brief banner advertisement consisting of three scenes. At the end of each scene, the Go To action is used to send the playhead to the next scene. In this way, the movie creates a circular loop. Many banner advertisements can be created using scenes in this manner. Use the Control | Test Movie option to view the entire animation, or use the Control | Test Scene option to test the current scene.*

# ▪▪▪ Movie Explorer

One of the new items in Flash 5 that will become more important as you start dealing with more complex movies is the Movie Explorer. One of the problems that has existed in prior versions of Flash is that there was no way to get an overall snapshot of the elements in a movie. Sure, the library provides a limited amount of information, such as the symbols that exist in the movie and the frequency of use (usage count), but it does not reveal information relative to the timeline.

For example, if you wanted to quickly find out what was in frame X, you had to move the playhead to frame X to find out what was there. Similarly, you could not search for a particular item, such as a movie clip called "cat." Instead, you would have to rely on memory to find the frame in which the item occurred.

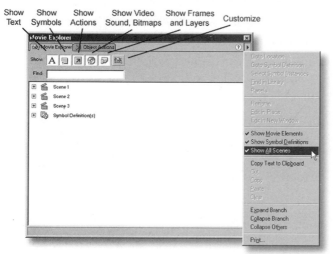

Show Text | Show Symbols | Show Actions | Show Video Sound, Bitmaps | Show Frames and Layers | Customize

As shown in figure 8-3, the Movie Explorer shows two major things about the movie. First, it shows all of the scenes currently in the movie, and second, it shows all the symbols that exist in the movie. Thus, it provides a quick way of examining all elements in a movie and how they are arranged in the movie. You can customize which elements are shown in the panel by using the menu or the buttons displayed across the top part of the panel.

*Figure 8-3   The Movie Explorer shows the scenes and symbol definitions in the current movie.*

In addition to providing an overview, the Movie Explorer allows you to quickly perform two very important things. First, you can use the Movie Explorer to find, select, and modify almost every aspect of a text element or action. For example, imagine you played back your movie, only to find a typographic error. In the past, you would have had to figure out which frame or symbol the mistake was in, move the playhead to the frame or access the symbol, and then edit the text. With the Movie Explorer it is much quicker. Let's do a quick exercise to see how you can quickly change text in a movie.

## CD-ROM Exercise

To examine how the Movie Explorer works, open the file *ch8-02.fla* located in the *F5gai/chapter8* folder, installed from the companion CD-ROM.

1.  As many of the items are in Flash 5, the Movie Explorer is yet another panel. Open the Movie Explorer using Window | Movie Explorer. You will find that it is opened in the same window as the Actions panel.

Once the Movie Explorer is open, use the menu (see figure 8-3) to make sure the Show all Scenes option is selected. Also ensure that all of the optional buttons on the upper part of the panel (Show Text, Show Symbols, and so on) are selected. The Customize button should be the only one that is not pressed in.

2. With the Explorer open, double click on the Symbol Definition icon to expand it, or single click on the small plus sign to the left of it to expand it.

3. Expand the CG Text Flyin graphic symbol.

4. Expand the Layer 1 item and then the Frame 1 item.

5. Click on the Computer Graphics text item. Use the Text menu to change the font to some other font you have on your machine.

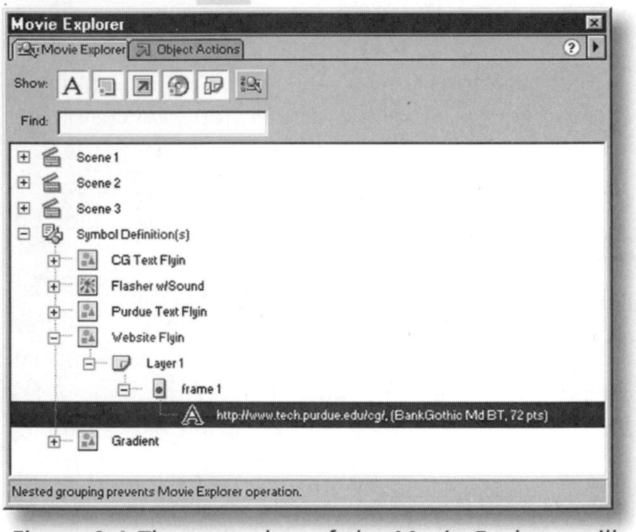

Note that if you double click on the text in the last step you could also edit the actual text. However, due to the way this movie is set up (small flashes of gold are aligned to each letter in the text), changing the text would require realigning the flasher elements.

Make sure you pay attention to the status bar of the Movie Explorer, as it will provide important information to you, as shown in figure 8-4. For example, when a text element is grouped, you cannot use the Movie Explorer to edit it.

*Figure 8-4 The status bar of the Movie Explorer will reveal to you important information.*

6. As an example, try it by accessing the "Purdue Text Flyin" symbol or the "Website Flyin" symbol. Note that neither of these can be edited because they are in a nested group.

Earlier in the book you read that when actions are attached to buttons, no visual identifier is shown in the timeline or stage. When actions are attached to frames, an *a* is shown in the frame. You can access text items with the Movie Explorer, and you can quickly view and access their actions, finding both their location in the movie structure and the ActionScript associated with them.

7. Click on the Scene 1 item shown at the top of the Movie Explorer item list.

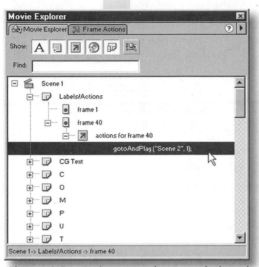

*Figure 8-5 Actions can be revealed and immediately opened into the Actions panel using the Movie Explorer.*

8. Expand the Labels | Actions item, frame 40 item, and actions for frame 40 items, as shown in figure 8-5. If you double click on an action in the Movie Explorer, the Actions tab will reveal the action so that you can edit it.

The last thing to be done is to use the Movie Explorer to find various items. Proceed with the following steps.

9. Collapse all expanded items so that all you see are the three scenes and the symbol definitions item.

10. Enter *Purdue University* in the Find field. Notice that the Movie Explorer automatically reveals the element to you. Thus, you can use the Find field to find almost any item in the movie structure.

In general, there are many things you can do with the Movie Explorer. However, most of these things are better understood in the context of particular operations. Therefore, you will explore the Movie Explorer further as you move through the applied examples in the later half of this book.

## ▪ ▪ ▪ Multilevel Movies

Multilevel movies give you the ability to load one movie into another movie. You do this by using the Load Movie and Unload Movie actions from a given frame. Because any action can be called from any frame, the Load Movie or Unload Movie action can be used in the main timeline or within a symbol.

 **NOTE:** *The Load Movie and Unload Movie actions work in movies embedded within web sites, as well as within SWF files that are played back inside the Flash Player.*

The Load Movie action is used to display several movies at the same time. It can also allow the user to switch between two movies without loading a new HTML document into the browser. When you load a movie, the stages of the two movies are overlaid on top of one another in layers similar to Dynamic HTML (DHTML) or Cascading Style Sheets (CSS).

As you learned in Chapter 6, *_level0* is associated with the main movie timeline, as is *_root*. It is the bottom layer, or the layer that is behind all others. Subsequent movies are layered in front of level 0 and can be assigned to any layer. For example, you could load a movie into level 2 (_level2_) and then another to level 1 (_level1_), or vice versa. However, level 0 (the main movie timeline) cannot be reassigned to a new level.

As logic dictates, because layers are defined as _level0_, _level1_, _level2_, and so on, you can easily use Tell Target to send commands or information from one movie to another. Loaded movies can control the main timeline. Similarly, the main timeline can control the loaded movies. Tell Target commands with the appropriate Tell Target path specified can also be used to control movie clips embedded within any movie.

 **NOTE:** *All targets used with multilevel movies are absolute. You cannot use relative references with loaded movies.*

The following section examines how to set up movies to use the Load and Unload Movie actions. It can be tricky, particularly when using Tell Target actions to load several movies or control various movies and the main timeline. The next section looks at a basic example, one that simply loads and unloads two other accompanying movies. This is followed by a more complex example that shows how to control a movie and its movie clips from the main timeline. The complex example also demonstrates how the loaded movie can control the main timeline and its movie clip.

# ▪ ▪ ▪ **Loading and Unloading Movies**

Setting up a basic load and unload scenario in Flash is relatively easy, as long as you know the rules. Two of the first questions that should come to mind are "How are the stages of the two movies aligned?" and "What is, and where is, the registration point?"

 **NOTE:** *The Load Movie and Unload Movie actions are located in the Action list (as opposed to the Basic Actions list) in the Actions panel's Toolbox list.*

## **Stage Attributes and Frame Rate**

In general, the main movie, which loads the other movies, is paramount when it comes to several of the settings at playback. The main movie defines the stage size, background color, and frame rate that will be used for all movies. Therefore, when the movies you load have different stage sizes, background colors, or frame rates, the main movie will override these settings.

Concerning registration, the upper left corner becomes the registration point of all the movies, even if they are not all the same size. If a movie with a smaller stage size is loaded into a movie with a larger stage size, the upper left corner point in both movies serves as the registration point, and the smaller movie will fit within the larger. If the reverse is true (that is, a larger movie loaded into a smaller movie), the loaded movie will be cropped to the size of the smaller. Thus, it is easiest to design all movies with the same stage size to avoid registration problems. To further examine how multilevel movies work, see the following CD-ROM exercise.

 ## CD-ROM Exercise

To examine how multilevel movies work, open the file *ch8-03.fla* located in the *F5gai/chapter8* folder, installed from the companion CD-ROM. The companion files that will be loaded into *ch8-03.fla* are named *ch8-03-1.fla* and *ch8-03-2.fla*. It is the SWF versions of these files that are loaded. Examine the process of loading and unloading movies a little closer by performing the following steps.

1. Begin by testing the movie to see how it works. Use the Control | Test Movie menu option.

As with testing movie clips, the Load Movie and Unload Movie actions can only be tested using Control | Test Movie. Additionally, the movies to be loaded must be SWF files created using the Export Movie or Publish menu options. You cannot load an FLA file.

2. Use the Load Movie 1 and Load Movie 2 buttons to load the "child" movies into the current movie.

3. Use the Unload Movie 1 and Unload Movie 2 buttons to unload the movies.

4. Close the Flash Player window to examine other important things you can do with loaded movies.

5. Use Modify | Movie to view the main movie's properties. Realize that the main movie's frame rate, stage size, and stage background color define the settings that will be used throughout the Load and Unload Movie process. Mentally note these settings or write them down. Then, close the Movie Properties dialog box.

6. Use File | Open to open the file *ch8-03-1.fla*.

7. Once this file is open, notice that the background is black, even though when it was loaded you saw an animation in the main movie. As you read earlier, the background color established in the "child" movie does not apply when the child movie is loaded using the Load Movie action. The main movie's settings override the child movie's setting.

8. Close *ch8-03-1.fla* so that you can examine the Load Movie actions in the main movie.

9. In the file *ch8-03.fla*, right-click on the button next to the "Load Movie 1" text in the upper part of the small controller and select Actions from the context menu.

10. In the Actions panel, note how the movie is referenced, as shown in figure 8-6. Realize that the Load Movie action works only on SWF files. Thus, when trying to test and "connect" the movies, you must generate SWF files of the movies you want to load. The Load Movie action will have no effect on an FLA (native) Flash file.

When developing and testing a set of movies using the Load and Unload Movie actions, it is best to store all files in a single directory. As long as the parent and child movies reside in the same directory on the web server, you do not have to worry about changing the URL setting to a lengthy absolute HTTP address (such as *http://www.tech.purdue.edu/cg/facstaff/jlmohler/ch8-03-1.swf*). You can simply leave it as a relative directory.

If the movies will reside in different directories and you want to specify relative directories rather than repetitive HTTP addresses, use *../* to step back a directory and */foldername* to specify a folder deeper in the structure, similar to the techniques used in a DOS or UNIX command line interface.

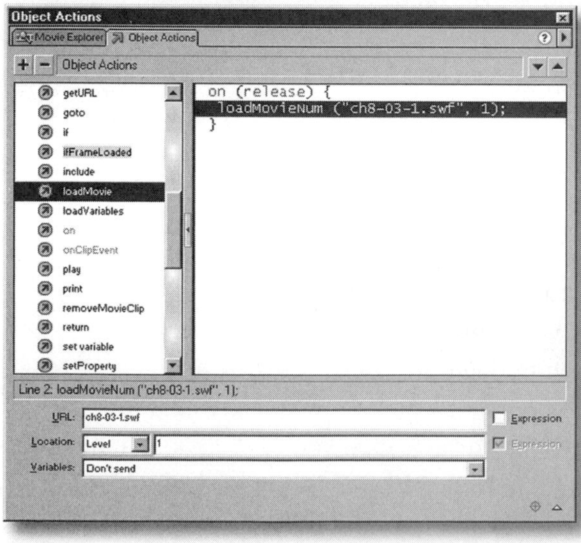

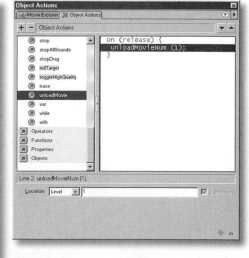

*Figure 8-6  SWF versions of movies are referenced in the Load Movie action.*

*Figure 8-7 You unload movies based on their level, not on the movie file name.*

**NOTE:** *Web-ready Flash (SWF) files can be generated using the File | Export Movie, File | Publish, or the Control | Test Movie menu options. See Chapter 9 for more details.*

11. Before leaving the Load Movie action, notice the Level field. You can load a movie into any level and you can unload any level (including *_level0*). Therefore, movies can be nonlinearly loaded; that is, loaded in any order, using the Load Movie action.

12. Before leaving this example, take a look at the Unload Movie action. With the Actions panel open, click on the button next to the "Unload Movie 1" text.

13. As shown in figure 8-7, note that you can only unload movies based on their level number, because in Flash only one movie can be loaded per level.

**NOTE:** *If you load a movie to a layer that already has a movie on it, the newly loaded movie will replace the previous movie on that layer.*

In both the Load and Unload Movie actions you will notice that you can pass variable values from one movie to another. As discussed in Chapter 6, with the Get URL action, variables and their data can be sent using either POST or GET methods, with POST being the preferred method. You will return to this issue in Chapter 13, where you will examine the use of variables in more detail.

## Levels Revisited

As you read in Chapter 6, keeping track of the hierarchy of objects in your movies is important. Because you cannot load multiple movies on a single layer, you must keep track of which movie is where. Assigning a new movie to a layer that already has something on it may cause you problems (that is, the loaded movie will replace the existing one), particularly where complex structures are concerned. If you are going to use loaded movies in your site, you may want to jot down the hierarchical structure and the layer numbers of the movies to help you with designing and testing.

## Designing Movies

Due to the dependency of loaded movies on the parent or main movie, designing loaded movie structures will be easier if you begin by designing the main movie. Once the main movie is created, use it as a template for all other movies to be loaded. This will keep you from designing child movies with erroneous stage sizes. It will also enable you to put together the child movies with some knowledge of where the objects in the main movie are located. Use the following suggestions as a guide for creating the parent and child movies:

- Lay out and design the elements that will appear in the main movie.
- Make a copy of the main movie to use as a template for all other movies.
- If you have a complex layout, it may be useful to convert the main movie, in its entirety (as well as subsequent child movies) to a movie clip symbol for insertion as you are working on the design.

If you have a timeline that has many layers and many frames you want to make into a symbol, you cannot simply select everything on the stage and press the F8 function key to convert it to a symbol. Rather, select all frames (in all layers) in the main movie timeline by turning on Edit Multiple Frames. Then, right-click in the frames in the timeline and use Copy Frames from the context menu. Use Insert | New Symbol to create the symbol, and select Movie Clip as the behavior. Right-click in the first keyframe in the newly created symbol and select Paste Frames. All layers and frames will be pasted into the new symbol.

# ▪ ▪ ▪ Controlling Loaded Movies

The ability to load and unload child movies into a parent movie is a very useful feature. However, if you use the Tell Target command, there is more you can do. For instance, you can control either the main movie timeline or the child movie timeline. This section examines how to use Tell Target in several ways. Understanding the hierarchy of elements is paramount to getting Tell Target to work.

## Hierarchy Revisited

The example in the following CD-ROM exercise takes a look at a main movie that loads a child movie. Both the main movie and the child movie have three sets of looping frame segments. Each also has buttons (to control the other), as well as a basic movie clip symbol. The hierarchical structure for the movie scenario is shown in figure 8-8. The visual representation is shown in figure 8-9.

## Setting Up Tell Targets

In the following CD-ROM exercise, the buttons within the main movie timeline control the child movie, as well as its nested movie clip. The buttons within the child movie will, conversely, control the main movie timeline and its nested movie clip.

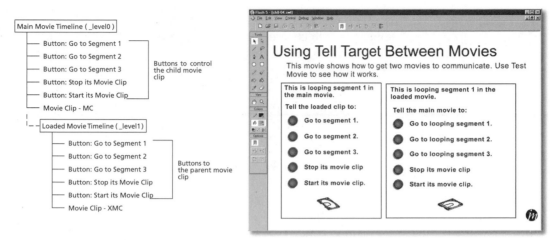

*Figure 8-8  The hierarchical structure for the sample movie.*

*Figure 8-9  The visual representation for the sample movie.*

### CD-ROM Exercise

To examine how multilevel movies work, open the file *ch8-04.fla* located in the *F5gai/chapter8* folder, installed from the companion CD-ROM. The file loaded into it is named *ch8-04-1.fla*. Begin examining this example by performing the following steps.

1.   Use Test Movie to see how the movies work. Close the Flash Player to return to the Flash application when you are done.

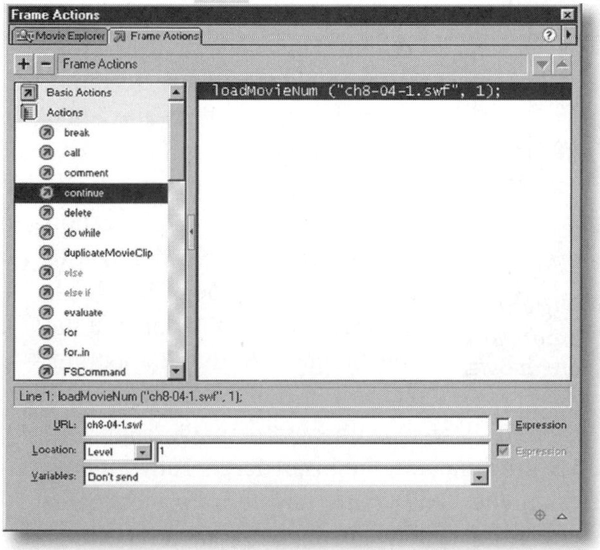

2.   One of the first things you should have noticed in the main movie timeline is the action assigned to frame 1. This action loads the child movie into the main movie. If you right-click on that frame and select Actions from the context menu, you can examine the action, as shown in figure 8-10. The child movie is loaded into level 1.

Notice in figure 8-10 that the URL in the Load Movie action is assigned to an SWF file. The most frequent error when learning to use the Load Movie action is in trying to load an FLA file. Loaded files must be web-ready SWF files.

*Figure 8-10 The frame action assigned to frame 1 immediately loads the child movie into level 1.*

3. The main movie timeline is divided into three looping segments, which are set up using labels and Go To frame actions. In this example, the child movie (*ch8-04-1.fla*) is set up in a similar way. The first three buttons in the main movie and in the child movie control which set of frames is playing in the other movie. Examine the Tell Target associated with the "Go to Segment 1" button. Right-click on the button and select Actions to do so.

4. When you click on Begin Tell Target in the Actions panel, try using the Insert Target Path window to view the available objects you can target. Click in the Target field and then click on the Insert Target Path button at the bottom of the Actions panel. Notice that the Insert Target Path window reveals "an object," as shown in figure 8-11. However, this is not the object you want to talk to. Keep in mind that the Insert Target Path window shows targets in the current movie, not the loaded movie you actually want to target. To "speak" to the movie timeline that will be loaded at runtime (i.e., the child movie), you need to manually enter the level number in the Target field in the Tell Target action. The target you want will not appear in the target preview window because it is not currently available in the environment. Consequently, to target the movie timeline in the child movie, target *_level1* because level 1 is the level on which the child is loaded. The Go To action assigned within the Tell Target in the example goes to label XLoop1, which is the name of the label assigned to the first looping segment in the child movie.

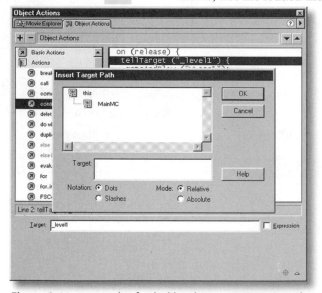

*Figure 8-11 Do not be fooled by the Insert Target Path window; it only shows targets in the current movie and at the current level.*

When you are using Tell Target with nested movie clips (see Chapter 6) or with loaded movies, the Insert Target Path window is relatively useless if the items being targeted are in another movie, or if the items being targeted are higher in the movie hierarchy. The window only shows movie clips in the current movie and at the current "level" (or below) in the main timeline.

**NOTE:** *Be mindful that the preview window does not trick you.*

Before you look at the last two buttons that control the movie clip in the child movie, open the child and see how you can target the main movie's timeline from the child.

5.  Open the file *ch8-04-1.fla*. In it, access the actions attached to the button next to the "Go to looping segment 1" text.

6.  If you access the Insert Target Path window in the Actions panel (figure 8-12) you will see that, similar to the Target in the main movie, the target window does not show the main movie target. To "speak" to the main movie from the child, manually enter *_level0* in the Target field. The Go To action goes to label Loop1, which is the label assigned to the first set of looping frames in the main movie.

7.  The Start and Stop movie clip buttons control the movie clip in either of the two movies. The child's buttons control the main movie's movie clip. The main movie's buttons control the child's movie clip. As you learned in Chapter 6, this process requires that you name the instance of the movie clip. Look at the instance name of the child's movie clip. Minimize the Actions panel if it is open. Right-click on the movie clip at the bottom (the CD-ROM casing) and select Panels | Instance.

8.  In the Instance panel, notice that the Name field is set to LoadedMC. Minimize the Instance panel and use Window | *ch8-04.fla* to switch back to the main movie (assuming both files are open).

9.  In the main movie, right-click on the button next to the "Stop its movie clip" text and select Actions from the context menu. Examine the Target associated with the *tellTarget* statement, as shown in figure 8-13. To control the movie clip in the child (from

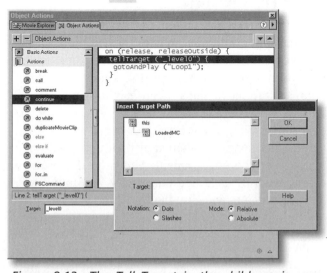

*Figure 8-12   The Tell Target in the child movie uses _level0 as the target to be able to control the main movie timeline.*

the parent), you add the name of the instance to the end of _level1, separated by a period for dot syntax or by a slash (/) for slash syntax. This allows you to send commands from the parent to the child. It also allows you to send commands from the child to the parent.

10. To finish reviewing these movies, examine the instance name of the main movie's clip and compare it to the target used in the child movie.

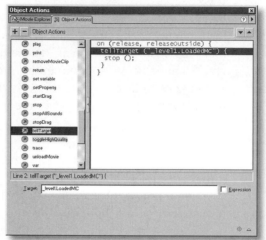

*Figure 8-13 To target the child's movie clip, you add the instance name at the end of the level information.*

## Loading Movies into Movie Clips

As you have been working with Tell targets in this chapter, most of your time has been spent on examining movies loaded into levels. However, within Flash you can also load movies into movie clips, which is particularly useful for printing movies. You need to know a couple of things about loading movies into movie clips before moving on.

The biggest difference between loading a movie into a level, as opposed to a movie clip, concerns registration. As previously stated, when you load movies into levels, all movies are aligned by their upper left-hand corner, which is the origin for the environment. Similarly, the primary movie (_level0) is the determiner of stage size, stage color, and frame rate.

When you load a movie into a movie clip, the first thing you will note is that the loaded movie will be imported at the size, location, and orientation of the originating movie clip. Thus, if a movie clip is small, the loaded movie's stage will be fitted to the area already being used for the movie clip and will therefore also be small. The same is true of issues concerning location and orientation.

As you have seen throughout this book, the registration point of a movie clip usually appears in the center of the work area when you begin creating a new movie clip symbol. Similarly, when you convert items on the stage to a movie clip, the registration point defaults to the center of the selected items. Thus, the upper left-hand corner of the loaded movie's stage will be aligned with the movie clip's registration point. Therefore, you may need to design your movie clip so that its content is down and to the right of the registration crosshairs.

 **CD-ROM NOTE:** *To see an example of loading movies into a movie clip, open the file* ch8-05.fla *located in the* F5gai/chapter8 *folder, installed from the companion CD-ROM. The files* ch8-05-1.fla *and* ch8-05-2.fla *are SWF versions of the movies, loaded into the movie clip.*

## Rules for Using Tell Target

Setting up Tell Targets, particularly when you start nesting movie clips or movies, can be tricky. To help, keep in mind the following two rules for getting the Tell Target paths to work.

- Name the movie clip instances you want to target. If you have movie clips nested within one another, to target them you must name every one so that you can direct Flash to the one you want to control.

- You cannot control movie clips nested within buttons or graphic symbols. Button and graphic symbols will "break" the hierarchical chain. You can work around this by changing the stage's definition, but in general you cannot target through a graphic or button symbol.

# ▪ ▪ ▪ Summary

This chapter examined two of the overall organizational strategies for your movies: scenes and multilevel movies. Both are powerful, and your choice of which to use will depend on what you are trying to accomplish. As you have read, loading and unloading movies can be somewhat tricky, particularly if you forget how you have structured movie clips you want to control in those movies. Generally, if there is a problem and you cannot "talk" to an element in your movies, review the Tell Target rules and examine the hierarchy of your movie clips. Errors are most likely related to one of these two items.

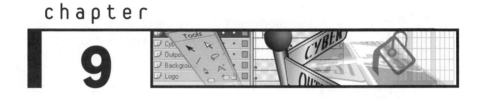

# 9

# Testing, Integration, and Distribution

### ∎ ∎ ∎ **Introduction**

This book has discussed many things concerning the creation of Flash movies, but has not dealt with testing, integration, and distribution issues. Indeed, to be an exceptional Flash developer requires not only the ability to aesthetically design but the ability to critically analyze, test, and debug movies. Knowing how to integrate Flash movies and having a sense of when there is "too much stuff in your movies" are also important.

This chapter begins by focusing on how to test movies. Regardless of whether you are developing movies for delivery over the Web or on other media as projector files, testing will be a vital step. Testing is not a "one-shot" occurrence. It occurs over and over, all the time.

Additionally, this chapter will familiarize you with the HTML code for integrating movies into your pages. Flash provides an integrated feature called *Publish* that can automate much of the process of integration. However, basic HTML tags and attributes that relate to Flash are also covered. Sometimes it may be preferable to code by hand. In fact, you might want to code material using Notepad, or Simpletext, two text editors that let you know exactly what is going on in your pages. Nevertheless, knowledge of both methods is necessary.

Flash also provides the ability to critically analyze the way your movies download over the Web. Flash's Size Report feature and Bandwidth Profiler, combined with several other features, can be used to optimize your movies.

This chapter concludes by reviewing the most important things that have to do with optimizing the graphics, bitmaps, and sounds that may find their way into movies.

# Objectives

In this chapter, you will:

- Learn methods for testing your movies in Flash
- Discover the three methods for distributing movies, including how you can specifically develop for each mode of delivery
- Examine the differences between the native FLA file format and the Web-ready SWF format
- Use the Export Movie command to create web-ready SWF files
- Learn to convert an SWF file into an executable file called a projector
- Find out about the Publish feature and how it can be used to automate the integration process
- Determine the HTML tags and attributes used to integrate Flash SWF files into web pages
- Use the Size Report and Bandwidth Profiler tools to critically analyze the data within a Flash movie
- Discover optimization techniques that can be used to decrease the size of movies

# Test, Test, and Test Again

Testing is one of the most critical aspects of developing successful Flash movies and sites. Testing is critical because of the range of variables with which you have to deal. The audience's connection, browser, browser version, RAM, video RAM, and processor can all change the way your movies are played back. The main goal in testing is to ensure that a large portion of the potential audience is not eliminated. It is often the end user's hardware, software, or connection that presents limitations. Without keeping these variables in mind, you can quickly develop something that does not run, or runs poorly, for your audience. Without testing, you make assumptions that will most likely be detrimental.

As it relates to web development, two main types of testing occur: *concurrent testing* and *compatibility testing*. Concurrent testing takes place the entire time movies are being developed. When completing the exercises throughout this book, you completed this type of testing when you used the Control | Play and Control | Test Movie menu options. Most often developers are the ones who perform concurrent testing. It occurs continually during the entire development process.

On the other hand, compatibility testing is done to determine if the product works under various technical scenarios. Do the page and its movies work in Internet Explorer and Netscape Communicator? Does it work in older versions of these browsers? What about the user's connection speed? Are the movies so large that it takes many minutes to download or is response instantaneous? All of these are questions answered through compatibility testing.

You will never be able to accommodate every scenario that exists in the browsing community. There will always be somebody who cannot get that plug-in installed or somebody who is so petrified of computer viruses that downloading anything from the Web is unthinkable. Nevertheless, the goal is to accommodate the middle 50 percent of the distribution. The middle of a normal distribution is more alike than different. This is the audience for whom you should conduct testing.

# Testing in Flash

Flash provides two methods for performing concurrent testing, both of which occur within the application environment. The Control | Play or the Control | Test Movie commands can be used. You have used these to run the movies included with this book, but all of their settings have yet to be discussed. Nonetheless, as reiterated here, which method you use depends on what your movie contains. Keep in mind that movie clips do not play when you use the Play command. To see and hear movie clips that are inserted into the main timeline, use the Test Movie option instead of the Play option.

## Playing in Flash

When a movie does not contain movie clip symbols, use the basic Control | Play command to test the movie. This allows you to see the playhead move across the timeline as elements appear on the stage.

 **TIP:** *To quickly play and stop a movie that does not contain movie clips, press the Enter key.*

When testing this way, other options found in the Control menu apply.

- *Rewind*, *Step Forward*, and *Step Backward*: Allow you to control the playhead, which changes what is displayed on the stage.

- *Loop Playback*: Forces the movie to loop when it reaches the end of the scene or movie.

- *Play All Scenes*: Forces the movie to play every scene, even if no action is assigned to jump between scenes.

- *Enable Simple Frame Actions*: Implements any actions assigned to frames in the movie. By default, frame actions are not enabled.

- *Enable Simple Buttons:* Allows buttons to function so that you may interact with them. Turn this on to see the states of a button. Turn it off to scale, position, or orient a button on the stage.

- *Mute Sounds:* Disables sounds associated with the main movie timeline when play is used.

### Using Test Movie and Test Scene

The most frequent command used for testing movies is the Control | Test Movie menu option. This command allows you to see all of the movie clips and other symbols within the movie function. The Enable Simple Buttons, Enable Simple Frame Actions, and Mute Sound options have no effect when using Test Movie. Rather, the settings used for Test Movie are established in the Publish Settings menu option found in the File menu.

When the Test Movie menu option is selected, Flash quickly generates a web-ready Flash file with an SWF extension. SWF stands for Shockwave Flash. The SWF file is instantly opened into the Flash Player, directly in front of the stage of the currently open movie. The speed of this process depends on the complexity of the movie. The SWF file that is generated is placed in the same directory as the FLA file and has the same name. Each time you use Test Movie, the SWF file is updated and displayed in the player.

If you are developing movies on the Macintosh, be very careful when using the Test Movie option, as well as the Export Movie and Publish options described later in this chapter. Make sure you save your native Flash files with an extension (.fLA).

 **WARNING:** If you do not save files with an extension, the native FLA file will be overwritten with the SWF file when you use the Test Movie or Export Movie commands. Consequently, if the SWF is protected (via Export Movie), you will render the file useless. The FLA file will be overwritten with a protected SWF file that cannot be reopened into the Flash application. In short, even if you are on a Mac and have no intention of going to PC, use file extensions!

## ∎ ∎ ∎ Distributing Your Movies

Macromedia Flash files can be distributed to your audience in one of five ways. The mode chosen is determined by how much content can be realistically included in the intended delivery mechanism. Flash files can be distributed as:

- An SWF file to be played back in the stand-alone Flash player, apart from the Web

- A projector file that has all code necessary for playback of the Flash movie (does not require the Flash player or the Flash application)
- A QuickTime 4 file
- A RealPlayer file
- An SWF file to be played back in the browser using a plug-in or ActiveX component

As it relates to multimedia and hypermedia development, realize that your delivery system is only as strong as the weakest link. For your movie files to be perceived as effective, you must design around the limitations that exist for each method of delivery.

When delivering on the Web, the user's connection is usually the weakest link. Lengthy audio segments or many bitmaps will make download times significant. If your audience has a direct network connection, you may be able to get away with larger file sizes. Yet, if your audience has the typical consumer-level modem connection, you must judiciously design movies within the bounds of what is realistically deliverable.

If movies are to be distributed via diskette or CD-ROM, you are less restricted, but still limited in how much audio and graphics can be delivered, even from a CD-ROM or hard drive. Always keep the end user in mind during your decision-making process.

 **NOTE:** *To help you better understand the impact of bandwidth and data rate on the delivery of information, Appendix A presents a table (also shown in Chapter 1) that shows the common bandwidth and data rate of various devices. With it, you can determine the best-case scenario for delivery of information.*

## Using the Player

The first method for distributing Flash files is to provide your audience members with web-ready SWF files. These SWF files can be played back on the user's computer either in the stand-alone player or in the browser's player (as a result of a plug-in ActiveX component). Thus, one of the assumptions you make when providing SWF files is that the audience has the Shockwave Flash Player in one form or another.

This method of distributing Flash movies is generally used for viewing movies apart from the Web, although the SWF file could very well be integrated into a web page as well. For example, you can show your Flash files to a colleague or friend in the SWF format. Realize that as long as the user has the Shockwave Player, they do not have to have Flash to view your movies. Conceptually, this is the same idea behind Microsoft's PowerPoint viewer. The viewer allows you to open and play the file, but you cannot edit it.

**NOTE:** *The Flash Player for both the PC and Mac platform are located on the software installation CD-ROM. Additionally, you can freely distribute the Flash Player with your movies, much like the PowerPoint presentation player can be freely distributed with your PowerPoint files.*

## Creating Projectors

If you are unsure whether or not your audience has the Shockwave Flash Player (and you do not want to have to worry about it), open a Flash file into the Flash Player and create a projector file. This is probably the best technique if you are going to be distributing your movies via CD-ROM or diskette and are not sure if the person you are giving it to has the player.

Similar to Director's capability of the same name, making an SWF file into a projector converts the file into an executable application that can be run on any computer (of the same platform), regardless of whether the user has the Shockwave Player. When you convert an SWF file to a projector, the Flash Player adds the appropriate code to the file so that it can "play itself." The file will increase in size slightly when you convert it to a projector. But again, this method is predominantly used to distribute movies apart from the Web, so you have more flexibility in regard to file size. Projectors can be included on most media, such as CD-ROM, DVD, or diskettes.

Projectors created via the player are not cross-platform capable. Thus, a projector created on the PC cannot be run on a Mac, and vice versa. However, Flash's Publish command will allow you to create projectors for both platforms, but you must tell it that you want it to do this.

**NOTE:** *For more details concerning cross-platform issues, pay close attention to the "Cross-Platform Issues" section later in this chapter.*

## QuickTime 4

Another means of delivery that can be used on the Web or on CD-ROM media is made possible by QuickTime 4. QuickTime is one the most far-reaching software technologies that exists. It is installed on millions of computers and helps cross the great divide between Macs and PCs as it relates to the delivery of multimedia assets.

The latest version of QuickTime allows for Flash data to be integrated directly within it. Realize that the QuickTime format is much more than a format for digital video. It includes a wide range of data and support for over 30 file formats, not the least of which is Flash movies. Think of QuickTime as more of a "container." Flash elements can be intermixed with digital video data, virtual reality components (QTVR), and several other types of assets. For more information concerning the specifics of QuickTime 4, see Apple's web site.

NOTE: *For the QuickTime 4 Publish option to work, as well as for you to be able to import some of the file formats mentioned in Chapter 1, you must have QuickTime 4 or higher installed before installing Flash 5. For more information concerning QuickTime 4 or to get the player and required system files, see Apple's site* (http://www.apple.com).

Within the application, Flash provides the ability to save directly to Apple's QuickTime 4 format. The Publish command allows you to generate QT4 files quickly and easily while you are also generating the other files required for publishing your Flash files. Although this book does not delve into great detail on the use of QuickTime, it is important that you understand the breadth of QuickTime and how it can help you in your development ventures. Just as Flash SWF files are integrated into web pages, so too can QuickTime movies, using the EMBED HTML tag. Appendix E discusses how to integrate generated QuickTime 4 files into an HTML page.

As discussed in Macromedia's literature, all of the interactivity of the Flash file should be retained in the resulting QT file. However, if you decide to use the QuickTime 4 distribution option, make sure you test early and often. QT versions of Flash files may work better on the Macintosh than on a PC.

## RealPlayer Format

A newly supported format in Flash 5 is the RealPlayer format. Much like the QuickTime format, the RealPlayer format should be thought of, as previously mentioned, as more of a "container" than a specific format. Nonetheless, two limitations exist when using RealPlayer for delivery. First, Flash files must be stored in Flash 4 format to be output as RealPlayer files. This means you loose some of the ActionScript capabilities of Flash 5. Second, RealPlayer version 8 or higher must be installed on the user's end.

NOTE: *For more information on the RealPlayer, see* http://www.realplayer.com.

## Web Delivery

The final means for distributing your movie, and the most common, is via an HTML page. To do this, generate an SWF file and then include a reference to it using HTML. Although the HTML tags for including Flash files are different and can be more complex, the process is similar to creating references to graphic images within a web page.

To write the required HTML code, you can use the Publish utility that automates the HTML coding process, or you can write the code by hand, using an ASCII-based text editor. Both of these methods are covered later in this chapter.

Once the HTML code has been written, the referenced SWF file will play directly in the browser, assuming the user has the Flash plug-in. When writing the appropriate HTML, you have several options concerning visual placement and formatting of the Flash elements on the web page. The relative HTML attributes and tags are reviewed later in this chapter.

# SWF Versus FLA

Regardless of which delivery means you use, each begins with exporting the native Flash file (FLA) as a Shockwave Flash (SWF) file. When an FLA file is converted to an SWF file, a couple of things occur. First, Flash removes extra data that may be contained in the FLA file. For example, bitmaps and sounds that are not used within the movie timeline are ignored and are not written in the SWF. Aside from these omissions, the process also applies compression to the sound and bitmap assets within the file, reducing the resulting SWF file size as much as possible.

Realize that *Shockwave* is actually an all-encompassing term used with many Macromedia products. It simply means that the movie file is optimized (as much as possible) for the Web. Flash and Director both provide the ability to generate Shockwave (web-ready) files. They are all Shockwave files, even though they are generated from different applications. What you can put in each type of Shockwave file depends on the application used to create it.

The SWF file format has the option of being "protected," so as to restrict others from opening the file back into Flash. SWF files generated from Macromedia FreeHand are not protected. Thus, you can import and use them in Flash. However, when you generate movies for the Web from Flash, make sure you generate protected SWF files. Otherwise, anyone could load and illegally use your Flash elements in their own movies. The Protect Movie option, discussed in the sections that follow, is provided in the Export Movie and Publish dialog boxes.

# Using Export Movie

Once you have a completed movie and are ready to prepare (Shock) it for the Web, use the File | Export Movie option. When using this option, you are first required to provide a name for the file. On the PC, the SWF extension is automatically applied to the file. On the Mac, you should get in the habit of adding the .SWF extension to the end of the file. Once the file is named, the Export Flash Player dialog box is presented, as shown in figure 9-1. The optional settings are described in the sections that follow. Once the desired settings are established, click on OK to generate the SWF file.

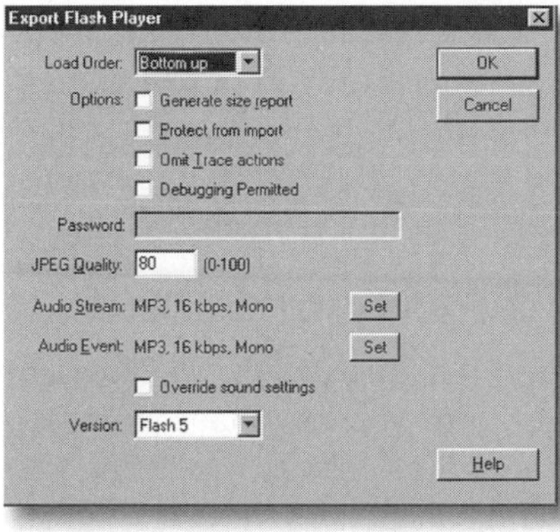

![Export Flash Player dialog box showing Load Order set to Bottom up, Options checkboxes for Generate size report, Protect from import, Omit Trace actions, Debugging Permitted, Password field, JPEG Quality 80 (0-100), Audio Stream MP3 16 kbps Mono with Set button, Audio Event MP3 16 kbps Mono with Set button, Override sound settings checkbox, Version Flash 5, and OK, Cancel, Help buttons]

*Figure 9-1 The Export Flash Player dialog box presents the optional settings that affect the generated SWF file.*

# Load Order

The first option presented is the Load Order drop-down. This option affects how each frame is rendered as the file is loaded. This is most evident in the first frame of the movie when the user is connecting via a slower connection such as a modem.

Because Flash files are streaming files, as portions (frames) of the file are downloaded and become available, they can be immediately rendered to the screen, even though the rest of the frames from the file have yet to be downloaded. Selecting the Bottom Up option will cause layers further down in the layering order (farthest back in the screen order) to be displayed first. The Top Down option does the exact opposite. Use the Load Order option to set which layers will be rendered first over slower connections.

## Generate Size Report

Size reports are one of the most impressive parts of Flash. If you select the Generate Size Report option, Flash automatically generates a text file that provides details about the size of each frame and the elements that occur within the movie. See the "Closely Examining the Size Report" section later in the chapter.

## Protect from Import

As mentioned earlier, SWF files have the option of being protected. When an SWF is protected, it cannot be loaded back into Flash for editing. If left unchecked, the generated SWF can be imported into Flash and made to yield its graphical and structural components.

 **WARNING:** Again, when using a Macintosh, save your files with extensions. Otherwise, an exported SWF may accidentally overwrite an FLA file.

Something new in Flash 5 is the Password Field. When you select the Protect from Import option, the Password Field can be used. This allows you to create protected SWF files that can be reused. This is a convenient safety feature in that if you use the Password field, you always have an editable version of your movies, even if the FLA is lost or corrupted.

## Omit Trace Actions

The trace action, which you will learn about later, can be used to reveal behind-the-scenes information concerning variables and the state of the application in the Output window. These actions, particularly if there are many of them, can increase the file size of your resulting SWF files. Trace actions do nothing in the resulting SWF file; that is, the information they generate is not shown in the Flash Player or in the browser. However, when you generate your SWF files, you should select the Omit Trace Actions checkbox so that trace actions are not recorded in the resulting SWF file.

## Debugging Permitted and Password Field

A new capability in Flash is the ability to debug within the browser. If you select the Debugging Permitted checkbox, you can choose to password protect your movie so that you are the only one who can debug the movie remotely. The Debugger is explored in Chapter 13.

## Image Compression

The JPEG Quality field controls the amount of JPEG compression applied to bitmap images. If no images are included in the file, the setting has no effect. Lower settings yield smaller file sizes and poorer visual results concerning the output image. Generally, it is best to experiment with various settings to get the best results, because compressibility and data loss with the JPEG compressor depends on the similarity of colors in the image.

If you change the Compression drop-down list in the Bitmap Properties dialog box (in the library) to Lossless, rather than Default, the JPEG Quality field will have no effect on the exported images in the SWF file. Use the Lossless setting only on bitmap images that must retain complete resolution. Taking advantage of the Lossless setting in the Bitmap Properties dialog box may result in very large file sizes.

Even if a JPEG setting is established in the library using the Bitmap Properties dialog box, the setting entered into the JPEG Quality field at the time of export will override the Library setting. This allows flexibility by allowing various qualities to be used at the time of export.

See figure 9-2 and color plate B-11 for an idea of how the JPEG Quality setting affects two images at various qualities. Their associated file sizes also change because of the JPEG Quality setting. Realize that results will vary, depending on the image being compressed.

 **CD-ROM NOTE:** *As the printing process often masks the true effects of screen data, the versions of the images shown in figure 9-2 are provided in the* ch9-01.fla *file located in the* F5gai/chapter9/jpeg/ *folder, installed from the companion CD-ROM.*

## Audio Compression

As you read in Chapter 7, sounds in Flash are either defined as streaming sounds or event sounds. The Audio Stream and the Audio Event Set buttons apply to how these two types of sounds are stored in the SWF file.

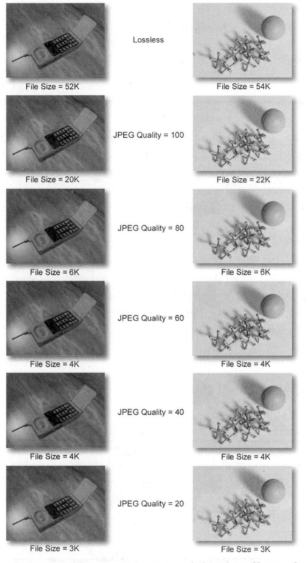

Lossless
File Size = 52K

File Size = 54K

JPEG Quality = 100
File Size = 20K

File Size = 22K

JPEG Quality = 80
File Size = 6K

File Size = 6K

JPEG Quality = 60
File Size = 4K

File Size = 4K

JPEG Quality = 40
File Size = 4K

File Size = 4K

JPEG Quality = 20
File Size = 3K

File Size = 3K

*Figure 9-2 These two images exhibit the effects of the JPEG Quality setting on file size and quality. (See also color plate B-11.)*

Again, streamed sounds are interleaved with frames as they are saved in the SWF file. This allows the sound to start playing almost instantaneously. Any delay in streaming will be perceived as a pause in the audio. Event sounds are associated with an event and are downloaded in their entirety before playback. If the stream of data over the Web pauses, event sounds are not affected.

Regardless of the type of sound, the Set buttons can be used to modify the output audio rate, even if the sound is stored in the FLA file at a higher sampling rate. This allows for flexibility as you generate SWF files. You can test various rates to compare file size to audio quality.

You can define the amount of compression used for audio with the Compression drop-down menus associated with the Audio Stream and Event Set buttons. Again, Flash can use either Adaptive Differential Pulse Code Modulation (ADPCM) or Motion Picture Experts Group 3 (MP3), both of which are lossy compression schemes.

**TIP:** *Use the Override Sound Settings checkbox to overrule the audio settings established in the Library Sound Properties dialog box. If this option is selected, the Export Flash Player Audio Stream and Audio Event settings will override the library settings.*

Remember that similar to JPEG compression, ADPCM and MP3 compression loses a certain amount of data to attain higher compression ratios (smaller files). Consequently, the more audio compressed, the less it is like the original file. Experimentation is key to getting the best mix. Just like the JPEG quality setting and colors in an image, audio compressibility is dependent on the range of amplitudes and the number of redundant amplitudes within the sound file.

**CD-ROM NOTE:** *To hear the effect of various compression rates on audio, examine the file in the* F5gai/chapter9/audio/ *folder, installed from the companion CD-ROM. Open the file ch9-02.fla, which presents three examples: one voice sample, one music sample, and one sound effect.*

## Versions

Finally, in the Export Flash Player dialog box is the Version drop-down menu. This menu allows you to export movies as older version Flash files. This feature is particularly useful for exporting Flash movies for use in other programs such as Director. When you select an older version, features supported in newer versions of Flash are disabled.

Macromedia Director 7 supports all Flash 3 SWF features. Director 8 supports all Flash 4 features. We will have to wait and see how soon support for Flash 5 is available in Director and Authorware.

 **TIP:** *When you open a Flash 4 file into Flash 5, you will find that the Export Flash Player dialog box defaults to Flash 4, rather than Flash 5. It is recommended that anytime you open an older Flash file into version 5, immediately go to the File | Publish Settings | Flash tab and set the default to version 5.*

# ▪▪▪ SWF to EXE (Projector)

Once you have an SWF file, quickly and easily convert the file to a projector using the Flash Player. Once a file is a project, the Flash Player is no longer needed to run the file. All of the needed player code is compiled into the projector so that it can be played anywhere. However, note that the generated projector can only be played on the platform on which it was compiled. To generate a projector for multiple platforms, use the File | Publish command. The CD-ROM exercise that follows provides practice in generating a projector file.

 ### CD-ROM Exercise

Open the file *ch9-03.swf* (located in the *F5gai/chapter9 folder*, installed from the companion CD-ROM) into the Flash player. To convert the SWF file to a projector, perform the following steps.

1. Open the SWF file into the Flash Player.

2. In the Flash Player, use the File | Create Projector menu option.

3. Name the file and click on OK. The generated projector (executable application) can now be ported to any computer that has the same operating system for playback.

# Exporting Images

Aside from exporting movies, there may be times when you will want to export a static image capture of a particular frame. Flash provides the ability to save in many vector and raster formats. Most of the raster formats are pretty straightforward. The formats include Windows Bitmap (PC), PICT (MAC), JPG, GIF, and PNG.

As far as vector export, this can be somewhat tricky. Of the files that exist on the computer, vector files (and even more particularly, metafiles) can be troublesome. Metafiles are those formats that can store raster data, vector data, or both simultaneously. Because metafiles can store data in a variety of ways (depending on the application that is writing the file), getting image A from package B to package C using metafile format D is difficult. Realistically, to find the best path between two packages will require some trial and error with the various vector formats available.

# Cross-platform Issues

Aside from the "which browser" question, one of the most important variables you have to deal with is the user's platform. When trying to accommodate users, consider how the operating system will affect your movies. If you want to use or provide SWF or projector files on both Mac and PC, as well as other platforms, how do you do it?

The Web was designed to be platform independent. As wonderful as this sounds, it is not always the case, especially when you are the developer trying to ensure that movies will work on multiple platforms. Although this section is not intended to be an all-encompassing list of problems you may encounter, it does answer some of the most frequently asked questions, and the major hurdles you might encounter.

First, understand that the SWF file format is intended to be platform independent. For example, you should be able to play SWF files generated on the PC in the Macintosh Flash Player, with few, if any, problems. Keep in mind that font definitions, bitmaps, and sounds should play back and display normally. They are stored within the SWF format. Using "sneakernet" (floppy disks or other media) as well as the Web, you can port an SWF file to any platform and play it back, as long as a player exists on that platform.

Developers may discover one caveat concerning sound. In some movies, effects assigned to "Custom" (in the Sound panel) within the PC FLA file will cause the sound (in the PC-generated SWF) to play erroneously when played back on the Macintosh. The sound plays back as meaningless feedback. The only instance of this in the development of this book has been with the Streaming sound in the Chapter 7 file named *ch7-02.fla*. This may be a rare occurrence, but it is worth noting. Make sure you not only test your movies in multiple browsers and versions but on multiple platforms.

Native Flash FLA files are platform independent. However, fonts assigned on the opposing platform can cause problems. Whereas the SWF file retains the font outline for playback, FLA files do not. Thus, the traditional problem of the unavailability of a font on one platform or the other still exists when porting FLA files cross-platform.

For example, if you design an FLA file with a particular font on the PC and save the FLA to the Mac for editing, the specific font must also reside on the Mac. If not, Flash will tell you that the font is not available. Consequently, your text will be substituted with some other font of the system's choosing.

However, even if the font used does reside on the other platform, you will likely have some editing to do. Although the name of a particular Mac and PC font may be the same (even if they visually appear the same), often the size, kerning, letter spacing, and other type attributes will vary. You will almost always have some editing to do when you go cross-platform, so make sure you budget some time for it. In this author's opinion, it is best to do all development on one platform or the other.

 **NOTE:** *Keep in mind tips concerning importing media elements presented in prior chapters of this book. In the PC version of Flash, WAV files are the preferred file format for sound files. In the Macintosh version of Flash, AIF files are the preferred file format for sound files. Remember that the support of some of the file types for importing and exporting is dependent on having QuickTime 4 installed.*

One final note related to cross-platform differences concerns the creation of projectors. When creating a projector file from the Flash player, the SWF file is compiled or prepared for playback on the platform on which it was compiled. Therefore, an SWF compiled on the PC (converted to a projector) can only be played back on the PC. An SWF compiled on the Macintosh can only be played back on the Macintosh. The Publish feature in Flash, however, allows you to create projectors for both platforms.

 **TIP:** *To create a set of projectors that accommodate both platforms, compile each projector on each platform or use the Publish command. Dual projectors are needed when creating hybrid HFS/ISO9660 CD-ROMs for multimedia distribution.*

## ▪ ▪ ▪ Delivery over the Web

Because most work in Flash ends up being delivered over the Web, the rest of this chapter deals with delivery and optimization techniques for Flash files. If the Web is your chosen vehicle, file size is a paramount concern. It does not take a lot of creative thinking to quickly use up bandwidth. What bandwidth you do have can quickly be eaten away by a few sound files, a couple of bitmaps, or a lot of vectors.

## Integration Versus Optimization

Before looking at optimization, consider integration. There are two ways of linking your Flash files to an HTML page. Both methods can yield the same results. Nevertheless, which method you choose should depend on your experience with HTML and web-based scripting languages.

If you are new to HTML, consider using the Publish command, Macromedia's automated integration engine. This command makes it easy to embed SWF files. It provides some nice features as well, such as generating projectors, static images, and other files. If you are more of the scripting sort, the later portion of this chapter is for you (as well as chapters 13 through 17). However, it is well worth being able to employ both methods.

## Publishing with Flash

The Publish feature replaces the software utility called Aftershock, which was distributed with earlier versions of Flash. All of the functionality of Aftershock can now be found within Flash. In fact, the Publish feature is more extensive because it allows the developer to create custom "template" HTML pages that can be used.

However, as its primary function, Publish provides a quick means of getting movies into a web page. With little if any knowledge of HTML code, you can set all of the EMBED and OBJECT attributes required to get your Flash movies up and running in both browsers. You can also generate a range of other assets that may be needed. The File | Publish menu option provides several powerful capabilities:

- Add a Shockwave movie to a new page.
- Provide a Java version of your movie.
- Generate static or animated GIFs, and static JPEG or PNG images of your movies, predominantly for those audience members who happen on your site without the Shockwave plug-in.
- Quickly generate QuickTime or RealPlayer versions of your Flash movies.
- Generate a script that detects the Shockwave Plug-in or ActiveX control. If the browser add-on is not found, the user is directed to display a GIF or to get the plug-in.
- Create the code required to give the user a cookie that stores their browsing settings for your site.
- Add code hooks for search engines.

    • Create template pages that can be used in the Publish command.

In addition to the tabs described in this section, if you have Macromedia Generator installed, a tab named Generator will exist in the Publish Settings dialog box.

 **NOTE:** *For more information about Macromedia Generator, see Appendix D.*

# ▪▪▪ The Publish Settings

Setting up the parameters for publishing your files is established using the File | Publish Settings command. Much like the tabbed dialog box found in the old Aftershock utility, you determine the media elements you want to generate and the characteristics of those media elements by selecting checkboxes and other controls.

## The Formats Tab

When you select the Publish Settings menu option, the dialog box in figure 9-3 is shown. In the Formats tab, select the items you want to output. There is a correlation between the tabs shown at the top of the dialog box and the selected checkboxes. For example, if QuickTime (.*mov*) is not checked in the Formats tab, the QuickTime tab does not appear.

As shown in figure 9-3, note that the name of the media elements shown in the grayed fields to the right of the items are the same as the name of the current FLA file. Additionally, the files are output to the same directory as the FLA file.

You can change the default names by deselecting the Use Default Names checkbox. Then, enter a name for the asset being generated. Just be aware of the names you use so that you do not accidentally overwrite existing files. Remember: even on the Macintosh, use file extensions.

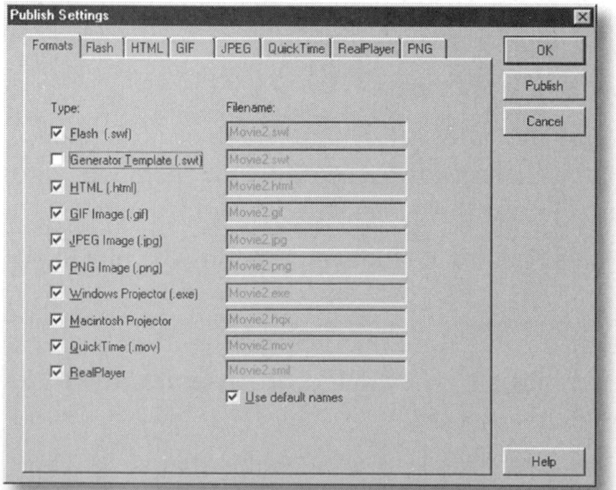

Generally, the HTML file created by the Publish command is good for inserting individual Shockwave elements onto your page. However, if you want to do further editing, such as adding other HTML elements or scripting, you will have to "know the code" or be familiar with a site creation and page-editing tool such as Macromedia Dreamweaver. Tools such as Netscape Composer, Microsoft FrontPage, and Adobe PageMill can be used, but they

*Figure 9-3 The Format tab is used to indicate the elements to be published.*

may not recognize the code inserted by the Publish command, or even recognize the Flash object itself.

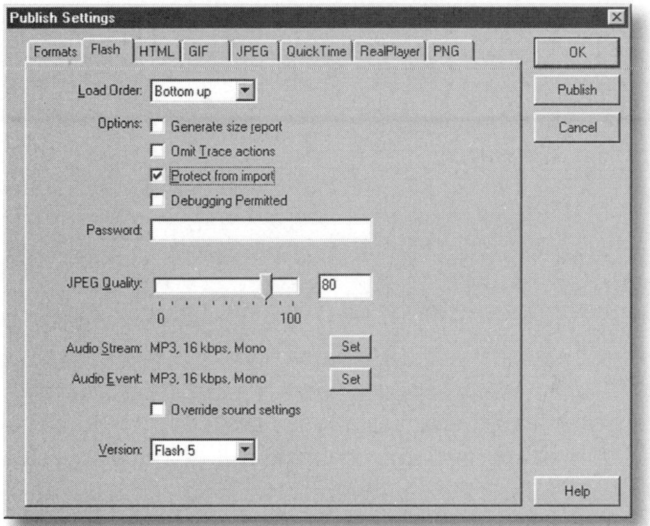

*Figure 9-4 The Flash tab resembles the Export Movie dialog box, where you establish the properties of the exported SWF file.*

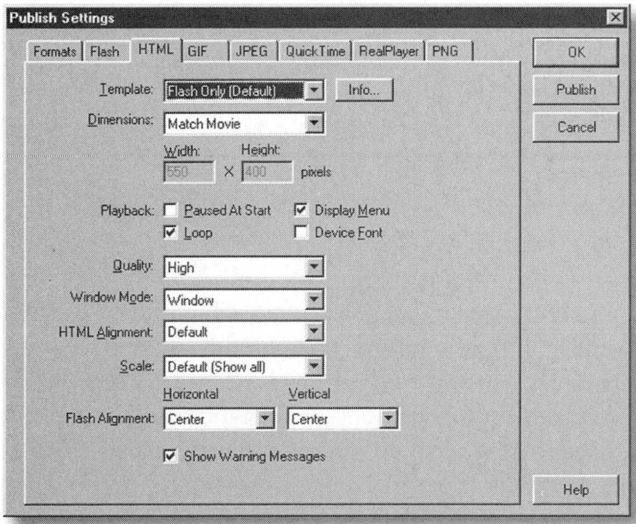

*Figure 9-5 The settings in the HTML tab determine the HTML code (and scripting) that will be added to the HTML file that is generated.*

## The Flash Tab

The content of the Flash tab, shown in figure 9-4, should look familiar, because it is the same as that shown in the Export Movie dialog box. As noted in that discussion, the settings established in the Publish Settings are used as the defaults for the Export Movie, Test Movie, Test Scene, and Publish commands. Use the elements displayed in the Flash tab to set the properties of the generated SWF file. Review the previous section "Using Export Movie" for detailed descriptions of the options found here.

## The HTML Tab

The HTML tab, shown in figure 9-5, provides the controls necessary to define how the Flash file will be integrated into an HTML page. The Template drop-down provides several default "template" schemes that can be used to quickly assign the most common scripted elements. You can use any of the default templates or create your own. The remaining controls in the dialog box are used to define the HTML attributes used in the < EMBED > and < OBJECT > tags.

**NOTE:** *Because Publishing templates require knowledge of HTML code and some special symbols, discussion of them is reserved for later in this chapter. See the section "Working with Publish Templates" later in this chapter for more details.*

Ignoring the Templates drop-down for now, examine the other controls available in the HTML tab. The first control, Dimensions, is used to define the WIDTH and HEIGHT attributes of your Shockwave element. As with other HTML elements, such as raster images, the size can be based on pixels or percentages. When pixels are specified in the Dimensions drop-down, the element is inserted at a fixed size. If the browser display is smaller than the fixed size, scrolling will be necessary.

The Match Movie option is also based on pixel size and is helpful in that you do not have to remember or write down the size of your movie. Selecting Percent (percentages) allows the size of the movie to change as the size of the browser window changes. The object is proportionally scaled to fit into the area of the browser window when percentages are used.

### Playback

The Playback checkboxes provide several controls over the movie's playback conditions. Paused at Start and Loop are self-explanatory. The Display Menu checkbox controls the context menu pop-up, which is displayed when you right-click on an embedded movie in the browser. There is no way to totally get rid of the context menu. At the minimum, About Flash 5 will always be available in the context menu when the user right-clicks on the movie in the web page.

The Device Font option, which only applies to the Windows platform, substitutes anti-aliased system fonts for fonts that are not installed on the user's system. This is not a recommended option because it may negatively affect playback and is not supported on all platforms. In addition to the playback parameters, you are provided with six very important drop-down menus (though one applies to Internet Explorer only, as you will see).

### Quality

The first drop-down menu is the Quality setting. As mentioned in earlier chapters, you can toggle between various view modes to increase performance within the Flash application. When machine speed slows, you can reduce the view complexity to speed up performance by turning off anti-aliasing. As your Flash movies play in a page, adjust the visual quality based on machine performance to achieve the same results. The Quality setting provides the following options for visual quality:

- Auto High tries to balance playback speed and appearance equally. However, if performance decreases, visual quality is sacrificed to increase speed. In general, playback will begin with anti-alias turned on. Yet, if machine speed degrades, anti-aliasing is turned off to improve playback speed.

- Auto Low tries to balance speed and appearance as well. By default, Auto Low starts with anti-aliasing off. If performance is favorable, anti-aliasing will be turned on.

- The High setting favors appearance and continually plays with anti-aliasing on.

- The Medium setting tries to favor both appearance and performance by anti-aliasing objects and ignoring text.

- The Low setting favors performance and continually plays with anti-aliasing off.

- Best attempts to choose from among the previous options to display the SWF file based on performance.

### Window Mode

The second of these options is the Window Mode. This is an exceptional feature; however, currently it only applies to movies played back in Internet Explorer. Nonetheless, it is worth mentioning.

One of the common questions asked is "How do you make the background of a Flash movie transparent so that the background color of the web page shows through it?" This is what the Window Mode is all about. Window Mode provides three options:

- *Default:* Sets the WMODE parameter of the <OBJECT> tag to WINDOW. This plays the movie "normally" and provides the fastest animation performance.

- *Opaque Windowless:* Sets the WMODE parameter to OPAQUE and allows you to fluidly move elements behind Shockwave Movies without the moving objects showing. This is typically used in conjunction with Dynamic HTML (DHTML).

- *Transparent Windowless:* Sets the WMODE parameter to TRANSPARENT and allows the elements behind the Shockwave movie to show through the blank areas of the movie. Although this is a neat feature, animation performance may decrease when this mode is used.

Currently, if you use the Window Mode setting, WMODE will be added to both the <OBJECT> and <EMBED> tags, as a PARAM in OBJECT and an attribute in EMBED. Currently, the WMODE attribute is not recognized by Netscape Navigator or Communicator.

### HTML Alignment

The Alignment drop-down controls the alignment of other elements on the page in relationship to the Shockwave element. Valid options for the Alignment drop-down include LEFT, RIGHT, TOP, and BOTTOM.

## Scale

The Scale drop-down menu controls how the Shockwave movie will fit into the area allotted within the Dimensions drop-down. The Default is

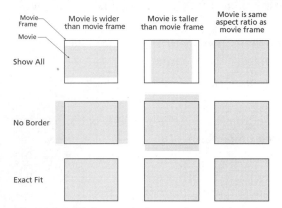

Show All. Figure 9-6 shows the results of the various settings on a movie that is wide and a movie that is tall. If the movie is the exact size specified in the HEIGHT and WIDTH (that is, you are using exact pixel dimensions), a scale will probably not be necessary. Thus, use the default of Show All. However, if you are using screen percentages for your dimensions and your movie has a different aspect ratio than the screen area, a scale setting will probably be required.

*Figure 9-6  If the movie is not the same aspect ratio as the defined HEIGHT and WIDTH (dimensions), a scale setting may be necessary.*

## Flash Alignment

The final two drop-down menus in the HTML tab allow you to control alignment when the movie does not completely fill the defined area. These two-drop downs are used in conjunction with the Scale drop-down when percentages are used for the dimensions.

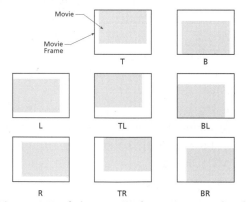

Figure 9-7 shows the various results of the Flash Alignment settings. In the HTML code, the single SALIGN attribute defines the alignment. Thus, if a movie is aligned left and top, the SALIGN attribute is set equal to LT. If the movie is aligned right and top, SALIGN is set equal to RT. The default when no SALIGN attribute is included is center horizontal and center vertical.

*Figure 9-7  If the movie does not completely dill the defined area, the SALIGN attribute controls the placement of the movie.*

## Show Warning Messages

The final checkbox in the HTML tab, Show Warning Messages, is used to indicate any problems that may occur when the Publish command is executed. With so many publishing options, some settings may conflict with one another. If the Show Warning Messages checkbox is selected, Flash will prompt you with errors if they occur. One such message is the QuickTime alert. If you do not have QuickTime 4 installed and you select the QuickTime checkbox in the Formats tab, Flash will prompt you that it cannot create a QuickTime movie.

## The GIF Tab

As you prepare your movies for web distribution, you always have to consider that there may be users that do not have the Flash plug-in. If so, they will see that ugly broken link icon in place of your SWF file. For cases when the user cannot view Flash elements, the Publish utility allows you to generate a static GIF, JPEG, or PNG representation of the first frame of your movie, or an animated GIF.

Although the primary use of the GIF, JPEG, and PNG images is for alternative images (when the user does not have the plug-in), you can also use it to create image maps from your Flash movies. The section "Using the Publish Command" discusses this in more detail.

When the GIF, JPEG, or PNG options are selected in the Format tab, use the Ad 5 Banner template option in the HTML tab so that the appropriate HTML code is added to the generated HTML file. Note that you will usually only generate one type of image, not all three at once.

The alternate image generated from Flash is only necessary for Netscape browsers that do not have the plug-in. If Internet Explorer does not have the ActiveX component to interpret the Flash element, it will automatically prompt the user to obtain the plug-in. Consequently, it will automatically show the broken link.

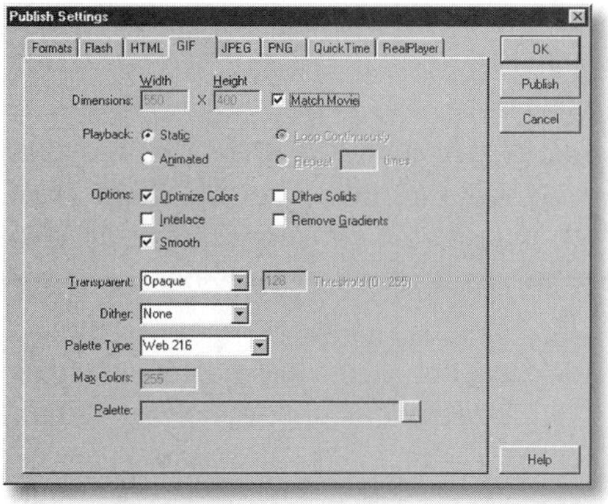

Figure 9-8 The GIF tab is used to define the static or animated GIF that will be automatically generated.

If you selected the GIF image option in the Formats tab, the GIF tab is used to define the properties of the file that will be generated, as shown in figure 9-8. As with the size of the embedded SWF file, you begin by defining the dimensions of the image. You then establish whether you want to use a Static or Animated GIF. If you choose Animated, you can control the number of loops it plays by either selecting the Loop Continuously option or by entering a number of repetitions.

## The GIF Format and Options

There are three things you should note about using animated GIFs. First, Graphic Interchange Format (GIF) is a graphic file format limited to 256 colors. Thus, you have to define the color characteristics for the file in the lower part of the dialog box. Consequently, the color fidelity of your images will not be as robust as that you see in Flash. Options related to color fidelity are discussed shortly.

Second, because animated GIFs consist of raster or bitmap images, the files generated may be quite large, particularly if your Flash movie is very lengthy. Watch your file sizes. It is safe to assume that if a user does not have the Flash plug-in, he or she may be a home user and will likely be connecting via a slower modem connection.

Finally, GIF is the only format that provides animation capability. Although free of many of GIF's weaknesses, JPEG and PNG files cannot store multiple images. They cannot be used for animation. If you want an animated image as an alternative to the SWF file, you must deal with the color limitations of the GIF format.

Other important options shown in figure 9-8 include the following specifications, which affect how the GIF file is generated, as well as how it is saved. Many of these options deal with reducing the colors of the image or animation down to a set of 256 that GIF can define.

- Optimize Colors attempts to reduce the number of odd colors found in the image. By reducing outlier colors via averaging, the colors of the image can be more easily made to fit the 256-color restriction of GIF.

- Dither solids attempts to reduce colors by replacing solid colors with dithered complements as much as possible. This reduces the total number of colors required by the image.

- Interlace allows you to specify that the GIF file is written so that it can be progressively viewed during download. Progressive images give the perception that the file downloads from the Web more quickly. Interlacing images neither increases nor decreases file size significantly.

- Much like the Dither Solids checkbox, Remove Gradients attempts to replace gradients with dithered combinations of color to reduce the number of colors required by the image.

- Smooth anti-aliases vector elements before creating the GIF file.

- Transparent provides the ability to select a color or colors (using Threshold) that will be transparent. Keep in mind that GIF transparency is 1-bit, meaning that a pixel can only be 100 percent transparent or 100 percent opaque. The Transparent option sets the background of the image to 100 transparent. The Threshold option allows you to choose a number between 0 and 255. Any color in the image with luminosity falling below the number entered will be assigned as transparent.

- Because GIF files can only contain 256-colors, Flash must reduce the colors in the image. The Dither option makes the resulting color reduction less noticeable by dithering adjacent pixels. By default, no dithering occurs. The Ordered option presents a patterned replacement, whereas Diffusion presents a fractal or random replacement. Generally, Diffusion will provide the best results.

- When developing images for the Web, you must acknowledge that some users may be limited to a 256-color display. When this is the case, the browser uses a default set of colors, called the Web or browser-safe palette, to display all images. Any color used by an image that is not in the Web palette is interpolated to the closest available color that is in the palette. This means that colors that do not exist in the palette will not display as you designed them. Use the Palette Type option to assign the palette to be used for the 256-color image. The Web 216 option should be used if you are likely to encounter users browsing at 8-bit (256-color). The Web 216 option is the palette of browser-safe colors and will force the generated GIF image to use only those colors. If you are not limited by your audience's display, you can use the Adaptive option, which generates a palette of colors from the colors needed in the image. The Web Snap Adaptive option yields colors that are an intermixing between those generated by Adaptive and those that exist in the browser-safe palette. The Custom option allows you to load Photoshop ACT (Swatch) files for use as the image's palette.

## The JPEG Tab

As you have already learned, the Joint Photographic Experts Group (JPEG) format uses a lossy compression scheme. Within the JPEG tab, shown in figure 9-9, you set the dimensions for the image to be generated, as well as the quality of compression. Higher numbers equate to lower compression, larger file sizes, and more visually pleasing images. Lower numbers equate to higher compression, smaller files, and less pleasing images. The Progressive checkbox can be used to create an interlaced JPEG image. Much like the interlaced GIF, progressive JPEG images appear to download more quickly because they can be instantaneously read even though the entire image has not been downloaded.

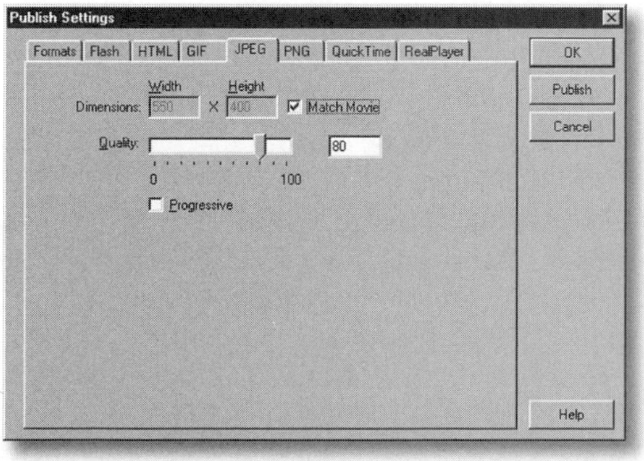

*Figure 9-9  The JPEG tab is used to define the parameters for the generated JPEG image.*

## The PNG Tab

The Portable Network Graphics (PNG, pronounced "ping") format is a relatively

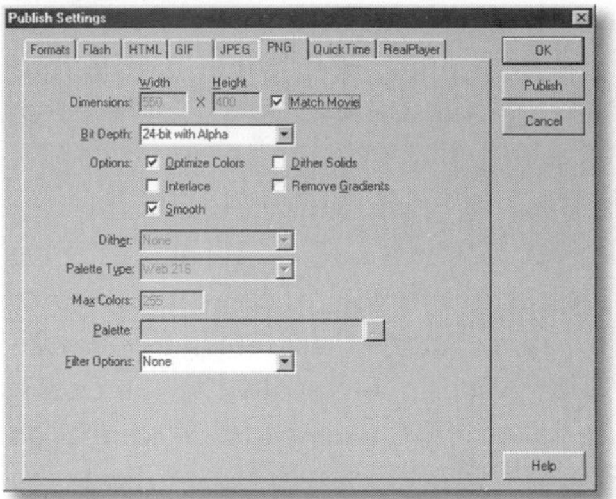

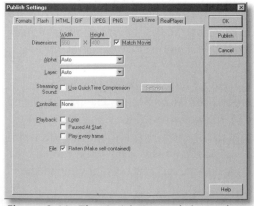

*Figure 9-10 PNG provides most of the features of GIF and JPEG, except for GIF's multiple image capability.*

new format to the Web. Developed as a response to developers wanting a patent-free format, it provides most of the capabilities of GIF and JPEG in one format. Again, it does not support multiple images (animation).

The PNG tab, shown in figure 9-10, contains most of the controls found in the GIF and JPEG tabs. The primary difference between PNG and JPEG images is that PNG's compression is a lossless scheme. This means that PNG's compression does not lose data and creates an exact replica of the original file when uncompressed.

Different, too, are the color capabilities of the PNG format. PNG can contain 24-bit data or 8-bit data. Realistically, GIF is limited to 256, whereas JPEG is usually limited to near 24-bit data. Thus, PNG can do both, and you will find that the Bit Depth drop-down found in the PNG tab allows you to select either. The color options found at the bottom of the dialog box are enabled only when you select the 8-bit option from the Bit Depth drop-down menu.

## The QuickTime Tab

As shown in figure 9-11, the QuickTime tab provides control over several aspects of the resulting digital video movie. As with other tabs, Dimensions specifies the image size for the video clip. The Alpha drop-down permits you to define portions of the Flash movie as transparent. This is useful if you decide to composite generated QuickTime movies in other packages and technologies. The Layer drop-down lets you set the layer on which the SWF information will reside.

Although Flash uses its own compression techniques for audio, the Use QuickTime Compression option allows you to choose from any one of the many QuickTime-accessible compressors that may be on your machine. Codecs (short for compressors/decompressors) such as Sorenson, QDesign, or Qualcomm can be chosen. If you are a digital video developer as well, you will find that the ability to use QuickTime's compressors may provide more flexibility and possibly better compression. The remaining checkboxes within the QuickTime tab are standard elements you can control:

*Figure 9-11 The QuickTime tab is used to define the parameters for the MOV file generated.*

- Use the Controller drop-down to select the type of control you would like for the movie to display. Options include None (No Controller), Standard, and QTVR.

- Loop and Paused at Start are self-explanatory.

- Use Play Every Frame to ensure that graphic components of the QuickTime clip are not dropped to attain synchronization.

- The File option allows you to flatten the generated movie. When working on the Macintosh, QuickTime movies can be made to store data outside the QuickTime movie. This increases playback performance. For movies to be cross-platform, however, make sure you use the Flatten checkbox.

## The RealPlayer Tab

As mentioned earlier, the ability to output RealPlayer files from Flash is a new feature. When the RealPlayer option is selected in the Formats tab, the RealPlayer tab appears in the Publish settings, as shown in figure 9-12.

Keep in mind that the Flash tab's version drop-down must be set to Flash 4 for you to be able to output RealPlayer versions of your file. Additionally, end users viewing those files must have version 8 of the RealPlayer. The RealPlayer tab provides access to the following controls:

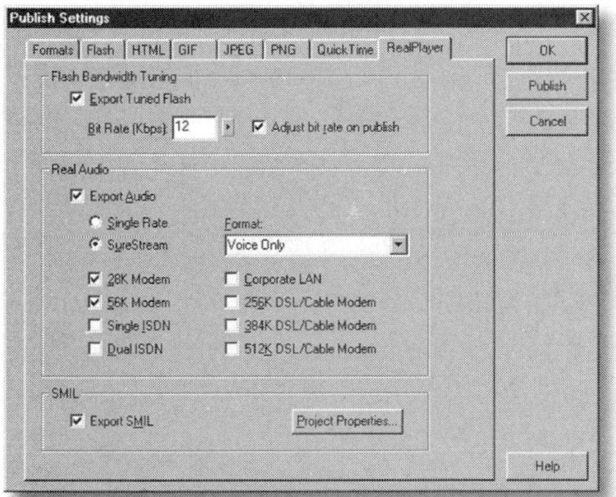

- Flash Bandwidth Tuning allows you to define the bit rate used for delivery of the Flash file. Choose a higher bit rate for faster connections, and a lower bit rate for slower connections.

- RealPlayer files excel at being able to deliver content based on user connection speeds. RealPlayer uses content negotiation to determine the user's connection speed, and then delivers content appropriate for the end user. The Export Audio section allows you define the speeds that will be included or "targeted" by the player.

*Figure 9-12 Use the RealPlayer tab to set the options for the generation of RealPlayer files.*

- The Export SMIL checkbox allows you to generate a SMIL (pronounced "smile"), Synchronized Multimedia Integration Language, file. SMIL is a markup language that allows you to define multimedia presentations consisting of a variety of elements using an HTML-like language. For more information on SMIL, see *http://www.w3.org/AudioVideo/*.

## The Generator Tab

If you have access to a server that is running Macromedia Generator, you will find that the Generator checkbox (in the Formats tab) is available.

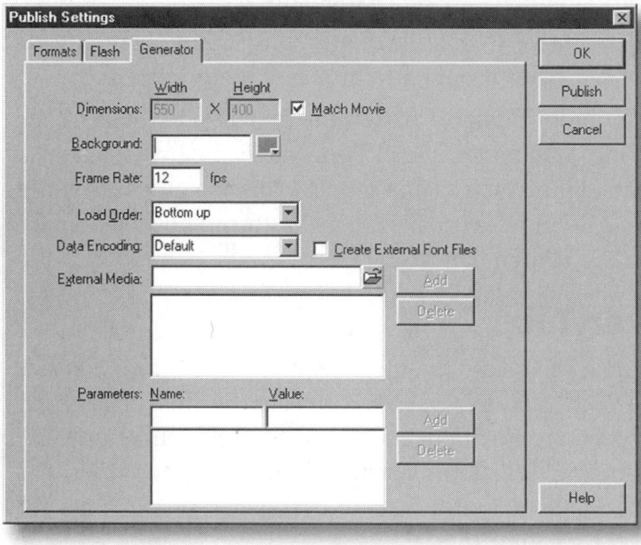

Generator allows you to create Flash movies that are templates; that is, Flash movies that are customizable in that they receive data from other sources (such as databases, Java applets, and so on) at run-time. Flash's Publish command allows you to generate Flash templates for use with Generator, the output options for which are revealed in the Generator tab, shown in figure 9-13.

The Dimensions and Load Order options shown in the Generator tab are similar to those found in the Flash tab, and function similarly. The Background and Frame Rate options are similar to the corresponding items in the Modify | Movie Properties dialog box. All four of these items override settings in the Flash tab and the Movie Properties. The other options in the Generator tab include:

*Figure 9-13 The Generator tab provides access to settings for templates.*

- Data Encoding, which determines the encoding method used when the template sends or receives data from external sources such as databases or Java applets.

- Create External Font Files tells Generator to create font files for the respective Flash template. With certain versions of Generator, font files can be cached to increase performance.

- When using Generator, Flash templates can dynamically import and use symbols from external sources. The External Media section specifies the name of the template that contains the symbols you want to use.

- The Parameters section of the dialog box is where you define variables to be used for remote testing.

## ■ ■ ■ Using the Publish Command

Once you have established the Publish settings, selecting the File | Publish menu option generates the selected files. The generated files will be created in the same directory as the Flash FLA file, with the names defined in the Formats tab of the Publish Settings dialog box. Again, remember that it is vital that you name your files with extensions.

 **WARNING:** As soon as you select the Publish menu option from either the File menu or the Publish Settings dialog box, the respective files are generated. There is no prompt asking if you are sure you want to publish. This is true even if a series of files with the same names already exists in the current directory. Be careful you do not overwrite files you want to keep.

# ▪ ▪ ▪ Writing HTML

Although this section is not intended to be an extensive HTML indoctrination, knowing enough HTML to be able to integrate a Shockwave element is straightforward. The two main tags used to integrate Shockwave movies in HTML are <EMBED> and <OBJECT>. The difference between these two may not be readily apparent because both are a means of integration.

Yet, it boils down to what is used to support the Shockwave element in the browser (as far as software components are concerned) and which browser is being used. The difference between the <EMBED> tag and the <OBJECT> tag really centers on implementation. Both tags can also be used for media elements other than Shockwave.

## Embed Versus Object

To successfully integrate a Shockwave Flash movie into a page so that it will work on both Netscape and Internet Explorer requires the use of both the <EMBED> and the <OBJECT> tags. The <EMBED> tag forces the browser to use a plug-in to support the Shockwave element, whereas the <OBJECT> tag forces the browser to use an ActiveX control.

Thus, the <EMBED> tag provides the needed information for Netscape, which uses only plug-ins, and the <OBJECT> tag provides the necessary information for Internet Explorer, which predominantly uses ActiveX components. Both tags are used simultaneously within one another so that, regardless of browser, only one of the two linked Shockwave files is displayed in the page.

## Plug-ins Versus ActiveX Components

"What is the difference between a plug-in and an ActiveX component," you may ask. Both plug-ins and ActiveX components are designed to extend the capabilities of HTML because alone the browser supports only JPEG and GIF images. Through add-on software components (plug-ins and ActiveX components), developers can add almost any type of media element, not the least of which is Shockwave.

Basically, the difference between plug-ins and ActiveX components relates to scope. Plug-ins are software components that can be used only by the browser. End users download and install a plug-in, which is added to the browser itself. ActiveX components, on the other hand, are much broader in scope. When an ActiveX component is installed to the user's computer, it becomes part of the operating system (Windows). Thus, ActiveX components can be used by (at least theoretically) all applications on the system because they are installed at the system level rather than the application level.

Microsoft's vision was to increase the scope of extensibility by allowing its version of the plug-in (the ActiveX component) to be used in every application, not just the browser. Although the implementation of ActiveX components in applications other than the browser can be tricky, it is an inventive concept nonetheless.

To integrate a Flash file into your web page, use the <OBJECT> and <EMBED> tags within the <BODY> section of the web page. Internet Explorer interprets the <OBJECT> information and ignores the <EMBED> information. Netscape ignores the <OBJECT> information and reads the <EMBED> information. Therefore, it does not matter which browser you are using; only one Flash element will be inserted into the browser. Additionally, depending on what is contained within the Flash file, you may use a variety of attributes within the tags, as discussed further in the next section. Code example 9-1, which follows, provides a basic implementation.

## Code Example 9-1  Use of <EMBED> and <OBJECT> Tags to Integrate Flash Files in HTML

```
<HTML>
 <HEAD>
  <TITLE>A Simple Example</TITLE>
 </HEAD>
 <BODY>
  <CENTER>
  <OBJECT ID="shadow" classid="clsid:D27CDB6E-AE6D-11cf-96B8-
444553540000"codebase="http://active.macromedia.com/flash2/cabs/swflash.
cab#version=5,0,0,0" width="250" height="300">
  <PARAM NAME="Movie" VALUE="ch9-03.swf">
  <PARAM NAME="Quality" VALUE="High">
  <PARAM NAME="Loop" VALUE="TRUE">
  <PARAM NAME="Play" VALUE="TRUE">
  <EMBED NAME="shadow" src="ch9-03.swf" type="application/x-shockwave-
```

```
flash" width="250" height="300" Quality="high" Play="true"
loop="true"PLUGINSPAGE=
"http://www.macromedia.com/shockwave/download/index.cgi?P1_Prod_Version=
ShockwaveFlash">
    </EMBED>
    <NOEMBED>
     <IMG src="ch9-01.gif" width=250 height=300>
    </NOEMBED>
    </OBJECT>
  </BODY>
</HTML>
```

The following CD-ROM exercise makes use of the code shown in code example 9-1. In this exercise, you will enter the code into Notepad (or other text editor) and then save the file and open it in a browser. Further notes on the code contained in code example 9-1 follow the exercise.

 *CD-ROM Exercise*

Open the file *ch9-03.swf* located in the *F5gai/chapter9/* folder, installed from the companion CD-ROM. Enter the code shown in code example 9-1 into Notepad or another ASCII text editor. Then save the file with the .HTML extension, place it in the same location as the SWF file, and open it in a browser to see the results.

Take a look at the code shown in code example 9-1. Notice how the typical HTML sections are defined:

- < HTML > ... < /HTML > defines the document as an HTML document.

- < HEAD > ... < /HEAD > is known as the header. Miscellaneous document settings are presented here, such as the title that will appear in the browser's title bar.

- < BODY > ... < /BODY > is the actual content that will be rendered in the browser.

This simple web page contains nothing but the Flash element that is integrated with the < OBJECT > and < EMBED > tags. The < OBJECT > tag contains the relevant information for Internet Explorer. The optional parameters, listed as < PARAM > statements, control settings such as the display quality, looping, and autoplay for the Flash file. The < EMBED > tag contains the information pertinent to Netscape browsers. There should be congruency between the parameters set for the < OBJECT > tag and the attributes within the < EMBED > tag. Often a similarity will exist between these two; however, some optional settings may apply to only one browser or the other.

Keep in mind that HTML is not case sensitive. The only exception to this rule is embedded URLs, such as the URL assigned as the CODEBASE in the <OBJECT> tag and the URL assigned as the PLUGINSPAGE in the <EMBED> tag. All URLs in HTML are case sensitive.

 **TIP:** *As far as HTML code is concerned, it is a good idea to adopt some sort of consistent method of capitalization for readability.*

One of the most critical things you should notice in the implementation in code example 9-1 is that the <EMBED> tag is nested within the opening and closing <OBJECT> tags. This makes the scheme work. It is due to this nesting that Internet Explorer or Netscape Communicator/Navigator ignores the opposing command (<EMBED> and <OBJECT>, respectively). If the <EMBED> is not encased within the <OBJECT> tag, errors or two Flash representations may be rendered in the resulting HTML page.

The last thing you should notice is the <NOEMBED> tag. This tag provides backward compatibility for older browsers, as well as browsers that do not have the plug-in. If you are manually coding your pages, do not forget this tag. Although you will have to manually create the associated GIF file, the <NOEMBED> tag provides a mechanism for supporting rather than eliminating a portion of the web audience.

## EMBED Attributes/Object Parameters

The previous section discussed a simple implementation of the <OBJECT> and <EMBED> tags for Flash elements. Depending on the features your files use, you may need to add more or less optional parameters for your Flash files. Some of the optional settings apply to a particular browser only. Thus, some apply to <OBJECT> only or to <EMBED> only. Table 9-1 shows the settings that can be used with both the <OBJECT> and <EMBED> tags. The various parameters and attributes of the <OBJECT> and <EMBED> tags are specified in HTML documents. The required parameters in the table are denoted with an asterisk (*). The remaining settings are optional, but they are frequently included.

Table 9-1 *Various parameters and attributes of the <OBJECT> and <EMBED> tags specified in HTML documents*

| < OBJECT > | < EMBED > | Function | Description |
|---|---|---|---|
| MOVIE* | SRC* | Provides the URL for the Flash movie that is being included. | Can include both relative and absolute references. |
| WIDTH* | WIDTH* | Defines the width of the Flash movie window. | Can be specified as a fixed pixel size or a percentage. |
| HEIGHT* | HEIGHT* | Defines the height of the Flash movie window. | Can be specified as a fixed pixel size or a percentage. |
| CLASSID*, CODEBASE* | PLUGINSPAGE* | Provides the URL and information for acquiring the ActiveX component or plug-in. | CLASSID is specified as a version number, CODEBASE and PLUGINSPAGE are defined as URLs. |
| ID | NAME | Specifies a name for the element for scripting. | Permits the object to be controlled via scripting. |
| N/A | SWLIVECONNECT | Specifies whether Java should be loaded when the Flash Player loads. | A TRUE setting forces Java to load. FALSE prevents Java from loading. This is required for use of FS Commands and JavaScript. |
| N/A | MAYSCRIPT | Identifies that the object may use scripting. | MAYSCRIPT="MAYSCRIPT" is required to use JavaScript and FS Command actions. |
| PLAY | PLAY | Determines whether the movie plays automatically. | True causes the movie to play after the first frame is loaded. False stops the movie at the first frame. |
| LOOP | LOOP | Determines whether movie loops when it reaches the last frame. | True causes the movie to loop. False cause the movie to stop on the last frame. |
| QUALITY | QUALITY | Controls the display quality of the movie during playback. | Options include Autohigh, Autolow, High and Low described earlier in this chapter. Best is an undocumented value that allows the Flash Player to choose the quality based upon performance at playback. |
| BGCOLOR | BGCOLOR | Determines the background color of the movie. Note that this attribute is used it will override. the background color assigned in the movie. | Six digit hexadecimal values are entered, two values representing each of the RGB. components. See Appendix E for more information. |
| SCALE | SCALE | Determines how the movie resizes to fit the space allocated by the browser (area defined by HEIGHT and WIDTH). | Can include SHOWALL, NO BORDER, and EXACT FIT described earlier in this chapter. |
| SALIGN | SALIGN | When the movie's aspect ratio does not match the area aspect ration, this controls the placement of the movie within the area. | Options include T, B, L, R, TL, TR, BL and BR described earlier in this chapter. |
| BASE | BASE | Defines a reference URL/address for relative URLs in a movie (similar to the BASEREF HTML attribute). | The value is defined as a URL from which all other relative URLs are based. |
| MENU | MENU | Defines what options appear in the context menu when the user right clicks on a flash movie in a web page. | A value of TRUE displays all the menu option and a value of FALSE displays the About Flash 5.0 option only. |
| WMODE | N/A | Provides additional features in Internet Explorer 4.0, including positioning, layering, and transparency. | Options include WINDOW, OPAQUE and TRANSPARENT. Window is the default wherein the movie simply plays in its window. OPAQUE allows objects to pass behind the opaque Flash movie. TRANSPARENT allows objects to pass behind a Flash movie whose background area is transparent. |

In Chapter 15, nearly all of these attributes are used on one way or another. The ID, NAME, SWLIVECONNECT, and MAYSCRIPT tags are of particular utility because they allow you to use JavaScript and VBScript to control Flash movies in web pages.

 **NOTE:** *Chapter 16 discusses the ID, NAME, SWLIVECONNECT, and MAYSCRIPT tags in depth, with applied examples.*

# ▪▪▪ Working with Publish Templates

One of the most interesting features of the Publish command is the ability to use and create templates for integration. Realizing that getting an SWF file into a page is sometimes laborious, Macromedia has attempted to make it easier to get your pages onto the Web.

When you select the HTML tab in the Publish Settings dialog box, you will note that there are several default templates available in the Template drop-down menu. Because coding different functionality requires different tags and scripting, there are several templates. For example, if you use the FS Command action in your movie, special tags are required in the web page. Thus, there is a template for Flash with FS Command. However, if you do not use FS Command, the simple Flash Only template may be all you need. The Templates provided in the Publish Settings include the following:

- Ad 3 Banner creates an HTML file that embeds a version 3 SWF file into the page. Note that features of Flash 4 will be disabled. Flash 3 with Image also incorporates intelligent code that determines if the user has the plug-in. If the user does not have the plug-in, a < NOEMBED > tag that is included causes a GIF, JPG, or PNG image to be displayed instead. When selecting this template, you must make sure you select SWF, HTML, and one of the image options (GIF, JPEG, or PNG) in the Formats tab.

- Ad 4 Banner is identical to the Flash 3 with Image, except that it uses a version 4 SWF file. It also requires that the SWF, HTML, and one of the image options be selected in the Formats tab.

- Ad 5 Banner is the same as the prior two except that it uses a Flash 5 file.

- Flash Only Default includes the tags ( < EMBED > and < OBJECT > ) for integrating the SWF file into the web page with no additional coding.

- Flash with FS Command includes the tags (Embed and Object) that integrate the SWF file into the web page. It also sets up a scripting section in the header of the HTML file for detecting the FS Command action used within the Flash movie. Even so, manual coding is required to create the functionality called by the FS Command option. Manual coding is discussed in detail in Chapter 16.

- The Template listing includes several specific templates for use with Generator.

- Most often, image maps are generated using small utility programs. Yet, with the Image Map template, you can quickly create image maps using Flash. The HTML file created contains no link to the generated SWF file. Instead, the created GIF, JPEG, or PNG file is defined in the HTML file as a client-side image map. If the Flash file has buttons, the buttons become the hot links defined in the map area.

- The Java Player template creates the code that includes the SWF file as a Java Applet instead of a compiled Flash file (Applet tag). Applets are effective in situations where a major portion of the audience does not have the plug-in. Yet, realize that Java Applets, because they are interpreted rather than compiled, start up more slowly than SWF files played by the Flash Player.

- The QuickTime option, similar to the Java Player option, uses a QT4 file instead of a Flash SWF file. The code generated in the page uses the < EMBED > tag to include the QuickTime 4 file. To successfully use this option you must ensure that QuickTime 4 is installed and that you select the QuickTime checkbox in the Formats tab.

- The User Choice template includes any and all coding that may be required by any Flash SWF file in the HTML file. When you use this template, you can go back and manually edit the ASCII HTML file in an editor such as Notepad or Simpletext to remove the coding you do not need.

In addition to the variety of templates provided, you can generate your own templates for use in the Publish Settings dialog box. The files used in the Template drop-down are contained in the *Program Files/Macromedia/Flash 5/HTML* folder on the PC. The location is similar on the Macintosh within the Flash folder.

# Examining and Creating Templates

The HTML files used in the Template capability are special in that they use special characters to represent values substituted during the Publish command. These special characters are a combination of the dollar sign symbol ($) and other alphanumeric characters. Thus, they are "custom" HTML files, but follow the general rules of normal HTML files.

To see what these files look like, open the *Default.html* file located in the *Macromedia/Flash 5/HTML* directory into an ASCII editor. The code for the Default template is shown in code example 9-2. Notice the token values represented by the dollar signs ($). These values are replaced when the Publish command is executed.

---

### Code Example 9-2  Default Template File Used in the Publish Settings Dialog Box

```
$TTFlash Only (Default)
$DS
Use an OBJECT and EMBED tag to display Flash.
$DF
<HTML>
<HEAD>
<TITLE>$TI</TITLE>
</HEAD>
<BODY bgcolor="$BG">
<!- URL's used in the movie->
$MU
<!- text used in the movie->
$MT
<OBJECT classid="clsid:D27CDB6E-AE6D-11cf-96B8-444553540000"
codebase="http://active.macromedia.com/flash2/cabs/swflash.cab
#version=5,0,0,0" WIDTH=$WI HEIGHT=$HE>
$PO
<EMBED $PE WIDTH=$WI HEIGHT=$HE TYPE="application/x-shockwave-
flash" PLUGINSPAGE="http://www.macromedia.com/shockwave/
download/index.cgi?P1_Prod_Version=ShockwaveFlash"></EMBED>
</OBJECT>
</BODY>
</HTML>
```

In code example 9-2, note the first two lines. The first line, preceded by $TT, is the name of the Template as it will be shown in the Publish Settings dialog box. Note the second line, which begins with $DS and ends with $DF. The text between will be shown when the Template Info button is selected in the Publish Settings dialog box.

Using the substitution values, you can create your own templates to be used within the Publish Command. You can copy the existing files and use them as a starting place, or write your own from scratch. Table 9-2 shows the token characters used with the template HTML files and the values they represent. Once you have created a template, all you need do is copy it to the *Macromedia/Flash 5/HTML* directory to begin using it. Its name will appear in the Template drop-down in the Publish Settings dialog box.

*Table 9-2 Symbol Combinations Used as Placeholders Within HTML Template Files*

| Name | Symbol | Associated With... |
|---|---|---|
| Template Title | $TT | Template Definition |
| Template Description Start | $DS | Template Definition |
| Template Description Finish | $DF | Template Definition |
| Movie Width | $WI | Embed/Object WIDTH attribute/parameter |
| Movie Height | $HE | Embed/Object HEIGHT attribute/parameter |
| Movie Source | $MO | Embed/Object SRC attribute/parameter |
| HTML Alignment | $HA | Embed/Object ALIGN attribute/parameter |
| Looping | $LO | Embed/Object LOOP attribute/parameter |
| Parameters for OBJECT | $PO | Location for the OBJECT parameters to be written in the HTML |
| Attributes for EMBED | $PE | Location for the EMBED attributes to be written in the HTML |
| Play | $PL | Embed/Object PLAY attribute/parameter |
| Movie Quality | $QU | Embed/Object QUALITY attribute/parameter |
| Movie Scale | $SC | Embed/Object SCALE attribute/parameter |
| Movie Alignment | $SA | Embed/Object SALIGN attribute/parameter |
| Movie Device Font | $DE | Embed/Object DEVICEFONT attribute/parameter |
| Movie Background Color | $BG | Embed/Object BGCOLOR attribute/parameter |
| Image Width | $IW | IMG tag WIDTH attribute |
| Image Height | $IH | IMG tag HEIGHT attribute |
| Image Source | $IS | IMG tag SRC attribute |
| Image Map Name | $IU | IMG tag USEMAP attribute |
| Image Map Tag Location | $IM | MAP and AREA tags (used for client-side image mapping) |
| Movie Text (location in HTML file to write movie text) | $MT | Flash movie text insertion point; test insert into HTML comment tags <!— —> |
| Movie URLs (location in HTML file to write movie URLs) | &MU | Flash movie URL list insertion point; text inserted as blank anchor tags |
| QuickTime Width | $QW | EMBED WIDTH of the QuickTime element |
| QuickTime Height | $QH | EMBED HEIGTH of the QuickTime element |
| QuickTime Filename | $QN | EMBED SRC movie file name |
| GIF Width | $GW | WIDTH specified in <IMG> tag |
| GIF Height | $GH | HEIGHT specified in <IMG> tag |
| GIF Filename | $GS | SRC specified in <IMG> tag |
| JPEG Width | $JW | WIDTH specified in <IMG> tag |
| JPEG Height | $JH | HEIGHT specified in <IMG> tag |
| JPEG Filename | $JN | SRC specified in <IMG> tag |
| PNG Width | $PW | WIDTH specified in <IMG> tag |
| PNG Height | $PH | HEIGHT specified in <IMG> tag |
| PNG Filename | $PN | SRC specified in <IMG> tag |
| Generator Variables OBJECT Tag | $GV | Variables specified as OBJECT parameters |
| Generator Variables EMBED Tag | $GE | Variables specified as EMBED attributes |

# ▪ ▪ ▪ Streaming, Testing, and Playback

As mentioned earlier, Flash SWF files are a streaming file format. This means that the playback of files can begin before the file is completely downloaded. In reality, for the Flash Player to play any frame, all of the elements used in that frame (including vector shapes, bitmaps, and event sounds) must be downloaded.

Although there are many fast connections on the Web, streaming is limited by the slowest connection through which the downloaded frame data must travel. Often, the slowest connection is the user's computer. Network traffic or other variables can also affect this "link." Nevertheless, the speed of the end user's connection often dictates what is reasonably deliverable.

Thus, it is vitally important to closely examine the content of your movies to make sure that the end user perceives what you do. Flash provides a couple of tools that make examining movies much easier, which are described in material to follow.

The perceived effectiveness of Flash's streaming capability during playback depends solely on the amount of data required to render each frame. For smooth playback, the size of the data for each frame should be as small as possible. This is performed through analysis and optimization.

Additionally, the amount of time required to download a series of frames should take no longer than the amount of time required to play those frames. When it takes longer to download a series of frames than to play it back, noticeable pauses or gaps may appear in the presentation, and likely where you do not want them to occur. The goal in analysis and optimization is to reduce any lapses, or at least to control when those lapses occur.

Before you can control or prevent pauses in your presentation, first figure out where they might occur. The next two sections provide a detailed look at the facilities within Flash that allow you to identify potential problems related to downloading and playback.

## Closely Examining the Size Report

One of the two most import features for creating efficient and effective movies is the Size Report option. When you export an SWF file from Flash, you have the option of generating an ASCII text file that provides valuable information about the file. Use Size Report to help you figure out where the bandwidth intensive portions of your file are, as well as information concerning where some "fat" could be trimmed away.

## CD-ROM Exercise

Open the file *ch9-4.fla* located in the *F5gai/chapter9* folder, installed from the companion CD-ROM. To practice generating a size report, perform the following steps.

1. Select File | Export movie.

2. Name the SWF file that will be created.

3. In the Export Movie dialog box, make sure that Generate Size Report is selected.

4. An ASCII text file will reside in the same location as the generated SWF file.

5. Open this into any ASCII text editor, such as NotePad or SimpleText. The generate file should look similar to code example 9-3. The size report for the simulated shadow Flash file (*ch9-04.fla*) allows you to perform extensive frame examination.

## Code Example 9-3  Size Report for the Simulated Shadow Flash File

```
Movie Report
------------

Frame #    Frame Bytes   Total Bytes   Page
-------    -----------   -----------   ---------------

1             1214        1214          Scene 1
Page                      Shape Bytes   Text Bytes
------------------------  -----------   ----------

Scene 1                        0             0
Symbol                    Shape Bytes   Text Bytes
------------------------  -----------   ----------

Broken Piece 1            150             0
Broken Piece 2            168             0
Broken Piece 3            162             0
Dot                        75             0
Ellipse                    80             0
Rotating                    0             0
Sphere                    114             0
Sphere Movie                0             0
```

The size report generates a frame-by-frame examination of the file, showing entries for Frame Number, Frame Bytes, Total Bytes, and Page (see code example 9-3). The Frame Bytes section reports the number of bytes required for download before the frame can play. Because this sample movie has a movie clip inserted into the main timeline and has only one frame, one frame is reported. This example was used for brevity to show the format of a size report.

In addition to the frame-by-frame information, Flash also reports the total file size of each scene and the file sizes of each symbol. Because this example file is quite brief, there is not much "fat" to trim from the file.

 **CD-ROM NOTE:** *Look at a more complex example to see how the size report can be used to find out where the most bandwidth will be needed. To do this, generate a size report for the file* ch9-05.fla *located in the* F5gai/chapter9/ *folder, installed from the companion CD-ROM. Use the sample file to generate your own size report, or follow along with the explanation in the book.*

The following size report has been broken into "chunks," omitting the irrelevant portions. To see the entire report, generate an SWF file using the file *ch9-05.fla* located in the *F5gai/chapter9/* folder, installed from the companion CD-ROM. Make sure to select Generate Size Report in the Export Movie dialog box.

Code example 9-4 shows a portion of the frame-by-frame report from a much larger Flash movie. The movie uses a streaming sound, so the Frame Bytes entry associated with each frame is somewhat larger than the previous example. Notice in code example 9-4 that frame 19 has a spike and requires much more data than the previous frames. During testing under target conditions, this spike may indicate a place where there is a lag or problem during playback. If such problems occur during testing, revision of the content of the frame may be necessary, such as optimizing curves (or other techniques).

## *Code Example 9-4  Partial Report with Spikes in Data*

```
Movie Report
- - - - - - - - - - -

Frame #   Frame Bytes   Total Bytes   Page
- - - - - -   - - - - - - - - - -   - - - - - - - - - - -   - - - - - - - - - -
      1         1190          1190      Scene 1
      2         1158          2348      2
      3         1158          3506      3
      4         1158          4664      4
      5         1158          5822      5
      6         1158          6980      6
      7         1158          8138      7
      8         1158          9296      8
      9         1158         10454      9
     10         1158         11612      10
     11         1158         12770      11
```

```
12        1158        13928        12
13        1158        15086        13
14        1158        16244        14
15        1158        17402        15
16        1158        18560        16
17        1158        19718        17
18        1158        20876        18
19        3878        24754        19
20        1158        25912        20
21        1158        27070        21
```

Code example 9-5 shows a more significant spike in the needed data. Take a closer look at frame 126 and notice that it is requiring a tremendous amount of data for playback. This frame may cause problems on slower machines and should be addressed and optimized. Ultimately, some data should be reduced if the file is to be delivered over the Web.

## Code Example 9-5  Frame 126 with High Data Requirement for Playback

```
124        1169        146897        124
125        1169        148066        125
126      192261        340327        126
127        1158        341485        127
128        1158        342643        128
```

Finally, as shown in code example 9-6, the required bytes for each of the bitmap and sound elements is presented (as is the required byte information for the symbol and font elements). The bitmap elements are the main contributors to the size of the file, because originally they were defined as Lossless in the library. Because these graphic elements only appear for a short time on screen, reducing their quality to JPEG = 50 will more than likely decrease the overall size of the file, as well as the bytes required for frame 126.

## Code Example 9-6 End of the Size Report

```
Bitmap                        Compressed  Original   Compression
----------------------        ----------  ----------  -----------
web2 copy.bmp                   30629      120000     Lossless
raster2 copy.bmp                45124      120000     Lossless
raster3 copy.bmp                36183      120000     Lossless
web1 copy.bmp                   24371      120000     Lossless
raster1 copy.bmp                52979      120000     Lossless
Stream sound: 22KHz Mono 5 bit ADPCM
```

```
Event sounds: 11KHz Stereo 5 bit ADPCM
Sound Name                    Bytes      Format
----------------------        --------   --------
sustain.wav                   110505     11KHz Stereo 5 bit ADPCM
```

Using the Size Report feature, you can easily troubleshoot and optimize your movies. By providing detailed information about your movie's media elements, you can visually determine the trouble spots and attempt to deliver quality appropriate for the given circumstance.

 **CD-ROM NOTE:** *To see the effect that reducing the bitmap qualities had on the resulting SWF files, open the file* ch9-06.fla *located in the* F5gai/chapter9/ *folder, installed from the companion CD-ROM. Generate a report. Compare this report to the report generated from the* file ch9-05.fla. *Although not all spikes in the data have been addressed, the main problem at frame 126 has been significantly reduced.*

## Bandwidth Profiling

The Bandwidth Profiler is the second tool that is quite valuable when you are preparing, testing, and optimizing your movies. A component of the Test Movie command, the Bandwidth Profiler shows a graphic of the amount of data required for the movie over time, as shown in figure 9-14. To turn on the Bandwidth Profiler, use Control | Test Movie to start the movie. Then use View | Bandwidth Profiler to view the profiler.

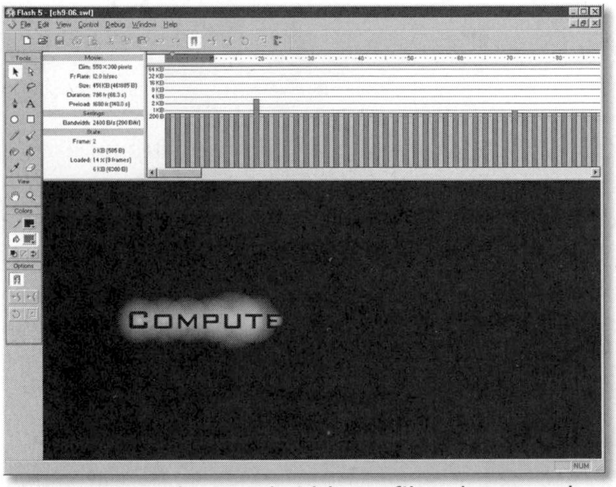

The most powerful feature of the Bandwidth Profiler is the View | Show Streaming option. This option provides a means of getting a more accurate simulation of performance over the Web because it takes into account the downloading of the file.

*Figure 9-14   The Bandwidth Profiler shows a chart representing the amount of data within each frame. (See also color plate B-12.)*

To use the View | Show Streaming option, select a data rate in the Debug menu. Use Control | Rewind and then View | Show Streaming (or Ctrl + Enter) instead of Play. The file will begin to play automatically once enough of the file has been downloaded, which is represented by the green bar.

The Show Streaming option, when selected, reveals a green bar at the top of the timeline in the Bandwidth Profiler. The bar represents how much data has been downloaded over time, using the connection setting in the Debug menu. Once enough of the file has been downloaded to start playback, the playhead begins to play the file while the green bar continues to move. If the playhead reaches the end of the green bar, you know for sure that there will be problems (a pause in the presentation) when the user views it over the Web. This is probably the most effective means of testing, aside from uploading the files to a live server for testing.

Let's examine this a little more closely. With the Bandwidth Profiler open, each bar in the graphic represents the amount of data for that frame, as shown in figure 9-15. The red line through the middle of the graph represents the current target data rate for the end user. Bars that extend above the red median indicate frames that will require greater download times.

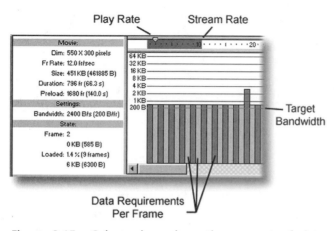
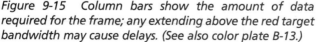

Also shown in figure 9-15 is the comparison of the play rate (represented by the playhead) to the stream rate (represented by a green bar). The stream rate is based on the current connection rate. In general, you do not want the playhead to overtake the stream rate during playback. The number of frames that extend beyond the target bandwidth (the number of frames whose data requirements are greater than the target bandwidth) determines if and when the play rate will overtake the stream rate.

*Figure 9-15   Column bars show the amount of data required for the frame; any extending above the red target bandwidth may cause delays. (See also color plate B-13.)*

If the playhead "runs into" the stream rate, the movie will pause. This is particularly problematic when streaming sound is involved. In these instances, provide extra time for the data to download by using preloading sequences, called *preloaders*.

 **NOTE:** *The next chapter discusses preloaded movies and how to create them.*

When using the Bandwidth Profiler, you may, at any point in the playback of the movie, click any bar in the profiler and access the frame. This allows you to determine which sections are the most data intensive. You can then return to the Flash movie and attempt to optimize the frame.

The View menu allows you to view by either a frame-by-frame graph or a streaming graph (the default). The streaming graph shows which frames may cause the movie to pause due to delayed download. The frame-by-frame graph visually illustrates the amount of data in each frame.

The Bandwidth Profiler allows you to specify several data rates, against which you can compare the content of the movie. Use the Debug menu to access various default modem settings (data rate settings). Select the Debug | Customize option to open the Custom Modem Settings dialog box, as shown in figure 9-16a. Or, you can add your own settings, as shown in figure 9-16b.

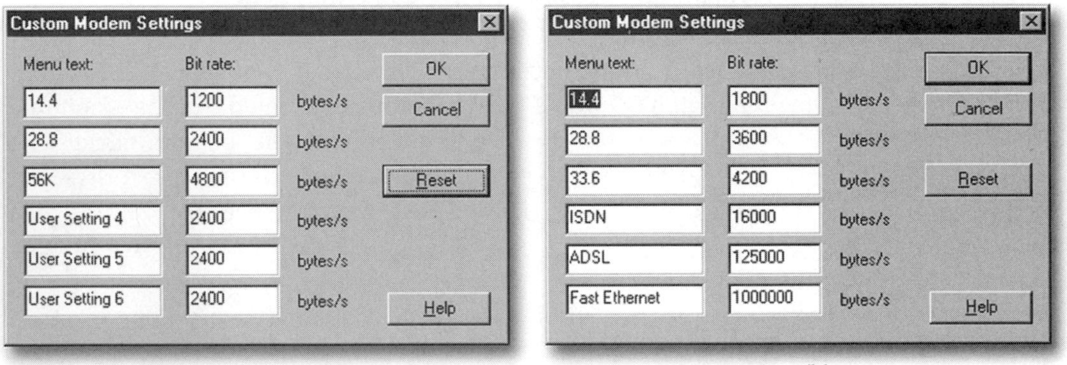

(a)                                              (b)

*Figure 9-16  Use the Bandwidth Profiler to (a) access the default modem settings (data rate settings) or (b) create your own custom settings using the Debug | Customize menu option.*

Again, to create movies that play seamlessly, the primary goal is to make sure the playhead of the movie never intercepts the streaming of data (that is, the normal flow of data from the server over the network connection). If the playhead overtakes the flow of data, the presentation will pause. Because there is no straight pipe from one computer to another on the Net, there will always be the possibility that the presentation may be interrupted. Yet, the Bandwidth Profiler and the Show Streaming options are among the best tools for minimizing the likelihood of this happening.

# ▪▪▪ Optimizing Your Files

A significant portion of this chapter has been devoted to finding problems in your presentation. Features such as the Bandwidth Profiler and the Show Streaming option are used to locate areas where optimization may be necessary. Nevertheless, you can do other things to optimize your files and reduce the data needed to play back your presentation.

In general, the weightiest items in your files will be bitmap images and sound files. Note that as you are constructing the vector elements in your file there are several additional things you can do to help reduce the overall file size. Although optimization of bitmaps and sound files will show the most dramatic effects on file size, optimizing even the vector elements is prudent. When dealing with web delivery, every little "bit" counts.

It is really never too early to start using the Test Movie, Bandwidth Profiler, and Show Streaming features. Often, most problem areas in a movie can be addressed much easier if they are caught early in the development. It is much more difficult to come back and try to optimize than it is to optimize during the process. Concurrent testing should be an integral part of development.

 **TIP:** *One overriding tip that always applies is to test early and test often.*

The sections that follow provide guidelines for maximizing the outcome of optimization. These sections include general tips and tips for bitmaps, audio snippets, and vector elements, which are among the largest contributors to file size.

## General Tips

The following are tips for maximizing the effect of optimization overall.

• Use shared libraries as much as is possible.

Shared libraries can provide a significant file size savings because they allow you to share symbols across multiple files, including sound, bitmap, and font symbols.

• Do not use or import too many fonts.

If you add a significant number of fonts to your files, you will find that your files grow quickly.

## Tips for Bitmaps

The following are tips for maximizing the effect of optimization regarding bitmaps.

• First and foremost, use bitmap images sparingly.

The more bitmaps you add to a Flash file, even with JPEG compression, the larger the file size. Use bitmaps only if they are necessary and cannot be easily achieved using vector components.

• Import bitmap images at sizes that are as small as possible.

Size your bitmaps to the exact size needed before importing them into Flash, just as you would if you were creating bitmaps for the Web. Do not import more data than you need.

• Reduce image quality as much as possible.

Unless complete resolution needs to be maintained, use JPEG compression in Flash. Because the JPEG compression algorithm discards a certain amount of data to attain smaller file sizes, JPEG compression should be used unless an exact representation of imported bitmap is needed in the presentation. Try various settings for the JPEG Quality to get the optimum size-to-quality ratio. Lossless should be used only if you must retain the exact visual quality and resolution of an image.

- Avoid animating bitmaps at all costs.

Like most multimedia authoring programs, bitmap images do not scale or rotate very well because of the real-time interpolation and extrapolation that must occur. Additionally, these operations require CPU time to render to the screen. Each time you rotate or scale a bitmap in Flash, you can expect some type of slowing in the playback, because the bitmap must be redrawn through each step.

- Reduce computation (playback) time by turning off the Smoothing option for an image.

In the Bitmap Properties in the library, you can speed up the rendering of bitmaps to the screen by deselecting the Smoothing checkbox. Although this should not affect file size, it will increase playback speed, depending on the size of the bitmap image.

- Watch the size report for spikes that may be a result of bitmap images.

As demonstrated with the example earlier in this chapter, one of the spikes in the size report was due to a series of bitmap images that flashed on the screen. After viewing the size report, quality was sacrificed for the sake of delivery. If you have a movie that has bitmaps in it, use the Size Report feature.

## Tips for Audio Snippets

The following are tips for maximizing the effect of optimization regarding audio snippets.

- Use the lowest sampling rate and bit depth required.

As mentioned in Chapter 7, the sampling rate, bit depth, and number of channels (mono versus stereo) can significantly impact the size of an audio clip, which is transferred to the Flash file. As with raster images, test various quality settings to find the optimal ratio of quality to file size.

- Brevity is the key to efficient and effective sounds.

Even though Flash offers ADPCM and MP3 compression, the longer the clip, the poorer the quality and the larger the compressed file. Try to loop sounds as much as possible. Looping is often a feasible alternative to a large, long-playing sound clip.

- Use the Size Report feature to locate spikes caused by sounds.

Event sounds do not play until they are loaded in their entirety. Thus, the size report of a movie often shows spikes before the playing of an event sound. Be cautious of bottlenecking caused by several event sounds (look at frame numbers near the location of keyframes that contain event sounds).

In some instances, consider using preload techniques, such as those discussed in the next chapter, to ensure that event sounds are loaded well before they are needed.

## Tips for Vector Elements

The following are tips for maximizing the effect of optimization regarding vector elements.

- Use symbols exclusively.

Anytime you have a set of repeating elements, even if they are only repeated once, they should be converted to a symbol. Grouped items, even though they act as a single unit, do not share the symbol's reusable nature. Copied groups add size to a file no matter how simple. Symbols should be used as frequently as possible.

- Use preload techniques to ensure symbol data is present when needed.

Flash can only render a frame if all of the frame components are downloaded. Similar to problems with bitmaps or audio, even some complex symbols (or having many symbols in a single frame) may cause the movie to pause while the symbol(s) is downloaded. The next chapter discusses some ingenious methods of making sure, through the use of preloading, that your symbols are present when needed.

- Use Flash's Modify | Optimize command.

Imported elements from Adobe Illustrator and other packages can often bring with them much extraneous information that is not really needed. This is indicative of many of the processes described in Chapter 11. Make sure to at least attempt to use the Optimize feature of Flash. Additionally, imported images can often be simplified by reducing the number of lines. Fills imported from other programs also frequently cause problems regarding file size. Inspect all of these options as you are working. Again, it is much easier to optimize an image the moment you import it, rather than waiting until it is animated and the movie is half completed.

- Avoid using too many complex tweening operations at a time.

Although tweening does not necessarily affect file size, it does affect playback. The more complex tweens you have, particularly motion and color effects, the greater chance you will have of significantly slowing playback. Additionally, moving or changing large areas of the screen can also be problematic. Be aware of how many effects you are accruing.

- Avoid breaking apart text or using too many curve modifications.

Breaking text apart converts outline text into individual line and arc components. The Lines to Fills, Expand Shape, and Soften Edge commands (found in the Modify | Curves submenu) all increase the number of vector elements in your movies. If at all possible, leave text as editable outlines. Be mindful also of the number of curve effects you use. Line and arc components and curve effects can dramatically affect file size.

# ∎ ∎ ∎  Summary

This chapter examined the major issues concerning testing, integration, and distribution of your movies. Designing Flash movies is one thing; compiling and preparing them for delivery is another. To be a successful Flash developer you must know how to do both.

As you have read, the new Publish utility goes a long way toward getting Flash movies on the Web. Indeed, it is an ingenious tool that can do most of the basic coding. Yet, knowing the code is also important. As far as coding goes, this chapter is just a start. Later chapters will pick up where this chapter left off, and will look at how to use external coding with JavaScript and VBScript to create complex sites.

part two:

# The
# Implementation

# 10

# Creating Preload Sequences

### ▪ ▪ ▪ ▪ Introduction

Throughout the previous chapters, the subject of preloaders has been mentioned several times. As you read in the last chapter, before a frame can play its graphics or sounds, the content of the frame must be fully downloaded. The Size Report feature and Bandwidth Profiler can be used to determine trouble spots within your movie. Often, you will be able to optimize a file and correct these areas.

However, a preloader will usually be needed for the beginning elements, particularly for those who are cursed with a slow Internet connection. As end user connections get faster, the need for preloaders will probably decrease. Nevertheless, for now, preloaders provide you with a means of indicating to the user that the site is downloading and how long that download will take.

This chapter describes the importance of preloaders. It also describes several ways preloaders can be generated. The preload sequences used in your movies can range from simple flashing, "Loading" indicators to more complex, pre-movie introductions. Regardless, the most important aspect is to ensure that the audience has something to look at and has some indication of the amount of time required to load your site. The most frequent reason for skipping a site is download time. A close second is not knowing how long it will take to load the site.

### ▪ ▪ ▪ ▪ Objectives

In this chapter, you will:

- Examine Flash's streaming capability and understand why preloaders are even possible at all

- Learn to create a basic preloader using a movie clip and the If Frame Loaded action
- Review advanced preloaders that indicate progress of elements being downloaded
- Understand how to create pre-movie introductions that serve as preloaders

# ▪ ▪ ▪ Flash and Streaming

Due to the way they are written, Flash files are a streaming file format. The term streaming describes the way in which data flows from the HTTP server to the end user's computer. Normally, before a browser can render a graphic, text, or other element to the screen, the entire file must be downloaded from the Web. Thus, if a slow connection exists somewhere between the end user and the server, content loads very slowly because the file has to be fully downloaded before it can be viewed.

Flash files, however, are written sequentially; that is, frame 1 is written, then frame 2, and so on. Therefore, as soon as the data associated with frame 1 is downloaded, it can be played, even if the remainder of the file is not downloaded.

Streaming in multimedia files (such as Flash files, QuickTime movies, or RealPlayer files) is akin to interlaced graphics. As you learned in Chapter 9, graphics that are interlaced (progressive, in the case of JPEG) are written so that the file may be gradually viewed. When loaded, an interlaced image begins on screen as a blurry (usually pixelated) image. As more data is downloaded, the image becomes clearer and clearer, much like focusing a camera lens. Streaming file formats share this characteristic. However, instead of becoming "clearer," their content begins to play before a complete download.

Yet, streaming multimedia files over the Web will only play smoothly (without noticeable pauses) if the rate of playback is less than or equal to the rate of downloading. Any time the rate of playback is faster than the rate of download, a noticeable pause may occur, because the multimedia asset must stop and wait for more data to load.

Flash movies always stream. The effectiveness of *.swf* streaming ultimately depends on the amount of data required for each frame. If large bitmaps or lengthy sounds are present, the data requirements for the frame become quite large and can negatively affect the streaming process. Although optimization may yield some decrease in file size, often it is not enough to avoid a presentation pause. In these scenarios, preloaders provide a means of presenting something on-screen during the time required for downloading. They can also be used to indicate the amount of remaining download time.

# • • • **The Basics of Preloaders**

Preloaders are simply a set of frames in the beginning of a normal movie file (or in an introductory scene in a movie file) that loops or plays while the remainder of the movie file is downloaded. Setting up a basic preloader requires three things:

- Elements somewhere in the file that make a preloader necessary. With all the creative things Flash can do, this is not usually a problem.

- A set of frames to loop while waiting for the content to load. This can be just about anything, as you will see.

- An If Frame Is Loaded (*IfFrameLoaded*) action that is assigned to jump to a certain frame or label once a particular frame is loaded.

The *IfFrameLoaded* action is deprecated in Flash 5, meaning that it will likely not be available in future versions of the product. The recommended item to use in place of the *IfFrameLoaded* action is the *_framesloaded* property, within an If action. Thus, both methods are examined in this chapter.

In the following sections, you will create a simple preload movie from scratch. This will get you familiar with the basics. Directly following this, you will add a preload sequence to an already existing movie clip. Exercise 10-1, which follows, takes you through the process of creating a basic preloader.

 **CD-ROM NOTE:** *If you want to preview what you will be creating, the finished preloader can be opened from the* F5gai/chapter10/ *folder, installed from the companion CD-ROM. The file is named* ch10-01s.fla. *You must use the Show Streaming option and Bandwidth Profiler to be able to see the preloader.*

## *Exercise 10-1 Creating a Basic Preloader*

To begin examining how preload sequences are created, perform the following steps.

1.  Begin by opening Flash and starting a new movie.

2.  In the movie, add a layer, named Actions/Label, to the timeline. This layer will be used for the labels and actions you will add. Rename the other layer Content.

3.  Using the F5 function key (Insert Frame), extend the blank frames of the two layers out to frame 10.

4.  Right-click in frame 10 of the Content layer and select Add Keyframe.

5.  One of the requirements for using a preloader is to have a need for a preloader. Thus, you will insert a bitmap graphic and a sound clip into frame 10. This should provide enough file size to your movie to be able to see the preloader work on your local machine.

6.  Import the sound file named music.wav or music.aif from the *F5gai/chapter10/* folder, installed from the companion CD-ROM. Also, import the graphic file named *image.bmp* or *image.pct*.

As you are testing your movies, you must understand that pre-loaders you create may be undetectable if you test them from your local machine using the basic Test Movie option (without the Bandwidth Profiler). Additionally, if you have a direct network connection to the Internet, you may not be able to see the pre-loader when testing from the network, because it loads too quickly. Preloaders are detected only when the connection is slow.

In the example you are working on, the bitmap and sound clip (which are relatively large) are inserted so that you can see the preloader while testing it on your local machine. However, in the real world, to adequately test a preloader, use the Bandwidth Profiler with the Show Streaming option (as described in the last chapter). An alternative is to empirically test the file by loading it to the server and then accessing it on a slow connection (a modem).

7.  When you inserted the bitmap image, it should have automatically been added to frame 10 of layer Content. Right-click on frame 10 and select Panels | Sound from the context menu.

8.  In the Sound panel, assign the music clip to the frame. Set the Sync drop-down of the music clip to Start, and the Loop field to 999.

9.  Before you move on, add a label to frame 10 of the Content layer. Right-click in frame 10 and select Panels | Frame. Type *Start* into the Label field in the Frame panel.

Now that you have some content that needs to be preloaded, you can set up the preload sequence.

10.  Right-click in frame 1 of the Labels/Actions layer and select Panels | Frame from the context menu.

11.  In the Frame panel, enter *Preloader* into the Label field.

12.  Insert a keyframe in frame 9 and in frame 10 of the Labels/Actions layer.

13. Right-click in frame 9 and select Actions from the context menu.

14. Using the Actions panel, add a Go To action to the frame. Set the Label drop-down to the Preloader label. Make sure you select the Go To and Play checkbox. If you do not, the preloader will not work.

15. Now you must create the movie clip that will play while the content in the rest of the movie will be loading. Use Insert | New Symbol to create a new movie clip symbol named Loading.

16. In the new symbol, add some text that says *Loading* that is of generous point size (12 points or larger).

17. Create a short animation in the symbol's timeline. You can make the text flash on and off, or anything else you want it to do, while the content is loading. The movie clip will be inserted so that it continually repeats while the preload function is occurring. Once you are finished, click on the Scene 1 link in the Edit Path to switch back to the main movie timeline.

18. In the main timeline, open the library and insert the Loading movie clip into frame 1 of the Content layer.

19. Right-click on frame 1 of the Content layer and select Actions from the context menu.

20. In the Actions panel, insert an *IfFrameLoaded* action from the Actions group in the Toolbox list. Enter 10 in the number field.

21. Insert a Go To action inside the *IfFrameLoaded* action. Assign the Type drop-down list to Frame Label and the Frame drop-down to Start, as shown in figure 10-1. Make sure the Go To and Play checkbox is not selected.

22. Select Test Movie from the Control menu. Depending on the speed of your computer, you may or may not see the Loading movie clip.

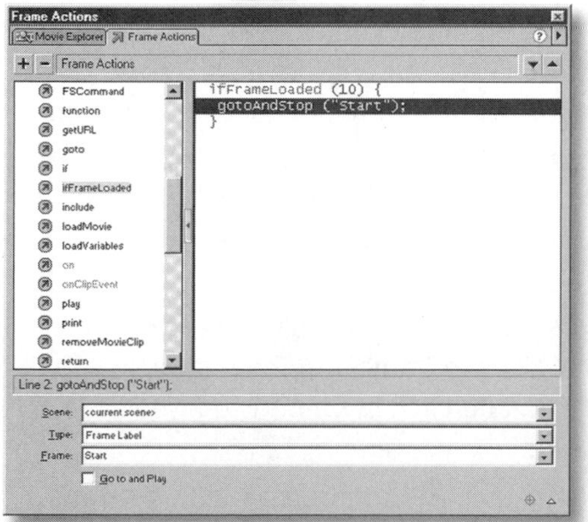

*Figure 10-1 Set up the Go To action within the IfFrameLoaded action.*

23. To really see what the end user will detect, while still in Test Movie, select 28.8 from the Debug menu and Bandwidth Profiler from the View menu.

24. Select Show Streaming from the Control menu. Doing this will limit playback to the data rate defined in the modem settings. Now you can see that the preloader is doing its job.

Realize that the preloader shown here is rather poor. The example is simply to show you how a preloader is constructed. Really, the only thing this preloader does is tell the user that your movie is loading. They could already determine by the lights on their modem, the indicator in the Windows status tray, or the lengthy pause that would follow, that something is going on. Thus, this preloader has little value.

Preloaders can do much more, such as indicate the amount that has been downloaded or the items that are being downloaded. However, before examining how this is accomplished, let's look at adding a preloader to a better (and a more complex) example.

## Adding to an Existing Movie

In the last example, a large bitmap and a sound clip were inserted into a file so that a preloader is necessary. Although this gave something that could be waited on, concerning downloading, a more realistic example is in order. In the following exercise, you will add a preloader to an existing file by inserting it at the beginning of the file.

### CD-ROM Exercise

Begin by opening the file *ch10-02.fla* located in the *F5gai/chapter10/* folder, installed from the companion CD-ROM. The file already contains the movie clips that will be used for the preloader. You may want to test the movie to see the existing movie for which the preloader will be created. If you want to preview what you will be creating, the finished sample preloader can be opened from the *F5gai/chapter10/* folder. The file is named *ch10-02s.fla*.

1.  Begin by creating some "space" at the beginning of the timeline for the preloader. Click in frame 1 in the Labels/Actions layer, hold the Shift key, and click in frame 1 in layer 8. This selects the first frame in every layer.

2.  Use Insert | Blank Keyframe (F7) to insert a blank keyframe in every layer.

3.  Move the playhead to frame 1 and make sure no frame in any layer is selected.

4.  Use Insert | Frame (F5) to scoot the existing frames out to frame 11, as shown in figure 10-2.

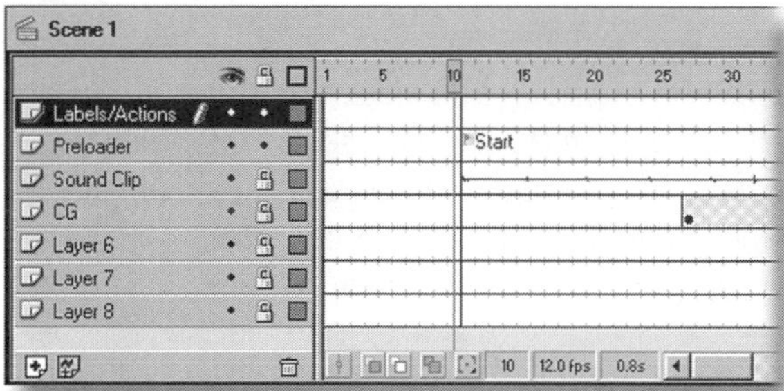

*Figure 10-2 Adding the space in the timeline for the preloader.*

5. Right-click in frame 1 of the Labels/Actions layer, select Panels | Frame in the context menu, and add a label named Preloader.

6. Double click in frame 1 of the Preloader layer and remove the label that was added by the click-dragging operation.

7. Right-click in frame 10 and add a blank keyframe in layer Labels/Actions.

8. Add a Go To action to frame 10 in the Labels/Actions layer that jumps back to the Preloader label. Make sure you select the Go To and Play checkbox!

9. Add the elements that will be displayed while the movie is waiting to be loaded from the Web. Use Window | Library to open the current movie's library.

10. With frame 1 of the Preloader layer selected, find the *CG Flash2* movie clip symbol and drag it to the upper part of the stage.

11. Find the Preloader movie clip in the library and drag it to the stage also. Figure 10-3 shows the arrangement on the stage.

*Figure 10-3 Place the two movie clips from the library onto the stage.*

Now you must set up the *IfFrameLoaded* action. Because this movie clip has a streaming sound, and because the sound is quite long, the *IfFrameLoaded* action will be used to wait until a significant amount of the sound is loaded.

12. Right-click in frame 1 of the Preloader layer and select Actions from the context menu.

13. In the Actions panel, add an *IfFrameLoaded* action and enter *100* in the Number field.

14. Add a Go To action beneath the If Frame Is Loaded event handler and set it to go to label Start, as shown in figure 10-4. Make sure the Go To and Play checkbox is selected in the Go To action.

*Figure 10-4 Add the IfFrameLoaded action based on frame 100.*

15. Save your file so that you can return to it later.

 **TIP:** *When creating preloaders, make sure you select the Go To and Play checkbox in the repeating loop, as well as the Go To action assigned inside the* IfFrameLoaded *action. This is the most common reason for preloaders not working.*

# Testing a Preloader

Now let's see how effective this preloader is. You know that this file, because it has a lengthy audio clip, is quite large. Your goal with this preloader is to make sure the movie does not start playing until enough of the sound file is downloaded. Additionally, you do not want it to inadvertently stop or pause during the presentation (due to the playhead overtaking the streaming). Use the Bandwidth Profiler in exercise 10-2, which follows, to test and see what a user on a 28.8 modem would see and hear.

## Exercise 10-2  Using the Bandwidth Profiler

To test a preloader, perform the following steps.

1. Use Control | Test Movie to start the Flash Player.
2. Select Bandwidth Profiler from the View menu and make sure Streaming Graph is selected in that menu as well.
3. In the Debug menu, make sure that the 28.8 option is selected. This is the constraint that makes the movie run as if it were coming off the Web, even though it is not.
4. Select Show Streaming from the View menu and watch the presentation. At some point, the presentation should pause as the playhead overtakes (catches up to) the streaming bar (green), probably about frame 133. This is not what you want to happen.
5. Close the player and double click on frame 1 in the Preloader layer. This will quickly open the Actions panel.
6. Change the *IfFrameLoaded* frame number to 200 instead of 100 and click on OK.
7. Use the Bandwidth Profiler again to see if the playhead intercepts the streaming marker. Does it? If you have the bandwidth set to 28.8, the playhead should still intercept the stream, at about frame 290.
8. Change the *IfFrameLoaded* action to wait until frame 300 is loaded. Then test the movie again. Once again, you should

see that the movie is interrupted. This occurs later in the presentation, but the movie still pauses.

In the previous example, due to the amount of data, the *IfFrameLoaded* action would have to wait until frame 550 for no pause to be evident. This is a long time to wait, but there is also much data to be delivered.

The file you are working with was not really designed for the Web, or at least it is not meant for users on a 28.8 modem. However, it does show how you can use the *IfFrameLoaded* action with the Bandwidth Profiler to find the optimum time you would have to make the audience wait. Use the Debug menu to select various bandwidths, or the Customize option to enter your own custom parameters. Again, your primary concern is to keep the playhead from intercepting the data stream, represented by the green bar. It is when these two run into each other that a noticeable pause will occur in your movies.

# ▪ ▪ ▪ Advanced Preloaders

In the prior examples, the preloaders that were created do provide an on-screen notification to the end user about what is going on; that is, the file is being downloaded. However, preloaders can be made more useful. In the next three sections you will examine a few more advanced preloaders. The first uses a progress bar to show the percentage of loading that is left. The second shows the elements being downloaded, and the last shows a "pre-movie" before the "real movie."

## Showing Load Progress

By using multiple *IfFrameLoaded* actions, you can create a movie that shows an indicator bar. This provides more information to the end user concerning how much longer they will have to wait. There are many ways to do this, but this example will use a simple indicator bar consisting of 10 blocks.

 **CD-ROM NOTE:** *Due to limits on the size of this book, you will simply review the important points from an already created file. Open the finished preloader from the* F5gai/chapter10/ *folder, installed from the companion CD-ROM. The file is named* ch10-03s.fla. *You may want to use Test Movie to see how it works. Make sure you use the Bandwidth Profiler and the Show Streaming option to see the preloader.*

The example you will look at has two important things that are needed. First, the *IfFrameLoaded* action is included multiple times (10 times, to be exact). As a certain frame farther down in the movie is loaded, the *IfFrameLoaded* action in that looping segment jumps to the next *IfFrameLoaded* segment. Because the movie has a streaming sound, the

*IfFrameLoaded* frames are simply equally spaced numbers of frames.

The main part of the movie runs from frames 62 to 620. These are the frames that must be loaded before the movie plays. Thus, the first *IfFrameLoaded* waits until frame 62 is loaded. Then it progresses to the next *IfFrameLoaded*. The second *IfFrameLoaded* is waiting on frame 124. The third waits on frame 186, and so on.

For the sake of time, in this example the increments are calculated based on number of frames that occur rather than the amount of data required by the frames. If you really wanted the progress bar to be indicative of download time, you would want to calculate increments based on the data required by each frame, rather than by simple frame count. This is because the amount of data for each frame varies. As you have seen earlier, frame 128 required quite a bit of data. If you want to be completely accurate, use the Size Report feature to calculate where the If Frame Is Loaded increments should be based on frame size rather than frame count.

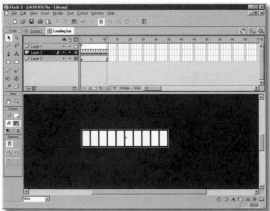

Figure 10-5 The progress meter has a stop in the first layer sprite, which keeps the movie clip from playing through.

The second important thing that occurs in each *IfFrameLoaded* segment is a Tell Target that tells the progress meter to go to the next frame. The progress meter is nothing more than a movie clip symbol whose instance name is Bar. You can check this out by right-clicking on the symbol instance on the stage and selecting Edit from the context menu. As shown in figure 10-5, the progress meter's timeline has a stop action in the first layer sprite, which applies to every frame. This keeps the movie clip from playing through (from frame 1 to 11).

If you right-click on frame 1 of the Labels/Actions layer and select Actions from the context menu, you can review the Tell Target action associated with the *IfFrameLoaded* action, as shown in figure 10-6. Note that once frame 62 is loaded, the Bar movie clip is progressed to the next frame and the main movie timeline jumps to the next preloader segment. The second If Frame Is Loaded segment progresses the bar one more frame and jumps to the next preloader segment. Once the last preload action frame is loaded, the movie jumps to the first real content frame and begins to play the movie.

Keep in mind that this example would be more effective if the Size Report feature were used to determine the segment breakpoints based on data requirements instead of frame count. The Size Report feature could be used to determine the amount of data required for frames 62 to 620, collectively. The resulting byte size could then be divided by 10, provid-

*Figure 10-6 The* IfFrameLoaded *action, once sat-isfied, tells the progress bar to go to the next frame, and tells the main movie timeline to jump to the next looping segment.*

ing the data increment at which each step of the progress bar should relate to. Then, using the Size Report feature, you could determine where the real interim points should be for the *IfFrameLoaded* actions.

For the sake of time, simple frame increments were used in the example. However, if you play the animation using the Bandwidth Profiler and the Show Streaming option, you will see that the increments of the progress meter are not very accurate. Some "blocks" take more time than others, due to the variation of the amount of data required in the frames. Calculating the *IfFrameLoaded* increments based on the data required by each frame would provide a more accurate progress bar.

## Showing What Is Loading

Although they have now moved to a different design, one of the preloading techniques used at many sites previews the items being downloaded as the download is taking place. The first place this technique appeared was

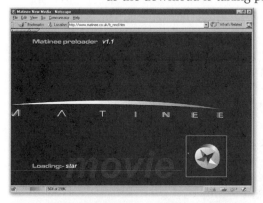

*Figure 10-7 The masters of Flash at Matinee Sound and Vision were the first to use preview preloaders.*

at Matinee's web site (*http://www.matinee.co.uk/*). As shown in figure 10-7, the preloader displayed the items being loaded in the lower right-hand corner. As an introductory effect, the sound effects complement this preloader.

Creating a preview preloader is similar to the technique used in the progress bar from the previous example. Multiple preload segments are established. However, special frames that contain specific elements are used as the basis for the *IfFrameLoaded* action. In the following CD-ROM exercise, you will examine a sample that uses multiple *IfFrameLoaded* actions in this manner.

### CD-ROM Exercise

Open the file *ch10-04s.fla* located in the *F5gai/chapter10/* folder, installed from the companion CD-ROM. Perform the following steps to understand how it works.

1. Begin by using Test Movie to see how this preloader works. Make sure you use the Bandwidth Profiler and the Show Streaming option to see the preloader. Notice that the movie shows in the small preview window the elements that have been loaded during the test. To make this example a little more fun, a flashing loading signal and a progress bar also exist.

As you begin this exercise, note that this movie is a small game that was created for elementary students. It is similar to the old television game "Concentration." Students match animals behind the doors. Creating a match reveals a small piece of a picture behind the doors. The goal is to match the animals to be able to guess what the background animal is. After guessing ten correct background animals, a small animation plays. Later in the book you will examine how it works. For now, let's focus on the preloader.

To see the entire thing work, open the file *noahFS.html* located in the *F5gai/chapter10* folder, installed from the companion CD-ROM. Load this file into Internet Explorer or Netscape Communicator. Note that the game will not work unless you open the web page in a browser (it uses FS Command actions and JavaScript). Thus, the web page contains the brains for it to work.

If you open this page, you will likely not see the preloader, because it is loading locally. Nonetheless, you can see how the game works. In Chapter 14 you will return to Noah's Memory Game to see how the game can be created entirely in Flash using ActionScript. In Chapter 17, you will use the FS Commands feature and JavaScript to create the same thing.

2. In the timeline, notice that there are 18 preload (*IfFrameLoaded*) segments. The first 16 load all animal symbols used in the movie. The remaining segments wait for remaining graphics and buttons to load, as well as the sound clips used in the movie.

3. Examining one of the preload segments reveals the secret to doing it. Examine the action attached to frame 1. It is labeled Pre1 and has an action assigned to it. Right-click on frame 1 in the Labels/Actions layer and select Actions from the context menu.

4. As shown in figure 10-8, notice the typical Go To and Play surrounded by the *IfFrameLoaded* action. The important element here is the label assigned in the *IfFrameLoaded* action.

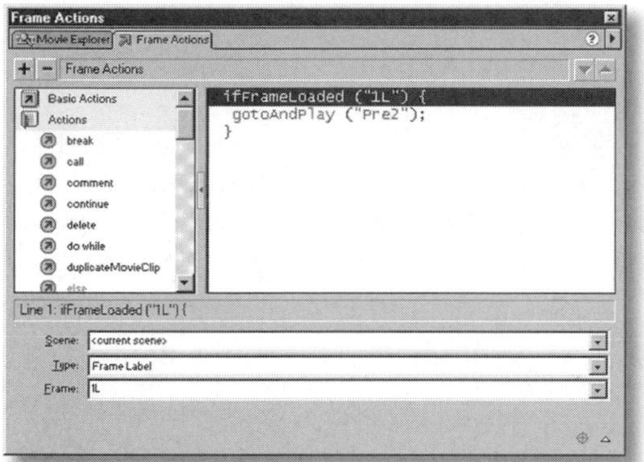

Figure 10-8 A special labeled but unseen frame is used to preload the elements.

Instead of referencing a frame in the content further down in the movie, it references a special frame set up specifically for the preloader (1L). Let's examine frame 1L.

5. Minimize the Actions panel and click on frame 7. This frame is labeled 1L. It has specific elements that have been placed in the timeline on which the *IfFrameLoaded* action is based. The stage reveals the elements that have been inserted. Note that the end user never sees this frame. It is used for preloading purposes only. Similarly, the last frame of each preload loop has the same type of frame; that is, a frame used for preloading purposes only.

> **NOTE:** *You should also note that the* IfFrameLoaded *segments in this example are based on frame labels rather than frame numbers. Again, whenever possible, you should reference labels in all Go To and* IfFrameLoaded *actions in case you need to add frames at any point in the timeline.*

6. In addition to the "hidden" frame used for graphic components, the last preload segment ensures that the sound clips used in the movie are downloaded using the same technique. However, because a frame can have only one sound clip associated with it, all sounds have been inserted into a movie clip symbol. Click on frame 135 in the Instructions/Questions layer.

7. On the stage, you see a black square indicating a symbol that has no graphic components. Right-click on the element and select Edit from the context menu.

Symbols that have no graphic components appear as black squares when selected. If they are deselected, they appear as white circles.

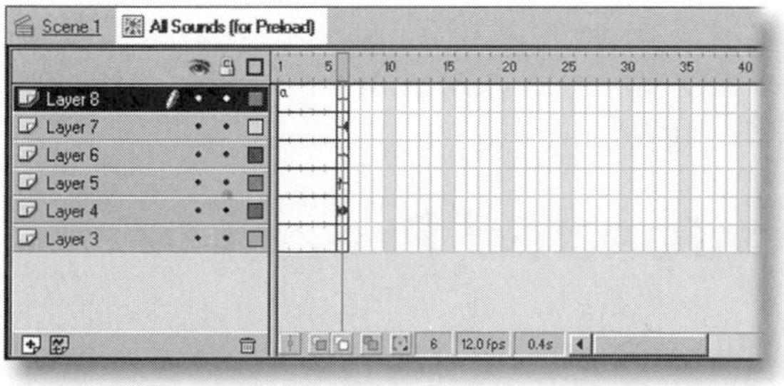

Figure 10-9 A movie clip that contains all sound elements is used as the basis for the IfFrameLoaded action. In the main movie, this movie clip does not play but does ensure that all sounds are loaded.

8. As shown in figure 10-9, the All Sounds (for Preload) symbol contains all sounds needed by the movie. By placing the movie clip symbol in the main movie timeline,

you can ensure that all sound clips are loaded. In this segment, the If Frame Is Loaded is based on all sounds being completely downloaded.

9. The last thing you should note is that the flashing text that appears during the preloader and the progress bar are controlled the same way as in previous examples. The Tell Target action, interspersed within the preload sections, makes these items change during the life of the preloader.

The first real starting frame for the Noah's Memory Game does not occur until frame 136. Indeed, preview preloaders are one of the most difficult and complex to construct. Frames 1 to 135 are for the preloader only. The remaining frames in this movie are for the game itself. Later chapters discuss how the game functions. Here, the example is presented to show a complex preloader. Realistically, anything is possible, given enough time.

## Creating a Show Before the Show

In addition to the previous methods, you can also create brief pre-show preloaders. Many sites use this technique. However, you have to be careful that the pre-show does not become so large that it makes waiting on the real show a joke.

 **CD-ROM NOTE:** *To see an example of a pre-show preloader, open the file the file* ch10-05s.fla *located in the* F5gai/chapter10/ *folder, installed from the companion CD-ROM. Use Test Movie with the Bandwidth Profiler and the Show Streaming option.*

By combining scenes and preloader capabilities, you can create pre-shows that keep the audience occupied while you download what they actually came for at your site. Ultimately, this is what it is all about: buying time. Effective preloaders occupy the audience's attention. The best preloaders make you believe that the preloader is the show until the rest of the site is loaded. Some of the most effective preloaders are as simple as they are interesting. Planning and knowing your audience is the ultimate key to designing effective preloaders.

# ∎ ∎ ∎ Using the *_framesloaded* Property

This chapter has focused on the specific use of the *IfFrameLoaded* action. Realize, however, that with the If action and the *_framesloaded* property you can also set up preload scenarios using ActionScript. Indeed, using an If action with the *_framesloaded* property is now the preferred method of creating preloads.

It was mentioned earlier in the chapter that the *IfFrameLoaded* action is deprecated in Flash 5. The next version of Flash will probably not offer the *IfFrameLoaded* action. Thus, you should understand how to use regular If actions as well. By using an If action with the condition of *_framesloaded*, you can achieve the same effect as the *IfFrameLoaded* action.

Later chapters cover ActionScripting in more detail. Extensive review of the If action is found in those chapters. However, If versions of the prior preloaders are included here so that you can review them to see how they are different (see the following CD-ROM Note).

 **CD-ROM NOTE:** *Access the* book/chapter10/ifs/ *folder to examine the prior preload examples using the If action and the* _framesloaded *property. As you will see, there is really not that much difference between the two methods. The only real difference is understanding how to describe the scenario you are testing against using the Condition field. Chapter 13 reviews this and other items in more detail, but you will no doubt find the conditions pretty easy to understand.*

One other difference about the *_framesloaded* property is noteworthy. Recall from Chapter 8 that you can use the Load Movie action to load a movie file (.*swf*) into a movie clip. This technique is primarily used for printing. For example, when loading a movie into a movie clip for printing purposes, you want to make sure the movie is totally loaded into the movie clip before you actually initiate the print action. Thus, the ability to use the *_framesloaded* property on movie clips, as well as the main movie timeline, is important.

# ▪ ▪ ▪ **Summary**

In this chapter you have examined the *IfFrameLoaded* action. You have seen how you can create looping segments that repeat until a certain portion of a movie has been downloaded. Indeed, you can do much more than what is presented here, especially when you add ActionScript's *_frameloaded* property. Both frames and specific actions can be made to take place following the loading of a frame.

However, before you delve into the practical details of ActionScript, the next chapter will highlight one of the most sought-after effects in Flash 3D animation. Indeed, there have been some interesting developments lately as it relates to generating 3D for Flash. The following chapter examines some further animation techniques. In Chapter 13 and following, you will delve further into Actions and ActionScript examples.

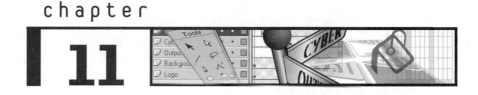

# 3D Animations and Flash

### ▪ ▪ ▪ **Introduction**

Many times in this book, you have read about how Flash can do almost anything. However, no software is strong in every area, and the content of this chapter focuses on one of the weaker points of Flash: its inability to efficiently incorporate 3D animation without the aid of other programs. Although it can be manually created in Flash, from scratch, 3D animation can be very time consuming, to the point that it is not worth the means required. Understand that when you create a web site that includes 3D animation, the most time-consuming aspect will be the creation of the 3D animation.

Why does it take so long to create 3D animation with Flash? It is because "3D animation" in Flash does not mean rendering out a series of raster images and importing them, as with a package such as 3D Studio Max or form-Z. Although this is one way of getting 3D into Flash, it is not the preferred method, because raster images quickly expand the size of Flash movies. The most effective means of creating 3D in Flash is to use elements that are vector, not raster.

Nevertheless, how do you get the vector representations that appear on the screen in a 3D modeling, animation, or rendering package into Flash in a vector form? Additionally, what about using GIF animations? Which is the most bandwidth savvy, while maintaining maximum visual appeal?

The content of this chapter covers a variety of methods of getting 2D representations of 3D elements into Flash. You will examine which methods of transference are the most effective, as well as which are the most time consuming. You will soon see the correlation between these different priorities. Since the release of Flash 4, two software packages now on the market (Vecta3D and Swift3D) make it easier to get 2D representations from 3D environments into Flash. However, if you are going to use 3D extensively, you need to be sure to include a little extra money in your budget so that you can pick up a copy of one of these software programs.

# Objectives

In this chapter, you will:

- Examine the rules of the road for using corporate identities and logos
- Discover the primary means of incorporating 3D into Flash
- Learn how to use bitmap graphics as a basis for generating vectors
- Find out how to export vector representations from modeling packages such as AutoCAD and Pro/Engineer (Pro/E) for use in Flash animations
- Compare three new plug-ins/programs that allow you to use models and animation files from 3D Studio Max
- Take a closer look at how other packages (such as Adobe Streamline, Adobe Dimensions, ITEDO IsoDraw, Microsoft Word, and Viewpoint LiveArt) can assist in the generation of 3D-for-Flash projects
- Explore the advantages, disadvantages, and tips and tricks of using various graphic file formats with Flash

# Rules of the Road for Identities

One of the most basic elements web designers (and designers in general) work with is the corporate identity. In the traditional sense, most of the rules associated with logos are in relation to colors, spacing, and fonts. Yet, when using logos in a dynamic media, the rules may become somewhat gray.

This section provides a brief overview of the main things to consider when creating logo animations. If you are an experienced designer, you may want to skip this section. However, for new designers, the following information can save you many headaches, as well as hours of rework time.

## Find Those Usage Guidelines

If you are presented with the need to animate an existing logo, you must first ascertain usage guidelines. Most corporations have manuals defining the context in which a logo can be used. These instructions provide key information, such as what colors can be used to render a logo, what fonts must be used, how much spacing must be allotted, and how large or small the logo may be.

Further information may be specified, depending on the logo's complexity and the rigidity of the owner of the logo. It is very tempting to immediately take a logo and start conceptually animating. However, usage guidelines for any identity must be examined before you start brainstorming. Quite often, aspects of a logo satisfy legal requirements, such as the inclusion of copyright, trademark, and registered trademark symbols.

## Planning Your Logo Animation

With guidelines in hand, the next step is to begin brainstorming, sketching, and planning the animation. Storyboarding and sketching skills are absolutely necessary. It is amazing the number of computer graphics people who have traded their pencil for a bar of soap (mouse). Pencil-and-paper sketching should precede any digital work. Paper and pencil are still the fastest means of carrying out conceptual and developmental work.

Typically, the developmental or storyboard sketches become the main mode of communication between the developer and the client. Thus, the sketch quality should match the level needed for effective communication. Sometimes storyboard sketches may need to be fully rendered. At other times, only basic sketches are required for communication. Intended use determines the level of quality needed for communication.

## Flowing with the Corporate Identity

Probably one of the most difficult aspects of designing dynamic logos is retaining the genre of the original logo. Keep in mind that small changes in the dynamic aspect of a logo can significantly affect the audience's perception of what the logo represents and portrays about the company.

For many years, designers have followed rules that govern the interpretation of a symbol. In relation to logo design, most of the decision making is based on prior research and experiential knowledge concerning the use of abstraction in static design. Yet, in comparison to print media, dynamic design is still very young. Approach logo animation creation with caution. Many corporate logos, such as the Disney silhouette of Mickey Mouse, cannot be altered in "look" at all, as the logo itself can be a corporate identity and/or legally a corporate trademark.

## Approvals Will Save Your Hide!

As a final note, particularly for freelancers, make sure to get approvals from your clients for all of your Flash work, particularly for logos. Ultimately, approvals provide at least two things. First, getting a client to approve design work provides a mechanism (and paperwork) to prove that the client accepts your animation design. This can be a vital piece of evidence if any legal actions are ever necessary.

Second, and more importantly, using approval documents helps reduce endless design cycles. Multimedia projects are notorious for extending well over their projected timelines. As a freelancer, every extra hour spent revising a design cuts into profit margins. As a contracted entity, the same hours have to be justified (always an unpleasant experience for the client liaison) or "eaten," which will rarely go down well with your management. Use approvals as a mechanism for curtailing endless design cycles.

# ▪ ▪ ▪ Methods of Creating/Simulating 3D

The use of 3D effects and objects in animations is a design trend appearing across the Internet. One of the most frequent questions asked by designers relates to how these effects are generated. It is not as simple as constructing a 3D animation or object in a package such as 3D Studio or form-Z and then rendering out the frames. All rendering packages, including 3D Studio and form-Z, render frames as raster images, not vector. Thus, a method must be established for converting the raster images from these packages to vector. The alternative is to construct 3D animations from scratch in Flash, which is not a simple task.

To create a 3D Flash animation, you will have to construct, photo trace, or capture the needed vectors in one form or another. Although it is a lot of work, the results of 3D animation in Flash movies have been well received. Hopefully, future versions of Flash will simplify this job. But for now, construction, photo tracing, and capturing are the means of obtaining 3D vector animations in Flash. Table 11-1 outlines the primary means, as well as the positives and negatives, of each method.

In general, all of the methods described in this chapter provide a means of getting the baseline work of an animation into Flash. Aside from directly integrating a series of raster images, in several cases there is no method that will automatically create or transfer an animation into Flash for you. Only two packages currently offer this capability: Swift3D and Vecta3D. When using the other techniques, the best-case scenario is that you will be able to transfer the basic line work of an animation into Flash. From that point, you will then have to render the frames of the animation, or the objects, in Flash.

## Construction

As logic dictates, 3D animations in Flash can be constructed using both traditional cel animation techniques and other facilities, such as motion paths and symbols. In general, this is the most time-consuming method. It can also be tricky to figure out how to implement a specific animation using the capabilities in Flash.

Ultimately, whether or not you can construct an animation in Flash depends on the complexity of the animation. There is no way to work with true 3D elements in Flash. Yet to a certain extent, realize that you can simulate 3D in Flash. Due to the amount of time input, this is not a widely used means. You can read more on this topic in the section "Advanced Layer Guides" in Chapter 12. The methods presented examine how to fake 3D with

*Table 11-1  Methods of Creating Flash 3D Animations*

| Method | Required Software | Advantages | Disadvantages |
|---|---|---|---|
| Construction | Flash Only | High visual quality | Has greatest time input<br><br>Complex 3D constructions are difficult<br><br>Matching color transformations is difficult |
| Bitmap: Direct Integration | Raster editor, GIF animator, modeling, animation or rendering package | Fastest method<br><br>Very accurate geometry | Largest file size (raster)<br><br>Images may appear grainy due to compression or color depth |
| Bitmap: Manual Tracing | Modeling, Animation or Rendering Package | High visual quality<br><br>Small file size | Large time input<br><br>Trace each frame (monotonous)<br><br>Matching color transformations is difficult |
| Bitmap: Automatic Tracing | Modeling, Animation or Rendering package, Adobe Streamline | High visual quality<br><br>Medium file size<br><br>Can generate very stylized images<br><br>Can automate rendering | Time consuming<br><br>Files may have many points (larger file size)<br><br>Cannot always control rasterization process |
| 3D Environment/ Static Extraction | Modeling package & a converter (depending on file type) | High visual quality<br><br>Small file size<br><br>Effects, such as farcles, can be added<br><br>Direct generation of vectors<br><br>Extremely detailed 3D objects<br><br>Easy extraction of animated vectors<br><br>Direct to SWF file | Frames are manually output<br><br>Intermediate file formats and conversion software may be needed<br><br>Modeling packages are expensive<br><br>Modeling packages may be limited to certain platforms |
| 3D Environment/ Dynamic Extraction | 3D Studio Max and purchased plugin (Illustrate! 4.0, Swift3D or Vecta3D) | Maintain true arcs and Bezier curves | Requires knowledge of 3D animation package<br><br>Generally spline based, as opposed to polygon based |
| Other: LiveArt | ViewPoint LiveArt98 (Adobe Streamline also required) | Very stylized images (preset artistic styles)<br><br>"Import" existing models<br><br>Full 360 degree rotation of object and lighting | Only exports raster (tracing required to complete)<br><br>Difficult to obtain line only representations |
| Other: Dimensions | Adobe Dimensions, FreeHand (optional) | Extrusions and revolution used to generate 3D<br><br>Can determine light source and direction | Limited to simple geometry<br><br>Fills are blended shapes and lines<br><br>Cause Flash to generate many symbols |
| Other: Word | Microsoft Word, FreeHand (optional) | Very easy<br><br>Readily available package (MS Word) | Extrusion-only<br><br>Limited rotation<br><br>Gradients produce large file sizes |

Flash through the use of layer guides. Some impressive techniques for tasks you may want to accomplish are also provided.

One program of note is ITEDO IsoDraw. This program is well known among technical illustrators in many fields. However, the general publishing and design crowd is often unaware of its existence. This program is magnificent for constructing vector axonometric and perspective draw-ings. Although it is expensive, the assistance this specialized package pro-vides for constructing drawings is priceless.

 **NOTE:** *If you are creating a lot of mechanical, architectural, or other non-organic illustrations, take a look at this tool (*http://www. isodraw.com/*).*

## Raster Images

The first method of creating 3D animations in Flash is through the use of raster images. As highlighted elsewhere in this book, Flash is very capable as it relates to importing raster images, albeit raster images can quickly make file sizes grow. You can quickly and easily import a series of raster images into Flash, or import a GIF animation to get "3D in Flash." If you have a 3D modeling, rendering, or animation package, ren-der out a series of BMP or PCT files to import into Flash. However, if the animation is lengthy, you will find that the movie's file size will grow quickly.

Although you can import GIF animation into Flash, more often than not the subsequent Flash movie will have a larger file size than the GIF anima-tion. The results of a test showed that an *.swf* file was 10 KB larger than the GIF animation. This is presumably because GIF animations store data at 256 colors, versus Flash, which stores data in near 24-bit quality using the JPEG compressor. The lossless compression fared no better. In addition, GIF images frequently look poor in Flash if JPEG compression is used. This is because the JPEG compressor does not compress 256-color data very well.

## Vector via Manual Tracing

Another method of creating animations in Flash is to use bitmap images as a basis for manual tracing, a technique developed by traditional technical illustrators called photo tracing. This method is faster than from-scratch con-struction and provides better on-screen representation than simply integrat-ing raster images. It also provides smaller file sizes than the integration of raster images. Exercise 11-1, which follows, takes you through the process of creating animations using the tracing technique.

 ### Exercise 11-1  Creating Animations with the Tracing Technique

To create an animation in Flash using the tracing technique, perform the following steps.

1.  Construct an animation, scene, or object in a 3D package. Render out an animation from the package as a series of

images in BMP or Macintosh PCT (PICT) format. In general, you will want to render the images at a pseudo-high resolution, such as 800 x 600. This way, when you trace the vectors, an adequate amount of detail will be retained.

In addition to the size of the images, you will also want to make sure you render the images with shadows on and in "Phong" mode. Generally, raytracing and radiosity are not needed, nor are they recommended.

2. Import the raster images into Flash on a single layer and lock it.

3. Create a new layer and trace the edges and elements in each frame of the animation. In general, the Pen tool works best for this operation.

4. Using the raster image layer as a reference, render the frames using the painting and drawing tools in Flash. The Dropper and Paint Bucket are the main tools you will use for this operation. Do not forget about the Lock Fill and Transform Fill modifiers, because they will be very useful as you render each frame.

5. Once you have finished rendering the frames, open the library for the current file (Window | Library) and delete the raster images.

 **TIP:** *When using the tracing technique, do not forget to open the library and delete the raster images when you are done. If you do not delete the raster images, the FLA file will be unnecessarily large.*

Although the tracing method is a valid technique for creating animations, it is by no means the fastest or the most accurate in relation to color transformations across multiple frames. It is very difficult, no matter what technique is used, to get gradients and fills to transform naturally across multiple frames. Using the tracing technique is also laborious because it requires each frame to be traced. Tracing is most effective when the number of frames is few, such as less than 30. As it relates to 3D animations, although the process of tracing is laborious, the typical end results are worth the effort.

# Vector Rasterization: Automatic Tracing

Raster-to-vector converters can also be used to generate vector images for 3D animations created in Flash. In general, this technique provides an efficient means of creating vector representations, yet some control over the resulting vector drawing is lost. Raster-to-vector conversion still has a long way to go concerning accuracy. Yet in many cases this process can reduce the time input required for generating source material for 3D animations.

The first place to look for raster-to-vector conversion is in traditional illustration packages. Macromedia FreeHand and Adobe Illustrator both offer autotrace capabilities. In both packages you can import a raster image and then use the autotrace feature to generate a vector representation. Yet, based on testing of these facilities, they are only best for very simple line drawings. When raster images contain fills and other complex gradations, the autotrace tools perform poorly at best.

However, Adobe Streamline is a software package specifically designed for changing bitmaps to vector images. The latest version (4.0) provides several advanced features:

- Support of major formats such as TIF and BMP
- Multilevel color support, including black-and-white to unlimited colors
- Adequate control over line recognition, accuracy, and path characteristics
- Ability to save both color and conversion settings as a composite setting
- Batch processing capability that can be used to convert multiple images at a time
- Path tools that can be used to edit generated vectors
- Ability to preview and view both raster and vector representations as overlays or individually
- An affordable price for such a powerful tool
- Ability to export in Adobe Illustrator AI format, which can also be successfully imported into Macromedia FreeHand and CorelDraw!

As with the manual tracing process, if you use Adobe Streamline you should with raster images that are 800 x 600 pixels or larger. If you use an automated raster-to-vector process, do not forget to use the Modify | Optimize command to reduce the point count in your files. If the animation is frame-by-frame animation (likely, it will be), use optimization on each frame to decrease file size. Examination of versions 3.0 and 4.0 of Adobe Dimensions shows that version 4.0 is significantly better in many aspects.

 **TIP:** *If you are creating 3D Flash animations, Adobe Dimensions may be a smart investment, potentially saving you a tremendous amount of time (and money) in the long run.*

 **CD-ROM NOTE:** *There are several examples in the* F5gai/chapter11/Streamline Process *folder (installed from the companion CD-*

*ROM) that demonstrate Flash animations that took significantly less time to generate due to Adobe Streamline.*

# Vector from 3D Packages

Of all the means for creating 3D animation, probably the most promising as it relates to extremely complex objects is the capture of vector components from a 3D environment. If you have access to packages such as AutoCAD, Pro/E, or another modeling environment, capturing the vectors for use in Flash is much easier.

Additionally, new plug-ins released for 3D Studio Max are advantageous for generating Flash animations. This is not to imply that there are no problems with some of these methods or that it is a one-step process even with the new 3-D Studio Max plug-ins and standalone programs. Nevertheless, these programs do provide the means for using complex images, derived from models or environments, within Flash without having to photo trace.

## Static Extraction

The specifics for capturing the vectors from a 3D environment will vary, depending on the modeling package used. This is predominantly because each CAD-focused modeling package outputs various file formats. The basic procedure is outlined in exercise 11-2, which follows.

### Exercise 11-2 Capturing Vectors from a 3D Environment

To capture vectors from a 3D environment, perform the following steps.

1.  Create a model and orient the viewing angle to a pleasing view.

2.  Capture a hidden-line-removed version of the vectors shown on-screen by exporting in a vector format, copying and pasting, or using a plot file.

3.  Rotate the object to the next "frame" in the animation and repeat step 2.

4.  Continue rotating and capturing until the entire "loop" or animation has been captured.

5.  Import the captured files into FreeHand (preferably) or Flash and render.

The following sections provide further detail on the process of obtaining vectors from two of the most common modeling packages: AutoCAD and Pro/E. Pointers for other modeling packages are included.

### Extracting Vector from AutoCAD

In exercise 11-3, which follows, you will create an animation using the 3D AutoCAD environment.

## Exercise 11-3  Using the AutoCAD Environment to Create an Animation

To use the 3D AutoCAD environment to create an animation, perform the following steps.

1. Create an object you want to animate, as shown in figure 11-1. Using this technique, you can have the object rotate around any of the three primary axes. Additionally, you could have it rotate simultaneously around all three. This example focuses on a simple rotation around one axis.

The basis for the 3D model shown in figure 11-1 was created in FreeHand. To get vector images into a modeling program such as AutoCAD, the *.ai* (Adobe Illustrator) file format works rather well. Once the line work was in AutoCAD, it was converted to a special line, called a polyline or pline, and extruded.

*Figure 11-1  Use a program such as AutoCAD to create a 3D object to be transferred to Flash.*

2. Choose a pleasing view in the modeling environment. Although this example will be a trimetric view, note that most modeling packages (AutoCAD included) can create isometric, dimetric, trimetric, and perspective views.

In this example, the logo shown in figure 11-1 will rotate around the Z axis. As with most modeling programs, the location of the object in relation to the origin for rotation is important. In AutoCAD, you can rotate around any point. However, to automate the generation from AutoCAD, the object has been located so that the center of the logo is at the origin (0,0,0). Thus, 0,0 can be entered when a base point for rotation as needed. Keep in mind that in AutoCAD rotation always occurs around the Z axis. If you want to rotate the object in another way (around absolute X or Y), you must reorient the coordinate plane so that the Z axis is aligned parallel to the axis around which you want the object to rotate.

3. Before you start extracting and rotating the object, place a locator object in the drawing, such as two intersecting lines. This will be used as a registration point. As shown in figure 11-1, you will notice a pair of crosshairs in the upper right

corner. This is important when you start piecing together the animation in FreeHand.

4.  Use the Hide command to generate a hidden-line-removed version of the screen image.

5.  Use the File | Export command and select Metafile (*.WMF) from the Save as Type drop-down menu. Name the file and click on OK.

You must determine the number of frames desired for the final animation. To determine the rotation of the object in the modeling environment, divide 360 by the number of frames. Keep in mind that more frames yield a smoother animation, but increase file size and the number of frames you must render in Flash.

6.  In this example, the animation will be 12 frames. Therefore, a WMF file will be saved for every 30 degrees of rotation. Using the Rotate command, rotate the object 30 degrees, and save as a WMF file. Repeat this process for each of the 12 frames.

Because the extracted WMF files from AutoCAD have tessellation lines (lines that define the polygons along the sides of cylinders and other objects), the extracted WMF files will be imported into FreeHand. There they can be aligned, cleaned up, and then exported into Flash for color rendering. If you import the WMF files directly into Flash, many symbols of small line segments will be created automatically. Importing into FreeHand first reduces the number of symbols generated when you get to Flash.

7.  Once all of the WMF files have been extracted, import each of the WMF files into FreeHand, and place each one on a separate layer.

8.  With all layers turned on, use the Align feature to align the images to the upper right (to the registration point).

9.  Turn off all layers and begin working on getting rid of the tessellation lines on each layer, as shown in figure 11-2. Cleaning up the drawings in FreeHand will significantly reduce the file size of the resulting Flash animation.

10. Once all layers are cleaned up, export the file as a Flash Movie, with the Animate Across Layers checkbox selected.

11. In Flash, import the animation file and then use the Paint Bucket to render each frame.

If you use *.wmf* or *.eps* files from AutoCAD (and some other a CAD packages), you will likely find that all arc segments are

Figure 11-2 Importing the *.wmf files into FreeHand allows you to remove the tessellation lines and align the images.*

imported as small line segments. As noted earlier, this significantly increases the resulting Flash file size. In addition, you may find that the drawings exported in these formats provide reduced accuracy. For example, arcs often become "wavy" rather than remaining as smooth Bezier curves.

To provide more accuracy, you may find that using Hewlett-Packard Graphics Language (HPGL) files from AutoCAD yield better end results, although it does take longer because you have to print, rather than export, the files. An HPGL file is the format normally sent to a plotter or printer. However, by plotting the file to the hard drive, you can actually use it as a method of transferring flat vector drawings out of a CAD package.

In actuality, any CAD package that can print or plot could use this method. However, an added benefit to HPGL files is that FreeHand will attempt to recognize line segments representing arcs and circles, replacing them with true arcs and circles. In this manner, HPGL files may prove to be more effective from AutoCAD, and quite possibly, other modeling programs. Exercise 11-4, which follows, takes you through the process of setting up AutoCAD to output appropriate HPGL files for import to FreeHand.

### Exercise 11-4  Setting Up AutoCAD HPGL Files for FreeHand Import

To set up AutoCAD HPGL files for import in FreeHand, perform the following steps.

1. Use the File | Printer Setup menu option to open the Preferences dialog box.

2. Use the New button to configure a new printer.

3. In the Add a Printer dialog box, select the Hewlett-Packard (HP-GL) ADI 4.2 driver and click on OK.

4. Select the 7574 model and press Enter. Other printer models may also work.

5. Accept the remaining default options by pressing the Enter key several times.

6. Once you are returned to the Preferences dialog box, you should find the new printer configuration listed in the window. Click on OK to close the dialog box.

Once the printer driver is configured, extracting the HPGL files is a relatively easy process, as outlined in exercise 11-5, which follows.

## Exercise 11-5  Extracting HPGL Files Imported into FreeHand

To extract HPGL files from FreeHand, perform the following steps.

1. Make sure the entire object is displayed in the current window, and then select File | Print. You can change the zoom level in AutoCAD using the View | Zoom menu options.

2. In the Print dialog box, change the Device and Default Information area to the new printer driver you just configured.

3. In the Additional Parameters area, make sure the Hide-Lines and Plot to File checkboxes are selected.

4. Click on the File Name button and assign a path and file name to the HPGL file. Keep in mind that you will be outputting several of these, so choose a name that lends itself to incremental naming.

5. Click on OK. AutoCAD will output a plotter file (HPGL file) to the hard drive.

6. Rotate the object (as before) and use the File | Print menu option to output the remaining "frames" for your animation.

7. To finish the HPGL-to-animation process, import the files in a manner similar to the WMF process. Use the FreeHand Import feature, with the Files of Type drop-down set to HPGL Plot File.

8. Place each HPGL file on a separate layer and then, with all layers visible, align the images using the registration point you created.

9. Clean up each of the layers by removing the tessellation lines, and then export a Flash file from FreeHand.

10. In Flash, use the Paint Bucket to render each of the frames in the animation.

 **CD-ROM NOTE:** *Sample files from the AutoCAD process are located in the* F5gai/chapter11/AutoCAD Process/ *folder, installed from the companion CD-ROM. The original FreeHand, AutoCAD, and Flash files are available. Due to the inaccuracy of the WMF file, the HPGL file was used instead. This process produced far more accurate arcs and circles in the resulting Flash files.*

### Extracting Vector from Pro/Engineer

Using Pro/E to extract your animation data is similar to the AutoCAD process, except that a different format for transfer of the data must be used. Realize that Pro/E and AutoCAD differ significantly in the way they create models. AutoCAD uses constructive geometry, whereas Pro/E is a parametric-based modeler. Additionally, AutoCAD models are polygonal, and Pro/E models are spline based. Nonetheless, if you have even remote experience in either package, you should at least be able to open a model and extract the basic data needed for a Flash animation. Exercise 11-6, which follows, takes you through the process of extracting vector information from Pro/E.

### Exercise 11-6  Extracting Vector Information from Pro/Engineer

To extract vector information from Pro/E, perform the following steps.

1. Begin by creating or opening your model or scene into Pro/E, such as that shown in figure 11-3.

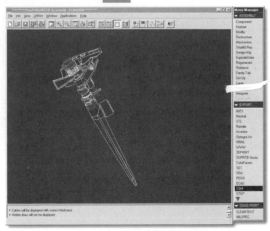

2. Use Utilities | Environment to turn off labels (such as datum plane notes, axis names, and object names) shown on the screen. If you do not turn them off, they will appear in the files you output (and subsequently increase the file's size tremendously).

3. In the menu bar at the top, set the display mode to Hidden Line Removed.

4. Choose an appropriate view for your animation using View | Spin/Pan/Zoom. This will bring up the dialog box shown in figure 11-4. Set the Type to Dynamic Orient and then use the sliders to get the object into an appropriate view.

*Figure 11-3  Models in Pro/E can also serve as a basis for Flash animations (courtesy of Shylo Diskey, Cory Shively, Matt Siddall, Adrienne Meech, and Chris Creager, Purdue University).*

In this animation, a simple "rotate around a single axis" will be performed. As with the AutoCAD process, you can rotate around any axis of the object, or around the origin. In this object, the rotation was set around the center of the object. Once you know what you want to do with the object, decide how many frames you want in the animation. Divide 360 by the number of frames to yield the degrees of rotation for each increment.

*Figure 11-4 View | Spin/Pan/Zoom brings up a dialog box in which you can set the starting orientation of the object.*

5. Capture the first frame in the "starting" orientation and save it as a CGM file. In Pro/E, you do this using File | Export | Model. In the Menu Manager, select CGM | Cleartext | Abstract and enter a file name at the bottom of the screen. Keep in mind that you will be exporting multiple images, so your file name should lend itself to incremental naming.

If you are unfamiliar with Pro/E, understand that Pro/E works in a default directory called the Working Directory. The CGM files you save will be stored there.

**TIP:** *If you want your CGM files to be stored in a specific location, use File | Working Directory to set the working directory before you export the CGM files.*

6. Rotate the model to its next orientation (360 divided by number of frames) using View | Spin/Pan/Zoom. For example, if you wanted 12 frames, the rotation would be 30 degrees.

7. Capture another CGM file.

8. Repeat this process until you have all frames for the animation.

In both the AutoCAD and Pro/E processes, if you have multiple objects that need to rotate simultaneously, you may find it easier to rotate the view than the objects. Efficiency will depend on how the objects being captured were created.

**CD-ROM NOTE:** *Sample files from the Pro/E process are located in the* F5gai/chapter11/Pro-E Process *folder, installed from the companion CD-ROM. Two animation files are available. One rotates the object around one axis; the other rotates around all three at one time.*

## Other 3D Environments

If you are using a package other than AutoCAD or Pro/E, you will likely find that there is at least one way to capture the vectors. If the package can output to a printer, you can at least use a printer (HPGL) file.

Another package worth noting as it relates to 3D models is a viewing and "rendering" program called LiveArt98 from ViewPoint DataLabs (*http://www.viewpoint.com*). This relatively inexpensive utility allows 3D models to be viewed in various illustration styles. The most useful feature of the program is that the model can be completely manipulated within the viewer; that is, you can view it from any angle, similar to VRML or VR files.

Originally, the purpose of this program was to provide those who knew nothing about modeling with the ability to use models in the documents they produce on a daily basis. Thus, LiveArt models can be embedded within all sorts of programs, not the least of which is Microsoft Word. An added (and undocumented) feature is the ability to drag and drop your own 3DS and DXF files into the viewer, which will render the files using the preset styles.

The one caveat to this program is that there is no way of capturing or outputting the vectors the viewer displays. If there were, all developers using Flash would undoubtedly purchase this program, because it would provide one direct way to go from a 3D model to a 2D vector representation. The only output from the program is the print capability and exporting TIF, GIF, JPG, and PNG (all raster). Due to this limitation, the program has not yet reached its full potential.

If you do much 3D work in Flash, you need to examine this program, regardless of its limitations. When you combine TIFs from LiveArt with Adobe Streamline's vector conversion capability, you can quickly generate very stylized Flash animations.

Several of the techniques mentioned in this chapter (including the AutoCAD, Pro/E, and Streamline tracing processes) add many symbols to your file when you import the images into Flash. If you use Break Apart to separate the individual frame images from their symbols, you can then delete these extraneous symbols. To delete a large number of symbols without having to right-click on each symbol and delete the symbol in the library, use Window | Library to open the current file's library. Then select multiple symbol names in the window, access the Options menu, and select Delete. This will let you delete multiple symbols easily.

If you have a modeling program other than AutoCAD or Pro/E, there is likely at least one way of obtaining vectors. In general, you should look for the following features:

- Support for exporting a vector format, such as EPS, CGM, or AI. These formats are the most widely supported intermediate file formats for 3D-based packages. Generally, these three formats can be imported into FreeHand or Flash. Yet, with the wide variety of graphics file formats available, be prepared to spend a little extra cash for a conversion program such as Hijaak Pro or Debabelizer. Some 3D programs do not support these standard metafile formats.

- Support of copy-and-paste functionality. In this scenario, you can select the screen representation of the modeling vectors and copy them to the clipboard. You then paste them into FreeHand or Flash. Some modeling programs do support copy and paste; however, the routine generates bitmaps rather then vector representations. In addition, the complexity of the object(s) being copied and the amount of RAM available may limit the use of this technique.

- HPGL (printer) output support. Even though the software can generate hardcopy prints, this is the method that will most likely work for almost any 3D modeling environment. By setting up a printer/plotter driver to write an HPGL file to the hard drive, you can then import the resulting file into FreeHand or Flash for editing to remove any extraneous data. Again, it is preferable to load the file into FreeHand and then export to Flash.

The previous method has one severe caveat: all arcs are plotted as individual line segments. This factor exponentially increases your file size because of the number of points used. When importing an HPGL file into FreeHand, it will attempt to recognize arc components consisting of line segments and replace them with true arcs. However, many arcs will still remain as individual line segments. In this scenario, the best effort is to manually replace arcs in FreeHand.

 **TIP:** *If you have to use the HPGL process, the latest version of FreeHand has many facilities that can help you. The Cleanup | Simplify filter is invaluable, as is the ability to join and work with layers.*

### Dynamic Extraction

3D Flash animations began appearing on the Web not long after the release of Flash 3. Everyone wanted a simple, straightforward method for quickly generating Flash animations from a 3D model. Until lately, all of the other techniques in this book were the only way to generate 3D Flash animations, and they are anything but quick!

Following the release of Flash 4, three supplementary plug-ins/programs that can generate 3D animations in the Flash SWF format were released. They are Illustrate! 5 by Digimation, Inc. (*http://www.digimation.com*); Vecta 3D by IdeaWorks3D (*http://www.ideaworks3D.com/*); and Swift3D by Electronic Rain (*http://www.swift3D.com*). All three solutions will generate flat, animated vector files for Flash. As of this writing, Swift3D and Vecta3D are the only solutions that will output gradients. The solution will output flat colors only. Swift3D or Vecta3D might be your best bet.

 **NOTE:** *Several of the developer sites mentioned in Chapter 2 provide a variety of information about these two programs. Demonstration versions of Swift3D and Vecta3D are found on the companion CD-ROM.*

## Vector from Other Packages

As ingenuity is the mother of invention, depending on what software you have available, you could probably discover many ways of creating animations in Flash. Undoubtedly, Swift3D and Vecta 3D should be used if you have many 3D animations to create.

However, for those who are not blessed with finances or software packages and utilities, other programs can also be used to help you more quickly and more easily generate animations. Some packages you may have, and some you may not. Nevertheless, these ingenious methods are worth a brief mention if nothing else.

### Microsoft Word

If you are familiar with the data tracked by sites such as MediaMetrix (*http://www.mediametrix.com*), you know that Microsoft Office is one package that most people are likely to have. You may not have AutoCAD or Pro/E, but most likely, you own or otherwise have access to Word.

With Microsoft Word's 3D tools, you can create, albeit simple, animations. Although it really was not designed for it, you can use Word to generate basic 3D line work from which you can create Flash animations. Exercise 11-7, which follows, takes you through the process of using Word to generate 3D images.

**NOTE:** *Keep in mind that this method has two problems. It works with very simple shapes only, and Word can rotate a shape up to 180 degrees only.*

### Exercise 11-7  Using Word to Generate 3D Images

To use Word's 3D tools to generate 3D images, perform the following steps.

1. Open Word's drawing tools by right-clicking on one of the toolbars at the top of the screen. Select the Drawing option in the context menu that appears.

2. Use the draw menu to create a polygon, or paste a polygon from another package, such as FreeHand or Flash. Figure 11-5 shows a shape that is simple enough for Word to manipulate.

Realize that Word can deal only with very basic, singular polygons. If you have two closed shapes, peculiar overlapping will occur because Word is not really designed for the creation of 3D animation. Keep in mind that Word can handle basic shapes only, such as the shape shown in figure 11-5.

*Figure 11-5  A simple shape that can be manipulated in Word.*

3. In the Drawing toolbar, turn on 3D by clicking on the 3D icon on the far right. Select 3D Settings from the menu that pops up.

4. Use the 3D Settings toolbar to set a Depth, Direction, Lighting, Surface, and 3D Color.

5. Once you have the first "frame" defined, copy the object to the clipboard and paste it into Flash.

6. Back in Word, use the Tilt options in the 3D Settings toolbar to rotate the simple object.

7. Again, copy and paste the new image to the clipboard. Repeat these steps until all frames are in Flash.

If you decide to use the Word process, it is probably best to use the Wireframe Surface option and then render the object in Flash. The gradients created by Word will generally make files quite large.

### Adobe Dimensions

There has been much talk on the Web concerning Adobe Dimensions as a possible tool for outputting material for 3D animations in Flash. No doubt, one of the goals for the program was to easily work in 3D with vector-based, 2D objects. However, Dimensions has several problems. In general, Dimensions works well for simple geometry and basic transformations. It will also handle some animation tasks. Yet, it is a somewhat difficult program to use. Additionally, the files the program outputs require rerendering, because their gradients consist of line and shape blends instead of fills.

Many Flash developers like using Dimensions. However, version 1.0 of the program was better than 3.0 in terms of use with Flash. In addition, as with many of the procedures discussed in this chapter, using many of the automatically generated symbols is a way of reducing file sizes. Unfortunately, Dimensions is notorious for adding hundreds.

## ▪▪▪ What Format? What Purpose?

Although vector graphics have many advantages on the Web and for print, file formats related to vector graphics are often tricky. The biggest problem is that vector formats such as Encapsulated PostScript (EPS), Computer Graphics Metafile (CGM), Windows Metafile (WMF), Enhanced WMF (EMF), and Macintosh Picture format (PICT) can contain more than just vector data. This is why many of them are called (and even have in their name) *metafile* formats.

Metafile formats are special in that they can contain vector, raster, or both. As if this were not enough, there are also different "flavors" of a format; that is, the way in which a format is written. For example, you may have an EPS file that favors Adobe Illustrator and dislikes Macromedia FreeHand, or vice versa. Generally, to find the best path from software A to software B requires some trial and error. In an effort to assist you in this area, reference the following tips and tricks related to file formats:

- In general, the Adobe Illustrator EPS format and the Macromedia FreeHand EPS format are different "flavors." If you import an EPS file into FreeHand and it is placed as a box with an X in it, understand that you are dealing with an Adobe Illustrator EPS file.

- Windows Metafiles (WMF) do not retain arcs and circles. These elements are broken into individual line segments, similar to an HPGL file. It is preferable to avoid this format if possible. Use an Enhanced WMF (EMF) file instead. This format does retain arcs and circles. As a side note, it allows you to create images that are completely scalable, with no degradation, in Microsoft products.

- Although the PICT format works very well on the Macintosh, it can be somewhat unpredictable on the PC. Obviously, you can take a Photoshop PICT on the Mac to Photoshop on the PC with little difficulty. However, in general, PC applications do not care for PICT files because of PICT files' capacity to contain metadata.

- Computer Graphics Metafiles (CGM) are characteristic formats from high-end workstations or programs. For desktop users, CGM format may present many of the same "flavor" differences as the EPS format. Just because your program will read CGM does not mean it will be able to parse every CGM file. Yet, if you use the Pro/E method for capturing vectors, use of the CGM format is required. Perhaps the best program for interpreting Pro/E's CGM files is CorelDraw!. It is not necessarily the best for drawing and creation, but it supports a wide array of file formats for importing and exporting. It is worth purchasing even if you only use it as a file translator.

- When taking static vector images from Flash to FreeHand, use the Adobe Illustrator (AI) format. Note that mask layers will not transfer. Thus, they will not retain their "paste inside" effect, regardless of which vector format is chosen.

- Frequently, when you export from FreeHand to the SWF format, FreeHand will tell you that you have fills, lines, or strokes that Flash does not support. This message can appeareven though you have not used a paste inside, arrowheads, line styles, or custom fills. Nonetheless, even when you are prompted with this message, the generated SWF file will probably still contain the mainstay of your FreeHand drawing.

- When exporting static images from Flash for use in Microsoft products, use the EMF format. This format retains arc and circle properties and is scaleable.

# ▪ ▪ ▪ Summary

In this chapter, you have examined a wealth of methods for generating 3D Flash animations. Indeed, the best method for creating 3D animations depends on time, task, and the software resources available. Keep in mind that the end results of 3D animations in Flash are usually very impressive, even if the means seem contrived and monotonous. Ultimately, for each project that seems to demand 3D, evaluate that need based on the difficulty of achieving it. Make sure you need 3D before you spend hours generating a Flash representation of it.

# chapter 12

# Creating Animated Effects

## ▪ ▪ ▪ Introduction

While examining "how-to" examples created in Flash, one of the significant aspects is animated effects. How are transitions and cool text effects created? What about methods for creating background effects and advanced guide layers and masks?

Chapter 4 included simple examples of how Flash can be used to create basic animations. This chapter provides many examples of more complex animations. From text effects and transitions to advanced guide layers and mask layers, these examples should get your creativity flowing.

Indeed, this chapter's examples may not be visually astounding because the focus is more on the *how* than refining the end product. Animations can be tweaked for hours to get an end product that has that special look. Yet, from a procedural perspective, the examples in this chapter should still be impressive. Apply what is explained in this chapter to create any number of things. More than likely, you will think of some things not included here. When animating in Flash, the imagination is the only real limit.

 **CD-ROM NOTE:** *Many samples on the companion CD-ROM are not covered in the book. Make sure to examine the* F5gai/chapter12 *folder, installed from the companion CD-ROM. These examples include more tips, techniques, and nuggets of how-to information.*

## ▪ ▪ ▪ Objectives

In this chapter, you will:

- Learn how to create various text effects such as hard blurs, soft blurs, rolling credits, and more

- Find out how to simulate transitions using masks, including fades and dissolves

- Discover how to use masks to create more realistic spotlight effects and magnification effects

- Understand how to use closed-path guide layers to create closed-path animations, as well as simulate 3D , shadows, and reflections

# Animated Text Effects

One of the benefits of working with text objects in Flash is that once a single text effect is constructed, it can generally be reused over and over. When the basis of a text effect is a graphic symbol, a series of text blocks can be created that uses the same effect, without having to recreate the effect multiple times.

This section describes three common text effects used on the Web. Granted, not every effect possible can be described in this book. Nevertheless, with the information provided, you should be able to get started. The *chapter12* folder, installed from the companion CD-ROM, contains other samples.

 **TIP:** *A new software application, called SWiSH, allows you to more quickly create text effects. See* http://www.swishzone.com *for more information. If you are using a PC, a demonstration version is available. There is no Macintosh demo available.*

## Hard Blurs

One of the most basic text effects is the hard blur. This is generally used on a mouse-over or some other menu or button effect. Realize that most of these effects are components that are intermixed with other items, such as buttons. Few of these effects stand alone. These effects are generally part of a larger animation, which is why they are created as symbols. As such, they can be easily inserted into other movies. Exercise 12-1, which follows, takes you through the process of creating a hard blur effect.

 **CD-ROM NOTE:** *To visually understand what a hard blur looks like when animated, open the file* hardblur.fla *located in the* F5gai/ chapter12/text effects/ *folder, installed from the companion CD-ROM. Consider starting there if you learn better by dissecting movies.*

---

 *Exercise 12-1 Creating a Hard Blur Effect*

To create a hard blur effect, perform the following steps.

1.  Start a new movie in Flash.

2. Select Insert | New Symbol (Ctrl + F8) to create a new symbol. This symbol will be the text on which the movie symbol (which will actually be the effect) will be based. Select Behavior as Graphic and name the symbol Hard Blur.

3. Use the Text tool to insert some text into the Hard Blur symbol. Center the text on the crosshairs on the stage. You may also want to adjust the size, color, or font of the text element. Then click on the Scene 1 link in the Edit Path to switch back to the main movie timeline.

4. Select Insert | New Symbol again, and select Movie Clip as the Behavior. Name the symbol Hard Blur MC.

5. Open the library for the current movie by selecting Window | Library.

6. In the library preview window, click-drag the graphic symbol Hard Blur to the stage. Line up the two sets of crosshairs. Close the library window.

7. The symbol you just placed is on layer 1. Rename layer 1 Static.

8. Click-drag the duration of the sprite, or use the F5 function key to insert frames in the timeline, to extend the sprite to frame 10.

9. Set up the top and bottom blurring tweens. Insert two layers and place one above, and one below, the Static layer in the timeline. Name the upper layer Top Blur and the lower layer Bottom Blur.

10. Right-click on the sprite in the Static layer and select Copy Frames from the context menu.

11. Paste the copied frames in frame 1 of the Top Blur layer. You may need to adjust the endframe marker so that the Top Blur layer ends at frame 10.

12. Repeat Step 11 on the Bottom Blur layer.

13. Hide the Static layer.

14. Insert a keyframe in frame 10 in the Top Blur layer and the Bottom Blur layer.

15. Select frame 10 in the Top Blur layer and use the arrow keys or the Info panel to move the text on the Top Blur layer up 30 pixels and to the right 30 pixels.

16. Select frame 10 in the Bottom Blur layer and use the arrow keys or the Info panel to move the text on the Bottom Blur layer down 30 pixels and to the left 30 pixels.

*Figure 12-1 Move the text to create the blur effect.*

17. When you turn on the Static layer, the stage should look as it does in figure 12-1.

18. If you turned the Static layer on, hide it again. Also hide the Bottom Blur layer.

19. In frame 10 in the Top Blur layer, right-click on the symbol (on the stage) in the Top Blur layer and select Panels | Effect from the context menu. Set the instance's Alpha to 0, which should make it "disappear" from the stage.

20. Repeat step 19 for the symbol on the Bottom Blur layer.

21. Right-click on frame 1 in the Top Blur layer and select Create Motion Tween.

22. Repeat step 21 on the Bottom Blur layer.

23. Turn the Static layer back on.

24. Click on the Scene 1 item in the Edit Path to return to the main movie timeline.

25. Insert the movie clip symbol you just created onto the stage.

26. Use Control | Test Movie to play the animation and see the effect.

Before finishing this example, take a look at one more thing. Note that because you built your movie clip based on a graphic symbol, any changes you make to the graphic symbol will appear in the movie clip.

27. Access the Hard Blur graphic symbol using the Symbol list button.

28. Change the color of the text to a 40-percent gray by selecting on it and using the Fill color swatch in the Colors section of the toolbar or the Fill panel.

29. Switch back to Scene 1 and then test the movie again. Notice how the modification to the graphic symbol is automatically incorporated into the movie clip symbol. This is one of the powerful things about using symbols for everything!

30. To finish this movie, add some sound effects to add interest. A gong sound was added to enhance the CD-ROM example. Do not forget about the aural element. It adds a new dimension to movies!

> **TIP:** *If you only want the clip to play once, place a Stop action in the last frame of the movie clip.*

## Soft Blurs

Similar to the last example, a soft blur can be created by adding more tween layers to a movie clip. In exercise 12-2, which follows, you will create a graphic and movie clip symbol, similar to the previous exercise. However, this time the movie clip will have more layers, to create a softer effect.

> **CD-ROM NOTE:** *To see what a soft blur looks like when animated, open the file* softblur.fla *located in the* F5gai/chapter12/texteffects/ *folder, installed from the companion CD-ROM. This file was developed according to the procedure outlined in exercise 12-2.*

---

### Exercise 12-2  Creating a Soft Blur Effect

To create a soft blur, perform the following steps.

1. Start a new Flash file.
2. Make a graphic symbol that contains a string of text, similar to the last exercise.
3. Create a movie clip symbol and insert the graphic symbol on the stage of the movie clip.
4. Name the existing layer in the movie clip Main.
5. Build three new layers, named Fade, Medium, and Tall.
6. Copy the Soft Blur symbol from the Main layer.
7. Use Paste in Place (Ctrl + Shift + V) to paste the symbol to the three new layers.
8. Extend the duration of the four layers to frame 25.
9. Insert keyframes at frames 15 and 25 in the Medium and Tall layers.
10. Add a keyframe at frame 15 of the Fade layer.
11. Turn off all layers except for the Fade layer. Your environment should look like that shown in figure 12-2.
12. Prepare the fade-in for the text. Change the Alpha of the symbol instance in frame 1 in the Fade layer to 0 using the Effects panel. Then, right-click on frame 1 and select Create Motion Tween from the context menu.

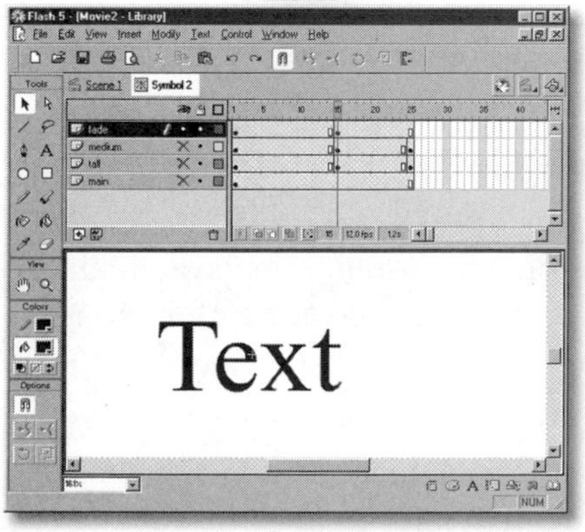

*Figure 12-2 Set up the keyframes and hide the layers.*

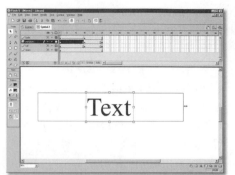

*Figure 12-3 Scale the instance of the text on the Medium layer.*

*Figure 12-4 Scale the instance of the text on the Medium layer, using the corner point.*

*Figure 12-5 Scale the instance of the text on the Tall layer.*

13. Hide the Fade layer.

14. Unhide the Medium layer and click on frame 1. Scale the instance of the text, as shown in figure 12-3. Make sure to grab the handle on the edge, not on the corner.

15. Change the Alpha of the symbol instance in frame 1 in the Medium layer to 0.

16. Right-click on frame 1 in the Medium layer, copy it, and paste it into frame 25.

17. In frame 25, scale the instance up slightly by using the Arrow tool and a corner of the instance, as shown in figure 12-4.

18. Right-click on frame 1. Select Create Motion Tween from the context menu.

19. Right-click on frame 15 and select Create Motion Tween from the context menu.

20. Hide the Medium layer.

21. Unhide the Tall layer and click on frame 1. Scale the instance of the text, as shown in figure 12-5. Notice that the symbol is scaled more than that of the Medium layer.

22. In frame 1 in the Tall layer, change the Alpha of the symbol instance to 0. Right-click on frame 1, copy it, and paste it into frame 25.

23. In frame 25, slightly scale up the instance using the Arrow tool and a corner of the instance, similar to step 12.

24. Right-click on frame 1 and select Create Motion Tween.

25. Repeat step 24 in frame 15.

26. Hide the Tall layer and reveal the Main layer.

27. Right-click on the instance in layer Main. Select Panels | Effect and set its Alpha to 30 percent.

28. Reveal all layers.

29. Because the animation is a movie clip, insert it into the main movie timeline and use Control | Text Movie to see the animation.

**TIP:** *To stop the clip from looping when it plays, add a stop in frame 25 of the Tall or Medium layer.*

After completing the soft blur, try to modify the text. Access the graphic symbol the movie clip is based on and change the text. Reinsert the symbol into the main movie and play it again. This is how you can create one effect and reuse it over and over, simply by changing the text!

# Rolling Credits

Of all the text effects you will want to create, rolling credits is one of the easiest to do. Many people see this effect and believe it is achieved with a mask layer. However, it is much simpler. Exercise 12-3, which follows, takes you through the process of creating rolling credits.

## Exercise 12-3 Creating Rolling Credits

To create rolling credits, perform the following steps.

1. Create a layer named Background.

2. Create a solid fill that spreads across the entire stage. Use the Rectangle tool and set its Stroke to No Color. Set its fill color to one of the existing swatches in the color palette.

3. Draw a rectangle consisting of lines only (no fill) in the area of the screen where you want the rolling credits to appear, as shown in figure 12-6.

4. Because the stroke rectangle and fill rectangle reside on the same layer, the stroke will "cut into" the fill, allowing you to delete the fill area that falls within the stroke. Select the fill area inside the stroke and delete it, as shown in figure 12-7. (See also color plate B-14.)

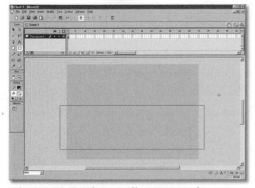

*Figure 12-6 The smaller rectangle cuts the background fill.*

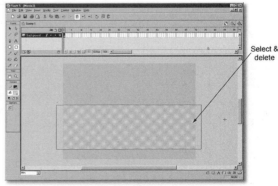

*Figure 12-7 Select and delete the portion of the fill inside the stroke. (See also color plate B-14.)*

Now you will fill this area with a linear gradient that fades from the background color to 100 percent transparent and back to the background color. However, first you must create a transparent swatch to be used in the gradient.

5. Open the Mixer panel.

6. Enter *255, 255,* and *255*, respectively, into the R, G, and B fields.

7. Enter *0* into the Alpha field.

8. Select Add Swatch from the Mixer panel's menu.

9. Open the Fill panel to create a gradient color that fades from the color of the fill (whatever color you chose in step 2) to 100 percent transparent (the "color" you just defined) and back to the fill color, as shown in figure 12-8. (See also color plate B-15.) To add color markers to the gradient definition, click along the gradient bar. To change the color of one of markers, use the swatch drop-down list that appears.

*Figure 12-8 Define the linear gradient with solid colors on the ends and transparent colors in the middle. (See also color plate B-15.)*

10. Fill the rectangle with the new gradient. Use the Transform Fill option for the Paint Bucket to modify the fill to your liking. You will need to at least rotate the fill so that it goes from top to bottom, as opposed to left to right, as shown in figure 12-9. (See also color plate B-16.)

11. Double click the on lines that surround the gradient and delete them so that you see no outline around the gradient area.

12. To simplify things, lock the Background layer.

13. Create a new layer for the animated text and create a graphic symbol of the body of text you want to animate.

14. Create a motion tween of the text passing over the gradient area. When setting up the tween, the text should start and end outside the place where the transparency begins.

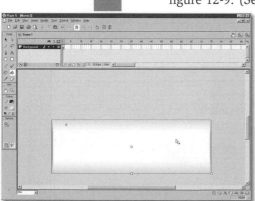

*Figure 12-9 Fill the rectangle with the gradient and modify it so that it goes from top to bottom. (See also color plate B-16.)*

15. Once the tween is set up, move the text layer behind the Background layer and play the animation by press Enter.

**CD-ROM NOTE:** *Examine the file* rolling.fla, *and several other text effects in files located in the* F5gai/chapter12 *folder, installed from the companion CD-ROM. Text effects included are the following animations:*

- *Flipping text*
- *Stretching text*
- *Blooming text*
- *Tumbling text*
- *Exploding text*
- *Rippling text*
- *Shifting text*

# A Mask for Any Occasion: Transitions

Unlike other animation and authoring programs, Flash does not have its own built-in transitions. Transitions must be created using tweened effects and masks.

## Fading and Dissolving

The first transition to examine is the creation of a fade or a dissolve. Earlier you read about how to adjust the transparency (Alpha) of a symbol on the stage. To create a fade-in or a fade-out, use the transparency settings, directly on the object, combined with a motion tween. Exercise 12-4, which follows, takes you through the process of creating a fade transition.

### Exercise 12-4  Creating a Fade (Dissolve) Transition

To create a fade-in or fade-out, perform the following steps.

1. Start a new Flash file.

2. Begin with some object, such as an imported graphic. Change it into a graphic symbol.

3. Set up a series of frames during which you want the object to fade in or fade out, such as a fade-in over 10 frames. Place a keyframe at the beginning (frame 1) and ending (frame 10) of the frame series.

4. To have the object fade in, set the Alpha at frame 1 to 0 percent. To make the object fade out, set the transparency at frame 10 to 0 percent.

Remember, right-click on an object in the stage and select Effect from the context menu to set the transparency via the Effects panel. The Alpha of an object is a property of the instance on the stage.

5. After specifying the transparency of the objects on the stage, right-click in a frame between frames 2 and 9. Select Create Motion Tween from the context menu.

6. Test the transition by pressing the Enter key.

> **CD-ROM NOTE:** *View an example of a fade (dissolve) transition by referencing the file* fade.fla *located in the* F5gai/chapter12/transitions/ *folder, installed from the companion CD-ROM.*

## Wipe or Reveal

Create a wipe, or reveal-type, transition by using an animated mask. All of the transitions that use layer masks require that the mask be a symbol. Keep in mind the rules that govern the use of motion tweens; mainly that symbols are required. Exercise 12-5, which follows, takes you through the process of creating a wipe transition.

### Exercise 12-5  Creating a Wipe (Reveal) Transition

To create a wipe transition, perform the following steps.

1. After you have created the object you want to transition on the stage, change it to a graphic symbol.

2. On a new layer, draw a rectangular or circular fill. It will be used as the mask. The shape of the mask determines how the final transition will look. Additionally, ensure that the mask is large enough to completely cover the object you want to reveal. Make the fill a symbol in order to animate it.

3. Once the fill is defined as a symbol, animate it using a motion tween. In a reveal transition, the mask moves over the top of the object to reveal it. Thus, to define the animation for the mask, create a motion tween animation in which the mask moves over the top of object, as shown in figure 12-10.

> **NOTE:** *Keep in mind that the mask and the object(s) to be masked must reside on different layers.*

4. Once the motion tween for the mask is specified, double click on the layer name to open the Layer Properties dialog box. You can also access this dialog box using the Modify | Layer menu option.

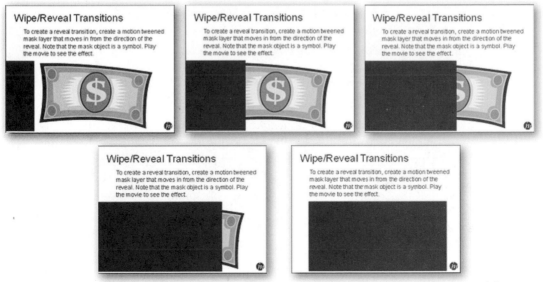

*Figure 12-10 Define the movement of the mask for the reveal transition.*

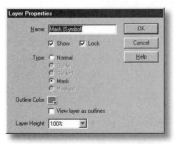

*Figure 12-11 Setting the layer to mask using the Layer Properties dialog box.*

5. In the dialog box, select the Mask radio button, as shown in figure 12-11. Click on OK. When you do this, the layer beneath the layer set to Mask should be set to Masked automatically. This is visually displayed in the timeline by the small arrows that replace the layer icons (see figure 12-12).

*Figure 12-12 The timeline shows which layer is set to Mask and which is set to Masked.*

6. Play the animation to show the reveal transition.

Keep in mind that the mask layer affects the layer directly beneath it. However, a single mask layer may affect multiple layers if you want. Use the Layer Properties dialog box to set the layers that should be masked. Additionally, both the mask and its respective layers become locked when mask or masked is chosen in Layer Properties. If either layer is unlocked, the mask will no longer function.

**CD-ROM NOTE:** *To see an example of a fade (dissolve) transition, reference the file* reveal.fla *located in the* book/chapter12/transitions/ *folder, installed from the companion CD-ROM.*

## Push/Cover

Another type of transition worthy of noting is push or cover. In this transition, one object appears to push or cover a background object, as shown in figure 12-13. When creating this transition in Flash, use two masks that simultaneously animate to cover and reveal objects on different layers. Exercise 12-6, which follows, takes you through the process of creating a push transition.

*Figure 12-13 The push or cover transition pushes or covers one object over another.*

 **CD-ROM NOTE:** *To view an example of the transition in exercise 12-6, check out the file* push.fla *located in the* F5gai/chapter12/transitions/ *folder, installed from the companion CD-ROM.*

### Exercise 12-6 Creating a Push (Cover) Transition

In this exercise, you will create an animation in which the faucet stays on stage for five seconds. Then a cover animation occurs over five frames, revealing the telephone, which remains on-screen for five frames.

1. First, create two objects on two different layers. In this example, the telephone character will push or cover the water faucet character, as shown in figure 12-13. Note that this transition works best if the two objects are close to the same size.

2. Once the two objects are on different layers, turn off one layer, preferably the object that is being covered. In the example, the telephone will cover the faucet; therefore, the faucet layer is turned off.

3. Make a symbol to use as the mask for the animation. Use the same mask for both objects. Make sure the mask is big enough to completely cover both objects.

4. Place the mask symbol over the top of the first object, but on a different layer. This cover will occur over five frames, beginning in frame 5 and ending in frame 10. The mask will be completely over the telephone in frame 10, and in frame 5 the mask will be to the left of the telephone, as shown in figure 12-14.

Frame 5                                              Frame 10

*Figure 12-14 Placement of the mask for the first object (telephone).*

5. Create a motion tween for the mask to animate it. Right-click in a frame between the keyframes and select Create Motion Tween.

6. To make the mask work, use the Layer Properties dialog box on the layer that contains the animated mask and set it to Mask. One half of this transition is now set up. Press Enter to play the animation to see how it is developing.

7. To finish the second half of this transition, create a mask for the faucet that moves from center to right of the faucet while the mask for the telephone moves from left to center. In the timeline, both masks are tweened at the same time.

8. Make the layer that contains the mask for the telephone the current layer and unlock it. This temporarily turns off its mask characteristics. Click on frame 10 in the timeline. This should be where the mask is in the center of the screen. Select the mask on the stage and copy it.

9. Hide the telephone layer and lock its mask. This enables you to see the mask but keeps you from inadvertently changing it.

10. Turn on the Faucet layer and create a new layer above it. The new layer will be used for the Faucet's mask.

11. In the newly created layer, click in frame 5 and create a keyframe. Use the Edit | Paste in Place menu option to paste the copied mask symbol into the center of the screen. The new pasted mask and the already existing mask should be next to each other on the stage.

12. Create a keyframe in frame 10 of the faucet's mask layer. Turn off the telephone's mask layer and use the right arrow key to nudge the faucet's mask to the right.

13. Turn on the telephone's mask layer. Click in frame 10 and nudge the faucet's mask to the right so that its left edge is adjacent to the right edge of the telephone's mask.

14. Set the faucet's mask layer to mask mode and lock the telephone and its mask. Press Enter to view the resulting cover transition.

## Shape Defines Transition

When it comes to mask transitions, note that the shape of the mask defines the transition. In prior examples, plain rectangular masks were used. Note that you can make the shape of a mask any shape you want, with only a couple of limitations. You cannot use a color blend tween on a mask. If you want an object to fade in or out, make it a symbol and apply the transparency tween to the object. Remember that no matter what the opacity of the object you use as the mask, the mask will always be 100 percent opaque. The second limitation: you cannot use a shape tween on a mask.

 **CD-ROM NOTE:** *To see an example of circular mask transition, reference the file* circular.fla *located in the* F5gai/chapter12/transitions/ *folder, installed from the companion CD-ROM.*

# ■■■ More on Masks

In addition to text effects and transition effects, masks provide three other effects worth noting. These include a more realistic spotlight using partially transparent fills, magnification effects, and rolling credits.

 **NOTE:** *The magnification effects described here are a simulated effect as a result of animation and masks. This should not be confused with a movie's ability to zoom via ActionScript or FlashScript Player commands, which are discussed in more detail in chapters 16 and 17, respectively.*

# A More Realistic Spotlight

In Chapter 4, you saw the basics of how a spotlight effect could be created using a plain circular fill as a mask. The result was not very realistic. Although plain fills can be used as masks, take it one step further by using a mask and another fill object. A second fill object softens the edges of the mask, creating a much more aesthetically pleasing effect. Exercise 12-7, which follows, takes you through the process of creating a push (cover) transition.

 **CD-ROM NOTE:** *To view an example of spotlight trick described in exercise 12-7, open the file* realspotlight.fla *located in the* F5gai/chapter12/masks/ *folder, installed from the companion CD-ROM.*

## Exercise 12-7  Creating a Push or Cover Transition

To create a push transition, perform the following steps.

1. Begin by importing or creating an image that you can "reveal" using your spotlight. In this example, the spotlight reveals a cityscape image of Seattle, Washington.

2. Create a new symbol and draw a filled circle with the Oval tool. Make the fill color something other than black.

When creating spotlight effects, make sure the spotlight reveals a large enough portion of the background image. If you do not let the audience see enough of the background through the spotlight, they will not able to tell what the image is.

3. Make the second object to create the soft edge around the spotlight. Double click on the line that surrounds the oval and cut it (Ctrl + X or Command + X). This will be used as the basis for the second object.

4. Make a new graphic symbol and paste the copied circle in place so that its position is exactly the same as the previous symbol.

5. Create a new radial gradient that blends from black to transparent. Remember that before you can create a gradient that uses transparency, you must create a transparent color and swatch in the Mixer panel. You can then use the Fill panel to create the gradient. Use the settings to produce a new gradient, as shown in figure 12-15.

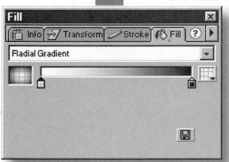

*Figure 12-15 Creating the radial gradient to be used for the spotlight.*

6. Select the Paint Bucket and fill the circle with the new gradient. Make sure the gradient is perfectly centered within the circle. Then delete the outer line.

7. Switch back to the main movie timeline. Use the mask symbol to create the typical spotlight animation that has sharp edges. Open the Library window and place the mask symbol on the stage. Set the positional keyframes and tween them. Then set the layer's mode to Mask. This process is just like the one used to create the spotlight animation, as in the example in Chapter 4.

8. To finish the effect, use the soft edge fill you created and place it over the top of the mask, having it move the same way as the mask. Align the key positions of the second symbol exactly over the mask and tween it. You may have to unlock the layer mask so that you can position the upper object.

9. Change the background color of the stage to black to finish the effect.

## Magnify

Another effect that is quite easy to create using masks is a magnification effect. By building on the previous example, you can create a movie that has a magnifying glass pass over it. As it does so, the image will appear to magnify right before the viewer's eyes. It is really nothing more than a combination of a mask that reveals a background image and an enlarged image with a more complex symbol for the second object.

 **CD-ROM NOTE:** *To dissect the magnification example to see how it works, reference the file* magnify.fla *located in the* F5gai/chapter12/masks/ *folder, installed from the companion CD-ROM. Also in this folder is an example of how to use masks for reflections. View the file* reflect.fla.

# ■ ■ ■ Advanced Guide Layers

Aside from the advanced animations that use masks, guide layers provide the capability for complex creations. Chapter 4 described the basics. Here, you will read about using closed-path guide layers and how to control elements that move along them. Additionally, you will discover ways to simulate 3D objects, shadows, and reflections.

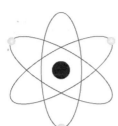

# Atom Animation

To demonstrate how to use closed-path guide layers, examine a basic animation of a 2D atom, as shown in figure 12-16. In exercise 12-8, which follows, you will animate the looping ball around the layer guide, create one path, and then reuse the path via symbols.

*Figure 12-16  Use guide layers to create an animated atom.*

## Exercise 12-8 Creating a Closed Guide Animation

To create a closed guide animation, perform the following steps.

1. Import or draw the basic image, as shown in figure 12-16. All you need is the black fill in the center, one ellipse (in a vertical orientation), and the small ball on the ellipse. These three elements should be graphic symbols so that they can be reused.

2. Begin by placing the center dot in the stage. Then place the ellipse symbol three times, orienting it as shown in figure 12-16. Do not place the "electrons" on the ellipses. You may need to switch to View | Outlines to line up the items. Use the Modify | Transform | Scale and Rotate selection to enter numeric information for the rotation of the ellipses.

3. Create a new movie clip symbol named Rotating. This will be the symbol that will be used on the stage for the three rotating electrons. Assign the default layer the name Electron.

4. Use Window | Library and place the "electron" on the stage.

5. Using the Add Guide Layer button, create a guide layer for the Electron layer.

6. Click-drag the ellipse symbol from the Library window to the Guide layer.

7. With the ellipse selected on the stage, select Modify | Break Apart. This "detaches" the ellipse from the symbols, making it an object rather than an instance. Then use Modify | Ungroup on the ellipse to make it a stage object.

 **NOTE:** *When using guide layers, they must be stage-level objects to work properly. You cannot use a grouped element or a symbol as a guide layer.*

8. Extend the two existing keyframes out to frame 20. The loop of the electron around the ellipse will occur over 20 frames.

9. With Edit | Snap to Objects enabled, drag the electron to the uppermost point on the ellipse, as shown in figure 12-17. When Snap is on, the electron will snap to the ellipse (guide layer).

10. Create a keyframe at frames 5, 10, 15, and 20. In each of these frames, drag the electron to the following locations:

   • Frame 1: 12:00 position

   • Frame 5: 9:00 position

   • Frame 10: 6:00 position

   • Frame 15: 3:00 position

   • Frame 20: 12:00 position

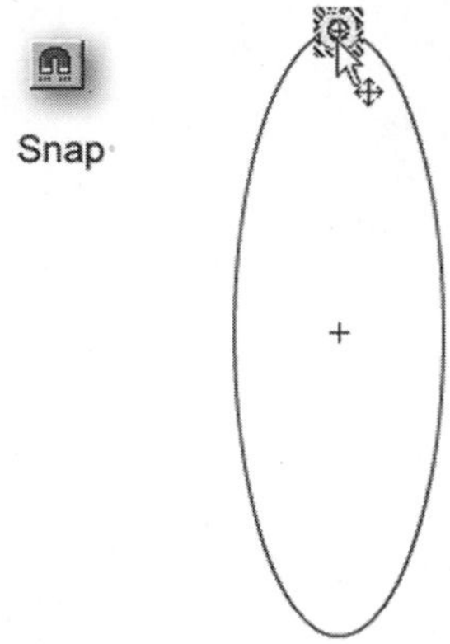

*Figure 12-17  With Snap enabled, the object will snap to the guide layer.*

11. After the electrons are in place, set up the tweening between each key position. Press Enter to see the electron pass along the ellipse. If you want to get rid of the pause that occurs between frame 20 and frame 1, insert a keyframe at frame 19 and delete frame 20.

12. Switch back to scene 1. Use Window | Library and place the movie clip you just created on the stage. Position it over the top of the existing vertically oriented ellipse.

13. Copy the movie clip and orient it for the other two ellipses. Scale and Rotate can be used to enter numeric information for the rotation.

14. Select Test Movie to view the results.

 **CD-ROM NOTE:** *To examine the previous example to see how it works, reference the file* atom.fla *located in the* F5gai/chapter12/ guides/ *folder, installed from the companion CD-ROM.*

## Simulating 3D

The prior example demonstrated how you could create a flat representation. When creating 3D effects, the difficulty is dependent on the content to be animated, because these effects are simulated 3D in Flash. For example, figure 12-18a shows an animated object. Figure 12-18b demonstrates how the illusion was created. Because a broken piece of the sphere was placed above the ellipse, the electron appears to pass behind the sphere.

**CD-ROM NOTE:** *To see how this illusion works, check out the file* sim3D .fla *located in the* F5gai/chapter12/guides/ *folder, installed from the companion CD-ROM.*

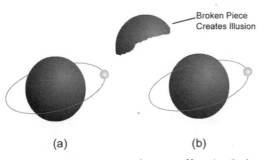

(a)                              (b)

*Figure 12-18 To create the 3D effect in Flash requires (a) the creation of an illusion and (b) using a broken piece of the sphere.*

In actuality, this broken technique alone is not enough to do "everything." However, by combining this idea with the ability to create masks, almost anything is possible, as seen in the example in figure 12-19. In each case, masks hide the "behind" area for the elliptical elements.

**CD-ROM NOTE:** *To see how this illusion works, reference the file* sim3D _2.fla *located in the* F5gai/chapter12/guides/ *folder, installed from the companion CD-ROM.*

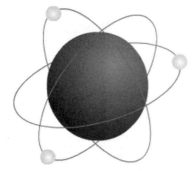

*Figure 12-19 Use masks and guides to create more complex illusions.*

## Shadows

Using the techniques described earlier in this chapter, you may already understand how to make shadows and reflections. The 3D effect shown in figure 12-19 can be enhanced by the creation of a simple shadow.

Using the file *sim3D _2.fla*, quickly create a shadow. First, change the image displayed on the stage to a symbol. Although this is not as easy as pressing the F8 function key or using Insert | Convert to Symbol, it is not a complex process. Once the sphere is created and its rotating electrons are made a symbol, the shadow part is easy! The following CD-ROM exercise takes you through the process of creating the shadow.

### CD-ROM Exercise

Open the file *sim3D _2.fla* located in the *F5gai/chapter12/guides/* folder, installed from the companion CD-ROM. Perform the following steps.

1. Unlock the layers.

2. Use Edit | Select All (Ctrl + A or Command + A) to select everything.

3. Right-click on one of the frames in the timeline and select Cut Frames.

4. Select Insert | New Symbol and make a movie clip symbol named Sphere Movie.

5. In Sphere Movie symbol, right-click in frame 1 and select Paste Frames. Lock all the layers except the bottom layer (layer 7).

6. Switch back to Movie mode and delete everything, layers and all, leaving one layer. Name the remaining layer Sphere Symbol.

7. Use the Window | Library menu option and click-drag the Sphere Movie symbol onto the stage.

8. Copy the Sphere Movie symbol, create a new layer named Shadow, and paste the copied symbol instance.

9. Right-click on the pasted symbol (the copy) and select Panels | Effect.

10. In the Effect panel, access the Advanced option and make the settings match those shown in figure 12-20.

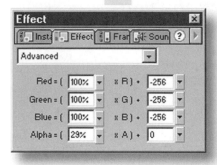

*Figure 12-20  Set the Effect panel to Advanced, with the settings shown.*

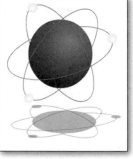

*Figure 12-21  Who says Flash cannot do cool 3D tricks? (See also color plate B-17.)*

11. Arrange the elements on the stage to match figure 12-21. (See also color plate B-17.) Use Test Movie to view the results.

 **CD-ROM NOTE:** *To see a finished example of the 3D shadow, reference the file* sim_shadow.fla *located in the* F5gai/chapter12/ guides/ *folder, installed from the companion CD-ROM.*

## Reflections

Just as you can create interesting shadows, you can create reflections using the technique described for shadow creation, as shown in figure 12-22. (See also color plate B-18.) By adjusting the Special settings or using the Alpha settings, you can also produce reflections. The key is the ability to take items that exist on the stage and convert it all into a symbol.

*Figure 12-22  Reflections are as easy as shadows. (See also color plate B-18.)*

**CD-ROM NOTE:** *To see a finished example of the 3D reflection, check out the file* sim_reflection.fla *located in the* F5gai/chapter12/guides/ *folder, installed from the companion CD-ROM. In addition, this chapter just touched on some of the effects possible with Flash. Included on the CD-ROM are many more examples of special effects you can examine to learn tips and tricks. The* F5gai/chapter12/other/ *folder contains files showing the following effects:*

- *Clouds*
- *Fog*
- *Smoke/fire*
- *Rain/snow*

*In the* chapter12 *folder on the companion CD-ROM, you will find a* misc *folder that contains some miscellaneous effects, such as lens flares and other items.*

# ▪ ▪ ▪ Summary

By taking a look at the various effects that can be used for animation creation, this chapter explained some of the advanced uses of tweening, guide layers, masks, and other techniques. Even if you do not use these specific techniques, they have more than likely sparked your imagination as to what is possible with Flash. The following chapters discuss uses for these animations in the production of interactive elements and interfaces. Although few of the animation techniques presented in this chapter stand alone, they are fundamental components of interesting buttons and unique interfaces.

# 13

# Understanding ActionScript

## ∎ ∎ ∎ Introduction

Since Chapter 6, you have been reviewing a variety of items, many of which deal directly or indirectly with actions and ActionScript. You were exposed to the rudiments of OOP theory in Chapter 6. This chapter provides an in-depth examination of programming fundamentals, specifically in the context of ActionScript. Subsequent chapters build upon the information provided. Take the time to digest the examples and the content presented.

Prior to version 4 of Flash, all scripting developers desired had to be performed outside the Flash environment. For example, storing variables, generating random numbers, If statements, and basically anything that required any programming at all meant that external technologies such as JavaScript and VBScript had to be employed.

These external technologies were accessed using the FlashScript FS Command action. Data was sent back into Flash using Flash Player methods. Although the FS Command action is still alive and well, much of what used to be accomplished with external scripting can now be done internally. As previously stated, Flash is now on the same plateau as Director in that there is really no limit to what you can do in it.

ActionScript is the title given to Flash's internal scripting capabilities. ActionScript is not a singular feature or command. Rather, it is a feature set integrated throughout many of the new and previously available actions, thus the name ActionScript. In prior versions, actions were the only means of getting to scripting in Flash. Thus, the tool was predominantly aimed at the non-programmer. However, you can now directly type in your own ActionScript code. And all the programmers said "Amen."

ActionScript and FlashScript are two of the most powerful and advanced features of Flash. Thus, they have been reserved for the later chapters of this book. Though Flash can generate a wide range of graphical assets, if you can understand and master the use of ActionScript and FlashScript and their integration with browser languages such as JavaScript and VBScript, your skills will be highly desired in the marketplace. Most novices can figure out how to use the basic Flash capabilities over time, but it is knowledge of ActionScript and FlashScript that sets the serious (and highly paid) developer apart.

This chapter explores advanced skills by closely examining ActionScript and related concepts and principles of programming. Although prior chapters of this book have briefly touched on various components of ActionScript, this chapter explores the feature in depth. This chapter begins with an overview of ActionScript, analyzing variables, operators, commands, methods, and properties. Most of the exercises in this chapter are simple, with the goal of presenting programming constructs in ActionScript in an easily understood manner. Subsequent chapters present more advanced examples.

# Objectives

In this chapter, you will:

- Examine and understand what ActionScript is, how it is used, and how it compares with the JavaScript Core Programming language
- Learn the difference between programming (extrinsic) objects and environmental (intrinsic) objects
- Establish what variables are and how they are used
- Find out about ActionScript operators and how they are used
- Discover ActionScript's general commands and control of flow commands
- Learn about methods that return values and those that do not return values

# An Overview of the ActionScript Language

Chapter 6 spent some time examining specific terminology related to object-oriented programming (OOP). For review and clarity, let's review the terminology established. You will undoubtedly remember that Macromedia's use of terms differs from the usage in this book. Again, Macromedia has attempted to make scripting in Flash easier by basically lumping many of the actions together and by generically using programming terms. The following is a review of terms as they are used in this book:

- *Classes* define the methods, properties, and event handlers of objects.

- *Objects* are specific instances of a class in the environment.

- *Methods* are the things an object can do (action verbs for the object).

- *Properties* are the characteristics or attributes of the object (adjectives that describe the object).

- *Event handlers* (technically methods) are the events to which an object can respond.

You will recall that in Chapter 6 distinctions were made among methods, functions, and commands.

- *Methods* are predefined functions that generally tell the object to do something or that do something to the object.

This chapter further defines methods as of two types, both of which "do something." One type of method returns a value; the other does not. The important thing to remember for both types is that they are both *predefined* for the object. This is what makes both different from a function.

- *Functions*, like methods, are designed to do something in the environment in relation to an object. However, functions, unlike methods, are not predefined. Rather, the programmer declares them by writing them in code.

Note that in some languages, such as the JavaScript core language specification, the term *function* can also mean a method primarily used to convert one type of data to another, such as the conversion of text data to a number. Nonetheless, this book will continue refer to functions as special code segments, written by the programmer, that are design to do something to or for an object.

- *Commands*, like functions and methods, are code that does something in the environment. Sometimes, these are simply called statements. Nevertheless, what makes them different is that they work independently of any object.

Like methods, there are two types of commands in the environment: general commands and control-of-flow commands.

- *Arguments,* sometimes called *parameters*, are optional bits of information you send to methods and functions. Usually, a method or a function will use the data sent to it in some way and may return a value to whatever called it.

As you progress through this chapter, you will note discussion of the following additional definitions. These are reiterated where appropriate throughout the chapter.

- A *variable* is a container for data and is defined by a scope (length of existence) and a data type [such as string (text) or numeral]. *Global variables* are variables that are active and accessible during the entire movie. *Local variables* are temporary variables used within the context of specific objects, methods, or functions.

- A *string* is any data element that consists of text, whereas a *numeral* is an actual number on which mathematic operations may be executed.

- *Operators* are programming elements that perform calculations (operations) or comparisons on two values to reach a third value.

- An *expression* is a combination of code statements that may include variables, functions, methods, properties, and operators. Usually, expressions must be evaluated.

- An *array* is a special type of variable that can store multiple values.

## A Macro-organizer for ActionScript

In an effort to make the ActionScript language holistically easier to understand, examine table 13-1. This table shows the language in light of the terminology used in this book. Although the chapter structure of this book is not organized according to these areas (discussed as applicable within a given chapter), table 13-1 provides a convenient macro-organizer for the ActionScript language.

 **NOTE:** *For simplicity sake, programming objects available in ActionScript are omitted from table 13-1. See table 13-2 for the programming object hierarchy.*

Make sure you specifically note the asterisked items in table 13-1. These are termed *deprecated* items. Rather than completely deleting carryover items from prior versions, which would make the learning curve for transitioning to the new version quite steep, software manufacturers leave legacy commands in new versions and identify them as deprecated. This also allows some level of backward compatibility with older, native files.

Deprecated generally means that the item will not exist in the next version of the software, and thus that you should find other ways of performing what you are doing. In most instances of deprecated items discussed in this book, the new or preferred way of performing the task is also presented.

*Table 13-1 An Environment Macro-organizer of the ActionScript Language*

### Event Handlers & Associated Events

- on ( )
  - dragOut
  - dragOver
  - keyPress
  - press
  - release
  - releaseOutside
  - rollOut
  - rollOver
- onClipEvent( )
  - data
  - enterFrame
  - keyDown
  - keyUp
  - load
  - mouseDown
  - mouseMove
  - mouseUp
  - unload

**String Escape Characters**

| | |
|---|---|
| \b | Backspace |
| \f | Form-Feed |
| \n | Line-Feed |
| \r | Carriage Return |
| \t | Tab |
| \" | Double Quotation |
| \' | Single Quotation |
| \\ | Backslash |
| \000-\377 | An Octal Byte |
| \x00-\xFF | A Hexadecimal Byte |
| \u0000-\uFFFF | A 16-bit Unicode Char in hexadecimal |

### Commands (Statements)

**General**
- /* (Comment) */
- // (Comment)
- break
- continue
- delete
- evaluate
- function
- new
- return
- trace
- var

**Control of Flow**
- do...while / while
- for / for...in
- if / else / else if
- with

### Methods (Actions)

- call
- duplicateMovieClip
- fscommand
- getURL
- gotoAndPlay
- gotoAndStop
- ifFrameLoaded
- loadMovie
- loadVariables
- nextFrame
- nextScene
- play
- prevFrame
- prevScene
- print
- printAsBitmap
- removeMovieClip
- set (variable)
- setProperty
- startDrag
- stop
- stopAllSounds
- stopDrag
- tellTarget*
- toggleHighQuality
- unloadMovie
- updateAfterEvent

**Special**
- #include

**Keywords**
- Infinity
- NaN
- newline
- null
- this
- void

### Methods (Functions)

**Boolean**
- chr*
- escape
- eval
- getProperty
- getTimer
- getVersion
- int*
- isFinite
- isNaN
- length*
- mbchr*
- mblength*
- mbord*
- mbsubstring*
- number
- ord*
- parseFloat
- parseInt
- random*
- string
- substring*
- targetPath
- typeof
- unescape

### Operators

**General**

| | |
|---|---|
| "" | String Delimiter |
| () | Parentheses |
| , | Comma |
| . | Dot Delimiter |
| ?: | Conditional |
| [] | Array access |
| {} | Object Initializer |
| : | Value or property delimiter |

**Numeric**

| | |
|---|---|
| + | Addition |
| * | Multiplication |
| / | Division |
| % | Modulo |
| - | Subtraction |
| ++ | Increment |
| -- | Decrement |

**String**

| | |
|---|---|
| + | Concatenate |
| add | Concatenate** |
| eq | Equality* |
| ge | Greater Than Equal to* |
| gt | Greater Than* |
| le | Less Than* |
| lt | Less Than Equal to* |
| ne | Not Equal* |

**Bitwise**

| | |
|---|---|
| & | Bitwise And |
| \| | Bitwise Or |
| ^ | Bitwise Xor |

**Logical**

| | |
|---|---|
| && | Logical AND |
| \|\| | Logical OR |
| ! | NOT |
| and* | |
| not* | |
| or* | |

**Comparison**

| | |
|---|---|
| < | Less Than |
| > | Greater than |
| <= | Less than or equal |
| >= | Greater than or equal |

**Equality and Assignment**

| | |
|---|---|
| == | Equality |
| != | Inequality |
| <> | Inequality* |
| = | Assignment |
| += | Addition and assignment |
| -= | Subtraction and assignment |
| *= | Multiplication and assignment |
| %= | Modulo and assignment |
| /= | Division and assignment |
| <<= | Bitwise shift left and assignment |
| >>= | Bitwise shift right and assignment |
| >>>= | Shift right zero fill and assignment |
| ^= | Bitwise Xor and assignment |
| \|= | Bitwise Or and assignment |
| &= | Bitwise And and assignment |

### Properties

- _alpha
- _currentframe**
- _droptarget**
- _focusrect (global)
- _framesloaded**
- _height
- _highquality (global)
- _level**
- _name
- _parent**
- _quality
- _root**
- _rotation
- _soundbuftime (global)
- _target**
- _totalframes**
- _url**
- _visible
- _width
- _x
- _xmouse**
- _xscale
- _y
- _ymouse**
- _yscale
- _maxscroll**
- scroll

*deprecated in Flash 5
**Cannot be changed

## ActionScript Versus JavaScript

ActionScript is now closely modeled after the JavaScript Core Programming language. Thus, if you are familiar with JavaScript you will find the syntax and structure of ActionScript very familiar. However, even if you have no prior JavaScript experience, you should find ActionScript easy to pick up as you progress through these later chapters.

 **TIP:** *As acknowledged in the Using ActionScript reference manual, one of the best resources for information on the core JavaScript language is located online at* http://developer.netscape.com/docs/manuals/js/core/jsguide/index.htm. *An additional resource is JavaScript Developer Center at* http://developer.netscape.com/tech/javascript/.

The *Using ActionScript* reference acknowledges several key differences between ActionScript and JavaScript. The following are the primary differences you should understand at this point.

- At this time, some objects in JavaScript, logically enough, are not supported in ActionScript. These include items such as the Window, Document, and Anchor objects.

- ActionScript supports special syntax that is not necessarily available in JavaScript. Items such as *tellTarget*, *ifFrameLoaded*, and slash syntax are a carryover from Flash 4. As acknowledged elsewhere, commands and syntactical items such as these should be avoided as you develop your movies. They will likely be removed from the next version of Flash.

- ActionScript does not support some JavaScript control of flow statements such as *switch*; t*ry, catch,* and *throw*; and *label* statements.

As you progress through this and other chapters, you will note that other differences between ActionScript and JavaScript, as listed in the *Using ActionScript* reference, are acknowledged at appropriate times.

 **NOTE:** *The Using ActionScript reference says that ActionScript does not support the function constructor and the continue statement. This is erroneous, as both are available in the Actions panel.*

## Programming Objects Versus Environment Objects

The JavaScript Core Programming Language incorporates two generic types of objects: environment objects and programming objects. Environment objects are items that can be seen on the screen such as in the browser window. These objects are such things as a document in the browser window, a form that may be a part of a document, and so on. All of these are objects that have methods, properties, and event handlers associated with them, which you can access and utilize in various ways.

In a similar manner, as you are writing coding, there are what might be called "theoretical objects," which contain data and can also be used to do perform specific tasks. These theoretical objects (that is, programming objects) are just as tangible as the objects you can see. Examples of programming objects in JavaScript include the *date* object, the *math* object, the *string* object, and so on.

Similar to JavaScript, ActionScript, too, provides access to objects you can use to manipulate data. To be exact, ActionScript provides 15 special programming objects that can be used to manipulate data via code. One of them, the *MovieClip* object, straddles the environment/programming object divide in that it exists and is accessible via both avenues.

To help you grasp the programming objects and their methods and properties, table 13-2 serves as a macro-organizer for these objects. As you look at the table, note that all of the objects have methods you can use to get the object to do something. However, note that not all of the objects have properties you can access or manipulate.

# Tools for Scripting in Flash

As you are working in Flash, there are several tools to help you write, check, and debug your scripts. You have seen two of these previously: the Actions panel and the output window. A third, the Debugger, is examined later in this chapter.

## *Actions Panel*

As you have already seen, the Actions panel provides a means of working in two editing modes: Normal and Expert. When in Normal mode, you simply select "actions" from the Toolbox list and double click on them to add them to the actions list on the right side of the Actions panel. You then set the parameters for the action using the lower portion of the panel, called the parameters area.

When you working Expert mode, the primary difference is that you can manually write your own actions and statements in the Actions panel. You still have the ability to select and add actions from the Toolbox list; however, the parameters area of the Actions panel is not shown. When in Expert mode, you will also find that the minus sign (remove action from list) and the Up and Down arrows (for arranging actions in the Action list) are disabled, as shown in figure 13-1.

Table 13-2 An Object Macro-organizer of the ActionScript Language

| Name | Method | Properties | Name | Method | Properties | Name | Method | Properties |
|---|---|---|---|---|---|---|---|---|
| Array | | | Key Cont'd | | | Number | | |
| | .concat | | | .isDown | CONTROL | | .toString | MAX_VALUE |
| | .join | | | .isToggled | DELETEKEY | | .valueOf | MIN_VALUE |
| | .length | | | | DOWN | | | NaN |
| | .pop | | | | END | | | NEGATIVE_INFINITY |
| | .push | | | | ENTER | | | POSITIVE_INFINITY |
| | .reverse | | | | ESCAPE | | | |
| | .shift | | | | HOME | Object | | |
| | .slice | | | | INSERT | | .toString | |
| | .sort | | | | LEFT | | .valueOf | |
| | .splice | | | | PGDN | | | |
| | .toString | | | | PGUP | Selection | | |
| | .unshift | | | | RIGHT | | .getBeginIndex | |
| | | | | | SHIFT | | .getCaretIndex | |
| Boolean | | | | | SPACE | | .getEndIndex | |
| | .toString | | | | TAB | | .getFocus | |
| | .valueOf | | | | UP | | .setFocus | |
| | | | | | | | .setSelection | |
| Color | | | Math | | | | | |
| | .getRGB | | | .abs | E | Sound | | |
| | .getTransform | | | .acos | LN2 | | .attachSound | |
| | .setRGB | | | .asin | LOG2E | | .getPan | |
| | .setTransform | | | .atan | LN10 | | .getTransform | |
| | | | | .atan2 | LOG10E | | .getVolume | |
| Date | | | | .ceil | PI | | .setPan | |
| | .getDate | | | .cos | SQRT1_2 | | .setTransform | |
| | .getDay | | | .exp | SQRT2 | | .setVolume | |
| | .getFullYear | | | .floor | | | .start | |
| | .getHours | | | .log | | | .stop | |
| | .getMilliseconds | | | .max | | | | |
| | .getMinutes | | | .min | | String | | |
| | .getMonth | | | .pow | | | .charAt | length |
| | .getSeconds | | | .random | | | .charCodeAt | |
| | .getTime | | | .round | | | .concat | |
| | .getTimezoneOffset | | | .sin | | | .fromCharCode | |
| | .getUTCDate | | | .sqrt | | | .indexOf | |
| | .getUTCDay | | | .tan | | | .lastIndexOf | |
| | .getUTCFullyear | | | | | | .splice | |
| | .getUTCHours | | Mouse | | | | .split | |
| | .getUTCMilliseconds | | | .hide | | | .substr | |
| | .getUTCMinutes | | | .show | | | .substring | |
| | .getUTCMonth | | | | | | .toLowerCase | |
| | .getUTCSeconds | | Movieclip | | | | .toUpperCase | |
| | .getYear | | | .attachmovie | | | | |
| | .setDate | | | .duplicateMovieClip | | XML | | |
| | .setFullYear | | | .getBounds | | | .appendChild | docTypeDec1 |
| | .setHours | | | .getBytesLoaded | | | .cloneNode | firstChild |
| | .setMilliseconds | | | .getBytesTotal | | | .createElement | lastChild |
| | .setMinutes | | | .getURL | | | .createTextNode | loaded |
| | .setMOnth | | | .globalToLocal | | | .hasChildNodes | nextSibling |
| | .setSeconds | | | .gotoAndPlay | | | .insertBefore | nodeName |
| | .setTime | | | .gotoAndStop | | | .load | nodeType |
| | .setUTCDate | | | .hitTest | | | .lonLoad | nodeValue |
| | .setUTCFullYear | | | .loadMovie | | | .parseML | parentNode |
| | .setUTCHours | | | .loadVariable | | | .removeNode | previousSibling |
| | .setUTCMilliseconds | | | .localToGlobal | | | .send | status |
| | .setUTCMinutes | | | .nextFrame | | | .sendAndLoad | xmlDec1 |
| | .setUTCSeconds | | | .play | | | .toString | |
| | .setYear | | | .prevFrame | | | | |
| | .toString | | | .removeMovieClip | | XMLSocket | | |
| | .UTC | | | .startDrag | | | .close | |
| | | | | .stop | | | .connect | |
| Key | | | | .stopDrag | | | .onClose | |
| | .getAscii | BACKSPACE | | .swapDepths | | | .onConnect | |
| | .getCode | CAPSLOCK | | .unloadMovie | | | .onXML | |
| | | | | | | | .send | |

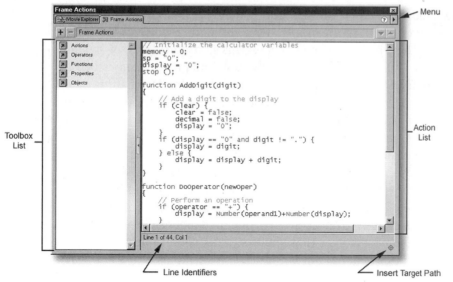

Figure 13-1 Several of the Actions panel controls are disabled in Expert mode.

To this point, you have basically used the Actions panel in Normal mode, not really being concerned with writing your own custom ActionScript. Similarly, you have not dealt in detail with the colors used for such purposes as highlighting. As you move through the remainder of the book, it will become important for you to be familiar with the Export mode of entry, as well as other features of the Actions panel.

To be proficient with ActionScripting requires that you be able to work in either mode, and to be able to work in Expert mode requires intimate knowledge of ActionScript and the Actions panel. Thus, one of your goals as you progress through these later chapters is to become proficient writing ActionScript directly into the Action list. However, before looking at syntactical issues (the rules for writing ActionScript), let's examine some rules for working with the Actions panel.

## Normal Versus Expert

You can easily switch from Normal to Expert mode using the Actions panel menu. However, reverting back to Normal once you have been working in Expert mode is a little more difficult. However, it is possible to go back and forth between the two modes.

When you switch from Expert mode to Normal mode, note two important things. First, the Actions panel will reformat your scripts and will strip away any white space or indenting you have added that is different from its "Normal" mode formatting. You will find that as you get more comfortable with writing ActionScript, you will probably develop a "style" or method for formatting scripts. Understand, however, that if you switch back to Normal mode, any custom formatting or styling of scripts will be removed. This can be good and bad.

The removal of custom formatting or styling is good from the standpoint that if you need to "clean up" messy formatting, you can switch to Normal and then back to Expert mode. This is a quick way of having Flash clean it up for you. However, the reformatting that occurs is bad if your style of formatting is unlike Flash's Normal mode of formatting! You will loose all of your own styling. Although it is recommended that you write scripts in the style of the Normal mode, as you will do throughout this book, take note of this reformatting issue.

The second thing you must note when reverting to Normal mode is that as you write scripts in Expert mode, there is always the possibility of an error. Even the best are prone to writing erroneous code, either due to logical errors or syntax errors (spelling or language). The Actions panel menu does indeed have a Check Syntax command that can be used to validate what you have entered. However, you must tell it to do it.

The reason this is important is because if a script has errors in it, you will not be able to revert to Normal mode until the error is corrected. The Actions panel normally does a pretty good job of identifying errors (using a red highlight to specify them), but there is always the chance of the Action panel not catching slight errors.

## Compatibility and Deprecation Highlighting

As you worked with the Actions panel in prior chapters, you may have noticed the colorization of certain items. The Actions panel does two very important things as it relates to colorization. First, the actions shown in the Toolbox list may be displayed as green or yellow at different times. Generally, highlighting that occurs in the Toolbox list concerns compatibility issues or deprecation. Which color is shown depends on settings in the Version drop-down list in the File | Publish Settings | Flash tab, as follows:

- If you have the Version drop-down list set on Flash 5, certain actions will be highlighted with green, indicating that the actions are deprecated. Again, deprecated actions will likely be gone in the next version of Flash.

- If you have the Version drop-down list set on Flash 4, certain actions will be highlighted with yellow, indicating that the actions are not able to be used in a version 4 Flash file.

In addition to the colors revealed in the Toolbox list, as you write ActionScript in Normal mode, errors in syntax are highlighted in red. If you move your cursor over the red highlight, a tooltip will display the error. When you are working in Expert mode, error highlighting is not shown. Compatibility and deprecation highlighting, however, are shown in Expert mode.

## Syntax Highlighting

You may have noticed in your prior dealings with the Actions panel that the scripts displayed in the Action list are colorized. The highlighting in the Action list denotes the various aspects of the ActionScript language. The colors used are:

- *Blue:* For commands, keywords, and both types of methods
- *Green:* For properties
- *Magenta:* For comments
- *Gray:* For strings denoted by double quotation marks

 **TIP:** *Although it is not recommended, you can turn off syntax highlighting using the Actions panel's menu.*

Particularly as you begin learning about ActionScripting, as well as programming in general, pay close attention to the colorization. Indeed, half the battle of programming is searching for errors or bugs in your scripts. Syntax highlighting can help in this regard.

## Other Features for Scriptwriting

Other features of the Actions panel should be noted. When you are in Expert mode, line and column numbers are shown directly beneath the Action list. When you use the Check Syntax menu option (from the Actions panel menu) a pop-up dialog box reveals whether or not there are errors in your scripts. If there are errors, the lines on which the errors occur will be revealed in the output window. For example, if you have an error, something like the following will be revealed:

```
Scene=Scene 1, Layer=Layer 1, Frame=1: Line 18: Unexpected
'}' encountered

    }
```

Thus, line numbers become important. The previous message tells you that line 18 of a script in frame 1, layer 1, scene 1 is causing problems. The latter part (following *Unexpected*) of the message attempts to indicate the problem. Sometimes the information provided will be helpful and sometimes not. More important than the error message is the line number. Quite often, knowing the location of a problem is more important than knowing the nature of the problem.

In chapters 6 and 8 you examined the Insert Target Path window, which is associated with the Insert Target button (see figure 13-1). When in Expert mode, you can select the Insert Target button anytime you want. Remember that you can use it to reveal the current object structure from an absolute or relative perspective. You will find this a handy item as you begin authoring your own movies.

A final note concerning working in Expert mode is that you do not have to use the Actions panel to write your scripts. You can author script files outside Flash and import them using the Import from File option in the Actions panel's menu. Generally, script files are basic text files that follow the normal ActionScript syntax conventions. They are identified with an *.as* extension. This is particularly useful for programmers who are used to a particular editor. The only drawback to this is that you do not see syntax checking. However, for advanced work, this is a convenient feature.

Flash provides an advanced action called *#include* that can be used to include external script files at the time of *.swf* file generation. If you use the *#include* action, you identify the *.as* file containing ActionScripting that you want compiled with the Flash *.swf* file. At the time of *.swf* file generation (when you use Export Movie or Publish), the *.as* file specified in the action must be available.

The advantage that such an action would provide is the ability for multiple programmers to work concurrently on complex scripting, or for programmers to set up default script files for specific functionalities. This is much like using *#include* in languages such as C or C++, as well as the same ability in JavaScript, where an externally linked file contains all JavaScript code for a set of pages.

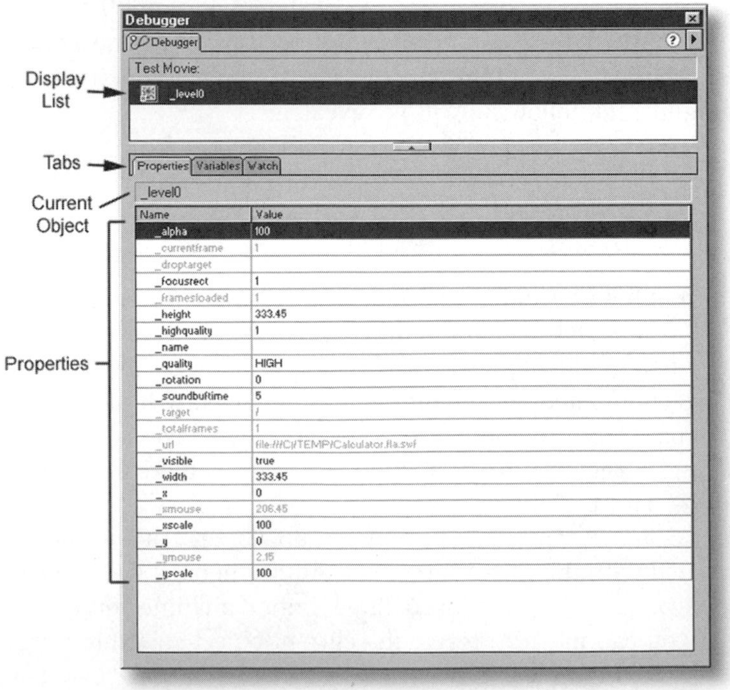

## The Debugger Window

A final tool worth mentioning is the Debugger window, shown in figure 13-2. With it you can track and watch various aspects of a movie while the movie itself plays in the Flash Player. You can also debug movies while they are playing live from a server.

*Figure 13-2*
*The new Debugger window can be used to watch all variables or properties in a movie, or specific variables or properties.*

## Debugging in Flash

The Debugger is a highly useful new feature of Flash. For those familiar with Director, you will find Flash's Debugger similar. Exercise 13-1, which follows, takes you through the process of using the Debugger in Flash.

### *Exercise 13-1  Using Flash's Debugger*

Open Flash and access the Help | Samples | Calculator movie.

1. Once it is open, use Control | Debug movie to start the Flash Player. The Debugger window will be automatically opened.

2. When the Debugger window opens, you must select on an object in the Display list (see figure 13-2). This identifies the object about which you desire information.

The movie being debugged in figure 13-2 has only a single object, the main movie timeline. If you debug a movie with more objects, the movie hierarchy will be displayed, including all movie clips, similar to the Insert Target Path window.

3. Click on the Properties tab. It will reveal information specific to the object you selected in the Display list, as shown in figure 13-3.

4. Click on the Variables tab. This tab reveals all of the variables and their current values in the player.

5. Click on some of the buttons in the calculator's interface. Note that the values in the Debugger change as you click on various buttons. This is how you track the state of variables in the movie.

Realize that the Debugger is not just for outputting data. You can also modify the value of variables in real time as the movie plays.

6. In the Variables tab, enter a numerical value in the value column next to display, as shown in figure 13-4. Note that the item associated with the display variable (the LED of the calculator) changes in the player. Thus, you not only see the state of variables with the Debugger but can dynamically change them.

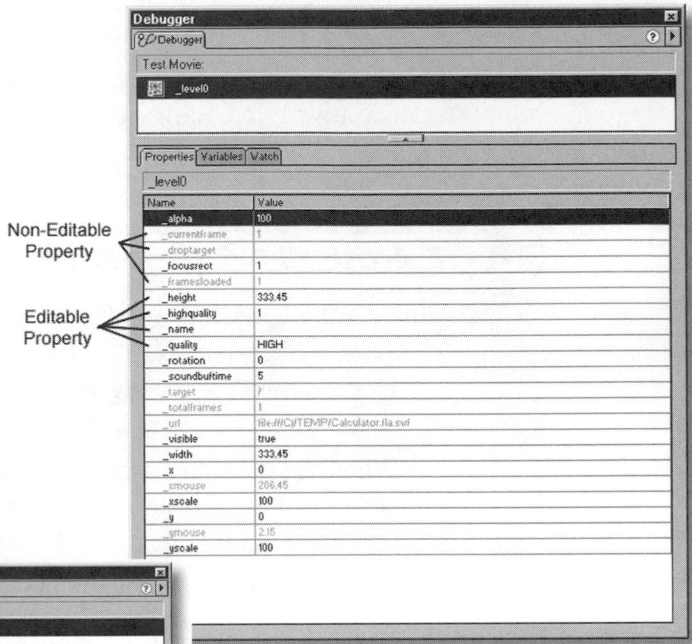

Figure 13-3 *The Properties tab reveals in the Display list information about the object selected.*

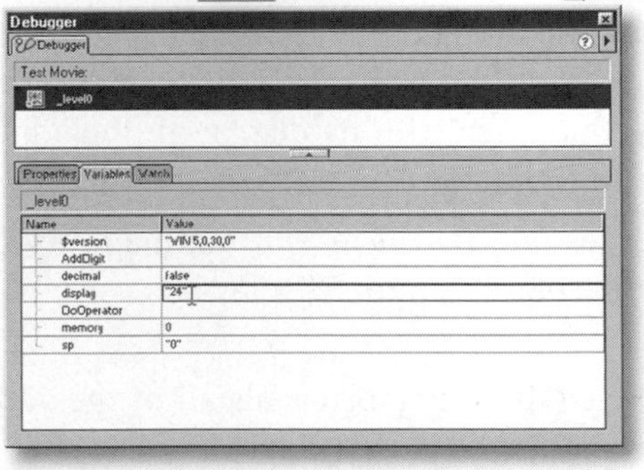

Figure 13-4 *You can dynamically modify the value of properties and variables displayed in the Debugger.*

 **TIP:** *Just as you can modify variables, you can dynamically enter different values for properties in the Property tab. Properties that appear grayed out are displayable only. As you will learn a little later, some properties cannot be set; they can only be retrieved.*

One final note about the Debugger is that you can use the Watch tab to specifically view a single variable. It is not uncommon to have many variables in complex movies. Thus, the Variables tab may show more than you want. In the Watch tab, you can enter a specific variable (or property) you want to view.

### Using the Debugger in a Web Browser

If you recall from Chapter 9, when you use the Publish or Export Movie commands, a checkbox is provided for you to enable or disable debugging in the browser. If you enable debugging, you can load your Flash movie to a live server and test it directly under the conditions it will be operating. If you perform a "live debug," remember to enable the Debugging Permitted checkbox when you generate the *.swf* file.

Once you have uploaded your movie to your server for testing, access the page that contains the movie. Once the movie is playing in the web page, right-click on the Flash movie. Select Debugger from the context menu. Because the Debugger option is contained in the Flash context menu in the web page, do not forget to set the MENU attribute (for the Embed tag) and the MENU parameter (for the Object tag) in your HTML coding. Otherwise, you will not be able to access the Debugger context option!

## Syntax Issues

When dealing with any language, whether it is a spoken language or a programming language, there are rules you must follow so that the receiver understands, for example, a request. Although the book to this point has spent a lot of time on constructs of OOP, syntax is just as important.

As previously mentioned, there are two types of errors in programming: logical and syntactical. Logical errors are resolved or overcome through knowledge of programming constructs. Syntactical errors, those wonderful "needle-in-a-haystack" types of problems, are overcome by carefully paying attention to the rules regarding the language and vehemently adhering to them. When dealing with Flash, there are four things you need to pay attention to in regard to syntax.

- Structural details such as braces, semicolons, and parentheses
- Case sensitivity issues
- Comments and what they are for
- Target paths and the methods for specifying them (dot versus slash syntax)

The sections that follow examine each of these points in more detail. In regard to syntax errors, it cannot be stressed enough that failing to follow one of the foregoing items is the most frequent cause of errors in scripts. You cannot depend on Flash to catch all of these problems. The help it offers regarding error codes placed in the output window will often point you in the right direction and tell you the line the error occurs on, but it seldom provides the exact solution to the error. This is where knowing the syntax issues and being able to quickly see them in code is important.

### Braces, Semicolons, and Parentheses

One of the first things you probably noticed since Chapter 6 is that curly braces ({}) are now used in ActionScript coding. There is really nothing mysterious about these characters, and indeed JavaScript, Java, and many other languages use them. Much like the logic of HTML carrots ( < > ), which enclose tag keywords, curly braces are used to denote logical blocks of code that function as a single unit. In this regard, and like the JavaScript standard ActionScript is built upon, curly braces are always used in matched pairs in coding. Most often, curly braces are used to define function definitions (i.e., code subroutines and/or handlers you write) and control structures (such as If statements).

As you write ActionScript or JavaScript, the location of the curly braces in code is not that important, as long as they enclose (delimit) lines of code that should function together. For example, the three items in code example 13-1 would all be valid and interpreted by Flash the same way. The physical location of curly braces is not imperative, as long as a pair encloses logical code groupings.

 **NOTE:** *The two small slashes (//) in code example 13-1 are used to denote comments, discussed later in this section.*

### Code Example 13-1  Use of Curly Braces

```
//Item 1
tellTarget ("myclip") {
        gotoAndPlay (1);
}
//Item 2
tellTarget ("myclip")
{
        gotoAndPlay (1);
}
//Item 3
tellTarget ("myclip") { gotoAndPlay (1);}
```

The main thing to keep in mind when writing ActionScript is that curly braces must be in matched pairs. When you are working in Expert mode, it is not uncommon to forget one, particularly when you start interjecting If statements, *tellTargets*, or *ifFrameLoaded* actions. Even though you can write scripts such as any of the three shown in code example 13-1, it is recommended you develop the style represented by Item 1, because it is a de facto standard (at least as far as the JavaScript community is concerned). It also makes going back and forth between Expert mode and Normal mode in the Actions panel easier.

Another syntax issue you must deal with in Flash is the use of the semicolon (;). Semicolons are not important if you are dealing with the first two methods of writing scripts shown in code example 13-1 (Item 1 and Item 2). Although code example 13-1 shows semicolons following the *gotoAndPlay (1);* methods, you could omit these. However, if you are using the last style of notation, semicolons are important because they identify where one method ends and another begins, as shown in the following.

```
tellTarget ("myclip") { gotoAndPlay (1); play();}
```

The issue of semicolons and their appearance in Flash and JavaScript is a carryover from Java, where semicolons are required to separate commands and a variety of other things. The only scenario in Flash or JavaScript where semicolons are imperative is when you are writing multiple commands in a single line. Unless you are writing ActionScript in a single-line field in Normal mode, you probably will not have to deal with this.

## Case Sensitivity

A common programming question has to do with case sensitivity. It is always a good idea to be consistent in your capitalization of items, regardless of the rules of a particular language. Macromedia states that only keywords are case sensitive. However, in truth, most, if not all, ActionScript code words are case sensitive. Properties are the only items that are not case sensitive. Thus, only the items in the Properties column in table 13-1 are not case sensitive. All other code words found in the table are case sensitive.

## Comments

A common practice in programming is to include internal documentation in code. Comments allow you to leave notes for yourself or others in your code so that you can remember what something does, or anything else concerning the code you might later forget. Comments entered into code are ignored by the Flash Player and do not appear when the user views your movie.

In Flash 5, single-line comments are identified by double slashes that precede them. Code example 13-1 used comments to identify the sections of code that were highlighted. If you need to include multi-line comments, you use a special set of characters. A slash followed by an asterisk (/*) begins the comment, whereas an asterisk followed by a slash (*/) ends the comment. Code example 13-2 shows an example of a multi-line comment format containing these conventions.

## *Code Example 13-2 Multi-line Comment Format*

```
/* This is an example of a multi-line comment.
All of the items written here are ignored by the
player. */
tellTarget ("myclip") {
    gotoAndPlay (1);
}
```

If you are familiar with HTML, multi-line comments are created with the following characters:

```
<!--This is a comment in HTML -->
```

## *Dot Versus Slash Syntax Revisited*

In earlier chapters you read about the difference between Flash 4's slash syntax (which models DOS or UNIX command line navigation and referencing) and Flash 5's dot syntax (which models JavaScript's method of notation). Dot syntax in ActionScript uses a period to separate components of a hierarchical reference, whereas slash syntax uses a slash (/) character. Dot syntax can actually be traced all the way back to the C language, where it originated. Certain aspects of C were used in Java. Certain aspects of Java are found in JavaScript and thus exist in ActionScript. Slash syntax, on the other hand, is a carryover from DOS or UNIX, and is also apparent in URL structures.

Do not confuse slash syntax used for scripting purposes with "slash syntax" used in URL references. URL references will always use slashes, such as *../mypage.html* to access a web page further up in the file hierarchy or *foldername/mypage.html* to access a web page further down in the file hierarchy. You cannot use dot syntax in URL fields unless you are constructing a URL from an expression; in which case, regardless of syntax, the resulting output to the browser is slash based. Dot syntax applies to target paths used to identify movies and movie clips, as you have already seen. It is also used when you want to access a method, function, property, or variable that belongs to an object.

You will recall that regardless of whether you are working with dot syntax or slash syntax, you can create absolute references or relative references. Remember that absolute references use the main movie timeline as the reference point, whereas relative references use the current object the script is being attached to as the reference.

All absolute references in dot syntax [whether target paths (which you saw in chapters 6 and 8), references to variables, or references to properties, and so on] start with the most global scope (the uppermost object being the main movie timeline, referenced as _root) and narrow the focus with each successive dot delimiter. Thus, to reference a movie clip named MC1 existing in the main movie timeline, you would use _root.MC1.

With absolute referencing, you do not have to really worry about the location of the object performing the targeting, because the point of reference is the main movie timeline. Thus, the absolute reference from a button in the main movie timeline to an object, and a reference from a button buried somewhere in the movie hierarchy to that same object, will be exactly the same. If this does not make sense, go back to Chapter 6 and review the information late in the chapter that discusses this. It is very important!

"Why go over the same ground again?" you might ask. Much like referencing objects (movies and movie clips), these concepts also apply to your ability to access variables, properties, methods, and functions of objects. As you move through this chapter and begin taking a deeper look at methods, variables, and properties, this will become more evident. However, prior to a discussion of these items, you need to understand the syntax of references and what they mean. Let's take a look.

### *Paths to Methods, Properties, and Variables*

To access a method, property, or variable that belongs to a particular object, you use a specific target structure. For example, a new programming object you will learn about is the *Math* object, which allows you to perform a variety of tasks. One such task is the generation of random numbers. For this purpose, the *Math* object has a method called *random*.

### Dot Syntax

In dot syntax, to access the *random();* method of the *Math* object you use *Math.random();*. To access any method, you use the following form:

```
object.method();
```

In most programming language source code, methods are distinguished from properties or variables by the parentheses that follow them. Later you will learn that you can send data to a method (or function) by placing values in the parentheses. Such data are called arguments or parameters.

You use similar syntax to access properties and variables. For example, if you want to access the *_alpha* property of an object named MC1 residing in the main movie timeline, you would use *_root.MC1._alpha*. The dot syntax form for such a reference is:

```
targetpath.property
```

Finally, if you wanted, for example, to access a variable *myvar* belonging to movie clip MC1, you would use *_root.MC1.myvar*. The form for accessing variables is:

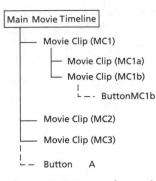

Figure 13-5  A sample movie structure based on tables 13-3 and 13-4.

```
targetpath.variablename
```

To give you comparative examples with variables and properties, table 13-3 outlines a variety of references from button A and button MC1B to a variety of elements (see figure 13-5). The table lists valid target paths for retrieving properties and variables from nested movie clips and the main movie timeline using dot syntax (see figure 13-5).

Remember that relative dot syntax uses _parent to go up one timeline in the hierarchy. The main timeline is identified as _root, and the current timeline referenced as this. Note that both relative and absolute references are provided in dot syntax. The nature of variables and properties is dealt with shortly. For now, simply pay attention to the syntax for referencing them.

Table 13-3 Valid Target Paths Using Dot Syntax

| From Button A | | |
|---|---|---|
| **Relative** | **Absolute** | **Description** |
| MC1.MC1a._x | _root.MC1.MC1a._x | Gets the X location (relative to the main movie) of movie clip MC1a |
| MC2._alpha | _root.MC2._alpha | Gets the alpha of movie clip MC2 |
| MC3._visible | _root.MC3._visible | Gets the visible property (binary value) of MC3 |
| MC1.MC1a.MYVAL | _root.MC1.MC1a.MYVAL | Retrieves the value of the variable MYVAL (created and held in movie clip MC1a) |
| **From Button MC1b** | | |
| **Relative** | **Absolute** | **Description** |
| _parent.MC1a._x | _root.MC1a._x | Gets the X location (relative to the parent movie) of movie clip MC1a |
| _parent._parent.MC2._visible | _root.MC2._visible | Gets the visible property (binary value) of MC2 |
| _parent._parent.MC3._alpha | _root._alpha | Gets the visible property (binary value) of MC3 |
| _parent..MC1a.MYVAL | _root.MC1a.MYVAL | Retrieves the value of the variable MYVAL (created and held in movie clip MC1a) |

## Slash Syntax

Although it is not recommended that you use slash syntax, as it probably will not be available in the next version of Flash, for users making the transition from version 4 it may be helpful to see what the prior items would look like in slash syntax.

The primary difference between dot and slash syntax is that slash syntax uses a slash delimiter (/) instead of a dot. Absolute position is specified by _level0. Stepping up one timeline in the hierarchy is achieved using `..`/. In all cases, properties, variables, and methods are separated from the target path by a colon ( : ). The form for accessing a method in slash syntax is:

`object:method();`

The form for extracting the value of a property or variable from some object in a movie structure is:

`targetpath:property`

> or

`targetpath:variable`

Table 13-4 outlines references to various properties and variables using slash syntax. Both relative and absolute target paths are provided.

*Table 13-4 Valid Target Paths Using Slash Syntax*

| From Button A | | |
|---|---|---|
| **Relative** | **Absolute** | **Description** |
| /MC1/MC1a:_x | _level0/MC1/MC1a:_x | Gets the X location (relative to the main movie) of movie clip MC1a |
| /MC2:_alpha | _level0/MC2:_alpha | Gets the alpha of movie clip MC2 |
| /MC3:_visible | _level0/MC3:_visible | Gets the visible property (binary value) of MC3 |
| /MC1/MC1a:MYVAL | _level0/MC1/MC1a:MYVAL | Gets the value of the variable MYVAL (created and held in movie clip MC1a) |
| **From Button MC1b** | | |
| **Relative** | **Absolute** | **Description** |
| ../MC1a:_x | _level0/MC1a:_x | Gets the X location (relative to the parent movie) of movie clip MC1a |
| ../../MC2:_ visible | _level0/MC2:_ visible | Gets the visible property (binary value) of MC2 |
| ../../MC3:_ alpha | _level0/MC3:_ alpha | Gets the visible property (binary value) of MC3 |
| ../MC1a:MYVAL | _level0/MC1a:MYVAL | Gets the value of the variable MYVAL (created and held in movie clip MC1a) |

# ▪ ▪ ▪ Programming Fundamentals

Although this section is devoted to a discussion of programming fundamentals, you have already had some exposure to the general terminology and basic modus operandi of ActionScripting in Flash. The sections that follow deal with a few more conceptual issues, and include simple examples that help with an understanding of these programming concepts, which in the chapters to follow combine toward the creation of complex programs.

## Variables

One of the fundamental concepts associated with any scripting or programming language is that of variables. Variables are nothing more than containers for data. Throughout the life of a program, variables are used to store information such as the user's name, the date or time, as well as a wide range of other bits of information that need to be tracked.

Variables are dynamic in that the content they hold can change over time. For example, you could use a variable to keep track of a score in a computer game. As the user kills more beasties or solves more problems, the variable keeps track of such information. At the end of the experience, the score can then be retrieved and presented to the user. You could also dynamically display the score as the user progresses through the game. This would be accomplished by creating a text field that shared the variable's name.

### *Rules for Variables*

In most programming and scripting languages there are many rules associated with the use of variables. The three main concerns in Flash are the variable's name, the scope of the variable, and the type of data contained in the variable. Scope simply signifies how long the variable and its data are active. The data type signifies what type of data is in the variable. Let's examine variable naming first.

### Variable Names

You may think it silly, but the way you name your variables is important. In Flash, variables can generally be anything, but it is recommended you develop a scheme for naming your variables. Flash variable names must adhere to the following rules:

- All characters in a variable's name must be a letter, number, underscore ( _ ), or dollar sign ( $ ). Thus, you cannot use other symbol characters, such as an asterisk ( * ) or a slash ( / ), in a variable's name.

- Variable names cannot be any of the reserved ActionScript words. (See table 13-1.)

- All variable names must be unique within their scope (see the section "Variable Scope" that follows).

## Data Types

In many programming languages, you must specify the type of data contained in the variable before you can use it. This is not as simple as specifying a variable as simply a string (text) or a numeral. In most languages, there are several specific data types for string and numeral data. For example, in Java, a variable designed to hold a number can take various forms, such as *byte*, *short*, *int*, or *long*. You must define the variable as one of these forms before you can use it.

Fortunately in Flash, you do not need to worry about multiple types of strings or numerals, or any other data contained in a variable. Flash determines this the moment you assign data to a variable. For example, say you define the following two variables by assigning a variable name to a value.

```
myvar1=10
myvar2="potato"
```

When Flash sees the first assignment, it sees that *myvar1* is assigned to a number and automatically establishes that the variable *myvar1* should be designed to hold numbers. When Flash sees the second assignment, it sees that *myvar2* is assigned to a string (signified by the matched set of double quotations). Thus, the program designs the variable *myvar2* to hold string data. You do not have to worry about telling Flash the general data type, nor any specific data type, for the variable.

There is, however, one exception to the rules governing variables. When a variable or a property has a binary value (on or off), its value can be referenced either as a keyword (TRUE or FALSE) or as a numerical value. Thus, if a variable or property is binary (Boolean), you can refer to its value as either TRUE or 1 (on) or FALSE or 0 (off). In this respect, binary variables (and properties) are different.

One final note in this section is that you must understand the difference between a *string* and a *numeral*. In essence, strings are nothing more than basic text elements. With them you can perform special operations, such as searching for specific characters or words in a paragraph, joining two strings (called concatenation), or truncating or extending the characters in a text element. Numbers, on the other hand, can be used to perform mathematical operations and comparisons, as well as a wide variety of other tasks.

Many newcomers think they understand the difference between strings and numerals; that is, until they actually start writing their own code. To get to the fundamental difference, examine the following two statements:

```
myvar=1
myvar="1"
```

Although the prior two statements look similar, they are not the same. The first is a numerical, and the second is a string (text). The fundamental difference between strings and numerals is pointed out here: the first line means the numeral 1, whereas the second means the character *"1"*.

As stated early in this section, you do not necessarily have to worry about the intricacies of data types typical of other languages. However, understanding the basic differences among generic data types is important, particularly when you start modifying properties and working with methods.

Methods and properties will expect a certain type of data to be provided to them. For example, if you want to change the *_alpha* property of a movie clip, Flash will expect you to provide it with a number (numeric value), not a string. This is where it is important to understand the difference between strings and numerals. Later in this chapter you will see how to convert a string to a numerical using the *number();* method, and how to convert a numeral to a string using the *string();* method.

## Variable Scope

In most languages, scope refers to the length of time a variable is active or accessible. *Local variables* are normally active only for a brief period, serving as temporary storage, and are typically used in a function or object script. When the object ceases to exist or the script is finished executing, the variable, too, is removed from memory. *Global variables*, on the other hand, are usually alive and active during the entire duration of a program, no matter what object initiated them, or when.

To create a variable, you generally do something called *declaring* the variable. In some languages, you have to declare a variable to reserve space in memory for it, while at the same time specifying its data type. Some programming languages are *very* stringent in this regard. Flash is not. Although it is good and common practice, you do not have to declare a variable before you use it.

 **TIP:** *Even though you do not have to, it is recommended that you always use comments to describe the intended use of the variables you create. It is a good practice to do this at the first instance of a variable.*

You can define both global and local variables in Flash. How you write the code determines whether a global or local variable is created. Let's first look at global variable declaration in Flash. There are two methods of defining a global variable in Flash. The first is to use the Set Variable action in Normal editing mode. The second is to create an expression in Expert mode. Although you cannot define two variables in the same scope with the same name (remember naming rules), for the sake of comparison, the following two lines of code say the same thing:

```
myvar=1;
set (myvar, 1);
```

Similarly, the following two lines of code say the exact same thing:

```
myvar="Jamie";
set (myvar, "Jamie");
```

In both of the previous sets of instances, the variable *myvar* is created. The first two lines create a global variable that contains numerical data, and the second set of lines creates a global variable that contains string data. Anytime you use the set variable action from the Toolbox list, or manually use an expression, the variable becomes a global variable, accessible by any other object in the movie.

Let's talk scope for a moment. Global variables created in Flash are scoped according to timelines. Thus, when a variable is created by the main movie or a movie clip, it is "owned" by that object. To pass or access the variable data from another movie or movie clip requires the use of a target path for accessing or modifying the data in the variable. This is what the prior section concerning target paths was all about.

You must also keep in mind that a variable created by a movie clip will exist in the movie only as long as the movie clip is on the stage. The same is true of loaded movies. If you instantiate a variable in a movie clip or loaded movie, the variable exists only as long as the movie clip or loaded movie remains in the environment. For example, if a movie clip named MC1 creates a variable named *gfinal*, accessing the variable's data could be done using an absolute target path, such as the following:

```
_root.MC1.gfinal
```

If you wanted to use a relative path, the entry would be dependent on the relative position between the object trying to access the variable and MC1. A global variable can be accessed from anywhere in the hierarchical structure if you know the movie or movie clip to which the variable belongs, as well as the name of the variable. Exercise 13-2, which follows, provides practice in working with variables.

**CD-ROM NOTE:** *To see an example of how variables are created and incremented, open the file* ch13-01.fla *located in the* F5gai/chapter13/ *folder, installed from the companion CD-ROM.*

## Exercise 13-2 Using Variables

To practice using variables, perform the following steps.

1.  With file *ch13-01.fla* open, note the following. First, the *myval* variable is initialized in frame 1. Right-click on frame 1 and select Actions.

2.  Notice in the Actions panel, shown in figure 13-6a, that the action's value field is set to Expression. To be able to enter numbers into Action fields in Normal mode, you must enable the Expression checkbox. If not, Flash will treat the entered data as a string, not a number. Notice in figure 13-6b the quotations added to the Action's list if Expression is deselected. With Expression deselected, the value entered is treated as text.

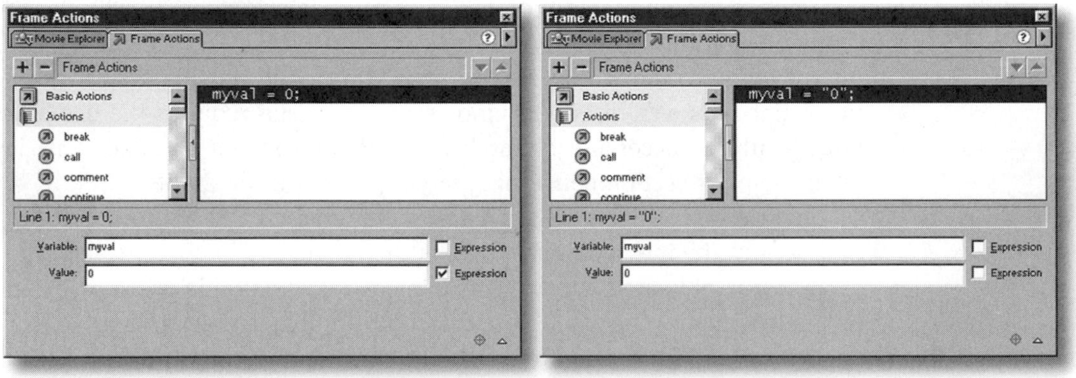

|            |            |
| :--------: | :--------: |
| (a)        | (b)        |

*Figure 13-6  The Expression checkbox is very important. With it selected, (a) the value entered is treated as a number. With it deselected, (b) the value entered is treated as a string.*

**NOTE:** *See the sidebar "Ye Ole' Flash 4 String Literals" following this exercise for more on the workings of the Expression checkbox.*

3.  Now let's look at the scripting that actually does the variable incrementing. With the Actions panel open, click on the red button on the stage. Note in the Action list that the variable is incremented by using *myval = myval + 1*.

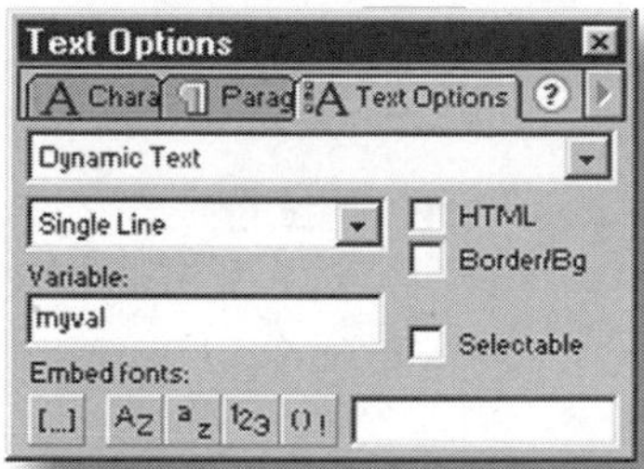

*Figure 13-7 The text field is associated with the variable using the Text Options panel.*

When you click on the button, the variable is incremented. But what makes the text field change? The answer: the field is linked to the variable.

4. Right-click on the text field and select Panels | Text Options from the context menu.

5. In the Text Options panel, shown in figure 13-7, note that the text element is set to Dynamic Text and that the variable *myval* has been associated with the text element. This is how you create dynamic text fields: by associating them with variables. Thus, anytime the variable changes, the text field changes as well.

**CD-ROM NOTE:** *An alternative method for incrementing variables (or decrementing variables) is shown in the file* ch13-02.fla *located in the* F5gai/chapter13/ *folder, installed from the companion CD-ROM.*

# Ye Ole' Flash 4 String Literals

The Expression checkbox that appears in the parameters area of the Actions panel is shown only when you are in Normal mode. In Expert mode, no parameters area is shown, let alone the Expression checkbox.

Basically, the Expression checkbox allows you to enter numbers and expressions into a single text field. This is partially a carryover from Flash 4, but it is also what allows Macromedia to provide a convenient front end to scripting while allowing some programming capability as you work in Normal mode in the Actions panel.

When you work in Normal mode, almost everything you enter into the fields in the parameters area is a string (called a *string literal* in Flash 4). Think back to the actions you have worked with and the fields you entered data into. Target paths, frame labels, URLs, and so on are all strings. The only time you entered numbers were frame numbers for the *Goto* action and the *ifFrameLoaded* action.

Did you realize you were entering numbers as opposed to strings? Probably not, because the distinction did not make a difference. Flash knew that you meant them to be numbers, because of other settings you chose. For example, in the *Goto* action, when you select *Frame number* in the Type drop-down, Flash assumes the data in the Type field is a number. If you select *Frame label* in the Type drop-down list, Flash assumes the information is a string.

The difference the Expression checkbox makes is important. When you start working with variables, whether or not the Expression checkbox is selected becomes important, because it determines what type of data is in the variable. Students commonly exclaim that "variables don't work in Flash."

Similar comments are made concerning the Set Property action. The answer to such exclamations is that if you plan to use variables in your movies (not using them is like having a car with no engine), you cannot mindlessly enter data into action fields and expect the software to understand. Software is not intelligent. You are!

In summary, by default, all fields in the Actions panel assume the data you are entering into them are strings. If you wish to use variables or modify properties, pay attention to the type of data you want to use (variables) or the type of data Flash is expecting (properties).

To enter a number (a true numeral), or an expression to be evaluated, you must select the Expression checkbox. Chapter 6 (see file *ch06-1.fla*) presented an example of this in which a URL was constructed for the Get URL action using concatenation (joining of two strings). For Flash to evaluate the expression that was entered, the Expression checkbox had to be selected.

In addition, but not necessarily recommended as an alternative method, you can enter strings, with the Expression checkbox selected, by simply surrounding the data with double quotations. Thus, theoretically, you could enable the Expression checkbox in every field and in every action in Normal mode. As long as you understood the difference between a numeral and a string, as well as what the software was expecting you to enter, and made your entries accordingly, everything would work out fine.

This process would be less confusing if all fields defaulted to Expression. You would then simply have to keep in mind the difference between the two types of expressions and have an understanding of which type Flash expects to be entered. Currently, the combination of the Expression checkbox, Normal mode, Expert mode, and so on is more confusing than it might otherwise be designed.

## Variables, Scope, and Target Paths

One of the important things to keep in mind concerning variables is scope. Remember that the timeline in which the variable is defined owns the variable. In the prior two examples, the button(s) and the text field resided in the main movie timeline. Thus, when referencing the variable, no target path was necessary. However, if a variable is instantiated within a movie clip or another movie in a different hierarchical location, target paths are required to be able to point to the file. This concept is very important because it, like the difficulty with strings versus numerals, causes no end of trouble for beginners.

Let's review one more example. Examine figure 13-8. This example was used in Chapter 6 and earlier in this chapter. However, this time a variable

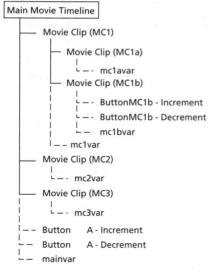

Figure 13-8 A movie structure in which a variable is defined in each timeline. How do you reference each variable from the two buttons? See table 13-5 for the answer.

has been added to each of the movie clip timelines, as well as to the main movie timeline. As previously examined, what would the target paths to the variables from the two buttons look like? Table 13-5 reveals the answer.

 **CD-ROM NOTE:** *To see an applied example of figure 13-8 using absolute targets, open the file* ch13-03.fla *located in the* F5gai/chapter13/ *folder, installed from the companion CD-ROM. To see an applied example of figure 13-8 using relative targets, open the file* ch13-04.fla *located in the* F5gai/chapter13/ *folder.*

Now that you know what scope means in Flash, keep in mind that one of the rules of variables is that all variables that belong to a specific timeline (movie or movie clip) must be uniquely named. In other words, a single timeline cannot have two variables with the same name. Table 13-5 outlines valid target paths for accessing the variables from the buttons using dot syntax (see figure 13-8).

Table 13-5 Valid Target Paths for Button Variables Using Dot Syntax

| From Button A (Increment) | | | | |
|---|---|---|---|---|
| **To** | **Relative Path** | **Relative Expression** | **Absolute Path** | **Absolute Expression** |
| *mainvar* | *this.mainvar* | *++this.mainvar* | *_root.mainvar* | *++_root.mainvar* |
| *mc1avar* | *this.MC1.MC1a.mc1avar* | *++this.MC1.MC1a.mc1avar* | *_root.MC1.MC1a.mc1avar* | *++_root.MC1.MC1a.mc1avar* |
| *mc1bvar* | *this.MC1.MC1b.mc1bvar* | *++this.MC1.MC1b.mc1bvar* | *_root.MC1.MC1b.mc1bvar* | *++_root.MC1.MC1b.mc1bvar* |
| *mc2var* | *this.MC2.mc2var* | *++this.MC2.mc2var* | *_root.MC2.mc2var* | *++_root.MC2.mc2var* |
| *mc3var* | *this.MC3.mc3var* | *++this.MC3.mc3var* | *_root.MC3.mc3var* | *++_root.MC3.mc3var* |

| From Button MC1b (Increment) | | | | |
|---|---|---|---|---|
| To | Relative Path | Relative Expression | Absolute Path | Absolute Expression |
| mainvar | _parent._parent. mainvar | ++_parent._parent. mainvar | _root.mainvar | ++_root.mainvar |
| mc1avar | _parent.MC1a.mc 1avar | ++_parent.MC1a.mc 1avar | _root.MC1.MC1a.mc 1avar | ++_root.MC1.MC1 a.mc1avar |
| mc1bvar | this.mc1bvar | ++this.mc1bvar | _root.MC1.MC1b.mc 1bvar | ++_root.MC1.MC1 b.mc1bvar |
| mc2var | _parent._parent. MC2.mc2var | ++_parent._parent. MC2.mc2var | _root.MC2.mc2var | ++_root.MC2. mc2var |
| mc3var | _parent._parent. MC3.mc3var | ++_parent._parent. MC3.mc3var | _root.MC3.mc3var | ++_root.MC3. mc3var |

As you can see, global variables are indeed important, but what about local variables? Does everything need to be a global? Not really. In fact, each global variable you create does require a certain portion of RAM memory. Thus, creating too many global variables can consume considerable amounts of RAM, not to mention having to keep track of so many variables.

In ActionScript, you can define local variables using the *var* action. To define a local variable, you simply instantiate it from within a function or event handler. When the event handler or the function is finished executing, the local variable is discarded.

## Expressions

Expressions in Flash are sequences of operators and operands (variable names, functions, properties, and so on) used to compute numerical or string results. Although at this point extensive examples might be more confusing than productive to an understanding of expressions, you should be aware of what is meant by the term *expression*. In table 13-5 the expressions listed use the increment operator to change the value of a variable. When Flash encounters an expression, either in ActionScript code or in a field associated with an action (set on expression), it evaluates it to a resulting value.

For example, you could create a string expression that concatenates (joins) the user's first and last name, such as "James" + " Mohler." The resultant would be the string result "James Mohler." A numeric expression could be used to add two straightforward numbers, such as *5 + 3*, or increase the value in a variable, such as *gscore + 1*. In the prior examples, you encountered two "shorthand" operators: *increment* and *decrement*. As you can see, operators are vitally important to being able to do anything in ActionScript.

# Operators

At the heart of expressions are operators. Depending on the data, and on the results you are trying to obtain, different operators are used. Thus, there are specific operators that apply to numerical expressions only, and specific operators that apply to string expressions only. There are also general, comparison, logical, and bitwise operators. The operators are discussed in the sections that follow.

**NOTE:** *You may find it helpful to reference table 13-1 as you progress through the discussion of specific ActionScript items.*

## General Operators

The general operators include several delimiter items, of which the following have been discussed.

- *String delimiters:* Sets of double quote marks ( " " ) used to signify string data elements
- *Parentheses:* Used to offset arguments that are sent to functions or methods
- *The dot delimiter ( . ):* Used to reference hierarchical object order in target paths
- *Curly braces ( { } ):* Used to denote logical code groupings

General operators not previously discussed include the comma, conditional, and array access operators. The latter two are discussed later in this chapter. The comma delimiter is used when multiple arguments are sent to a method or function. For example, when you use a Get URL action, the URL and the target window are sent to the Get URL method as follows:

```
getURL ("http://www.somesite.com", "_blank");
```

Note that a comma is used to separate the values being sent to the method. This works the same way in regard to functions. Imagine you wrote a function to add two numbers and return a result, such as the following:

```
function addme (x, y) {
    x + y = z
    return z;
}
```

Note in this function that the comma is used to separate data being received in the function. To call or utilize this function you would write the following inside some handler:

```
myvar = addme(1,3);
```

Notice again the comma being used to separate the values being sent to the *addme();* function. In short, the previous function is written so that it receives values when it is called, which are assigned to two local variables (*x* and *y*). The values that will be substituted for *x* and *y* are those located within the parentheses when the function is called. Therefore, in essence, the values in the call to the function (*1* and *3*) are substituted for *x* and *y* when the function executes. The function then returns the value *z*, which is placed within *myvar*.

 **CD-ROM NOTE:** *To see an example of this, open the file* ch13-05.fla *located in the* F5gai/chapter13/ *folder, installed from the companion CD-ROM.*

### *Equality Versus Assignment Operators*

The assignment and equality operators are pretty straightforward. One of the biggest issues concerning the use of operators is the issue of equality versus assignment. ActionScript follows the JavaScript rule where a single equal sign represents "set this equal to this" and where a double equal sign means "does this equal that." Thus, the following lines do not mean the same thing:

```
myvar = 1
myvar == 1
```

The first of the previous lines is assigning the value 1 to the variable *myvar*, whereas the second line is asking, "does *myvar* equal a value of 1?" As you begin writing your code, this is important to remember. Already you have seen examples of assignment (via the variable exercise). Equality ( = = ) operators are examined in greater detail later in this chapter, under a discussion of conditional statements.

As you peruse the listing of equality and assignment operators, beyond equality, assignment, and inequality you will find that the remaining operators are shorthand methods for performing certain tasks, called compound operators. They allow you to do two things (usually a mathematical operation and assignment) at the same time.

For example, if you wanted to subtract a known value from a variable, and at the same time assign the new value to the variable, you can write it in a shorthand way. For example, the following pairs of expressions do the same thing:

$x = x + 7$ and $x + = 7$

$y = y * 245$ and $y * = 245$

$a = a / b$ and $a / = b$

### Numeric and String Operators

Numeric expressions are most often used to perform math operations on numbers. These include addition ( + ), subtraction ( – ), multiplication ( * ), and division ( / ). Flash 5 now also includes Modulo ( % ), as well as Increment ( + + ) and Decrement ( – – ), which you have already examined. When the function itself returns a numerical value, numeric expressions may also integrate functions. Examples of this include *eval*, *int*, and *random*, which are deprecated in Flash 5, as well as *parseFloat*, *parseInt*, and *number*. Properties, also, may be used with operators when their values yield numbers.

Already you have seen some basic numeric expressions in examples and in the text. Generally, numeric expressions follow the standard rules governing mathematics. Thus, multiplication and division occur before addition and subtraction. Parentheses can be used to specify operations that should occur before multiplication and division. Dividing by zero results in an error presented by the keyword *Infinity*.

If you use a string in a numeric expression, Flash will attempt to concatenate the string and number before performing the evaluation. For example, adding *6 + "3"* ("3" being a string) will result in the number *63*. Similarly, *"DOG" + 3* results in *dog3*. Similarly, string operations are performed on string values. Any set of characters surrounded by double quotation marks (" ") is evaluated as a string. Empty strings are identified as quotations separated by a space (" "). The only true operational evaluation of a string is concatenation, in which two string portions are added.

### Logical

Logical operators differ from other operators in that they are used to conjugate two comparison statements. The prior version of Flash used *and*, *or*, and *not*, which are now deprecated. Instead, you should use the double ampersand ( && ) for logical *and,* double pipes ( | | ) for logical *or*, and the exclamation mark ( ! ) for logical *not*. For example, to see if a variable's value resides between two numbers, you could use the following expression in the condition of an *if* action:

```
myscore < 10 && myscore > 100
```

This expression would determine if the variable *myscore* were between 10 *and* 100. You could use the *or* operator to determine if the variable *userpassword* were a certain value, as in the following:

```
userpassword == "dogfight" || userpassword == "chicken"
```

If *userpassword* equaled *"dogfight"* or *"chicken"*, the appropriate actions could be executed. Finally, you could use the *not* operator to allow all values except a specific one to respond, by entering the following:

```
myvalue < 100 ! myvalue == 77
```

In this scenario, all values less than 100, except for 77, would evaluate as true. You will see other examples of logical operators later in this book.

### Comparison

Comparisons (as well as logical operators) are elements used most commonly within *if* statements and conditional loops. Comparison operators compare two elements, such as shown in table 13-6. The result of a comparison operation is a binary value of either TRUE (1) or FALSE (0). When integrated into an *if* or a conditional loop, appropriate actions are either initiated or ignored.

*Table 13-6 Numerical and String Expression Comparison Operators*

| Comparison | Type | Statement | Result |
|---|---|---|---|
| Two values | Numerical | *1 >= 2* | FALSE |
| Variable and value | Numerical | *myscore >= 3* | Depends on value in *myscore* |
| Variable and variable | Numerical | *myscore > highscore* | Depends on values in *myscore* and *highscore* |
| Property and value | Numerical | *_currentframe == 10* | Depends on the current frame |
| Two strings | String | *"James" == "Mohler"* | FALSE |
| Variable and value | String | *firstname != "Mohler"* | Depends on value in variable *firstname* |
| Variable and variable | String | *password == userentry* | Depends on values in variables |
| Property and value | String | *_droptarget == "/MC1"* | Depends on value in *droptarget* property |

### Bitwise

Bitwise operators are used to internally manipulate floating-point numbers by changing them into 32-bit integers. Bitwise calculates are useful for advanced mathematical operations. Unfortunately, space does not permit a lengthy discussion of them in this book.

### Operators in Summary

As you can see, with operators you can create almost any expression that can be evaluated and reacted to. The main point to keep in mind is to pay attention to the syntax you are using if you are working in Expert mode. If you are working in Normal mode, make sure you use the Expression checkbox when entering values for variables and properties.

When you are working with strings or string literals, there may be times when you want to use special characters in your strings. For example, strings are identified by double quotations. How do you define a double quotation inside a string? To do this requires the use of special sequences of characters, called escape sequences, within the string. Flash supports the following escape sequences:

\b for backspace

\f for form feed

\n for line feed

\r for carriage return

\t for tab

\" for double quotations

\' for single quotations

\\ for backslash

The following are examples of the use of these characters. *My dog's name is \"Winnie\"* would result in the following string:

```
My dog's name is "Winnie"
```

The code *My name is:\nJames Mohler* would result in the following string:

```
    My name is:
    James Mohler
```

Although you may never use some of the sequences, \n, \t, \", and \' are very common. The string escape sequences are included in table 13-1 in the lower, left-hand corner.

## Controlling Flow with Commands

Being able to respond to certain conditions allows you to control the program flow. There two general types of flow control statements: conditional loops and repeats. In Flash, you can use the If construct to react to a specific condition in the program. With the *do...while/while, for/for...in,* and *with* constructs you can create repeating segments. Conditional statements allow you to create sets of actions that may or may not execute, which depends on the condition. Repeats allow you to create sets of actions that repeat themselves with various settings, which in essence is a means of shortening ActionScript code segments.

### if, else, and else if

The *if* construct provides a tremendous capability within Flash. As a basic programming capability, the *if* statement allows you to write a set of statements that executes if a particular condition is found to be true or false. It also allows you to set up alternatives to the condition. Thus, you can create binary conditions, as well as conditions that respond to a variety of conditions.

For example, if you have a button you want to go to certain URL locations based on the current frame, you could use the If action and a single button. For example, say you want the URL to go to one web site if the playhead is in frame 10. If the current frame is anything else, you want the URL to go to a different web site. The basic *if* structure in simple English would look like the following:

```
If the current frame equals 10 then
      Get this URL
If it does not (Else)
      Get a different URL
End If
```

In Flash, you set up a conditional statement by adding an If action to an element. In this example, the element is a button. When you select the If action in Normal mode, the Actions panel is displayed, as shown in figure 13-9. When you use the If action, the Condition field is automatically

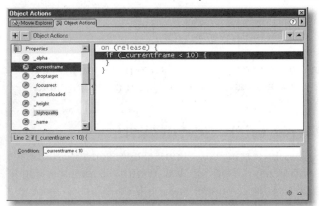

set to expression. You will notice no expression checkbox available, meaning that Flash expects a valid expression to be entered. Once you establish the condition, you add the actions you want to execute if the condition is found to be true, and then any alternatives and their respective actions. Let's examine how to set all of this up.

*Figure 13-9 Setting up an If action requires a condition, in the form of an expression, to be entered into the condition field.*

One of the changes from version 4 is that there is no longer an Expression Editor. Instead, you use the Toolbox list with the Condition field by simply clicking in the Condition field. In the Toolbox list, you then select a property you want to test against, and it will be added to the Condition field.

In the example, you want to test the current frame to see if it equals 10. Use the Toolbox list to find Properties | *_currentframe*, which is a property that stores the current frame. Click on it in the list and then append "less than 10" ( < *10* ) to the end of the expression, as shown in figure 13-9. Actions following this first line will now execute only if the current frame is less than 10.

 **TIP:** *At any point in your code writing, you can use the Check Syntax option in the Actions panel menu to make sure what you wrote is syntactically correct.*

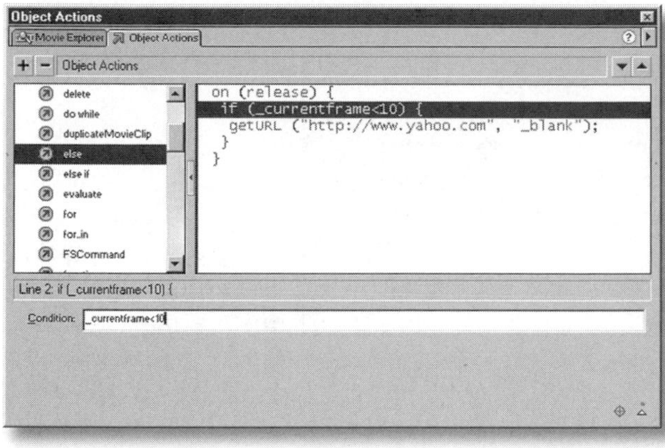

Figure 13-10 Once the condition is established, you add actions for the condition.

Once you have entered a condition, you can add to the Action list the actions you want to execute for that condition. Notice in figure 13-10 that a Get URL has been added and that it is embedded within the *if* structure, in a manner similar to that of the *tellTarget* structure in Chapter 8.

Now you must set up the alternative situation (if the current frame is greater than or equal to 10). Select the If action you just created in the Action list and then select the Else action in the Toolbox list. Then insert a *getURL* under the *else* and enter the alternative location (that is, where you want to go if the current frame is greater or equal to 10). The finished *if* statement should look like that shown in figure 13-11. Keep in mind that to add Else or Else If actions (the alternatives to the condition), you must click in the *if* statement in the Action list to select the Else and Else If actions in the Toolbox list.

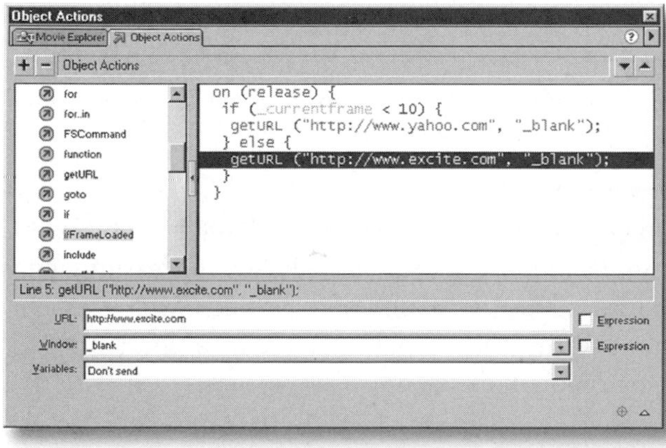

Figure 13-11 The completed conditional statement for the button.

When you are working with If actions, there are four basic scenarios for your statements. They include the scenarios shown in figure 13-12. Because Flash allows both *else* and *else if* clauses to be added to an If statement, you can test a condition for any value. When an *else* statement exists, it is a catchall set of statements. If none of the other conditions specified in the *if* or else *if* statements are found to be true, the Else statements are executed.

 **CD-ROM NOTE:** *To see a simple example of using the If action, open the HTML file ch13-06.html located in the F5gai/chapter13/ folder, installed from the companion CD-ROM. This shows how a single button can be used to go to different places using the If action.*

In many programming languages, a second conditional construct is provided. In JavaScript it is called *switch*; in Director, *case*. In essence, when you use an *if* that has many values you want to test for (let's say greater

| (a) | (b) | (c) | (d) |
|-----|-----|-----|-----|
| if (condition) {<br>   statements<br>} | if (condition) {<br>   statements<br>} else if (<br>   statements<br>} | if (condition) {<br>   statements<br>} else if (condition) {<br>   statements<br>} | if (condition) {<br>   statements<br>} else if (condition) {<br>   statements<br>} else {<br>   statements<br>} |

*Figure 13-12*
*The scenarios that can be established using the If action.*

than 5), you may notice a lag when you run the program. This is because the program must check the condition for each segment of the *if* statement, not to mention that writing lengthy *if* statements can become laborious and confusing (if you have *If* statements nested inside *if* statements).

Thus, *switch* and *case* statements are designed to speed up the evaluation of multiplicative conditions, as well as to provide a shorter way of writing the code. Unfortunately, Flash does not provide either *case* or *switch*. Complex conditional statements must be constructed with nested *if* statements, or with multiple *else if* clauses.

 **CD-ROM NOTE:** *To see another example of using the If action, open the file ch13-07.fla located in the F5gai/chapter13/ folder, installed from the companion CD-ROM. This has a button increment, a variable, and an associated field. Using an if, when the variable is incremented to a certain number, the main movie timeline reacts.*

The previous discussion of general operators did not include the conditional operator consisting of a question mark and a colon ( ? : ) This operator allows you to create conditional statements quickly and easily when there are only two possible values for a condition. In other words, if you have a binary condition, use the conditional operator as a shortcut. The form for the use of the condition operator is:

```
condition ? do_this_if_true : do_this_if_false
```

Examples of the use of the conditional operator follow.

- `myval == 1 ? gotoAndPlay(1) : gotoAndStop(3);`

  In this example, if *myval* equals 1, the movie will go to and play frame 1. If *myval* does not equal 1, the movie will go to frame 3 and stop.

- `_framesloaded < 100 ? gotoAndPlay("Loop") : gotoAndPlay("Start")`

  In this example, if the *_framesloaded* property (the number of frames loaded) is less than frame 100, the movie returns to a label named Loop. If the *_framesloaded* property is greater than frame 100, the movie goes to the frame label Start.

- MC1._x <= 75 ? MC1._x=0 : MC1._x=200

In this example, if the *x* location of the movie clip MC1 is less than or equal to 75, the *x* location of movie clip MC1 is assigned to 0. If not, the *x* location of movie clip MC1 is set to 200.

**NOTE:** *To use the conditional operator you must work in Expert mode. If you revert from Expert to Normal mode in the Actions panel, conditional operators are "erased."*

Let's look at the prior examples you have worked with to see the difference. For example, in the file *ch13-06.fla*, the following code was used for the condition:

```
on (release) {
  if (_currentframe < 10) {
    getURL ("http://www.yahoo.com", "_blank");
  } else {
    getURL ("http://www.excite.com", "_blank");
  }
}
```

A shorthand method for writing the same thing using the conditional operator would be:

```
on (release) {
  _currentframe < 10 ? getURL ("http://www.yahoo.com",
"_blank") : getURL ("http://www.excite.com", "_blank")
}
```

Note the position of the question mark and the colon. As previously mentioned , the use of semicolons is not critical unless you are writing several statements back to back. When you use the conditional operator, it is recommended that you not use semicolons. For example, in the file *ch13-07.fla*, the following code was used for the condition:

```
on (release, releaseOutside) {
  // this increments the variable
  myval = myval+1;
  if (myval>=10) {
    gotoAndPlay ("End");
  }
}
```

A shorthand method for writing the same thing using the conditional operator would be:

```
on (release, releaseOutside) {
 // this increments the variable
 myval = myval+1;
 myval >= 10 ? gotoAndPlay ("End") : gotoAndPlay ("Loop1")
}
```

In this example, note that a second *gotoAndPlay* had to be added to complete the command. You cannot use a conditional operator unless there are specified resultants for both cases. In this scenario, it causes no ill effects.

 **CD-ROM NOTE:** *See applied examples of conditional operators in the files* ch13-08.fla *(which mirrors* ch13-06.fla*) and* ch13-09.fla *(which mirrors* ch13-07.fla*) located in the* F5gai/chapter13/ *folder, installed from the companion CD-ROM. The file* ch13-10.fla *shows an additional example that displays a movie clip that reacts to the main movie timeline.*

A final note concerning conditional operators is that you can combine conditional operators with other items to achieve quite a range of things. In the chapter that deals with FS Command action, you will see conditional operators used in additional ways in JavaScript. The nice thing is all of this is related. If you learn and understand ActionScript coding techniques, understanding and using JavaScript should become easier too!

## for *and* for...in

As you write ActionScript, you often want to perform an operation upon several items at once, or repeat a section of code multiple times. The *for* and *for...in* repeat loops let you repeat something a specific number of times using a counter. The form for creating an incrementing or decrementing counter would be:

```
//incrementing counter
for ( var i = minvalue; i <= maxvalue; ++i ) {
     statements you want to repeat with the value of i
}
//decrementing counter
for ( var i = maxvalue; i >= minvalue; −i ) {
     statements you want to repeat with the value of i
}
```

For example, imagine you wanted to repeat something a certain number of times, such as turning a series of movie clip symbols to invisible or duplicating a certain number of movie clips. In as much as you are aware

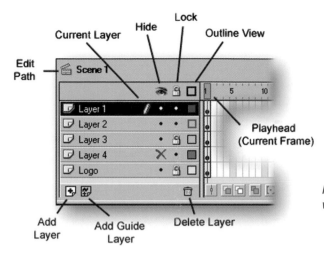

Edit Path

Current Layer    Hide    Lock    Outline View

Scene 1

Layer 1
Layer 2
Layer 3
Layer 4
Logo

Playhead (Current Frame)

Add Layer    Add Guide Layer    Delete Layer

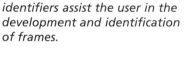

*Plate B-1  The timeline controls allow you to work with the layers in your movie scene.*

Keyframe Indicator    Endframe Indicator    Playback Head

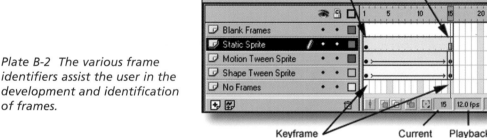

Scene 1

Blank Frames
Static Sprite
Motion Tween Sprite
Shape Tween Sprite
No Frames

*Plate B-2  The various frame identifiers assist the user in the development and identification of frames.*

Keyframe    Current Frame    Playback Speed    Duration at Current Speed

Original Position

New Position

*Plate B-3  The hands are moved and rotated into position.*

Position Frame 1

Position Frame 2

Position Frame 11

*Plate B-4  The hands are moved and rotated a little more.*

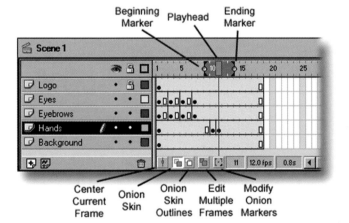

Beginning Marker  Playhead  Ending Marker

Center Current Frame  Onion Skin  Onion Skin Outlines  Edit Multiple Frames  Modify Onion Markers

*Plate B-5  Using the Onion Skin feature allows smoother animations to be created in Flash.*

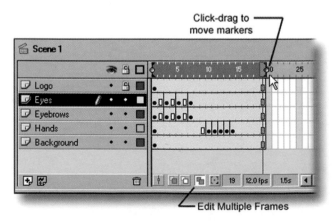

Click-drag to move markers

Edit Multiple Frames

*Plate B-6  The beginning and ending markers can be moved while in Edit Multiple Frames mode.*

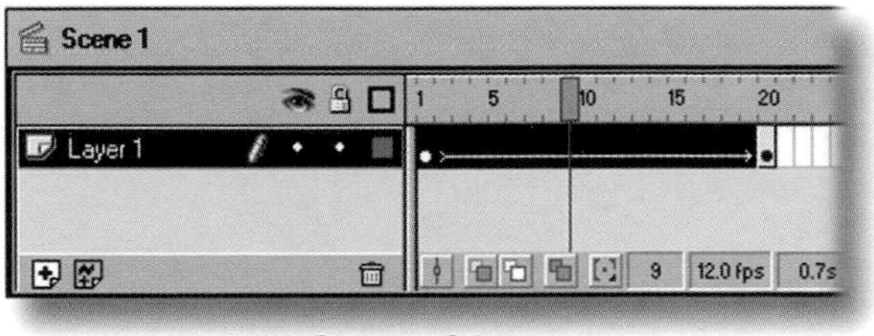

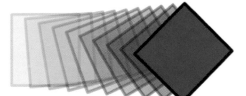

(a) Successful tween

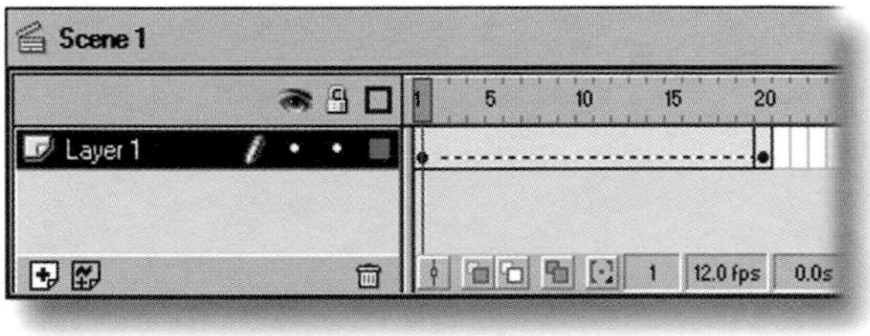

Plate B-7 The Tween frame identifier shows that a tween animation was (a) successfully applied or (b) unsuccessfully applied.

(b) Unsuccessful tween

Plate B-8 Shape tweening allows you to produce elements that morph from one thing to another.

Beginning
Keyframe

Ending
Keyframe

Plate B-9 Shape hints allow you to control shape metamorphosis.

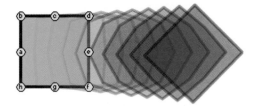

Plate B-10 Eight shape hints perform the shape tween in this example.

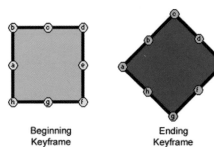

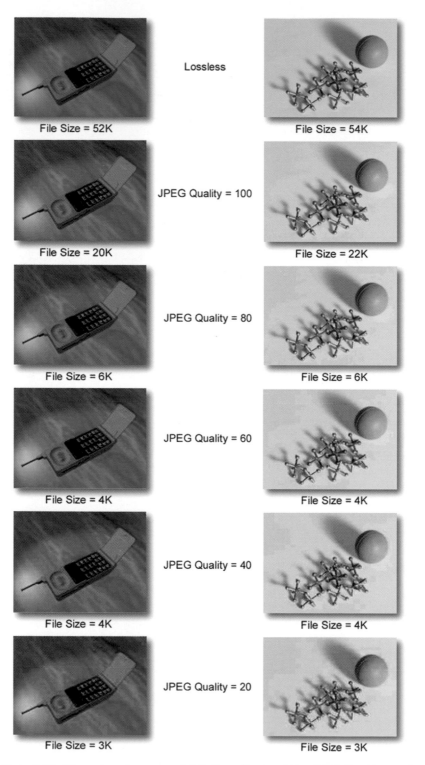

*Plate B-11 These two images exhibit the effects of the JPEG Quality setting on file size and quality.*

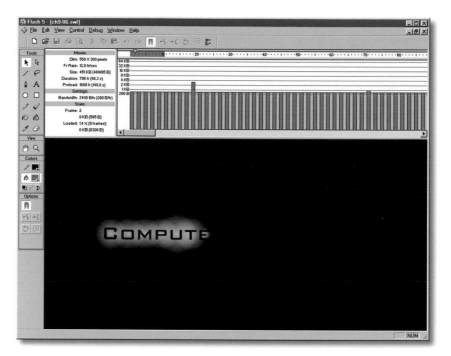

*Plate B-12  The Bandwidth Profiler shows a chart representing the amount of data within each frame.*

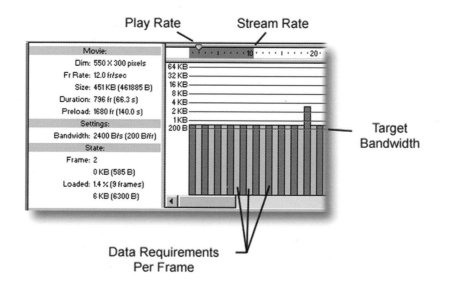

Play Rate    Stream Rate

Target
Bandwidth

Data Requirements
Per Frame

*Plate B-13  Column bars show the amount of data required for the frame. Any extending above the red target bandwidth may cause delays.*

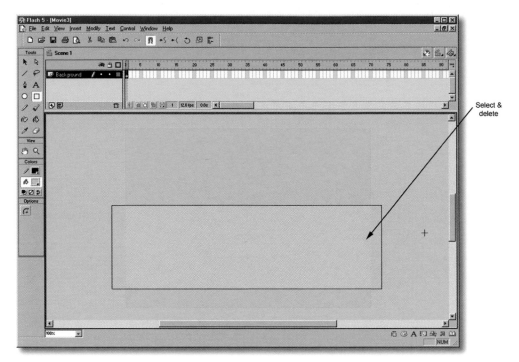

Plate B-14  Select and delete the portion of the fill within the stroke.

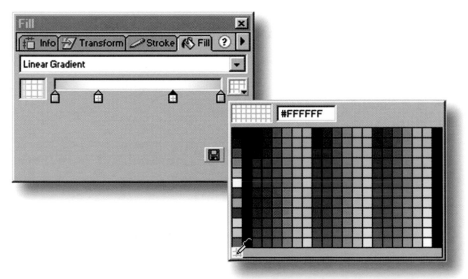

Plate B-15  Define the linear gradient with solid colors on the
ends, and transparent colors in the middle.

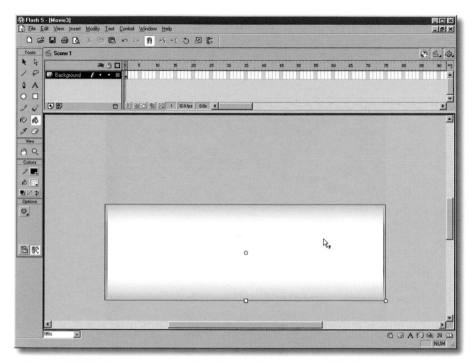

*Plate B-16  Fill the rectangle with the gradient and modify it so that it goes from top to bottom.*

*Plate B-17  Who says Flash cannot perform cool 3D tricks?*

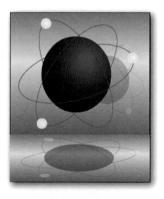

*Plate B-18  Reflections are as easy as shadows.*

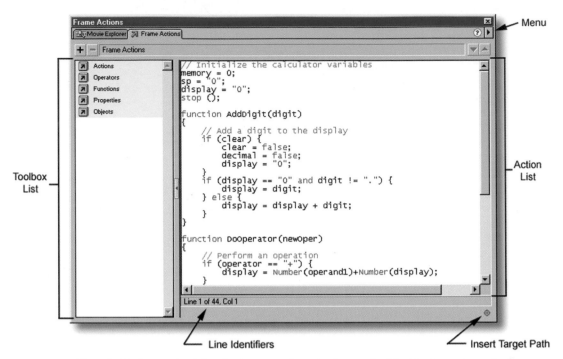

*Plate B-19  Several of the Action panel controls are disabled in Expert mode.*

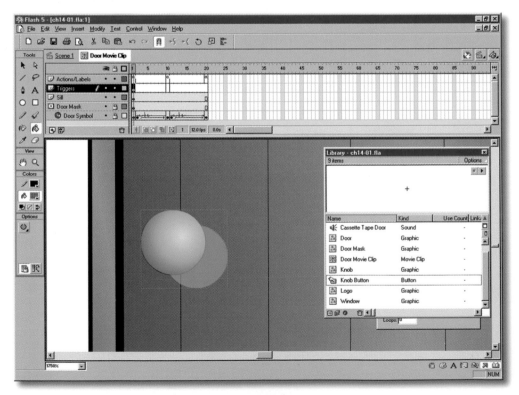

*Plate B-20  Position the trigger over the door.*

right now, the only way to do it is to write multiple lines that manually set each of the items to invisible. With the *for* repeat loop, however, you can create a set of looping code that repeats a specific number of times and does the same thing, such as changing the visibility property.

 **CD-ROM NOTE:** *To see an applied example of the* for *repeat loop, open the file* ch13-11.fla *located in the* F5gai/chapter13/ *folder, installed from the companion CD-ROM.*

The *for* repeat loop can be used for quite a number of things. You would think the *for* repeat loop could be used to incrementally modify the *_alpha* property to create a transition. However, in Flash the screen is only updated when a frame is encountered and there is no way to use ActionScript to forcibly redraw the screen. Another thing along these lines that you should be aware of: the data that is output to the Output window is also dependent on the refreshing of the display. Thus, if you put a Trace action inside a repeat loop you will not see the Trace output in the Output window. We can only hope for a refresh command or action in the next version of Flash (similar to Director's *updateStage* command).

 **CD-ROM NOTE:** *To see an example of use of the* for *loop, open the file* ch13-12.fla *located in the* F5gai/chapter13/ *folder, installed from the companion CD-ROM. Notice that even though the* for *loop is incrementally adjusting the* _alpha *property, because the stage cannot be forcibly redrawn, you do not see a smooth transition.*

The primary difference between the *for* and *for...in* actions is that *for...in* allows you to find out or modify things relative to a specific object. When you begin working with programming objects such as the *Array* object, *for...in* becomes more important.

## while *and* do...while

The *do...while* and *while* loops repeat a set of actions as long as a particular condition is true. Whereas the *for* and *for...in* loops provide a counter and respond to that internal counter's condition or state, the *do...while* and *while* loops assume a condition is TRUE and continually repeat the code statements until the condition is FALSE. *While* loops are pretty easy to understand. The following is an example.

```
while ( condition ) {
     statements to perform
}
```

In general, as long as the condition is evaluated as true, the statements will react. The minute the condition no longer exists, the statements cease. The main thing to keep in mind is that the condition must be TRUE upon encountering the *while* statement; otherwise, the statements inside will not execute. The *do...while* repeat looks like:

```
do {
        statements to perform
} while ( condition )
```

The primary difference between the two types is that *do...while* allows you to execute the statements once before the condition is examined. Thus, the condition would not have to be true for the statements to execute once. However, the condition would have to be true for the statements to execute multiple times. When you just use the *while* repeat, the condition must be true for the statements to ever execute.

### *with*

The last item is similar to the others in that it lets you control flow. However, it is different in that it allows you to target several commands to a single object, very similar to the *tellTarget* action. In Chapter 8, you used the *tellTarget* action. However, the *with* [operator, action, variable] can be used instead. For example, instead of using:

```
tellTarget ("StoppedCD") {
  gotoAndPlay (1);
}
```

use

```
with ("StoppedCD") {
        gotoAndPlay(1);
}
```

**CD-ROM NOTE:** *To see applied examples, examine the files* ch13-13.fla, ch13-14.fla, *and* ch13-15.fla, *located in the* F5gai/chapter13/ *folder, installed from the companion CD-ROM. These are synonymous, respectively, with the files* ch6-09s_adv.fla, ch6-10.fla, *and* ch6-11.fla.

## Other Commands

One of the things you should have noticed when examining the repeat loop commands available is that you must be careful you do not get your users caught in an endless looping scenario. For example, if a user encounters a *while* loop, you need to make sure there is indeed a way to change the condition causing the loop. In addition to those associated with this issue, several other utility commands are available. These are discussed in the sections that follow.

### break and continue

*break* and *continue* are predominantly used with repeat loops. For example, you may find that for a particular value in a *for* loop, you want to break out of the loop when the particular case is found. This is very common when using arrays. *Arrays* are nothing more than variables that can contain multiple values. Most programs call them arrays; however, in Director they are called lists.

Nevertheless, arrays do give you some special capabilities, such as being able to sort the values in an array or search for a particular value in the array. When you search or a value in an array, *break* becomes important. For example, imagine you have an array named *grocerylist*, which contains a series of grocery items. Let's say you know that one of the values in the array is *potatoes*. You could create a *for* loop in a function that searches for the value in the array, breaks out of the *for* loop when it finds the value, and returns the index number (position in the list) of the item. The code for creating the array would look like:

```
grocerylist = new Array();
grocerylist[0] = "apples"
grocerylist[1] = "oranges"
grocerylist[2] = "potatoes"
```

The function would look like:

```
function finditem (myitem) {
      var i
      for ( i = 0; i < grocerylist.length; ++i ) {
            var item = grocerylist[i]
            if ( item == myitem ) {
                  break
            }
      }
      return i
}
```

To call the function and find the index number of *potatoes* you would enter:

```
myindexnum = finditem ("potatoes");
```

When this line calls the *findItem* function, it passes the value *potatoes* to the function. When the function *findItem* receives the value, it sticks it inside the local variable *myitem*. The code inside the function sequentially pulls an item out of the array and compares it to the content of *myitem*. If the item from the list matches *myitem* (that is, the item you were looking for is found), the *break* command is initiated and the loop ceases.

Notice the last line, *return i*. This makes the function return the value in *i* to the line that originally called it, *myindexnum = finditem ("potatoes");*. Thus, the value in *i* is inserted into the variable *myindexnum*. The important thing to remember about *break* is that once you have found the item or value you want, it keeps the loop from continuing needlessly. Even though the example array contains just three values, arrays can be extremely long. Using the *break* command saves time funneling through array items unnecessarily.

 **CD-ROM NOTE:** *To see an applied example of the break command, examine the file* ch13-16.fla *located in the* F5gai/chapter13/ *folder, installed from the companion CD-ROM.*

*continue*, like *break*, serves a special purpose when dealing with looping code segments. *continue* basically tells the repeat to skip the statements contained within it for a particular value. Code that contains a *continue* would look something like the following:

```
for ( var i = 10; i <= 50; ++i ) {
   if ( i == 15 ) || ( i == 25 ) {
      continue
   }
   loop statements to be executed with i
}
```

In this code, the variable *i* is incremented from 10 to 50, one value at a time. At each increment, except 15 and 25, the associated statements are executed. When *i* is found to be 15 or 25, the loop is told to *continue*, meaning skip the statements and repeat the loop without executing them for the current value of *i* (15 or 25). *continue* basically means continue the next loop with the next counter value.

### delete

As you start working with variables and objects such as arrays, you have to keep in mind, particularly with large arrays, that they take up memory. It is possible to create so many arrays or variables that you bog down the machine or cause the application to lock up due to using too much RAM.

The *delete* command, however, allows you to free up memory by deleting the specified variable, array, or other object from memory. It is good and common practice to free up memory by deleting variables or arrays you are no longer using.

Generally when you delete an object, Flash will return a Boolean TRUE if the operation was successful. Therefore, if you wanted to see if an object was successfully deleted from memory, such as the *grocerylist* array used earlier, you could create a temporary variable and check its value to see if it was successfully deleted. The following code does this, using a Trace action to print the results of the *delete* command to the output window:

```
var tempvar = delete grocerylist;
trace tempvar
```

If you tell Flash to delete an object and it is unsuccessful, a Boolean FALSE will be output. You cannot delete predefined objects, properties, or local variables.

### evaluate

The *evaluate* command is used when you work in Normal mode in the Actions panel. Already you have seen two examples that utilized functions written by the end user. The *evaluate* command (action) allows you to call a function in Normal mode.

### function and new

*function* and *new* are two special commands that let you define a function and create a new instance of an object, as you have already seen. Both of these were used in the prior CD-ROM Note examples. You will continue to encounter examples of these items as you move through the rest of this book.

### return

*return* is generally used in combination with functions. More often than not, functions are written so that they receive values, do something to those values, and return the results to the script that called them. Some programming languages refer to functions as subroutines. Regardless which terminology you use, they normally return their results.

Again, prior CD-ROM exercises have shown how to use *return* to send a value back to the script that called it. You will see more examples of this as you progress through this and chapters 15 and 16.

### Trace

*Trace* is used to send data from the Flash Player to the Output window. Note that it only works in the Flash authoring environment. Trace commands are ignored by the player in the browser, as well as the stand-alone Flash Player.

Whatever parameters (arguments) you place in the parentheses of the Trace action will be evaluated and output in the Output window. The main thing to keep in mind when using the Trace action, particularly when you are in Normal mode, is that you must make sure you select the Expression checkbox. If you do not, the arguments in the parentheses will be evaluated as string data rather than an expression to be evaluated. Consequently, whatever is written will be spit to the Output window.

# Dealing with Methods

Let's look in detail at the special items called *methods*, as well as the attributes of objects, called *properties*. In the next three sections, you will continue to build your knowledge of ActionScript by examining these three components: methods that do not return values, methods that do return values, and properties.

Methods can be divided into two major groups: (a) methods that do not return values and (b) methods that do return values. Macromedia generally calls the former "actions" and the later "functions." Table 13-1 at the beginning of this chapter shows both the categorization used in this book and Macromedia's organization.

Macromedia's terminology usage is not necessarily wrong; it is just looking at it differently. As a matter of fact, the use of the term *function* is a carryover from the JavaScript Core Language (JCL) specification. Regardless, as previously stated, the terminology used by Macromedia as well as the JCL does not really coincide with the typical language used in OOP. OOP stresses that functions are generally user defined and related to objects, as followed in this book. However, you can look at the term another way. Some people refer to functions as components that convert data of one type to another, such as converting a string to a number, or vice versa.

## Methods That Do Not Return Values (Actions)

This section deals with the methods in ActionScript that are designed to do something but do not return a value. You have already looked at several of these methods in Chapter 6. These include *gotoAndPlay, gotoAndStop, play, stop, toggleHighQuality, stopAllSounds, getURL,* and *tellTarget.* Similarly, *stopAllSounds* was discussed in Chapter 7; *tellTarget, loadMovie,* and *unloadMovie* were discussed further in Chapter 8; and *ifFrameLoaded* was discussed in Chapter 10.

Similarly, the set variable action was discussed earlier in this chapter. Thus, these items will not be duplicated in this continuing discussion. However, some simple examples will help round out your knowledge of the remaining methods. Chapter 15 deals further with many of these methods, in the context of more complex applied examples.

 **NOTE:** *The FS Command method is discussed in Chapter 16.*

### call

The *call* method provides the ability to create sets of actions that can be called and executed from anywhere in the movie; a subroutine, if you will. This is a carryover from Flash 4 and basically does the same thing as writing a function name to call it (as previously shown in regard to the *additem* function). Keep in mind that the *call* method is deprecated and will likely be unavailable in the next version of Flash.

To use a *call* method, you set up a frame in the movie that contains a series of frame actions you wish to execute. You then assign a frame label to the frame. The *call* method can then be used to reference the frame and execute its actions, by calling the label associated with the frame, as shown in figure 13-13. Information supplied to the Frame field is entered in a manner similar to that used for the Go To action. All entries that are valid for the Go To action are valid for the Call method. In addition, when a frame is called using the *call* method, the frame's stage content is not displayed. Only the called frame's frame actions are executed.

*Figure 13-13  Entering a frame label into the Call action.*

 **TIP:** *If you are working in Normal mode in the Actions panel, you will probably use the* call *method. If you are working in Expert mode, use the* function *command. It is preferable to use the* function *command instead of the* call *method.*

### duplicateMovieClip *and* removeMovieClip

The *duplicateMovieClip* method allows you to make duplicate copies of movie clips on the stage. The *removeMovieClip* method allows you to remove copied clips. These methods are particularly useful for, among other uses, drag-and-drop types of games, for which a duplicate copy of an object may be needed. When you access the *duplicateMovieClip* method, the dialog box shown in figure 13-14 is displayed. Within it you must define the target movie clip you wish to copy, the new name for the copied instance, and the depth (level) for the new object.

When a new instance is generated using *duplicateMovieClip*, the depth of the object becomes important. The simple way of thinking about this is that the copied instance is layered above the original within the parent layer and movie. The instances become part of the parent movie. If the

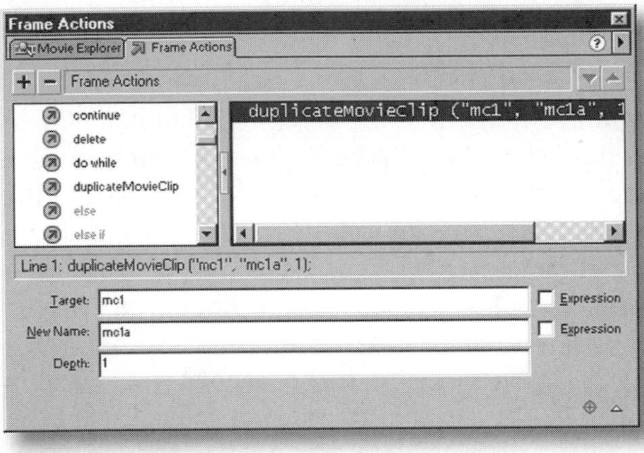

*Figure 13-14 Using the* duplicateMovieClip *method in the Actions panel.*

parent movie is unloaded, the instances will also be unloaded.

Specifically, the first generated instance of a movie clip starts at layer offset 16382 (0x400 hexadecimal). If the depth is specified as 1, the layer offset of the object is 16382 + 1. A depth of 5 is 16382 + 5. The main thing to keep in mind is that duplicated instances are placed above the original object. Because the *duplicateMovieClip* and *removeMovieClip* methods are based on an instance name, only movie clip symbols may be duplicated.

## loadVariables

In version 4 of Flash, the *loadMovie* and *loadVariables* capabilities were wrapped into a single action. In Flash 5, they are now separate entities. The *loadVariables* method allows you to load data from a text file, or from text generated by a technology such as PHP, ASP, or CGI, as shown in figure 13-15. The data being imported must be URL-encoded. For example, recall the Get URL example from Chapter 6 that used GET to pass data to ASP. URL-encoded data looks much like the end of a GET, where data is presented in name and value pairs, separated by ampersands ( & ).

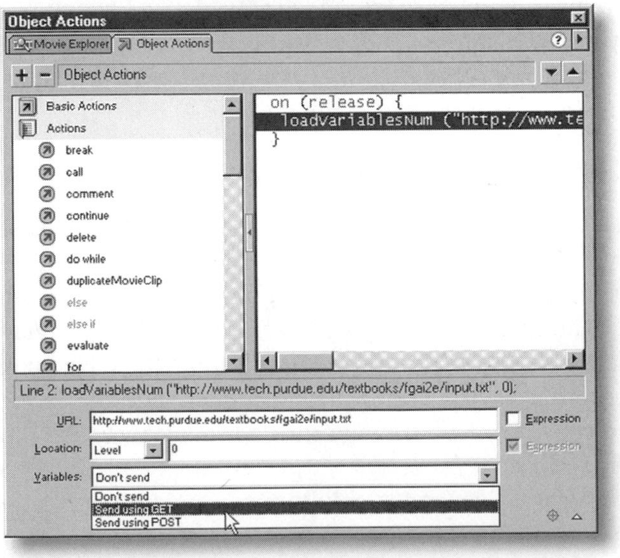

Recall that some characters are replaced by other entities. For example, spaces are replaced with plus signs ( + ). Because humans do not commonly write text in a "URL-encoded" method, ActionScript provides two actions: one to encode to URL-encoded data (escape), and one to decode URL-encoded data (unescape). These commands were used to write the URL-encoded entries for the following CD-ROM Note.

*Figure 13-15 Using the* loadVariables *action to retrieve data from a text file.*

**CD-ROM NOTE:** *To see an applied example of how to load data from an external text file, examine the file* ch13-17.fla *located in the* F5gai/chapter13/ *folder, installed from the companion CD-ROM. The text file loaded (input.txt) is also included in the* F5gai/chapter13/ *folder. Note that you do not have to understand how to write URL-encoded data. The section later in this chapter concerning Escape and Unscape demonstrates a little utility that allows you to quickly encode and decode URL-encoded strings. Note that you have to be connected to the Web for the Load it (from web) button to work!*

You can use the *loadVariables* method in combination with the Get URL technique you learned about in Chapter 6. In the prior CD-ROM Note, the file loads a static text file. However, notice in figure 13-15 that you can send data to a technology (such as ASP or CGI), have it do something to the values, and return the results just by using a single *loadVariables* action. See the following CD-ROM Note for an example.

 **CD-ROM NOTE:** *To see an applied example of how to send data to an external technology, have it process the data, and send something back, examine the file* ch13-18.fla *located in the* F5gai/chapter13/ *folder, installed from the companion CD-ROM. The ASP files for the exercise are also included in that directory. Note that you have to connect to the Web to make the example work.*

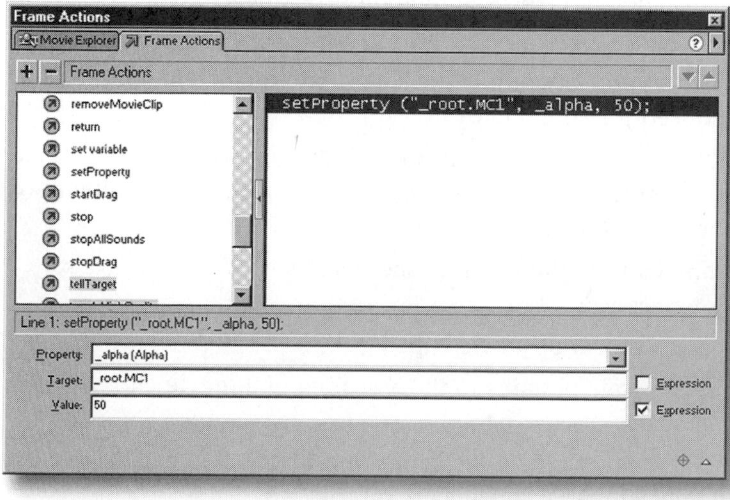

*Figure 13-16  Using* setProperty *to change a movie clip's alpha.*

## setProperty

As you have already read, properties are the attributes of objects. Both objects in your movie, as well as the movie itself, have properties that can be tested and set during playback. When you select the *setProperty* action, you are presented with the dialog box shown in figure 13-16. Within the dialog box, use the Property drop-down list to select the property you wish to change, and the Target field to specify the object to which the property belongs. The Target field should contain a valid target path. The Value field is used to enter the new value for the property of the object. The Value field will often need to be an expression, as many of the properties are numerical values.

 **NOTE:** *All properties in Flash, except for maxscroll and scroll, are preceded by an underscore.*

Two types of properties exist in Flash: global properties, which apply to the entire movie, and local (or movie clip) properties, which apply to movie clip instances currently on the stage. The Set drop-down list provides access to the following properties (which are settable):

- *_alpha:* Alpha allows the transparency (opaqueness) of an object to be changed. The value is entered as a percentage, with 0 being fully transparent and 100 being fully opaque.

- *_focusrectangle:* Show Focus Rectangle is a binary value determining whether the focus rectangle of buttons is displayed.

- *_height:* Height is the height of the referenced object in pixels.

- *_highquality:* High Quality is a binary movie property associated with the display quality during playback. High Quality (Anti-alias) equals 1, and the Fast display setting equals 0.

- *_name:* Name is the name of the symbol instance on the stage.

- *_quality:* A string value specifying one of the following concerning display quality: *LOW, MEDIUM, HIGH,* or *BEST.*

- *_rotation:* Rotation sets the rotation of a movie clip. The value is entered in degrees.

- *_soundbuftime:* Sound Buffer Time determines the size of the buffer used for sound clips.

- *_visible:* Visibility is a binary value indicating whether the movie clip is visible. A visibility of 0 hides the object, and a visibility of 1 shows the object.

- *_width:* Width is the width of the referenced object in pixels.

- *_x:* X Position changes the X position of a movie clip relative to the parent movie or movie clip.

- *_xscale:* X Scale pertains to the X scaling of a movie clip. A value of 1 indicates no scaling.

- *_y:* Y Position modifies the Y position of a movie clip relative to the parent movie or movie clip.

- *_yscale:* Y Scale relates to the Y scaling of a movie clip. A value of 1 indicates no scaling.

Realize that in addition to the settable properties associated with your movies, there are several properties that can be tested (but not set). These properties apply only to the *getProperty* method and conditional statements such as *if*. They include the following:

- *_currentframe* indicates the current frame of the movie.

- *_droptarget* indicates the target path of an object beneath an object that is being dragged. This permits the developer to determine intersections between two movie clips for such things as drag-and-drop games or exercises.

- *_framesloaded* can be used to determine if a frame has been loaded.

- *_level* refers to the level number of the movie you are referring to, such as *_level0* (the *_root* movie).

- *_parent* references a relative step-up in the movie timeline hierarchy.

- *_root* refers to the main movie timeline. This is the same as *_level0*.

- *_target* is the name of a movie clip instance. Note that *_target* provides the reference in slash syntax.

- *_totalframes* reveals the total number of frames in the movie.

- *_url* contains the URL location from which the movie was loaded.

- *_xmouse* is the *x* location of the cursor.

- *_ymouse* is the *y* location of the cursor.

When in the Set Property action, properties that cannot be set are not shown in the Set drop-down menu. When setting up a conditional action based on a property, all properties are shown and can be tested.

 **NOTE:** *Chapter 15 discusses advanced uses for setting properties. You have seen the use of _alpha and other properties.*

### startDrag and stopDrag

The *startDrag* and *stopDrag* methods allow you to create entities within your movie that can be manipulated with the mouse. The *startDrag* method is used to start the drag operation, and the *stopDrag* method is used to cease it.

When you select the *startDrag* method, the dialog box shown in figure 13-17 is displayed. Within it, you enter the object target you want to drag. Note that once a drag is initiated, it will continue until a *stopDrag* or another *startdrag* method is encountered. Note that two dragging operations cannot occur at the same time. If a drag is initiated while one is already underway, the new drag will override the old.

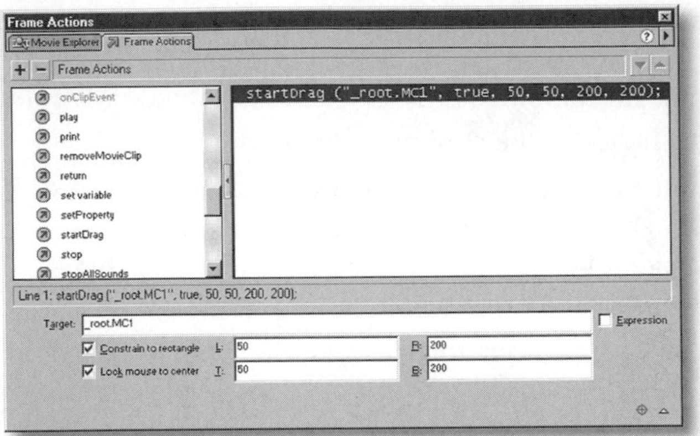

*Figure 13-17 Setting up a drag operation using the Drag Movie Clip method.*

The *startDrag* method requires a target object to drag. This can be defined using a standard target path or using an expression. The *Constrain to rectangle* option permits the definition of a constraining rectangle for the object. The coordinates for the rectangle are based on the parent movie's stage coordinates and can be absolutely or relatively defined.

The *Lock mouse to center* checkbox determines where the movie clip appears in relation to the user's mouse. If the checkbox is not selected, the point of the movie clip the mouse was over when clicked is the registration point between the mouse and the movie clip. If the checkbox is selected, the center of the movie clip will follow the mouse position.

One of the properties mentioned earlier directly relates to the *startDrag* and *stopDrag* methods. The *_droptarget* property is constantly updated while a drag operation is taking place. By checking the *_droptarget* property immediately following a *stopDrag*, you could determine if the released item intersected another movie clip on the stage. Use the *_droptarget* property to create drag-and-drop games and similar interactive components.

**NOTE:** *For more information on creating draggable movie clips, see chapters 14 and 15.*

### updateAfterEvent

The *updateAfterEvent* action is specifically designed for drag-and-drop scenarios. In essence, it allows you to keep objects that are being dragged from flickering during the drag operation. You will see an example of its use in Chapter 15.

## Methods That Return Values (Functions)

In addition to methods generally used to perform operations in the Flash environment, specific methods are designed to receive data, do something to that data, and return the results. Macromedia, as well as other languages, call these functions. Here they are referred to as methods that return values.

### Boolean

The *Boolean* method or function converts the specified value or expression to a Boolean result. The Boolean values of TRUE or FALSE are returned. For example, if you had a variable you created somewhere in your movie, using the Boolean function, you could "ask Flash" if the value was a certain thing. The function would return a TRUE or FALSE. The following code demonstrates this:

```
var x=5
var myresult=Boolean(x==10)
trace (myresult)
```

The result of the *trace* output would be false because the variable *x*, set prior to the variable *myresult*, equals 5, not 10.

### chr and ord

The *chr* method converts an ASCII code representation to an alphanumeric character, whereas *ord* converts an alphanumerical character representation to ASCII code. *chr* and *ord* are deprecated in Flash 5. Therefore, you should use *String.getCharAt();* instead of *chr*. Unfortunately, there is no string method equivalent of *ord*. Instead, you have to use the Key object's *getAscii* method ( *key.getAscii();* ). There are some caveats to this because the Key object tracks only the last key pressed. Nonetheless, an example comparing the items is available.

 **CD-ROM NOTE:** *To see an applied example of the* chr *and* ord *methods, examine the file* ch13-19.fla *located in the* F5gai/chapter13/ *folder, installed from the companion CD-ROM.*

### escape and unescape

The *escape* and *unescape* methods are specialized functions for encoding and decoding strings to URL-encoded formats. When this is done, all alphanumeric characters are escaped with various hexadecimal sequences. You would use this function in association with the loadVariables action, or when you use POST or GET to send data in and out of Flash. The following CD-ROM Note points to an example file that is helpful when you want to encode or decode text strings to the URL-encoded format.

 **CD-ROM NOTE:** *To see applied examples of the Escape and Unescape functions, examine the file* ch13-20.fla *located in the* F5gai/chapter13/ *folder, installed from the companion CD-ROM.*

## eval

The *eval* method can be used to retrieve the value of a variable, property, object, or movie clip by entering the respective name as the expression. The *eval* method provides a means of referring to an object's name in code. In Flash 4, it was also used for the purpose of simulating arrays. However, the new *Array* object should now be used for that purpose. For example, *eval("x")* retrieves the value contained in *x*. If *x* is a variable or property, the value of the item will be returned. If *x* is anything else, the reference to the object is returned.

 **NOTE:** *The* eval *method in Flash is not the same thing as the* eval *method in JavaScript. Eval in Flash cannot be used on expressions.*

Note that *eval* is a deprecated method in Flash 4. Even so, an example is provided in the following CD-ROM Note.

 **CD-ROM NOTE:** *To see applied examples of the Eval method, examine the file* ch12-21.fla *located in the* F5gai/chapter13/ *folder, installed from the companion CD-ROM.*

## getProperty

As previously mentioned, there are many properties in Flash, some global and some local. Similarly, some properties can only be tested against. Others can only be set. The *getProperty* function allows you to retrieve any of the properties listed in the previous section. For example, when you create drag-and-drop scenarios, you may want to use the *getProperty* method to determine if the clip you were dragging intersected another clip. You would do this using the *getProperty* function, to see what the *_droptarget* property contained.

When you select the *getProperty* method, you must enter a target (the object the property belongs to) and the property you want to get, as shown in figure 13-18. In the illustration, the *getProperty* method is being used to extract the *_droptarget* property.

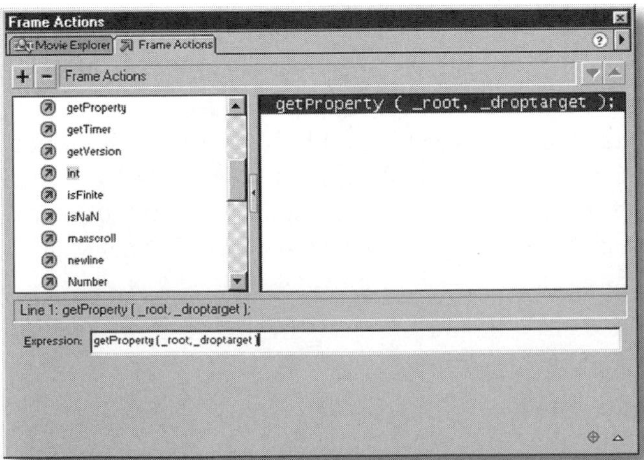

*Figure 13-18 Using the* getProperty *method to retrieve a value.*

For now, the *getProperty* method will not be examined further, because an advanced project would be necessary. Later you will use this method in a variety of ways. Simply remember that the *getProperty* method takes the following form:

```
getproperty( target, property );
```

### getTimer

The *getTimer* method provides a facility for measuring time that has elapsed within a movie. It is measured in milliseconds and is based on elapsed time since the movie started playing. The *getTimer* method returns a numerical value.

 **CD-ROM NOTE:** *To see applied examples of the getTimer method, examine the file* ch13-22.fla *located in the* F5gai/chapter13/ *folder, installed from the companion CD-ROM.*

### getVersion

The *getVersion* method is simple. It returns the current version of the Flash Player, as well as the platform the player is running on. Note that it will not work when you use Test Movie. However, you can easily see what the output of *getVersion* would be by using the Debugger. Click on the main movie and look at the Variables tab.

### int

The *int* method generates an integer number from the value passed to it. For example, *int(16.89)* yields a value of 16; *int(-25.567)* yields –25; and *int(.678)* yields zero (0). The *int* method has been deprecated in Flash 5. Therefore, it is recommended you use the *Math.floor()* method instead. The CD-ROM Note that follows points to examples of the use of the *int* method.

 **CD-ROM NOTE:** *To see applied examples of the* int *method, examine the file* ch13-23.fla *located in the* F5gai/chapter13/ *folder, installed from the companion CD-ROM.*

### isFinite and isNaN

The *isFinite* and *isNaN* (not a number) methods are designed to help you evaluate the value of variables, properties, or expressions to determine if they are finite numbers (*isFinite*) or if they are numbers at all (*isNaN*).

### length

*length* allows you to determine the number of characters in a string element, such as a variable or other item. *length* is deprecated in Flash 5. As an alternative, you should use the *String.length* property. The following CD-ROM Note examines both methods.

 **CD-ROM NOTE:** *To see applied examples of the* length *method, examine the file* ch13-24.fla *located in the* F5gai/chapter13/ *folder, installed from the companion CD-ROM.*

### number and string

The *number* and *string* methods allow you to convert between strings and numbers. Their forms are as follows:

```
Number(x);
String(x);
```

Here, *x* may be a string, Boolean, or expression. Understand that *number* and *string* methods are not the same thing as Number and String programming objects. For example, the following items are not equivalent:

*new String(); and* string *(mystring);*

*new Number(); and* number(myval);

See the following CD-ROM Note for examples that uses the *number* and *string* methods.

 **CD-ROM NOTE:** *To see applied examples of the Number and String methods, examine the file* ch13-25.fla *located in the* F5gai/chapter13/ *folder, installed from the companion CD-ROM.*

### parseFloat and parseInt

*parseFloat* and *parseInt* are functions designed to be used with numerical entries. They can be used to evaluate strings, numbers, or expressions. *parseFloat* attempts to convert a string to a floating-point number, whereas *parseInt* attempts to convert the string to an integer. See the following CD-ROM Note for examples of these methods.

 **CD-ROM NOTE:** *To see applied examples of the* parseFloat *and* parseInt *functions, examine the file* ch13-25.fla *located in the* F5gai/chapter13/ *folder, installed from the companion CD-ROM.*

### random

The *random* function allows you to generate a random number. The value inserted in parentheses is one number greater than the maximum value that may be generated. For example, *random(25)* will generate a random number between 0 and 24. To generate a number between 1 and 25, use *random(25) + 1.*

*random* is a deprecated item in Flash 5. Thus, you should use the *Math.random* method instead. The interesting thing about the *Math.random* method is that it only generates a value between 0.0 and 1.0. Therefore, you must multiply and round the resulting value to get a specific integer. For example, to generate a number between 1 and 25 you would use:

```
Math.Round(Math.random() * 25)
```

Note in this expression that the *Math.random()* method is used within the *Math.round* method. This is so that you do not end up with a decimal number to infinity. See the following CD-ROM Note for an example.

 **CD-ROM NOTE:** *To see applied examples of the* random *function, examine the file* ch13-27.fla *located in the* F5gai/chapter13/ *folder, installed from the companion CD-ROM.*

### substring

*substring* allows you to extract a portion of a string variable by defining the string, the index (starting position for extraction), and the count (ending position for extraction). Again, *substring* is deprecated in Flash 5. Therefore, you should use the *String.substring* method. The following CD-ROM Note points to examples of both methods.

 **CD-ROM NOTE:** *To see applied examples of the* substring *and* String.substring *methods, examine the file* ch13-28.fla *located in the* F5gai/chapter13/ *folder, installed from the companion CD-ROM.*

### targetPath

The *targetPath* method provides another means of retrieving and pointing to the target path of the object specified by the argument. In theory, the *targetPath* function should be equivalent to the *tellTarget* action. The primary difference is that *targetPath* requires dot notation and *tellTarget* requires slash notation.

### typeOf

The *typeOf* method provides you with a quick means of evaluating a string, movie clip, object, or function. When you use it, it returns a string describing what the object is.

# ▪ ▪ ▪ Rules of the Road for Writing Scripts

For those who are new to scripting and programming, your first ventures into ActionScript may be somewhat frustrating. There are several programming-related tips you can use to make the experience a little more enjoyable. This section is for you. On the other hand, if programming is old hat for you, you may already practice, or at least be aware of, these guidelines. However, it might be a good idea to review them. It never hurts to remind yourself of the common practice principles, even if you do not follow every one. We all develop our own style, but our approach is more often alike than different. The following general guidelines, therefore, can be helpful, particularly for beginners.

- Keep in mind the rules governing the use of ActionScript.

The most common errors are syntactical. Keep a watchful eye that you follow the rules presented early in this chapter concerning syntax.

- Do not write a mile of script; test it, and then just hope it all just works out.

If you are trying to write complex ActionScript, add a little scripting and then test it. Add a little more, and test again. It is much easier to debug scripts by adding a little bit at a time than it is to test complex, lengthy scripts all at once.

- Isolate the problem.

If you are having difficulty getting a particular item to work, start a new file and separate from the main file the function or whatever it is that you are trying to do. Test code snippets in blank files to get them to work. Once they work in a simple environment, move them to your working file. This will help you determine where problems may lie.

- Use the Trace action to post information to the Output window.

The Debugger is a nice feature, but is overkill for a lot of things. The Trace action is the quickest, simplest way of finding out what is going on. If you have a more complex problem or more complex code, use the Debugger.

- Use comments to provide internal documentation within your movies.

Comments are vital to a program, particularly when you come back to it several months later or if you must pick up where someone else left off. Good programmers leave a "comment trail" in their code both for themselves and others.

- Develop and follow a consistent manor of labeling for variables, functions, and so on.

Develop a consistent style of variable naming. You may want to begin all global variables with $g$ or $g\_$ for easy identification. In addition, use meaningful names for variables, particularly global variables. Keep in mind that you are not in DOS. Use more than eight characters if you have to for clarity's sake.

- Save early and save often.

No explanation needed!

# ▪ ▪ ▪ Summary

In this chapter, you have taken a further step into the "technoweenie" world of Flash programming. Indeed, if you are able to garner and retain the information in this chapter you are well on your way to making big money as a Flash programmer. I recognize that not everybody wants to be a programmer. However, in today's world, and every historical period I know of, everybody would like to make more money. And in the Flash development community, as well as the web development community at large, the quickest way today is through greater experience and understanding of programming.

This is a main reason so much of this book deals with programming. It is also the reason Macromedia has refocused Flash. The real power is in understanding programming and being able to apply that knowledge to do something beneficial for your web audience or clients. With the fundamentals now under your belt, let's move on to applied professional examples you can dissect and examine.

chapter

# 14

# Interactive Techniques and Smart Clips

## ■ ■ ■ Introduction

Of the many things you can do with Flash, creating interfaces and interface components is one of the most exciting. For quite some time developers have been trying to create sites that provide unique navigation controls, much of which has been done using raster graphics and other technologies. However, file size is a detrimental factor in regard to these raster techniques. With Flash, however, almost anything you would typically see on a multimedia CD-ROM can now be incorporated in material designed for the Web.

This chapter focuses on using Flash as a basis for navigation controls. The chapter first examines what makes a good interface and why effective affordances are important. The chapter also examines the wealth of buttons, sliders, and other interface elements that can be used for a variety of purposes. In addition, you will learn how to create sliders and menus. You will see how the new text field capability can be used to collect information via Flash-based forms, as well as its use for creating combo boxes. Also of importance is the new drag-and-drop capability, which allows any button to become a moveable element on the stage.

# ▪ ▪ ▪ Objectives

In this chapter, you will:

- Examine the issues surrounding interface design
- Look at what makes an effective affordance
- Create custom buttons, such as for an opening-and-closing door
- Discover how the text field element works, and how it can be used to pass data from one movie or page to another
- Understand the use of drag-and-drop actions
- Learn about smart clips and how they can be used to create menus and sliding button controls

# ▪ ▪ ▪ The Value of an Affordance

Affordances are those things that clue the user to functionality. They are recognizable components, such as a push button or the handle on a slider, a user identifies with interaction. In this case, the handle (the affordance) indicates what the control (the slider) is used for.

Much research has been devoted to examining the affordances associated with computer and software interfaces. We are just now beginning to apply the same approach to the "face of the Web," in large part due to the speed and efficiency attributed to vector graphics. When raster graphics were the primary mechanism for graphics in web design, it was inefficient to develop complex interfaces because download time was wasted on the interface and not spent on content. With vector graphics and their very small file size, it now makes sense to put interfaces on web sites.

## Effective Affordances

The effectiveness of any affordance (control) is based on several things. First, affordances must be recognizable. As you begin building collections of affordances (interface controls), each control must be self-explanatory. If an affordance is not obvious, the user will likely need help to understand its workings.

If you use standard controls such as push buttons, drop-down menus, and the like, most users familiar with computers will have no problem telling what the controls do. However, if you depart from the norm and use unique or custom-designed controls, make sure the affordance clues the user as to functionality. For example, one way of achieving this is through the use of changing states via color, shape, or size, or combinations of these. An example of this is a button that changes from an inactive state to an active state, where it appears "pushed in."

Recognition of an affordance is most often associated with experience and knowledge. Thus, the success of a particular gadget in an interface is based on the premise that the user is familiar with the object being mimicked (such as a real push-button). Successful interface components are most often modeled on elements in the physical world with which a majority of your audience is familiar. Although almost anything is possible in Flash, be careful you do not design controls (affordances) that are difficult to use. Historically, there is a correlation between unsuccessful software products and their ease of use.

## Metaphors and Interfaces

As you begin putting a face on your web sites, frequently the components (as well as the overall look and feel) of your site may use a similarity or likeness to something else. This is called a metaphor. Metaphors are used in creating the controlsand many other components of an entire interface.

A metaphor often implies a likeness to some device a user has an intuitive familiarity with. An affordance styled accordingly will quickly orient the audience as to its purpose. For example, if you give your web interface a VCR look, you are assuming your audience is familiar with a VCR and its workings. Thus, they should be able to easily use your interface. A prime example of this is the QuickTime controller or the Windows Media Player, which both use a simple VCR-like control panel. Interface metaphors draw on a user's familiarity with the world around him or her, making for ease of interface navigation and quicker access to desired information.

Although some sites use metaphors, an increasing number of sites do not. An interface does not necessarily have to be like anything else. Several Flash sites listed in this book do not necessarily look like a VCR, PDA, or other digital device. In fact, many use design themes totally unrelated to anything else. We are seeing the Web develop its own genre and its own look.

However, with this freedom as a web developer, you have to be careful that you do not design a site that looks wonderful but is difficult to navigate or understand. As noted in Chapter 1, utility and navigability are of the utmost importance. In most cases, people do not just come to navigate. They came to consume information or to get something of value. Navigation and navigation controls should be as transparent and easy to use as possible.

## Successful Interfaces

Much research has been done concerning interface design, mainly related to software development. However, many of the design rules transfer to the Web. Five human factors can be identified concerning the evaluation of an interface:

- *Time to learn:* For example, how long does it take to figure out how to navigate?

- *Speed of performance:* How long must you wait for a response?

- *Rate of errors:* For example, how often does the user encounter a dead end and have to back up?

- *Retention over time:* Does the user remember that this item or that performs a certain function?

- *Subjective satisfaction:* Do the layout, fonts, controls, and other components make it easy for the user to get what they need from your site?

Typically, these five points are central to the evaluation of an interface. However, an overriding factor to keep in mind is human diversity. The fact that each user is different in experience, age, professional level, skill level, and so on is what makes interface design so complex. To design a successful interface requires knowing the task you want to accomplish and the information that must be accessed, usually summed up in a task profile. Additionally, knowledge of the audience is usually described in a usage or audience profile. With these in mind, a successful interface is right around the corner.

# The World of Interaction

There are several different ways to interact with the computer. With today's graphical user interfaces, the basic WIMP construct is used. WIMP is an acronym for Windows, Icons, Menus, and Pointers. Interaction in a WIMP environment can occur in one of five ways.

- Manipulation
- Menus
- Form text boxes
- Command language
- Natural language

Within this chapter, you will examine the first three of these using Flash. Manipulation includes buttons, sliders, and drag-and-drop components. Menus and form boxes are standard components you will also see implemented in Flash. Command language interaction is usually reserved for developers and for programming environments.

End users seldom encounter command language systems, unless they are still using command-line interfaces such as DOS or UNIX. As a developer, if you use ActionScript or JavaScript, you are actually using command language interaction. Natural language (i.e., non-technospeak nomenclature) is a rapidly evolving area and is used in Microsoft's help system. As an extension to and sometimes replacement of command language, natural language helps both end users and developers create and use interactions.

# Custom Buttons: A Sliding Door

In Chapter 5, you saw how basic push buttons could be created using Flash symbols. By defining an Up, Over, Down, and Hit states, push buttons can be quickly and easily generated. However, note that almost any control can be created with the button facility, particularly with the advent of smart clips. In this section, you will examine how to create a sliding door, which is a custom button type. In the next two chapters, this door will be used with Noah's Memory Game.

In the CD-ROM exercise that follows, you have the opportunity to practice creating a custom button. First, however, a note on terminology. The term *trigger* is used frequently in this chapter. A trigger is a button that contains no Up, Over, or Down state. When a button symbol has a Hit state only, it is invisible during playback. However, the user can still roll the mouse over the button symbol (whereupon the cursor changes to a hand) and click on it. When triggers (invisible buttons) are placed on the stage, they are displayed in a cyan color. The cyan color is displayed only during authoring. When Test Movie is executed, the cyan object is not shown, even though it is still there.

## CD-ROM Exercise

Open the file *ch14-01.fla* located in the *F5gai/chapter14/* folder, installed from the companion CD-ROM. Use the file in performing this exercise. If you want to see the finished file first, open the file *ch14-01s.fla*. Use Test Movie to see how the button works. To create a custom button, perform the following steps.

1. With the start-up file open, use Window | Library to open the library. Note that there are already symbols in the library. You will use these to construct the sliding door.

2. Begin by creating the trigger. Use Insert | New Symbol to create a symbol named Knob Button. Select Button as the behavior and click on OK.

3. Add a blank keyframe to the Over, Down, and Hit states.

4. Select the Hit frame and drag the Knob symbol from the library to the Hit frame.

5. With the Knob symbol selected on the stage, use Modify | Break Apart to separate the instance from the symbol.

6. Edit the element so that it is nothing but a black fill. Delete the gradient and the portion of the arc that separates the gradient from the shadow. Use the Paint Bucket to fill the white area and the existing gray fill. This should cause the two fills to union (merge). Delete the remaining arc portion and click on the Scene 1 link in the Edit Path to close the symbol.

> **NOTE:** *You may think it unnecessary to modify the hit area. Indeed, you could have just inserted the Knob symbol and left it as the hit area. However, it is acceptable practice to use only singular fills for hit areas, as this reduces file size.*

With the Hit frame modified, you have completed the trigger. Keep in mind that a trigger is nothing more than an "invisible" button; that is, a button with only a hit area defined. When placed on the stage in the authoring environment, the trigger will be displayed as a cyan-colored element (in the shape of the hit area). To create the door movie clip, continue as follows.

7. Use Insert | New Symbol to create a new symbol. Name the symbol Door Movie Clip and select Movie Clip as its behavior. Click on OK.

8. Create five layers and name them as indicated in figure 14-1. Extend frame 1 in all layers to frame 20.

9. In the Actions/Labels layer, insert a keyframe in frames 2, 10, 11, and 20.

10. Enter *Closed* as a label for frame 1.

11. Enter *Close* as a label for frame 11.

12. Add a Stop action to frames 1 and 10.

13. Insert a Go To action in frame 20. Deselect the Go To and Play checkbox. Set the action to go to label Closed.

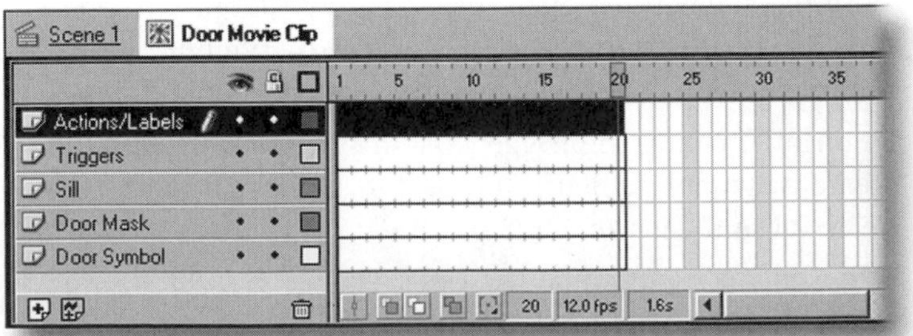

*Figure 14-1  Adding and naming the five layers for the door button.*

14. Click on frame 1 of the Sill layer and drag the Window symbol from the library to the stage. Line up the crosshairs of the Window symbol with the crosshairs of the stage.

15. Click on frame 1 of the Door Mask layer and drag the Door Mask symbol from the library to the stage. Line up the crosshairs of the symbol with the stage.

16. Hide the Door Mask layer.

17. Click on frame 1 of the Door Symbol layer. Drag the Door symbol from the library to the stage and align the crosshairs.

18. Add a keyframe in frames 2, 10, and 20 of the Door Symbol layer. Remember that you have to hold down the Ctrl key (Command in Mac) to be able to select a single frame in a sprite.

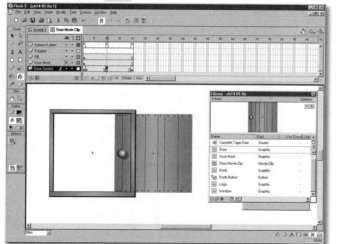

*Figure 14-2 Moving the door to the open position.*

19. Click on frame 10 and move the door to an open position, as shown in figure 14-2. Note that you want to make sure the doorknob remains visible. If it is hidden behind the windowsill, or is off the stage, there will be no way of closing it!

20. Add a keyframe to frame 11 of the Door Symbol layer.

21. Right-click on the sprite between frames 2 and 9 and select Create Motion Tween from the context menu. Repeat this between frames 11 and 19.

As you were adding the keyframes to the Door Symbol layer, note that you waited to add the keyframe in frame 11. This is to minimize the work you had to do. Had you added a keyframe to frame 11 when you added keyframes to frames 2, 10, and 20 you would have had to define the position of the door in multiple frames.

 **TIP:** *Whenever you are creating tween animations, think about the process before you start. You can save yourself a lot of steps (and time).*

22. Right-click on frame 2 and open the Sound panel. Assign the Cassette Tape Door sound to the frame. Set the Sync drop-down list to Start. Repeat this in frame 11.

23. Unhide the Door Mask layer and right-click on the layer name. Select Mask from the context menu. Now if you move the playhead you will see that the door appears to be opening and closing (sliding).

The final thing that must be inserted is the trigger. The trigger is what makes the door function. Although the animated segments exist, there is nothing to react to the interaction. The trigger is inserted apart from the animated door so that the user can click on the doorknob only when the door is stationary (open or closed).

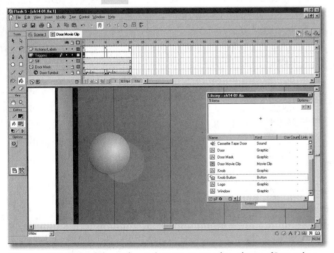

Figure 14-3 Position the trigger over the door. (See also color plate B-20.)

24. Insert a keyframe in the Triggers layer in frames 2, 10, and 11.

25. Select frame 1 of the Triggers layer, and then drag and drop the Knob Button from the library to the stage, as shown in figure 14-3 and color plate B-20. Align it perfectly over the top of the actual doorknob. You will notice that when you drop it on the stage it appears in a cyan color, denoting that it has only a hit area defined.

26. Select frame 10 of the Triggers layer and repeat the process. Place the Door Knob symbol from the library directly over the doorknob.

27. Now assign a simple Play action to the trigger in frame 1.

28. Assign a Play action to the trigger in frame 10.

29. Click on the Scene 1 link in the Edit Path and insert the Door Movie Clip symbol from the library to the main timeline.

30. Use Test Movie to see the door work.

There are myriad buttons you can create in Flash. Macromedia has included many categories of button libraries in Flash. Make sure you check them out, as they provide a good opportunity for learning. To do this, access Window | Common Libraries | Buttons.

# Creating Sliders

There are two methods of creating sliders. One method is to use triggers, which is a carryover technique from Flash 4. This is still a completely valid way of creating a slider. With this technique, as with the creation of the door, multiple triggers are inserted into a file. However, you must tell Flash to track the trigger as a menu option, rather than as a button, as you will see. The second method is to create slider components using ActionScript programming. Let's begin by looking at the former.

## Trigger-based Sliders

Triggers, as you have already learned, are buttons that contain nothing but a Hit state. By using multiple triggers adjacent to one another, and by attaching actions that control a movie clip, you can easily create a sliding control. The following CD-ROM exercise demonstrates this technique.

### CD-ROM Exercise

Open the file *ch14-02.fla* located in the *F5gai/chapter14/* folder, installed from the companion CD-ROM. Use the file in performing this exercise. If you want to see the finished file first, open the file *ch14-02s.fla*. Use Test Movie to see how the button works. To begin creating the slider control, perform the following steps.

1. Use Insert | New Symbol to create a new symbol. Name the symbol Slider and set Behavior to Movie Clip.

2. Open the library and drag the Bar symbol to the stage. Use the Info panel to align the registration points. Set the bar's X to 0 and Y to –16. This will perfectly align the graphic symbol's registration point to the newly created movie's registration point.

   **NOTE:** *When you start creating interface components, realize that accuracy related to sizes and position on the screen (in relation to the registration point) become very important. You will find that you will use the Info panel quite a lot when creating interface components.*

3. Extend the duration the sprite to frame 10.

4. Insert a new layer, named Ball, and drag the Ball symbol from the library to frame 1 of the new layer. Align the Ball

instance so that its center resides directly over the first tick mark of the Bar instance. Again, use the Info panel to set -13 for the ball's X and −13 for the ball's Y.

5. Add a keyframe to frame 10 of the Ball layer and drag the ball to the other end of the slider. Align the center of the ball over the last tick mark. Again, use the Info panel and set the ball's Y on 239 (the length of the bar, 252, minus the radius of the ball, 13).

6. Set up a motion tween for the ball so that it passes from one end of the bar to the other. You should notice that once the tween is set up, the ball falls on each of the already established tick marks.

Although the tween is working, when you actually use the slider you do not want it to play the entire animation. Thus, you need to create one more layer that has a Stop action, so that animation does not play through.

7. Create a new layer and name it Stop. In frame 1 of the new layer, assign a Stop action. This will cause the playhead to stop at every frame, because copied instances exist for the duration of the existing slider frames.

Next, you must create the trigger that will be used for the slider. Again, a correctly sized symbol already exists for you to use. When you are creating your own sliders, you can construct the hit area for the slider based on the width between two vertical tick marks.

8. Use Insert | New Symbol to create a new symbol. Name the symbol Trigger and select Button as its behavior.

9. Add a keyframe to the Over, Down, and Hit frames in the Trigger symbol.

10. In the Hit frame, drag the Hit Area graphic symbol from the library to the stage.

11. Save your file.

Now you will composite all of the elements within a new movie clip symbol. By compositing the elements in a movie clip, the component will be portable and can be used for a variety of things.

12. Use Insert | New Symbol and name the item Slider-component. Select Movie Clip as the behavior.

13. Drag the Slider Movie Clip from the library to the stage.

14. Use the Info panel to perfectly align the registration points. The registration point for the Slider movie clip should be –13, -16.

15. Right-click on the Bar movie clip on the stage, open the Instance panel, and name its instance Slider. To make the slider's ball react to the trigger, you will need to reference the object using the *with* (preferred) or *tellTarge*t action. Again, to target a movie clip, the instance must be named.

16. Drag the Trigger symbol to the stage from the library. There will eventually be 10 copies of the trigger on the stage. However, before you add all of them, you will add actions to the first trigger. Then you will copy and paste the trigger onto the stage so that you have less to do.

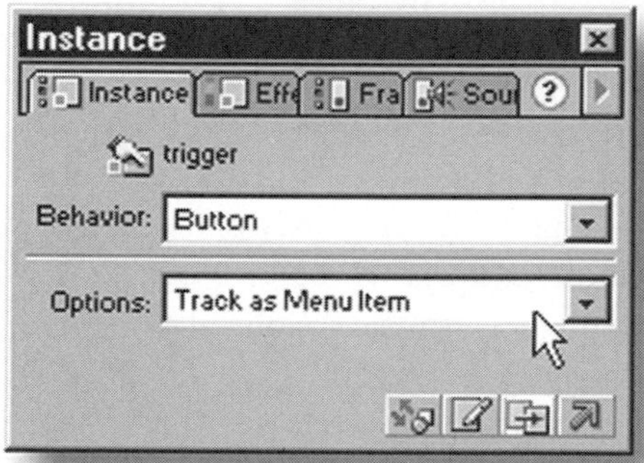

17. To make a slider (as well as a menu) work, you must tell Flash to track the trigger in a special way. As shown in figure 14-4, notice that the Track as Menu Item option is selected from the Instance panel's Options drop-down list. Select this option to make the slider trigger act as a menu item instead of as a button.

*Figure 14-4 Select the Track as Menu Item option in the Instance panel to make the item function correctly.*

**NOTE:** *The previous step is vital. Anytime you are creating a slider or a menu, you must set the triggers to Track as Menu Item. If you do not, the slider or menu will not work!*

18. Open the Actions panel and click on the trigger on the stage.

19. In the Actions panel, use the *with* action and use *this.slider* in the Object field.

20. Set the *on* event handler to both Release and Drag Over, as shown in figure 14-5.

When viewing figure 14-5, notice the mouse events assigned to the actions. Both Release and Drag Over are selected. When you want a slider to react to a drag operation only, specify the Drag

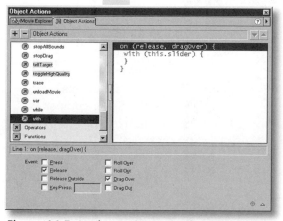

*Figure 14-5 In the Actions panel, add the with action and set the on event handler to both Release and Drag Over.*

Over option only. In this scenario, if the user clicks on a tick mark, the slider will do nothing. When Drag Over is the only mouse event specified, the user must drag. When both the Drag Over and Release options are selected, if the user click-drags or clicks, the slider's ball will move.

21. Add a Go To action (frame 1 and stop), as well as a set variable action. Use *sliderno* for the variable name and set it to 1, as shown in figure 14-6. Note that the Expression checkbox is checked for the Value field.

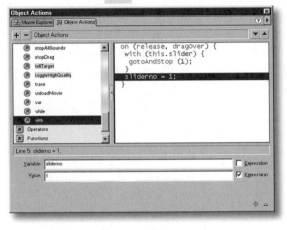

*Figure 14-6  Add a gotoAndStop and a set variable action.*

22. Copy and paste the trigger. Line up the triggers adjacent to one another, as shown in figure 14-7. Ten copies of the trigger should be generated.

23. Once all triggers are in place, you must go back and modify the Go To action and set variable associated with each trigger. Note that you assigned the action to the first trigger before copying, so that the action would be copied as well. Select the second trigger and change its action so that it tells the slider to go to frame 2 and sets the *sliderno* variable to 2.

24. Change the third trigger's actions to go to frame 3 and set *sliderno* to 3. Repeat this for each of the triggers up to 10.

25. Once you have modified all actions, place the Slider-component movie clip on the stage.

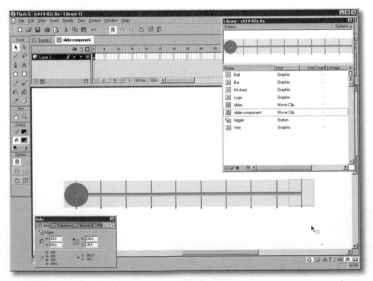

*Figure 14-7*
*After assigning the actions to the first trigger, copy and paste it so that there are a total of 10 triggers adjacent with one another.*

26. Save your file.

27. Use Test Movie to see the resulting slider function.

The slider created in this exercise can now be used for a variety of purposes. You can use a slider such as this for a scenario in which you need a control with 10 "states." Feel free to change its look and feel to something else. Later, you will see this type of slider integrated into a couple of real-world scenarios. However, let's first examine how you can program a slider using ActionScript.

## ActionScript-based Sliders

In creating an ActionScript-based slider, you have to pay careful attention to the positioning of elements on the stage and within symbols. In the last example, you started using the Info panel to accurately place elements on the stage. In the following CD-ROM exercise, where you want to use programming to set the location of elements on the stage, you must pay even closer attention to coordinate details.

In this exercise, you will create an movie clip slider that has 11 increments, instead of 10. This example is most appropriate where you have an element, such as a volume slider, that has 10 levels plus a zero level (thus 11 specific settings). See the following CD-ROM exercise for practice creating this type of slider.

---

 ### CD-ROM Exercise

Open the file *ch14-03.fla* located in the *F5gai/chapter14/* folder, installed from the companion CD-ROM. Use the file in performing this exercise. If you want to see the finished file first, open the file *ch14-03s.fla*. Use Test Movie to see how the button works.

1. You will begin creating this example by setting up the drag-and-drop element. Use Insert | New Symbol to create a new movie clip symbol. Name the symbol *horiz_slide*.

2. In the new symbol, drag the Bar graphic symbol to the stage and use the Info panel to position it at 0, –10 exactly.

3. Drag the Ball Graphic symbol to the stage and, using the Info panel, position it exactly at –13, –13.

4. You will be using the *onClipEvent* handler to detect and position the ball on the slider (instead of using a tween, as in the previous exercise). Select the ball on the stage and use Insert | Convert to Symbol to encase the graphic

symbol inside a movie clip symbol. Name the new movie clip symbol Ball MC and set Behavior to Movie Clip.

5. Right-click on the ball on the stage and select Edit in Place. Now you are working inside the Ball MC movie clip. The Edit Path should read *Scene 1/horiz_slide/Ball MC*.

6. Select the ball graphic symbol, which is currently within Ball MC, and select Insert | Convert to Symbol. Select Button as the behavior and name the button Ball Button. The scenario you now have for the "ball element" is a graphic (Ball Graphic) in a button (Ball Button) in a movie clip (Ball MC) in a movie clip (*horiz_slide*).

7. With the Ball Button object selected on the stage (you should be in movie clip Ball MC; check the Edit Path), right-click on it and open the Actions panel.

8. In the Actions panel, add a *startDrag* action to the button. StartDrag is located within the Actions group in the Toolbox list.

9. In the target field for the *startDrag*, enter *this* and enable the Expression checkbox. Flash will set the current movie clip (Ball MC) to draggable when you use the slider.

10. You will notice that the *startDrag* action is automatically placed within an *on* event handler. Change the *on* event handler to Press.

11. In the *startDrag* action, enable the *Lock mouse to center* checkbox.

12. Now you must also set up the *stopDrag* action. Click on the ending curly brace in the Action list. Select *stopDrag* from the Actions group in the Toolbox list and make sure the *on* event handler for the *stopDrag* section is set to Release and Release Outside. The complete set of actions should look like that shown in figure 14-8.

13. Access Scene 1 from the Edit Path and drag *horiz_slider* from the library to the stage.

14. Save your file and then use Test Movie to see what you have created thus far.

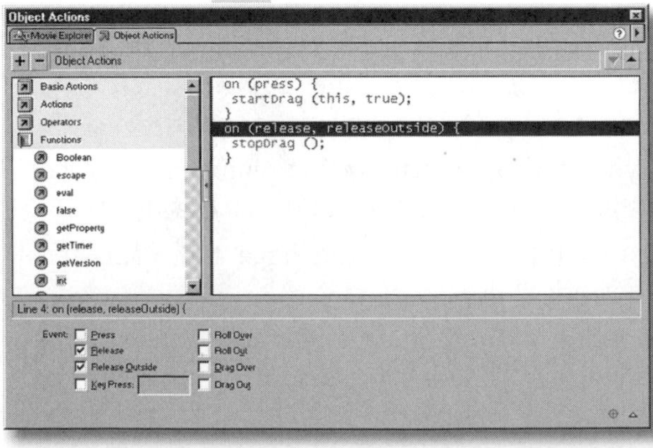

*Figure 14-8 Assign the* startDrag *and* stopDrag *actions to the button.*

When you test the movie, you will notice that the ball can currently be freely dragged over the screen. Let's examine how to constrain it.

15. Right-click on the *horiz_slider* symbol and select Edit in Place.

16. Right-click on the Ball MC movie clip and open the Actions panel.

You will use the new *onClipEvent* handler to set the constraints using the Ball MC movie clip. The constraints will be extracted from the Ball MC movie clip's position (when it loads) and stored as variables. The variable values will be accessed by the drag action when the user initiates the drag.

17. Add an *onClipEvent* handler to the movie clip. The *load* event is the default, which is what you will use.

18. Now you will create four variables that define the top, left, right, and bottom constraints. Use the set variable action to add a variable named *top*, with a value of _y. Enable the Expression checkbox. This will cause a variable to be created that will hold the value of the *y* position of the Ball MC movie clip. Concerning its scope, the variable will be owned by the Ball MC movie clip.

19. Create three more variables using three more set variable actions, as follows: *left* = _x, *right* = _x + 200, and *bottom* = _y. In each, make sure you enable the Expression checkbox for the Value field. You will note that the right constraint is set to _x + 200. The slider is 200 pixels wide. This is what will let the ball slide from left to right. If you did not modify the right constraint, the ball would not slide at all because it would be constrained to a single point.

20. Now that you have set up the variables that will be used for the constraints, you must make the *startDrag* action attached to the Ball Button symbol inside the Ball MC movie clip use these variables. Assuming you are currently accessing the *horiz_slider* movie clip, right-click on the Ball MC symbol on the stage and select Edit in Place.

21. Open the Actions panel and select the ball on the stage. You should see the *startDrag* and *stopDrag* actions you just created. Click on the *startDrag* action.

22. Enable the Constrain to Rectangle checkbox and enter *top*, *left*, *right*, and *bottom* in the parameters area, as shown in

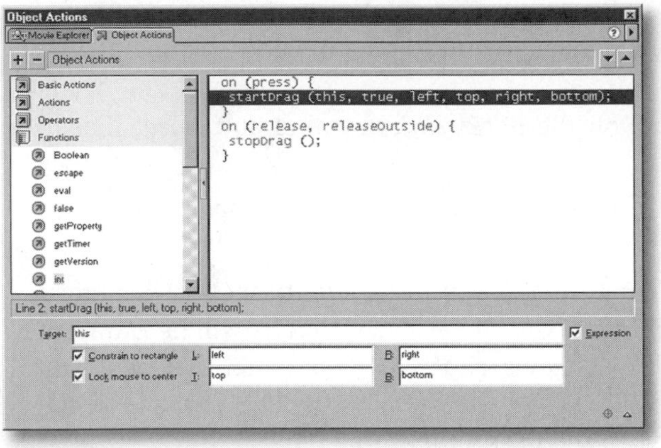

*Figure 14-9 Enter the variable names as the constraints for the drag operation.*

figure 14-9. Note that because the variables belong to Ball MC, and because Ball Button resides in that timeline, no target path to the variables is necessary.

23. Save your file.

24. Use Test Movie to see how you are progressing.

If you test your movie you will see that the ball indeed is constrained to the horizontal. This scenario works because the bar graphic is exactly 200 pixels long (recall how specifically you lined up all of the items using the Info panel). When creating an item such as this, it is important that you specifically plan the layout of items so that the programming will work logically and correctly.

In some instances, it may be nice just to have a slider that smoothly travels along the bar as you drag. For example, you could create a text field that receives the X position, if you simply wanted to view it, or you could add actions to do something based on the values. The possibilities are quite endless.

However, here you have tick marks. Thus, you need to make the slider snap to the increments, which is not too difficult. Let's start setting this up. To begin, you need to create a binary variable (a variable that is simply on or off) to keep track of whether the user is trying to drag the item. Continue with the following steps.

25. While accessing the Ball MC movie clip, click on the Ball Button on the stage and open the Actions panel. Beneath the *startDrag* action, add a set variable action that sets the *_parent.dragging* variable to *_parent.dragging = true*. Make sure you enable the Expression checkbox for the variable value so that *true* is interpreted as a Boolean keyword. You are going to scope the *dragging* variable to the movie clip *horiz_slider* instead of to the movie clip Ball MC, thus the reason for *_parent.dragging*.

26. Beneath the *stopDrag* action, add a set variable action that sets *_parent.dragging* to *false*. Again, enable the Expression checkbox for the variable value. The actions attached to the button should now look like those shown in figure 14-10.

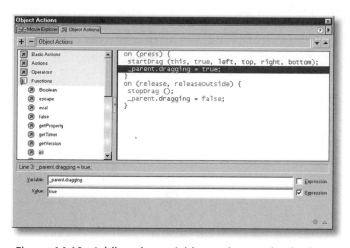

*Figure 14-10 Adding the variable used to track whether or not the user is peforming a drag.*

27. In the Edit Path, click on *horiz_slide*.

28. In frame 1 of *horiz_slide*, add a set variable action that initiates the *dragging* variable. Enter *dragging = false*. Make sure you do not enter *_parent.dragging*. If you do, you will have two variables named *dragging*, one owned by the main movie timeline and one owned by movie clip *horiz_slider*!

The next thing you are about to do will seem a little odd, but it is the only way to go about doing this. In theory, you should be able to attach ActionScript code to the Ball MC movie clip that forces the ball to snap to the increments along the bar graphic.

However, the *drag* action overrides any movie clip code set up, using *onClipEvent(mouseMove)*, to force the ball to snap to specific points. If you try it, the ball "sputters" across the screen in an unattractive manner, because the drag action tries to override the content of the *onClipEvent(mouseMove)* content. Recall the discussion of precedence in Chapter 6. Here is an example of where precedence negatively affects your movies. However, never fear! There is a workaround.

The basic workaround is this: you create (1) a transparent element that is actually the object that is dragged and (2) a dummy object that is seen but is controlled by the transparent object. In essence, you are creating the illusion of the scenario working correctly. Let's take a look.

29. Begin by right-clicking on the Ball MC movie clip in the *horiz_slider* movie clip, and use the Effect panel to change the item to about 30 percent transparent. This will eventually be the transparent object representing the "brains" of the control.

30. Use the Instance panel to rename the Ball MC movie clip to Trans.

31. Create the dummy object. Use Insert | New Symbol and create a movie clip symbol named Ball Dummy.

32. Open the library and place the Ball Graphic symbol on the stage.

33. Using the Info panel, exactly position the placed symbol at –13, –13.

34. Switch back to the *horiz_slide* movie clip.

35. Insert the Ball Dummy object onto the stage and use the Info panel to set its location to –13, –20. You will notice that you are purposely leaving the Ball Dummy object below the transparent ball. You will come back later and make the *Trans* object 100 percent transparent and move the opaque ball directly over the top of the transparent ball. With the balls in these positions, it will be easier to see what is going on as you add the coding.

 **TIP:** *As you start working with exact placement of objects on the stage, you may find it more efficient if you place the Info panel in the same panel group as the Instance, Effect, Frame, and Sound panels. Just click-drag the Info panel to the other group to add it.*

36. Use the Instance panel to name the opaque ball's instance Ball.

37. Now let's add the guts of the code to the *Trans* object that will eventually be used to control the opaque ball. While accessing movie clip *horiz_slider*, click on the Trans instance on the stage with the Actions panel open.

38. In the Actions panel, enter the code in listing 14.1. Note that it may be easier if you enter it in Expert mode and then revert to Normal mode. Code example 14-1, which follows, shows the code for the *Trans* object. Make sure you use the exact case for entries, as shown in example 14-1.

## *Code Example 14-1 Trans Object Code*

```
onClipEvent (mouseMove) {
    if (_parent.dragging == true) {
        if (_parent._xmouse<=10) {
            setProperty (_parent.Ball, _x, 0);
        } else if (_parent._xmouse<=30) {
```

```
                                setProperty (_parent.Ball, _x, 20);
                        } else if (_parent._xmouse<=50) {
                            setProperty (_parent.Ball, _x, 40);
                        } else if (_parent._xmouse<=70) {
                            setProperty (_parent.Ball, _x, 60);
                        } else if (_parent._xmouse<=90) {
                            setProperty (_parent.Ball, _x, 80);
                        } else if (_parent._xmouse<=110) {
                            setProperty (_parent.Ball, _x, 100);
                        } else if (_parent._xmouse<=130) {
                            setProperty (_parent.Ball, _x, 120);
                        } else if (_parent._xmouse<=150) {
                            setProperty (_parent.Ball, _x, 140);
                        } else if (_parent._xmouse<=170) {
                            setProperty (_parent.Ball, _x, 160);
                        } else if (_parent._xmouse<=190) {
                            setProperty (_parent.Ball, _x, 180);
                        } else if (_parent._xmouse>190) {
                            setProperty (_parent.Ball, _x, 200);
                        }
                    }
            }
```

Before continuing with the exercise, let's dissect the code in code example 14-1. First, note that the code is inserted into an *onClipEvent* handler with the *mouseMove* event. By default, the *mouseMove* event makes the handler execute whenever the mouse moves. If it were not for the next *if* statement, the lines of code would execute every time the mouse moved. However, the *if* statement will let the handler code execute only if *dragging* = = *true*. Recall that earlier in the exercise you set up the *dragging* variable so that it would be true only when the drag operation were executed. Thus, even though this lengthy code snippet is in a *mouseMove* event, it will execute only when dragging is true.

Another note about the dragging variable is that the reference is preceded by the *_parent* property. Note that the *dragging* variable is scoped to (owned by) the *horiz_slider* movie clip. When you use the *onClipEvent* handler, referenced variables are assumed to be scoped in (owned by) the movie clip to which the handler is attached. Thus, if the *if* action used *dragging* = = *true* as opposed to *_parent.dragging* = = *true*, Flash would assume that the Ball MC movie clip owned the variable. In reality it does not, so to access the variable in *horiz_slider* you must preface the variable name with *_parent*.

The last thing to notice is the lengthy *if* statement that determines the location of *_xmouse*. Basically, this *if* statement determines the *x* location of the mouse in relation to the *horiz_slider* movie clip (thus the reason for *_parent._xmouse* as opposed to just *_xmouse*). Then, based on the *x* position, it tells the dummy object to go to a specific location. To make this easier (and this is where the positional accuracy of objects on the stage becomes important), the slider is 200 pixels long and is based on 20-pixel increments. If the *_xmouse* is within 10 pixels of the tick marks (in either direction), the dummy ball snaps to the respective tick mark.

One final note. You will notice that the *if* statement only checks the upper boundary on each tick mark. When you use an *if* statement, once a matching condition in the *if* structure is found, the remaining conditions are ignored. Thus, you only have to check for the upper boundary, as opposed to checking to see if the *_xmouse* is between two values. Continue with the following steps.

39. Save your movie and use Test Movie to see that indeed the movie clip is working. Note why the two balls were offset from one another: it allows you to see what is going on. However, you will note that at times the dummy object and the transparent object do not exactly line up. In this scenario, it is not detrimental, but is sloppy. Let's fix it.

40. Access the Ball MC movie clip and click on the Ball button in it.

41. Open the Actions panel, where you had entered the *startDrag* and *stopDrag* actions.

To fix the alignment between the *Trans* and *Ball* instances, you need a single statement that, once the drag stops, sets the position of the *Trans* instance to the position of the *Ball* instance. This is valid because once the drag ceases, you can control the position of the transparent ball.

42. Below the *_parent.dragging = false* line, add the following:

```
_parent.trans._x=_parent.Ball._x
```

This line of code sets the *_x* position of the *Trans* instance to the *_x* position of the *Ball* instance.

43. Save your file and use Test Movie to see that the two objects stay adjacent to each other when you release the mouse.

44. To finish this example, you need to make the *Trans* object completely transparent, and move the two objects over each other. Click on the *Trans* instance and use the Effects panel to set its Alpha to 0%.

45. Before moving the *Ball* instance, you need to move the *trans* instance to the front of the stage order. When you move the two items over each other, if the *Trans* instance ends up in the back you will not be able to interact with the controller. Select the *Trans* instance and use Modify | Arrange | Bring to Front.

46. Click on the *Ball* instance and use the Info panel to set its coordinates to exactly –13, –13.

47. Save your file and use Test Movie to see the finished slider.

Note that because you created the slider as a movie clip, you could actually use it anywhere. You could scale it up, scale it down, and so on and it would still work.

# ■ ■ ■ **Using Sliders**

You have seen how to create slider controls using triggers as well as using ActionScript. In the following examples, let's put them to use by integrating them into some sample projects. In the next three sections, examine the examples, which present a couple of methods of integrating sliders into movies.

## **Fake Zooming**

In other chapters of this book, you have read that there are two ways to zoom an image in Flash. One is really a way to fake it, whereas the other truly capitalizes on the zooming capability of Flash. In the following CD-ROM exercise, you will see how fake zooming is accomplished. Along with it, you will see how a slider can be used to control the "zooming."

### *CD-ROM Exercise*

Open the file *fakezoom.fla* located in the *F5gai/chapter14/fake-zoom/* folder, installed from the companion CD-ROM. Use the file in performing this exercise. To create "fake zooming," perform the following steps.

1. Use Test Movie to see how the movie works.

2. As you can see, the slider makes the map appear to zoom. The map is nothing more than a movie clip symbol with motion tweening assigned to it. Use Window | Library to access the Zoom 1 symbol. Notice that the map is a straight-forward tween in which the scale of the map changes. Notice also the Stop (frame) action assigned, which keeps the Zoom 1 movie clip from playing through.

3. Close the Zoom 1 movie clip. Double click on any one of the triggers associated with the slider on the stage, to open the Actions panel and examine the associated actions. By adding a *with* action that points to the map instance (*ZoomMe*), the trigger controls the map as well as the slider.

4. One final note concerning zooming as a result of scaling: so that the map does not consume the entire screen, a fill has been inserted to hide the outer portions of the map during scaling. This fill element is on the Mask layer (not to be confused with a layer mask, which it is not). If you change the background color of the stage from white to something else, you will see the "mask." With the stage color changed, hide the Mask layer.

Zooming as a result of scaling is really a carryover effect from Flash 3. More than likely, if you want to perform scaling in Flash 5, use the real zooming feature, which is easy to set up.

 **TIP:** *When you use special mask effects or bitmaps in a movie file, use an FS Command action in the first frame of the movie to set the allowscale property to* false. *This will keep your movies from scaling during playback, which could negatively affect presentation.*

## Real Zooming

You have already seen how to use the Load Movie action to load one movie into another. In the following CD-ROM exercise, you will see how one movie can change the properties of another. The focus here is on the X and Y scale of a movie. Nevertheless, you can change any of the other movie properties as easily as you can change scale.

Before you start dissecting the files, a brief explanation is in order. This example consists of two movies. The first movie contains the map at its base size. The map movie then loads the second movie, which contains the slider bar, instructional text, and mask.

### CD-ROM Exercise

Open the file *map.fla* located in the *F5gai/chapter14/action-zoom/* folder, installed from the companion CD-ROM. Use the file in performing this exercise. To see how one movie can change the properties of another, perform the following steps.

1. Within this movie is nothing but a static image of the map and a frame action in frame 1. The map is a movie clip, and the instance is named Map. The frame action is a Load Movie action that loads the second file, *sliderbar.swf*, into *_level1*. You will see in a moment why the map loads the controls, instead of the other way around.

2. Open the file *sliderbar.fla*.

Once the movie is loaded, you can see the white mask (because the grid is turned on), as well as the slider control. Note that the slider in the movie on *_level1* (*sliderbar.fla*) tells the movie on *_level0* (the map) to zoom. You will find that this movie uses a rendition of the ActionScript-based slider. Let's look at how it modifies the map on level 1. Continue with the following steps.

3. Right-click on the slider and select Edit in Place. You will notice immediately that this slider is horizontal, not vertical! One of the cool things about movie-clip-based controls in Flash is that if you design them right you can do anything with them. Recall that the coding performed previously was self-contained; that is, everything was relative to the movie clip. Therefore, you can actually use the single slider in either orientation.

4. Click on the ball on the stage (symbol: Ball MC, instance name: *Ball*). Open the Actions panel, which will reveal the coding for the element, as shown in figure 14-11.

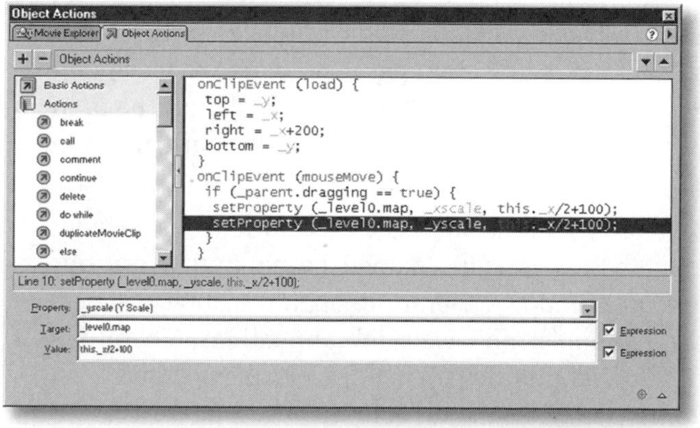

*Figure 14-11 The slider actions that modify the x scale and y scale of the map.*

The only difference in this example, from the previous, is the *setProperty* actions being used to set the *x* and *y* scale of the map in the other file. Everything else is the same. Note the math equation for letting the ball's position be translated into a scale for the map. Because the control is 200 pixels wide, you can generate the scale for the map using _x/2 + 100. This means "get the x position of the ball instance (*this*), relative to its timeline, divide by 2, and add 100. Then set the x scale and y scale of the movie clip 'map' in level 0 to the resultant."

# The Interactive Axonograph

A final example of using sliders involves use of the *interactive axonograph*. Those familiar with the area of technical illustration and visualization will find this example refreshing. The CD-ROM exercise that follows presents and example containing two sliders that allow you to control the elevation and rotation (azimuth) of a small cut block. Although this might seem straightforward, it is somewhat tricky.

## CD-ROM Exercise

Open the file *jlmaxon.fla* located in the *F5gai/chapter14/axonograph/* folder, installed from the companion CD-ROM. Use the file in performing this exercise. To see how the interactive axonograph is used, perform the following steps.

1.  Use Test Movie to see how the movie functions. Note that part of the trick of making the axonograph work will be visible. You may want to play the .*swf* file outside Flash to see what the user would see.

The tricky part of this example is not so much the sliders but changing the cut-block movie clips. The images of the block were generated from a modeling package, with the viewpoint oriented in various positions. Because either slider can be used at any time, the cut-block movie clips had to be constructed in a special way.

2.  The Elevation rotations were each constructed as individual, animated movie clips named by azimuth (rotation) position. Use Window | Library to open the library. Access the *Rotations* folder and view the animations. There is a movie clip of various elevations for each azimuth position. Put another way, the movie clips themselves are the different elevations of the block at the azimuth position.

3.  All of the Elevation movie clips' positions were inserted into a single movie clip, named *AxonogrMC2*. This allows all movies to be updated concurrently via the *with* action, even

though they are not all displayed concurrently on the stage. Thus, as the Elevation slider changes, all movie clips are changed to the correct elevation, regardless of whether they are currently shown. Access the symbol named *AxonogrMC2* to see that indeed all movie clips exist in one movie clip.

4. The *AxonogrMC2* movie clip was inserted into another movie clip. A fill was created to serve as a mask. This allows the displayed portion of *AxonogrMC2* to change based on selected azimuth. Select the *AxonogrMC* movie clip in the library. View its timeline and move the playhead. Notice that each frame displays a different portion of the *AxonogrMC2* movie clip. These frame positions are synchronous with the azimuth slider.

The secret to the Axonograph movie is the *AxonogrMC* movie clip, which contains the *AxonogrMC2* movie clip. You cannot target movie clips that are not presently on the stage. Thus, for the elevations and azimuths to be updated concurrently, they all have to be present on the stage. The elevations are represented by *AxonogrMC2*. Azimuth is represented by *AxonogrMC*.

As the elevation slider changes, all elevation movies are updated. When the Azimuth slider changes, the current frame (and currently displayed portion of *AxonogrMC2*) changes. By allowing the azimuth triggers to control frame position in *AxonogrMC2*, and the elevation's triggers to control the movie clips in *AxonogrMC*, the sliders can work simultaneously. That is the secret to this trick.

The reason for the complexity of this movie is that you want neither slider dependent on the other. If this is still confusing, try exercise 14-1, which follows.

## Exercise 14-1 Examining Sliders That Work Independently

Using the work performed in the previous CD-ROM exercise, to see how sliders work independently, perform the following steps.

1. Change the background color of the stage to something other than white, black, or cyan.

2. Access the *AxonoMC* movie clip.

3. Zoom out and delete the fill being used as a mask. It resides on the Stop layer.

4. Test the movie. Notice that as the Azimuth slider changes,

a different portion of *AxonoMC2* is shown because the azimuth slider tells *AxonogrMC* to go to a specific frame. Set the azimuth slider to −15.

5. Change the elevation slider. Notice that all of the blocks are changing at the same time. Examine the actions associated with the elevation and azimuth sliders to further examine how this movie works.

# ▪ ▪ ▪  Creating Menus

Creating menus within Flash requires two basic steps:

- Use Track as Menu Option for a series of elements you want to be "menu options."
- Combine menu options within a single movie clip. Additionally, use a trigger to open and close the menu when the user rolls over and off it.

## Where's the Smart Clips?

Having begun delving into the creation of menus and away from sliders, you may be asking "So where's the information on smart clips?" Anyone who has seen a Macromedia dog-and-pony show about Flash 5 at a conference or tradeshow has undoubtedly heard about smart clips. "Why demonstrate the creation of menus, sliders, and base components? I heard that with smart clips you do not have to worry about creating menus or any of that other stuff," you may say. The fact is, smart clips are still based on the simple construction techniques of the past.

Do not view smart clips as solving all of the world's development problems or performing and correcting all the work for you when it comes to creating things in Flash. Indeed, using smart clips will save you some time with certain elements; that is, if you have a smart clip for what you want to do, and know how you want to do it.

However, as you advance as a developer, seldom will you take one of these components as is, not wanting to modify it in some way for customized use. Only 1 percent of the time will a particular smart clip (or other similar item in another package) do everything you want, exactly how you want it. Like the current fad among other packages (such as Behaviors for Director, Extensions for Dreamweaver or UltraDev, Xtras for FreeHand, and so on), Macromedia is continuing to create more convenient front ends so that all you have to know is how to manipulate, rather than create, your own entities.Or at least that is what people believe when they hear talk about such features!

There is still tremendous power in understanding how things work and being able to create your own stuff. Smart clips are an innovative feature, but do not be deceived that knowing how to use them is all you need to get by. If you want to be a highly paid Flash developer, you must understand how they work, as well as how to create and use them. In the discussion of smart clips at the end of the chapter, you will see that the basics of creating the components of a smart clip are still based on the existing techniques for creating sliders, menus, and buttons presented in the early parts of this chapter.

In this section, you will run through a quick exercise to see how menus are created. In exercise 14-2, which follows, you will create a drop-down menu to be inserted into the main movie timeline.

## Exercise 14-2  Creating a Drop-Down Menu

To create a drop-down menu, perform the following steps. You will first create a symbol to be used for the list items.

1.  Open a new blank file and use Insert | New Symbol to create a new symbol. Name as the symbol List Button, and set Behavior to Button.

2.  In the Up state, create a rectangle and fill it with a color or white. Do not leave the rectangle with no fill, because it will cause problems later.

3.  Use the Info panel to make the button width and height an easy set of numbers to work with, such as 200 wide by 40 tall. Set the X and Y locations so that the object is centered with the registration points of the symbol in the center. If you use 200 wide by 40 tall for the size, the location will be –100, –20.

4.  In the Over state, add a keyframe and fill the rectangle with a different color.

5.  Insert a blank keyframe in the Down state. This button will serve as an indicator only of what the user is rolling over in the menu you are creating, so you do not need anything in the Down state.

6.  In the Hit frame, copy the filled rectangle from either the Up or Over state and use Edit | Paste in Place to position the rectangle at the right location.

7.  Now you will create the menu movie clip, which is really the "brain" of the control. Click on the Scene 1 link in the Edit Path.

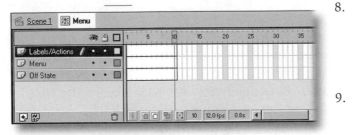

*Figure 14-12 Creating and naming the layers for the Menu movie clip.*

8. Select Insert | New Symbol and name the symbol Menu. Select Movie Clip as the behavior and click on OK.

9. Create three layers, labeled Labels/Actions, Menu, and Off State. Extend the duration of frame 1 in the timeline to frame 10, as shown in figure 14-12.

10. Label frame 1, in the Labels/Actions layer, Hide.

11. Insert a blank keyframe in frame 6 of the Labels/ Actions layer and name it Show.

12. Insert a keyframe in frames 5 and 10.

13. Add a *gotoAndPlay* action to frame 5 that loops to label Hide.

14. Add a *gotoAndPlay* action to frame 10 that loops to label Show.

15. Open the library and drag the List Button symbol into frame 1 of the Menu layer.

16. Use the Info panel to align the Button symbol perfectly over the movie clip registration point.

17. Right-click on the List Button instance on the stage and open the Instance panel.

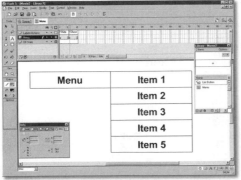

*Figure 14-13 The instance is copied five times; one for each menu item.*

18. In the Instance panel, select Track as Menu Item from the Options menu.

19. Add some text on top of the Menu instance. This will be the text displayed for the menu item.

20. Insert a keyframe in frame 6 of the Menu layer. Copy the existing instance of the List Button symbol for as many menu options as you require. As shown in figure 14-13, the example will have five menu options. Add text on top of the menu items, as you did for the word *Menu* in step 19.

**TIP:** *If snap is turned on, you can easily align the instances to one another. After you paste one, grab*

*the midpoint on the side of the pasted instance. A small circle will appear. Click-drag close to the object you want to align it to and it will snap to it.*

21. For the menu to expand, you must set up an action that jumps to the Show label when the user rolls over the Menu button. Click on frame 1 of the Menu layer. Right-click on the symbol instance and select Actions.

22. Assign a Go To action to go to the label Show. The mouse event for the action should be set on Roll Over only.

23. Now you must set up the object, and the action that closes the menu. The object will be a trigger. Create a keyframe in frame 6 of the Off State layer.

24. Click on frame 6 in the Menu layer and draw a rectangular fill (with no line) that completely surrounds the menu elements, as shown in figure 14-14.

25. Select the fill, and select Insert | Convert to Symbol. Name the symbol *off_trigger* and select Button as its behavior.

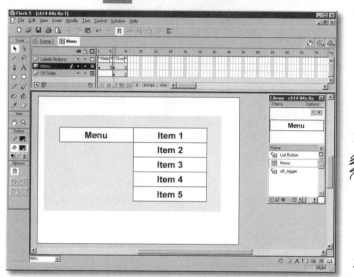

*Figure 14-14 Creating the trigger that will close the menu.*

26. Access the *off_trigger* symbol.

27. As with previous triggers, the Up, Over, and Down states of the symbol should have nothing in them. Cut the fill from the Up frame.

28. Add blank keyframes to the Over and Down frames.

29. In the Hit frame, create a keyframe.

30. Click on the Hit frame and use Paste in Place to insert the fill. Then, click on the Menu link in the Edit Path to return to the Menu movie clip symbol.

31. Click on frame 6 of the Off State layer.

32. Right-click on the *off_trigger* symbol instance and select Instance.

33. In the Instance panel, set the Options drop-down list to Track as Menu Item.

34. With the *off_trigger* instance selected, open the Actions panel.

35. Add a Go To action that goes to label Hide. Make sure the mouse event is set to Roll Over only.

36. Click on Scene 1 in the Edit Path.

37. Open the library and insert your newly created menu into the main movie timeline.

38. Use Test Movie to see the results.

 **CD-ROM NOTE:** *To see a finished example of the previous CD-ROM exercise, open the file ch14-04s.fla located in the* F5gai/chapter14/ *folder, installed from the companion CD-ROM. Complete this menu scenario by adding functionality, using actions. To do it you would simply assign actions to the List Button instances in the Menu movie clip.*

 **TIP:** *Menus constructed in the manner outlined in the previous CD-ROM exercise usually work well. However, sometimes if the user sporadically moves or clicks the mouse outside the menu area, the menu may remain inadvertently open. To solve this, you can create a trigger, equivalent to the size of the stage, that closes the menu.*

Macromedia has included a sample file (Help | Samples | Advanced Buttons) that shows several other types of controls, including radio buttons, checkboxes, drop-down menus, and a scrollbar. All of these controls are based on techniques such as those presented in the previous CD-ROM exercise. Make sure you check it out!

# Setting Up Drag-and-Drop Scenarios

A feature added in Flash 4 and present in Flash 5 is the *startDrag* and *stopDrag* actions. With them, any range of drag-and-drop games or other scenarios can be set up. See the following CD-ROM exercise for practice in creating a draggable element.

 ### CD-ROM Exercise

Open the file *ch14-05.fla* located in the *F5gai/chapter14/* folder, installed from the companion CD-ROM. Use the file in performing this exercise. To create a draggable element, perform the following steps.

1. The first step is to create a button symbol that will be used to start the dragging operation. Frequently, the button itself is the item being dragged, although this is not always the case. Use Insert | New Symbol to create a new symbol. Name it P1 and set Behavior to Button.

2. The file you are working with already has a puzzle piece you will make draggable. Open the library and drag the "puzzle piece" component to the stage.

3. Align the crosshairs by nudging the puzzle piece with the arrow keys, or by using the Info panel.

4. Insert copied frames into the Over, Down, and Hit states by clicking on each frame and pressing the F5 function key. Once you are done, click on the Scene 1 link in the Edit Path.

5. Because only movie clips can be dragged, you will insert the button into a movie clip symbol. Use Insert | New Symbol and name the symbol MC1s. Set Behavior to Movie Clip.

6. Once you are accessing the MC1s timeline, open the library and drag the P1 button to the stage. Once you are done, click on Scene 1 in the Edit Path.

7. In the main movie timeline, drag the newly created MC1s symbol to the stage. The *startDrag* action will target the instance of the MC1s symbol that resides in the main movie timeline. Thus, you must give the instance a name. Right-click on the instance in the main movie timeline and select the Instance panel. In the Instance panel, enter *MC1* in the Name field.

Now you must go back and add the *startDrag* and *stopDrag* actions to the button in the MC1s movie clip. Realize that you could have done this earlier, but seeing the Instance Name of the movie clip first makes more sense of the *startDrag* action's target.

8. Access the MC1s movie clip symbol by right-clicking on the instance on the stage and selecting Edit in Place from the context menu.

9. Right-click on the button on the stage and select Actions.

10. In the Actions panel, add a *startDrag* action.

11. Insert MC1 in the target field and enable the Expression checkbox.

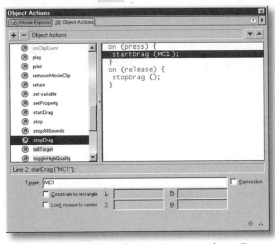

12. Select the on (Release) item in the Action list and change the option to Press rather than Release. You want the dragging to start when the user presses.

13. Click on the ending curly brace in the Action list and add a *stopDrag* action. The two actions should resemble those shown in figure 14-15.

14. Click on Scene 1 in the Edit Path.

15. Use Test Movie to test your draggable button.

*Figure 14-15 Adding the* startDrag *and* stopDrag *actions to the button.*

If you have problems, compare your file with the file *ch14-05s.fla* located in the *F5gai/chapter14/* folder, installed from the companion CD-ROM. The three most common errors with the Drag action are:

- Not naming the movie clip instance on the stage
- Not correctly referencing the named instance of the symbol you want to drag in the *startDrag* Target field
- Not setting the mouse event for the *startDrag* action to Press (instead of Release)

 **CD-ROM NOTE:** *Examine the file* ch14-06s.fla *located in the F5gai/chapter14/ folder, installed from the companion CD-ROM. This file contains many components, all of which are movable.*

As you start working with moveable elements, realize that any number of draggable elements can be set up. In Chapter 15, you will add some ActionScript to the example in the previous CD-ROM exercise so that the components either snap to their correct location (assuming they are placed correctly) or return to their starting position (if incorrect). For now, just observe how drag functionality is established.

When you are working with multiple draggable objects, only one object can be dragged at a time. If you are in the process of dragging and a second drag is encountered, the first will automatically terminate. In addition, when you start to drag an object, it is not moved to the front of the layering order. Thus, if an object is layered behind another, either as a consequence of layering or group arrangement, the moving object will pass behind and not in front of the other object. Layering and ordering do not change when you drag.

> **NOTE:** *Macromedia has included a sample drag-and-drop movie with the program's installation files. Access the Help | Samples | Eggplant menu option to open the file named* eggplant.fla. *This file has a Mr. Potato Head look-alike that displays drag-and-drop capability.*

## ▪ ▪ ▪ ▪ Input and Dynamic Fields

One of the most commonly employed methods of collecting information from web surfers is via the use of a text box. In times past, HTML form fields were the most common means of collecting such data. However, with Flash Input field capability, you can gather information with Flash and use it within a movie or pass the data to an external technology such as CGI or ASP.

By default, when you use the Text tool, text is entered normally as straightforward strings of text, simply called static text. However, with the Text Options panel, you can transform any static text item into a user-input field (Input Text), where the user can enter data, or a dynamic field (Dynamic Text), where data from some other source is used to populate the field. The Text Options panel is used to set these characteristics.

### Input Text

Once a text element is located on the stage, use the Text Options panel to set the text characteristics. If you select Input Text from the available drop-down list, several properties can be established, as shown in figure 14-16.

Line Type

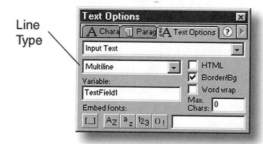

*Figure 14-16 When you select* Input Text *in the Text Options panel, several settings are available.*

As shown in figure 14-16, the Variable field is used as the container for the value entered into the text field by the user. As discussed in Chapter 6, a variable is simply a container for data. When you use a text field, the string content of the field is automatically placed in a variable. That variable can then be used for other purposes, such as concatenation with other string variables or passage to another technology. The other optional settings found in the Text Field Properties dialog box are:

- *Line Type:* Defines whether the user is constrained to a single line, multiline, or password entry. If Password is selected, the field displays asterisks for the text entered. Additionally, text entered into fields set to Password cannot be copied or pasted. Note that when

Multiline is enabled, word wrap is available. Word wrap inserts line breaks when the text reaches the right margin of the field.

- *HTML checkbox:* Allows you to define whether HTML elements can be defined in the field.

- *Border/BG checkbox (draw border and background):* Controls whether the border and background for the text field are shown.

- *Max Char (maximum characters):* Permits the developer to limit the number of characters the user can enter in the field.

- *Embed Fonts buttons:* Allows the developer to control whether font descriptions are stored in the SWF file for the field. Use caution, however, as the more font descriptions that are stored, the larger the resulting Flash movie.

## Dynamic Text

The primary difference between input text and dynamic text is that fields set to Dynamic Text are designed to receive data from another source, such as from a variable in the current movie, from a variable in another movie, or via the *loadVariables* action. Recall from the previous chapter, as well as Chapter 6, that data can be pushed in and out of Flash pretty easily.

When you select the Dynamic Text option from the Line Type drop-down list in the Text Options panel, there are three differences between what you then see and what you see when you access the Input Text option. First, you can set dynamic text fields so that they are selectable or not selectable, using the Selectable checkbox, as shown in figure 14-17. With Selectable enabled, the user can select and copy the text. Second, you will notice in the Line Type drop-down list that there is no Password option. Dynamic fields cannot be used as password fields. Finally, there is no Max Character option, as users do not place text in dynamic fields.

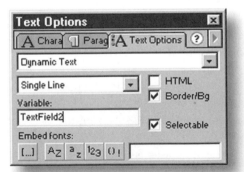

*Figure 14-17 When you select Dynamic Text in the Text Options panel, there are only a few differences from what you see when you access Input Text.*

## Using Text Fields

Setting up input or dynamic fields is a relatively easy process. Realize that the variables associated with text fields can be used in two ways. First, when the user inserts data into a text field, the string data is inserted into the variable. If any other text field shares this variable definition, such as a dynamic field, it is automatically updated as the variable is updated. The CD-ROM exercise that follows takes you through the process of working with text fields.

## CD-ROM Exercise

Open the file *ch14-07.fla* located in the *F5gai/chapter14/* folder, installed from the companion CD-ROM. Use the file in performing this exercise. To see how text fields work, perform the following steps.

1. Click on the Text tool and create a text element on the stage.

   Note that when you create a text field, the small square that usually appears in the upper right is displayed in the lower right. This identifies it as a dynamic or input field. You do not necessarily have to enter a starting value for a field. Unlike normal text elements, if you do not enter text into the entry box, the field will remain on the stage.

2. Right-click on the text element and select Panels | Text Options from the context menu.

3. In the Text Options panel, set the Line Type drop-down to Text Input.

4. Enter *myfield* in the Variable field. If you wish to modify any of the other options, you may.

5. Before testing the movie, set up a Trace action to track the content of the *myfield* variable. Right-click on frame 1 and open the Actions panel.

6. Select the Trace action and set the Message field to *myfield*. Make sure you select Expression from the drop-down, as shown in figure 14-18.

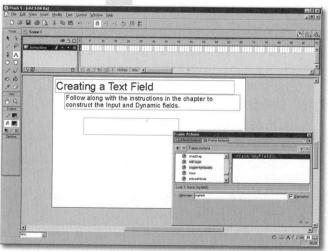

*Figure 14-18 Set up a Trace action to reveal the content of the variable* myfield.

The Trace action will reveal the value of the message displayed in the output window during testing. If the Expression checkbox is not selected, the word *myfield* will be repeatedly displayed, instead of the value within the variable *myfield*.

7. In the Control menu, select Loop Playback. You do this so that when you test the movie the Trace action is repeatedly encountered due to the loop.

8. Use Test Movie and enter some text in the text field. As you enter the information, the data should be displayed in the Output window. As you enter text into the text field, the variable is updated. The Trace action then posts that data to the Output window.

Before you close the file, realize that in addition to posting data to the Output window via a Trace action, you can also pass the data to any number of other text fields quite easily. By creating an additional text field (set to Dynamic Text) and setting its Variable field to *myfield*, data entered into the first field is posted to the second.

9. Add a second text element to your file, just below the existing one on the stage.

10. Right-click on the new field and select Panels | Text options.

11. In the Text Options panel, set the element to Dynamic Text and enter *myfield* in the Variable field.

12. Test your movie again to see that the value entered into the upper text field is passed to the lower text field.

 **CD-ROM NOTE:** *To see a finished example of the previous CD-ROM exercise, open the file* ch14-07s.fla *located in the* F5gai/chapter14/ *folder, installed from the companion CD-ROM.*

## Rich Text and HTML in Text Elements

One of the new features in Flash 5 is that text elements can now preserve rich formatting in text boxes set to Dynamic Text or Input Text. Similarly, these text boxes support a limited range of basic HTML tags. From the developer's perspective, this means you can create text elements in which specific elements are used as hyperlinks. It also means that you can use the rudimentary HTML formatting capabilities in the text elements in your movie. Flash supports the following basic HTML tags:

- < A > *(anchor):* Used to add hyperlinks to your text boxes.
- < B > *(bold):* Used to bold text.
- < FONT COLOR > *:* Changes the color of the text.
- < FONT FACE > *:* Changes the typeface used in the element.
- < I > *(italic):* Used to italicize text.

- <P> *(paragraph):* Allows you to define paragraph blocks. Remember that in HTML adjacent paragraph blocks are separated by a carriage return (line feed), which causes a blank line to be inserted between the paragraphs.

- <U> *(underline):* Used to underline text.

If you use the anchor tag, you will need to also use the <FONT COLOR> and <U> tags. When you insert an anchor in a dynamic field, the link does not automatically display as a different color, and is not underlined as it is in a web browser. You must manually set these parameters using all three tags together.

To get the paragraph tag to work, you must close the tag. When people code HTML by hand, they often ignore closing the </P> tag. However, Flash follows the rules of "well-formedness" associated with XML. Thus, you must follow those rules. One of them states that all tags must be closed.

 **CD-ROM NOTE:** *To see a finished example of a file that utilizes HTML tags in dynamic fields, open the file* ch14-8s.fla *located in the* F5gai/chapter14/ *folder, installed from the companion CD-ROM.*

# ▪ ▪ ▪ **Smart Clips**

One of the new features of Flash 5 is called smart clips. Smart clips are movie clip symbols designed for use by those without extensive scripting skills. Creating them does, however, require a pretty extensive understanding of ActionScripting and related concepts. With the background from other chapters, as well as the information provided here, you should be able to create your own smart clips.

The idea behind smart clips is to provide programmers the ability to create complex reusable components (controls) using in-depth ActionScripting. The programmer can associate "need-to-know" information with such controls and then pass the controls to designers, who (although the author does not subscribe to this idea) would not need to know about code. The designer simply has to add a bit of contextual information to the element, not having to deal with ActionScripting at all.

For example, a programmer could create an interface component such as a slider or other component using techniques discussed thus far in this chapter. The programmer could then add the ActionScripting necessary for the slider to function. Additionally, he or she would add special variables, called *parameters*, which would establish the information the smart clip would need to function.

In essence, except for the parameters sent to the smart clip, everything is self-contained. Regardless of what it is for, an effectively designed smart clip is set up so that it can be used ad infinitum. The intelligence of a smart clip (that is, the code necessary for it to work) should be context independent. Thus, only context independent items are appropriate for smart clips. If you need an item that is context dependent, a smart clip may or may not work, depending on the circumstance.

## Creating Smart Clips

Creating smart clips can take a significant amount of time, depending on what you are trying to do. Before immediately thinking *I must create a smart clip,* think about what you want to do. Is there an advantage to making the item a smart clip? Is it worth the investment in making the item usable in other contexts?

A slider is a good example of an element to examine in terms of reusability. In general, the sliders you saw in prior examples in this chapter basically function the same as a slider for a volume control would, right? Thus, it might very well make sense to create a slider that is a smart clip.

On the other hand, an issue you would have to consider in this scenario is that various sliders may have differing increments (number of tick marks on the slider). If this were the case, the sliders would be created as contextual. Thus, you have to consider all parameters of functionality in determining if designing an item as a smart clip will have utility later on, or for other immediate tasks. The CD-ROM exercise that follows takes you through the process of creating a slider as a smart clip.

 **CD-ROM Exercise**

Open the file *ch14-9.fla* located in the *F5gai/chapter14/* folder, installed from the companion CD-ROM. Use the file in performing this exercise, in which you will create a volume slider that is a smart clip. You may want to use Test Movie to refresh your memory about how this slider works.

You will begin where you left off with the file *ch14-03.fla.* Realize that the creation of most smart clips starts with the basic techniques previously covered. The process of creating smart clips does not eliminate having to construct basic elements, as previously noted.

Many have the misperception that smart clips mean you do not have to, for example, construct menus and other items. This is false. You still use the basic construction techniques. Then you take the results and further modify them to make them a smart clip. To modify the slider so that it is a smart clip, you need to add a some code to the movie to control the volume, as well as add a sound clip.

1. Begin by importing either the *.aif* or *.wav* file named *loop_ main* into the file.

2. Click on frame 1 in the main movie timeline and extend the sprite to frame 10.

3. Right-click on frame 1 and select Panels | Sound to open the Sound panel.

4. Assign the *loop_main* sound to frame 1. Select Start as the Sync option, and set the Loop value to 999. You now have something you can control with a smart clip slider.

5. Delete the slider movie clip from the stage.

6. Using either the Library window or the Symbol list, access the *horiz_slide* movie clip.

7. Click on the ball symbol on the stage and open the Actions panel.

8. You need to add some code to the movie clip so that it will control the volume. You may find it easiest to add the code in Expert mode. Add the code shown in code example 14-2, which follows this exercise. Some of the code will already exist in the Action list. Thus, you will need to enter only portions of the code shown in code example 14-2.

9. Once you have added the code, use Check Syntax from the Actions panel menu to ensure there are no typographic (syntax) errors in your script.

10. Save your file.

Code example 14-2, which follows, is the code to be entered at step 8 in the previous CD-ROM exercise. This is the code added to the Ball MC symbol instance.

## Code Example 14-2 Code Added to Ball MC Symbol Instance

```
onClipEvent (load) {
    top = _y;
    left = _x;
    right = _x+200;
    bottom = _y;
    var temp = _parent.startvol*2;
    setProperty (_parent.Ball, _x, temp);
```

```
        setProperty (_parent.trans, _x, temp);
}
onClipEvent (mouseMove) {
        if (_parent.dragging == true) {
                if (_parent._xmouse<=10) {
                        setProperty (_parent.Ball, _x, 0);
                        _parent.startvol = 0;
                } else if (_parent._xmouse<=30) {
                        setProperty (_parent.Ball, _x, 20);
                        _parent.startvol = 10;
                } else if (_parent._xmouse<=50) {
                        setProperty (_parent.Ball, _x, 40);
                        _parent.startvol = 20;
                } else if (_parent._xmouse<=70) {
                        setProperty (_parent.Ball, _x, 60);
                        _parent.startvol = 30;
                } else if (_parent._xmouse<=90) {
                        setProperty (_parent.Ball, _x, 80);
                        _parent.startvol = 40;
                } else if (_parent._xmouse<=110) {
                        setProperty (_parent.Ball, _x, 100);
                        _parent.startvol = 50;
                } else if (_parent._xmouse<=130) {
                        setProperty (_parent.Ball, _x, 120);
                        _parent.startvol = 60;
                } else if (_parent._xmouse<=150) {
                        setProperty (_parent.Ball, _x, 140);
                        _parent.startvol = 70;
                } else if (_parent._xmouse<=170) {
                        setProperty (_parent.Ball, _x, 160);
                        _parent.startvol = 80;
                } else if (_parent._xmouse<=190) {
                        setProperty (_parent.Ball, _x, 180);
                        _parent.startvol = 90;
                } else if (_parent._xmouse>190) {
                        setProperty (_parent.Ball, _x, 200);
                        _parent.startvol = 100;
                }
                mysound = new Sound();
                mysound.setVolume(_parent.startvol);
        }
}
```

You will notice in code example 14-2 that there are three main things added to the existing code. First, in the *onClipEvent(load)* section, notice the following lines:

```
var temp = _parent.startvol*2;
setProperty (_parent.Ball, _x, temp);
setProperty (_parent.trans, _x, temp);
```

Basically these lines of code extract the current volume level (stored in a variable) and set the starting position of the slider appropriately. Thus, if the volume is 70 percent, the slider ball will begin at position 7.

The first line creates a local variable named *temp* and sets it equal to the variable *startvol*, which is owned by the parent timeline of the movie clip *horiz_slide*. *Temp* is then used as the *x* location for the *Ball* instance and the *Trans* instance. Remember that the *Trans* instance is a draggable, transparent item that sets the position of the visible slider ball (*Ball* instance).

The volume in a Flash movie is measured in percentages from 0 to 100. You will recall that the positions of the slider range from 0 to 200. Thus, the position of the ball is twice the value of the volume. This is why the *temp* variable is set to twice the variable *startvol*. The second thing you will note is that the *startvol* variable [in the large *if* statement in the *onClipEvent(mouseMove)* handler] is set appropriately in each *if* condition by being referred to as follows:

```
_parent.startvol = 0;
```

The last item you need is the last two lines in the *onClipEvent(mouse-Move)* handler, as follows:

```
mysound = new Sound();
mysound.setVolume(_parent.startvol);
```

The first line creates an instance of the *sound* object. Notice that the instance of the *sound* object is set to a variable name. Once this is done, to execute any of the *sound* object's methods (or to access appropriate properties), you would preface the request statement with a variable name containing the instance of the *sound* object.

The *sound* object can be used for a variety of things. Here, you will use it to change the volume of the entire movie. Notice in the second line of the previous code that the *setVolume* method is called and is passed the *startvol* variable value. Generally, the *setVolume* method can receive two arguments: a target and a value. If you specify only a value, as you are doing here, the method is applied to the entire movie's sound.

Now that you have the complete functionality set up for the slider, you need to change the movie clip so it is identified as a smart clip. Do this by adding parameters to the clip in the Library window, as discussed below.

**CD-ROM NOTE:** *A finished example of the previous CD-ROM exercise is available. Open the file* ch14-9s.fla *located in the* F5gai/chapter14/ *folder, installed from the companion CD-ROM. Compare your file against the example.*

# Defining Parameters

The primary difference between a movie clip and a smart clip is that a movie clip uses global variables to set certain things, whereas a smart clip uses parameters, which are really nothing more than variables. However, smart clip parameters may also include arrays or objects that are needed by the clip.

The slider in the previous CD-ROM exercise is dependent on the variable *startvol*. You will note that when you were adding code in the previous exercise you did not establish a starting value for the *startvol* variable. For the slider in this exercise as well, you want to make the slider a smart clip that can be reused, and more than likely the end user of the smart clip will want to define his or her own starting value. Thus, you will use a parameter and allow the end user to define the starting value.

## CD-ROM Exercise

Open the file *ch14-10.fla* located in the *F5gai/chapter14/* folder, installed from the companion CD-ROM. Use the file in performing this exercise, in which you will turn a movie clip into a smart clip. If you performed the previous exercise, you could continue by using that file. To make the movie clip a smart clip, perform the following steps.

1. Open the Library window and click on the *horiz_slide* movie clip.

2. Access the Define Clip Parameters menu option from the Library window's Options menu. This will open the Define Clip Parameters window, shown in figure 14-19.

3. For this movie clip, you want to add a parameter named *startvol*. Click on the Plus button (see figure 14-19) to add a parameter to the list.

4. Enter *startvol* as the name of the parameter by double clicking in the Name column and entering the name using the keyboard.

5. Double click in the Value column and enter *70* as the default value. This will be the value used if the end user does not

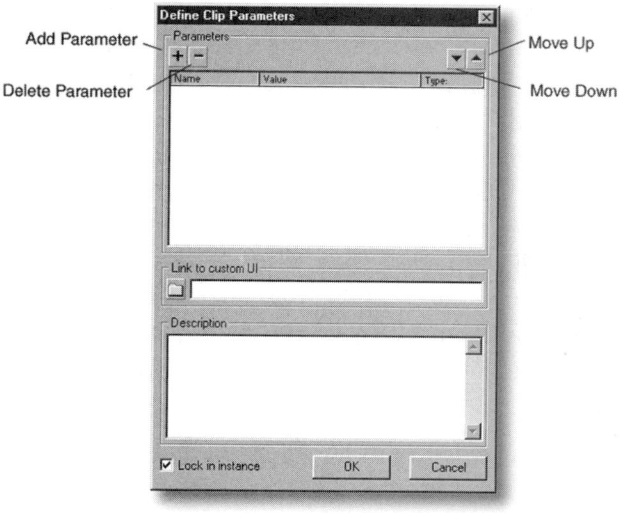

*Figure 14-19 The Define Clip Parameters window is used to define the parameters of the smart clip.*

enter a value when they use the smart clip. Leave the remaining column (Type) as it is. Click on OK to close the Define Clip Parameters window.

6. You have now created a smart clip. Even though there is only a single parameter for this smart clip, it is still a smart clip. Notice in the Library window that the icon used to represent the *horiz_slide* element has changed. This identifies the item as a smart clip.

7. Save your file.

**CD-ROM NOTE:** *A finished example of the previous CD-ROM exercise is available. Open the file* ch14-10s.fla *located in the* F5gai/chapter14/ *folder, installed from the companion CD-ROM. Compare your file against the example.*

## Using Smart Clips

Smart clips share the characteristics of all other symbols. You can use them in the current file, drag them to a new file, or use them in shared libraries. When you want to use a smart clip, you drag it to the stage, just as you do for a normal graphic, button, or movie clip symbol. However, with smart clips, you must define the starting values for their parameters. The CD-ROM exercise that follows provides practice in using smart clips.

### CD-ROM Exercise

Open the file *ch14-11.fla* located in the F5gai/*chapter14/* folder, installed from the companion CD-ROM. Use the file in performing the following steps regarding the smart clip. If you performed the previous exercise, you could continue by using that file.

1. Open the Library window. Select the *horiz_slide* smart clip and drag it to the stage.

2. Right-click on the instance of the smart clip and select Panels | Clip Parameters from the context menu.

3. In the Clip Parameters window, you will notice that the *startvol* parameter is shown with the starting value you defined earlier in the smart clip. For now, you will leave the value as is.

4. Close the Clip Parameters panel and use Text Movie to see (and hear) the slider work. When you do, note that the slider displays the ball in the 70 percent location. Recall that when the clip is loaded, the *Ball* and *Trans* instances where told to go to the location related to whatever the value of the variable *startvol* was.

5. Before closing this clip, let's make a modification to help you understand why a smart clip is beneficial. Close the player.

6. Right-click on the instance of the smart clip and open the Clip Parameters panel again.

7. Change the value of the *startvol* variable to 50 instead of 70.

8. Test the movie again. Note that the slide now starts at 50 percent instead of 70.

 **CD-ROM NOTE:** *A finished example of the previous CD-ROM exercise is available. Open the file* ch14-11s.fla *located in the* F5gai/chapter14/ *folder, installed from the companion CD-ROM. Compare your file against the example.*

As you saw at the end of the last CD-ROM exercise, the advantage of smart clips and the parameters associated with them is that you can quickly and easily modify certain settings associated with a smart clip without having to go inside the clip's symbol structure and find the appropriate actions to be modified. Smart clips exist exactly for this reason.

 **NOTE:** *In the next chapter you will see another example of a smart clip; in this case, one used within Flash to simulate panoramic movies, which are similar to QuickTime VR movies.*

# ▪▪▪ Summary

In this chapter you have examined how to create a wide variety of interface components. Key points of this chapter include the creation and use of triggers, the Track as Menu Item option, drag actions, the capability of text fields, and the creation and use of smart clips. Concepts covered in this chapter are revisited in the last three chapters of this book, as these concepts are foundational to many of the advanced examples presented in the chapters that follow.

# 15

# An Introduction to Advanced ActionScripting

## ■ ■ ■ Introduction

Previous chapters have had as their focus getting you up to speed with ActionScript via relatively simple exercises. The basic constructs thus far presented are the building blocks of Flash programming. In an effort to help solidify these concepts, and to show you how to put them together to create more complex movies, this chapter focuses on four applied projects. You will have the opportunity of "tear apart" the components of these exercises and closely examine the ActionScript code underlying them.

Toward learning both ActionScript and FlashScript, in Chapter 16 you will manipulate some of the same examples using the FS Command action and JavaScript. This will also allow you to compare the two types of scripting, toward understanding how and why ActionScript and JavaScript are purposely similar.

## ■ ■ ■ Objectives

In this chapter, you will:

- Learn to create an interactive graphic that can be colored using ActionScript
- Examine a drag-and-drop puzzle game, and learn how ActionScript is used to add intelligence to its puzzle pieces

- Find out how to build a pseudo smart clip for integrating seamless panoramic images in Flash
- Discover a complex ActionScript game

# A Word About the Exercises

To help you better understand how ActionScripting works, the exercises in this chapter are explained from a conceptual standpoint. Important aspects of associated scripting code and structure are also highlighted. Unfortunately, the limits of this book do not permit an exhaustive, from-scratch building of these projects. However, the discussion provided should be enough to get you started.

It is recommended that you spend a significant amount of time digesting these larger and more complex examples. This book covers the basic rules concerning ActionScript, which are not difficult. However, it is the application of these concepts into a complete structure that presents difficulty for most people. Examine, review, and dissect these examples and exercises to learn more.

# An Exercise in Coloring

The first example is based on a coloring-book type of illustration for which the user can choose a color and then paint the image, as shown in figure 15-1. The user selects a color from the left-hand side of the screen and then applies it to an object on the right-hand side. As you will see, the color swatches from which the user can choose can be customized by you, the developer. The colors in the swatches are defined using the *Color* object, as opposed to being assembled via color fills.

Before you dive in and start examining this first CD-ROM exercise, however, consider the following. The following points constitute an overview of how the exercise works.

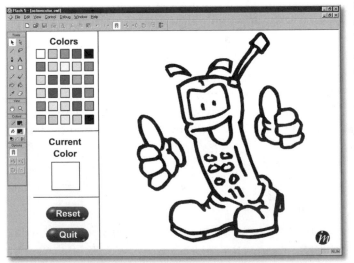

*Figure 15-1  The coloring example allows the user to choose a color and then paint the image.*

- The color swatches on the left-hand side of the screen are all generated from a single movie clip. Thus, there are multiple copies of the same movie clip placed on the stage. However, the instances all have different names.

- Note that the outlines of the swatches are not included within the movie clip. Rather, the only things in the movie clip are a single fill and a trigger. When the movie starts, the *Color* programming object is used to set the color of each movie clip to something different. The *Array* object is used in this process as well.

- When the user clicks on one of the swatches, ActionScript code gets the color from the selected swatch and sets the color of the Current Color swatch to match the small, selected swatch.

- Once a current color is selected (white is the default), the user clicks on one of the areas in the illustration. Each blank area (such as the hands, feet, or telephone body) is a movie clip. Similar to setting the color of the swatches, when the user clicks on an area in the illustration, the selected component of the illustration is assigned to the color from the Current Color swatch.

In the following CD-ROM exercise, you will examine the coloring process.

## CD-ROM Exercise

Open the file *actioncolor.fla* located in the *F5gai/chapter15/* folder, installed from the companion CD-ROM. Begin examining the coloring process by performing the following steps.

1. Begin by testing the movie (Test Movie) to see how it works.

2. Close the Flash Player and examine the color swatch buttons. Select any one of the cyan-colored color swatches in the upper left. Although the swatches look like triggers, the triggers are actually within a movie clip. Therefore, know that it is a movie clip that resides on the stage.

3. Right-click on one of the triggers and select Panels | Instance from the context menu.

4. Regardless of which swatch you choose, you will find that they are all instances of the Small Swatch movie clip, as shown in figure 15-2. The only difference among them is that each is named differently.

5. Before you examine the coding that fills the movie clips with color, let's examine what is inside the color swatch

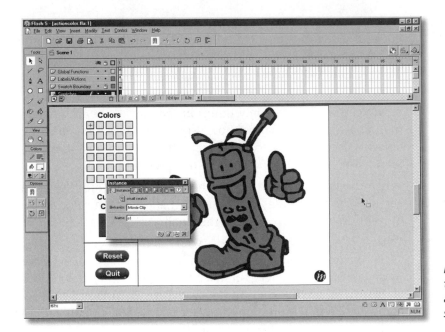

*Figure 15-2  All of the color swatches are instances of the same movie clip.*

movie clips. Right-click on one of the swatches and select Edit in Place from the context menu.

6.  Once you are accessing the timeline of one of the Small Swatch movie clips, you will notice two layers. The upper layer contains the trigger, and the lower layer contains a stage-level fill element. As previously mentioned, the *Color* programming object is used to set the color of the movie clip instances on the stage. The *Color* programming object can affect movie clips only (or the main movie), and affects all objects in the movie or movie clip (except triggers or other symbols). If you happen to have the Actions panel open, for now do not worry about the single line of code attached to the trigger in the movie clip. This is discussed later in the chapter.

7.  Note that the telephone image on the right-hand side of the screen consists of nine movie clips. If you were to access any of these telephone movie clips you would find a situation similar to the small color swatches. That is, within each telephone part symbol is a trigger and a fill.

8.  Click on Scene 1 in the Edit Path to return to the main timeline.

Before moving on to an examination of the "guts" of the code for this example, let's take a look at the procedure. Figure 15-3

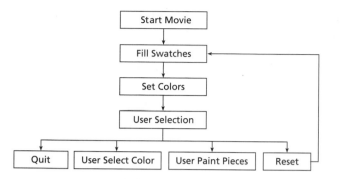

Figure 15-3 *A procedural flowchart of what does, and can, happen in the coloring example.*

shows a procedural flowchart for what should happen when the user plays this movie. Parts of the interaction should happen automatically, and other parts should occur as a result of user action.

When the movie starts, the first thing that should happen is filling of the color swatches with color. In the following material, this will be the first part of the code you examine. The second thing that happens is that the colors for the current color swatch and the telephone parts are established. The default color for all of them is white, but it could be any color.

Initialization of the swatches, Current Color swatch, and telephone parts happens very quickly (so quickly, in fact, that you should not be able to perceive this taking place). Once all initialization is complete, the user can begin working. The user can perform one of four tasks: select a color, paint a piece of the phone with the current color, reset the environment, or quit. The first two of these tasks are set up as functions, which are sets of code that can execute at any time. The latter two items are buttons that have the appropriate actions associated with them. Now that you understand how the program works, let's look at the code segments in the order in which they are executed.

9.  Locate the Labels/Actions layer and right-click in its first frame. Select Actions from the context menu.

10. In the Actions panel, you will see four lines of code. The first two lines are statements that "call" the initiating functions. You are already familiar with the nature of the latter two lines.

As you recall from figure 15-3, when the program starts, you want to set up the colors in the color swatches and set the default start-up colors for the telephone parts. Note that the reset button uses these functions as well. Instead of having to write the same code twice, and having to place it in two different locations, functions can be used to store reusable code snippets in a common location. Thus, this movie has a function for establishing the color swatch colors and for initializing the colors for the telephone image and the Current Color swatch.

The movie has two other functions, which will become apparent as the exercise progresses. Let's begin by looking at the code that builds the swatches, which is contained in the function *buildswatches();* (see code example 15-1). Continue with the following steps.

11. Locate the Global Functions layer and right-click on its frame 1. Select Actions to open the Actions panel.

Functions are normally stored in frames. To create global functions (functions accessible in the entire movie), you should create a layer that spans the length of the movie in the timeline. Functions are accessible only when the frames (or objects) to which they are attached are current.

12. In the Actions panel, scroll down and find the *buildswatches()* function, shown in code example 15-1, which follows. Note that a portion of the code in code example 15-1 has been truncated for manageability.

## Code Example 15-1  Code for the buildswatches(); Function

```
function buildswatches() {
//build the color swatches using temp array
        swatchlist = new Array();
        swatchlist[0] = 0xFFFFFF

        ...
        swatchlist[30] = 0xF45FFF
        for (i=0; i<29; i++) {
                myswatchitem = new Color("c" + (i+1));
                mycolor=swatchlist[i];
                myswatchitem.setRGB(mycolor.valueOf());
        }
        delete(swatchlist);
        delete(myswatchitem);
        delete(mycolor);
}
```

One of the first things you will notice in code example 15-1 is the use of an array for storing the color values (in hexadecimal format). (For more information about hexadecimal colors, see Appendix C). As you will recall, an array is simply a special variable that can store multiple values. The values in an array are indexed by position. The first array position is 0 through however many items are in the array.

**NOTE:** *When you work with arrays, understand that the computer starts counting at 0. Thus, the first item in an array is at position 0, not 1. The last position in the array in code example 15-1 is 29. However, there are 30 items in the list because it starts at 0.*

Setting a variable equal to an object, using the *new()* command, creates an *Array* object. The *new()* command creates an instance of an object in memory, allowing you to refer to the object by referring to the variable. For example, in code example 15-1 you see the array named *swatchlist*. If you wanted to find out the length of the array (number of items in it), you would use *swatchlist.length*.

The main reason an array is used in code example 15-1 is to keep the number of lines of code to a minimum, as well as to provide an easy means of defining the colors in the code. Notice the *for()* loop in the center of the function. If it were not for the array, the three lines of code within the *for()* loop would have to be written 30 times (3 x 30 = 90 lines of code). By using an array, combined with a *for()* loop, you can use the value of the counter associated with the *for();* loop (e.g., $i$ in this example ) to pull items out of the array by index number.

One of the other keys to this example is the naming of the movie clips on the stage. Recall that the movie clips are named c1, c2, c3, and so on. Just as $i$ is used to pull items from the array, it is used in the referencing of the movie clip. Let's examine the *for()* loop more closely to see what happens in it, so that this makes sense. The use of *for()* loops and arrays is one of the most widely employed constructs, which can reduce the amount of code typing necessary, if you understand how this works.

Once the array and its values are established, the *for()* loop is encountered. This *for()* loop will begin with $i=0$ and repeat the lines of code contained within it, up to 29. The first time the *for()* loop is encountered, $i=0$. The first and third lines in the *for()* loop are responsible for setting the swatches color. The second line is responsible for getting (from the *swatchlist* array) the color the swatch should be set to. Thus, the first time the *for()* loop is encountered, the first line reads:

```
myswatchitem = new Color("c1")
```

The *Color* object is used, among other purposes, to set or get colors associated with movie clips or the main movie. Thus, as indicated within its parentheses, the *Color* object expects to find a movie clip instance name or reference. Note that *i* is used within the *Color()* constructor. The movie clip instance name is constructed using the value of *i* (the *for()* loop counter), adding 1 (because this movie clips out on the stage start at c1 not c0), and concatenating the resulting value with the letter *c*, resulting in the string *c1*. As with the first line, the second line of code uses *i* again, as follows:

```
mycolor=swatchlist[0];
```

Recall that to talk to an instance of an object you refer to the variable associated with it. Thus, the second line creates a variable named *mycolor* and sets it equal to the value found at index position 0 in the *swatchlist* array. If you look back up in the coding you will find that the value at position 0 is 0xFFFFFF (white). When you tested the movie, you should have found that the first swatch was white.

The last line of code in the *for()* loop does not use *i*, but it does use the instance of the color object, *myswatchitem*, as well as the value in *mycolor*. The last line takes care of setting the value of *myswatchitem* (which is actually the color of movie clip *c1*) to the value of the variable *mycolor*, which was pulled from the *swatchlist* array. Note the *valueOf()* method used at the end of the *mycolor* variable. This ensures that the data provided to the *setRGB()* method is a number, because that is what it is expecting. If you wanted to ensure that an entry was a string, you would add *toString()* to the end of the entry's variable.

Note that to this point you have examined the *for()* looping just to the first value of *i*. The three lines of code within the loop, because they are contained in a *for()* loop, would continue through the remaining 29 values of *i*.

The last three lines in this function are simply "good-house-keeping" items. Whenever you use objects or variables and you know you are done with them, it is always a good idea to delete them rather than leaving them floating in memory. In many ways, this is just good practice. Moreover, in some languages, if you accidentally redefine a new object in memory (using the same name as an existing object), you can cause the system to lock up or crash.

You will notice in the *for()* loop that *myswatchitem* was used repeatedly, with different references in its parentheses. In some languages, this would cause the software to crash, but

Flash seems to have no problems with it. However, you should still delete variables and objects from memory when you are done with them.

13. Now that you have examined the *buildswatches()* function, let's review the *resetcolors()* function, shown in code example 15-2, which follows. The *resetcolors();* function sets the default starting color for all coloring items to be colored, as well as for the current color swatch.

## Code Example 15-2 Code for the resetcolors(); Function

```
function resetColors() {
// reset the colors
    selectedColor = 0xFFFFFF;
    currentcolor = new Color(currentC);
    currentcolor.setRGB(selectedColor.valueOf());
    lefthandcolor = new Color(lefthand);
    lefthandcolor.setRGB(selectedColor.valueOf());
    righthandcolor = new Color(righthand);
    righthandcolor.setRGB(selectedColor.valueOf());
    eyescolor = new Color(eyes);
    eyescolor.setRGB(selectedColor.valueOf());
    eyebrowscolor = new Color(eyebrows);
    eyebrowscolor.setRGB(selectedColor.valueOf());
    antennacolor = new Color(antenna);
    antennacolor.setRGB(selectedColor.valueOf());
    mouthcolor = new Color(mouth);
    mouthcolor.setRGB(selectedColor.valueOf());
    rightshoecolor = new Color(rightshoe);
    rightshoecolor.setRGB(selectedColor.valueOf());
    leftshoecolor = new Color(leftshoe);
    leftshoecolor.setRGB(selectedColor.valueOf());
    phonebodycolor = new Color(phonebody);
    phonebodycolor.setRGB(selectedColor.valueOf());
}
```

Overall, the *resetcolors()* function should be a little easier to understand than the *buildswatches()* function. In general, this function begins by creating a variable named *selectedColor*, setting this variable equal to 0xFFFFFF (white). The remaining paired lines of code simply create an instance (linked to one of the elements on the stage) of the *Color* object and then set the color of the object to *selectedColor*. *CurrentC* is the instance name of the current color swatch on the stage. The remaining items (such as *lefthand*, *righthand*, and so on) are the parts of the telephone.

As with the *buildswatches()* function, the *value.Of()* method is used in the second line of each pair to make sure the value being inserted into the *setRGB* method is a numerical hexadecimal representation and not a string.

The *buildswatches()* and *resetcolors()* functions, which you have just examined, are the items that execute the minute the movie starts. So what happens when the user clicks and interacts with the movie? Let's take a look.

14. Because the first thing the user will probably do is click on a color swatch, let's look at that first. Right-click on one of the color swatches on the stage and select Edit in Place.

15. Right-click on the trigger on the stage and select Actions from the context menu.

16. In the Actions panel, you will see a single, simple line of code contained in an event handler, as follows:

```
on (press) {
    _parent.changecolor(_name);
}
```

When the user clicks on the button, a function in the parent timeline of the movie clip that contains the trigger (that is, the main timeline) is told to execute the function *changecolor()*. The parent timeline function is also passed an argument (sometimes called a parameter). The argument is the value represented by *_name*. Take note of this. Remember that buttons do not have names. Thus, the name that will actually be passed to the function is the instance name of the movie clip that contains the button.

Depending on which swatch you selected on the stage, "cX" will be passed, where X is a number character, such as c1, c2, c3, and so on. Because the code attached to the trigger references a function contained in the main timeline, you must go there to see what actually happens.

When you want to call a function that exists in another timeline, you must preface the function name with the path to it. In the previous code, *_parent.changecolor()* was used, which is a relative reference. You can also use an absolute reference, such as _root.changecolor().

When a function is called, the currently executing timeline or script is interrupted to execute the code in the function called. Thus, if you call a function while something in the current timeline is animated, or within a set of procedures in a local script, you may find that the animation (or local script) will pause until the called function is complete. The complexity of the function determines whether or not a pause is noticeable. Continue with the following steps to see how the *changecolor();* function works.

17. Click on Scene 1 in the Edit Path and access the actions associated with frame 1 of the Global Functions layer.

18. Locate the *changecolor()* function, the code for which is shown in code example 15-3, which follows. The *changecolor();* function receives the movie clip instance name and changes the color of the current color swatch to the selected color.

---

### Code Example 15-3 Code for the changecolor(); Function

```
function changecolor(myswatch) {
        tempcolor = new Color(myswatch);
        tempval = tempcolor.getRGB();
        currentcolor.setRGB(tempval);
        delete(tempcolor);
        delete(tempval);
}
```

Recall that when the *changecolor()* function is called, the name of the movie clip in which the button resides is passed to the function. When the function receives the value, it creates a variable whose name is defined within the function's parentheses. Thus, *changecolor()* places the instance name of the movie clip into *myswatch* and then uses that variable in its own code.

The first thing the *changecolor()* function does is create a new instance of the *Color* programming object associated with the swatch that called the function. Note that the value of *myswatch* is used within the *Color* constructor. The instance is named *tempcolor*. When access is requested to any of the properties or methods of the *Color* object, *tempcolor* is used as the reference, as evident in the second line of code example 15-3.

Also in the second line, the variable *tempval* is created to hold the color value (in hexadecimal format) of the swatch that was clicked on (*myswatch*). Once the color value is obtained, the Current Color swatch on the stage is set equal to the color that was selected. This is what makes the Current Color swatch on the stage change to whatever small color swatch is selected.

At the end of code example 15-3, again you will notice that the *delete* command is used to delete the temporary color object (*tempcolor*) and the temporary color value (*tempval*). These items do not need to remain once the Current Color swatch's color has been changed. It is standard practice to delete variables if you will not again need the values contained in them.

> **NOTE:** *Be careful in regard to how many instances of a particular object you use at a single time. You can run out of RAM memory in most programming environments if you create too many object instances.*

The process for changing the telephone's image areas to a new color is basically the same process as changing the Current Color swatch to whatever small swatch is selected. Nonetheless, let's also look at this process by continuing with the following steps.

19. Right-click on one of the two hands in the telephone image area and select Edit in Place from the context menu.

20. Like the color swatches, take a look at the action assigned to the trigger.

21. As you can see in the Actions panel, the action conforms to the structure of the action associated with the color swatches, except that it calls a different function. Let's examine the *changepict()* function.

22. Click on Scene 1 in the Edit Path to return to the main timeline.

23. Access the actions associated with frame 1 of the Global Functions layer.

24. Locate the *changepict()* function, which is also shown in code example 15-4, which follows.

### Code Example 15-4 Code for the changepict(); Function

```
function changepict(mypart) {
    tempval = currentcolor.getRGB();
    tempcolor = new Color(mypart);
    tempcolor.setRGB(tempval);
    delete(tempcolor);
    delete(tempval);
}
```

In the *changepict()* function, you will notice (as with the *changecolor()* function) that the name of the movie clip instance being used is passed as an argument to the function. The primary difference between the *changepict()* function and the *changecolor()* function is that the *changepict()* function retrieves the value of the current color swatch on the stage and then sets the telephone part referenced by *mypart* to that color. Again, the *delete* command is used to remove the object and variable from memory.

The last part of this movie that is important is the actions associated with the Reset and Quit buttons. The Quit button uses the FS Command action to send the command *quit* to the Flash Player. (The next chapter delves into FS Command actions in more detail.)

The action associated with the Reset button is basically a call to the *resetcolors()* function. You will notice that no preceding target path is necessary to call this action from the Reset button, because the Reset button exists in the main movie timeline, where the function is stored.

 **NOTE:** *Macromedia has included several sample files of examples that use functions, variables, and the Math object. See the Help | Samples directory for the files named Calculator, Finance Calc, and Roll Dice.*

## ▪ ▪ ▪ The Puzzle

In regard to drag-and-drop environments, the previous chapter discussed the puzzle exercise that follows. In this exercise you create a puzzle game that detects the *_droptarget* upon release of a piece of the puzzle. As noted in the previous chapter, creating a drag-and-drop element requires that a button be inserted into a movie clip. When pressed, the button in the movie clip (the movie clip having been inserted onto the stage) tells the stage to make the movie clip draggable. When the button is released, it tells the stage to stop the drag operation.

**NOTE:** *Macromedia has included a sample puzzle with Flash as well. Access the Help | Samples | Puzzle menu option to view this example.*

Adding the functionality for the drag-and-drop game is relatively easy. Most people will find setting up the drag the difficult part. The CD-ROM exercise that follows takes you through the process of setting up this game.

### CD-ROM Exercise

Begin by opening the file *puzzle1.fla* located in the *F5gai/chapter14/* folder, installed from the companion CD-ROM. To set up the game, perform the following steps.

1.  Use Test Movie to see how the movie works.

The first step was to set up the buttons for the drag and drop. These buttons are found in the library folder named *Buttons*. Next, the buttons where inserted into movie clips. These elements are found in the *Movie Clips (of Buttons)* folder in the library. Actions were then assigned to the buttons (in the movie clips) so that the movie clips would be made draggable, similar to what you saw in the last chapter.

2.  Access the symbol named MC2s in the *Movie Clips (of Buttons)* folder. Right-click on the puzzle piece and access the Actions panel. Notice the *startDrag* and *stopDrag* actions. You will note other actions, which are explained below.

Because the movie begins with the first puzzle piece in place, there is no button or movie clip in the *Movie Clips (of Buttons)* folder for the first piece. The first piece begins in place and is not movable.

Next, an additional set of movie clips was created for each puzzle piece so that code could be established to detect the *drop target* property. These movie clips contain the graphical components of the buttons, but not the buttons themselves. Thus, the buttons were inserted into each additional movie clip, and then broken apart to separate the graphical components from the buttons. These movie clips are located in the *Movie Clips (Static)* folder.

In retrospect, it would have been more efficient to create a graphic symbol of the puzzle graphic. The graphic could have been used in the buttons, as well as in the static movie clips used to detect the drop target. However, stage-level elements were used within buttons and static movie clips. File size may be larger as a result.

Once these additional movie clips were created (*Movie Clips (Static)*), they were placed on the stage in the correct final locations. This is why you see both the completed picture and the pieces for the game.

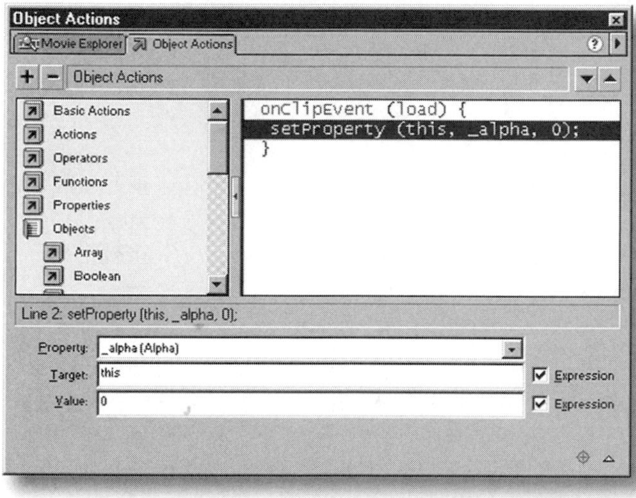

As shown in figure 15-4, each of the static puzzle pieces (those in final position) has code associated with it that sets its own *_alpha property* to 0 (transparent).

As shown in figure 15-4, the *onClipEvent (load)* handler is used so that as soon as the clip is loaded it is turned transparent. Note that the instance name of the static movie clips takes the form MC2a, MC3a, MC4a, and so on ("a" for answer).

*Figure 15-4  The static pieces have associated code that makes them turn themselves invisible as soon as they are loaded.*

When the user drags the moveable puzzle piece over to the solution area and lets go, the *_droptarget* property is detected to see if the draggable piece (MCX) intersects with the non-draggable, transparent piece (MCXa). If the dragged-piece name matches the solution-piece instance name, the draggable piece is turned off (made invisible) and the alpha of the solution piece is set to 100 (opaque). This is how the game is given some intelligence.

3.   Before exiting this example, let's return to the release event associated with the draggable buttons. Access the symbol named MC2s located in the *Movie Clips (of Buttons)* folder in the library.

4.   Select the button and access the Actions panel to see the associated actions, shown in code example 15-5, which follows. This is the ActionScript code associated with the buttons within the movie clips.

### Code Example 15-5 ActionScript Code Associated with Buttons Within Movie Clips

```
on (press) {
    with (_root) {
```

```
            setpieceloc(this);
        }
    startDrag (this);
}
on (release) {
    stopDrag ();
    _parent.checkDrop(eval(this), eval(
    _droptarget));
}
```

As you examine code example 15-5, you will notice two additional things you saw earlier. Notice that the *with()* command is used to communicate to the *_root* movie. The *with()* command tells the main timeline to execute the function *setpieceloc()*, and sends (via *this*) it the object's path. If you examine the *setpieceloc()* function, located in frame 1 of the Global Functions layer, you will see that this function records the starting *x* and *y* location for the puzzle piece. This locational information is used to put the puzzle piece back in its original starting location if the place the user drops the puzzle piece is not correct.

The code that sets the piece in its original location, or solves for the piece if the user drops it in the right place, is the *checkDrop()* function, also located in the main movie timeline. Note in code example 15-5 that once the drag ceases, the *checkDrop* function is executed. It is sent the name of the object (via *this*) and the current *_droptarget* property. You will notice that the arguments sent to the *checkDrop()* function are first evaluated with the *eval()* method. This is so that the data being received by the *checkDrop()* function is evaluated in the context of the current movie clip and not the main timeline. Let's take a look at the *checkDrop()* function, as it is the "brains" of the puzzle game.

The *_droptarget* property is immediately updated following a *stopDrag*. The data in the *_droptarget* property will remain until the next *stopDrag* has occurred.

5.  Click on Scene 1 in the Edit Path.

6.  Access the actions in frame 1 of the Global Functions layer.

7.  Locate the *checkDrop()* function, shown in code example 15-6, which follows. The *checkDrop()* function receives the movable puzzle piece's target path (*myname*) and the drop target property data (*dtarget*).

## Code Example 15-6 Code for the checkDrop() Function

```
function checkDrop (myname, dtarget) {
    if (String(dtarget) == String(myname+"a")) {
        setProperty (myname, _visible, 0);
        setProperty (myname+"a", _alpha, 100);
    } else {
        setProperty (myname, _x, myoriginX);
        setProperty (myname, _y, myoriginY);
    }
}
```

Code example 15-6 shows how the data from the _droptarget_ property is compared to the moveable clip to determine if the piece was dropped in the right place. A simple comparison is made to see if the string evaluation of _dtarget_, which contains the data from the _droptarget_ property, equals the string evaluation of the moveable item's reference. You will notice that the second part of the _if_ condition uses _myname_ + "a". The only difference between the moveable puzzle pieces and the static ones is the addition of "a" at the end of the instance name ("a" meaning answer).

If _dtarget_ equals _myname_ + "a" (MC2a = = MC2 + a), the visibility of the draggable piece is set to 0 (MC2), and the transparency of _myname_ + "a" (MC2a) is set to 100 percent. If the items do not equal each other, the location of _myname_ (MC2) is set back to its original position. If you will recall, the original position is set by calling the _setpieceloc()_ function, which you saw earlier.

A final note before leaving this example: Realize that alpha and visibility are not the same thing. For the _droptarget_ property to work, the solution piece cannot be invisible. If it is, _droptarget_ will not detect anything because there is nothing there. However, if the solution piece is instead transparent (alpha = = 0), _droptarget_ will detect the solution piece even though it is transparent.

 **CD-ROM NOTE:** *Realize that you can also use the* MovieClip *programming object to create a drag and drop, by using the* startDrag *and* stopDrag *methods of that object. The only problem with this method is that the cursor does not automatically change to a hand (indicating a hot element). To see an example of this alternative method, open the file* puzzle2.fla *located in the* F5gai/chapter15/ *folder, installed from the companion CD-ROM.*

## Cursor Parameters in Flash

This book has not spent time examining the many things you can do with the cursor because, compared to packages such as Director, the time that it takes to set up cursor changes in Flash is usually not worth the effort. Nonetheless, this sidebar and the following CD-ROM Note are about changing the cursor.

Cursor changes in Flash are effected by calling the *Mouse* object's *hide()* method and then attaching a movie clip to the cursor using the *setProperty* action (or some other similar technique). This is usually done in an *onClipEvent* handler, associated with *mouseUp*, *mouseDown*, and *mouseMove* events. The movie clip usually contains a static element. Yet, some people have put a twist on this by making a movie clip that duplicates itself and is animated. Thus, items such as snowflakes, sparkles, and so on seem to magically appear, emanating from the cursor.

However, a word of caution concerning these techniques is in order. Indeed they are novel, interesting, intriguing, and so on, but if you overdo the use of such techniques, your users will probably be cursing you for messing with their cursor! Be judicious in the use of such features.

If you are interested in mouse cursor techniques, there are many open source examples located at *http://www.flashzone.com* and *http://www.flashkit.com*. Rather than spending significant amounts of time in this book on already well-documented techniques, you are referred to these sites for examples.

**CD-ROM NOTE:** *To see an example of a cursor-change technique, open the file* puzzle3.fla *located in the* F5gai/chapter15/ *folder, installed from the companion CD-ROM.*

**NOTE:** *Macromedia has included a sample file with Flash that demonstrates mouse-tracking techniques. Access the Help | Samples | Circular Motion menu option to view this example. You may also want to see their Duplicate Movie Clip example as well.*

# ■ ■ ■ The Flash PanoPlayer

One of the techniques found in other authoring packages and in other programming languages is the implementation of interactive images to simulate an environment, called a *panoramic movie*, or to simulate the manipulation of an object, called an *object movie*. In the former, the camera is at the center looking out, whereas in the latter the camera moves about an object.

With the new ActionScript capabilities in Flash, you can now create a Flash-based panoramic image player. In this section, you will work through an exercise that examines the programming behind the Flash PanoPlayer. In addition, PanoPlayer is "almost a smart clip" (you will understand why the term almost is used later), you will learn how you can use it with your own panoramic images.

 **CD-ROM NOTE:** *To see an example of a panoramic movie, open the file* pano_sampe.swf *located in the* F5gai/chapter15/ *folder, installed from the companion CD-ROM. You can click-drag in the image to look around, click-drag and release to make the image spin and slow down, or use the spacebar and arrow keys to manipulate the image.*

The first technology to allow this type of interactive media asset was QuickTime, called QuickTimeVR. Thus, most people still associate panoramic images with QuickTime, and indeed Apple was the first to bring it to the desktop computer. However, many other technologies have since followed. Some are based on stitched panoramic images, as shown in figure 15-5, whereas others are based on true 3D models. The panoramic image player described and used in the exercise in this section is based on the stitched panoramic image. In this section, you will examine the code and setup for this type of movie, and you will learn how you can reuse the player for any panoramic image.

*Figure 15-5 A sample panoramic image created from special stitching software.*

# Creating Seamless Panoramic Images

Creating panoramic images requires that multiple photographs (12 to 28) be taken in a circular pattern around the camera. The number of photos required depends on the focal length of the camera lens and the quality desired in the final panoramic image. The photographs are stitched together to create a single seamless (panoramic) image using special software, such a Apple's QuickTimeVR Authoring Toolkit, PictureWorks Spin PhotoObject, or VR Workx. Although most of these tools are designed to generate QuickTimeVR movies, a by-product of the process, which can be used in the Flash PanoPlayer, is a seamless image.

When taking the source photographs, the camera must be precisely positioned so that photographs are taken at exact degree increments. If the photographs are not at correct increments, they will not be stitched together properly. Creating seamless panoramic images is not difficult and at a minimum all you really need is a basic camera (preferably digital), a tripod, and some software to stitch the images together. If you have many panoramic images to create, you might want to invest in additional hardware, such as a specialized tripod head and balancer to facilitate the picture-taking process.

Before you dive into the code that makes the PanoPlayer work, let's examine the overall structure for it. As shown in figure 15-6, there are three primary elements used in the PanoPlayer. The first is a draggable movie clip that contains a trigger. Additionally, the draggable movie clip is transparent (alpha = = 0), and therefore you never actually see it. The second and third elements are a mask object and the panoramic bitmap image. The only logical way to keep the panoramic image confined to an area, so that it does not consume the stage, is to use a mask layer. Thus, the mask layer will reveal only a portion of the panoramic image.

If you tried out the sample panoramic image in the previous CD-ROM Note, you saw that as you click-drag, the panoramic image responds to what you do. As you move the image you see no seam in the image at all, although you know that the image must have a "beginning" and an "end-

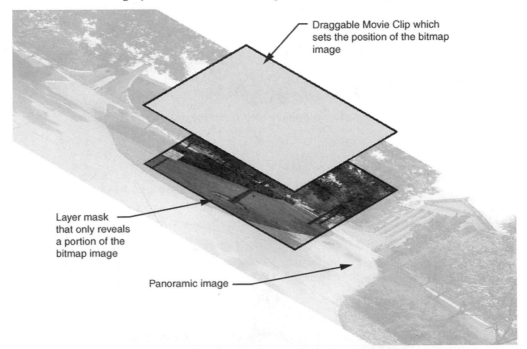

Draggable Movie Clip which sets the position of the bitmap image

Layer mask that only reveals a portion of the bitmap image

Panoramic image

*Figure 15-6 The structure of the PanoPlayer includes a transparent, draggable movie clip, a mask, and the panoramic image.*

ing." There are two parts to this illusion. The first is the fact that as the end of the panorama reaches the right-hand side of the mask, code in the movie automatically tells the image to change its location back to the begging. Thus, you never see the end of the image.

As is discussed in the section "Prepping Images for the PanoPlayer," you must copy and paste part of the panoramic image from the beginning of the image to the end of the image to make this work. The width of the copied area is based on the width of the mask used to reveal the panoramic image. This is discussed further later in the chapter.

The second thing to note about this illusion is that in reality the panoramic image is not the object being dragged. Rather, you are actually dragging the forward transparent movie clip, which in turn changes the $x$ and $y$ location of the panoramic image on the stage. You might think this could be accomplished by attaching the drag code directly to the panoramic image, and in fact this is what was originally tried in creating the illusion. However, when a drag occurs, everything else related to the object being dragged stops, making it impossible to set $x$ and $y$ locations needed to make the image appear to be seamless in a circular fashion. Thus, the use of a forward, transparent, draggable object was necessary.

## Examining the PanoPlayer Code

Of the examples presented thus far, use of the PanoPlayer code is probably the most complex. The most difficult thing to understand will be where the code segments are placed (attached to a movie clip, in a frame, and so on), and why it is imperative for the code to be in that exact location. These issues are discussed as you examine the code in the following CD-ROM exercise. Let's get down to business examining the code!

 *CD-ROM Exercise*

Open the file *panoplayer_code.fla* located in the *F5gai/chapter15/* folder, installed from the companion CD-ROM. Follow along as the code that makes this example work is discussed. Note that in this first file, the movie clip that makes the entire scenario work is a basic movie clip, not a smart clip. In the next section, you will see the difference the smart clip structure has on the movie clip.

1. With the file open, start by opening the Movie Explorer to reveal the structure for the symbols. As shown in figure 15-7, turn on the Show Buttons, Movie Clips, and Graphics buttons only.

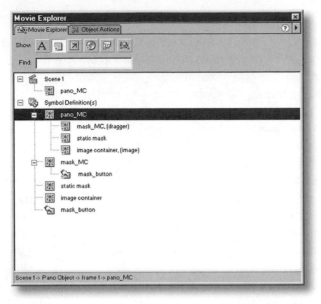

*Figure 15-7  Using the Movie Explorer to examine the structure of the PanoPlayer.*

2. With the Movie Explorer open, in the Symbol Definitions section, notice that the main movie clip is the *pano_MC* symbol. It contains the *mask_MC* symbol (whose instance name is *Dragger*), a movie clip named Static Mask, and a symbol named Image Container (whose instance name is *Image*).

**NOTE:** *Throughout the discussion of the code, movie clips (Dragger and Image) are referred to by their instance names so you know which item is being referring to. The static mask will simply be called the mask.*

3. Use either the Movie Explorer or the Symbol list button to access the *pano_MC* movie clip. This is where you will start examining the code.

4. In the *pano_MC* movie clip, you will notice that there are only three frames in the movie clip, each with actions associated with it. Access the actions attached to frame 1. The actions there set the main variables used in the movie. These variables include:

   • *dragging*: Tracks whether the user is currently dragging Dragger.

   • *lastMouseX* and *lastMouseY*: Keep track of the mouse position in relation to the main movie stage. When the user drags, these variables are compared to the current mouse position to determine which way the user is dragging.

   • *displaceX* and *displaceY*: While the user is dragging the Dragger movie clip, these variables are used to store the amount of offset between *lastMouseX* and the current *x* position of the mouse, and between *lastMouseY* and the current *y* position of the mouse. The Image movie clip is then offset by *displaceX* and *displaceY*.

- *toplimit* and *bottomlimit*: Store the upper and lower stage limits for the panoramic image so that the image does not slide beyond the upper and lower limits of the mask.

- *spinme*: If you tested the movie, or viewed the example, you noticed that the movie automatically starts the movie panning. In addition, if you tried the arrow keys you noticed that using them speeds up the pan or changes the pan direction. The *spinme* variable determines the rate of pan and the rate by which the pan speeds up.

- *imagewidth*: Stores the default size of the image without the copied addition at its end. The section on prepping images describes the addition of the piece in more detail. The *imagewidth* variable must be absolutely correct for the PanoPlayer to correctly pan the image.

- *friction*: If you tested the movie, again you saw that when you click, drag, and release, the panoramic image spins freely and then gradually slows down. The degradation of the spin is controlled by the *friction* variable. A larger friction number will make the image slow down more quickly, whereas a smaller number will make it slow down at a lesser rate.

5. Before continuing with the code, let's make the movie a little easier to understand by making the transparent mask partially visible. Click on the Moveable Mask layer, which contains Dragger, and open the Effects panel.

6. Set the Alpha for the Dragger object to 30 percent. Now you should be able to see the mask on the stage.

7. To see what is really going on, use Test Movie. Notice that it is actually the Dragger movie that is being dragged.

8. Now let's examine the code associated with the Dragger movie clip instance. Right-click on it on the stage and open the Actions panel. For now, you will examine only the code that executes when the clip loads, which is shown in code example 15-7.

## Code Example 15-7  Code for Drag Constraints

```
onClipEvent (load) {
    top = _y+((_parent.image._height-_height)/2);
```

```
left = _x-_width;
right = _x+_width;
bottom = (-_y)-((_parent.image._height
-_height)/2);
_parent.toplimit=top
_parent.bottomlimit=bottom
}
```

As you can see in code example 15-7, the code shown there sets 6 variables. The first four constrain the Dragger, and the last two constrain the Image. The *top*, *left*, *right*, and *bottom* variables, which constrain the Dragger, are set based on various elements. They are written so that Dragger can be any size and so that the panoramic image can also be any size. It is assumed that the Image's height will always be greater than or equal to the Dragger. It is also assumed that the Dragger and mask will always be the same size.

 The button within Dragger, which is examined shortly, uses the first four variables to determine and set the dragging constraints. The top variable is set based on the *y* position of the Dragger movie clip plus half the difference between the Dragger height and the Image. The same is true for the *bottom* variable. This allows the Dragger to move only vertically outside the mask area, by half the difference between the Image height and the Dragger.

In this example, the Image is 240 pixels high, and the Dragger 200 pixels high. Thus, the Dragger can be dragged up 20 pixels and down 20 pixels only. However, because the *top* and *bottom* variables are defined this way, Dragger and the image could be any size and the image and the variables will still be set properly.

**NOTE:** *Unless a property is preceded by* _parent, *it is assumed to be referring to the property of the current object. Items such as* _x, _y, _width, *and* _height *refer, respectively, to the x position, y position, width, and height of Dragger. When you see* _parent.image._height, *it refers to Image's height (*image._height*), which is one step up from Dragger (*_parent*).*

The *left* and *right* constraints for the Dragger are based on the width of the Dragger movie clip. In this scenario, the Dragger is 300 pixels wide. Thus, you can drag Dragger –300 pixels and +300 pixels because the Dragger's *x* is 0. Again, regardless of the size of Dragger, as long as its *x* and *y* location is 0,0, the Dragger can be any size. Just keep in mind that it must always be the same size as the mask object that reveals the Image.

The last two variables, *toplimit* and *bottomlimit*, are set based on *top* and *bottom*. You could simply use *top* and *bottom* at the appropriate time, instead of using *toplimit* and *bottomlimit*. It was preferred in this example, however, to separate the limits for Dragger and the limits for the Image to bar any unforeseen problems that might arise in sharing a single set of variables.

9. Now that you have examined the actions executed when the Dragger movie clip loads, let's examine the actions attached to the button within Dragger. If you are currently accessing the *pano_MC* movie clip (see the Edit Path), right-click on the Dragger movie clip on the stage and select Edit in Place. In the *mask_MC* movie clip (the library name of Dragger), click on the button (which is a big blue fill) and access the Actions panel.

Just for clarification, up to this point the button in the Dragger has been called a trigger for simplicity's sake. It is not really a trigger; rather, it is a button with a big blue fill in the first frame. Had it been a trigger, you would not have been able to modify its transparency on the stage or see it work in the main movie.

The actions associated with the button within Dragger, shown in code example 15-8, do several things. Let's begin by analyzing the actions associated with the *on (press)* handler that are attached to the button within Dragger.

## Code Example 15-8 Actions Associated with the on (press) Handler

```
on (press) {
    if (parent.spinme<>0) {
        _parent.spinme = 0;
        _parent.displaceX = 0;
    }
    _parent.dragging = true;
    _parent.lastMouseX = _parent._xmouse;
    _parent.lastMouseY = _parent._ymouse;
    startDrag (this, false, left, top, right,
bottom);
}
```

When the user presses the mouse, the *on (press)* handler first determines if the panoramic image is spinning. Recall that when the movie starts, the image automatically starts to pan, based on the *spinme* variable. The first *if* statement makes sure that if the panoramic image is spinning, it stops the moment the user presses the mouse. The *if* statement does this by setting the *displaceX* and *spinme* variables to 0.

In general, the *dragging* variable determines whether or not the panoramic image needs to be updated because of the dragging of the Dragger movie clip. Thus, when the user clicks on the button (within Dragger) the next line, *_parent.dragging = true*, tells the main movie that the user has begun to drag the Dragger movie and that the panoramic image's position will need to be updated.

The next two lines record the *x* and *y* location where the user clicked to begin the dragging operation. This is so that the movie can track the relative position of the mouse during dragging in relation to where the click was actually initiated. The difference between these two locations, as you will see in another script, is used to displace the panoramic image.

Finally, the last line in the *press* handler initiates the drag of the Dragger movie clip. Note that this is used to signify that the Dragger movie clip should be the item dragged. Also notice the use of the *left*, *top*, *right*, and *bottom* variables defined in the last script.

10. Now let's examine the content of the actions associated with the *on (release, releaseOutside)* handler that are attached to the button within Dragger, as shown in code example 15-9, which follows.

### Code Example 15-9  Actions Associated with the *on (release, releaseOutside)* Handler

```
on (release, releaseOutside) {
    _parent.dragging = false;
    stopDrag ();
    setProperty (_parent.dragger, _x, 0);
    setProperty (_parent.dragger, _y, 0);
}
```

The first thing to notice in code example 15-9 is the use of both the *release* and *releaseOutside* events. When the movie was originally created, only *release* was used. However, when the user clicked, dragged, and released (a "free spin"), occasionally the release would occur outside the button. Presumably the computer was having difficulty keeping up with the "spin." To fix this problem, *releaseOutside* was added so that no matter where the mouse button was released, the button would still stop the drag.

The first thing that is done in this handler is the stopping of the drag. Thus, the *dragging* variable, owned by the main movie timeline, is set to *false*. In addition, a *stopDrag* action is used to cease the dragging of the Dragger object.

The last two lines are pretty important. When the user ceases the drag, the Dragger movie clip must be returned to its original position so that the next time the user starts to drag the item is not somewhere off in space or off the location. This is a key to making the illusion work. Keep in mind that the user does not even know that they are interacting with a different movie clip. They think they are actually manipulating the panoramic image directly, which to some degree is true. However, the manipulation is achieved through another object.

Now that you have looked at the code that initiates the drag scenario, it is time to look at the real brains of the operation. They are located in the second frame of the *pano_MC* movie clip. The third frame of the *pano_MC* movie clip simply contains a *gotoAndPlay* action that continually returns to the second frame. Continue with the following steps.

11. Click on the *pano_MC* link in the Edit Path.

12. Using the Actions panel, access the actions associated with frame 2. Note that the actions are located there so that they are constantly executed due to the looping action defined in frame 3.

13. Once you are accessing frame 2 of the *pano_MC* movie clip, note that there are three major sections of code denoted by *if* commands. You will examine each of these separately. Code example 15-10 shows the first, and longest, of these segments.

### Code Example 15-10  First Part of pano_MC's Frame 2 Actions

```
if (dragging == true) {
      displaceX = _xmouse-lastMouseX
      lastMouseX = _xmouse
      displaceY= _ymouse-lastMouseY
      lastMouseY = _ymouse
} else if (dragging==false && spinme==0) {
      displaceY = 0
      //this degrades the spin over time
      if (dragging == false) {
            if ( displaceX > 0 ) {
                  displaceX = displaceX-friction
                  if ( displaceX < 0 ) {
                        displaceX = 0
                  }
            } else if (displaceX < 0) {
                  displaceX = displaceX+friction
                  if ( displaceX > 0 ) {
                        displaceX = 0
                  }
            }
      }
} else if (dragging==false && spinme<>0) {
      displaceX = spinme
}
```

As shown in code example 15-10, there are three main conditions for which this section checks. First, it checks to see if the user is currently dragging the Dragger movie clip. The *dragging* variable is used to determine this. If the user is dragging, the section constantly updates the displacement variables. Note that this section does not use the variables to set the image. Rather, it just tracks the mouse and determines a displacement based on it.

The second major condition detected is if the user is not dragging and if the panoramic image is not set on "autospin" (*spinme* = =0). If this is found to be true, the current displacement is reduced by the *friction* value. Basically, this section of code degrades the spin so that when the user performs a free spin (quickly clicks, drags, and releases), the panoramic image does not spin infinitely.

The last, rather short, section checks to see if dragging is false and *spinme* is not equal to 0. This basically means that the panoramic image should be in free-spin mode. The amount of displacement here is based on *spinme*.

In all three of the previous code sections, note that none of them actually sets the panoramic image location. They set only the variables that will be used to set the image location. In reality, the next two code segments handle the image displacement. The first, shown in code example 15-11, handles the horizontal displacement. The second, shown in code example 15-12, handles the vertical displacement.

## Code Example 15-11 Code for the Horizontal Displacement of the Panoramic Image

```
//this makes the image spin (horizontal)
if (displaceX<>0) {
      newimageX = image._x+displaceX;

      if (newimageX<imageX-imageWidth) {
           newimageX = newimageX+imageWidth;
      }
      if (newimageX>imageX) {
           newimageX = newimageX-imageWidth;
      }
      image._x = newimageX;
}
```

The code shown in code example 15-11 takes the horizontal displacement values determined in the first part of the script and uses them to change the *x* location of the image on the stage. The first line, *newimageX = image._x + displaceX*, creates a new variable to hold the summative value of where the image currently is (*image._x*) and where it needs to be moved (*displaceX*).

Keep in mind that *displaceX* is based on the difference between the starting point where the user clicked, which was set in the Dragger button's script, and the current *_xmouse* location. The script then takes the value of *newimageX* and determines the proper location for the image placement, so that the seam of the image is never perceived. It then sets the image's *x* location to *newimageX*.

## *Code Example 15-12  Code for the Vertical Displacement of the Panoramic Image*

```
//this takes care of vertical
if (displaceY<>0) {
      newimageY = image._y+displaceY;
      if (newimageY>toplimit) {
            newimageY=toplimit
      } else if (newimageY<bottomlimit) {
            newimageY=bottomlimit
      }
      image._y = newimageY
}
```

As shown in code example 15-12, the last portion of the script determines and sets the *y* location of the panoramic image. Here, instead of worrying about the seam, what you have to be concerned with is making sure the bottom of the panoramic image does not move above the bottom of the mask. Similarly, you have to make sure the top of the image does not move below the top of the mask.

Once the new location for the image (*newimageY*) is set (based on the sum of the image's current *y* and the *y* displacement), it must be checked against *toplimit* and *bottomlimit*. If the new location is found to be greater than *toplimit*, *newimageY* is set equal to *toplimit*. If the new location is found to be greater than *bottomlimit*, *newimageY* is set equal to *bottomlimit*. Once the limits are checked, the image's *y* location is set to *newimageY*.

Aside from the code details, one of the more holistic things to realize is that this entire script is encountered many, many times. This is what makes the image spin and what makes the drag scenario work. Because the frame continues to play while the drag is executing, the code causes the image to be constantly updated.

Now that you have examined the brains of the code, let's return to the code that makes the keyboard able to control the *autospin* that occurs when the user is not dragging. Continue with the following steps.

Click on the Dragger movie clip (the partially transparent item on the stage) and view its actions in the Actions panel. Recall that earlier the discussion of the *load* actions skipped over the *keyDown* events associated with this movie clip. Let's now turn our attention to them. Code example 15-13 shows the code.

### Code Example 15-13  Code for Controlling the autospin Capability

```
onClipEvent (keyDown) {
    temp=Key.getCode();
    //Right Arrow
    if (temp==39) {
        _parent.spinme-=2;
        if (_parent.spinme==-22) {
            _parent.spinme=-20;
        }
    } else if (temp==37) {
    //Left Arrow
        _parent.spinme+=2;
        if (_parent.spinme==22) {
            _parent.spinme=20;
        }
    //Space Key
    } else if (temp==32) {
        if (_parent.spinme<>0) {
            _parent.spinme=0;
        } else {
            _parent.spinme=2;
        }
    //up arrow
    } else if (temp==38) {
        if (_parent.image._y+2<_parent.toplimit) {
            _parent.image._y+=2
        } else {
            _parent.image._y=_parent.toplimit
        }
    //down arrow
    } else if (temp==40) {
        if (_parent.image._y-2>_parent.bottomlimit) {
            _parent.image._y-=2
        } else {
            _parent.image._y=_parent.bottomlimit
        }
    }
}
```

To be able to respond to keyboard events, two things are required. First, an element has to be set up to detect a keypress. You will recall from earlier chapters that you can use the *on (keypress)* handler to create quick keys for the buttons in your movie. In the scenario, however, you want to be able to determine specific keys when the user presses any keys. To do this, the *onClipEvent(keyDown)* handler is quite helpful.

The second thing required is use of the *Key* programming object. By using the *Key.getCode()* method, you can determine the exact key pressed. Thus, the first thing the code in code example 15-13 does is place the value retrieved by the *Key* object into a variable. *If* statements are then used to react to specific keys.

 **NOTE:** *Appendix G shows the key code values and what keys they represent.*

The *if* sections in code example 15-13 associated with the left and right arrow keys modify the *spinme* variable to either increase or decrease its value. Because no variable is associated with the *y* position of the image on the stage, the up and down arrows directly interact with the image's position on the stage. The spacebar toggles the *spinme* variable. If the image is not currently spinning, the spacebar starts it spinning. If the image is currently spinning, the spacebar stops the spin. In both cases, the spacebar is used to modify the value of *spinme*, similar to the arrow keys.

## Making the PanoPlayer a Pseudo Smart Clip

The example PanoPlayer movie clip might have been created as a smart clip, in which the end user could import an image and set some parameters. This way, many things could be parameters, including:

- The size of the panoramic image (*imageWidth* and *height*)
- The panoramic image reference itself
- The size of the mask and dragger (the area through which the panoramic image is viewed)
- The *friction* and *spinme* variables

To a large extent, the PanoPlayer can be used in this way. However, some limitations do exist. The center two items, the reference of the bitmap in its movie clip (Image) and the size and location of the mask object, cannot be dynamically manipulated with parameters. Thus, the PanoPlayer is a "pseudo" smart clip. The size of the image and the *friction* and *spinme* variables are parameters. However, when using the PanoPlayer, the user must manually insert the bitmap image into the Image movie clip. Likewise, the size and location of the mask and dragger must be manually set. In the next two sections you will see how you can use the PanoPlayer pseudo smart clip.

To make the PanoPlayer a smart clip, or at least as close as it can be, the *spinme*, *friction*, and *imageWidth* variables were removed from frame 1 of the *pano_MC* movie clip. They were defined as Clip Parameters in the library window.

## Prepping Images for the PanoPlayer

The key to creating images that will work with the PanoPlayer is to open a stitched panoramic image in Photoshop (or other raster image editor) and copy a portion of the beginning of the image to the end of the image. The size of the portion copied is based on the size of the window in which you will play the image. For example, if you have an image that is 1450 pixels wide by 240 pixels high, and you want to play it through a mask that will be 400 pixels wide by 300 pixels high, you need to copy and paste a piece from the beginning of the image that is 400 pixels wide and paste it at the end of the image. The CD-ROM exercise that follows takes you through the process of prepping an image for use with the PanoPlayer.

 *CD-ROM Exercise*

For this exercise, follow along using the CD-ROM files to see how to prep an image for use with the PanoPlayer. The author has included several panoramic images in the *F5gai/chapter15/ pano_images/* folder, installed from the companion CD-ROM. You must have a raster image editor to do this exercise. Note that the sample images from the companion CD-ROM are in JPEG format. Generally, you do not want to use JPEG when you go into Flash. However, for the purposes of the exercise, JPEG will suffice.

1. Open an image editor such as Photoshop and open the panoramic image you wish to prep. Write down the initial width of the image; you will need this when you bring the image into Flash. In Photoshop, you can use the Info tab or the Image | Image Size dialog box to retrieve this information.

2. In this exercise, it is assumed you want to make the mask that will reveal the panoramic image 400 pixels wide. In Photoshop, you would use the mask tool to select a 400-pixel-wide segment at the beginning of the panoramic image so that you can copy it. Photoshop provides a nice feature whereby you can constrain a mask to a specific size. This is located in the Options tab when the mask tool is selected. With the mask set, select the beginning portion of the panoramic image, as shown in figure 15-8, and copy it.

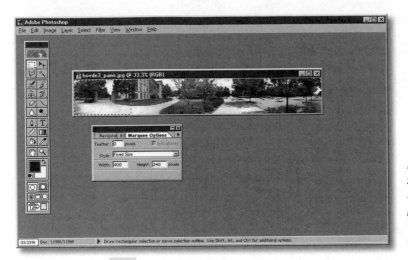

*Figure 15-8 Make a selection of the beginning portion of the panoramic image that is the size of the mask you intend to use in Flash.*

3. If you are in Photoshop, use Image | Canvas Size to increase the width of the canvas by 400 pixels.

4. Paste the copied piece into the image.

5. When you paste in Photoshop, the pasted piece is placed on a new layer. Drag the pasted object to the right-hand end of the image and position it so that you cannot see any white space between the pasted piece and the original image.

6. In Photoshop, use Layer | Flatten image.

7. Save the file as a non-lossy compressed format, such as TIF or BMP.

8. You are now ready to use the image in Flash.

## Using the PanoPlayer

Once you have prepared an image for use in the PanoPlayer, you will find that it does not take very long to insert your images and start enjoying them in Flash. Insert the image, position it, set a few parameters, and you are ready to go. In this final CD-ROM exercise on the PanoPlayer, you will import an already prepared image into Flash for use with the PanoPlayer.

### CD-ROM Exercise

Open the file *panoplayer_sc.fla* located in the *F5gai/chapter15/* folder, installed from the companion CD-ROM. To import an image into Flash for use with the PanoPlayer, perform the following steps.

1. Once you have the *panoplayer_sc.fla* file open, the first thing to do is import a prepared panoramic image. Import the image *hovde3_ready.bmp* located in the *F5gai/chapter15/ pano_images/* folder.

2. When you import the file, it will automatically be placed on the stage. You do not want it on the main stage, so delete it.

3. Open the library.

4. Double click on the Image Container movie clip to access its timeline. In it you will notice an existing image.

5. Delete the existing image.

6. Delete the old image from the library.

7. Drag the *hovde3_ready.bmp* file from the library to the stage.

8. For the panoramic image to work, it must be placed in an exact position on the stage. Open the Info panel.

9. With the Info panel open, select the image and place its *x* at 0 and its *y* at negative one-half the height of the image. If the image is 240 pixels tall, its *y* should be at –120, as shown in figure 15-9.

10. With the image positioned, click on the *pano_MC* smart clip in the library to access its timeline.

11. Remember that this panoramic image should be displayed in a window that is 400 by 200 pixels. Now you must set the Dragger object and the mask object so that they are exactly that size. In the *pano_MC* smart clip, click on the Moveable Mask layer.

12. Access the Info panel and set the width of the object to 400 pixels and the height to 200 pixels.

13. Similar to the panoramic image, the *x* and *y* location of the Dragger movie clip must be 0 for *x* and negative, one-half the height for *y*. Thus, for this clip, *x* should be 0 and *y* should be –100.

*Figure 15-9 In the Image Container movie clip, exactly position the image on the stage using the Info panel.*

14. Hide the Moveable Mask layer.

15. Unlock the Static Mask layer.

16. Select the mask object on the stage and use the Info panel to make the width, height, and x and y settings of the mask match those of the Dragger (*width = 400*, *height = 200*, *x = 0*, and *y = –100*, respectively).

17. Lock the Static Mask layer and make all other layers visible.

18. Click on the Scene 1 link in the Edit Path to return to the main movie timeline.

19. Because you changed the size of the viewing window, you may need to reposition the smart clip on the stage.

20. The last thing you must do is set the Clip Parameters for the instance of the smart clip on the stage. Right-click on the *smart clip* instance on the stage and select Panels | Clip Parameters from the context menu.

21. You need to change the *imageWidth* value to the number you wrote down when you were working in Photoshop. If you forgot to write it down, you can retrieve the current width of the bitmap by double clicking on the image in Flash's library. Then subtract the width of the mask or Dragger to find out what the original width of the image was. Once you have the size, enter it in the Clip Parameters panel in the value field next to the *imageWidth* variable.

22. Close the Clip Parameters panel and use Test Movie to see your working panoramic image.

 **CD-ROM NOTE:** *A finished version of the previous CD-ROM exercise is included. Open the file* panoplayer_sc_finished.fla *located in the* F5gai/chapter15/ *folder, installed from the companion CD-ROM.*

A final note about the PanoPlayer is that you will find that it performs better if you do not allow the end user to scale the player stage. Playing any raster image too large will cause it to play less smoothly. If you want to ensure that users cannot scale the stage, add an FS Command action to the first frame of the main timeline. Use the Commands for Standalone Player drop-down list to select *allowscale*. Set the argument field to *false* instead of true.

 **NOTE:** *The Panoramic Image Player is predominantly based on movie clip properties. Macromedia has included two samples that demonstrate property control. Access the Help | Samples menu and select the Pan Zoom and Set Property examples.*

# ▪ ▪ ▪ **Noah's Memory Game**

The final exercise in this chapter is Noah's Memory Game. This game was actually first designed with FS commands, which you will explore in the next chapter. However, it presented a good opportunity to push ActionScript to the limit and really exhibit the complex things that can be done within Flash. It also makes a good learning opportunity by comparing an example done with ActionScript to one done with FS Command actions and JavaScript. As this book has stated throughout, if you have gotten really familiar with ActionScript and never used JavaScript, you should find that it will look and feel very familiar, for obvious reasons.

This example is indeed a complex one, and the scope of this book again limits an exhaustive analysis of the example. In the remainder of this chapter, you will examine the major things that make this example different from prior examples in this chapter.

Before dissecting the example, an overview is needed. The game does several things. First, there is a set of basic preloader frames used to show a progress bar while the game is loading. You reviewed this aspect in Chapter 10, so it will not be examined here. The game itself comprises sets of frames that contain 15 small doors, as shown in figure 15-10.

The goal of the game is to match a set of doors. As matches are made, a picture behind the doors is revealed. Once three matches are made, the player is prompted to guess at what the hidden animal is. They can either guess or continue matching until all doors are open. Whenever the user makes a guess, they are prompted whether they got it right or wrong. A right answer adds 1 to their score. A total of 10 background animals constitutes a game. However, the number of rounds of the game can be modified.

To make the game interesting, there are 31 animals that can appear behind the sets of doors, and the doors that are matched (of which there are also 31) change, depending on the current frame. There are 31 sets of frames in the timeline that

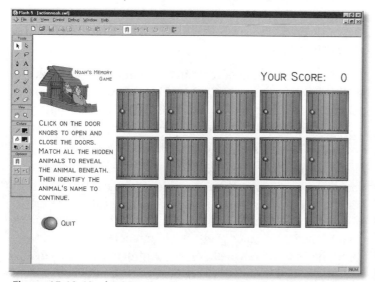

*Figure 15-10 Noah's Memory Game resembles the television game show Concentration!, except this game is for elementary children.*

correspond to the "behind the doors" animals. When the user starts the game, a random animal (set of frames) is selected using a function.

Once the user guesses the animal behind the doors, they are prompted as to whether they got it right or wrong. Then another random animal is chosen, the doors are closed, and they start matching again. Once 10 sets of doors (10 background animals) have been presented, the game shows a brief closing segment and tells the user how many animals they got right.

Before you start dissecting the game, note the architecture of the game, as shown in figure 15-11. The illustration is a flowchart of what happens in the game. You may want to refer to this chart as you progress through the discussion in the CD-ROM exercise that follows.

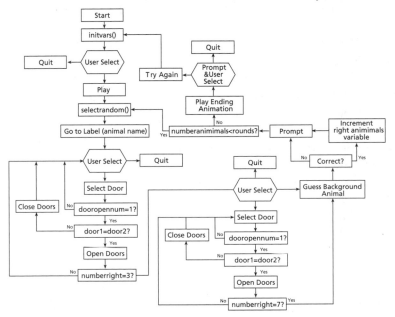

*Figure 15-11   A procedural flowchart for what happens in Noah's Memory Game.*

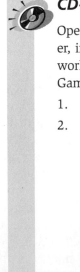

## CD-ROM Exercise

Open the file *actionnoah.fla* located in the *F5gai/chapter15/* folder, installed from the companion CD-ROM. Follow along as you work through this exercise. To examine how Noah's Memory Game works, perform the following steps.

1.  Use Test Movie to see how it works.

2.  In the game, there are several variables that are used to track various things. As with prior examples, the Global Functions layer contains functions that are called at various points in the movie. When the movie starts, the *initvars()* function is called. Let's begin by looking at the variables that are established. Access the actions associated with frame 51 of the Global Functions layer. Code example 15-14 shows the code from this function. For brevity, the inner content of the array has been omitted.

---

### Code Example 15-14 Variables Initialized in the initvars() Function

```
function initvars() {
        door1 = null;
        door2 = null
        dooropennum = 0;
        rightanimals = 0;
        numberanimals = 0;
        rounds=10;
        numberright = 0;
        answer = 0;
        animallist= new Array();
        animallist[0] = "Camel";
        ...
        animallist[30] = "Zebra";
}
```

As you can see in code example 15-14, several variables are defined when the *initvars()* function is called. Generally, this function is called only when the game starts. The first screen image the user is presented with is shown in figure 15-12. When the frame is encountered, the variables are initialized. The are also reinitialized when the user has completed the game and wishes to play again.

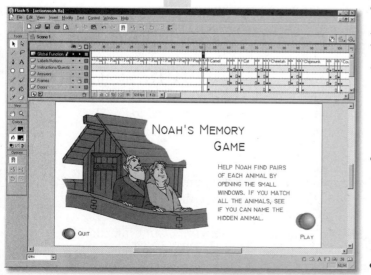

Figure 15-12 The initvars() function is called in the first frame of the game (frame 51).

The action in frame 51 of the Labels/Actions layer calls the function. The variables used in the game are:

- *door1* and *door2*: Used to store the instance name of the doors that are opened so that a comparison of them may be made at the proper time.

- *dooropennum*: Keeps track of how many doors are open at a single time. By using the value in this variable, the movie allows only two doors to be open at a single time.

- *rightanimals*: Used to store the number of background animals the user has correctly answered.

- *numberanimals*: Used to store the number of background animals the user has played.

- *rounds*: Determines the number of background animals the user must play; determines the number of rounds in the game.

- *numberright*: Keeps track of how many door matches the user has made in a single round. When *numberright* reaches 3 (three pairs of doors solved), the user is prompted to see if they can determine the background animal. When *numberright* reaches 7 (seven pairs of doors solved), it means all the matches have been made and one door remains closed. At this point, the remaining door is forced open and the user must determine the name of the background animal.

- *answer*: Used when the user guesses at a background animal. If he or she chooses the correct answer, answer is set to 1. If not, answer is set to 0.

- *animallist*: An array that holds the names of all background animals. When the user starts a round, a random number is generated and the corresponding array item (animal name) is pulled from the array. The user is then sent to that label name.

3.  Once the variables for the game are initialized, the game sits and waits for the user to press the Play button (see figure 15-12). When the user presses the Play button, a second function, *selectrandom()*, is called. This function generates a random number, pulls an animal name from the *animallist* array based on the random number, and then sends the user to the respective label in the movie that correlates to the animal name. The action attached to the Play button looks like the following:

```
gotoAndPlay (selectrandom());
```

Notice that the function call is placed within the *gotoAndPlay* method. Thus, this should tell you that the *selectrandom()* function will return something that will be used in the *gotoAndPlay* method. Indeed, the *selectrandom()* function returns an animal name, which is used in the *gotoAndPlay()* method. Code example 15-15 shows the code for the *selectrandom()* function.

### Code Example 15-15 Code for the selectrandom() Function

```
function selectrandom() {
      door1 = null;
      door2 = null;
      dooropennum = 0;
      numberright = 0;
      numberanimals++;
      var temp = Math.round(Math.random()*
animallist.length)
      myselection=animallist[temp]
      animallist.splice(temp, 1);
      return myselection;
}
```

In the *selectrandom()* function, note that it begins by resetting the *door1*, *door2*, *dooropennum*, and *numberright* variables. The first time *selectrandom()* is called, these variables do not really need to be reset because *initvars()* has just been called. However, the *selectrandom()* function is used multiple times (each time a new round begins). Thus, each time a new round begins, the variables related to each round do need to be reset. Thus, even though a reset is not necessary in the first round, it is in subsequent rounds of the game.

The next variable, *numberanimals*, keeps track of how many rounds (background animals) the user has played through. Thus, each time *selectrandom()* is called, it is a new round and the *numberanimals* variable is incremented. This variable is used later on to see how many rounds the user has played, so that they do not have to play through all 31 background animals.

The next four lines are the real "brains" of the *selectrandom()* function. The first of these four creates a local variable named *temp*, which is set equal to a random number generated between 0 and the number of items in the array *animallist*. The reason the length of *animallist* (the number of array items in *animallist*) is used for the upper limit for the random number is that once a particular background animal screen has been played, you do not want the user to play it again in the current game.

Each time a random animal's name is extracted from the array, the animal name will be deleted from the array. Thus, the length of the *animallist* array will change as you progress through the game, as will the upper limit for the random number.

The next line of code creates a global variable that will hold the value of the item pulled from the array. For example, if the random number generated from the previous line is 0 (temp = = 0), *myselection* would be set to the value found in the *animallist* array at index position 0 (*animallist[0]* = = "*camel*"). You access the values in an array by placing after the name of the array in square brackets ( [ ] ) the index number of the item you want to access. The value found there (*animallist[0]* ) is "*camel*" (see code example 15-14).

The next line of code removes the retrieved item ("*Camel*" ) from the array using the *splice()* method of the array object. This is done so that the user does not encounter the *camel* a second time as the background animal in the current game.

The last line, *return myselection*, returns the value of the variable *myselection* to whatever script called the *selectrandom()* function. Recall that *selectrandom()* was inserted into a *gotoAndPlay()* method. Thus, the *gotoAndPlay()* method would be *gotoAndPlay("camel")* when the value is returned from the *selectrandom()* function.

4. Once you are done looking at the *selectrandom()* function, minimize the Actions panel so that you can see the timeline.

5. Now that you know how the random animal is selected, let's examine one of the sets of frames that constitute one round of play (one background animal). Click on the frame named Camel (frame 53).

In each of the sets of animal screens, different doors appear. One of the most important items for planning and creating this game was a matrix showing which animals were on the stage at which times, as shown in table 15-1. When it came to editing, this chart was vital.

 **CD-ROM NOTE:** *A copy of the matrix in Excel format is available in the* F5gai/chapter15/ *folder, installed from the companion CD-ROM. The file containing the matrix is named* noah.xls.

6. Once in the Camel frame, right-click on the upper left door and select Panels | Instance from the context menu. Notice the instance name of the item, *Chipmunk1*. Also notice that it is referenced to the symbol named *Door-Chipmunk1*.

*Table 15-1  Matrix of Door Appearances on the Stage*

| X=Used / O=False Answer | Camel | Cat | Cheetah | Chipmunk | Cougar | Cow | Deer | Dog | Elephant | Fox | Frog | Giraffe | Gorilla | Hippopotamus | Kangaroo | Koala | Lamb | Lion | Monkey | Mouse | Panda | Pig | Porcupine | PrarieDog | Rabbit | Raccoon | Rhino | Squirrel | Tiger | Weasel | Wolf | Zebra |
|---|---|---|---|---|---|---|---|---|---|---|---|---|---|---|---|---|---|---|---|---|---|---|---|---|---|---|---|---|---|---|---|---|
| Camel | | | | | X | | | | X | | | | | O | | | X | | | | | | X | | X | | | | | X | | |
| Cat | | | O | | | | | X | | X | | | | | X | | | X | | | X | | | | | | | X | | | X | |
| Cheetah | | | | X | | X | | | | | X | | | X | | | O | | | | | | | X | | X | | | X | | | |
| Chipmunk | X | | | | | X | | X | | | | | | X | | | O | | | | | | | X | X | | | | X | | | |
| Cougar | | X | | | | | O | | X | | | | | | | | | | X | X | | | | | | | | X | | | | X |
| Cow | | | | X | X | | | | | X | | | X | | | | | | O | | | X | | | | X | | | | | X | |
| Deer | | | X | | | X | | | | | X | | | X | | | | | | O | | | X | | X | | | | X | | | |
| Dog | | | X | X | | | | | | | X | | | X | | | | X | | | O | | | | | | X | | | X | | |
| Elephant | X | | | | | X | | | X | | | | X | | | | X | | | | O | | | | X | | | | | | | X |
| Fox | | X | | | | | X | | | X | | | | X | | | | X | | | O | | X | | | | | | | | X | |
| Frog | | | X | | | X | | | | | X | X | | | | | | X | | | | O | | | X | | X | | | X | | |
| Giraffe | X | | | X | | | | | | X | | | | X | | | | X | | | | X | | | O | | | | | | X | |
| Gorilla | | | X | | O | | | | X | | | | | X | | | | X | | | | X | | | X | | | | | X | | |
| Hippopotamus | | X | | | X | | | | | X | | | | X | | X | | | | X | | | | | O | | | | | X | | |
| Kangaroo | | | X | | | X | | | | | X | | X | | | | | | | X | | | X | | | | O | | X | | | |
| Koala | | | X | | | | X | | X | | | | | X | | | | X | | | X | | | | | | | O | | X | | |
| Lamb | X | | | | | | | X | X | | | | | X | | X | | | | | | | X | | | X | | | | O | | |
| Lion | | | X | | | X | | | | | X | X | | | | | | | X | | | X | | | X | | | | | O | | |
| Monkey | | X | | | | | | X | X | | | | | O | | | | X | | | X | | | | | | | | X | | | X |
| Mouse | | | X | | | | X | | X | | | | X | | | | X | | | | | | | X | X | | | | | | O | |
| Panda | | | | O | | | | X | | | X | | | X | | | | | | X | | | X | | | X | | | | | | X |
| Pig | X | | | | O | | | | | X | | | | | X | | X | | | | | | X | | | | | | X | X | | |
| Porcupine | X | | | | X | | | | O | | | | | X | | | X | | X | | | | | | X | | | | | | X | |
| Prairie dog | | X | | | | | X | | | | X | | | | O | | | | X | | | | | X | | X | | | | | X | |
| Rabbit | | | X | | | | X | O | | | | | | X | | X | | | | | | | X | | | | | | X | | | X |
| Raccoon | | | | X | | | X | | O | | | | X | | | | | | | X | X | | | | X | | | | | X | | |
| Rhino | | O | | X | | | | | X | | | | | X | | X | | | | | | | X | | | | | X | X | | | |
| Squirrel | O | | | | | | | X | | X | | | X | | | | | X | | X | | | | | | X | | | | | X | |
| Tiger | | | X | | | X | | | | | O | | | X | | | | X | | X | | | X | | X | | | | | | | X |
| Weasel | | | X | X | | | | | | X | | | | X | | | | | X | X | | | | | | | | X | | | | O |
| Wolf | | X | | | | O | | | | | X | | | X | | | | X | | | | | X | | X | | | X | | | | X |
| Zebra | X | | | | | | | X | | X | | | O | | | | | X | | | | | | | X | | | X | | X | | |

7. Now click on the fourth door in the bottom row of doors. Notice that its instance name is *Chipmunk2* and the symbol it is referenced to is the same as the prior door, *Door-Chipmunk1*.

When the user opens two doors, the instance names are compared to see if they match. If they do, the doors are opened. If not, the doors are closed. Because the instance names are what is compared, both instances of the door can be based on the same symbol. In each screen of doors, there are seven doors that have a match and one door that is the odd (or discriminator) door.

The table 15-1 matrix shows the doors that appear in each background animal screen. The odd door is shown with an O (capital "oh"). Now let's look inside one of the door symbols to see how they are made. In Chapter 14, you saw how the door was constructed. Here, you have added a bit of code to give it some intelligence.

8. Right-click on the upper left-hand door (*Chipmunk1*) and select Edit in Place to access its timeline.

9. In Chapter 14, you saw the basics of how this "button" was created. The important part is to look at the actions assigned to frames 5 and 9 in the Labels/Actions layer. Maximize the Actions panel and select frame 5. Code example 15-16 shows the code associated with frame 5. The code found here is the same in every door symbol.

---

### Code Example 15-16 *Code Associated with Frame 5 of the* Door-Chipmunk1 *Movie Clip*

```
if (_root.dooropennum==0) {
    _root.door1 = _name
    _root.dooropennum++
    stop();
} else if (_root.dooropennum==1) {
    _root.door2 = _name
    _root.checkdoor();
}
```

If you recall from Chapter 14, the button is set up so that it stops in the first frame. When the user clicks on the *door knob* trigger, the move plays to frame 5. When the symbol reaches frame 5, it checks with the main movie timeline to see what the value of the variable *dooropennum* is. If *dooropennum* equals 0, no doors are currently open. If *dooropennum* equals 1, a door is currently open.

If the script in code example 15-16 finds that *dooropennum* is 0, it stores its own instance name in the main movie timeline's variable *door1*. It also increments the variable *dooropennum* to 1, signifying that there is a door currently open. It then stops. If *dooropennum* is equal to 1, meaning that there is already a door open, the script stores its own instance name in the main movie timeline's variable *door2*. It then calls the function *checkdoor()* in the main movie timeline. This function actually does the comparison between the door names and then takes appropriate action.

As you proceed, realize that the script in frame 5 exists in every door symbol. Thus, each time a door is opened on the stage, the conditions shown in code example 15-16 are checked.

Before you look at the *checkdoor()* function, let's also look at the actions in frame 9. The actions in frame 9 are in case the user decides to shut a door. This can happen (where the user willfully shuts a door) only if there are no other doors open. The minute a second door is opened, the scripting takes over and does not allow the user to do anything.

10. Click on frame 9 and use the Actions panel to view the actions there. Code example 15-17 shows the actions found in frame 9.

## *Code Example 15-17  Actions in Door Symbols at Frame 9*

```
_root.door1 = null;

_root.dooropennum=0;

gotoAndStop ("Closed");
```

You will recall from Chapter 13 that when the door is open, a trigger exists that allows the user to shut the door. In the game, if the user shuts a door after they have opened it, a couple of the variables must be cleared out. Specifically, if the user shuts an open door, the *door1* and *dooropennum* variables must be reset. The *dooropennum* variable is the important one, because if it is not reset to 0, when the user opens the next door, the *checkdoors()* function will try to do an erroneous comparison.

Now let's look at the script that is the real "brains" of the game. The *checkdoor()* function is where the names of the two open doors are compared to see if they match. The script does a simple string comparison. If the names match, the two doors are told to go to the solved frame inside them. This frame is basically a blank frame. It is blank so that a portion of the background animal becomes visible. If the door names do not match, they are automatically forced back to their closed position.

11. Click on the Scene 1 link in the Edit Path.

12. Access the actions associated with frame 51.

13. Scroll down the list of actions and find the section named *checkdoor()*. The code for this function is shown in code example 15-18.

## *Code Example 15-18 Code for the* checkdoor() *Function*

```
function checkdoor() {
    var doorlength1 = door1.length-1;
    var tdoor1 = door1.substring(0, doorlength1);
    var tdoor2 = door2.substring(0, doorlength1);
    if (tdoor1==tdoor2) {
      numberright += 1
      tellTarget("_level0/" + door1) {
        gotoAndStop ("Solved");
      }
        tellTarget("_level0/" + door2) {
          gotoAndStop ("Solved");
        }
        if (numberright==3) {
        play();
        } else if (numberright==7) {
        play();
        }
    } else {
        tellTarget("_level0/" + door1) {
            play();
        }
        tellTarget("_level0/" + door2) {
            play();
        }
    }
    dooropennum=0;
    door1 = null;
    door2 = null;
}
```

The *checkdoor()* function uses the values of the *door1* and *door2* variables to see if the two doors that were opened are the same. Recall that if the two doors match, the only difference between their names should be the ending element (*Chipmunk1* versus *Chipmunk2*). Thus, to compare the doors, the first thing the *checkdoor()* function does is determine the length of *door1* (the number of characters in its value) and subtracts 1 from it.

The *checkdoor()* function then places the result in a local variable named *doorlength*. Then, using the variables *door1* and *door2*, the string object is used to extract the name portion of the doors based on the value in *doorlength*. The result is placed in two more local variables: *tdoor1* (truncated door1) and *tdoor2* (truncated door2). The variables for *tdoor1* and *tdoor2* are then compared.

If as a result of the comparison *tdoor1* and *tdoor2* have the same content, the *numberright* variable is immediately incremented, signifying that the user has matched a pair of doors. Then, the door instances (*door1* and *door2*) are told to go to their respective frames named *"Solved"*. This reveals a portion of the background animal.

The next section of code generally causes some confusion. When you tested the movie, recall that once you had made three door matches you were provided the opportunity to guess at the background animal, as shown in figure 15-13. The next section of code is what makes this happen. If *numberright* is found to be equal to 3, the main movie timeline is told to *play()*. If you were playing the *"Camel"* background animal, the *play()* method would cause the main movie to progress from frame 60 to frame 61, giving you an opportunity to guess at the background animal.

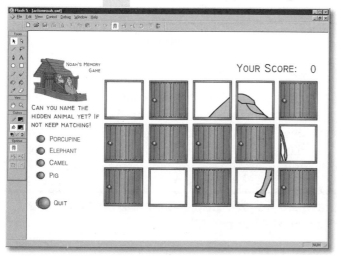

*Figure 15-13    Once three matches have been made (numberright=3), the user is given the opportunity to guess at the background animal by telling the main movie timeline to play.*

The second part of the previously mentioned *if* statement checks to see if *numberright* == 7. If *numberright* is found to be equal to 7, it means you have matched all doors that can be matched. Only one odd door remains. At that point, the end user must guess at the animal because there are no more doors to match. Similar to when *numberright* equals 3, the main movie timeline is told to play. If you were in the *"Camel"* set of frames, the playhead would move from frame 61 to frame 63, and the user would have to guess at the animal, as shown in figure 15-14.

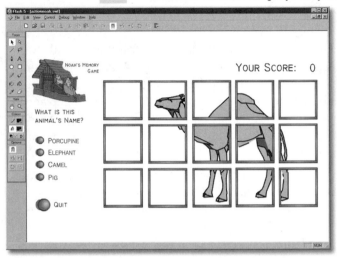

Note that because the name of the odd door changes in each background animal, the actions that cause the final door to open are actually contained in next-to-last frame of whatever animal you are playing. For example, in the *"Camel"* set of frames, the script that causes the odd door to open (which is *squirrel*) is located in frame 63.

*Figure 15-14    Once seven matches have been made (numberright=7), there are no more doors to be matched. Thus, the user is forced to answer the question.*

To complete the analysis of the *checkdoors()* function, notice the last part of the main *if* statement. If *tdoor1* does not equal *tdoor2* (a mismatch), the two open doors are simply told to close. In addition, regardless of whether the doors match or do not match, when the script ends, it resets the values of *door1*, *door2*, and *dooropennum*.

14. The last thing to analyze as it relates to an individual screen of play is the what happens when you answer the prompt in figure 15-13 or figure 15-14. Code example 15-19 shows the code associated with the correct answer, and code example 15-20 shows the code associated with the incorrect answer.

### Code Example 15-19 Code Associated with the Correct Animal Name

```
on (release, releaseOutside) {
  rightanimals++;
  answer = 1;
  gotoAndPlay (myselection+"A");
}
```

**TIP:** *On buttons it is usually a good idea to set the event handler to both release and releaseOutside.*

If the user selects the correct animal name under the conditions shown in either figure 15-13 or figure 15-14, the first thing that is done is to increment the *rightanimals* variable. This global variable keeps track of how many right background animals the user has correctly identified. The field in the upper right-hand corner, to the left of the text *Your Score:*, is also associated with the *rightanimals* variable.

Then the answer variable is set to 1 and the main movie timeline is told to *gotoAndPlay(myselection + "A")*. In a moment you will see how the *answer* variable is used. As for the variable *myselection*, remember that the variable *myselection* was set back in the *selectrandom()* function and is the name of the current background animal. The last frame of every set of animal frames is a frame labeled with the animal's name plus an *A* at the end (for *answer*). Thus, in the *"Camel"* section, the last frame is *CamelA*.

## Code Example 15-20  Code Associated with the Incorrect Name of the Animal

```
on (release, releaseOutside) {
    answer = 0;
    gotoAndPlay (myselection+"A");
}
```

Code example 15-20, like the code for the correct response, sets the *answer* variable and tells the main movie timeline to go to the answer label. The only thing the incorrect answer does not do is increment the *rightanimals* variable.

15. To finish looking at the frames associated with one round of play, access the *CamelA* frame (frame 64).

16. In the frame, which both the correct and incorrect responses send you to, you will find an action associated with the frame. Use the Actions panel to view the actions. Code example 15-21 shows the code. The code in the answer frame of each animal sets up the frame to display Right or Wrong, depending on the user's response to the question.

## Code Example 15-21  Code for Animal Answer Frames

```
if (answer == 0) {
    with(RW) {
        gotoAndPlay ("Wrong");
    }
} else {
    with(RW) {
        gotoAndPlay ("Right");
    }
}
stop ();
```

In the code in code example 15-21, you see that the *answer* variable, which was set in both the *right* and *wrong* answer buttons in the previous frames, is used. If *answer* equals 0 (an incorrect answer), a movie clip named *RW* in the current frame is told to go to label *"Wrong"*. If *answer* equals 1 (a correct answer), a movie clip named *RW* in the current frame is told to go to label *"Right"*. As shown in figure 15-15, there is an invisible movie clip on the stage. Notice the small circle in the lower part of the screen.

— The "invisible" movie clip

*Figure 15-15  An invisible movie clip is used to change the look of the last screen, based on the value in the* answer *variable.*

The small, blank movie clip that starts out blank is told by the *if* statement in the frame action to go to a specific frame, based on the value in *answer*. This is what allows a single frame to be used for both a correct and an incorrect response. Figure 15-16 shows the results of a correct response (a) and an incorrect response (b).

**NOTE:** *You may want to examine the movie clip named Right/Wrong to better understand the RW instance, or the movie clip named Score to better understand the Score instance.*

*Figure 15-16 The results of (a) a correct response and (b) an incorrect response.*

17. To this point, you have looked at the scripting through one round of play. Once the user has completed one round (and regardless of whether they got the answer correct), the Next button, shown in figure 15-16, is used to continue game play until 10 rounds have been executed. Code example 15-22 shows the code that makes this determination.

## Code Example 15-22  Code Associated with the Next Button

```
on (release, releaseOutside) {
    if (numberanimals<rounds) {
        gotoAndPlay (selectrandom());
    } else {
        gotoAndPlay ("Ending");
    }
}
```

As shown in code example 15-22, the Next button compares the *numberanimals* variable to the *rounds* variable. Recall that *numberanimals* is incremented each time the *selectrandom()* function is called. The *rounds* variable is a constant that was set in the *initvars()* function. If the number of background animals the user has played is less than the number of rounds specified, the *selectrandom()* function is called, similar to the action associated with the Play button in the first frame of the movie. If the user has played the number of rounds specified in the *rounds* variable, he or she is sent to the frame labeled *"Ending"*.

18. If you access the timeline and find the frame labeled *"Ending"* (frame 429), you will notice that there is a brief animation that plays.

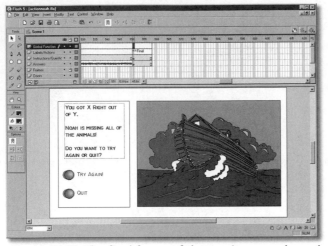

Figure 15-17 *The final frame of the movie uses a dynamic text field to provide feedback to the user.*

19. Scroll further down the timeline and find the frame labeled *"Final"* (at frame 551). Figure 15-17 shows the final frame of the game.

20. Access the actions associated with the Labels/Actions layer in frame 551. Code example 15-23 shows this script. The actions associated with frame 551 change the text in the dynamic text field using the values in the *numberanimals* and *rightanimals* variables.

## Code Example 15-23   Actions Associated with the Labels/Actions Layer in Frame 551

```
if (rightanimals>=0 && rightanimals <=.3*rounds) {

    myfield="You got " + rightanimals + " right out
of " + (numberanimals-1) + ".\r\nNoah is missing a
lot of animals!\r\nDo you want to try again or
quit?"

} else if (rightanimals>.3*rounds && rightanimals
<=.6*rounds) {

        myfield="You got " + rightanimals + " right
out of " + (numberanimals-1) + ".\r\nNoah is missing
a several animals!\r\nDo you want to try again or
quit?"

} else if (rightanimals>.6*rounds && rightanimals
<rounds) {

        myfield="You got " + rightanimals + " right
out of " + (numberanimals-1) + ".\r\nNoah is a few
animals short!\r\nDo you want to try again or quit?"

} else if (rightanimals=rounds) {

        myfield="You got all " + (numberanimals-1) +
```

```
" of the animals correct.\r\nVery Well done!\r\nDo
you want to try again or quit?"
}
stop ();
stopAllSounds ();
```

As shown in code example 15-23, depending on how many background animals the user answered correctly, appropriate feedback is provided. Note the use of the special characters (\r for carriage return and \n for line feed) in the string assignments for entering a blank line after each sentence. The variable *myfield* is used by a dynamic text field located on the stage (see figure 15-17). By updating it, the text on the stage is displayed, as shown in figure 15-18.

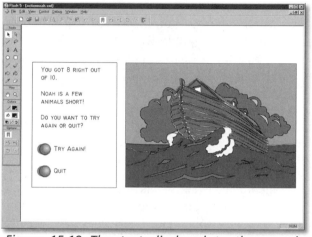

*Figure 15-18 The text displayed to the user is dynamically generated, based on how many answers they answered correctly.*

The last script to examine is the code associated with the Try Again! button. With the Actions panel open, click on the Try Again! button on the stage. The code attached to the button is shown in code example 15-24.

## Code Example 15-24 Code Associated with the Try Again! Button

```
on (release, releaseOutside) {
    delete(animallist);
    initvars();
    gotoAndPlay (selectrandom());
}
```

If the user decides to play the game a second time, three things happen, as shown in code example 15-24. Recall that as the *selectrandom()* function was called, animal names (array items) were deleted from the array so that the user did not encounter the same animal twice. To replay the game with all animals included, you must reinitialize the *animallist* array so that all items will be in it. Before you can do this, it is important that you first remove the old array item from memory. Thus, *delete(animallist)* clears the old array from memory. Then you call the *initvars()* function again and use the *selectrandom()* function, as you did in the first frame of the game.

Indeed, this exercise has been lengthy and somewhat complex. However, it just goes to show that Flash can now do just about anything. As has been stated elsewhere, Flash is now on the same level as Director, in that there is almost nothing you cannot do with Flash.

 **NOTE:** *Macromedia has included a sample game with Flash. Access the Help | Samples | Mosquito Killer menu option to view this example.*

# ▪ ▪ ▪ **Summary**

In this chapter, you have examined many of the important aspects of using ActionScript. Of primary importance is an understanding of the basic programming constructs: variables, strings, expressions, operators, functions, and properties. You discovered in the coloring book exercise how a coloring example could be created using the *array* object and the *color* object. The puzzle game demonstrated how to use and set properties, as well as how to detect the *_droptarget* property. The PanoPlayer demonstrated how you can simulate even relatively complex applications within Flash.

Finally, the memory game discussed random number generation and the use of arrays and functions. In the next chapter, you will again revisit some of these examples. However, they will be created using FlashScript Command actions and JavaScript rather than the ActionScript language of Flash. Again, these two advanced capabilities (ActionScript and FlashScript/ JavaScript) are vital for the intermediate to advanced developer who wishes to push the envelope and be more than a novice developer.

# 16

# Flash Player Methods and Browser Scripting

### ■ ■ ■ Introduction

Before ActionScript, most of the programming intelligence of web pages that used Flash had to rely on JavaScript or VBScript. In general, you would pass data out of Flash using the FS Command action. JavaScript or VBScript could be made to interpret and use the data, as well as to control a Flash element using Flash Player methods.

However, as you have seen throughout this book, there is much you can now do within Flash. In fact, there is really no limit to what you can do. When there was talk of advanced scripting capability within Flash, many developers feared the techniques that used Flash Player commands would no longer work. However, prior techniques with combinations of the FS Command action, Flash Player methods, and JavaScript or VBScript still work as before. This is refreshing, because it allows you to choose which method to use based on time, task, resources, and know-how.

This chapter provides a basic overview of using the FS Command action to call external JavaScript and VBScript functions. The primary focus is on using the FS Command action and Flash Player methods, not JavaScript. There are myriad books on the market that cover JavaScript, and you should explore these resources for further information.

However, this chapter serves as a basic JavaScript primer. The techniques presented in this chapter cover common tasks, such as opening pop-up windows, detecting various browser objects, and other functions.

# ▪▪▪ Objectives

In this chapter, you will:

- Obtain an general understanding of JavaScript and how it works
- Examine simple code examples for performing common tasks
- Examine how FlashScript commands can be used to pass data to JavaScript, as well as to initiate functions
- Learn about the Flash Player methods that can be used in JavaScript code to control a Flash movie
- Examine three applied examples of movies that interact with JavaScript

# ▪▪▪ A JavaScript Primer

JavaScript is a cross-platform scripting language that adds extended scripting capability to web pages. JavaScript can be used to do many things in addition to its uses associated with Flash elements.

In this chapter you will be examining client-side JavaScript. However, JavaScript can also be used as server-side scripting, usually as part of JavaScript Server Pages (JSP). JSP pages use JavaScript just as ASP (Active Server Pages) use VBScript. The main advantage of JPS over ASP is that JSP is not dependent on Microsoft Internet Information Server (MIIS). You will recall that if you want to use ASP on a UNIX server, you must obtain additional software for it to run. JSP, on the other hand, requires Java support only.

 **TIP:** *For an overview of client-side vs. server-side JavaScript and how they relate to the core JavaScript language, see* http://developer. netscape.com/viewsource/husted_js/husted_js.html.

Like most scripting languages, JavaScript is much easier to pick up than programming languages such as Java, PERL, or CGI. Throughout the previous chapters of this book, although you were working with ActionScript, it is actually modeled after JavaScript. Thus, as you begin this chapter you should find that JavaScript is very familiar, even if you have not used it before. The main difference you will find is that JavaScript provides access to additional objects you can work with in the HTML environment. HTML objects (such as the browser window, the HTML document in the window, and forms and other items) have methods, properties, and events associated with them that you can utilize.

 **TIP:** *For a detailed description of the JavaScript object hierarchy, see* http://developer.netscape.com/viewsource/goodman_roadmap/ goodman_roadmap.html.

As discussed in Chapter 6, methods, properties, and event handlers constitute an object. Just as all elements in ActionScript conform to this rule, so too do elements in regard to JavaScript. The primary difference you will find between JavaScript and core JavaScript is that the general JavaScript capabilities are much more expansive. That is, there are many more methods, properties, and event handlers you must be aware of.

In addition, there certain features of the JavaScript language that are custom to specific browsers. JavaScript is officially in version 1.3. However, browser manufacturers often add their own custom support for certain features. Thus, you do have to be careful what JavaScript methods, properties, or event handlers you use. This is probably the thing that makes working with JavaScript the most difficult: making it work seamlessly in both browsers. The previous tip points to a chart by Danny Goodman that describes the meticulous features of the JavaScript language and with what versions of the browser the features are compatible.

 **TIP:** *See* http://developer.netscape.com/docs/manuals/js/client/ js-guide/index.htm, *which provides an online book detailing the client-side JavaScript 1.3 language.*

In addition to the URLs previously presented, as you start working with JavaScript you may wish to examine the following resources:

- The JavaScript Source: *http://javascript.internet.com/*
- JavaScript.com: *http://www.javascript.com/*
- Ask the JavaScript Pro: *http://www.inquiry.com/techtips/js_pro/*
- WebCoder.com: *http://www.webcoder.com/*
- Doc JavaScript: *http://www.webreference.com/js/*
- Website Abstraction: *http://www.wsabstract.com/*
- JavaScript World: *http://www.jsworld.com/*

 **TIP:** *Perhaps the best book on JavaScript is the* JavaScript Bible, *by Danny Goodman (ISBN 0-7645-3188-3). This book is very well written and provides many sample scripts.*

# ▪ ▪ ▪ Writing JavaScript Code in Web Pages

JavaScript code can be integrated into a web page in one of two ways. Functions can be written almost anywhere in the document, but usually reside at the top of the HTML page, in the < HEAD > section. For example, a JavaScript function to open a pop-up window would look something like the script in code example 16-1.

### Code Example 16-1  JavaScript for Opening a Pop-up Window

```
<HTML>
<HEAD><TITLE>Pop-up Windows</TITLE>
<SCRIPT LANGUAGE="JavaScript">
<!--
function instructions() {
  iwin = window.open("popup.html","IWIN",

  "status=no,toolbar=no,location=no,menu=no,height=200,width
=300");
}
//-->
</SCRIPT>
</HEAD>
<BODY>
<H1>Pop-up Window</H1>
<HR>
This page demonstrates the use of a <A
HREF="javascript:instructions();">pop-up window</a>. The
window is created when the link is clicked, and disappears
when the OK button is pressed inside the window.
<HR>
</BODY>
</HTML>
```

The scripting in code example 16-1 should look quite familiar. Only a few things differ from coding you have already seen in Flash. Notice the opening and closing <SCRIPT> section. Note that the opening <SCRIPT> tag defines the type of scripting (JavaScript, VBScript, and so on). Between the <SCRIPT> tags are the <!-- and //--> tags. These two sets of tags are a safety net for older browsers, in case the user's browser cannot handle the scripting. The <!-- and --> tags are used to add comments to HTML code. The browser will typically ignore information between these tags. The double slash (//) is how you create a comment in JavaScript, so that the script interpreter does not try to read the --> tag.

 **NOTE:** *Although this code does not show it, you should also add the <NOSCRIPT> tag at the end of the file. Then add your own normal HTML coding to let the user know that they need to update their browser to see the scripting. The <NOSCRIPT> tag is similar to the <NOFRAMES> tag. Both are a means of providing information to older browsers.*

The actual JavaScript function (which opens a pop-up dialog box) is found between the comment tags. JavaScript functions begin with the word *function*, then the name of the function and opening and closing curly brackets ({}). The code that falls between can be any valid JavaScript code you want executed. All of this should be familiar to you, as it is written the same as ActionScript within Flash.

Realize that just because a function is written into a document's <HEAD> section does not mean it is automatically executed. As you will recall from previous Flash examples, something has to call the function. You can initiate JavaScript functions from just about anywhere. You can call the function from within an anchor tag, as shown in code example 16-1, or you can use JavaScript event handlers, which are much like Flash's event handlers. The line of code that reads *< A HREF="javascript:instructions();" >* could also be written as *< A HREF="#" onClick="instructions();" >*.

This alternative method uses the *onClick* JavaScript event handler to call the function. The pound sign in the HREF attribute satisfies the browser's need for something in the HREF attribute. Here, the JavaScript function would be interpreted, rather than the HREF element. JavaScript includes many event handlers, including *onClick*, *onLoad*, *onFocus*, and several others. You will find that there are many different ways to do the same thing in JavaScript.

 **CD-ROM NOTE:** *The companion CD-ROM includes a few examples of things people commonly want to know how to do in JavaScript. See the* index.html *file located in the* F5gai/chapter16/javascript/ *folder, installed from the companion CD-ROM. Subsequent folders that can be accessed from the file contain a variety of JavaScript examples.*

Although you can use JavaScript to call its own functions, when you are using FS Command actions from Flash, Flash calls the function. Thus, a web page that contains a Flash element that opens a pop-up window might look like the scripting shown in code example 16-2.

## Code Example 16-2  Code for a Flash Element That Opens a Pop-up Window

```
<HTML>
<HEAD><TITLE>Pop-up Windows</TITLE>
<SCRIPT LANGUAGE="JavaScript">
function button_DoFSCommand(command, args){
 var URL=window.location.href
 var mylocation=unescape(URL.substring(0,(URL.lastInd
```

```
exOf("/"))+1));
iwin=window.open(mylocation+"popup.html","IWIN",
"status=no,toolbar=no,location=no,menu=no,height=200,width
=300");
}
</SCRIPT>
<SCRIPT LANGUAGE="VBScript">
// Map VB script events to the JavaScript method—Netscape
will ignore this...
Sub button_FSCommand(ByVal command,ByVal args)
      call button_DoFSCommand(command,args)
end sub
</SCRIPT>
</HEAD>
<BODY>
<H1>Pop-up Window</H1>
<HR>
<P>Use the button below to open the pop-up window. Examine
the JavaScript code associated with this movie to see how
it works.
<center>
<OBJECT ID="button" CLASSID="clsid:D27CDB6E-AE6D-11cf-96B8-
444553540000"
CODEBASE="http://active.macromedia.com/flash2/cabs/swflash.
cab#version=5,0,0,0" WIDTH="56" HEIGHT="33">
<PARAM NAME="Movie" VALUE="ch16-01.swf">
<PARAM NAME="Play" VALUE="false">
<PARAM NAME="Quality" VALUE="best">
<PARAM NAME="menu" VALUE="false">
<EMBED NAME="button" mayscript="mayscript" SRC="ch16-
01.swf" swLiveConnect="true" WIDTH="56" HEIGHT="33"
salign="t" quality="best" play="false" menu="false"
TYPE="application/x-shockwave-flash" plug-
inspage="http://www.macromedia.com/shockwave/download/index
.cgi?P1_Prod_Version=ShockwaveFlash">
</EMBED>
</OBJECT>
</center>
<HR>
</BODY>
</HTML>
```

As shown in code example 16-2, the code for opening a pop-up window is a little more complicated than the previous example. First, note that there are two <SCRIPT> sections. The JavaScript section is read only by Netscape, and the VBScript section is read only by Internet Explorer. For Internet Explorer to be able to use commands sent from Flash, it must map its native VBScript commands to JavaScript. Thus the reason for the two <SCRIPT> sections. Code example 16-2 also reveals that all functions called by FS Command actions must be written in the form of:

```
function objectIdorName_DoFSCommand (command, args) {
        JavaScript commands

    . . .

}
```

Note in code example 16-2 that *Button* is the Object ID specified in the <OBJECT> tag, and is also the *Name* specified in the <EMBED> tag. For the function to respond to the FS Command action, you must make sure the function name uses the Object ID or Embed Name of the Flash file. The Object ID and Embed Name should be named consistently in every pair of <OBJECT> and <EMBED> tags. Two other lines you have not seen before are the following:

```
var URL = window.location.href
var mylocation =
unescape(URL.substring(0,(URL.lastIndexOf("/")) + 1));
```

To get Netscape to open a file into a pop-up window, you must use these lines of code. Note that the value of the variable *mylocation* precedes the HTML that is defined into the *window.open* function, as follows:

```
iwin = window.open(mylocation + "popup.html","IWIN",
"status=no,toolbar=no,location=no,menu=no,height=200,width=
300");
```

If you do not include these two lines of code, Internet Explorer will open the page, whereas Netscape just sits there. If you do include the lines, both browsers will open the related pop-up window.

Flash developers also typically want to know how to detect the Flash 5 plug-in, as well as other browser settings. Macromedia's web site details how to detect the Flash 5 plug-in (TechNote #14526) at *http://www.macromedia. com/support/flash/ts/documents/uber_detection.htm*. You may also want to review information about the Flash Deployment Kit, at *http://www. macromedia.com/support/flash/player/flash_deployment_readme/*.

# ■ ■ ■ The FS Command Method Versus Flash Player Methods

Usually when you start talking about FS Command actions in Flash, many people misunderstand what they are and what they are used for. Before moving into some examples, you need to understand the distinction between the FS Command method (or action) and the Flash Player methods that can be used outside Flash.

 **NOTE:** *Throughout this section, keep in mind that Macromedia simply calls the FS Command element in Flash an action. This text uses the OOP term method.*

The FS Command method in Flash is used to send data out of Flash to JavaScript or other technologies. In essence, the FS Command method causes a single JavaScript function to automatically execute when the FS Command is encountered in the Flash movie. The Flash Player knows that it should respond to an FS Command from a Flash movie because it has an event handler named FS Command. Remember that event handlers are things that happen in an environment that a particular object knows it should respond to.

Flash Player methods, on the other hand, are used in JavaScript to control, as well as send data into, a Flash movie. As you learned previously, a method is a predefined thing an object can do in the environment or to itself. The Flash Player, which in the browser is a plug-in or ActiveX component, is an object and indeed it has many methods you can use to manipulate any Flash movies in the current web page.

Similarly, the Flash Player has events, one of which is the FS Command event, which allows it to respond to the FS Command method called within Flash (as well as other things that may happen in the browser environment). In short, the FS Command method is for communication from Flash to JavaScript. Flash Player methods are for communication from JavaScript to Flash.

## The FS Command Method in Flash

Let's focus on the FS Command method for a moment. When you have a Flash movie embedded in a web page, you can define a JavaScript function in the HTML document that is directly related to the Flash movie. The JavaScript function associated with the Flash movie will be called anytime an FS Command is encountered in the Flash file. Thus, for each Flash movie in a web page, you can have one, and only one, function defined in JavaScript for it. A single Flash movie cannot have two associated JavaScript functions.

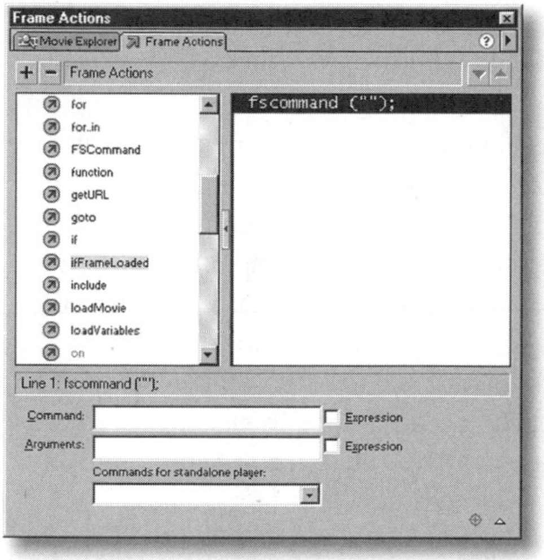

*Figure 16-1    The FS Command action provides two variables that can be passed to JavaScript:* command *and* arguments.

"Then how do you set up JavaScript code that will do different things for (or within) the same movie," you might ask. For example, if a Flash movie has two different buttons and you want each to do something different, how do you write the code, in that you can only have one JavaScript function per embedded Flash movie?

The answer is that the FS Command method has two values that can be sent from Flash to the associated JavaScript function. One value is contained in a variable named *command*, and the other is in a variable named *arguments* (usually abbreviated *args*), as shown in figure 16-1.

Whether or not these fields have data in them, when the FS Command method is encountered in the movie, the associated JavaScript function in the web page will execute the scripting contained within it. Keep in mind that it knows to do so because the Flash Player (plug-in or ActiveX component) has an event handler set up to handle the FS Command call from the Flash movie. As long as everything is named correctly, the Flash Player will automatically execute a function associated with a Flash movie. It is through properly naming the JavaScript function, as well as the Flash movie, that makes the entire scenario work. (This aspect is discussed in greater detail later in the chapter.)

If you want a single function to do different things for different items within the JavaScript function associated with it, you use the *command* and *args* variables to send data out of Flash. Then, in the JavaScript function, you write an *if* statement whose condition is based on either the *command* or *args* variable. Note that the *command* variable is the one normally used, but either variable do the same thing. Let's dissect a quick example to drive this point home.

### Working with the FS Command Method

To better understand the FS Command method, in the following CD-ROM exercise you will examine the button used in the previous code sample (code example 16-2).

---

### CD-ROM Exercise

Open the file *ch16-01.fla* located in the *F5gai/chapter16/* folder, installed from the companion CD-ROM.

1.  Right-click the button on the stage and select the Actions | FS Command method attached to the object, as shown in figure 16-1.

As you examine the FS Command method in figure 16-1, realize that the Command and Arguments fields correspond with the *command* and *args* variables within the JavaScript function (see code example 16-2). Generally, the *command* and *args* functions are used to simply pass name and value pairs to JavaScript. However, if you just want the JavaScript function to execute, no values are needed in the *command* and *args* variables. When values are present, JavaScript can do something intelligent with the variables, such as using a conditional statement to interpret the received values and respond accordingly.

2.  Once an FS Command action is set up in Flash, you are ready to implement it within the web page. Again, when you set up your JavaScript code, you must make sure the Class ID and Embed Name attributes are similar so that you can write one function for the object. Open the file *index.html* located in the *F5gai/chapter16/ch16-01/* folder, installed from the companion CD-ROM. Load this into a text editor such as Notepad or Simpletext.

3.  In the HTML file, notice that the ID attribute of the < OBJECT > tag and the Name attribute of the < EMBED > tag match. If they do not match, problems will arise later. Verify that these match.

4.  Also notice how the object and the embedded name are used in the JavaScript function: *button_DoFSCommand*. Whatever the Flash movie's name is, it needs to precede *_DoFSCommand*. Verify that this is the case.

5.  Finally, note in the VBScript code section that the name is used two more times. In all of these instances, the name of the Flash movie, followed by *_FSCommand*, must be written exactly as shown. Verify that this is the case.

6.  In the < EMBED > tag, notice the attributes *LIVECONNECT = "TRUE"* and *MAYSCRIPT = "MAYSCRIPT"*. In Netscape, LiveConnect is used to allow the Flash Player plug-in to talk to the Java Interpreter. You must include these two attributes in the < EMBED > tag for Netscape to be able to utilize the Flash Player methods and JavaScript. If you forget them, Netscape will just sit there and will not respond to any FS

Command methods in the Flash movie. Note that these attributes are not needed in the < OBJECT > tag section. Verify that these two attributes are present.

**CD-ROM NOTE:** *To see the button from the previous CD-ROM exercise work in the web page, open the* file index.html *located in the* F5gai/chapter16/ch16-01/ *folder, installed from the companion CD-ROM. Load this file into a browser.*

### Specific Commands for the Stand-alone Player

As you were setting up the FS Command method in the last exercise, you may have noticed the *Commands for stand-alone player* drop-down list associated with the FS Command method. Although most of the movies you develop in Flash may be for the Web, you can use the FS Command method to send specific commands to the stand alone Flash Player. In Chapter 9, you examined how you could play an *.swf* file in the Player, as well as create a projector file of your movie. The *Commands for stand alone player* drop-down list is for movies you intend to distribute in either of these two ways. Descriptions of the options found in the *Commands for stand alone player* drop-down follow.

- *fullscreen* is a binary variable that determines if the movie scales to fit the screen.
- *allowscale* determines if the user is permitted to scale the movie during playback. It is a binary variable.
- *showmenu* defines whether or not the Flash Player menu is displayed and is a binary variable.
- *trapallkeys* is a binary variable that controls whether or not the Flash Player locks all keyboard strokes.
- *exec* opens external files and runs external programs. The Args field must contain a path to an application or program file. Blank spaces in the path must be represented with a tab character.
- *quit* unloads the movie and causes the Flash Player to close.

In the following CD-ROM exercise, you will practice using the stand-alone player.

### CD-ROM Exercise

Open the file *ch16-02.fla* located in the *F5gai/chapter16/* folder, installed from the companion CD-ROM. Use the file to follow along with the exercise.

1. When you open the file *ch16-02.fla*, you will notice that the movie has elements that extend beyond the stage. Use Test Movie to see what the movie does.

When you test the movie, notice that you can see all elements in the movie, even those that extend beyond the stage. The fact that Flash movies can scale is a nice feature; that is, most of the time. When you are trying to render special effects, this aspect can be negative. However, the problem can be easily remedied with an FS Command method.

2. Close the Player and double click in frame 1 to open the Actions panel.

3. In the Actions panel, double click on the *FSCommand* method from the Actions group in the Toolbox list to add it.

4. In the *Commands for stand alone player* drop-down list, select the *allowscale [true/false]* option.

5. Using the keyboard, enter *false* in the Arguments field.

6. Use Test Movie to see the results. When you do, you will see little change from the previous test. The special FS Command settings do not work when you use Test Movie in Flash.

7. Close the Player and minimize the Flash application.

8. Locate the *.swf* file associated with the Flash file you just tested and open it into the Flash Player. You should be able to double click on the *.swf* file, which should open the external Flash Player.

9. In the Flash Player, the size of the stage area is now constrained and the movie plays without the work area showing.

 **CD-ROM NOTE:** *To see a finished example of the previous CD-ROM exercise, open the file* ch16-02s.fla *located in the* F5gai/chapter16/ *folder, installed from the companion CD-ROM.*

## Flash Player Methods

The Flash plug-in (or ActiveX component) is an object in the browser environment you can use to talk to Flash movies. Thus, knowing that it is an object, you should wonder what methods, events, and properties may be available. In reality, the Flash Player makes only methods and events accessible to the developer. In the previous sections, the Flash Player was responding to FS Command events sent from the Flash movie.

Let's look at the methods associated with the Flash Player, as well as two other events that exist for the Player. As previously stated, Flash Player methods are used to talk from some technology, usually JavaScript, to a Flash movie. The Flash Player methods include two major groupings: standard methods and *tellTarget* methods.

## Standard Methods

The standard methods for the Flash Player are generally associated with the main movie timeline or main movie environment. The standard Flash Player methods include the following:

- *GetVariable("variablename")*: Retrieves the value in the variable specified by the string *variablename*. For example, *GetVariable("myval")* would return the value in the variable *myval*, which would be owned by the main movie timeline.

The Flash Player methods can use slash syntax or dot syntax. You will recall that in dot syntax, to specify a variable that is owned by a particular timeline you simply include the reference at the end of the dot-separated path. For example, if a movie clip MC1 owns the variable *myname*, to access it you would enter the following path in dot syntax: *_root.MC1.myname*. In slash syntax, to access a variable, the variable is separated from the path by a colon. Thus, to access the *myname* variable, slash syntax would look like *_level0/MC1:myname*.

- *GoToFrame(framenumber)*: Sends the movie to a specific frame. Note that *framenumber* must be an integer. For example, *GoToFrame(23)* would send the main movie timeline to frame 23.

- *IsPlaying()*: Returns a binary response as to whether the movie is playing (True = playing). This is commonly used in a JavaScript If statement condition.

- *LoadMovie(level, "URL")*: Allows a movie to be loaded, similar to the *loadMovie* method. Level must be an integer and URL must be a string. For example, *LoadMovie(1,"mymovie.swf")* would load *mymovie.swf* onto level 1.

- *Pan(X, Y, mode)*: Allows the movie to be panned (only when zoomed in). X and Y must be integers. The mode is a binary variable allowing pixels to be entered (0), or percentages to be entered (1). For example, *Pan(25, 25, 0)* would pan the movie 25 pixels down *x* and 25 pixels down *y*.

- *PercentLoaded()*: Returns to the browser the amount of the file that has been streamed (ranges from 0 to 100). This, too, is commonly used in a JavaScript conditional statement.

- *Play()*: Plays the movie if it is currently stopped.

- *Rewind()*: Sends the playhead to the starting frame of the movie.

- *SetVariable("variablename", "value")*: Sets the value of the variable specified by the string *variablename* to the string value specified. For example, *SetVariable("myname", "Jamie")* would set a variable named *myname* (owned by the main movie timeline) to the string *Jamie*.

- *SetZoomRect(left, top, right, bottom)*: Permits JavaScript to change the zoom to the specific rectangle. Note that *left*, *top*, *right*, and *bottom* must be integers, and are specified in *twips* (1440 units per inch). To calculate *twips*, set the units in Flash to Points and then multiply all values by 20 (20 twips = 1 point). For example, *SetZoomRect(0, 0, 400, 400)* would set the zoom rectangle to 0, 0 (upper left corner) and 200, 200 (lower right corner), in pixels.

- *StopPlay()*: Stops the movie.

- *TotalFrames()*: Returns the total number of frames in the movie.

- *Zoom(percentage)*: Allows the zoom level of a movie to be changed based on a percentage, which must be an integer. Note that the percentage works like the drop-down in most applications, where 50 means 50 percent (stage size doubles/zooms in). A percentage of 200 would zoom out, making the stage area smaller.

### tellTarget Methods

In addition to controlling the main movie, you can also specifically target individual movie clips and command them. Keep in mind that you can also target the main movie timeline if you specify the target as *_level0* or as /. The following are descriptions of the Flash Player methods for controlling movie clips.

- *TCallFrame("target", framenumber)*: Executes the actions in frame *framenumber*, located in the target specified by *target*. The target must be a string, and the frame number must be an integer. For example, *TCallFrame("myMC", 5)* would execute the actions associated with frame 5 of *myMC*, located in the main movie timeline.

- *TCallLabel("target", "label")*: Allows the Call action to be executed by calling a label instead of a frame. Both *target* and *label* must be strings. For example, *TCallLabel("myMC", "initvars")* would call the actions associated with the frame label *initvars* in *myMC* (*myMC* would reside in the main movie timeline).

- *TCurrentFrame("target")*: Returns an integer representing the current frame number of the target. The target specification must be a string. For example, *TCurrentFrame("myMC")* would return the current frame number of movie clip *myMC*, located in the main movie timeline.

- *TCurrentLabel("target")*: Returns a string representing the current frame label of the target. The target specification must be a string. For example, *TCurrentLabel("myMC")* would return the current frame label of movie clip *myMC*, located in the main movie timeline. Keep in mind that for a label to be returned, the playhead must be in the exact frame in which the label resides.

- *TGetProperty("target", property)*: Retrieves a property value from the target. The target is specified as a string, whereas the property is an integer (see table 16-1). For example, *TGetProperty("myMC", 0)* would retrieve the current *x* position of movie clip *myMC*, located in the main movie timeline.

- *TGetPropertyAsNumber("target", property)*: Retrieves a property value as a number from the specified target (see table 16-1). For example, *TGetPropertyAsNumber("myMC", 10)* would return the rotation of movie clip *myMC* as an integer, rather than as a string.

- *TGotoFrame("target", framenumber)*: Tells the specified target to go to a specific frame. The target must be a string, and *framenumber* must be an integer. For example, *TGoToFrame("myMC1/myMC1a/", 5)* would tell the movie clip *myMC1a* (which is within *myMC1*) to go to frame 5.

- *TGotoLabel("target", "label")*: Tells the specified target to go to a specific label. Both the target and label must be strings. For example, *TGotoLabel("MC1/MC1a", "Print")* would tell movie clip *MC1a*, located within movie clip *MC1*, to go to the frame labeled Print.

- *TPlay("target")*: Tells the specified string target to play. For example, *TPlay("MC1")* would tell movie clip *MC1* in the main timeline to play.

- *TSetProperty("target", property, value)*: Allows external scripts to set a property in Flash. The target must be a string, whereas the property and value are defined as numbers (see table 16-1). For example, *TSetProperty("bfinder", 0, 200)* would set the *x* location of the movie clip *bfinder* to 200.

- *TStopPlay("target")*: Tells the specified string target to stop. For example, *TStopPlay("MC1")* would tell movie clip *MC1* in the main timeline to stop.

**NOTE:** *All of the string targets used by the Flash Player methods follow the standard rules for tellTarget paths. These string targets are specified in slash syntax.*

## *Property Numbers*

When setting or retrieving properties, you must use numerical values to represent the various properties that are available. Table 16-1 outlines the properties and their integer equivalents that can be called using *TGetProperty* and *TSetProperty*. Of importance for Flash Player methods are the property numbers on the left. The table also outlines which properties are settable and which are only gettable. This information was also presented in Chapter 6. For descriptions of the properties themselves, see Chapter 6.

*Table 16-1 Callable Properties/Integer Equivalents Using* TGetProperty *and* TSetProperty

| Nonglobal Properties | | | | |
|---|---|---|---|---|
| Property Number | Constant | Description | Settable | Gettable |
| 0 | X_POS | X Position (_x) | Yes | Yes |
| 1 | Y_POS | Y Position (_y) | Yes | Yes |
| 2 | X_SCALE | X Scale (_xscale) | Yes | Yes |
| 3 | Y_SCALE | Y Scale (_yscale) | Yes | Yes |
| 4 | CURRENT_FRAME | Current Frame (_currentframe) | No | Yes |
| 5 | TOTAL_FRAMES | Total Frames (_totalframes) | No | Yes |
| 6 | ALPHA | Alpha (_alpha) | Yes | Yes |
| 7 | VISIBLE | Visibility (_visible) | Yes | Yes |
| 8 | WIDTH | Width (_width) | No | Yes |
| 9 | HEIGHT | Height (_height) | No | Yes |
| 10 | ROTATE | Rotation (_rotation) | Yes | Yes |
| 11 | TARGET | Target (_target) | No | Yes |
| 12 | FRAMES_LOADED | Frames Loaded (_framesloaded) | No | Yes |
| 13 | NAME | Name (_name) | Yes | Yes |
| 14 | DROP_TARGET | Drop Target (_droptarget) | No | Yes |
| 15 | URL | URL (_url) | No | Yes |

| Global Properties | | | | |
| --- | --- | --- | --- | --- |
| Property Number | Constant | Description | Settable | Gettable |
| 16 | HIGH_QUALITY | High Quality (_highquality) | Yes | Yes |
| 17 | FOCUS_RECT | Focus Rectangle (_focusrect) | Yes | Yes |
| 18 | SOUND_BUF_TIME | Sound Buffer Time (_soundbuftime) | Yes | No |

### Flash Player Events

The Flash Player provides three standard events that it can respond to. The most widely used is the *FSCommand* event. However, two others also exist. For the sake of completeness, they are mentioned here. However, the techniques for using them are undocumented and not widely publicized. The two other Flash Player events are:

- *OnProgress(percent)*: Generated as the Flash movie is downloading. The value *percent* is provided as an integer.

- *OnReadyStateChange(state)*: Generated as the ready state of the movie changes. Values provided via state include *0 = Loading*, *1 = Uninitialized*, *2 = Loaded*, *3 = Interactive*, and *4 = Complete*.

# ▪ ▪ ▪ Getting Down to Business

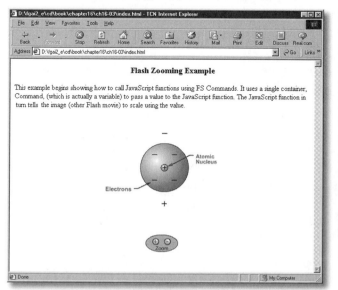

*Figure 16-2  A simple example of one movie controlling another using the* FSCommand *method, JavaScript, and the Flash Player methods.*

Now that you have examined the various Flash Player Methods and the *FSCommand* method, the next four sections will start building your knowledge of their use. Make sure you take the time to examine the code, sample files, and descriptions. They will help you better understand how to use the *FSCommand* method to call external functions.

## Passing Single Values to One Function

Figure 16-2 displays a simple example of a web page that contains two Flash movies. The controller is used to cause the upper movie to zoom. The CD-ROM exercise that follows and the remainder of this section describe how the coding works.

### CD-ROM Exercise

Open the file *index.html* located in the *F5gai/chapter16/ch16-03/* folder, installed from the companion CD-ROM. Load this file into a browser. Use the controls to change the zoom of the "atom" image so that you can see how it works.

1. Use the browser's View Source command to examine the code associated with the page. If you are in Netscape or IE, you should be able to right-click to the right of the atom image and select View Source from the context menu.

2. Once you have the code open, you will notice the typical arrangement of code in the HTML file. If you scroll to the bottom of the page, you will find two sets of < OBJECT > and < EMBED > tags. The upper one is the atom, whose Object ID and Embed Name is *cell*. The lower one is the zoom control, named *zoomer*. These two elements are separated by a line break tag < BR > so that there is a small space between them when viewed in the browser.

3. Scroll back up to the top of the source code and notice the script section. In the script section, you will find the code shown in code example 16-3. Note that the comments have been removed for brevity.

### Code Example 16-3 Script Section for First Zooming Example

```
<SCRIPT LANGUAGE="JavaScript">
<!--
var InternetExplorer =
navigator.appName.indexOf("Microsoft") != -1;
function zoomer_DoFSCommand(command) {
    var myimage = InternetExplorer ? parent.cell :
parent.document.embeds[0];
    myimage.Zoom(parseInt(command));
}
//-->
</SCRIPT>
```

The script section of this example file contains some very important things to note. The first line within the section is the following:

```
var InternetExplorer =
navigator.appName.indexOf("Microsoft") != -1;
```

This line of code is used to determine which browser is being used to view the web page. This is important because IE and Netscape use different means of identifying Flash elements. Fundamentally, it is the difference in the object models used by each browser that makes this necessary. As you will see in a moment, to be able to talk to an object requires defining a path to it. The *InternetExplorer* variable determines how the path to the Flash object is defined. The next line of code defines the beginning of the zooming function, as follows:

```
function zoomer_DoFSCommand(command) {
```

Note that the function begins with the word *function*, followed by the ID/Name of the Flash object, an underscore, and *DoFS-Command*. As noted earlier, the form of *function object IDorEmbedName_DoFSCommand* is required for the function to respond to the Flash movie.

The word *command* within the parentheses creates in the JavaScript environment a local variable named *command*. This variable is used to contain the data passed from Flash. In other words, the content of the Command field in the *FSCommand* method in Flash is placed in a JavaScript variable named *command*. You will see how this content is used in a moment. The next line of code is where the variable *InternetExplorer* is used, as follows:

```
var myimage = InternetExplorer ? parent. cell :
parent.document.embeds[0];
```

Because of the difference in the way IE and Netscape define objects, this line custom builds the path to the Flash object based on the browser. Basically, the line says that if the *InternetExplorer* variable exists, set the variable *myimage* to *parent.cell*. If the *InternetExplorer* variable does not exist, set *myimage* to *parent. document.embeds[0]*.

Notice the difference here. For IE, you define the path to the Flash element as simply the parent (the parent document of the *zoomer* Flash movie) plus the name of the object being identified. With Netscape, you cannot use the object name. Instead, Netscape uses the Embed index to find the object, which is similar to an array index number. Because the atom image is the first embedded element, the line is set to *embeds[0]*. The *zoomer* Flash movie would be *embeds[1]*. If you had more embedded elements, the index would simply increase.

Probably the most difficult part of getting Flash movies to work with FS Command actions and JavaScript is specifying the path to the object being controlled. If you work with frame documents (which you will see later), the path to the object becomes lengthier. The final line of code in this function actually performs the zooming operation, as follows:

```
myimage.Zoom(parseInt(command));
```

This line takes the content of the *myimage* variable and tells it to zoom. Thus, for IE this line would be interpreted as:

```
parent.cell.Zoom(parseInt(command));
```

For Netscape, it would be interpreted as:

```
parent.document.embeds[0].Zoom(parseInt(command));
```

In either case, note the use of the *Zoom()* method. The content of the *command* variable defined in Flash is used within it. Because the *Zoom()* method expects a numeral, the JavaScript *parseInt()* method is used on the data prior to sending it to the *Zoom()* method. Let's look inside the *zoomer* Flash movie to see what is defined within it. Continue with the following steps.

4.  Open the file *zoomer.fla* located in the *F5gai/chapter16/ch16-03/* folder, installed from the companion CD-ROM.

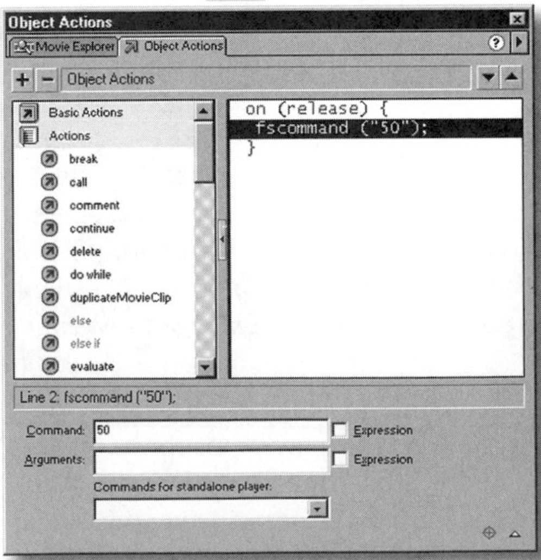

5.  Right-click on the Plus button on the stage and select Actions in the context menu.

6.  As shown in figure 16-3, the *FSCommand* method is used to send the characters *50* to the JavaScript function. As noted earlier, the *Zoom()* Flash Player method requires integers for the zoom value. Thus, in the JavaScript code, the JavaScript *parseInt()* method is used to convert the characters to numerals within the *Zoom()* FS Command action. If you access the action associated with the Minus button, you will see that the *FSCommand* method is set up in a similar manner.

*Figure 16-3 The* FSCommand *method sends the string "50" to JavaScript.*

Keep in mind that the numbers associated with the zoom are based on zoom level. Therefore, 50 is "zoom out" and 200 is "zoom in."

If the Command field were set to Expression, the value of the *command* variable in JavaScript would be a numeral. In this case, the JavaScript *parseInt()* function would not be required.

One of the last things you should note about code example 16-3 is the closing curly bracket (}). In this simple example, it may seem odd to make an issue of it. However, as the code examples get more complex, these are vitally important, because if they are not entered as sets, the coding will not work.

 **TIP:** *If you run into coding problems, always check syntax first. This includes spelling, as well as opening and closing brackets.*

In the previous example, you saw how a single value could be used to pass information to a JavaScript function. In the next example, you will see how to pass two values to a function using both the *command* and *args* variables.

In the previous example, make sure you examine the VBScript code section in the HTML file. Although the JavaScripting does not have to define the *args* variable, for VBScript to correctly receive information from the Flash movie, it must define both the *command* and *args* variables, even if they are not used. If only using a single value (*command*), make sure you still define the *args* variable in the VBScript section. If you do not, IE will inform you of an error.

## Passing Double Values to One Function

This second example, although somewhat contrived, shows you how to pass two values from an FS Command action. Use the following CD-ROM exercise to see how an *if* statement in JavaScript can be used to determine the value of the *command* variable. If *command* is *dozooom*, the zooming function is executed.

---

 ### CD-ROM Exercise

Open the file *index.html* located in the *F5gai/chapter16/ch16-04/* folder, installed from the companion CD-ROM. Use the controller to see that it functions in much the same way as the previous example. However, the coding is a little different.

1. Use the browser's View Source option to examine the code. The important part of this example is the scripting section, as shown in code example 16-4, which uses an *if* statement in JavaScript to determine the content of the *command* variable. Again, comments have been omitted for brevity.

## Code Example 16-4 JavaScript If Statement for Determining Content of the Command Variable

```
<SCRIPT LANGUAGE="JavaScript">
<!--
var InternetExplorer =
navigator.appName.indexOf("Microsoft") != -1;
function zoomer_DoFSCommand(command, args) {
     if ( command=="dozoom" ) {
          var myimage = InternetExplorer ?
parent.cell : parent.document.embeds[0];
          myimage.Zoom(parseInt(args));
     }
}
//-->
</SCRIPT>
```

Much of the coding in this example is similar to the first. However, notice the use of the *if* statement to check the value of *command*. If the *command* variable contains *dozoom*, the movie will zoom. Further down in the code, you see that the *args* variable is used to contain the amount of zoom, instead of the *command* variable, as in the previous example. Examine the *FSCommand* action set up in the *zoomer.fla* file for this web page.

2.  Open the file *zoomer.fla* located in the *F5gai/chapter16 /ch16-04/* folder, installed from the companion CD-ROM.

3.  Right-click on the Plus button on the stage and select Actions in the context menu.

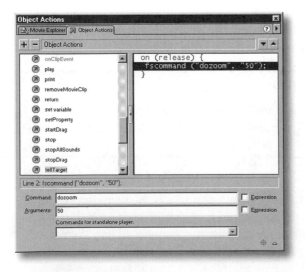

As shown in figure 16-4, the Command field is set to *dozoom*, whereas the Args field is used for the zoom percentage. Again, because the zoom percentage is set as a string, *parseInt* is used in the JavaScript coding to convert the string to a numeral.

The importance of this example is to note how to use an *if* statement to determine the value of *command*. Because you have two values to work with in the *FSCommand* method, you can set

*Figure 16-4 The FSCommand method is used to pass two pieces of information.*

one (*command*) to a string and then use an *if* statement in JavaScript to respond accordingly. The exercise that follows shows you how a single controller can perform multiple functions in this manner.

## Passing Two Values to Three Functions

The following CD-ROM exercise shows you how to call different functionalities using two *FSCommand* method values. Most often, there will be multiple functionalities you will want to call for a movie. In this example, the controller contains zoom buttons and pan buttons. Because you cannot have two JavaScript functions that relate to the same Flash movie, you must do everything with the *command* and *args* variables and an If statement.

### CD-ROM Exercise

Open the file *index.html* located in the *F5gai/chapter16/ch16-05/* folder, installed from the companion CD-ROM. Use the controller to see how the movie works. Note that the pan buttons will not work if the zoom is set at 100 percent.

1.  Use the browser's View Source option to examine the scripting in the page.

2.  The example displays a better reason to use the JavaScript *if* facility. Code example 16-5 shows the scripting from the web page. Examine this code.

### Code Example 16-5  Adding Multiple Functionalities to a Movie

```
<SCRIPT LANGUAGE="JavaScript">
<!--
var InternetExplorer =
navigator.appName.indexOf("Microsoft") != -1;
function zoomer_DoFSCommand(command, args) {
    var myimage = InternetExplorer ? parent.cell :
parent.document.embeds[0];
    if ( command=="dozoom" ) {
        myimage.Zoom(parseInt(args));
    } else if ( command=="dopanx" ) {
        myimage.Pan(parseInt(args), 0, 0);
    } else if ( command=="dopany" ) {
        myimage.Pan(0, parseInt(args), 0);
    }
}
//-->
</SCRIPT>
```

The first thing you will note about code example 16-5 is that the *else if* statement is used to react to specific entries in the *command* variable. Here you also see how the *Pan(X, Y, mode)* Flash Player method is used to change the viewed portion of the movie. Note that pan will only work when zoomed in.

You will also notice that the *InternetExplorer* variable is defined outside the function. In JavaScript, when a variable is defined inside a function it is a local variable, meaning that it ceases to exist after the function has executed. A global variable, on the other hand, remains as long as the page is open or until the page is reloaded. One of the caveats of JavaScript is that if the reload button is used, all global variables are cleared.

 **CD-ROM NOTE:** *Continue dissecting this example by opening the associated* zoomer.fla *file into Flash. See how the* FSCommand *method is used on the zoom and pan buttons.*

# Passing Double Values to Triple Functions

In the following CD-ROM exercise you will review an example that contains two controllers and two atom images. Each controller is uniquely named so that it may control one of the two atom images.

---

 *CD-ROM Exercise*

Open the file *index.html* located in the *F5gai/chapter16/ch16-06/* folder, installed from the companion CD-ROM. Use the controllers to see how the movies work.

1. Use the browser's View Source option to examine the code used in this web page.

2. Scroll to the bottom of the page to see that there are two atom images and two controllers (a total of four Flash movies) defined in the page. Notice also that each of the elements is uniquely named (ID/Name).

3. Scroll back up to the top to view the script section. There is one function set up for the first zoom controller, and a second for the other controller.

Because the two functions are similar in coding, only one will be closely examined. The main difference between the two functions is in the specification of the *myimage* variable. Note also that the *InternetExplorer* variable is defined outside the function, making it a global variable. This allows the *InternetExplorer* variable to be used by both functions without having to include the code in both functions. The code for the first function in this fourth zooming example is shown in code example 16-6.

### Code Example 16-6  Code for First Function of Fourth Zooming/Panning Example

```
function zoomer1_DoFSCommand(command, args) {
    var myimage = InternetExplorer ? parent.cell1
: parent.document.embeds[0];
    if ( command=="dozoom" ) {
        myimage.Zoom(parseInt(args));
    } else if ( command=="dopanx" ) {
        myimage.Pan(parseInt(args), 0, 0);
    } else if ( command=="dopany" ) {
        myimage.Pan(0, parseInt(args), 0);
    } else if ( command=="dogoframe" ) {
        myimage.Zoom(0);
        myimage.GotoFrame(parseInt(args));
    }
}
```

As with the previous example, the function shown in code example 16-6 uses *if* and *else if* statements to determine the value of the *command* variable. Based on its content, the appropriate code is executed.

Notice the last *else if* statement. JavaScript does two things to the movie if *dogoframe* is found in the *command* variable. First, the image is told *Zoom(0)*. This resets the zoom to 100 percent (true size). Then the *GoToFrame()* method is used to send the movie to a specific frame. Realize that you can initiate several commands from JavaScript to the same movie, one right after another. This allows tremendous flexibility in that you can do several things within one Else If section.

 **CD-ROM NOTE:** *To further analyze this example, view the source FLA files located in the* F5gai/chapter16/ch16-06/ *folder, installed from the companion CD-ROM. Again, all of the FS Command methods in these movies are set to strings; thus the need for the* parseInt() *JavaScript function shown in code example 16-6.*

## ∎∎∎ Applied Examples

To further extend your knowledge of Flash Player methods, several examples follow., Two of these are examples you have seen before in one form or another, which will help you see the difference between ActionScript

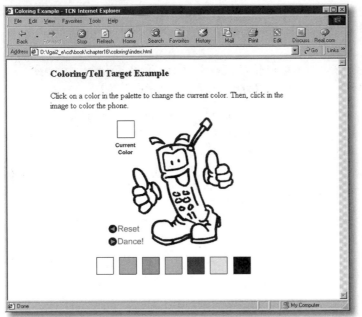

*Figure 16-5 The coloring example in this chapter is a little less complicated than the one from the last chapter.*

and Flash Player methods. Seeing them implemented with Flash Player methods and JavaScript should provide an excellent learning opportunity. The last example is the Purdue University Virtual Visit.

# A Coloring Example

In the previous chapter, you saw how the coloring example could be implemented with ActionScript. Here, you will see how JavaScript can be made to control and track the necessary information for the example to work. It is not quite as complex as the one from the previous chapter, but it will give you an opportunity to see how a similar example could be created using Flash Player methods and JavaScript. Figure 16-5 shows the example in the browser.

Once of the main differences in this example is that the color bar used for selecting color and the items to be colored are separate files. Similarly, the swatches do not use the Flash color object. The following CD-ROM exercise takes you through the process used to create this example using FS Command actions.

## CD-ROM Exercise

Begin by opening the file *index.html* located in the *F5gai/chapter16/coloring/* folder, installed from the companion CD-ROM. To refresh your memory, use the color swatches to choose a color. Then, color the telephone.

1. To begin examining this movie, open the file *colors.fla* located in the *F5gai/chapter16/coloring/* folder, installed from the companion CD-ROM.

2. Click on one of the color swatches and access the Actions panel.

3. Note that each color is assigned a number, 0 to 7. When the user clicks on a color, the *FSCommand* method sends the color number to the JavaScript function associated with the movie.

4. Open the file *colorme.fla* located in the *F5gai/chapter16/ coloring/* folder, installed from the companion CD-ROM.

5. This example assigns the colors to the telephone in a more simplistic way. Let's begin with the current color swatch. Its instance name on the stage is *SwatchX*. Right-click on it and select Edit in Place from the context menu.

6. The colors in the swatch and the colors in the telephone parts are changed, but not by the color object, as in the last chapter. Rather, these colors are changed by telling the swatch movie clip or the telephone parts to move to a different frame. Thus, the colors in each frame of the swatch (as well as the telephone parts) are different. The frame numbers in which each color occurs are directly related to the numbers used in the *FSCommand* method in the *colors.fla* file. Thus, in the *colors.fla* movie, the reddish color was assigned a number of 5. In the current color swatch movie clip (as well as in the telephone part movie clips), frame 5 contains that reddish color.

7. Click on the Scene 1 link in the Edit Path.

8. Access one of the telephone part timelines.

9. Notice in the timeline that there is a trigger and a colored fill (similar to the color swatch movie clip). Again, if you check frame 5 in any of the telephone part movie clips, you will find the reddish color. The frame numbers and the colors that occur within them are directly related to the swatches in *colors.fla* and the number sent to JavaScript.

10. While you are accessing one of the telephone part movie clips, click on the trigger on the stage and access the Actions panel. Notice that the triggers use the *FSCommand* method as well. The Command field in them says *change-color*, whereas the Arguments field uses the expression *this*, as shown in figure 16-6. The keyword *this* will be replaced by the instance name of the movie clip when the *FSCommand* method is executed.

Now let's turn our attention to the JavaScript code that receives the data from the movie. For this movie, there are two

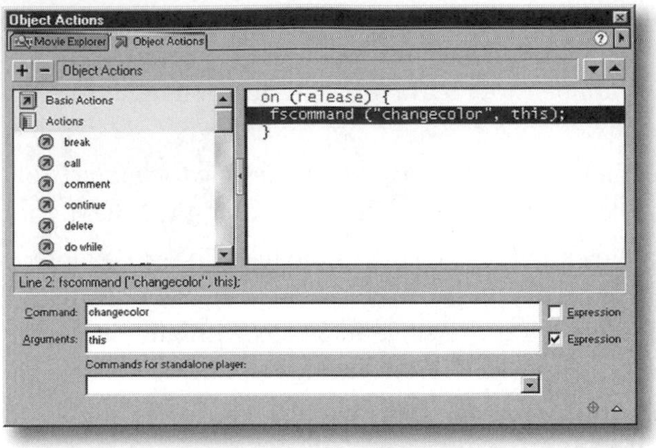

Figure 16-6  *The keyword* this *is used to refer to the movie clip's instance name on the stage.*

functions that are used. One is used to store the number passed to it from the "colors" movie. The function also tells the current color swatch movie clip to go to the appropriate frame. The second function used in this page assigns the selected color numbers, stored in JavaScript, to the telephone part in the image and tells them to go to the appropriate frame.

11. If you have the file *coloring.html* open in the browser, use the browser's View Source option to examine the code.

12. Scroll down to see the coding for the two Flash movies in the page. The color swatch movie's ID/Name is *colors*. The telephone movie is *colorme*. Thus, one function relates to the swatch movie and the other to the telephone.

13. One of the first things you should notice is the line that says:

    `var mycolor=0;`

This line is the variable used to store the color in JavaScript. You will see how the variable changes in just a moment. Before you do, however, note the VBScript section below the JavaScript section. Code example 16-7 shows the VBScript section. The VBScript section of the code must also have two subroutines, and it must define the global variable.

## *Code Example 16-7  VBScript Section*

```
<SCRIPT LANGUAGE="VBScript">
<!--
Dim mycolor
mycolor = 0
Sub colors_FSCommand(ByVal command, ByVal args)
    call colors_DoFSCommand(command, args)
end sub
Sub colorme_FSCommand(ByVal command, ByVal args)
    call colorme_DoFSCommand(command, args)
end sub
-->
</SCRIPT>
```

Because this web page contains two JavaScript functions, there are also two VBScript functions. As logic would dictate, for IE to be able to correctly map VBScript commands to JavaScript, two functions are necessary in the VBScript section. Yet, the variable *mycolor* also requires special treatment in the VBScript section. For it to properly track the color number, it must be defined for VBScript. The word *Dim* is used to define the global variable in VBScript. This variable is assigned a starting value.

14. The JavaScript function used to define the chosen color is shown in code example 16-8, and is described in more detail in the material that follows. The color selection function sets the *mycolor* variable and controls the current color swatch.

## Code Example 16-8 Code for the Color Selection Function

```
function colors_DoFSCommand(command, args) {
    var colormeMovie = InternetExplorer ? colorme :
document.embeds[0];
    mycolor=parseInt(command);
    colormeMovie.TGotoFrame("_level0.SwatchX",
mycolor);
}
```

The function shown in code example 16-8 does three things. The first line, which you have already learned about, sets the path to the Flash movie so that it can be controlled. The second line receives the value contained in the *command* variable, converts it to an integer, and then tells the color swatch in the telephone movie to go to a specific frame. The *mycolor* variable defined a line earlier is used as the frame number.

The second function used in the coloring movie does several things. It is listed in code example 16-9. The second function can do one of several things, depending on the value in *command*.

## Code Example 16-9 Code for the Second Function

```
function colorme_DoFSCommand(command, args) {
    var colormeMovie = InternetExplorer ? colorme :
document.embeds[0];
    var colorsMovie = InternetExplorer ? colors :
```

```
document.embeds[1];
   if ( command=="changecolor" ) {
     colormeMovie.TGotoFrame(args,mycolor);
   } else if ( command=="dancebaby" ) {
   colorsMovie.GotoFrame(2);
   } else if ( command=="resetbar" ) {
   colorsMovie.GotoFrame(0);
   } else if ( command=="resetcolors" ) {
   mycolor=0
   colormeMovie.TGotoFrame("_level0/SwatchX",mycolor);
   colormeMovie.TGotoFrame("_level0/AntennaX",mycolor);
   colormeMovie.TGotoFrame("_level0/EyesX",mycolor);
   colormeMovie.TGotoFrame("_level0/EyebrowsX",mycolor);
   colormeMovie.TGotoFrame("_level0/MouthX",mycolor);
   colormeMovie.TGotoFrame("_level0/LefthandX",mycolor);
 colormeMovie.TGotoFrame("_level0/RighthandX",mycolor);
   colormeMovie.TGotoFrame("_level0/LeftshoeX",mycolor);
   colormeMovie.TGotoFrame("_level0/RightshoeX",mycolor);
   colormeMovie.TGotoFrame("_level0/PhonebodyX",mycolor);
   }
 }
```

The first If section in code example 16-9 is used to change the color of the movie clips associated with each telephone part. Using *TGotoFrame*, the appropriate telephone part, as contained within *args*, is sent to the frame number defined in *mycolor*.

The first Else If section shown in code example 16-9 is used to make the telephone dance. If the Dance button is selected, an *FSCommand* method is executed, with *command* set equal to *dancebaby*, and the color bar is sent to a blank frame. This is so that the user is not selecting colors while the telephone is dancing.

When the telephone is dancing, an option to stop the dance is available. The *resetbar* Else If section is for this button. It tells the color swatch bar to return to frame 0, which is frame 1. This displays the color swatches again.

The last Else If section relates to the Reset button. If the Reset button is selected, all telephone movie clips return to their first frame (color: white), and the *mycolor* variable is set to 0. Additionally, the Current Color swatch is told to return to its first frame.

## Noah's Memory Game

The next example displays more complex JavaScript code in that it shows how to use JavaScript arrays, global and local variables, and complex *if* structures. Discussion in this section assumes you have read and understand the Noah's Memory Game exercise of the previous chapter. You may want to review it, as the predominant focus in this section will be on the JavaScript code. There are a few features that are a little bit different in this game. Specifically, the number of rounds per game is fixed at 10, the ending sequence does not use dynamic text fields, and the *animallist* array remains at a constant length.

### CD-ROM Exercise

Begin by opening the file *index.html* located in the *F5gai/chapter16/noah/* folder, installed from the companion CD-ROM. Click on the Load Game button and try the game to see how it works. It is very similar to what you saw in the last chapter.

1. Because the game opens a pop-up window with no menu or buttons, you must open the correct file to review the web page code. Close the pop-up if it is open and, in the main browser window, open the file *noah.html* located in the *Noah* folder. Use the View Source option to examine the coding.

2. One of the first things you will notice about the *noah.html* file is that its script section is very long. Because Noah's Game is a single Flash file, the coding is quite extensive. However, at the very top of the script section you will see that several variables are set. When you saw the example in the last chapter, these variables were set in ActionScript. Here, they are set in JavaScript, as everything will be tracked with it.

3. Of particular importance is the *animallist* array that is defined. Similar to what you saw in ActionScript, JavaScript supports true arrays, which provides extended capabilities when working with large amounts of data. Notice how the name of the array and its length are defined by the line that says:

```
var animallist = new Array(31)
```

After defining the array, the "animals" are loaded into it using an index number. This index number becomes important later, when a random number is generated. Another important attribute of the array is that because it is defined outside the function, it is global in nature.

You definitely do not want the array defined over and over, as it takes time to define it and it consumes memory. The more arrays that are defined, the more memory is consumed, so much that it is possible to eat up all available RAM memory with arrays. Be careful how many lists you use, and make them global if possible.

Like other examples you have seen, custom variables in your scripting require that the VBScript section mirror the JavaScript section. If you peruse the VBScript section, you will see that the array is defined for IE as well. This is necessary if you want your variables to work in IE.

Because the *noah_DoFSCommand* function is quite lengthy, it is examined by each If section. Although it may look unwieldy, most of it is simple, and represents a compilation of what you have already seen.

If you will recall from the last chapter, one of the first things Noah's Memory Game does is to define several variables used throughout the game. The first If section is for the initialization of the variables. In relation to the ActionScript example, this is basically the same information that was in the *initvars* function in the last chapter.

4. The first Else If section, *selectrandom*, uses the array defined earlier to select the random animal. Code example 16-10 shows the code that selects the random animal and then sends the movie to the appropriate frame. Examine this code.

### Code Example 16-10 Code for the selectrandom Section

```
} else if (command=="selectrandom") {
    door1 = "nothing";
    door2 = "nothing";
    dooropennum = 0;
    numberright = 0;
    if (numberanimals < 2) {
        tempval = Math.round(Math.random() *
animallist.length)
        var myloc = animallist[tempval]
        noahmovie.TGotoLabel("_level0/", myloc);
        noahmovie.TPlay("_level0/");
    } else {
```

```
noahmovie.TGotoLabel("_level0/", "Ending");
noahmovie.TPlay("_level0/");
}
```

The two most important lines in this section of code are where the *tempval* and *myloc* local variables are defined, directly below the nested If statement. The following line is important, as it allows a random number to be chosen:

```
tempval = Math.round(Math.random() *
animallist.length)
```

The second line then uses the generated number to choose one of the animals in the array, based on the index, as follows:

```
var myloc = animallist[tempval]
```

Following this, the Noah movie is sent to the appropriate frame label using the string within *myloc*. Recall that one round of the game is based on ten hidden animals. Thus, the need for the nested *if* statement. If ten rounds have been completed, the user is sent to the end of the movie.

The next *else if* section, *feedback*, is used at the end of the movie. Based on the number of animals the user got right, he or she is sent to the appropriate frame. The *command* variable is set equal to *feedback* using a frame action at the end of the short animation that plays.

Similar to the frame actions used for a restart, the JavaScript code in the next *else if* section resets the variables if the user restarts the game. In the ending feedback frames, the Restart button sets *command* equal to *restart* and executes this section of code.

The *rightanswer* and *wronganswer else if* sections are used when the user is guessing at the hidden animal. Again, much like the ActionScript example, these elements are called when the user clicks on the four animal names that appear during the matching of doors.

The next *else if* section is the most complex part of the JavaScript coding, and is the "brain" for making the doors work properly. Code example 16-11 shows the code that will be described. Examine this code.

### Code Example 16-11  Code for If Section That Tracks Doors

```
} else if (command=="dooropen") {
    if (dooropennum==0) {
        door1=args;
        dooropennum++;
    } else if (dooropennum==1) {
        door2=args;
        var varlength = InternetExplorer ?
door1.length : door1.length();
        reallength = varlength - 1
        for (i = 0; i < reallength; i++) {
        door1char = door1.charAt(i)
            door2char = door2.charAt(i)
        if (door1char != door2char) {
            temp = 0
                break
            }
                temp = 1
        }
        if (temp==1) {
            numberright = numberright + 1
            noahmovie.TGotoLabel('_level0/' +
door1,'Solved');
            noahmovie.TGotoLabel('_level0/' +
door2,'Solved');
            if (numberright==3) {
                noahmovie.Play();
            } else if (numberright==7) {
                noahmovie.Play();
            }
        } else {
            noahmovie.TPlay('_level0/' + door1);
            noahmovie.TPlay('_level0/' + door2);
        }
        door1="nothing";
        door2="nothing";
        dooropennum=0;
    }
```

The *dooropen* section is called anytime a doorknob is clicked on to open a door. As you will recall, the *dooropennum* variable is used to keep track of how many doors are open. If *dooropennum* equals 0, no doors are open. If a door is open, *dooropennum* equals 1.

When *dooropennum* equals 0 and the user clicks on a door, *dooropennum* is increased. The variable *door1* is set equal to the name of the door. Although this is fundamentally the same as the ActionScript technique, the difference is that the name of the open door is contained within *args*. Thus, *door1* is set equal to *args*.

If there is already a door open and the user opens another door, the second part of code example 16-11 is executed. Again, to find out if the two doors are the same animals, the values of *door1* and *door2* are compared. To do the comparison requires eliminating the number from the door name. The following code gets the length of the string in the variable *door1*. Note that the code for IE and Netscape differs in the way the length is gained. Thus, the reason for the conditional statement, as follows:

```
var varlength = InternetExplorer ? door1.length :
door1.length();
```

Following this, the length is truncated to get rid of the numeral at the end of the door name, as follows:

```
reallength = varlength-1
```

The following JavaScript code compares the individual characters in *door1* and *door2*, using a For loop. If they match, a temporary variable *temp* is set equal to 1. If not, *temp* is set equal to 0.

```
for (i = 0; i < reallength; i++) {
  door1char = door1.charAt(i)
  door2char = door2.charAt(i)
  if (door1char != door2char) {
    temp = 0
    break
    }
    temp = 1
  }
```

If the content of the variables *door1* and *door2* are found to be matching (*temp* = = *1*), *numberright* is increased, and the door movie clips are told to go to frame *Solved*. If the user has matched either three or seven sets of doors, the main movie timeline is told to play to the next stop frame. If the content of *door1* and *door2* do not match, the two doors are told to close.

One of the things that may seem odd is the difference between *temp = 1* and *temp = = 1*. In JavaScript, as in ActionScript, when a single equal sign is used, it means assignment. Thus, *temp = 1* assigns a value of 1 to *temp*. However, when double equal signs are used, it means you are testing for a value. Thus, *temp = = 1* means you are testing to see if *temp* equals 1.

5. The final Else If section in the *noah.html* file resets the *door1* and *dooropennum* variables if the user closes a door they have opened. This would only occur when the first of two doors is opened. When the second door is opened, prior code automatically executes, and either the two doors match or they do not. The *command* variable is set equal to *door-close* in the Open frame of each door. Examine this code.

**CD-ROM NOTE:** *To continue dissecting this example, open the file* noah.fla *located in the* Noah *folder on the companion CD-ROM. Examine where each of these code snippets is called using the* FSCommand *method.*

## Purdue University Virtual Visit

The final example in this chapter is the Purdue University Virtual Visit. In reality, the coding used in it is somewhat simpler than that of Noah's Memory Game. However, there are a couple of items that are worth mentioning. The CD-ROM exercise that follows takes you through an examination of this example.

**NOTE:** *Several portions of the Virtual Visit are not included on the companion CD-ROM; namely, the Apple QuickTimeVR movies. Additionally, the Virtual Visit got a major facelift not too long ago. Check out the latest version at* http://www.tech.purdue.edu/resources/map/.

---

### CD-ROM Exercise

Open the file *index.html* located in the *F5gai/chapter16/virtual visit* folder, installed from the companion CD-ROM.

1. Click on the *Go to the Virtual Visit* button in the *index.html* page in the browser.

2. Use the controls and click on the buildings to see how it works. Note that most of the code is nothing more than simple pop-up windows. Make sure you try the Building Finder button to see how these work.

3. The Virtual Visit consists of two movies. The two movies are in two frames. Therein lies the first complex part: identifying or locating movies that reside in frames. The upper frame is named *fw_map*, and the lower frame is named *fw_con*. If you open the *index.html* file into Notepad or SimpleText, you will see how they are named.

When using frames, the frame names must be used in the Flash location description in JavaScript. To "talk" to the map requires the following path:

```
var map = InternetExplorer ? parent. fw_map.map :
parent.fw_map.document. embeds[0];
```

To "talk" to the controller requires the following path:

```
var controller = InternetExplorer ?
parent.fw_con.controls : parent.fw_con.
document.embeds[0];
```

**NOTE:** *If you open the* map.html *file or the* controller.html *file, you will see the two previous paths in the JavaScript coding.*

Again, the most difficult part of controlling Flash movies from other Flash movies or elements is finding the location. The more frames and frame names that exist, the longer the path name. To be able to control an element embedded in frames requires that the frame the element is in, as well as the path to it, be named.

The only other difficult part of the Virtual Visit was getting the Building Finder, which is a separate HTML file and window, to be able to talk to the map in the other window. To do this required naming the main frame window when it opened. When you choose the Building Finder, it allows you to select a building name from the drop-down menu. The map Flash movie has a main frame in which all the buildings are present. Subsequent frames contain arrows that point to each building.

When the user chooses a building from the Building Finder, the Building Finder window must tell the map to go to a specific frame. The problem is that browser windows are not named by default. If you want to communicate between two windows, you must name the window when it is opened, so that it may be targeted. Thus, when you click on the *Go To the Virtual Visit* button in the *index.html* file, special code allows the Building Finder to find the main window.

4. Open the browser and open the file *index.html* located in the *F5gai/chapter16/virtual visit/* folder, installed from the companion CD-ROM.

5. Use the browser View Source option to examine the code.

Notice the line below the *window.open* statements that says *opencampus.opener = self*. This line names the window upon its opening, so that it can be targeted later. If this line were not there, the Building Finder would not be able to target the map.

6. Open the file named *bfinder.html* into Notepad or SimpleText. Note how it defines the map and controller variables. Both are preceded with *opener*. This is how you can allow one window to communicate with another: by naming the window when it is opened.

## ▪▪▪ Summary

In this chapter you examined how the *FSCommand* method and Flash Player methods are used to connect with external technologies. Indeed, the *FSCommand* method can be used to communicate a variety of things to the browser. It can be used as well to send specific commands to the Flash Player for execution. The main thing to keep in mind is the *FSCommand* method is used to pass data from Flash to some technology in the browser. Flash Player methods, on the other hand, are used to control a Flash movie and pass data to it, from some external technology.

# Glossary

**< A >** An HTML tag for creating links to other pages or resources; an anchor tag.

**< EMBED >** An HTML tag for including multimedia elements on web pages; causes the browser to use a plug-in.

**< H1 >** An HTML tag for creating headings of various sizes; importance of heading is denoted by number. 1 is the most important; 6 is the least important.

**< HR >** An HTML tag for creating horizontal rules.

**< IMG >** An HTML tag for including images within a web page.

**< OBJECT >** An HTML tag for including multimedia elements on web pages; causes the browser to use ActiveX components.

**< P >** A block-level HTML tag that creates a paragraph of text offset from other elements by a carriage return (line feed).

**24-bit color** Describes an image that can contain up to 16.7 million colors.

**2D animation** An animation file created using a package in which every frame's content is defined through either vector or bitmap descriptions.

**3D animation** An animation file generated from a 3D model or scene.

**3-D Studio Max** A 3D animation package created by Kinetix (*http://www.ktx.com*).

**8-bit color** Describes an image that contains up to 256 colors. All colors are described in a matrix called the Color Lookup Table (CLUT).

**acetate** Clear plastic film used to create traditional cel animation.

**achromatic colors** Include hues that have no true color, such as black, white, and gray.

**ACT** The extension assigned to save Photoshop color palettes.

**action** Feature of Flash that allows you to assign functionality to elements in a movie.

**ActionScript** Flash's internal scripting capability.

**Active Server Pages (ASP)** A server-side scripting language used in conjunction with Microsoft's HTTP server software, MIIS.

**ActiveX** Microsoft's approach to plug-ins, in which components are installed at the system level and accessible by all applications.

**adaptive differential pulse code modulation (ADPCM)** Compression algorithm commonly used in the WAV file format; a lossy sound compression format.

**additive colors** Color system used to create projected or displayed images via a cathode ray tube.

**additive primaries** Red, green, and blue.

**address field** The portion of a browser into which a universal resource locator (URL) can be typed.

**Adobe** A company well known for its raster and vector graphics applications (*http://www.adobe.com*).

**affordances** The controls in an interface that clue the user in as to functionality.

**Afterburner** Original name for the filter used to convert image and multimedia files created in Macromedia products to a form that is distributable over the Web. Most newer applications can convert data within the program and do not need the external converter.

**AI** The extension for an Adobe Illustrator file.

**algorithm** A mathematical or logical schemata for solving a problem.

**aliasing** Characteristic stair-stepped nature of vector lines on a display screen or in an extracted bitmap.

**alignment** The positioning of text bodies in relationship to other screen elements.

**alpha** Controls the transparency (opaqueness) of a symbol in Flash.

**alpha channels** A special part of high-resolution files that can contain masking and gamma information.

**alphanumeric character** A character (letter or number).

**ambient light** The amount of light present without any other light sources; representative of sunlight or moonlight; atmospheric light.

**analog data** Data consisting of a range of frequency variations; what the human senses are able to perceive.

**analog degradation** The decay of analog information as a result of copying an analog source to another analog device.

**analog source** A device, such as a VCR or a cassette tape, used to record or play back analog data.

**analog to digital conversion (ADC)** The process of converting analog data to digital data; often performed by a hardware chip or software.

**animation** The phenomenon of quickly changing images, which give the perception of movement or change over time.

**animator** The portion of a 3D animation package that allows the operator to define changes over time.

**anti-alias halo** Discolored pixels that occur around the edges of an object as a result of previous anti-aliasing.

**anti-aliasing** The process of blurring the edges of an image or object to make it appear smoother.

**Apple** Manufacturers of the Macintosh computer (*http://www.apple.com*).

**applet** A small, self-contained executable application created in the Java language.

**application development** The process of creating software designed to perform a task.

**array** A special type of variable that can contain multiple values.

**ASCII text** A standard and universal computer text format.

**ASP** See *active server pages*.

**asymmetrical balance** Describes a layout in which there is an unequal amount of visual elements on each side of a page.

**AU** See *Sun Audio*.

**Audio Interchange File Format (AIFF)** A digital audio file format predominantly used on Macintosh and Silicon Graphics machines.

**Authorware** An interaction-based authoring program created by Macromedia (*http://www.macromedia.com*).

**Autodesk FLI and FLC** A digital animation format that uses frame differencing to write the frames in the animation.

**avant garde** Generally viewed as a paradigm shift or something that is out of the ordinary.

**AVI** See *Video for Windows*.

**balance** The equal or unequal amount of visual elements on a page; described as either symmetrical or asymmetrical.

**banding** The visual stripes that can appear in 256-color images as a result of interpolation.

**bandwidth** The amount of data that can be pushed over a network connection; measured in kilobits or megabits per second.

**bandwidth profiler** Feature available when testing a movie in Flash that allows the developer to simulate performance of a movie by limiting the data delivery rate.

**Bezier curves** Special spline curves that have control points that can be moved, thus changing the shape of the curve.

**binary compression (BIN)** A standard Internet external compression scheme.

**binary data** Data described using series of 0s and 1s; digital data.

**binary variable** A variable that can contain one only of two values: 0 (False) or 1 (True).

**bit depth** Determines the number of physical bits that can be used to represent a sample from an analog source.

**bit rate** The size of the chunks of data that are compressed in an MP3 sound clip.

**bitmap** A graphic in which the smallest element is the pixel (picture element).

**bitmap editor** An application designed to edit bitmap images.

**bitmap fonts** Fonts described using bitmap images.

**bitmap graphics** See *bitmap*.

**blending** Merging two or more items to obtain steps between the items.

**BMP** See *Windows bitmap*.

**bookmark** A browser convention that allows the user to copy URL locations that can be used at a later time to instantly access a web site.

**Boolean operations** Logical operations that are used to create unique objects from a set of lower objects. The three primary operations are union, subtraction, and intersection.

**browser** A special application designed to view HTML pages from the WWW.

**bump mapping** A special feature of 3D animation programs that allows the user to specify textures through the use of other bitmaps. Depths are generated from grayscale values and applied to an object or surface.

**button symbol** A symbol that automatically behaves like a push-button control.

**byte** A series of 8 bits.

**cache** A special location on the hard drive at which a browser can temporarily store files for future use.

**cameras** A special view created in 3D animation programs for rendering a 3D scene; a perspective view.

**cascading style sheets (CSS)** A client-side web technology that provides templates that can be used for a series of web pages; also provides layering and positioning capability.

**cathode ray tube** A tube that allows images to be projected from special guns to create colored images.

**cel** A single frame from an animation; derived from celluloid, a substance on which animation frames were first created.

**cel animation** Traditional method of creating animations in which each frame was hand drawn and painted on a celluloid or acetate substance.

**channels** Special saved selections (raster editor); a track of music in an audio program (mono versus stereo).

**Chr** String function that converts an ASCII code representation to an alphanumeric character.

**chroma keying** A special compositing feature that allows one clip to substitute for a special color in the second clip.

**classes** Define the methods, preoperties, and event handlers of objects.

**clip art** Pre-generated and generally public-domain graphics that can be used in derivative works.

**clipping paths** Objects used to clip or limit the display of other objects; typical in illustration programs.

**CLR** The extension assigned to saved Flash color palettes saved out of the Colors dialog box.

**codec** Acronym for "compressor/decompression" generally used to describe the code that performs compression and decompression.

**color** The visual phenomenon that occurs as a result of absorption or projection of visible light.

**color cycling** An animation effect in which colors are substituted in an image, such as cycling from red to blue.

**color look-up table (CLUT)** The color matrix used in 8-bit images. Each color in the CLUT has a number, and each pixel in the image is associated with one number from the CLUT.

**color schemes** Sequences of color know to look visually pleasing when used together in images.

**color shifting** An unappealing visual affect in which colors shift from proper to inappropriate colors. Generally occurs when the computer has to interpolate colors.

**color space** The method of theoretically defining all colors that can be replicated or generated by a specific device.

**color wheel** A circular arrangement of all colors associated with a particular device.

**command line interface** An operating environment in which commands are typed in, one line at a time.

**comment** An action in Flash that permits the developer to add internal documentation to movies; are ignored by the player.

**common gateway interface (CGI)** A server-side technology that provides a bridge for communication between two dissimilar technologies.

**communication** The process of sending a message through a communication channel. The message must be received and interpreted correctly for communication to occur.

**compact disc read-only memory (CD-ROM)** A computer storage medium in which digital data is stored on a plastic-coated silver platter. CD-ROMs can contain from 550 to 650 megabytes.

**comparison operators** Operators used to compare two values, such as equal, greater than, or less than.

**compilation** A copyrightable work in which major portions of various works are used together to create a new work, such as combining songs from various artists to create a "Greatest Hits"-type CD-ROM.

**complementary** Colors that occur across the color wheel from one another such as blue and orange, red and green, and purple and yellow. Most color-blindness problems are the result of the inability to distinguish complementary colors.

**compositing** The effect of merging media elements into one media element.

**compression** The process of reducing digital file size by either deleting unneeded data or substituting for redundant data.

**compression ratio** A description of a codec's effectiveness; obtained by comparing bits before and after compression.

**concatenate** To join two string elements into a single string element, such as "James" and " Mohler." The resultant would be the string result "James Mohler."

**consistency** Describes reoccurring elements that appear across multiple pages of a web site.

**content** The media elements used to convey a message, including the message being conveyed.

**contrast** A description of the value differences between adjacent items or colors.

**cool colors** Colors that tend to recede in a graphic, such as green, blue, and violet.

**copyright** The method of protecting creative works in the United States.

**CYMK** Describes the colors used in four-color process printing.

**CYMK color model** The conceptual color space used to describe the gamut of colors for printed output.

**data rate** The speed of the delivery of data, usually inside the computer; measured in kilobytes or megabytes per second.

**data type** The nature of data contained within a variable; types include string and numerical.

**daughter card** An add-on computer interface card that connects to an existing card within the computer, rather than to the computer's main system board.

**Debabelizer** A program used to convert graphic, sound, and digital video files (*http://www.debabelizer.com/*).

**decibels** A measure of frequency variations that are not necessarily associated with loudness.

**deformation** The act of deforming; something that is malformed.

**device dependent** Descriptive of a media element that has a fixed resolution; designed for output on a specific device.

**device independent** Descriptive of a media element that does not have a fixed resolution; can be adjusted for output on any device.

**device resolution** The number of dots per inch for a specific device.

**digital audio** An audio file that describes a waveform bit by bit as it occurs over time.

**digital audio tape** (**DAT**) A digital recording and playback device used in the music industry.

**digital data** See *binary data.*

**digital signal processor (DSP)** A special processor found on most sound cards that allows the sound card to process audio functions and commands.

**digital to analog conversion (DAC)** The process of converting digital data to analog data so that it can be interpreted by humans.

**Director** A time-based authoring program created by Macromedia (*http://www.macromedia.com/*).

**dithering** The process of scattering pixels during interpolation to overcome banding.

**dots per inch (dpi)** A measurement of the number of displayable or printable dots per square inch.

**dub** A slang term for copying a medium, or the product thereof.

**dynamic** Describes animated graphics, as opposed to static or unmoving graphics.

**dynamic HTML** A client-side web technology that provides the ability to include dynamic text and graphics, as well as interactive components.

**easing** Speeding up or slowing down the beginning or ending of an animation.

**edutainment** Software with an educational purpose that is entertaining as well.

**electromagnetic spectrum** The range of waveforms that occur in the environment.

**e-mail** Electronic mail; the capability to send text messages and other digital files across the Internet.

**embedded programs** Self-contained applications that can be included in a web page.

**Enhanced Metafile Format (EMF)** A metafile format developed by Microsoft; predominantly used in Microsoft products.

**events** Something that occurs during the playback of a movie that can be responded to, such as the click of a button.

**executable application** A standalone program most often designed to perform a specific task. Requires no other programs for execution.

**Explorer** A web browser created by Microsoft.

**expression** Sequences of operators and operands (variable names, functions, properties, and so on) used to compute numerical or string results.

**Extensible Markup Language (XML)** A web technology that permits the data within a web page to be described to enable better search capabilities; does not refer to formatting.

**external file compression** Compression that occurs independently of any particular type of digital data.

**external link** A link in a web page that leads outside the current site.

**eyeflow** The direction in which a user's eyes are drawn or directed across a page.

**farcle** A sharp and intense flash of refracted light, similar to a starburst.

**field** A text element that is editable during playback.

**field of vision**  The range or cone of vision.

**file size**  The size of a digital file, usually in kilobytes or megabytes.

**File Transfer Protocol (FTP)**  An Internet service designed to distribute and retrieve files across the Internet.

**filter**  A special add-on program that allows the user to create a special effect or perform some special function.

**FLA**  The extension for a native Flash file that can be opened into Flash.

**Flash Player**  The stand-alone program that can be used to play back Flash SWF files.

**FlashScript command (FS Command)**  A specific action in Flash that allows two values to be passed to external web technologies such as JavaScript.

**flat shading**  Rendering in which the scene or model is represented by wires and flat polygonal colors.

**FLI**  See *Autodesk FLI and FLC.*

**font**  See *typefont.*

**four-color process**  Color printing technology that uses cyan, yellow, magenta, and black inks to create full-color reproductions.

**fps**  Frames per second.

**frame**  A single instance in time in an animation; one cel.

**frame number**  The total number of frames in a digital animation or video.

**frame rate**  See *fps.*

**FreeHand**  A vector-illustration program created by Macromedia (*http://www.macromedia.com/*).

**frequency**  A method of describing a particular sound; measured in hertz.

**frequency variations**  The fundamental basis for analog data; consist of waves.

**FrontPage**  An HTML generator and site management tool created by Microsoft (*http://www.microsoft.com/*).

**functions**  Special code words that receive a value, do something to that value, and then return the result.

**FutureSplash**  The original name of Flash when owned by FutureWave.

**FutureWave**  The original company that initiated the development of Futuresplash, Flash's predecessor.

**general MIDI mode**  The specification that states the standard MIDI channel and instrument numbers.

**generation**  Used to describe a hierarchy of copies in analog dubbing.

**GET**  A method of sending data from one web technology to another. When defined as a GET action, data is sent in the form *Query_String.*

**GIF 89a**  A special GIF file that can contain transparency data.

**global variable**  A variable that exists during the entire life of a program or web page.

**Gopher**  A text- and menu-based Internet search program.

**Gouroud**  A rendering technique in which polygonal faces are rendered using surface normals; no shades and shadows.

**graphic (symbol)**  Symbols that cannot include button symbols, interactivity, or sound. Graphic symbol instances stop playing when the main timeline stops.

**Graphic Interchange Format (GIF)**  A special file format developed by CompuServe that can contain 256-color data as well as transparency information.

**grayscale**  The scale of values from black to white.

**group**  The ability to temporarily cluster elements so that they may be edited as a single object.

**guide layers**  Special layers used as motion paths for symbols in motion tweening.

**handles**  Small, square boxes used in vector illustration programs to represent points.

**helper application**  An external application used to aid the browser in viewing certain types of files.

**hertz**  A measure of waveform cycles per second.

**hexadecimal color** A base 16 mathematical scheme used to define colors for a web browser.

**hierarchical linking** The ability to link one object to another so that changes to one object also affect the linked object.

**HLS** An acronym for hue, light, and saturation.

**HLS color model** A color model used to describe a gamut of colors by hue, light, and saturation.

**horizontal space** The width of the letter M in a font.

**hue** A characteristic of color that distinguishes it from other colors; the name of a color such as red, blue, and green.

**human-computer interface** An area of study that focuses on the development of effective interface design.

**hypermedia** Media that includes text, graphics, sound, animation, and video and is not confined to a single source medium.

**hypertext** Text that is nonlinear and nonsequential.

**Hypertext Markup Language (HTML)** The tag language used to describe the content of web pages; a derivative of the SGML language.

**icons** Graphic representations or abstractions.

**Illustrator** A vector illustration program created by Adobe (*http://www.adobe.com/*).

**image bit depth** See *bit depth*.

**image maps** Special graphics that can be used in web pages that are divided into regions; each region may be hotlinked to a different site or page.

**image resolution** A description of the number of pixels per inch in an image.

**image size** A description of an image's physical size in pixels.

**in-betweens** Frames that occur in between the key actions or movements in an animation.

**indexed** See *8-bit color*.

**inline image** An image inserted into a web page using the < A > tag.

**instance** The occurrence of a symbol on the stage.

**interactive multimedia** Any combination of text, graphics, sound, animation, and video that is controlled by the user and displayed by a computer.

**interface** The point of interaction between a user and a computer.

**interlaced** A file stored so that it may be downloaded and displayed a chunk at a time.

**internal file compression** File compression that occurs as a result of the data in a particular file format.

**interpolate** To derive values based on other values.

**interpreter** A program that executes lines of code a line at a time.

**intersection** A basic Boolean operation in which the overlapping area or volume of two objects becomes residual, with all remaining area (nonshared)deleted.

**intrasite link** A link that jumps you to another page in the current site.

**inverse kinematics** The study of interrelationships among mechanical objects and their movements over time.

**Java** A universal, platform-independent, object-oriented programming language.

**JavaScript** A scripting language that is a simplified derivative of the Java programming language.

**Joint Photographic Experts Group (JPEG)** A graphic image file format that uses lossy compression and can contain image data up to 24-bit.

**kerning** The amount of space between letters or between words.

**keyframe** A frame in an animation in which a key action or change is taking place; primary positions, colors, sizes, or orientations of objects defined within the timeline.

**kilohertz (kHz)** 1000 hertz.

**kinematics** The study of the relationship of movement as it relates to mechanical objects.

**kinesiology** The study of the relationship of movement as it relates to the human body.

**labels** Special markers associated with timeline keyframes that can be jumped to.

**layering** The capability of a graphics application to store objects distinctly and separately.

**leading** The spacing between lines of text.

**length** String function that determines the number of characters in a string.

**Lepel ZivWelch compression (LZW)** Lossless compression scheme most often used in the TIFF file format.

**letter spacing** The spacing between letters of a font.

**library** Collection of symbols; facility through which the symbols of any file may be accessed and imported into another file.

**license** A permission to use a copyrighted item, typically based on various parameters of use and for which a fee is paid.

**linear** Pertaining to progression or straight movement.

**linear array** An array in which each additional value is indexed by a number.

**local variable** A variable that exists only as long as the function that called it is executing.

**logical operators** Operators used to combine conditions within If and Loop actions.

**lossless** Compression programs in which no data is lost; the uncompressed file creates an exact replica of the original.

**lossy compression** Scheme in which certain amounts of data are sacrificed for higher compression ratios.

**Macintosh PICT** Native Macintosh metafile format that can house both vector and raster information.

**mapped** Pertaining to 8-bit color mapping.

**mask layers** Special layers used to mask out portions of other layers.

**metafile** A file format that can contain multiple types of data.

**modifiers** Optional settings for the tools in Flash.

**metaphor** A likeness, construct, or similarity to some other device that is used in an effort to more quickly familiarize the audience with an information device.

**methods** The things an object can do (action verbs for the object).

**modeler** The portion of a 3D animation package that is used to create or import modeling data.

**mono-aural** Describes a single-channel digital audio file.

**monochromatic** An image using only tints and shades of a single hue.

**monospaced fonts** Fonts in which there is no letter spacing variations from character to character.

**morph** The ability to smoothly interpolate between two or more images.

**motion guide** See *guide layers*.

**Motion Picture Experts Group (MPG)** A digital video format commonly found on the Web.

**motion tween** A tween animation based on position, orientation, size, or color changes.

**mouse events** See *events*.

**MOV** See *QuickTime*.

**movie clip (symbol)** A special timeline in a movie that permits any object to be inserted within it. Movie clip symbols continue to play even if the main movie stops.

**MPEG** See *Motion Picture Experts Group*.

**MP3** A compressed audio format for the Web; see also *Motion Picture Experts Group*.

**multimedia** Any combination of text, graphics, sound, animation, and video displayed and controlled by the computer.

**Multiple Master** A special type of vector font.

**multiprotocol** Descriptive of the capacity to communicate using various network protocols.

**Multipurpose Internet Mail Extension (MIME)** The method of associating Internet file types with specific extensions with applications that can open them.

**Musical Instrument Device Interface (MIDI)** A method of digitally describing audio using instrument and note descriptions.

**negative space** Describes white space, or areas without visual elements, on a web page.

**nested symbols** Symbols that contain other symbols.

**nonlinear** Nonsequential.

**nontransient information** Information that remains stable or accurate over a period of nine months to a year.

**Non-Uniform Rational B-Splines (NURBS)** A parametric modeling environment in which surface points may be easily edited; allows for very complex organic surfaces and objects.

**numerical operators** Operators that perform mathematical calculations.

**numerical value** A number.

**objects** Specific instances of a class in the environment.

**onion-skinning** A carryover technique from traditional cel animation in which the content of adjacent frames are composited to enable comparisons of motion.

**opacity** Describes the visual solidness of surfaces; transparent is the opposite of opaque.

**operators** Programming elements that perform calculations (operations) or comparisons on two values to reach a third resultant value.

**origin** In relation to the 3D coordinate system, the origin is the location 0,0,0.

**overlay** A theoretical organization level in Flash that contains groups, symbols, and text elements.

**palette** See *color look-up table (CLUT)*.

**palletized** See *8-bit color*.

**particle systems** A special function within a 3D animation program that allows the animator to create effects such as rain, snow, and tornadoes.

**path of motion** The path on which animated objects travel; defined by keyframe positioning and orientation.

**persistence of vision** The visual phenomenon of the eyes and brain perceiving an image after it has been removed from sight.

**perspective** A pictorial drawing in which the lines in the scene tend to converge to the horizon.

**phong** A rendering engine capable of generating smooth surfaces and calculate highlights and shadows based on lights positioned in the environment.

**Photoshop** A raster editing application created by Adobe (*http://www.adobe.com/*).

**PICT** See *Macintosh PICT*.

**pitch** The relative position of a tone in a scale, as determined by its sound-wave frequency.

**pixels (picture element)** The smallest element of a bitmap image, computer monitor, or television display.

**pixels per inch (ppi)** The number of pixels per square inch.

**plug-ins** Add-on programs that extend the capability of a web browser by allowing it to view a wide range of files, such as animations, digital videos, or multimedia elements.

**point size** Describes the size of a font in points.

**point** A unit of measurement for lines and text; 72 points equals 1 inch.

**polygonal mesh** A surface model that uses polygons, most often triangles, to define the surface of a model.

**Portable Network Graphics (PNG)**    A nonproprietary graphics format designed to unify the formats used on the Web. Boasts all of the features of both JPEG and GIF in a single format.

**positive space**    The areas of a web page that contain visual elements such as text or graphics.

**POST**    A method of sending data from one web technology to another. POST method is sent as a standard input stream.

**Postscript**    A page description language developed by Adobe that is used by most vector drawing programs.

**preloader**    An introductory portion of a movie that plays while the remainder of a movie is streamed to the end user.

**Premiere**    A digital video editing program created by Adobe (*http://www.adobe.com*).

**primary color**    The main colors of any given color system; all other colors in the system are derived from the primary colors.

**procedural mapping**    A method of adding surface textures to 3D objects through the use of algorithms.

**progressive JPEG**    A special type of JPEG image that allows the browser to begin viewing the image before it is fully down-loaded.

**projector**    A stand-alone Flash movie that is executable and does not require the Flash Player.

**properties**    Attributes of some object.

**property array**    An array in which each name and value pair can be uniquely iden-tified.

**public domain**    Media elements or works that can be used freely, without a license or release.

**quantization**    The process of averaging color based on subsampled blocks.

**QuickTime (MOV)**    A digital video format, created by Apple, originally designed for use on the Macintosh (*http://www.apple.com/*).

**radiant light**    A light source in which light is projected in all directions with no decrease in intensity.

**radiosity**    The most photorealistic type of 3D rendering; takes into consideration all light within a scene.

**random**    Numeric function that generates a random number.

**random access memory (RAM)**    The main memory of the computer that is used to temporarily store data.

**raster-based graphics**    See *bitmap*.

**raytracing**    A rendering technique that traces light rays within a scene; does not calculate scattered light rays.

**RCA-type**    A typical cable connector used with digital video and digital audio.

**reflected light**    See *additive colors*.

**reflectivity**    An object property that describes its shininess and how much of the scene is reflected in the surface.

**release**    A permission to use a copyrighted item without payment or fees; often usage has certain limitations.

**remapping**    Pertains to changing the color palette of an image.

**renderer**    The part of the 3D animation pro-gram that generates a raster image or ani-mation.

**rendering engine**    Special code that uses the 3D scene to create a flat raster image; includes wireframe, flat, Gouroud, phong, raytracing, and radiosity.

**resolution**    The photo-realism of an image; describes the ratio of image resolution to image size.

**RGB**    Acronym for red, green, blue.

**RGB color**    See *24-bit*.

**RGB color model**    Theoretical color space used to describe the range of colors avail-able on a computer monitor.

**roll**    Relates to rotation about the Z axis.

**run length encoding**    See *Windows bitmap*.

**S-Video** A video cable connector commonly found on U.S. devices.

**sampling** The process of converting analog data to digital data.

**sampling rate** Measure of how frequently samples in a sound clip or image occur.

**sans serif** Typefaces (fonts) without serifs. See also *serif*.

**saturation** Describes the purity of a color, or how much of a color is in a hue.

**Scalable Vector Graphics (SVG)** A web specification being developed by a W3C working group composed of a variety of leading companies, including Microsoft, Adobe, and Macromedia (*http://www.w3.org/TR/WD-SVG*).

**scan lines** The horizontal lines of pixels in a computer monitor.

**scenes** The main timelines within a movie.

**scope** The lifespan of a variable.

**serif** The stroke projecting from and finishing off the top and/or bottom of a character in some typefaces.

**serif fonts** Fonts displaying the serif characteristic.

**shade** Area of a surface opposite the light source.

**shadows** Areas of a surface blocked from a light source by another feature or object.

**shape hints** Reference points used within shape tweening to control the way one object morphs to another. See also *in-betweens* and *shape tweens*.

**shape tweens** Animations consisting of objects that morph.

**Shockwave** A plug-in created by Macromedia for viewing multimedia and vector elements on the Web. Shockwave components may be generated from Director, Authorware, or Flash.

**Shockwave Flash (SWF)** The generic movie format used to distribute movies on the Web; requires the Flash Player for playback; can be protected or unprotected.

**simple text** The standard Macintosh ASCII text editor.

**SIT** A compressed file create by Aladdin's Stuffit Deluxe.

**site map** A planning tool for charting the content of a web site.

**size report** An ASCII text file that details the file size requirements of the objects in a movie.

**SND** See *System 7 sound files (SND)*.

**solid model** A model that has theoretical volume and engineering properties.

**Sound Blaster Vocal Files (VOC)** A digital audio format designed by Creative Labs.

**spatial** Relating to 3D coordinate space or spacial relationships.

**spline** A curve with weighted control points.

**spot light** A directed light source.

**sprite** An element or object in a 2D animation program.

**stage** A theoretical organization level in Flash that contains ungrouped elements, basic objects (such as lines and fills), and broken elements.

**Standard Generalized Markup Language (SGML)** An advanced markup language commonly used to produce electronic versions of large texts such as encyclopedias and dictionaries.

**static** Pertaining to images that do not change or are not animated.

**stereo** A multiple-channel digital audio file.

**stereoscopic field of vision** The area created by the overlapping cone of vision from each eye; field in which depth is perceived.

**stereoscopic vision** The ability to perceive depth.

**storyboard** A thumbnail representation often used for planning an animation, multimedia, or hypermedia product.

**streaming** The process of delivering small chunks of a digital file over the Internet for instant execution.

**string literal** A value entered into an Action field; a variable that is text.

**string operators** Operators used to manipulate text. Flash has only one concatenate.

**string value** See *string literal*.

**Stuffit Expander** A compression program used on the Macintosh platform.

**subsampling** The process of breaking an image into component blocks that are then color averaged.

**substring** String function that extracts a portion of a string variable by defining a string, an index (starting position for extraction), and a count (ending position for extraction).

**subtraction** One of the basic Boolean operations; the volume or area of one object is subtracted from the volume or area of another.

**subtractive colors** Colors produced on a white page by applying hues.

**subtractive primaries** Cyan, yellow, magenta, and black.

**Sun Audio (AU)** Audio format predominantly used on the UNIX operating system.

**surface mapping** The process of applying qualities to 3D objects so that they look realistic.

**surface model** A model consisting of surfaces with no volume characteristics.

**symbol** A special reusable component in Flash that has its own timeline.

**symmetrical balance** Descriptive of a layout in which there is a relative balance of visual elements in the area of a page and/or between facing pages.

**synthesis** The ability to create a waveform (analog data).

**System 7 sound files (SND)** Standard Macintosh system sound format.

**system palette** The color palette or color look-up table associated with a 256-color environment.

**Tagged Image File Format (TIFF)** A raster graphic file format designed to contain high-resolution image data for print purposes.

**target path** The method for identifying objects in Flash; used within the Tell Target action.

**text editor** A program designed to edit plain ASCII text files.

**TIFF** See *Tagged Image File Format*.

**tiles** Bitmaps used as repeating segments over the background of a browser; a tiled background.

**tint** Adding white to any hue.

**transient information** Information that is rapidly changing; generally changes within nine months.

**translation** A basic manipulation of an object; includes move, rotate, and scale.

**translucent** The ability of light to pass through a surface.

**transparency** The ability to see through an object.

**triad** A color scheme using three colors that are equally spaced from one another on the color wheel.

**trigger** Slang for a button that has only a hit state.

**True color** See *24-bit color*.

**TrueType** A typical type of vector font.

**tweens** See *in-betweens*.

**Typeface (font)** A unique set of characters that have similar characteristics; examples are Helvetica, Geneva, and Times New Roman.

**typography** The study of type and its various characteristics.

**union** A basic Boolean operation in which overlapping volume or area between two objects is joined, or "welded," to create a single object.

**Universal Resource Locator (URL)** The unique naming address scheme used on the Web.

**value** Pertaining to the lightness or darkness of a color. Adding black to a hue creates a shade; adding white to a hue creates a tint.

**variable** A container for data.

**VBScript** A web-based scripting language.

**vector fonts** Fonts described using vector descriptions.

**vector-based graphics** Graphics in which the smaller drawing elements are points, lines, and arcs.

**vector markup language (VML)** An XML-based format for vector graphics, developed by Microsoft (*http://msdn. microsoft.com/standards/vml/*).

**Video for Windows (AVI)** A common digital video format created for use on the Windows platform.

**Virtual Reality Modeling Language (VRML)** A markup language designed to deliver 3D environment descriptions for viewing on the Web.

**visible light** The small portion of the electromagnetic spectrum that humans can perceive.

**VOC** See *Sound Blaster Vocal Files*.

**warm colors** Colors that tend to come toward the viewer; includes colors such as red, yellow, and orange.

**WAV** See *Windows Waveform Files (WAV)*.

**WebCGM** An ISO standard metafile format for the Web that can store raster data, vector data, or both. Currently, no browsers or authoring environments support it (*http://www.w3.org/TR/REC-WebCGM*).

**weight (of a font)** The thickness of the lines that constitute the characters of a font.

**white space** See *negative space*.

**Windows Bitmap (BMP)** Raster format created by Microsoft for bitmap images.

**Windows Waveform Files (WAV)** The standard Windows digital audio format.

**wireframe model** A model consisting of connecting lines and points but with no surfaces between these elements.

**wireframe rendering** A rendering in which the lines of the object are rendered but no surfaces are rendered.

**WordPad** The Windows 95 and Windows NT ASCII text editor.

**XML** See *Extensible Markup Language*.

**yaw** Rotation about the Y axis.

**ZIP** A compressed file created by PKWARE's PKZIP program.

# Understanding Bandwidth and Data Rate

Although high-quality media elements are limited on the Web, it must be noted that even low-quality multimedia elements can severely slow down web delivery, particularly at high-usage times during the day. Table A-1 outlines common connection speeds for various end-user technologies, as well as how long it takes to download 100 kilobytes of data using these technologies. The importance of this chart is that devices often claim a high connection rate or bandwidth when presented in marketing literature. Yet, actually the data rate is what is important.

Even moderate multimedia sound and video capability requires speeds of 200 kbps or greater for adequate playback. Devices appearing further up in the chart in table A-1 will provide unacceptable results, such as video that plays erratically or audio that inadvertently pauses.

You can easily calculate bandwidth from data rate, or vice versa. This allows you to determine how long it will take to download a certain amount of content over a particular connection. Given a bandwidth, divide by 8 to obtain the data rate. Then divide the file size by the data rate. Given a data rate, multiply by 8 to determine the bandwidth.

It must be noted that the connection speeds shown in table A-1 assume that a single user is connected to the data source. As more individuals attempt to access a site, the data rate is split across the number of multiple connections. This means that even though the user can download data at 188 KBps (assuming a 1.5-mbps connection), the server supplying the data may be serving 100 other users at the same time. This decreases the actual amount of data being served to each individual. In this instance, the server becomes the limiting element due to the number of connected users.

Many claim that for the Web to be as effective as CD-ROM media or video, it needs to support video and audio. In reality, this depends on your purpose and what type of content you want to deliver. Materials that depend heavily on full-screen graphics, video, or audio may be more effectively delivered on DVD, CD-ROM, video, or laser disk media. However, many new technologies, such as Macromedia Flash, are changing this.

*Table A-1 Web Connection Data Rates, Bandwidths, and Transfer Times*

| Connection | Data Rate | Bandwidth | Time per 100 KB (sec.) |
|---|---|---|---|
| 14.4 modem | 1.8 KB | 14.4 kb | 55 |
| 28.8 modem | 3.6 KB | 28.8 kb | 27 |
| 33.6 modem | 4.2 KB | 33.6 kb | 23 |
| 56-K modem | 7 KB | 56 kb | 14 |
| ISDN | 7-16 KB | 56-128 kb | 14-6 |
| Frame Relay | 7-64 KB | 56-512 kb | 14-1.5 |
| T1 | 32-193 KB | 256-1,544 kb | 3.1-.5 |

| Connection | Data Rate | Bandwidth | Time per 100 KB (sec.) |
|---|---|---|---|
| 1X CD | 150 KB | 1.2 mb | .66 |
| DSL | 188 KB | 1.5 mb | .53 |
| Cable modems | 188 KB | 1.5 mb | .53 |
| 2X CD | 200 KB | 1.6 mb | .5 |
| 4X CD | 450 KB | 3.6 mb | .22 |
| 10X CD | 1.2 MB | 9.6 mb | .08 |
| Ethernet | 1.25 MB | 10 mb | .08 |
| 16X CD | 2.4 MB | 19.2 mb | .04 |
| 24X CD | 3.6 MB | 28.8 mb | .02 |
| T3 | 5.5 MB | 44 mb | .01 |
| USB | 12 MB | 96 mb | .0083 |
| Firewire | 100-400 MB | 800 mb-3.2 gb | .001-.00025 |

appendix **B**

# Design Sizes for Web Browsers

The size of the browser display area changes, depending on browser and the viewing resolution. Although Flash movies are scaleable, it is helpful to know the sizes that can be used for development. Table B-1 presents the display area of the two major browsers (Netscape and Internet Explorer) at various sizes. Because the leftmost and topmost margins can never be zero, appropriate sizes for designs are also presented. Note that the sizes presented assume that the Taskbar is set to auto-hide.

*Table B-1  Netscape and Internet Explorer (IE) Browser Display Area Sizes*

| Browser | Version Resolution (pixels) | Display Resolution (pixels) | Exact Browser | Recommended Design Resolution (pixels) |
|---|---|---|---|---|
| Netscape | 3.X | 640 x 480 | 612 x 289 | 600 x 280 |
| Netscape | 4.X | 640 x 480 | 612 x 322 | 600 x 280 |
| IE | 4.X | 640 x 480 | 612 x 334 | 600 x 280 |
| Netscape | 3.X | 800 x 600 | 772 x 425 | 750 x 400 |
| Netscape | 4.X | 800 x 600 | 772 x 442 | 750 x 400 |
| IE | 4.X | 800 x 600 | 773 x 454 | 750 x 400 |
| Netscape | 3.X | 1024 x 768 | 996 x 593 | 990 x 585 |
| Netscape | 4.X | 1024 x 768 | 996 x 610 | 990 x 585 |
| IE | 4.X | 1024 x 768 | 996 x 622 | 990 x 585 |

# Hexadecimal Color

In web graphics, the definitions of colors in the image are a function of the raster or vector editor you use. Some allow you to use the RGB model and specify your colors by red, green, and blue. Others may use the HLS or CYM models for color specification. However, with graphics included on web pages, there is no direct color definition in the HTML file. The colors are defined in the image when you create it. Therefore, all colors are inherent to the image.

However, with text elements, backgrounds, and horizontal rules defined by the HTML coding, as well as some entities within Flash, you must work with something called hexadecimal color. Hexadecimal color is a base 16 mathematical numbering system used to define and describe HTML colors for the browser. Unless you have worked in some area of computer programming in the past, it is likely that this will be your first acquaintance with hexadecimal color.

As you will find, it is much easier to work with colors in a graphics editor than it is to work with colors in HTML coding. In an editor, colors are defined by simply picking them with the mouse. In HTML, however, you must mathematically define colors using abstract letters and numbers, such as FFFFFF for white or 000000 for black.

## Hexadecimal Color Code

All browser colors are defined using hex. Colored text, colored links, colored outlines, and anything that is not a graphic component must be defined using hexadecimal code. In reality, hexadecimal code is nothing more than three two-number sequences that represent our normal decimal numbering system. It sounds simple, but to many it is a point of confusion. Really the only thing you have to do is convert your normal method of representing graphic color (RGB) to a hexadecimal representation.

If you have used an image editor, you have probably seen how the environment defines colors. Using RGB or CYMK sliders, you combine additive or subtractive primaries to create a single color. In hexadecimal, however, each color requires a unique hexadecimal code to define it. To do the conversion, you will need to start with an RGB-based color definition.

For example, in RGB, white is defined as R:255, B:255, G:255. The hexadecimal representation is FFFFFF. For black, the RGB definition is R:0, B:0, G:0. The hexadecimal representation is 000000. Each hex digit counts from 0 to 9, and then A to F. Thus, the counting in hex is as follows: 0, 1, 2, 3, 4, 5, 6, 7, 8, 9, A, B, C, D, E, F. In the series of six hex digits, two values are used to represent each RGB value. The first two are for red components, the second two are for green, and the third set is for blue. Thus, you can think of a hex value as RRGGBB.

You will find that hex is an abstract way of representing color, and one that many despise. Probably the only hex values you will remember from memory are black, white, and "Netscape Gray" (CCCCCC). However, there is a quick method you can perform with a calculator that will give you accurate results every time. Note, however, that it will not make it any more fun!

# Calculating Hexadecimal Values

To calculate hexadecimal values, you will need twothings. The first is the RGB specification of the color you wish to convert to hex. For this, you can use a graphic editor. Choose a color visually and then write down the RGB color values shown in the editor. The second thing you will need is a scientific calculator. If you have a PC, you have it already (look in the Accessories group for the calculator). Unfortunately for Macintosh users, there is no system calculator that can work in scientific mode. There are, however, several shareware and freeware calculators that have this capability. To convert an RGB color to a hexadecimal color, perform the following steps.

- Find the red, green, and blue values for the color in your image editor. An RGB color defined by R:222, G:39, and B:151 is used for this example. However, any RGB color will do.

- Open the calculator from Window | Accessories.

- Select Scientific from the View menu.

- Make sure you are in DEC (Decimal) mode, and enter the red value into the calculator. From the sample color, you would use the red value of 222.

- Click on HEX, which will then show you the hex value of the red decimal value. Your red value of 222 gives you a hex value of DE. Jot this hex value down.

- Repeat steps 4 and 5 with the green and blue values. The green value of 39 should give you a hex value of 27. The blue value of 151 should give you a hex value of 97.

- Once you have converted the red, green, and blue values to hex, write your results as a single string. This is the hex value of the color. In the example, an RGB color of R:222, G:39, and B:151 is represented in hexadecimal code as DE3997. You would then use this value in your HTML code. If you wanted the background color of the browser to be this color, you would enter the following:

```
<BODY BGCOLOR="#DE3997">
```

- This makes the background of the browser the specified hex color. These hex values can be used in Flash, as well as in other graphic editors.

# Other Macromedia Tools

Although this is not meant to be an exhaustive review of the other Macromedia tools, this appendix provides some basic information concerning the advantage of using these other tools with Flash. For further information on these products, see Macromedia's web site at *http://www.macromedia.com*, which provides an in-depth look at the features of these products.

## Macromedia Authorware

Authorware is a longstanding Macromedia Product that provides an easy-to-use interface for creating interactive multimedia products. As an icon-based product, it is focused toward educational products, and provides many features that allow the developer to automatically track user response information. Generally, Authorware is used for CD-ROM projects, but may also be used to create web-distributable packets. Flash 4 movies may be fully integrated into the latest version of Authorware.

## Macromedia Director

As quite possibly holding the largest share of the multimedia market, Director is one of Macromedia's most popular programs. Not intended for the novice user, Director provides the ability to utilize a wide range of media elements, and has been mostly used for the creation of CD-ROM-based multimedia projects. With its internal scripting language Lingo, Director can be used to author very complex applications, not to mention the generation of Shockwave movies for the Web. As for Flash support, Director 8 supports Flash 4 features, Director 7 supports Flash 3 features, and older versions require a plug-in for Flash 3 support. Future versions of Director will likely support Flash 5 features.

## Macromedia Dreamweaver

Dreamweaver is Macromedia's web-site-creation and management tool. Similar to other tools that fit the site management category, such as Microsoft Frontpage, Dreamweaver allows you to generate HTML pages with all of the features common to HTML code. However, it provides extended features such as the support of Extensions, which automatically integrate complex JavaScript and DHTML code into the page. As with all site management tools, the goal is to provide an easy-to-use graphical user interface for creating complex web sites. Yet, Dreamweaver also permits the entry of custom code and does not revise or rewrite code that is added by the developer.

## Macromedia Fireworks

As a utility program for web site creation, Fireworks is designed to work with raster graphic elements for web pages. It provides the ability to optimize GIF graphics, create GIF animations, and preview and generate JPEG and PNG images for the Web. As a utility tool, it works well with Dreamweaver, as well as with several of Macromedia's other tools.

## Macromedia FreeHand

For the generation of static vector illustration, FreeHand is one of the two main tools on the market. Originally designed for printed materials, FreeHand is a very comprehensive vector illustration tool. However, in the past two versions several web-focused features have been added, such as the Release to Layers and Animate Layer/Pages commands. As a supplementary tool to Flash, FreeHand provides the typical Bezier approach to vector illustration.

## Macromedia Generator

Marcomedia Generator is a very powerful server and workstation product. The server version allows you to create Flash templates that provide the ability to include dynamically generated Flash graphics to your web pages. For example, you could create a Flash graphic whose content changed depending on user variables. When the user accesses the Flash movie, it is customized to the end user.

# Embedding QuickTime Files

Flash allows you to output QuickTime 4 files using the Publish command. Table E-1, which follows, presents the attributes that can be used within the Embed tag when QuickTime movies are defined as the source. More information may be found at Apple's site at *http://www.apple.com/quicktime/authoring/embed2.html.*

*Table E-1 Attributes Used with the <EMBED> Tag for QuickTime Movies*

| Attribute | Values | Version | Required | Function |
|---|---|---|---|---|
| AUTOPLAY=value | TRUE or FALSE | QT3 or later | No | Determines whether the movie automatically starts playing. |
| BGCOLOR=value | HEX Value (#000000 = black) or valid color name | QT4 or later | No | Determines the background color of any area not taken up by the movie. |
| CACHE=value | TRUE or FALSE | QT3 or later | No | Specifies whether the movie is stored in the browser cache. Only valid for Netscape 3 or higher. |
| CONTROLLER=value | TRUE or FALSE | QT3 or later | No | Determines whether the QT player control bar is shown. Default is FALSE. |
| CORRECTION=value | NONE or FULL | QT3 or later | No | Determines of a QTVR panorama is autocorrected. |
| ENDTIME=value | Numerically lists hours, minutes, seconds, frames in form H:M:S:F | QT4 or later | No | Specifies the last frame of the movie (duration). |
| FOV=value | Integer | QT3 or later | No | Defines the field of view for a QTVR movie. |
| HEIGHT=value | Integer (pixels) | All | Yes | Defines the height of the movie in the web page, defined in pixels. |
| HIDDEN | N/A | All | No | Controls the visibility of the movie. |
| HOTSPOTn=url | n=integer, url=String | QT3 or later | No | Defines the URLs associated with hotspots in a panorama (QTVR). |
| HREF=url | url=String | QT3 or later | No | Defines a URL for the movie, similar to defining an image to a URL. |
| KIOSKMODE=value | TRUE or FALSE | QT4 or later | No | When true, movie does not include pop-up menu and does not allow drag and drop for saving. |

| Attribute | Values | Version | Required | Function |
|---|---|---|---|---|
| LOOP=value | TRUE, FALSE or PALIDROME | QT3 or later | No | Allows movie to loop. PALIDROME plays forward and backward. |
| MOVIEID=name | String | QT4 or later | No | Allows one movie to target another using the MOVIEID. |
| NODE=value | Integer | QT3 or later | No | Defines the starting node in a multi-node (multi-movie) QTVR movie. |
| PAN=value | Integer | QT3 or later | No | Specifies the starting pan value in a QTVR movie. |
| PLAYEVERYFRAME= value | TRUE or FALSE | QT3 or later | No | When true turns off audio and plays every frame. |
| PLUGINSPAGE=url | String | All | No | Specifies the URL to get the plug-in. |
| QTNEXTn=url | n=integer, url=string | QT4 or later | No | Allows one movie to play after another. |
| QTSRC=url | String | QT4 of later | No | Forces the browser to use the QT plug-in regardless of MIME specification in the browser. |
| SCALE=value | TOFIT, ASPECT or number | QT3 or later | No | Allows size to be adjusted to HEIGHT and WIDTH attributes. |
| STARTTIME=value | Numerically lists hours, minutes, seconds, frames in form H:M:S:F | QT4 or later | No | Defines the starting frame of the movie. |
| TARGET=value | "QUICKTIME-PLAYER" | QT4 or later | No | Launches the QT Player as a helper application. |
| TARGETn=value | n=integer, value=string | QT3 of later | No | Specifies a frame name in conjunction with the HREF and HOTSPOT attributes. |
| TARGETCACHE= value | TRUE or FALSE | QT4 or later | No | Determines whether targeted movie is cached. |
| TILT=value | Integer | QT3 or later | No | Specifies the staring tilt value for a QTVR movie. |
| TYPE=value | String MIME type | All | No | Specifies MIME information for the embedded element. |
| VOLUME=value | Integer (0-100) | QT3 or later | No | Determines the starting volume for the movie. Default is 100. |
| WIDTH=value | Integer (pixels) | All | Yes | Defines the width of the movie in the web page, defined in pixels. |

appendix **F**

# Configuring Your Server

As you look at the wide range of multimedia elements that can be distributed on the Web, you will notice that they can be included in web pages in a variety of ways. Originally the browser could only interpret HTML code and plain GIF and JPEG graphics. Yet, as the functions users want to perform have gotten more complex, special capabilities have been added through add-on programs that allow multimedia elements to be embedded directly within HTML pages.

As you look at the brief history of the web browser, you will see the beginnings of web multimedia capabilities found in the use of helper applications. Helper applications are applications that are external to the browser (often created by a separate company) and are executed as certain media elements are encountered or downloaded from the Web. Even though the use of helper applications is decreasing, realize that many sites and end users still depend on them for playback of content.

For example, one of the first ways of utilizing digital video movies, such as QuickTime movies, was to use the QuickTime movie player application. In this scenario, when the browser encountered a page with a QuickTime video file, the user was required to click on a hotlink, which would then download the movie. Once the movie was downloaded, the browser would open an external application, Apple's QuickTime Movie Player, and play the movie. Any file that was foreign to the browser (anything other than HTML, GIF, or JPEG) required an external helper application.

## Enter MIME

The browser derives all of its application associations, the information that tells it how to view files (based on the three-character DOS file extensions), from an information list called Multipurpose Internet Mail Extensions (MIME). This list must be defined in the browser, as well as on the server used for distributing web files. The MIME information defines several important pieces of information for the browser or server concerning any given file type. This information includes:

- The file's type, such as text or image data.
- The application subtype, such as plain or JPEG.
- The three-letter extension for the file, such as *.txt* or *.jpg*.
- Information on what to do with the file. Options include View in Browser, Save to Disk, Prompt User, and Open Application.

Using the MIME entry information, the browser is able to look at the three-letter extension and then determine whether to try to view the downloaded file in the browser, save it to disk, or open it into another application (a helper application). On the server, MIME types define the file, type, and whether or not the file is distributable.

# Moving Up the Food Chain: Plug-ins

Even though helper-based multimedia was the first means of utilizing multimedia elements on the Web, many companies recognized the need to be able to directly integrate multimedia into the web page, rather than requiring an external application for viewing those elements. This lead to the advent of plug-ins that could be installed on the client machine to assist the browser in interpreting multimedia elements directly. These plug-in based multimedia elements, such as Shockwave movies, allow any range of media elements to be included on web pages.

Realize that certain media elements (such as digital video, animations, or digitized sound) can actually utilize either plug-in technologies or helper applications. Depending on how the user machine is configured (i.e., what MIME associations are established), the browser will determine whether a helper or plug-in is used.

## The Browser and MIME

Interpretation and delivery of Shocked media elements requires MIME entries for the various file extensions on both the client and server machine. Most often the client-side MIME types are set when plug-ins are installed for the browser. In general, your client-side MIME entries for Macromedia media elements should include the following:

- Director: *.dcr, .dxr, .dir*
- Authorware: *.aam, .aas*
- Flash: *.swf, .spl*

## The Server and MIME

The server-side MIME types must be set as recommended in your server documentation. If a MIME type does not exist for a particular file on the server, the user's browser may not know how to display the file and might ultimately display the broken image icon, rather than your Flash movie.

Note that each server requires that MIME types be established. However, they each do it a little differently. You should consult the server documentation for the specifics of implementation. Table F-1, which follows, presents the general MIME types and suffixes.

*Table F-1 MIME Types and File Suffixes*

| MIME Type | File Suffix |
|---|---|
| application/x-shockwave-flash | .swf |
| application/futuresplash | .spl |

If you are using a Macintosh server, you must also set the following:

- *Action:* Binary
- *Type:* SWFL
- *Creator:* SWF2

# Key Code Values

Tables G-1 through G-4 present key code values for alphanumeric, numeric keypad, function, and other keys associated with Flash.

## Alphanumeric Keys

Table G-1, which follows, presents alphanumeric key code values for Flash.

*Table G-1 Alphanumeric Key Code Values*

| Letter/ Number | Key Code | Letter/ Number | Key Code | Letter/ Number | Key Code |
|---|---|---|---|---|---|
| A | 65 | M | 77 | Y | 89 |
| B | 66 | N | 78 | Z | 90 |
| C | 67 | O | 79 | 0 | 48 |
| D | 68 | P | 80 | 1 | 49 |
| E | 69 | Q | 81 | 2 | 50 |
| F | 70 | R | 82 | 3 | 51 |
| G | 71 | S | 83 | 4 | 52 |
| H | 72 | T | 84 | 5 | 53 |
| I | 73 | U | 85 | 6 | 54 |
| J | 74 | V | 86 | 7 | 55 |
| K | 75 | W | 87 | 8 | 56 |
| L | 76 | X | 88 | 9 | 57 |

## Numeric Keypad Keys

Table G-2, which follows, presents numeric keypad key code values for Flash.

*Table G-2 Numeric Keypad Key Code Values*

| Numeric Keypad Key | Key Code | Numeric Keypad Key | Key Code |
|---|---|---|---|
| 0 | 96 | 8 | 104 |
| 1 | 97 | 9 | 105 |
| 2 | 98 | Multiply | 106 |
| 3 | 99 | Add | 107 |
| 4 | 100 | Enter | 108 |
| 5 | 101 | Subtract | 109 |
| 6 | 102 | Decimal | 110 |
| 7 | 103 | Divide | 111 |

# Function Keys

Table G-3, which follows, presents function key code values for Flash.

*Table G-3  Function Key Code Values*

| Function Key | Key Code |
|---|---|
| F1 | 112 |
| F2 | 113 |
| F3 | 114 |
| F4 | 115 |
| F5 | 116 |
| F6 | 117 |
| F7 | 118 |
| F8 | 119 |
| F9 | 120 |
| F10 | 121 |
| F11 | 122 |
| F12 | 123 |

# Other Keyboard Keys

Table G-4, which follows, presents other keyboard key code values for Flash.

*Table G-4 Other Keyboard Key Code Values*

| Key | Key Code | Key | Key Code |
|---|---|---|---|
| Backspace | 8 | Right Arrow | 39 |
| Tab | 9 | Down Arrow | 40 |
| Clear | 12 | Insert | 45 |
| Enter | 13 | Delete | 46 |
| Shift | 16 | Help | 47 |
| Control | 17 | Num Lock | 144 |
| Alt | 18 | ; or : | 186 |
| Caps Lock | 20 | = or + | 187 |
| Esc | 27 | - or _ | 189 |
| Spacebar | 32 | / or ? | 191 |
| Page Up | 33 | ` or ~ | 192 |
| Page Down | 34 | [ or { | 219 |
| End | 35 | \ or I | 220 |
| Home | 36 | ] or } | 221 |
| Left Arrow | 37 | " or ' | 222 |
| Up Arrow | 38 | | |

# About the Companion CD-ROM

The companion CD-ROM at the back of this book contains numerous instructional examples used throughout the text, as well as demonstration versions of Macromedia Flash 5, Swift3D, and Swish in their respective folders. The book folder contains the example files used in the various chapters. This appendix describes the files contained on the companion CD-ROM based on directory structure, as follows. Enjoy!

book/

chapter1/
- *sites.html*    List of sites that utilize Macromedia Flash

chapter2/
- *developer.html*    List of developer resource web sites
- *ch02_01.fla*    Sample Flash file used to see how playback is controlled
- *ch02_02.fla*    Sample file that demonstrates the use of scenes

chapter3/
- *ch03_01.fla*    Using the Arrow tool for shaping
- *ch03_02.fla*    Using the Arrow tool for moving
- *ch03_03.fla*    Using the Arrow tool for moving (fills & lines)
- *ch03_04.fla*    Using the Arrow tool for moving (add & subtract effect)
- *ch03_05.fla*    Working with groups (modify group by double-click)
- *ch03_06.fla*    Straighten and smooth modifiers
- *ch03_07.fla*    Rotate and scale
- *ch03_08.fla*    Using the Subselect tool
- *ch03_09.fla*    Using the Lasso tool
- *ch03_10.fla*    Experimenting with lines and the Stroke panel
- *ch03_11.fla*    Experimenting with ovals
- *ch03_12.fla*    Using the Line, Oval, and Rectangle tools
- *ch03_13.fla*    The Pencil versus the Brush
- *ch03_14.fla*    Working with Brush modes
- *ch03_15.fla*    Working with Eraser modes
- *ch03_16.fla*    Working with the Faucet option
- *ch03_17.fla*    Color and Gap Size modifiers
- *ch03_18.fla*    Paint Bucket and Transform Fill
- *ch03_19.fla*    Using the Ink Bottle
- *ch03_20.fla*    Using the Dropper
- *ch03_21.fla*    Using the Pen tool
- *ch03_22.fla*    Using the Text tool

- *ch03_23.fla* Using the Text panels
- *ch03_24.fla* Breaking text apart
- *ch03_25.fla* Using Align
- *ch03_26.fla* Using Trace Bitmap

chapter4/

- *ch04_01.fla* Example concerning layering and layer icons
- *ch04_02a.fla, ch04_02a.fla, ch04_02a.fla* Cyber Outpost frame-by-frame exercise files
- *ch04_03a.fla, ch04_03b.fla, ch04_03c.fla, ch04_03d.fla* Frame-by-frame telephone exercise files
- *ch04_04a.fla, ch04_04b.fla* Tween animation exercise files
- *ch04_05a.fla, ch04_05b.fla* Color Effect tween animation exercise files
- *ch04_06a.fla, ch04_06b.fla* Guide layer animation exercise files
- *ch04_07a.fla, ch04_07b.fla* Mask layer animation exercise files
- *ch04_08a.fla, ch04_08b.fla* Shape tween animation exercise files
- *ch04_09a.fla, ch04_09b.fla* Shape hints animation exercise files

chapter5/

- *ch05-01.fla* Working with symbols
- *ch05-02.fla, library.fla* Working with libraries
- *ch05-03.fla* The current file's library
- *ch05-04.fla, ch05-04s.fla* Creating a button symbol
- *ch05-05.fla, ch05_05s.fla* Animated buttons with movie clips

chapter6/

- *ch6-01a.fla, ch6-01b.fla, ch6-01c.fla, ch6-01d.fla* Examples of precedence: MC versus button mouse events
- *ch6-02.fla* Examples of precedence: MC versus button key events
- *ch6-03.fla* Examples of precedence: MC versus frame events
- *ch6-04.fla* Examples of precedence: Multiple movie clips
- *ch6-05.fla, ch6-05.swf, ch6-05.html* Examples of Get URL
- *frames/* Using frames and the Get URL action
- *ch6-06.fla, ch6-06.swf, ch6-06.html, get_test.asp* Sending values to a server (GET)
- *ch6-07.fla, ch6-07.swf, ch6-07.html, post_test.asp* Sending values to a server (POST)
- *ch6-08.fla, ch6-08s.fla* Using Play, Stop, and Go To actions
- *ch6-09.fla, ch6-09s.fla, ch6-09_adv.fla* Using Tell Target to control a movie clip
- *ch6-10.fla* Communication among elements (absolute paths), dot syntax
- ch6-11.fla Communication among elements (relative paths), dot syntax
- ch6-12.fla Communication among elements (absolute paths), slash syntax

chapter7/
- *ch7-01.fla*     Adding a sound to the library
- *ch7-02.fla*     Associating sounds with frames
- *ch7-03.fla*     The Event versus Start Sync options
- *ch7-04.fla*     Using the Stream Sync option
- *ch7-05.fla*     Library sound properties
- *ch7-06.fla*     Using Stop All Sounds
- *ch7-07.fla*     Tell Target and Stop All Sounds

chapter8/
- *ch8-01.fla*     Using multiple scenes
- *ch8-02.fla*     Using the Movie Explorer
- *ch8-03.fla , ch8-03-1.fla, ch8-03-2.fla*     Using the Load Movie action
- *ch8-04.fla, ch8-04-1.fla*     Using Tell Target between movies
- *ch8-05.fla, ch8-05-1.fla, ch8-05-2.fla*     Loading a movie into a movie clip

chapter9/
- *jpeg/*     Examples of images exported with various settings
- *audio/*     Examples of sounds exported with various settings
- *ch09-03.swf*     File to be embedded in an exercise
- *ch09-04.fla*     File to be used to generate a size report
- *ch09-05.fla*     File to be used to generate a size report
- *ch09-06.fla*     Optimized example file

chapter10/
- *ch10-01s.fla*     Simple preload example
- *ch10-02.fla, ch10-02s.fla*     Basic preload example
- *ch10-03s.fla*     Completed preloader with percentage bar
- *ch10-04s.fla*     Preloader for Noah's Memory Game
- *ch10-05s.fla*     Preloading across scenes
- *ifs/*     Preloading examples that use an If statement with the *_framesLoaded* property

chapter11/
- *AutoCAD Process*     Example files extracted from AutoCAD
- *Illustrate Sample*     Sample 3D animation using Illustrate 4 plug-in
- *Pro-E Process*     Example files extracted from Pro/Engineer
- *Streamline Process*     Example files generated using Adobe Streamline

chapter12/
  guides/
    - *atom.fla*     Simple layer guide example
    - *sim_reflection.fla*     Simulated 3D reflection
    - *sim_shadow.fla*     Simulated shadow
    - *sim3d.fla*     Simulated 3D animation

- *sim3d_2.fla*   More complex simulated 3D animation

masks/

- *magnify.fla*   Simulated magnification animation
- *realspotlight.fla*   Mask used to simulate a spotlight
- *reflect.fla*   Reflection in a logo

misc/

- *filmgrain.fla*   Simulated film grain
- *lensflare.fla*   Simulated lens flare
- *tvnoise.fla*   Simulated television static with a bitmap

other/

- *clouds.fla*   Animated bitmap used to simulate clouds
- *fire.fla*   Colorized bitmap used to simulate fire
- *fog.fla*   Grayscale bitmap used to simulate fog
- *rain.fla*   Movie clip used to simulate rain
- *smoke.fla*   Grayscale bitmap used to simulate smoke

text effects/

- *blooming.fla*   Text that blooms
- *blooming2.fla*   Another bloom effect
- *exploding.fla*   Exploding transparency text
- *flipping.fla*   Flipping letters across a vertical
- *hardblur.fla*   Hard/quick blur
- *rippling.fla*   Ripple explode
- *rolling.fla*   Rolling credits example
- *shifting.fla*   Shifting text on the stage
- *softblur.fla*   Soft blur example
- *stretching.fla*   Stretching text example
- *tumbling.fla*   Rotating text into place

transitions/

- *circular.fla*   Circular mask example
- *fade.fla*   Fade transition using mask
- *push.fla*   Push transition using mask
- *reveal.fla*   Reveal using rectilinear mask

chapter13/

- *ch13-01.fla*   Using variables
- *ch13-02.fla*   Increment and decrement
- *ch13-03.fla*   Accessing variables in the hierarchy (absolute)
- *ch13-03.fla*   Accessing variables in the hierarchy (relative)
- *ch13-05.fla*   Commas, functions, and passing values
- *ch13-06.fla*   Using the If action based on frames

- *ch13-07.fla*   Using variables (with an If)
- *ch13-08.fla*   Using conditional operators for file *ch13-06.fla*
- *ch13-09.fla*   Using conditional operators for file *ch13-07.fla*
- *ch13-10.fla*   Having a movie clip react to the main timeline
- *ch13-11.fla*   Using a For loop
- *ch13-12.fla*   Using a For loop for a transition
- *ch13-13.fla*   Using With to control a movie clip (with If)
- *ch13-14.fla*   Communication among elements (absolute paths), dot syntax
- *ch13-15.fla*   Communication among elements (relative paths), dot syntax
- *ch13-16.fla*   Using Break with the Array object
- *ch13-17.fla*   Using the *loadVariables* method
- *ch13-18.fla*   Sending data, crunching, and responding
- *ch13-19.fla*   Chr and Ord functions versus the Key object
- *ch13-20.fla*   Using Escape and Unescape
- *ch13-21.fla*   Using the Eval function
- *ch13-22.fla*   Using the GetTimer function
- *ch13-23.fla*   Using the Int function
- *ch13-24.fla*   Length method versus *String.length* property
- *ch13-25.fla*   String and Number methods
- *ch13-26.fla*   ParseFloat and ParseInt
- *ch13-27.fla*   Random versus *Math.Random* method
- *ch13-28.fla*   Substring versus *String.substring*

chapter14/
- *ch14-01.fla, ch14-01s.fla*   Creating a custom button
- *ch14-02.fla, ch14-02s.fla*   Creating sliders with triggers
- *ch14-03.fla, ch14-03s.fla*   Creating sliders with ActionScript
- *fakezoom/*   Simulated zooming controlled by a slider
- *actionzoom/*   Files used to create a functioning slider bar that controls another movie
- *axonograph/*   Example files showing how to create positional block using sliders
- *ch14-04s.fla*   A sample menu
- *ch14-05.fla, ch14-05s*   Creating a draggable element
- *ch14-06s.fla*   Example of multiple drag-and-drop elements
- *ch14-07.fla, ch14-07s.fla*   Creating a text field
- *ch14-08s.fla*   HTML Text
- *ch14-09.fla, ch14-09s.fla*   Basic smart clips (creating)
- *ch14-10.fla, ch14-10s.fla*   Basic smart clips (adding parameters)
- *ch14-11.fla, ch14-11s.fla*   Basic smart clips (using)

chapter15/

- *actioncolor.fla* Applied example that shows how to create a coloring book example using ActionScript
- *puzzle1.fla* ActionScript example that shows how to use the *_droptarget* property
- *puzzle2.fla* Uses movie clip methods for drag-and-drop instead of nested buttons
- *puzzle3.fla* Shows how to perform cursor changes within the puzzle game
- *pano_sample.fla* Shows a sample of how the PanoPlayer works
- *panoplayer_code.fla* Shows the basic code for the PanoPlayer
- *pano_images/* Folder containing five sample panoramic images that can be used with the PanoPlayer
- *panoplayer_sc.fla* A file with the PanoPlayer smart clip already set up
- *panoplayer_sc_finished.fla* A completed example of the PanoPlayer
- *Actionnoah.fla* Complex Action Script example of a children's game
- *noah.xls* An Excel spreadsheet showing the animals in Noah's Memory Game

chapter16/

- *javascript/* Various JavaScript examples
- *ch16-01/* Shows a basic example of the FS Command method
- *ch16-02.fla, ch16-02s.fla* Shows an example of the FS Command method being used to send commands to the stand-alone Flash Player
- *ch16-03/* Shows how to pass one value to JavaScript
- *ch16-04/* Shows how to pass two values to JavaScript
- *ch16-05/* Shows how to pass two values to two functions
- *ch16-06/* Shows how to pass values to two Flash movies
- *coloring/* FS Command rendition of the coloring book example
- *noah/* Shows a children's game implemented with FS commands and JavaScript
- *virtual visit/* Shows an applied example used at Purdue University

Macromedia/

- *flash5-trial.exe* Thirty-day trial evaluation copy of Flash 5

Swift3D/

- *Swift3D TrialAcer.exe* Trial version of Swift3D

Swish/

- *setupswitch151.exe* Trial version of Swish

Vecta3D/

# Index

# License Agreement for Delmar Thomson Learning

### Educational Software/Data

You the customer, and Delmar Thomson Learning incur certain benefits, rights, and obligations to each other when you open this package and use the software/data it contains. BE SURE YOU READ THE LICENSE AGREEMENT CAREFULLY, SINCE BY USING THE SOFTWARE/DATA YOU INDICATE YOU HAVE READ, UNDERSTOOD, AND ACCEPTED THE TERMS OF THIS AGREEMENT.

### Your rights:

1. You enjoy a non-exclusive license to use the software/data on a single microcomputer in consideration for payment of the required license fee, (which may be included in the purchase price of an accompanying print component), or receipt of this software/data, and your acceptance of the terms and conditions of this agreement.

2. You acknowledge that you do not own the aforesaid software/data. You also acknowledge that the software/data is furnished "as is," and contains copyrighted and/or proprietary and confidential information of Delmar Thomson Learning or its licensors.

### There are limitations on your rights:

1. You may not copy or print the software/data for any reason whatsoever, except to install it on a hard drive on a single microcomputer and to make one archival copy, unless copying or printing is expressly permitted in writing or statements recorded on the diskette(s).

2. You may not revise, translate, convert, disassemble or otherwise reverse engineer the software/data except that you may add to or rearrange any data recorded on the media as part of the normal use of the software/data.

3. You may not sell, license, lease, rent, loan, or otherwise distribute or network the software/data except that you may give the software/data to a student or and instructor for use at school or, temporarily at home.

Should you fail to abide by the Copyright Law of the United States as it applies to this software/data your license to use it will become invalid. You agree to erase or otherwise destroy the software/data immediately after receiving note of Delmar Thomson Learning termination of this agreement for violation of its provisions.

Delmar Thomson Learning gives you a LIMITED WARRANTY covering the enclosed software/data. The LIMITED WARRANTY follows this License.

This license is the entire agreement between you and Delmar Thomson Learninginterpreted and enforced under New York law.

This warranty does not extend to the software or information recorded on the media. The software and information are provided "AS IS." Any statements made about the utility of the software or information are not to be considered as express or implied warranties. Delmar Thomson Learningwill not be liable for incidental or consequential damages of any kind incurred by you, the consumer, or any other user.

Some states do not allow the exclusion or limitation of incidental or consequential damages, or limitations on the duration of implied warranties, so the above limitation or exclusion may not apply to you. This warranty gives you specific legal rights, and you may also have other rights which vary from state to state. Address all correspondence to: Delmar Thomson Learning, Box 15015, Albany, NY 12212 Attention: Technology Department

## LIMITED WARRANTY

Delmar Thomson Learning warrants to the original licensee/purchaser of this copy of microcomputer software/data and the media on which it is recorded that the media will be free from defects in material and workmanship for ninety (90) days from the date of original purchase. All implied warranties are limited in duration to this ninety (90) day period. THEREAFTER, ANY IMPLIED WARRANTIES, INCLUDING IMPLIED WARRANTIES OF MERCHANTABILITY AND FITNESS FOR A PARTICULAR PURPOSE, ARE EXCLUDED. THIS WARRANTY IS IN LIEU OF ALL OTHER WARRANTIES, WHETHER ORAL OR WRITTEN, EXPRESS OR IMPLIED.

If you believe the media is defective please return it during the ninety day period to the address shown below. Defective media will be replaced without charge provided that it has not been subjected to misuse or damage.

This warranty does not extend to the software or information recorded on the media. The software and information are provided "AS IS." Any statements made about the utility of the software or information are not to be considered as express or implied warranties.

Limitation of liability: Our liability to you for any losses shall be limited to direct damages, and shall not exceed the amount you paid for the software. In no event will we be liable to you for any indirect, special, incidental, or consequential damages (including loss of profits) even if we have been advised of the possibility of such damages.

Some states do not allow the exclusion or limitation of incidental or consequential damages, or limitations on the duration of implied warranties, so the above limitation or exclusion may not apply to you. This warranty gives you specific legal rights, and you may also have other rights which vary from state to state. Address all correspondence to: Delmar Thomson Learning, Box 15015, Albany, NY 12212 Attention: Technology Department

# FLASH Quick-Key Reference Guide

| Command | Menu/Submenu | Windows | Macintosh | Command | Menu/Submenu | Windows | Macintosh |
|---|---|---|---|---|---|---|---|
| 100% | View | Magnification | Ctrl+1 | ⌘+1 | Frame | Modify | Ctrl+F | ⌘+F |
| Actions | Window | Ctrl+Alt+A | ⌘+Option+A | Frame | Window | Panels | Ctrl+F | ⌘+F |
| Add Shape Hint | Modify | Transform | Ctrl+Shift+H | ⌘+Shift+H | Frame | Insert | F5 | F5 |
| Align | Window | Panels | Ctrl+K | ⌘+K | Group | Modify | Ctrl+G | ⌘+G |
| Align Center | Text | Align | Ctrl+Shift+C | ⌘+Shift+C | Hide Edges | View | Ctrl+H | ⌘+H |
| Align Left | Text | Align | Ctrl+Shift+L | ⌘+Shift+L | Hide Panels | View | Tab | Tab |
| Align Right | Text | Align | Ctrl+Shift+R | ⌘+Shift+R | Import | File | Ctrl+R | ⌘+R |
| Antialias | View | Ctrl+Alt+Shift+A | ⌘+Option+Shift+A | Increase | Text | Tracking | Ctrl+Alt+Right | ⌘+Option+Right |
| Antialias Text | View | Ctrl+Alt+Shift+T | ⌘+Option+Shift+T | Info | Window | Panels | Ctrl+Alt+I | ⌘+Option+I |
| Blank Keyframe | Insert | F7 | F7 | Instance | Window | Panels | Ctrl+I | ⌘+I |
| Bold | Text | Style | Ctrl+Shift+B | ⌘+Shift+B | Instance | Modify | Ctrl+I | ⌘+I |
| Break Apart | Modify | Ctrl+B | ⌘+B | Italic | Text | Style | Ctrl+Shift+I | ⌘+Shift+I |
| Bring Forward | Modify | Arrange | Ctrl+Up | ⌘+Up | Justify | Text | Align | Ctrl+Shift+J | ⌘+Shift+J |
| Bring to Front | Modify | Arrange | Ctrl+Shift+Up | ⌘+Shift+Up | Keyframe | Insert | F6 | F6 |
| Character | Window | Panels | Ctrl+T | ⌘+T | Last | View | Goto | End | End |
| Character | Text | Ctrl+T | ⌘+T | Library | Window | Ctrl+L | ⌘+L |
| Clear Keyframe | Insert | Shift+F6 | Shift+F6 | Lock | Modify | Arrange | Ctrl+Alt+L | ⌘+Option+L |
| Clear | Edit | Backspace | Delete | Lock Guides | View | Guides | Ctrl+Alt+; | ⌘+Option+; |
| Close | File | Ctrl+W | ⌘+W | Movie | Modify | Ctrl+M | ⌘+M |
| Convert to Symbol | Insert | F8 | F8 | Movie Explorer | Window | Ctrl+Alt+M | ⌘+Option+M |
| Copy | Edit | Ctrl+C | ⌘+C | New | File | Ctrl+N | ⌘+N |
| Copy Frames | Edit | Ctrl+Alt+C | ⌘+Option+C | New Symbol | Insert | Ctrl+F8 | ⌘+F8 |
| Cut | Edit | Ctrl+X | ⌘+X | New Window | Window | Ctrl+Alt+N | ⌘+Option+N |
| Cut Frames | Edit | Ctrl+Alt+X | ⌘+Option+X | Next | View | Goto | Page Down | Page Down |
| Debug Movie | Ctrl | Ctrl+Shift+Enter | ⌘+Shift+Enter | Open | File | Ctrl+O | ⌘+O |
| Decrease | Text | Tracking | Ctrl+Alt+Left | ⌘+Option+Left | Open as Library | File | Ctrl+Shift+O | ⌘+Shift+O |
| Default | File | Publish Preview | F12 | F12 | Optimize | Modify | Ctrl+Alt+Shift+C | ⌘+Option+Shift+C |
| Deselect All | Edit | Ctrl+Shift+A | ⌘+Shift+A | Outlines | View | Ctrl+Alt+Shift+O | ⌘+Option+Shift+O |
| Duplicate | Edit | Ctrl+D | ⌘+D | Paragraph | Window | Panels | Ctrl+Shift+T | ⌘+Shift+T |
| Edit Grid | View | Grid | Ctrl+Alt+G | ⌘+Option+G | Paragraph | Text | Ctrl+Shift+T | ⌘+Shift+T |
| Edit Guides | View | Guides | Ctrl+Alt+Shift+G | ⌘+Option+Shift+G | Paste | Edit | Ctrl+V | ⌘+V |
| Edit Symbols | Edit | Ctrl+E | ⌘+E | Paste Frames | Edit | Ctrl+Alt+V | ⌘+Option+V |
| Enable Simple Buttons | Ctrl | Ctrl+Alt+B | ⌘+Option+B | Paste In Place | Edit | Ctrl+Shift+V | ⌘+Shift+V |
| Export Movie | File | Ctrl+Alt+Shift+S | ⌘+Shift+Option+S | Plain | Text | Style | Ctrl+Shift+P | ⌘+Shift+P |
| Fast | View | Ctrl+Alt+Shift+F | ⌘+Option+Shift+F | Play | Ctrl | Enter | Return |
| First | View | Goto | Home | Home | Previous | View | Goto | Page Up | Page Up |
|  |  |  |  | Print | File | Ctrl+P | ⌘+P |

| Command | Menu/Submenu | Windows | Macintosh | Command | Menu/Submenu | Windows | Macintosh |
|---|---|---|---|---|---|---|---|
| Publish | File | Shift+F12 | Shift+F12 | Show Grid | View \| Grid | Ctrl+' | ⌘+' |
| Publish Settings | File | Ctrl+Shift+F12 | ⌘+Shift+F12 | Show Guides | View \| Guides | Ctrl+; | ⌘+; |
| Quit | File | Ctrl+Q | ⌘+Q | Show Shape Hints | View | Ctrl+Alt+H | ⌘+Option+H |
| Redo | Edit | Ctrl+Y | ⌘+Y | Snap to Grid | View \| Grid | Ctrl+Shift+' | ⌘+Shift+' |
| Remove Frames | Insert | Shift+F5 | Shift+F5 | Snap to Guides | View \| Guides | Ctrl+Shift+; | ⌘+Shift+; |
| Remove Transform | Modify \| Transform | Ctrl+Shift+Z | ⌘+Shift+Z | Snap to Objects | View | Ctrl+Shift+/ | ⌘+Shift+/ |
| Reset | Text \| Tracking | Ctrl+Alt+Up | ⌘+Option+Up | Step Backward | Ctrl | , | , |
| Rewind | Ctrl | Ctrl+Alt+R | ⌘+Option+R | Step Forward | Ctrl | . | . |
| Rulers | View | Ctrl+Alt+Shift+R | ⌘+Option+Shift+R | Test Movie | Ctrl | Ctrl+Enter | ⌘+Enter |
| Save | File | Ctrl+S | ⌘+S | Test Scene | Ctrl | Ctrl+Alt+Enter | ⌘+Option+Enter |
| Save As | File | Ctrl+Shift+S | ⌘+Shift+S | Timeline | View | Ctrl+Alt+T | ⌘+Option+T |
| Scale and Rotate | Modify \| Transform | Ctrl+Alt+S | ⌘+Option+S | Undo | Edit | Ctrl+Z | ⌘+Z |
| Select All | Edit | Ctrl+A | ⌘+A | Ungroup | Modify | Ctrl+Shift+G | ⌘+Shift G |
| Send Backward | Modify \| Arrange | Ctrl+Down | ⌘+Down | Unlock All | Modify \| Arrange | Ctrl+Alt+Shift L | ⌘+Option+Shift+L |
| Send to Back | Modify \| Arrange | Ctrl+Shift+Down | ⌘+Shift+Down | Work Area | View | Ctrl+Shift+W | ⌘+Shift+W |
| Show All | View \| Magnification | Ctrl+3 | ⌘+3 | Zoom In | View | Ctrl+= | ⌘+= |
| Show Frame | View \| Magnification | Ctrl+2 | ⌘+2 | Zoom Out | View | Ctrl+- | ⌘+- |

## Controlling layers and keyframes

| | Windows | Macintosh |
|---|---|---|
| To Select frames | Ctrl-drag | ⌘-drag |
| Link or unlink a layer to a mask or motion guides layer | Alt-click a layer icon | Ctrl-click a layer icon |

## Spring-loaded tools

Hold down the corresponding key listed below to temporarily activate certain tools. When you release the key, the tool you were using before reactivates.

| To temporarily activate this tool | Windows | Macintosh |
|---|---|---|
| Arrow | Ctrl | ⌘ |
| Hand | Spacebar | Spacebar |
| Magnifier zoom in | Ctrl+Spacebar | ⌘+Spacebar |
| Magnifier zoom out | Ctrl+Shift+Spacebar | ⌘+Shift+Spacebar |

## Switching tools

Press the keys listed below to switch to a different tool.

To switch to this tool    Press

| | | | |
|---|---|---|---|
| Arrow | V | Pencil | Y |
| Subselect | A | Brush | B |
| Line | N | Ink bottle | S |
| Lasso | L | Paint bucket | K |
| Pen | P | Dropper | I |
| Text | T | Eraser | E |
| Oval | O | Hand | H |
| Rectangle | R | Zoom | M,Z |

## Drawing shortcuts

| | Windows | Macintosh |
|---|---|---|
| To Set fill and line color simultaniously with the dropper tool | Shift-click with the dropper tool | Shift-click with the dropper tool |
| Create a new corner handle | Alt-drag a line with the arrow tool | Option-drag a line with the arrow tool |
| Move a selected element by one pixel | Arrow keys | Arrow keys |
| Move a selected element by 8 pixels | Shift+Arrow keys | Shift+Arrow keys |
| Change between zoom in and zoom out while the magnifier tool is active | Alt | Option |
| Drag a copy of the selected element | Ctrl-drag | Option-drag |